PROJECT CONTROL: SATISFYING THE CUSTOMER

Proceedings

of

ESCOM 2001

2-4 April 2001
London, United Kingdom

Proceedings of the 12th ESCOM (European Software Control and Metrics Conference) Conference including the SCOPE track on Software Product Quality.

Editors

Katrina D. Maxwell
Datamax, France

Serge Oligny
Université du Québec à Montréal, Canada

Rob J. Kusters
Eindhoven University of Technology & Open University,
The Netherlands

Erik P.W.M. van Veenendaal
Improve Quality Services & Eindhoven University of Technology,
The Netherlands

Printed in The Netherlands

ISBN 90-423-0148-1

Shaker Publishing BV
St. Maartenslaan 26
6221 AX Maastricht
The Netherlands
Tel.: +31(43)3500424
Fax: +31(43)3255090
http://www.shaker.nl/
info@shaker.nl

ESCOM 2001 CONFERENCE OFFICERS

General Chair
John Jenkins (Middlesex University, United Kingdom)
ESCOM Programme Chair
Katrina Maxwell (Datamax, France)
Associate Programme Chair
Serge Oligny (Université du Québec à Montréal, Canada)
SCOPE track Chair
Erik van Veenendaal (Improve Quality Services & Eindhoven University of Technology, NL)
Publications Chair
Rob. J. Kusters (Eindhoven University of Technology and The Open University, NL)
ESCOM-METRICS Co-ordinator
Adrian Cowderoy (Nexusworld.net, UK)
Conference Manager
Monica Kaayk (Escom Conference Ltd., UK)

ESCOM 2001 PROGRAMME COMMITTEE

Galtierro Bazzana, Onion, Italy
Miklos Biro, MTA SZTAKI, Hungary
Lionel Briand, Carleton University., Canada
A. Winsor Brown, USC, USA
Giovanni Cantone, University of Rome, Italy
John Elliott, DERA, United Kingdom
Fred Heemstra, Open University, The Netherlands
Ross Jeffrey, University of New South Wales, Australia
Pekka Forselius, STTF, Finland
Michael O'Duffy, Centre for Software Engineering, Ireland
Shari Lawrence Pfleeger, Software/Systems Inc., USA
Roberto Meli, Data Processing Organisation, Italy
Peter Mellor, CSR, United Kingdom
Ingunn Myrtveit, The Norwegian School of Management, Norway
Domenico Natale, SOGEI, Italy
Martin Shepperd, Bournemouth University, United Kingdom
Rini van Solingen, CMG, The Netherlands
Erik Stensrud, Stensrud Consulting, Norway
Richard D. Stutzke, SAIC, USA
Jos Trienekens, Eindhoven University, The Netherlands
June Verner, Drexel University, USA
Isabella Wieczorek, Fraunhofer (IESE), Germany
Claes Wohlin, Blekinge Institute of Technology, Sweden

Conference Office
Adrian Cowderoy, ESCOM Conference Ltd
30 Willow Tree Glade, Calcot, Reading
RG31 7AZ, UK.
Phone: +44(UK) 118 9 427 970
Fax: +44(UK) 118 9 542 591
Email: office@escom.co.uk
URL: http://www.escom.co.uk/

ESCOM 2001 SPONSORS
CSR, The Centre for Software Reliability, UK
ESCOM 2001 PARTNERS
The conference is held in association with SCOPE.
The conference is co-located with the IEEE 7th International Symposium on Software Metrics

Project Control: Satisfying the Customer

Preface

We are proud to present the proceedings of the 12th European Software Control and Metrics Conference (ESCOM). The conference this year also includes a Software Certification Programme in Europe (SCOPE) track. ESCOM was established in 1990 in order to support the metrics and management science communities in the software industry. The conference's focus is on the software-related issues of project and risk control, process improvement, quality and certification, cost estimation and productivity, and the measurement to support these activities. The annual conference provides a special opportunity for face-to-face contact between researchers, consultants and practitioners.

Contributions are peer reviewed to ensure that they reach high academic standards, and / or address practical needs. New ideas are shared and find support from inception through user acceptance – hence the conference slogan "You heard it first at ESCOM". The innovations first reported at ESCOM conferences are often expanded and published in prestigious academic journals.

Software is developed for people.
Customer participation has an impact on productivity and quality, and the wise management of requirements specification changes is key to project control and satisfied customers.

One theme that appears frequently in papers and discussions in the area of software control and measurement, and in particular software cost estimation, is the importance of requirements volatility. Even a slight change to requirements at a late stage in a project can have a disastrous impact on cost, schedule and quality.

Because of this, software engineers have been trying for years to manage requirements better. However, unless we are developing software for our personal use, we cannot control requirements, nor can we dictate the frequency or desirability of changes. What we can do is quantify the amount of change to re-negotiate cost and schedule estimates.

Nor must we lose sight of the fact that software is developed for people. A project in which requirements remain fixed may not be a success from the customer's viewpoint. Our goal should be to develop software on time, within budget and which satisfies the customer. While much research has been devoted to the cost and duration aspects, what are we doing to measure customer satisfaction?

To address these important issues we chose "Controlling Software Projects: Satisfying the Customer" as the conference theme this year. Thus in addition to traditional papers, several papers present pioneering work to better understand the human factor aspect of requirements volatility and its impact on software projects and product quality. The proceedings include experience reports, studies of best practice, new research concepts, and in-depth quantitative analyses.

Ultimately, the quality of the Conference depends on the quality of the contributions submitted and the processes that govern their review and selection. Many people helped to put the ESCOM 2001 program and proceedings together. In particular, we thank the authors for creating and submitting their work, and the members of the Program Committee for their prompt reviews and constructive comments.

Katrina D. Maxwell, Serge Oligny, Erik van Veenendaal, Rob J. Kusters

TABLE OF CONTENTS

TRACK A: FIRST NEWS

TRACK B: EXPERIENCE

Satisfying the Customer

SCOPE TRACK

Software Product Quality

Human Factors

Software Metrics

COCOTS: a Software COTS-Based System (CBS) Cost Model - Evolving Towards Maintenance Phase Modeling

Chris Abts, Barry W. Boehm, and Elizabeth Bailey Clark

Abstract

As the use of commercial-of-the-shelf (COTS) components becomes ever more prevalent in the creation of large software systems, the need for the ability to reasonably predict the true lifetime cost of using such software components grows accordingly. In using COTS software components, immediate short-term gains in direct development effort & schedule are possible, but usually as a trade-off for a more complicated long-term post-deployment maintenance environment. This paper discusses a COTS-based system cost model being developed as an extension of the COCOMO II cost model. This new model, COCOTS, attempts to predict the life cycle costs of using COTS components by capturing in its modeling parameters the more significant risks associated with using COTS components. A brief description of the COCOTS Development Phase model is presented, followed by a more detailed description of the proposed COCOTS Maintenance Phase model. The paper concludes with some suggested areas for further research that might offer a very useful return for those engaged in CBS planning and management.

1. Introduction

COCOTS is the acronym for the *COnstructive COTS* integration cost model, where COTS in turn is short for *commercial-off-the-shelf,* and refers to those pre-built, commercially available software components that are becoming increasingly important in the creation of new software systems.

The rationale for building COTS-based systems is that they will involve less development time by taking advantage of existing, market proven, vendor supported products, thereby reducing overall system development costs. But there are two defining characteristics of COTS software that drive the whole COTS usage process, and in any given development, they greatly influence whether up-front savings can be realized or not:

1) the COTS product source code is not available to the application developer, and
2) the future evolution of the COTS product is not under the control of the application developer.

(Note: in some cases, COTS software does come as source code, but for the purposes of our model, if the developer does anything to that code other than compile it unchanged into his own code, we treat that as a *reuse* item and model its usage as *adapted* code within COCOMO II itself.)

Because of these characteristics, there is a trade-off in using the COTS approach in that new software development time can indeed be reduced, but generally at the cost of an increase in software component integration work. The long term cost implications of adopting the COTS approach are even more profound, because you are in fact adopting a new way of doing business from the moment you start considering COTS components for your new system to the day you finally retire that system. This is because COTS software is not static, it continually evolves in response to the market, and you as the system developer must adopt methodologies that cost-effectively manage the use of those evolving components.

2. Model Description

2.1. Background

COCOTS is evolving. Initial research on the model addressed CBS development from just prior to requirements solidification and determination of Life Cycle Objectives (LCO) through Initial Operational Capability (IOC). This resulted in what is now called the COCOTS Development Phase (DP) model. As details of the DP model have been published elsewhere [1, 2], only a high level description will be repeated here. However, it has always been understood that just as with traditional software systems built from scratch, the overwhelming majority of costs realized over the total life span of a CBS through final retirement will be accrued during the post-deployment maintenance (sometimes called sustainment) phase. The ability to predict accurately these costs is then even more important than being able to predict initial development phase costs, and any truly credible analysis comparing alternate designs of COTS-based and custom-built systems must include a total life span estimate.

This is the rationale behind the development of the COCOTS Maintenance Phase (MP) model. The initial pass we've taken at defining the MP model will be described following the review of the DP model, along with some early insights we've gained into CBS maintenance phase issues.

2.2. The Development Phase (DP) Model

The DP model is composed of four related submodels, each addressing individually what we have identified as the four primary sources of development phase COTS software integration costs.

Initial integration costs are due to the effort needed to perform (1) candidate COTS component assessment, (2) COTS component tailoring, (3) the development and testing of any integration or "glue" code (sometimes called “glueware” or “binding” code) needed to plug a COTS component into a larger system, and (4) increased system level programming and testing due to volatility in incorporated COTS components.

(A fifth cost source was actually identified early in our research. This was the cost related to the increased verification and validation effort unrelated to COTS volatility but still usually required when using COTS components. But attempts have been made to capture these costs within the glue code and tailoring submodels directly rather than specify a fifth independent submodel.)

Assessment is the process by which COTS components are selected for use in the larger system being developed. *Tailoring* refers to those activities that would have to be performed to prepare a particular COTS program for use, regardless of the system into which it is being incorporated, or even if operating as a stand-alone item. These are things such as initializing parameter values, specifying I/O screens or report formats, setting up security protocols, etc. *Glue code* development and testing refers to the new code external to the COTS component itself that must be written in order to plug the component into the larger system. This code by nature is unique to the particular context in which the COTS component is being used, and must not be confused with tailoring activity as defined above. *Volatility* in this context refers to the frequency with which new versions or updates of the COTS software being used in a larger system are released by the vendors over the course of the system's development and subsequent deployment.

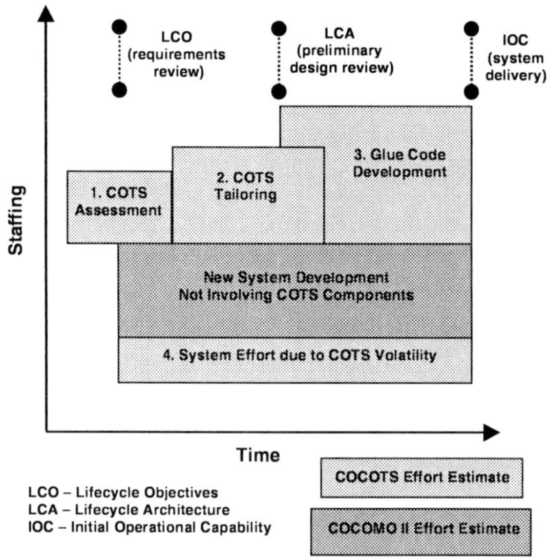

Figure 1. CBS Development Phase Sources of Effort

Figure 1 illustrates how the modeling of these effort sources in the COCOTS DP model is related to effort modeled by COCOMO II. The figure represents the total development phase effort required to build a software system out of a mix of new code and COTS components as estimated by a combination of COCOMO II and COCOTS. The central block in the diagram indicates the COCOMO II estimate, that is, the effort associated with any newly developed software in the system. The smaller, exterior blocks indicate COCOTS estimates, that effort associated with the COTS components in the system. The relative sizes of the various blocks in this figure are a function of the number of COTS components relative to the amount of new code in the system, and of the nature of the COTS component integration efforts themselves. The more complex the tailoring and/or glue code-writing efforts, the larger these blocks will be relative to the assessment block. Also, note that addressing the system-wide volatility due to volatility in the COTS components is an effort that will obtain throughout the entire system development cycle, as indicated by the long block running along the bottom of the figure.

The total development phase COTS integration effort then becomes the linear sum of the four identified sources of effort:

Total COTS Integration Effort =

Assessment Effort + Tailoring Effort + Glue Code Effort + System Volatility Effort

As an approximation, this works for now, but the true relationship between these terms is likely more complicated.

Finally, we caution the reader to not draw the erroneous conclusion that the various sources of effort being discussed can be as cleanly parsed as would appear to be indicated by the distinct boundaries drawn for each block in the figure. The reality is that rather than sharp lines, these boundaries would probably be more realistically shown as areas of different shading that blend into each other. This is particularly true for the boundary between the bottom volatility block and the larger system block.

2.3. The Maintenance Phase (MP) Model

The COCOTS MP model is in the early stages of development. Though not yet finalized, the initial MP model that we are proposing builds directly on the DP model. Figure 2 below illustrates how this is the case. On the left side of the figure, between the LCO and IOC life cycle anchor points, you can see the Development Phase model as detailed in Figure 1. Between the IOC and RRR (Requirements Readiness Review) anchor points, however, is a new phase labeled "transition." During this phase the completed system is being moved out of the development environment into the final, full deployment, end-user environment. Between the RRR and System Retirement anchor points, the system has entered the long-term maintenance or sustainment phase.

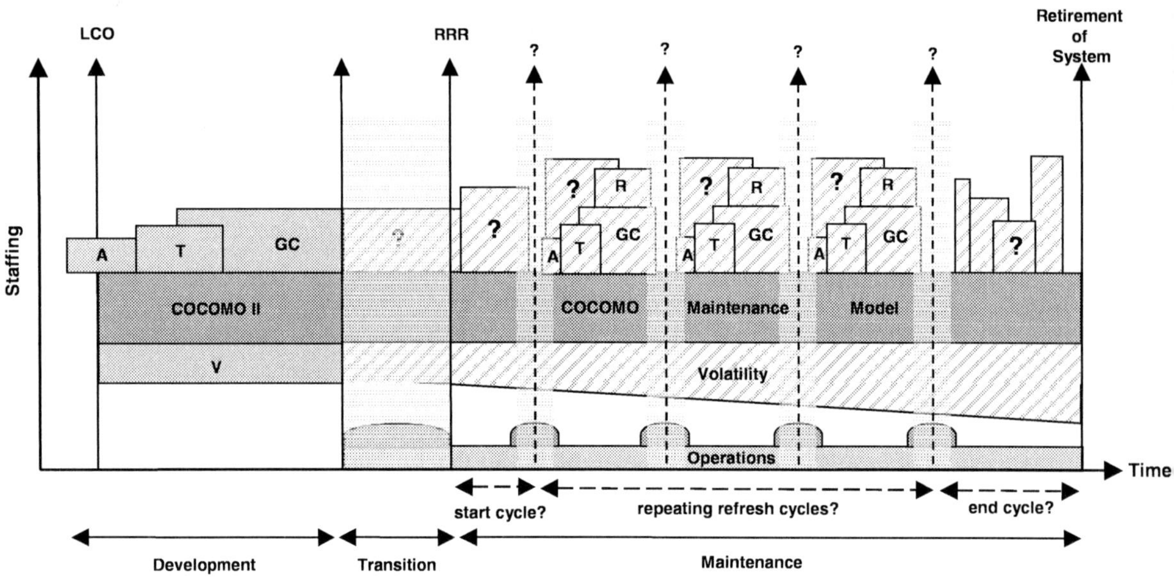

Figure 2. CBS Post-Deployment Modeling Horizon

The length of the initial transition phase and the effort and activities associated with that period are highly dependant on the size and complexity of the system, and also the nature of the end-user environment. For example, if only one copy of the final system is to be deployed, in a single location, then the transition phase will likely be relatively uncomplicated. However, if multiple versions of a very complex system need to be deployed to several different, geographically dispersed locations, the initial transition phase could be very effort intensive indeed. Transition effort in these cases will be spent on scheduling and coordinating new system installation activities at delivery sites to ensure the least disruption of existing operations at those sites. It will also include configuring and tuning each delivered copy of the system to all the unique site environments in which it must perform--even if all delivered systems are supposed to configured "identically," it is extremely rare that individual system tuning at each installation site will not have to be done.

Post-transition, the system has entered the maintenance phase. For custom-built software systems, the activities during this period are well understood. Usually these entail annual (or at least periodic) routine correction cycles of bugs and defects in the system that have been discovered and catalogued by the end-user while using the system operationally. Maintenance activities also usually include periodic enhancements or changes to the functionality of the system that were not included or requested at the time of initial system development. Such enhancements frequently first appear on a "wish list" at the start of each new maintenance cycle and then get negotiated down to deliverable requirements for that cycle between the system developer and client, usually as a function of the client's available budget for that current maintenance cycle. The staffing needed during such repeating maintenance cycles thus is usually easily predictable as a level-of-effort allocation of resources. The Maintenance model [3] within COCOMO II is available to estimate this kind of effort for custom-built systems.

COTS-based systems also typically go through repeating maintenance cycles between RRR and System Retirement. However, CBS maintenance cycles may not be anywhere near as stable or predictable as for custom-built systems. It may be harder to establish regular, uniformly lengthy maintenance cycles. The first and final maintenance cycles may differ qualitatively from all the other cycles in between. It may also be more difficult to smooth out maintenance expenditures at relatively uniform levels over several maintenance cycles.

Again, the reason for all this is that many of the components that make up significant portions of your system will be evolving independently in response to market forces beyond your control. It is during the maintenance phase that the profoundly different consequences of building CBS versus custom-built systems will become most apparent.

With the "wish list" approach to maintaining custom systems, the system developer and client generally get to pick and choose which system elements will be changed and when, and if the budget isn't currently available for some items on the list, then those items can often just be postponed until the next cycle. With COTS-based systems, it is the external market that may tell you which elements in your system will need to be changed in the current maintenance cycle, not your internally generated "wish list." You also may be forced to change things whether you have the budget available or not, because the consequences of retaining older versions of COTS components that the vendor decides no longer to support may be even more dire than having to cannibalize budgets from other projects.

The several question marks that appear in Figure 2 illustrate the ambiguity that still obtains when discussing CBS maintenance. The COCOTS Maintenance Phase model assumes that if you have to refresh existing COTS components during maintenance cycles, you will have to repeat to some degree the same assessment, tailoring and glue code writing activities that you performed during initial system development. You will also still be dealing with the consequences of COTS component volatility on the larger system, but even more so as time progresses, because it will likely become increasingly difficult to keep your diverse COTS components functioning in concert as they continue evolve in divergent directions. You may also have to completely replace or retire some COTS components, represented by the small boxes labeled "R" in the figure. But the question marks in some of the other boxes indicate that there may be other costs that we have yet to identify that also should appear in our model. The other question marks appearing above the arrowheads and after the small cycle labels found along the bottom axis indicate that the activities and schedule associated with individual CBS maintenance cycles are fluid and not yet well defined

Also, just as there is a significant transition phase after initial system delivery, there may be similar "mini" transition phases with similar kinds of costs associated with the completion of each maintenance cycle. These transition costs--both right after IOC and after each maintenance cycle--need to be accounted for, but may not all need to appear in parametric models such as COCOMO and COCOTS.

Finally, there will also be ongoing operations costs throughout the life span of the system, but these are not necessarily a direct function of the presence of the COTS components or other coded elements in the system. Again, like the transition costs, these costs need to be accounted for, but may not always be appropriate for parametric modeling.

Below then is our first cut at the COCOTS MP model:

CBS Maintenance Effort (for a Given Cycle Time T_M)

= COCOMO Application Maintenance + COTS Reassessment + COTS Retailoring + COTS Glue Code Evolution + COTS Volatility Effect on Application Effort + COTS Replacement

And a "brute force" procedure for determining an optimal maintenance or refresh cycle time length in terms of cost is proposed as follows:

1. Allow estimation parameters to change between each cycle T_M.
2. Test several T_M cycle lengths over your total planning horizon
   - i.e., 9 months, 12 months, 18 months, 24 months, 36 months, etc.
3. Select cycle length of least overall cost to schedule refresh efforts.

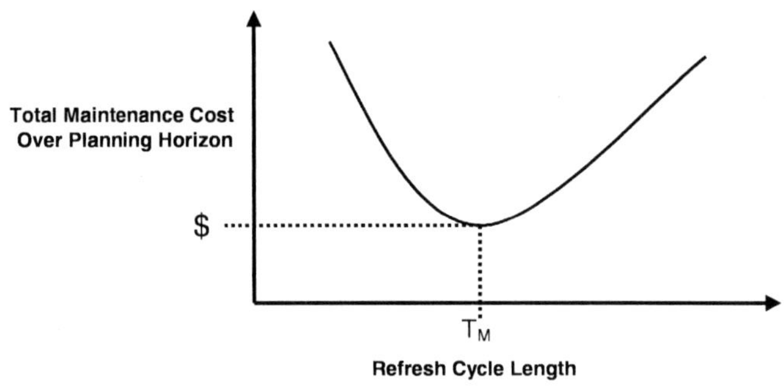

Figure 3. Determining Optimal Refresh Cycle Time

2.4. Other CBS Maintenance Insights

In addition to the model presented above, we also list below some potential CBS maintenance phase activities prioritized by effort involved and/or criticality. This list is not presumed to be exhaustive, but represents a distillation of ideas that were put forth at two FAA-sponsored COTS Maintenance workshops held last May and July [4] and at the 15th International COCOMO Forum held in October [5].

The list also indicates which of these activities are likely to be ongoing concerns throughout maintenance, and which activities are likely to spike in effort around the repeating maintenance cycle end points--in some cases, the activities are believed to do both.

Priority of CBS Maintenance Phase Activities by Effort Involved and/or Criticality

- Higher
  - training S C
  - configuration management C
  - operations support C
  - integration analysis S
  - requirements management S C
- Medium
  - certification S
  - market watch C
  - distribution S
  - vendor management C
  - business case evaluation S
- Lower
  - administering COTS licenses C

S - activity spikes around refresh cycle anchor points

C - activity is continuous throughout maintenance

SC - activity is continuous yet also spikes around cycle anchor points

3. Conclusions

In this paper we have presented a preliminary definition of a CBS Maintenance Phase cost estimation model. We have also identified some activities that are likely to be of concern during CBS maintenance, prioritized by relative criticality and/or effort involved. At this point we would like close by suggesting two other CBS modeling activities that may offer very useful returns if pursued.

The first research activity would be an effort aimed at clearly defining the CBS-oriented life cycle anchor points that should replace some of the question marks in Figure 2. This would include both the relevant, measurable milestones, and the activities leading up to the achievement of those milestones.

The second research activity would be the development of a detailed, standardized CBS Work Breakdown Structure (COTS WBS) that could be used in conjunction with a more traditional development WBS to estimate project costs.

4. References

[1] Boehm, B., Abts, C., Brown, A., Chulani, S., Clark, B., Horowitz, E., Madachy, R., Reifer, D. and Steece, D., *Software Cost Estimation with COCOMO II*, Prentice Hall, July 2000, p.237-253.
[2] Abts, C., Boehm, B. and Bailey Clark, E. "COCOTS: A COTS Software Integration Cost Model," *Proceedings ESCOM-SCOPE 2000 Conference*, ESCOM-SCOPE, Munich, Germany, April 2000.
[3] Boehm, B. et al., *Software Cost Estimation with COCOMO II*, p.27-28 and p.58-59.
[4] Summary Notes, US Federal Aviation Administration COTS Operations & Maintenance Issues Workshops, May 10-11, 2000, Ocean City, New Jersey and July 19-20, 2000, Herndon, Virginia.
[5] "COTS Breakout Group Summary Briefing," 15th International Forum on COCOMO and Software Cost Estimation, University of Southern California, Los Angeles, CA October 24-27, 2000.
[6] COCOTS website: http://sunset.usc.edu/research/COCOTS/index.html.

A Comparison of LAD and OLS Regression for Effort Prediction of Software Projects

Tron Foss, Ingunn Myrtveit, Erik Stensrud

Abstract

Accurate effort prediction of software projects is of concern to portfolio managers, customers, vendors as well as project managers. Ordinary least squares (OLS) regression is widely used to create software prediction models, and it seems to perform just as well or better than most other, non-regression, prediction models. Software data sets may however exhibit certain characteristics that do not always comply with the requirements of OLS. In particular, we may suspect industrial software data sets to be messy due to the cost and difficulty of gathering data. Thus, we should probably be prepared to expect the distribution of residuals to exhibit heavy tails, i.e. high kurtosis, and to be skewed. Under these circumstances, OLS regression may be less efficient than certain robust regression methods. In particular, it can be shown that the Least Absolute Deviation (LAD) regression method is more efficient than OLS when the distribution of the residuals exhibits high kurtosis. In general, it is also useful to apply more than one method to confirm that the initial model specification and results are reasonable. In this paper, we investigate empirically if LAD is more efficient than OLS on a data set of 87 ERP projects. The results suggest that: i) for this particular data set, LAD does not seem more efficient than OLS, ii) LAD does, however, confirm the initial OLS prediction model.

1. Introduction

Accurate effort prediction of software projects is of concern to portfolio managers, customers, vendors as well as project managers. Ordinary least squares (OLS) regression seems to perform just as well or better than most of the proposed prediction models including so called machine learning models [1]. Consequently, OLS seems to have emerged as the de facto standard against which other effort prediction models are compared. OLS has been generally adopted because of tradition and ease of computation. The latter property was an important practical matter in the early days when CPU cycles were expensive. Fortunately, this is no longer the case. This enables us therefore to investigate more sophisticated and CPU intensive regression techniques. Also, OLS has been accessible as opposed to LAD. All statistical software presumably includes OLS regression functionality.

Software data sets exhibit certain characteristics that may not always comply with the requirements of OLS. Two requirements concern *kurtosis* and *skewness*. Regarding kurtosis, OLS assumes that the distribution of the residuals is normal. However, software data sets may be messy. For example, the distribution of residuals may exhibit heavy tails, i.e. high kurtosis, or may be skewed. Under these circumstances, OLS regression may be less efficient than certain robust regression methods. In particular, Least Absolute Deviation (LAD) regression method may be more efficient than OLS when the distribution of the residuals is leptokurtic (high kurtosis).

Regarding skewness, the distribution of residuals of real data sets is not always completely symmetrical. If the distribution is skewed (for example by having a few large outliers on one side), LAD is less influenced by these outliers than OLS is.

In software engineering, when one observes unusual values, it is often difficult to determine whether this value is a wild value or just an unusual project. It is a wild value if the value is due to a punching error, a reporting error, or a large measurement error. It is an unusual project if this project just happened to perform unusually well or poorly. Since measuring and collecting data is costly and difficult in software projects, many values will contain smaller or larger measurement and reporting errors. Therefore, one will be in doubt whether one should consider some observations as outliers (i.e. having "large" measurement errors) that one should remove or rather consider the observations as unusual, but correctly reported, projects that one should keep. In such circumstances, LAD comes partly to your rescue because it matters less whether you keep or discard an outlying observation compared with OLS. LAD is a method that is less sensitive to these outlying observations than OLS.

There have been few studies in software engineering on the application of robust regression techniques. We are aware of only one study on LAD, the work by Pickard, Kitchenham and Linkman [7]. Our study differs from Pickard et al. in several respects: i) We explain theoretically when and why LAD is superior to OLS: the *kurtosis* issue. Pickard et al. simply applied LAD and reported the results, ii) We apply LAD to real industrial ERP data. They applied LAD to artificial data, and iii) We report which model is the more efficient (i.e. closer to the true model) in terms of t-values of the regression coefficients. Pickard et al. mainly used boxplots to assess the accuracy of the models.

In this paper, we investigate empirically if LAD is more efficient than OLS on a data set of 87 ERP projects. The results suggest that: i) for this particular ERP data set, LAD does not seem more efficient than OLS, ii) LAD does, however, confirm the prediction model. We assume, however, that other software data sets may lend themselves better to LAD. It also remains to discuss from a theoretical viewpoint whether software data sets should be expected to be leptokurtic and therefore lend themselves better to LAD than to OLS or not.

2. Data

The data set used for this investigation consists of 87 ERP projects. All the ERP projects in the sample implement ERP systems from one single ERP vendor, SAP, either the client-server version (R/3) or the mainframe version (R/2). Therefore, it is a homogeneous data set. There are four predictor variables (Users, Sites, Interfaces, Modules) and one response variable (Effort). Interested readers are referred to [9] for a definition of the variables. There are no missing values. Descriptive statistics is provided in Table 1. The data were gathered from 1990 to 1998 in a multinational consultant organisation with 70.000 employees. The projects span many industries and countries in all regions of the world. The data have been reported by project managers who themselves use the database to plan and estimate future projects. The company has a standard ERP methodology. Therefore, the data presumably have been reported in a consistent manner. See also [8][5] for an evaluation of the data quality.

Table 1. Descriptive statistics for ERP data set

Variable	N	Mean	Median	StDev	Min	Max
Users	87	966	300	2348	6	17000
Sites	87	29	5	73	0	500
Interfaces	87	28	13	48	0	270
Modules	87	5.2	5.0	2.6	1	13
Effort	87	10791	6000	14881	102	111420

3. Related work

To our knowledge, only one paper in software engineering, Pickard, Kitchenham and Linkman [7], has applied LAD regression. A few studies have reported the use of regression models other than OLS. They are generally referred to as *robust regression* in empirical software engineering. Robust regression aims to be robust against outlying observations thus addressing a potentially important issue in software engineering data. Robust regression is a family of regression techniques, not one special regression technique. LAD may be considered to belong to the class of robust regression techniques.

Pickard, Kitchenham, and Linkman [7] applied several prediction methods including LAD to five artificial data sets, each data set exhibiting a particular characteristic. The five data sets were: i) ideal, ii) skewed, iii) heteroscedastic, iv) with extreme outliers, and v) skewed plus heteroscedastic. Boxplots of residuals and sign tests based on residuals were used as model evaluation criteria together with a comparison of how close the estimated coefficients were to the true coefficients (or true equation). As opposed to our paper, Pickard et al. did not discuss the issue of *kurtosis*. Rather, their study is mostly explorative in the sense that they simply applied LAD and reported the results. Kurtosis is crucial to understanding when LAD is expected to be more efficient than OLS.

The use of simulation is generally useful to study specific properties in an isolated and controlled manner. Unfortunately, their simulation study suffers from some flaws casting doubts about the validity of their results:

- Heteroscedastic data sets must be transformed by some suitable transformation to satisfy the homoscedasticity requirement of OLS. It does not seem that Pickard et al. transformed the heteroscedastic data set before applying OLS. Thus, they violated one fundamental assumption of OLS.
- The data set with 5% extreme outliers (5% of the response variable values were multiplied by 10) had so extreme outliers that a person with knowledge of the data and common sense would likely consider these as wild values and do something about it, e.g. discard them. If such a traditional outlier detection and removal procedure had been used, the results would have changed.
- To our understanding, for each type of data set (heteroscedastic, skewed, etc.) they generated only one single data set, i.e. one skewed data set, one heteroscedastic, etc. It is not easy to draw any general conclusions from such a single simulation. In statistical science, it is common to generate not one, but rather thousands of such data sets of 100 observations each thereby creating a distribution of the estimators. By creating just one single estimator, it is to some extent arbitrary which model is closest to the true equation and therefore deemed "best".

Jeffery, Ruhe, and Wieczorek [2] applied a robust regression method that iteratively performs weighted LS regressions (WLS). It should be observed that Pickard et al. [7], too, applied WLS.

Miazaki, Terakado, Ozaki, and Nozaki [4] applied two variants of LMS (least median of squares) regression. LBRS (least-squares of balanced relative errors) regression minimises the sum of squares of balanced relative error. LIRS (least-squares of inverted balanced relative errors) regression minimises the sum of squares of inverted balanced relative error.

Gray and MacDonell [3] evaluated LMS and LTS (least-trimmed-squares) regression on three data sets.

Nesi and Querci [6] applied robust regression to predict the effort of three object-oriented systems coded in C++.

4. LAD

In the methods of least absolute deviations (LAD) the parameter estimates are chosen so that the sum of the absolute values of the residuals is as small as possible. That is, LAD parameter estimates are the values of the parameters that minimise

$$\sum |y_i - (a + bx_i)|$$

where a and b are the parameters in the simple regression case. This can be generalised to multiple regression. The concept of LAD estimation is no more difficult then the concept of OLS estimation. In fact it is simpler in so far as the absolute value of the residual is a more straightforward measure of the size of a residual than is the squared residual. In the actual calculation of the estimates, LAD is, however, more complicated. There are no formulas for the LAD estimates. Fortunately, there exist several algorithms for calculating them.

5. Method

We applied a log-log (also called log-linear) regression model in both the OLS and LAD cases. In this way, the data better conformed to the requirements of regression analysis, notably the homoscedasticity (equal variances of residuals) and linearity (in the parameters) requirements. We performed residual analysis combined with expert judgement to identify and remove outliers. The normality assumption of the residuals was tested using the Anderson-Darling normality test. The efficiency of the models was assessed primarily by the t-values of the coefficients. We also assessed prediction accuracy by means of MMRE and MdMRE since these evaluation metrics are widely applied and reported in software engineering. To calculate MMRE from the residuals of the log-log models, we back-transformed the residuals of the log-log models using the following formulas.

$$originalresidual = (1 - e^{-residual}) * actual\_effort$$

$$MRE = \left| \frac{originalresidual}{actual\_effort} \right|$$

6. Results

The OLS model using all 87 cases is given in Table 2, and the OLS model after removal of six outliers, i.e. using 81 cases, is given in Table 3.

In the latter OLS model, the normality test suggests the distribution of residuals is normal. See Figure 1. (P-value=0.5 of the Anderson-Darling normality test). There are no extreme outliers. (All standardised residuals are less than 2). There is no significant multicollinearity (VIF<=2, not reported). All predictor variables are significant (p<0.01). R2(adj) is 72%. The residuals are reasonably homoscedastic and linear (Plot of residuals vs. fits. Not reported.)

The LAD regression equation is given in Table 4. All 87 cases were used. Comparing the t-values of Table 2 (87 cases OLS model) and Table 4 (LAD), we observe that the OLS model seems slightly more efficient. The OLS t-values are somewhat higher for three out of four variables. Next, comparing the t-values of Table 3 (81 cases OLS model) and Table 4 (LAD), we observe that the OLS model with outliers removed is seems even more efficient than the LAD model. The OLS t-values are higher for all four variables. We observe, however, that the LAD model mostly confirms the OLS model although LAD casts some doubt about one predictor variable, Sites. Applying more than one model is therefore a useful quality assurance when one is unsure whether the model is correct or not.

LAD would be superior if the distribution of residuals is leptokurtic (high kurtosis). From Figure 1, we observe that kurtosis for the 81 cases OLS model is low (0.5). We therefore have no good reasons to believe that LAD is more efficient than OLS. Also, the t-values do not indicate that LAD is more efficient than OLS. Rather, the contrary seems to be the case. However, we cannot therefore conclude the opposite. OLS is not necessarily more efficient than LAD just because we found that its t-values are higher on this single sample. This result may be due to chance. To conclude that OLS is more efficient than LAD (or vice versa), one would have to carry out some test. Unfortunately, we are not aware of any useful tests to compare the efficiency of two regression models.

Table 2. OLS model results - 87cases

Predictor	Coef	SE Coef	T	P
Constant	4.65	0.39	11.9	0.000
LN(Users)	0.234	0.083	2.80	0.006
LN(Sites)	0.162	0.072	2.24	0.028
LN(Interfaces)	0.359	0.077	4.68	0.000
LN(Modules)	0.785	0.214	3.67	0.000
		R2(adj)	60%	

Table 3. OLS model results - 81 cases

Predictor	Coef	SE Coef	T	P
Constant	4.85	0.30	16.3	0.000
LN(Users)	0.275	0.063	4.35	0.000
LN(Sites)	0.153	0.055	2.77	0.007
LN(Interfaces)	0.289	0.058	4.94	0.000
LN(Modules)	0.732	0.164	4.46	0.000
		R2(adj)	72%	

Table 4. LAD model results - 87 cases

Predictor	Coef	SE Coef	T
Constant	4.79	0.44	10.8
LN(Users)	0.277	0.094	2.94
LN(Sites)	0.104	0.081	1.28
LN(Interfaces)	0.348	0.087	4.00
LN(Modules)	0.660	0.242	2.73

Table 5. Effort prediction accuracy of OLS and LAD models

	N	MMRE	MdMRE
OLS	87	0.81	0.40
OLS	81	0.48	0.36
LAD	87	0.82	0.38

In terms of MMRE and MdMRE prediction accuracy, the results in Table 5 suggest that the OLS (81 cases) model performs somewhat better. In terms of MdMRE, the differences are not significant, though. However, by removing six outliers one may be falsely lead into the belief that the prediction accuracy is higher than it really is. Comparing OLS-87 and OLS-81 illustrates this issue. Were we completely sure that the six removed observations were wild values, it would be safe to remove them and conclude based on the OLS-81 results. Unfortunately, we are not *that* sure they should be removed. We have had no way to find out whether the values of these six projects are due to erroneous reporting or if they just were projects that performed extremely bad or well, or if it is a combination. Regarding measurement errors, there is always an amount of it in this kind of projects, and it is hard to decide how large measurement errors are just too large.

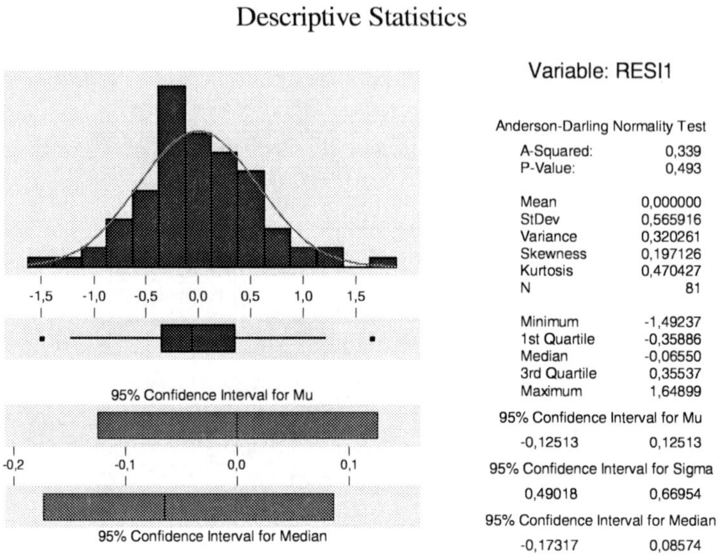

Figure 1. Summary statistics of residual for OLS model - 81 cases

7. Conclusions

The main purpose of this study was to investigate empirically if LAD is more efficient than OLS on ERP data. We used a data set of 87 ERP projects. A priori, we expected LAD to be more efficient than OLS on this data set based on expert knowledge of the ERP data and an initial visual inspection of the data. It seemed to indicate a bit messy data with a relatively large fraction of outliers. Thus, we suspected that the distribution of residuals might exhibit heavy tails (high kurtosis). This was one reason for investigating LAD. The other reason is that it generally is difficult to decide when to remove or not to remove an observation because an unusual observation may be due to either measurement errors or simply due to an unusually good or bad project, or a combination of the two. With LAD, it does not matter as much as with OLS whether an outlier is removed or not. Thus, in circumstances when one does not have sufficient in-depth knowledge to distinguish wild values (e.g. punching errors) from extreme projects (high performers or low performers), LAD may be safer to use than OLS.

Regarding the results, we found that LAD does not seem more efficient than OLS. Rather, the results weakly suggest that OLS may be more efficient. It is, however, not enough evidence in this investigation to conclude in either direction. By creating just one single estimator (and not a distribution of estimators), it is to some extent arbitrary which model is closest to the truth and therefore deemed "best".

We also found that LAD mostly confirmed the initial OLS prediction model in terms of predictor variables and the order of magnitude of the regression coefficients. Using LAD (or another method) as a "second opinion" is therefore useful to validate the model specification.

We agree completely with Pickard et al. [7] stating that "no single analysis technique is the best in all circumstances, and [] it is the nature of the dataset that determines which is the best analysis technique. Thus, we believe it is important to identify which technique to use in which circumstances."

Acknowledgements

This work was partly financed by Accenture's (formerly Andersen Consulting) Research Fund in Norway. Thank you Accenture!

8. References

[1] Briand, L.C. and Wieczorek, I., "Resource Estimation in Software Engineering", In: Encyclopedia of Software Engineering, Wiley, 2000.

[2] Jeffery, R., Ruhe, M. and Wieczorek I., "Using Public Domain Metrics to Estimate Software Development Effort", Forthcoming in Proc. METRICS 2001, IEEE Computer Society, 2001.

[3] Gray, A.R. and MacDonell, S.G, "Software Metrics Data Analysis - Exploring the Relative Performance of Some Commonly Used Modeling Techniques", Empirical Software Engineering, 4, 1999, pp.297-316.

[4] Miyazaki, Y., Terakado, M., Ozaki, K. and Nozaki, H., "Robust Regression for Developing Software Estimation Models", Journal of Systems and Software. Vol. 27, 1994, pp. 3-16.

[5] Myrtveit, I. and Stensrud, E., "A Controlled Experiment to Assess the Benefits of Estimating with Analogy and Regression Models", IEEE Trans. Software Eng., 25, 4, Jul/Aug 1999, pp. 510-525.

[6] Nesi, P., and Querci,T., "Effort Estimation and Prediction for Object-Oriented Systems", Journal of Systems and Software, vol. 42, 1998, pp. 89-102.

[7] Pickard, L., Kitchenham, B. and Linkman, S., "An Investigation of Analysis Techniques for Software Datasets", Proc. METRICS 99 Symposium, IEEE Computer Society, 1999, pp. 130-142.

[8] Stensrud, E. and Myrtveit, I., "Human Performance Estimating with Analogy and Regression Models: An Empirical Validation", Proc. METRICS'98, IEEE Computer Society, Nov 1998, pp. 205-213.

[9] Stensrud, E., "Estimating with enhanced object points vs. function points", Proc. COCOMO'13, Eds. B. Boehm, and R. Madachy, Univ. Southern California, Los Angeles CA, 1998.

BRACE: BootstRap based Analogy Cost Estimation: Automated support for an enhanced effort prediction method

Ioannis Stamelos, Lefteris Angelis, Evangelos Sakellaris

Abstract

Estimation by analogy is a technique that has been proposed since a long time as a valid alternative to algorithmic cost estimation and expert judgement. On the other hand, it is widely accepted that public domain software cost estimation techniques need to be calibrated, i.e. properly adjusted, to historical project data, in order to produce accurate estimates for new projects. Another important requirement for any modern cost estimation method is the ability to produce interval estimates, not mere point estimates. Statistical simulation techniques may be used for both purposes. The paper presents BRACE, a software tool that supports the practical application of the analogy based method using a simulation approach, namely bootstrap.

1. Introduction

Estimation by analogy is a technique that has been recognised since a long time as a valid alternative to expert judgement and algorithmic cost estimation. However, only recently ([10]) it has been presented in the form of a detailed estimation methodology and has been applied uniformly on a number of cost data sets.

The main aspect of the method is the utilisation of historical information from completed projects with known effort. Initially, it is necessary to characterise the new active project, with attributes identical to the ones of the completed projects registered in the database. Examples of project attributes are source code length, programming language and personnel experience. Attributes are distinguished as quantitative (such as source code length, measured in number of programming language instructions) or qualitative (such as personnel experience, measured in an ordinal scale with values, "low", "medium" and "high"). The form of the historical data set along with the new project can be seen in Table 1.

Table 1: Characterisation of an active project and its placement into a historical data set

	Actual Effort	Attribute 1	Attribute 2	...	Attribute k
Project 1	E_1	X_{11}	X_{12}	...	X_{1k}
Project 2	E_2	X_{21}	X_{22}	...	X_{2k}
Project 3	E_2	X_{31}	X_{32}	...	X_{3k}
....	...	...	...	...	...
Project n	E_n	X_{n1}	X_{n2}	...	X_{nk}
New Project	Unknown	Y_1	Y_2	...	Y_k

A basic notion is the *distance* between two projects. Distance measures how dissimilar the two projects are in terms of their attributes. A distance metric is used, based on the standardised values of the k attributes for these projects. The most known such distance metric is the *Euclidean* or *straight-line distance* which has a straightforward geometrical meaning as the distance of two points in the k-dimensional Euclidean space:

$$d_{new,i} = \left\{ \sum_{j=1}^{k} (Y_j - X_{ij})^2 \right\}^{1/2} , \quad i = 1, 2, \ldots, n$$

Other possible distance metrics are the *Minkowski distance,* the *Canberra distance*, the *Czekanowski coefficient* and the *Chebychev or «Maximum» distance* (see [3] for definitions). The Minkowski distance is provided as another example:

$$d_{new,i} = \left\{ \sum_{j=1}^{k} \left| Y_j - X_{ij} \right|^{\lambda} \right\}^{1/\lambda} \quad \text{where } \lambda \text{ is an integer, } i = 1, 2, \ldots, n.$$

Although the distance metrics require numerical data, it is possible to use them even for qualitative attributes. For example, if the j-th variable is ordinal or nominal, the term $Y_j - X_{ij}$ in the previous expressions can be calculated according to the formula:

$$Y_j - X_{ij} = \begin{cases} 1 & \text{if } X_{ij} \neq Y_j \\ 0 & \text{if } X_{ij} = Y_j \end{cases}$$

The estimation of the effort using analogies is based on the completed projects that are similar to the new one. The user of the method has to calculate the distances of the new project from all the database projects and identify few «neighbour» projects, i.e. those with relatively small distance value. The estimation of the effort is eventually obtained by some combination of the efforts of the neighbour projects. Typically, the statistic used is the mean (weighted or simple) or the median of these effort values. Missing values require further adjustment by the method of analogies. Since the relationship between effort and size is well established, the statistic may also be adjusted using the neighbour project size ([14]). For example, in the case of one neighbour, *linear size adjustment* is performed by the following formula:

$$EFFORT_{NEW} = \frac{SIZE_{NEW}}{SIZE_{NEIGHBOUR}} \times EFFORT_{NEIGHBOUR}$$

The calibration of the analogy-based method requires the detection of the best configuration of the available method options. The options that may be adjusted are (a) the distance metric by which the projects of the database will be sorted according to their similarity to the one under estimation (e.g. *Euclidean distance, Manhattan distance)*, (b) the number of closest projects (analogies), (c) the set of attributes for judging analogy, and (d) the statistic that will be computed from the efforts of the closest projects and will serve as estimation for the unknown effort. In addition, the statistic may be size-adjusted, as described above.

2. The bootstrap method

The method of analogies, as proposed in [10] and implemented in the *ANGEL* tool ([11]), foresees a method-tuning phase focusing on the search of the appropriate project attributes for the estimation procedure. The method also results in a *"point estimation"* for the unknown effort, i.e. a single value, which is computed from a particular sample (the historical data set) coming from a practically infinite population with unknown characteristics, i.e. the population of all possible software projects. A critical question is how valid the tuning activity may be and which is the accuracy and reliability of the generated estimation. In these cases, it is common practice to enhance the value of the point estimation with various measures of accuracy from its probability distribution. As the underlying probability distribution is unknown, we are constrained to use an empirical distribution in order to calculate accuracy measures. This can be achieved using statistical simulation techniques.

We will next describe briefly the bootstrap method, a simulation technique applicable in two different modes, namely the non-parametric and the parametric bootstrap. The first method is based entirely on the empirical distribution of the data set, without any assumption on the population distribution. The second method is based on the assumption that the data set comes from a theoretical distribution, which is approximated by a parametric model such as the normal distribution. A detailed account of the principles and the applications of the method can be found in [6].

The *non-parametric bootstrap* method is applied when we use a random sample of size n to estimate a certain parameter (in our case the effort of a new project) by a statistic which is calculated independently from the order of the sample. The idea is to draw a large number (say B) of samples from the original sample *with replacement* and to calculate the statistic for each one of these samples. By "sampling with replacement" we mean the procedure where a random number generator independently selects integers $j_1, j_2, \cdots, j_n$, each of which equals any value between 1 and n with probability $1/n$. These integers determine which members of the original sample are selected to participate in the new bootstrap sample. An obvious consequence of this sampling method is that in every new bootstrap sample there are data points, which appear more than once while others do not appear at all.

The *parametric bootstrap* differs in the way of sampling. Instead of sampling with replacement from the original data points, we draw B samples of size n (same size as in the original data) from a theoretical distribution that is assumed to have generated the data. Therefore, we need first to investigate the possibility that a known distribution (univariate or multivariate, according to our data) fits in a satisfactory way our original sample. Then, applying the appropriate algorithm we can generate random samples from this distribution. It is obvious that the parametric bootstrap is applicable only in cases where there is prior knowledge about the form of the underlying distribution.

The most common measures of accuracy that can be obtained from the bootstrap samples are the standard error, the bias (an indication of whether the produced estimation is an overestimation or underestimation of the unknown effort) and the confidence intervals (see [3]). In our case, the projects in the database are the data points that provide the bootstrap samples. Since the statistical inference based on the non-parametric bootstrap depends solely on the available sample, without any assumptions about the form of the underlying population, the method is particularly useful for data sets that are small and contain non-homogeneous data, a common situation for a software project cost data set. On the other hand, the parametric bootstrap is useful in cases where some knowledge about the form of the underlying population is available.

3. The BRACE software tool

The authors have implemented a software tool, called *BRACE* (BootstRap based Analogy Cost Estimation), that supports the practical application of the analogy based method using the bootstrap sampling method described above. In the first version of BRACE we have implemented only non-parametric bootstrap. Bootstrap is used for two purposes: first in order to calibrate the method of analogies choosing the optimal options (distance metric, number of analogies, statistic, size adjustment) and second to assess the accuracy of the estimations obtained by the method.

The tool provides a flexible interface that allows the user to experiment with the different calibration options. The main functions of BRACE are:

1. Typical input/output functions and file management facilities
2. Definition of attributes and project characterisation
3. Project/attribute management (e.g. exclusion of projects/attributes from calculations)
4. Choice of options to be considered for method calibration (with and without bootstrap)
5. Determination of the best attribute set (the one providing the better accuracy results according to some criterion)
6. Generation of estimations for a single project (with and without bootstrap)

In the calibration phase, the tool works on a data set of historical projects. It estimates each project's effort in turn using the other projects to find analogies (jack-knife). Accuracy is determined in terms of the MMRE and Pred(25) criteria ([5]). After the calibration phase the tool may estimate new projects using the method configuration that was found to be the best. Figure 1 provides a screenshot of BRACE with calibration results using bootstrap. The best configuration (i.e. the one producing the lowest mean MMRE value) consists of the Manhattan distance, size adjustment and one analogy.

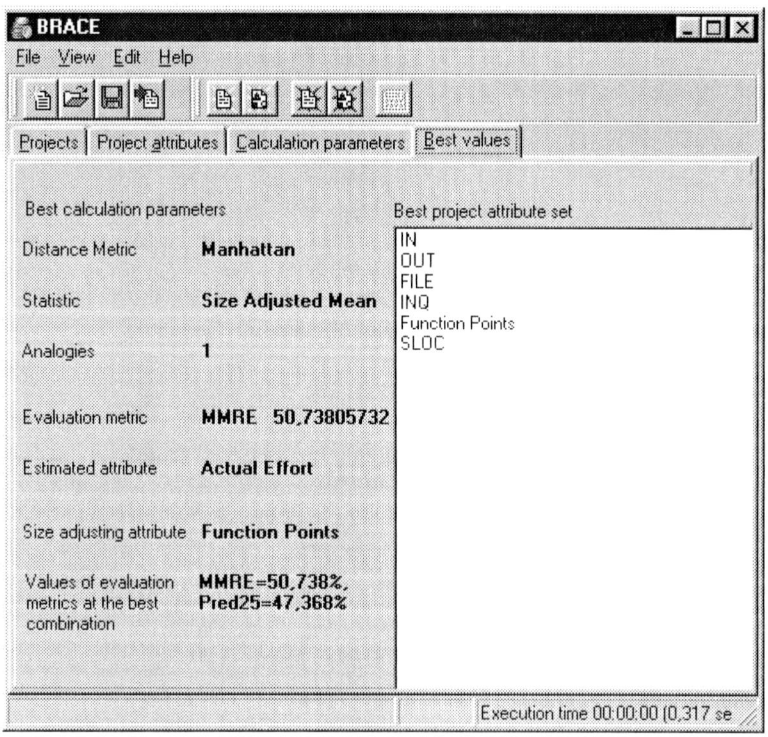

Figure 1. A screenshot of BRACE showing the results of a calibration session.

As an example of estimation, consider a real project that was measured using function points. Its size was found to be 216 FP with actual effort 2422 man-hours. The calibration phase found that the best configuration for the data set to which the project belongs was Minkowski distance with $\lambda = 3$, size adjustment and one analogy. The application of BRACE gave a prediction of 2322 hours with a 95% confidence interval ranging from 1232 to 2684. Considering the prediction of 2322 hours, the estimation error is approximately 4% with respect to the actual effort. The bootstrap procedure provides a probability distribution for our estimate. -The histogram in Figure 2, obtained as another output of BRACE, shows that the most probable estimate lies in the range 2000-2500 (65,1% probability), with a significant probability (23,1%) assigned to the range 2500-3000 and a much smaller probability (10,8%) assigned to the range 1000-1500. Practically this means that if a budget corresponding to 2700 man-hours were allocated for the project, cost overruns would have been avoided with an estimated probability of 99%.

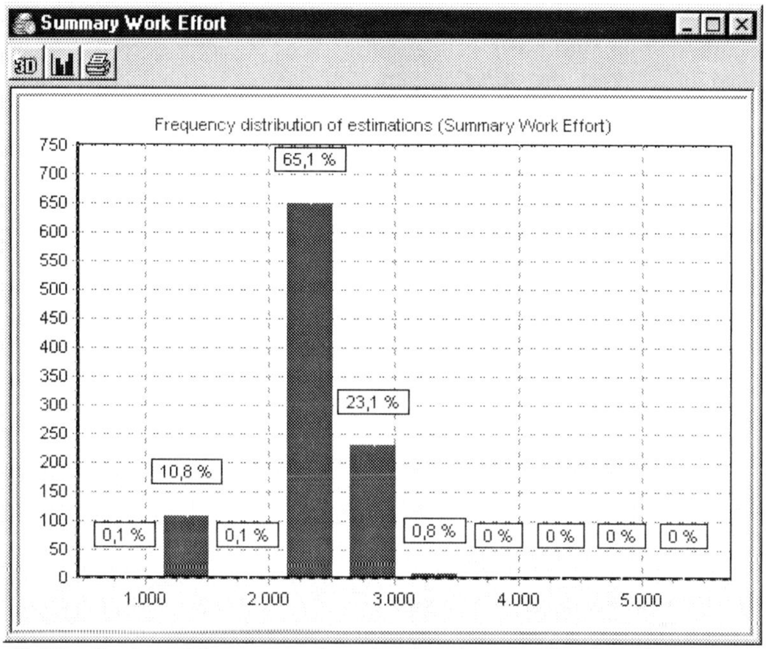

Figure 2. Distribution of the analogy-based estimation resulting from bootstrap samples

4. Preliminary Results and Future Work

BRACE was applied on various known data sets, in order both to evaluate the tool options and facilities and also to experiment with the analogy method. The tool has been tested on the Albrecht ([2]) and Abran & Robillard ([1]) data sets in order to reproduce the results reported in [3]. Next, the tool was applied experimentally to the data coming from the International Software Benchmarking Standards Group (ISBSG) data set ([7]).

The results that other researchers obtained using ANGEL (e.g. [8]) revealed that analogy does not always perform as publicised. This finding is an indication that analogy should be used with care and after a sufficient calibration procedure. In addition, the availability of large project data sets, such as the ISBSG database, poses a number of research issues in the area of analogy-based estimation. Some of these questions rising during a software cost estimation study are:

1. When should analogy be used?
2. Which historical projects (subset of the entire data set) should be used for analogy?
3. Which attributes should be taken into account?
4. Which trade-offs should be made between number of projects and number of attributes (when, for example, missing values may prohibit the use of certain projects or attributes)?
5. Should we use analogy in combination with some other cost method?
6. Which additional problems arise when the majority of the attributes are qualitative ([4])?

We are planning an explorative case study with the help of BRACE in order to investigate these open issues. We have already performed a preliminary case study concerning the application of analogy using BRACE on projects delivering information systems for the industry ([13]). We selected a sub-set from the ISBSG data set concerning manufacturing, logistics and inventory projects and we tried different estimation strategies. The best results were obtained by a strategy that aimed at a trade-off between the number of projects in the data set and the attributes used for the calculation of project distance. The MMRE and PRED(25) values were 23,84% and 70,37% respectively, revealing the potentiality of the analogy method.

Another interesting aspect of software cost estimation that can be explored with BRACE is the estimation of entire project portfolios. Kitchenham and Linkman in [9] have already emphasised the need for estimation of many projects in parallel. Stamelos and Angelis in [12] have shown how to assemble individually obtained estimates into a composite estimate for the entire portfolio employing bootstrap and Monte Carlo simulation. It would be interesting to apply such approach on the ISBSG data set and assess the precision of estimating artificial project portfolios composed from the available data base projects.

Finally, it would be interesting to explore hybrid estimation strategies, combining analogy with other estimation techniques such as least squares regression or regression trees. Such approach could be achieved through the generation of project clusters within the entire project data set. Then the strategy should identify which method gives best results for each one of the clusters.

We must emphasise that even with the assistance of BRACE, the analyst must make certain decisions when, for example, the computational complexity of examining all possible combinations between analogy options and attributes is prohibitively high. However, the existence of software tools such as BRACE is essential both for the successful application of the analogy method and for the exploration of new ideas.

5. References

[1] Abran, A. and Robillard, P.N., "Function point analysis: An empirical study of its measurement processes", IEEE Trans. on Software Engineering, 1996, pp. 895-909.

[2] Albrecht, A.J. and Gaffney, J.E., "Software function, source lines of code, and development effort prediction: a software science validation", IEEE Trans., 1983, pp. 639-648.

[3] Angelis, L. and Stamelos, I., "A Simulation Tool for Efficient Analogy Based Cost Estimation", Empirical Software Engineering, 2000, pp. 35-68.

[4] Angelis, L., Stamelos, I. and Morisio, M., "Building a Software Cost Estimation Model Based on Categorical Data", in 8th IEEE International Symposium on Software Metrics Proceedings, London, 2001.

[5] Conte, S., Dunsmore, H. and Shen, V.Y., "Software Engineering Metrics and Models", Benjamin Cummings, Menlo Park, Calif., 1986.

[6] Efron, B. and Tibshirani, R., "An Introduction to the Bootstrap", Chapman and Hall, New York, 1993.
[7] ISBSG, internet site http://www.isbsg.org.au.
[8] Jeffery, R., Ruhe, M., and Wieczorek, I., "A Comparative Study of Two Software Development Cost Modelling Techniques Using Multi-organisational and Company-specific Data", Information and Software Technology, 2000, pp. 1009-1016.
[9] Kitchenham, B. and Linkman, S., "Estimates, Uncertainty and Risk", IEEE Software, 1997, pp. 69-74.
[10] Shepperd, M. J. and Schofield, C., "Estimating Software Project Effort Using Analogies", IEEE Transactions on Software Engineering, 1997, pp. 736-743.
[11] Shepperd, M. J., Schofield, C. and Kitchenham, B.A., "Effort Estimation Using Analogy", in 18th Intl. Conf. On Softw. Eng. proceedings, Berlin, 1996.
[12] Stamelos, I. and Angelis, L., "Managing Uncertainty in Project Portfolio Estimation", submitted.
[13] Stamelos, I., L. Angelis, G. Bleris, M. Morisio, E. Sakellaris, "Controlling the Custom Software Development Cost of Information Systems for the Supply Chain: a Case Study", submitted.
[14] Walkerden, F. and Jeffery, R., "An Empirical Study of Analogy-based Software Effort Estimation", Empirical Software Engineering, 1999, pp. 135-158.

Measuring Change Requests to support effective project management practices.

Roberto Meli

Abstract

Some of the major reasons for software project failures relay in the area of the management of project objectives and requirements. In the actual "ever changing world", software requirements are subjected to continuous changes that might claim revisions of the allocated resources. Estimating effort, duration and costs from stable requirements is a difficult task, but estimating from "moving" requirements could simply be overwhelming. In a contractual market relationship between customer and supplier, the capability to measure Change Requests, for technical and managerial reasons, is critical and influences directly the Customer Satisfaction level as well as the profitability of the business for the Supplier. The standard IFPUG Function Point Analysis technique provides a mean to measure software from the external user point of view and is particularly effective in supporting contractual aspects. Unfortunately the original method is not satisfactory if applied to the Change Request measurement problem. This paper is focused on an operational approach to the functional measurement of Change Requests and on the related expected impact on the amount of additional effort and duration needed to implement them.

1. Introduction

There is a strong evidence [1] that some of the major reasons for software project failures relay in the area of the management of project objectives and requirements. This is still a software engineering field not yet adequately covered by standard methods, tools and widespread good practices. The main factors that negatively affect project outcomes are:

- User's problems are not adequately discovered, understood, described and communicated
- Project's goals are not adequately collected, stated, negotiated, approved, communicated and tested
- System Requirements are not adequately collected, described, negotiated, approved, communicated and tested
- Project resources are not estimated and/or allocated consistently with the goals, requirements and plan of activities established
- Goals and Requirements Changes are not adequately managed during the project life
- Resource allocation is not re-negotiated consistently with the accepted Change Requests

In the actual "ever changing world", software requirements are subjected to continuous changes for bad and good reasons. Examples of bad reasons are: stakeholder indecisions, poor requirement elicitation, changes in user's "taste", poor communications among the parties etc. Examples of good reasons are: the will to keep the system in touch with the evolving business, enhancement opportunities emerged during the project etc.

The real problem here is not that software requirements change during the life of a project, but that they usually change out of a framework of disciplined planning and control processes. If adequately managed, Change Requests (CR) may represent precious opportunities to achieve a better customer satisfaction and profitability. If not managed, instead, CR represent threats for the project success.

Since requirements are frequently subject to change, most of the Process Improvement frameworks include an effective requirements management process as a basic practice to be adopted by organizations that aim to improve the level of maturity of their software processes. To effectively manage CR the following conditions should be met:

- the organization should be familiar with project management culture, methods and systems;
- the organization should have in place a formal and well understood requirements management process;
- the (eventually internal) customer-supplier contractual approach should be consistent with a requirement management evolutionary framework – i.e. a freezed "budget to results" approach is not advisable;
- Change Requests should be measurable.

In the actual market conditions, developing a system just as it was stated in the original requirements documentation - in order to formally respect initial contracts and agreements - may lead to customer dissatisfaction, market share reduction, loss of future contracts etc. On the other hand, deciding to accept any single "fashion" driven CR might lead to continuous budget overruns and uncontrolled expenditure rates. What is really needed is a practical framework in which it should be possible to quickly understand the impact of any CR in term of technical aspects, duration of the change implementation, workloads, costs and benefits. Only knowing the previous information it would be possible to act on the basis of a priority based management system capable to support the identification of an adequate trade off between benefits and costs related to the eventual acceptance of a CR.

Many formal contracts include some terms to deal with the CR problem but they result inapplicable if it is not possible to measure the extent of any single CR. Subjectivity at the project level is usually considered negatively. Organizations need a more standardized and detailed approach in order to lessen (eliminating is not always possible) the subjectivity of judgement by means of a methodical appreciation of the basic factors involved.

Estimating effort, duration and costs from stable requirements is a difficult task but estimating from "moving" requirements could simply be overwhelming. In a contractual market relationship between customer and supplier, the capability to measure CR, for technical and managerial reasons, is critical and influences directly the Customer Satisfaction level as well as the profitability of the business for the Supplier.

2. Defining a Change Request

A Change Request is a set of one or more requirements related, in various way, to a set of existing requirements. A Change Request might concern an existing operational system, in which case is classified as a maintenance request, or it might concern a non-yet-developed system during one of its Life Cycle Phases preceding the delivery. Any "pure" CR may, then, be categorized as the need to:

- return the system in its correct operational state (corrective action);
- enhance the non-functional performance of the system (usability, maintainability, response time, user interface, use of resources, reliability etc.) leaving untouched the functionalities and data structures previously established (non-functional modification);
- enable the system to deliver the same functional capabilities in a changed technological environment (adaptive modification);
- extend or change the functional capabilities of the system (enhancement modification).

Many actual CR might be a mixture of "pure" CR types, but it should always be possible to distinguish logically the different components in order to treat them separately.

If we consider a software application from the functional (external) and technical (internal) point of view we may state that any CR affects the technical level but only some of them affect the functional level. This is because any change in the behaviour of the system must be reflected into the technical arrangements of software objects which implement the system (programs, modules, data tables, files, objects, GUI etc.). On the other hand only the last type of maintenance (enhancement maintenance) influences the functional features of the system adding, deleting or changing functionalities and/or data structures.

A CR is an issue strictly related to the Reuse subject, since any CR might be seen as the development of a new software "item" constructed on the basis of existing and partially adequate (or inadequate) software "items". "Reuse" is a word that could be attributed to two different software viewpoints: the logical organization and the technical organization. Both them are important and show a different aspect of reuse.

Functional reuse may be defined as the re-utilization of user recognizable and existent logical data structures and functionalities to build up new logical features. Depending on the particular architectural environment, we might have an extreme situation in which the functional reuse is very high but the technical capability of reusing existing "physical" software items is very low: we must re-build the desired logical item almost by scratch. This is the case, for example, when, in a multi level client-server architecture, we want to deliver a functionality logically similar to an existing one, but in a technical environment completely different from the original one.

Technical reuse may be defined as the re-utilization of existent physical data structures and software items (modules, objects, programs etc.) in order to build up new technical items to be used in the construction of new logical features. Depending on the particular functional requirements, we might have an extreme situation in which the functional reuse is very low but the technical capability of reusing existing "physical" software items is very high: we can build the desired new logical feature using almost effortlessly some existing technical "items". This is the case, for example, when we want to deliver a set of functionalities to manage (CRUD[1]) a number of logical files which are similar in structure (i.e. unique id.,

[1] Create, Read, Update and Delete

description, numerical values) but different in contents (i.e. money conversion table, time conversion table, length conversion table etc.).

Functional and Technical reuse may combine themselves in any possible way, as the figure shows here. The most significant savings due to a reuse strategy derive from the combination of both the reuse types.

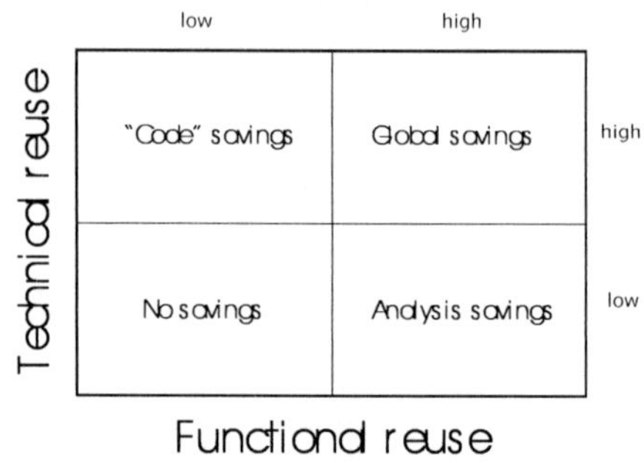

A CR may affect the system in two ways: it might require to create new logical functionalities or data structures and/or it might affect the way in which other logical functionalities or data structures are to be transformed. This means that starting from any CR directly related to a particular software item, we must conduct an impact analysis on the existing system components to understand the propagation of the change on the remaining structure: i.e. how many, which ones and how other functionalities and data structures are affected indirectly. An Impact Matrix like the one in figure below could be of some help in conducting this impact analysis. Any indirectly related object could be impacted in functional and/or technical terms.

	Changed or deleted		**New**		
Change Request	Func.1	Func.2	....	Func.n	Total CR
CR1	Effort	Effort	....	Effort	Effort
CR2	Effort	Effort	....	Effort	Effort
Total	Effort	Effort	....	Effort	Effort

In this paper we are interested only into the CR related to a not-yet-developed system seen as sources of deviation from the original contractual agreement established among the different project stakeholders. The key idea developed in the following sections of this document is to consider any CR originated during the different phases of a project life cycle as a maintenance request on a system partially constructed. In this manner we will be able to use the existing functional measurement approach proposed by the IFPUG FP Analysis for the Enhancement Count, specially tailored to a strongly "reuse" based development framework.

3. Functional measurement of Change Requests

How is it possible to quantify a CR in terms that are of interest in the customer-supplier relationship ? When should it be possible to claim a contract review in order to face with the excessive number and weight of CR ? How to prioritise the several CR that are issued to be incorporated in the system specifications ?

The standard IFPUG Function Point Analysis technique[2] [2] provides a mean to measure software from the external point of view (user view) and is particularly effective in supporting customer-supplier relationships [3] [4]. In a contractual context, indeed, any customer is not directly interested into a specific quantity of code (whatever it is defined) but in the resolution of his/her problems and, eventually, in the acquisition of the logical software features that are promised to be resolutive of those problems. For this reasons s/he will be interested into a measurement of the logical features more than of the technical aspects of the system. Logical features are much more related to user needs than technical features. The customer will tend to compare suppliers in term of capability in releasing logical functionalities and performances irrespective of technical issues (unless they represent established constraints). Function Point Analysis is commonly considered as a Functional Measurement Method. This

[2] See the appendix for a short introduction.

means that a Function Point measurement is related more to the "what" than to the "how" of a software system.

Unfortunately the standard IFPUG method (Counting Practices Manual - CPM rel. 4.0 or 4.1) is not resolutive with respect to the Change Request problem. In the latest revision of the CPM, the scope creep is defined as the "additional functionality that was not specified in the original requirements" and later on is written "It is essential to update application counts upon completion of the project. If the functionality changes during development, the function point count at the end of the life cycle should accurately reflect the full functionality delivered to the user." Unfortunately this approach is adequate only if we are concerned with an application type count (i.e. a quantification of the software organizational asset), but it is completely useless if we are interested into the measurement of the "quantity" of changes requested and incorporated into the system at all the development stages. If we measure the "scope creep" in terms of the difference between the final count and the initial one, we might incur in a situation where both them are equal to - let's say - 1000 FP but, for example, 50% of them (500 FP) were counted from completely different requirements found at the initial stage and at the delivery stage. Apparently there is no scope creep, no increase in functionality whereas we have probably almost doubled the cost of realization !

The solution that is proposed in this paper is to measure CR that are issued during the development stage as if they were maintenance requests asked on a system as it was finished and correcting then the measurements by some adjustment factors to keep in account the level of reuse that it could be assumed as applicable and/or the waste of effort due to the changed or abandoned requirements. The final CRFP (Change Request Function Point) measure could then be used to derive ratios or indicators for the changing environment. The CRFP may be derived for any type of software project conceived in the IFPUG FPA: new development or enhancement maintenance.

In order to count the CRFP measure for any software project it is needed an initial count that would correspond to the initial view of the functionalities and data structures that will be delivered by the project at the end of its execution. This will be assumed as the starting point and the baseline for the evaluation of the CR. Every time a single relevant CR or a set of CR are issued, they will be analysed in terms of functional impacts they have on the baseline as if they were enhancement requests on an already developed system using the following formula[3]:

$$CRFP = ADD + \Sigma_i (CHGA_i * CL_i * LCP) + CFP + \Sigma_i (DEL_i * CL_i * LCP)$$

where:

ADD are all the contributions from EI,EO,EQ,ILF,EIF that are added in the baseline if the CR is to be incorporated into the system;

CFP (Conversion FP) are all the contributions from EI,EO,EQ,ILF,EIF that are needed only once if the CR is to be incorporated into the system;

$CHGA_i$ (Changed after) is any single contribution from an EI,EO,EQ,ILF,EIF that is already present in the baseline and that will be changed if the CR is to be incorporated into the system; the numerical value corresponds to the complexity as it will be after the proposed change; it should be considered that, if the functionality was already present in the baseline and the CR is issued in an intermediate phase of the life cycle, there should be some semi

[3] In this paper we assume that the Value Adjustment Factor of the standard IFPUG method is not used any more since it is destined to disappear in the future to allow a compliance with the ISO standards on Functional Size Measurement Methods.

finished product that could be reutilized in order to produce the modified logical functionality; this is why the weight of any single modified EI,EO,EQ,ILF,EIF is corrected with the following two factors;

CL_i (Change Level) is a number between 0 and 1 representing the relative amount of logical change required on a particular functionality (EI,EO,EQ,ILF,EIF) already present in the baseline, if the CR is to be incorporated into the system; a CL_i close to 0 is associated to a situation where the proposed changes are impacting in a marginal way the existent functionality; a CL_i close to 1 is associated to a situation where almost nothing could be reused to implement the change. To reduce subjectivity in assigning change levels it is possible to refer to [5].

LCP (Life Cycle Progress) is a number between 0 and 1 representing the relative weight of the life cycle phase of the project in which the CR is issued; this corrective factor is needed to adequately keep in account the fact that changing a requirement when it has been completely realized is a lot different than changing it when it has only been elicited and almost no work has been already done on it.

After any particular CR has been accepted and incorporated to development then the Baseline Project Count should be updated using the standard IFPUG approach. Any new CR should be measured using the same technique described previously starting from the revised baseline.

At the end of the project, summing all the partial CRFP so far computed will produce the general measurement of CR issued to the project. In formula:

$$CRFP = \Sigma_j CRFP_j$$

If normalized to the total number of FP delivered by the project, this functional measurement of CR might be used, for example, to demonstrate the need to review some contractual terms and conditions. The Requirement Turnover Index may be conceived as:

$$RTI = [(\Sigma_j CRFP_j)/ FP] * 100$$

The CRFP measurement so defined is not particularly suggested to be used in order to estimate the additional effort required to deal with the CR. The following chapter is devoted to this aspect. The functional measurement of CR is a good mean to achieve and demonstrate an adequate comprehension of the very nature of the project "turbulence" and of the extent of some of its risks.

4. Effort, time and cost estimation related to Change Requests

How can a reasonable assessment of the impact caused by modifications to a project's requirements be made when they are required during the work? It must first be specified that this paper does not intend to deal with the technical aspects regarding changes in structure or functionality of the software application, but with the consequences in terms of resources use that the variation demands may bring.

Let us then assume that, after an initial definition of the requirements for a software project, the functionalities and data structures are classified using the FPA method. The result of applying this technique is therefore a Function Point initial count of the functional size of the software application to be developed. Using appropriate productivity and cost models connected to the specific development environment, we can forecast the project's effort, duration, and cost. Budget and deadlines can then be assigned in line with requirements, and the project can start on its way.

However, after a certain period of time, the stakeholders require important changes to the requirements, which necessitate revising both the functional and technical design and the project's work plan. At this point, how are we to evaluate whether resources have been correctly allocated or, if the original budget is maintained, whether the associated risk is increased or diminished?

It is necessary to obtain a new Function Point count for the new requirements configuration. Using this count with the same productivity models employed before, we obtain new time, effort, and cost forecasts. These forecasts, however, will regard a project as if it were starting from zero. Actually, since the requirements were modified while the work was in progress, the project has already committed a portion of those resources and yielded a portion of its results. The problem, therefore, is to obtain an assessment of the project's so-called "forecasts to complete," which is to say an estimate only of the resources needed starting from the moment the variation is made. The Earned Value (EV) technique is used to obtain this result. EV, a value that can be calculated at any time in the project's lifetime, is a cumulative indicator, which means that it outlines within itself the project's past history. It integrates the measurements of purpose, cost, and scheduling. Its proper definition is as follows: Earned Value is the budget value of the work actually accomplished at the date of reference (generally termed Time Now – TN). To use Earned Value properly, we must introduce the following terms:

- The budgeted cost, also called the budgeted cost of work scheduled (BCWS), is that portion of the approved cost estimate planned to be spent on the activity during a given period.
- The actual cost, also called the actual cost of work performed (ACWP), is the total cost incurred in accomplishing work on the activity during a given period.
- The earned value, also called the budgeted cost of work performed (BCWP), is a percentage of the total budget equal to the percentage of the work actually completed.

These three values are used in combination to provide measures of whether or not work is being accomplished as planned. The most commonly used measures are the cost variance (CV = BCWP – ACWP), the schedule variance (SV = BCWP – BCWS), and the cost performance index (CPI = BCWP / ACWP). The cumulative CPI (the sum of all individual BCWPs divided by the sum of all individual ACWPs) is widely used to forecast project cost at completion. In some application areas, the schedule performance index (SPI = BCWP / BCWS) is used to forecast the project completion date.

In substance, EV or BCWP represent the amount of resources in the original plan that have theoretically been consumed because they regard activities already performed or under way, regardless of how many resources that have actually been consumed, that is of the actual data. Comparing the BCWP and ACWP may permit us to know, in brief, whether the project is spending more or less than forecast, accomplished work being equal. On the other hand, comparing BCWP and BCWS may enable us to know, in brief, whether the project is early or late with respect to the original plans. It is not our purpose to illustrate this technique in detail, which can be learned elsewhere. [6]

The important thing, here, is to observe that if we remove the BCWP, calculated at the moment of revision, from the new estimate we have obtained following the variation of requirements (New Budget At Completion: NBAC), we will have a forecast "to completion" for the resources needed by the project, which may be "corrected" with an indicator of the degree of efficiency reached up to that moment (ACWP/BCWP). In effect, we must also consider that, of the work already accomplished (BCWP), a portion may still be valid even after the change in requirements, while another will be entirely useless because it will regard requirements that have been abandoned or modified. This can be taken into account by multiplying the BCWP by a percentage, R, which indicates the possible degree of reuse of the work already accomplished. To estimate R, we may ask ourselves the following question: "How much of the work already accomplished can be reused even after the requirements are changed?" If we can give this question a percentage value (for example, we believe that the work is 80% recoverable), the value to be subtracted from the new total forecast to obtain the final forecast will be 80% of the BCWP.

The following graphic may be of assistance for illustrating the proper analysis procedure. Even if the graphical arrangement is not accurate (for sake of simplicity), the relative positions of the curves are correct. The symbols used in the graphic are as follows: "a" is the curve for absorbing resources provided for in the original plan; "b" is the earned value curve; "c" is the curve for the new budget assessment after the requirements are changed; and "d" is the curve for the actual values and the budgets and forecasts for completion.

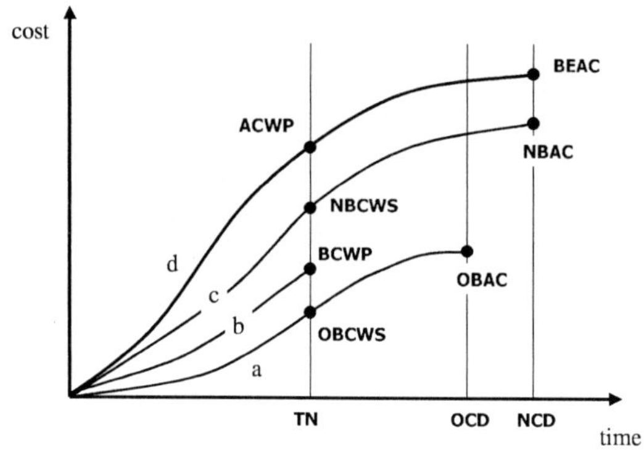

- ACWP represents the expenses actually incurred up to TN.
- NBCWS (New Budgeted Cost of Work Scheduled) is the new forecast of resource use at TN – that is, after the requirements are revised.
- BCWP represents the Earned Value calculated at TN, with reference to the original plan.
- OBCWS (Old Budgeted Cost of Work Scheduled) is the original forecast of resource use at TN.
- OBAC (Old Budget At Completion) is the total expense forecast of the original budget.
- NCD(New Completion Date) is the new project completion date.
- OCD (Old Completion Date) is the old project completion date.

Now then, the final forecast (Budget Estimated At Completion: BEAC) is given by the following formula:

BEAC = ACWP + (NBAC – BCWP*R) * (ACWP/BCWP)

The budget may then be suitably revised upon implementing the new requirements and for the productive behaviour shown up by the project up to that point.

In a contractual environment, where the actual behaviour of the project in terms of efficiency is not of interest for the customer (the risk is on the supplier), the only additional cost (AC) due to the Change Request may be calculated as:

$$AC = (NBAC - OBAC) + (1-R)\ BCWP$$

Where the last term [(1–R) BCWP] is the amount of work that will be wasted due to the CR implementation.

5. Conclusions

Change Requests represent opportunities and threats for any software project. Opportunities since their implementation allows the system to be more coherent with the users expectations and business needs. Threats since they could represent a source of waste and troubles to the project if not well managed. Two main questions arise to the attention: how to measure CR and the Requirement Turnover in a software project and how to predict the impact of a CR to the project budget, effort, duration and risk. This paper has tried to suggest answers to both the critical questions mentioned.

6. References

[1] The Standish Group - CHAOS: A Recipe for Success – 2000 http://standishgroup.com/visitor/chaos.htm

[2] IFPUG, "Counting Practices Manual rel. 4.1", International Function Point Users Group, 1999

[3] Meli, R - «Software reuse as a potential factor of database contamination for benchmarking in Function Points» - ISBSG workshop – Feb 12 1998 – Roma

[4] Meli, R - Functional and technical software measurement: conflict or integration ? – FESMA 2000 - Madrid

[5] "Function Point Analysis for Software Enhancement" - © NESMA, 2000 – www.nesma.org

[6] Project Management Institute – PMBOK : Project Management Body of Knowledge – www.pmi.org

[7] Poulin, Jeffrey S. – Measuring Software Reuse – Addison Wesley - 1997

7. Appendix: overview of the IFPUG Function Point Analysis

FP (Function Points) is a functional measurement method which is suitable for quantifying a software application from the user point of view.

The basic steps involved in function point counting include:

- Determine type of count (can be a new development project, an application/ base count or an enhancement project count).
- Identify the application scope and boundary (i.e., what transactions and logical files are included in the measurement?)
- Count the data function types: a) Internal Logical Files or ILFs, which are logical data groups maintained within the application boundary, and b) External Interface Files or EIFs, which are used only for reference by the application.
- Count the transactional function types: a) External Inputs or EIs, which are data entry processes, b) External Outputs or EOs, for example, reports, and c) External Queries or EQs, for example, browse order details. Several simple matrices based on data element types - DET (user recognizable, non-recursive data fields), together with record element types - RET (subsets of user recognizable data) or file types referenced – FTR (number of logical data groupings required to complete a process) are used to determine the complexity of each function as Low, Average or High.

	Low	**Average**	**High**
ILF (Internal Logical File)	7	10	15
EIF (External Interface File)	5	7	10
EI (External Input)	3	4	6
EO (External Output)	4	5	7
EQ (External inQuiry)	3	4	6

Table 1. Complexity weights with corresponding number of UFP.

- Determine the value adjustment factor (VAF) based on an equation
- (VAF = 0.65 + (Sum of General System Characteristics x .01)
- the 14 General Systems Characteristics being evaluated on a scale of 1 to 5.
- Group the resulting numbers (Unadjusted FP) into Added, Changed, or Deleted functions sets, and combine them with the Value Adjustment Factor (VAF) to obtain the final number of FP. A distinct final formula is used for each count type: Development Project, Enhancement Project or Application:

    - DFP = (UFP + CFP) * VAF
    - EFP = [(ADD + CHGA + CFP) * VAFA] + (DEL* VAFB)
    - AFP = ADD * VAF
    - AFP = [(UFPB + ADD + CHGA) - (CHGB + DEL)] * VAFA

Modelling and controlling changing requirements : a case study

M. Myers, C.Britton and A. Kaposi

Abstract

Constantly changing requirements demand a specification language that is readily intelligible to untrained users, but which also incorporates a degree of formality and supports well-structured specifications. In this paper we describe an industrial case study where an e-commerce application had to be introduced at relatively short notice. We show how using Product/process modelling (Kaposi and Myers, 2001) allows us to specify the changes to requirements effectively in the context of the existing system.

1. Introduction

We are fully aware, today, that requirements are dynamic and evolve constantly during development of a software system. Organisations are continually changing, in terms of their scope, their objectives, and their procedures. Moreover, development of a software system itself causes change and has an effect on the stability of requirements. In requirements engineering changes are the norm – what causes problems is our inability to deal effectively with these changes and stop them disrupting the development process. What we need to do is to accept that requirements will evolve and to develop tools and techniques that allow us to retain control of the development in spite of this.

At the centre of this problem is the requirements specification, which defines the system to be built and encapsulates the shared understanding of the stakeholders. Whatever form the specification takes, it must be both flexible enough to accommodate changing requirements and robust enough to maintain the structure and integrity of the developing system. In addition, it is crucial that any specification is readily intelligible to those people who have to read and validate it. The role of the specification as a corner stone of the development process, and the various demands made on it mean that the choice of specification language has a far-reaching effect on the ultimate success or failure of the development project. A number of authors have highlighted the importance of choosing an effective specification language for use in software development. These include Macaulay (1996), who identified the question of 'What representation format should be used?' as a significant one for practising software developers, and McCluskey et al (1995) who discussed the impact of choice of language on the specification of requirements for a decision support system for air traffic controllers.

In this paper briefly review the literature on what makes a good language for specification, and identify three criteria that most authors agree are important. Using a case study, we then illustrate how all three criteria may be reconciled in a single specification language, and how this language may be used to model the effects of changing requirements in a small system.

2. Criteria for effective specification languages.

Several authors have also identified criteria or properties of specification languages as being relevant in determining the suitability of a particular language for a particular project. Farbey (1993) covers criteria relating directly to languages, such as readability, modifiability and lack of ambiguity, and criteria relating to the language in use, such as the production of a well-presented specification, the cost in time to produce the representation, and the amount of support available. Davis (1993) also suggests a list of criteria pertaining to the effectiveness of representations and the choice of languages. Davis' list includes criteria relating directly to specifying languages, such as that the language should permit annotation and traceability, facilitate modification, and some that are expressed in terms of the software requirements specification (SRS). These include the criterion that "proper use of the technique should result in an SRS that is understandable by customers and users who are not computer scientists". Britton and Jones (1999) focus principally on the intelligibility of representations produced using a specification language. They identify six important properties of such languages, including the ability to exploit human visual perception and the amount of structure inherent in the language. Criteria for specifying languages in the STARTS guide (Department for Trade and Industry & National Computing Centre [DTI & NCC], 1987) incorporate properties such as rigour, suitability for agreement with the end-user and assistance with structuring the requirements. Rigour comprises four separate features: how precisely the syntax of the language is defined, the extent to which it is underpinned by maths and logic, whether the meaning of individual symbols is defined, and the extent to which the language supports consistency checking of the requirements themselves. Suitability for end-user agreement refers to ease of understanding of the language by an untrained user, and assistance with structuring the requirements assesses the extent to which the language supports hierarchical decomposition and separation of concerns in the representation. The STARTS guide also regards the range of requirements covered by the language as important, including functional, performance, interface, system development and process requirements. Finally, Admiral Training's (1995) guide to interactive multimedia development is similar to the STARTS guide in placing emphasis on what the language should be able to specify and on ease of understanding. Effective languages, according to Admiral, should be able to describe the current situation, the target audience, the actual and required level of user performance, the overall aim of the system, the environment, possible constraints and details of specific functions. Languages need to be easy to understand, not only for clients and users, but also for members of the multimedia development team who may not have a background in computer science.

As can be seen from the brief survey above, authors who have explored the topic of criteria for specification languages differ in their approach and in the weightings that they give to different properties. In general, and as might be expected, publications from industry focus on practical criteria aimed at producing an effective representation, whereas criteria chosen by academics tend to be more theoretically based. There are, however, certain criteria that are generally agreed by most authors to be important for effective specification languages:

- the language should be as easy as possible for untrained users to understand
- the language should incorporate a degree of formality and rigour
- the language should support well-structured specifications

In the rest of this paper we illustrate how these three, apparently incompatible, criteria can be reconciled in a single specification language. The method illustrated (Product/process modelling) is formal yet easily understood, sufficiently rigorous to support specification and amenable to translation into other specification languages suitable for particular technical fields. It is based on the generic definition of a system as a pair, a set of entities and a set of relationships over these entities. This definition and its consequences are fully explored in Kaposi and Myers (2001) as are all concepts introduced and used in the following sections.

3. The method by example

The case study involves a retailing organization that has expanded by incorporating various smaller businesses, each of which has evolved a systems infrastructure to suit its erstwhile requirements. The organization is now introducing e-commerce and needs to analyse its diverse current processes with their computerized system support and to integrate the new functions into a comprehensive overall system.

In this case the problem, the unsatisfactory current position, has been identified. The path to a solution becomes a two stage process:

- examine, understand and model the current structure;
- rationalize the current structure and introduce the new functionality with minimum disruption.

The process of establishing the model

The first stage in the establishment of a model is to portray the situation in a graphical representation, one understandable both to client and developer, yet sufficiently formal to be used by the latter in developing prospective solutions to the problem. The graphical component of product/process modelling (Kaposi and Myers, 2001) is just such a representation.

Overview of graphical representation

All entities in the real world can by modelled as systems, either product or process. We differentiate between product and process by recognising that processes have duration and products, (in the particular sense used in product/process modelling) have only an instantaneous existence.

Figure 1 represents an overall organizational process of start time t_1 and completion time of t_2 and hence of duration $t_2 - t_1$. The process has multiple input and multiple output products. The representation labels the various entities, products and processes and these labels serve as pointers to much more explicit information to be found in an accompanying document of which more later.

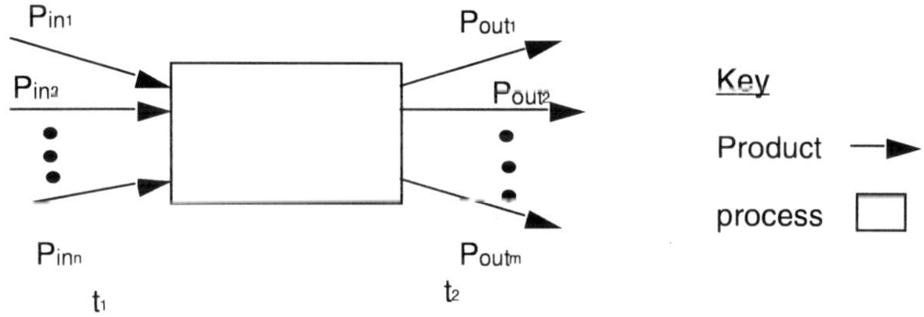

***Figure 1:** top level identification of inputs and outputs*

Figure 1 is understandable but contains far too little information to be useful, particularly in respect of the grouping of products. It may be that not all the products are available at time t_1 and not all the output products are produced at time t_2. In addition, it may be that only one of the inputs may be needed or only one of the outputs produced. The symbols of figure 1 do not provide a mechanism for resolving any possible ambiguities and provide no label pointing to resolution of the details. To provide such a label an extra symbol is added to the representation, that of a 'gate'. Figure 2 illustrates the use of gates. All input products needed for the process to initiate are collected into a single input product by a collection gate, and the single output product is distributed either into its components, or, if the output is broadcast information, as independent identical copies, by a distribution gate.

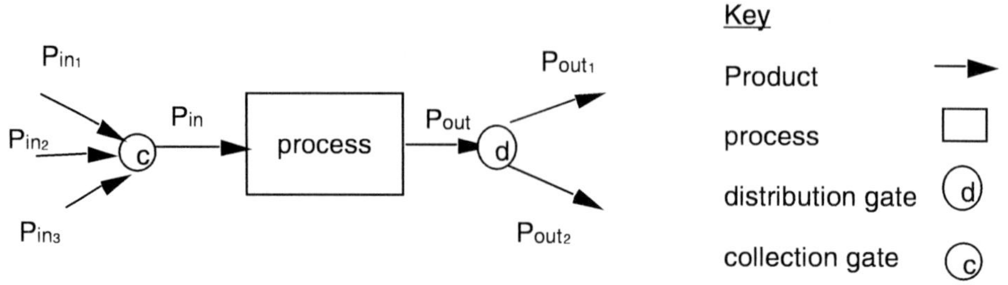

Figure2: Example of Product/process representation

The gate can then be defined in the accompanying document as AND, OR, EXCLUSIVE OR or M FROM N and in the last of these, any further information added to make its use explicit.

These are all the symbols needed at this stage of the representation.

Using the representation

Modelling the current marketing process of the organization as a series of sub-processes, the input from one forming part of the input to the next, we obtain the diagram of figure 3. The system developer will look at the processes of the various divisions to see if they can be accommodated in such a general structure. Where not, a further substructure is added to the graph.

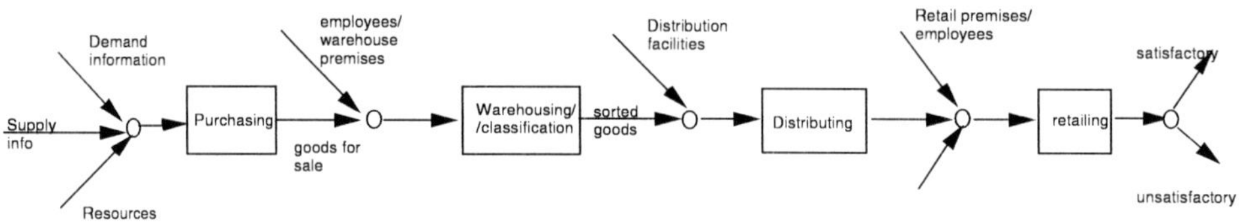

***Figure 3**: A series of processes leading from purchasing decisions to sales.*
Key as before, labelling incomplete.

Figure 3 shows a generalized view of the organization's supplier to customer chain of processes: purchasing, warehousing, distributing, retailing. We can show the purchasing process in more detail as a set of parallel processes within general 'purchasing'. Assuming three different sets of buyers, the composition of purchasing will have initially been as in figure 4 where the shaded area shows the composite process.

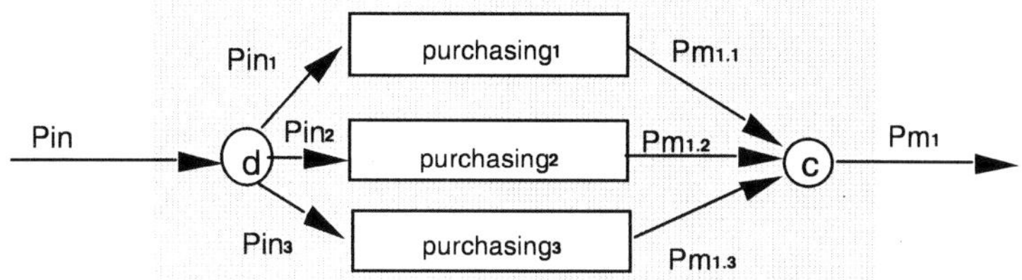

Figure 4: Parallel components of the purchasing process
Key as figure2

Extending the organization

The remit given to the systems developer was to incorporate on-line ordering using as many as possible of the existing processes. Having the product/process analysis of figure 3, or any fuller versions available, greatly simplifies the discussion between client and developer. Figure 5 shows that a first approach is to treat the e-tailing facility as yet another distribution point which shares the purchasing and warehousing facilities of the current enterprise. At the new distribution point the only extra facilities needed will be for the processing of customer information, payment handling and individual packing. Should the client disagree, an informed negotiation will follow. In such a case the analysis and its graphical representation forms an excellent basis for discussion between the domain-knowledgeable customer and the technically competent developer.

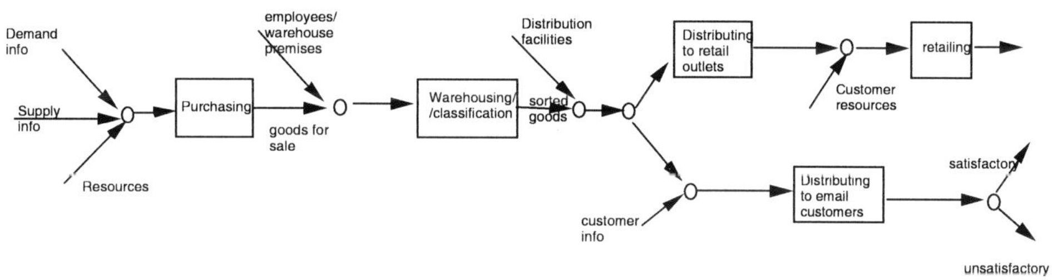

***Figure 5** : The extended series of processes leading from purchasing decisions to sales. Partially labelled diagram and key as above.*

Completing the model

As previously stated, and repeated for emphasis, the system approach adopted in product/process modelling models all real world objects (the referents) as pairs, a set of entities and a set of relations over those entities. In the black box model the entities are the measures of the referent's attributes and the relationships are a minimum of two, one which states that

- all the attributes belong to the same referent and the other that
- all attributes are measured at the same time instant.

The first of these is self-evident. The second follows from the definition of the product as an instantaneous model of the referent whose time stamp shows when the attributes were measured. We thus take cognisance of the fact that attribute values may change with time.

We now examine attributes of products and processes.

Product attributes

As a simple example taken from figure 4 we list some of the attributes of an on-line order. Each of these can be easily defined and measured and the scale of the measure identified as one of: nominal, ordinal, interval, rational or absolute.

Attribute	Measurement scale
Order number	absolute
Date/time	interval
Customer identification	ID or name and address or both
Items (a structure)	list of nominal
Total value.	currency (rational)
Credit card number	nominal
Credit card expiry date	interval

If any other attributes are relevant they will be added. All attributes are bound by the relationships that they all belong to the same unit **order** and were measured at the same time.

Now consider the input to the first process of figure 4, that of purchasing. The input has three components: 'demand information', 'supply information' and 'resources'. Supply information attributes should be available, consisting of supplier details, items, prices and delivery dates. 'Resources' will depend on the effort needed to gather the other details but may be subsumed into the cost of the other two products depending on the accounting policies of the organization. If not, then the main attribute may be cost or number of employee-hours spent and concomitant overheads. 'Demand information' attributes are more difficult both to identify and to quantify since their measures will, of necessity, be predictive. Nevertheless, the appropriate department or consultant will have produced a report and a careful reading of this should allow identification of attributes. This last example shows that we need to consider what is to be done when some of the attributes are deemed relevant but are not measurable. This is a common problem in the business world, where loosely defined and unmeasurable concepts abound. Such attributes are considered in the section dealing with hard and soft systems.

In some cases the value of the black box attributes may not be immediately available but will have to be aggregated over a structure. As a simple example consider the **order** product above. The value of the order will depend on the items it contains. We must therefore model how top level black box attribute values are derived from the values of the components. a structure is modelled as a bipartite structure tree as illustrated in figure 6. Bipartite graphs have two sets of nodes, elements of each alternating along any path in the tree. Each black node represents a black box model and each white node is a relationship between the lower level components. The top level value of any attribute should be available as a calculation of the values of that attribute in the components and the relationship with the next higher level. In the example of figure 6, the relationship is just '+'.

The ability to so calculate values is termed *constructivity*.

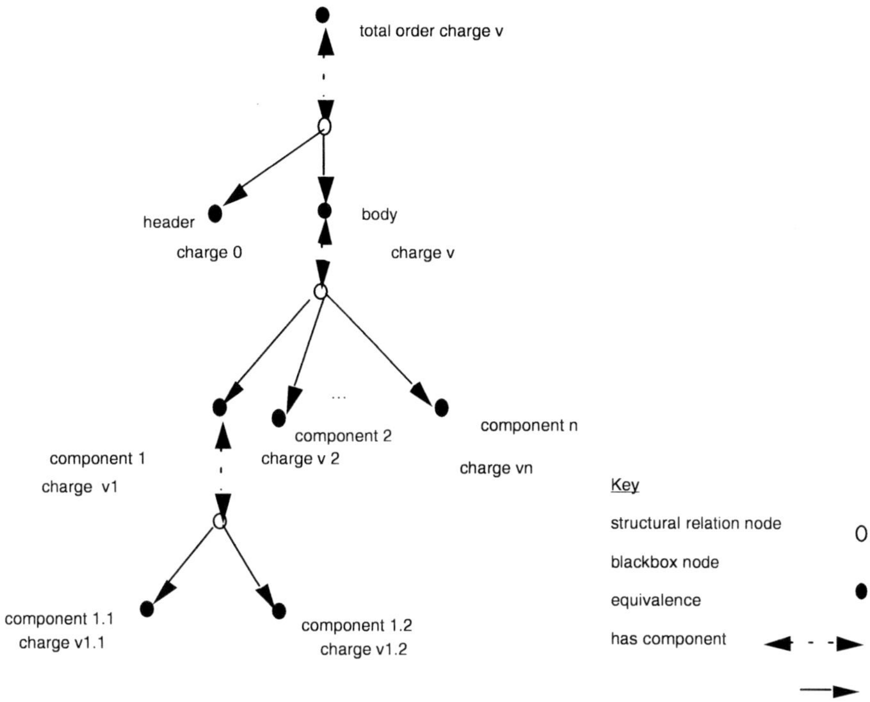

Figure 6: *Structural model showing aggregation of 'charge'*

In figure 6 the attribute value calculated is that of 'charge', the cost to the customer. In such as simple case it is probably not necessary to be so explicit but in more complicated examples, the ability to build up black box attribute values from the components is both useful and necessary.

As a final comment on products note that they may be classified as material –with attribute values in SI units, or information, with different attribute values including the ability to produce multiple copies at will.

Processes and their attributes

Several attributes are considered mandatory for the identification of processes. These are listed below.

- Input domain: The set of all allowable inputs to the process.
- Duration: >0 by definition of process
- Status: either free or busy (free or not to accept further input at a time instant)
- Owner: every man-made process should have an owner, who accepts responsibility for the process
- Transfer function: an engineering term which describes how input is transformed into output and which is represented as Output = f(Input).

There are other attributes which may be relevant, attributes such as

- Location: at which office is the report compiled, the product manufactured?
- Agent: person or machine carrying out the process.

Processes, like products, may show structure. Figures 3, and 5 show process sequence and figure 4 illustrates parallelism. In many well-defined processes attributes such as duration, input domain and owner may be aggregated over the structure. The subject is treated in greater detail in Kaposi and Myers (2001).

Gates

Gates are necessary to show groupings of products both for input and for output. They differ from the other product/process entities in that they do not model real life objects – hence they are designated virtual processes. Collection gates have many input arcs (figure 7(a)) and one output arc, distribution gates (figure 7(b)) have one input arc and many output arcs.

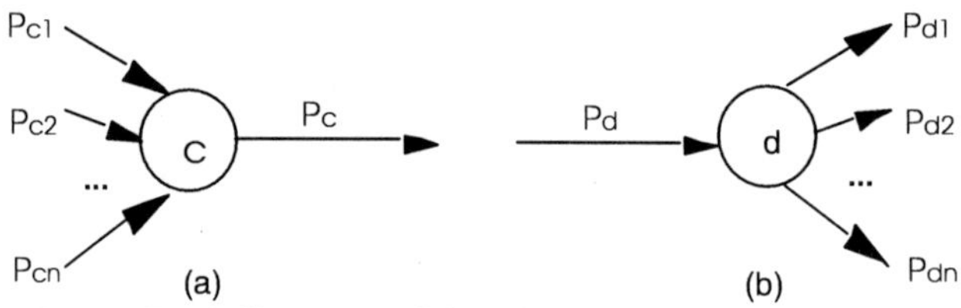

Figure 7 : Collection and distribution gates (usual key)

Gate rules

Collection gates

Each gate will have a rule associated with it governing whether the process can commence.

- AND rule: all inputs must arrive simultaneously at any instant t_{in} .
- EXCLUSIVE OR rule: one and only one input arrives at instant t_{in} .
- INCLUSIVE OR rule: any subset of inputs arrive at instant t_{in} .
- M from N rule: the gate has n inputs but m are necessary for the process to commence
- Other rules may be defined such that one or more of the inputs is necessary.

Distribution gates

- AND rule: All outputs are produced at instant t_{out}
- EXCLUSIVE OR rule: Only one output is present at instant t_{out}.
- INCLUSIVE OR rule: any subset of outputs are produced at instant t_{out}
- M from N rule: the gate as n outputs but only M are produced at instant t_{out}.
- Other rules may be defined.

Together, product, process and gate details give all required information for a complete representation of a system. Further, the compilation of such details leads to a deep understanding of the system under analysis or design.

Soft and Hard Systems

Product /process modelling is based on characterization by measurement. However, many abstract objects in the real world are not amenable to measurement. The so-called soft sciences such as economics, psychology or sociology have had their progress impeded by the lack of a reliable measurement system. However little is to be gained by considering such sciences to be relegated to a separate area and applying soft system methodologies to the exclusion of all else. We incorporate soft products and soft processes into product/process modelling by using extra definitions and symbols.

- A soft product is a product some of whose relevant attributes cannot yet be measured.
- A soft process is a process whose input products are soft.

By extension, those products and processes whose attributes can be measured can be labelled 'hard'. The symbols for soft products and processes are shown in figure 8.

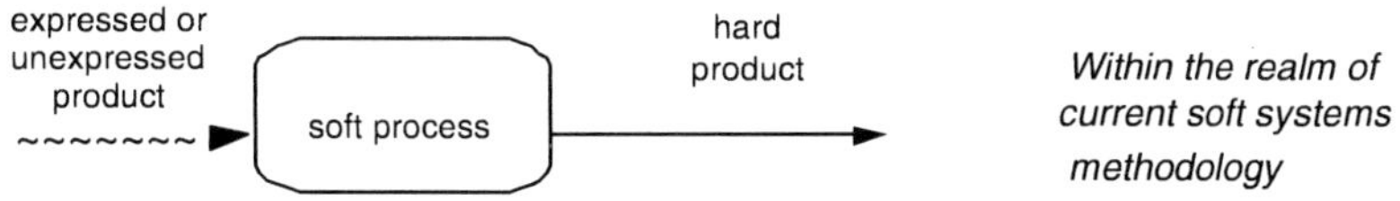

Figure 8: Soft product and soft process symbols

Examples

Advertising campaign has, as some of its black box attributes cost, media, effectivity. Here the first two attributes are measurable but the third will need a consensus definition before measurement is possible. Until such a definition is produced, advertising is a soft product.

Potential customers as an input product to a process, should be identified by the marketing people as possessing certain attributes which they should define and attempt to measure.

4. Summary

As we said at the beginning of this paper, the problem of evolving requirements demands a specification language that is as easy as possible for untrained users to understand, incorporates a degree of formality and rigour, and supports well-structured specifications. In the paper we have introduced Product/process modelling, a specification language which possesses all three of these properties. We have described an industrial case study where an e-commerce application had to be introduced at relatively short notice and have shown how using Product/process modelling allows us to specify effectively the changes to requirements in the context of the existing system.

References

[1] Admiral Training Ltd (1995). Multimedia design - A newcomer's guide.Department of Employment, Sheffield, UK.

[2] Britton, C. and Jones, S. (1999) The Untrained Eye: How Languages for Software Specification Support Understanding in Untrained Users, *Human Computer Interaction,* 14, pp. 191-244.

[3] Davis, A. et al. (1993). Identifying and measuring quality in a software requirements specification. *Proceedings of the First International Software Metrics Symposium*, 141-152. IEEE Computer Society Press.

[4] Department for Trade and Industry and National Computing Centre (1987). *The STARTS guide* (2nd ed.), volume 1, NCC Publications, UK.

[5] Farbey, B. (1993). Software quality metrics: considerations about requirements and requirement specifications. In R. Thayer & A. McGetterick (Eds.), Software engineering: a European perspective (pp.138-142). IEEE Computer Society Press.

[6] Kaposi A, Myers M (2001) Systems for All! To be published June 2001 Imperial College Press.

[7] Macaulay, L. (1996). Requirements for requirements engineering techniques. *Proceedings of ICRE96, the Second International Conference on Requirements Engineering*, IEEE Computer Society Press.

[8] McCluskey, T., Porteous, J., Naik, Y., Taylor, C. & Jones, S. (1995). A requirements capture method and its use in an air traffic control application. *Software Practice and Experience, 25 (1).*

Integrating Quality Modelling with Requirements Engineering

Paolo Donzelli, Ioana Rus, and Giovanni Cantone

Abstract

This paper introduces a structured goal-oriented agent-based process modelling framework, where advanced requirements engineering techniques are combined with software quality modelling approaches, to provide an environment within which the stakeholders and the analysts can easily cooperate to discover, verify and validate the new IT system requirements. It forces and assists the stakeholders, in particular the customer, to an early definition of the desired system functionality and quality attributes, improving our capability of achieving customer satisfaction.

1. Introduction

The successful implementation of a new information technology (IT) system relies on a firm understanding of its application domain and, above all, on our ability of envisioning the impact of the new system upon it [1, 2].

Introducing a new IT system in a company will affect, and usually lead to changes in, the business process of that organization and the IT system will be an "organic" component of this new process. We call the company after the deployment of the new system, the *to-be* company.

Envisioning the impact that a software system will have on its application domain, that is envisioning the *to-be* company, is a difficult task. Organisations are made of people, and the goals, the expectations, the needs of all the stakeholders, directly or indirectly involved (e.g. final users, customers, business and IT managers, procurements people, maintainers, developers, etc.), have to be explicitly addressed, analysed and "formalised" from the outset of the project. The software system and its application domain form a larger social-technical system that has to be treated and analysed as a whole: the overall needs of such social-technical system, eventually a *value-chain* [3], are the ones to be fulfilled [2]. Customer satisfaction becomes an organisation-wide concept, beyond the simple individual customer or user point of view.

To achieve this, we must move from "slow, reactive, adversarial, separated software engineering and systems engineering processes to unified, concurrent processes" [4], which will also include business process reengineering (BPR) [5].

Consequently, appropriate process modelling-based Requirements Engineering techniques are advocated [1,6,7], to provide a common conceptual framework within which both the stakeholders and the analysts (i.e., the process analysts and the requirements engineers) can easily work, to understand the application domain (i.e., the business process the new system has to support), envision possible solutions, compare feasible alternatives, and design the *to-be* company.

Building on such a perspective, this paper proposes a structured *goal-oriented agent-based process modelling framework* [7], where advanced *requirements engineering methods* are integrated with *software quality modelling approaches*. The framework is explicitly designed to support discovery, and verification and validation of both user-oriented and organisation-oriented requirements, by assisting negotiation among the stakeholders, or between the analysts and the stakeholders, and by providing reconcilable user-oriented views of the target software system in its application domain. While gathering requirements, the analysts can also build *measurement models* [8] of the relevant software quality attributes, thus capturing, formalising, and reconciling the different stakeholders' points of view on product and process characteristics.

Quality models such as [9,10,11] or specialised goal-oriented measurement identification methods, such as the Goal Question Metrics (GQM) approach [12] or the Measurement Model Life Cycle (MMLC) [8,13], can be used to address the customer satisfaction issue since the beginning of a new project. Customer satisfaction can be captured, formalised, and translated, since the inception of a new IT system, into implementable functionalities and constraints.

By using this framework, the quality attributes are defined and measurement for their achievement is facilitated. This supports validating not only the functionality of the system in the specific application domain, but also the negotiated quality attributes of the system (according to customer's desire and developer's constraints) [3,14].

This paper is organised as follows: Section 2 introduces the suggested process modelling framework, by briefly describing its main characteristics and capabilities. Section 3 elaborates some aspects introduced in Section 2, by showing extracts from a practical application, regarding the introduction of a workflow-based [15] software system into a public sector administration [16]. Finally, section 4 presents the conclusions.

2. The Process Modelling framework

The framework tackles process modelling by breaking activities down into more intellectually manageable components, and by adopting a combination of different approaches, on the basis of a common conceptual notation.

Agents are used to model the organisation [6,17]. The business process is modelled as a network of interacting agents (any kind of active entity within the process, e.g. teams, humans and machines, one of which is the target system), collaborating or conflicting in order to achieve both individual and organisational goals.

Goals are associated with agents and are used to link organisational needs to system requirements. In particular, once the goals to be achieved are identified, they are refined and implemented in social-technical terms. The outcome of the modelling process may in fact affect both the organisation (the business process, the personnel, for example in terms of tasks, responsibilities and required skills, and the pre-existing systems), as well as the new software system.

According to the nature of a goal, we distinguish between hard goals (functional) and soft goals (non functional). For a *hard goal*, the achievement criterion is sharply defined (e.g. "provide a help menu"); for a *soft goal*, it is up to the goal originator, or to an agreement between the involved agents, to decide when the goal is considered to have been achieved (e.g. "provide an *easy-to-use* and *complete* help menu"). In comparison to hard goals, soft goals can be highly subjective and strictly related to a particular context; they enable the analysts to highlight quality issues (e.g. easy-to-use and complete) from the outset, making explicit the semantics assigned to them by the stakeholders.

While a hard goal will lead to a set of functions (functional requirements) that the software system will have to provide, a soft goal will be refined into more precise sub-ordinate soft goals, for reducing its initial fuzziness, until, eventually, it can be expressed as a set of hard goals and constraints upon them (non-functional requirements). So, for example, the soft goal "provide an *easy-to-use* and *complete* help menu" will lead to the hard goal "provide a help menu" and to a set of constrains characterizing the help menu so that it will be easy-to-use and complete. In this case, for example, *easy-to-use* could lead to the implementation of a pull-down menu, using a technology similar to that adopted by other commercial products already known by the final users. In other words, for each soft goal, the resulting set of constraints represents the final and operationalised views of the involved quality attributes, i.e. the quality measurement models that formalise the attributes for the specific context [8, 12,13].

Separating goal modelling from organisational modelling, in this way, and then, further distinguishing between hard goal modelling and soft goal modelling helps to reduce the complexity of business process modelling [7]. The proposed framework, therefore, supports three inter-related modelling efforts: the organisational modelling, the hard goal modelling and the soft goal modelling (see Figure 1). For each area, the analysts may decide to employ a different technique, or a different set of techniques, that better serve the specific needs, and then to reconcile the results. In the remainder of this section we present the approach we decided to adopt for each modelling effort, and highlight some possible alternatives.

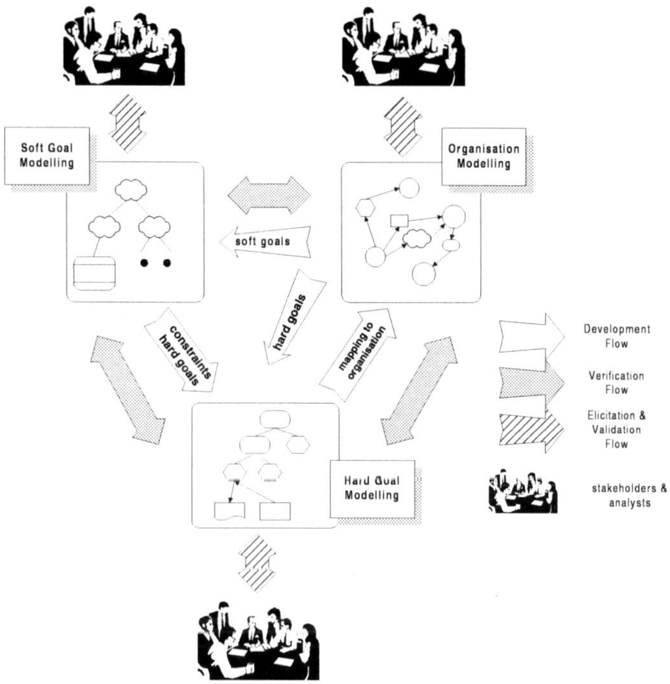

Figure 1. The Process Modelling Framework

2.1. Organisation Modelling

During *Organisation Modelling*, as already said, the organisation process is modelled as a network of interacting agents, operating as a whole to achieve the organisational goals. Of course, any agent may generate its own goals, may operate to achieve goals on the behalf of some other agents, may decide to collaborate with other agents for a specific goal, and might clash on some other ones.

At this stage, the analysts have all the mechanisms to envision, together with the stakeholders, possible solutions, select the feasible ones, and design the *to-be* company. By using business process reengineering techniques [5], the problem domain is analysed, the organisational needs are discovered, and the stakeholders and the corresponding goals are identified.

Our approach draws upon an agent-based process modelling framework [6]. This approach allows the analysts not only to deal with the *what* and the *how* of the application domain (i.e., the tasks and the way in which they are performed), but also to explicitly model the *why* (i.e. the underlying reasons for the *what* and the corresponding *how*), expressed in terms specific to the application domain goals. This enables the analysts to focus on the *right* system for a given application, to design (or re-design) the encompassing business process that fully exploits the system's capabilities [5], and to improve the capacity to identify, justify and validate the system requirements [2,6,18]. Unlike the original approach, the one we suggest spawns the other two modelling efforts, i.e., the hard goal modelling and the soft goal modelling, to simplify and better deal with the modelling problem, and allows the analysts to reconcile the emerging results. In particular, it recognises the need of explicitly modelling soft goals, by exploiting available quality modelling techniques, to translate quality issues into agreeable upon, and implementable functionalities and constraints.

2.2. Hard Goal Modelling

The *Hard Goal Modelling* seeks to determine *how* to achieve the hard goals, by decomposing them into more elementary subordinate hard goals and tasks. While a *hard goal* just defines an objective that an agent (someone or something within the organisation) has to achieve, without specifying *how* to do it, a *task* is a well-specified activity, leaving little room for initiative. Of course, the granularity of refinement of a hard goal into subordinate hard goals and tasks depends on the level of capability and autonomy of the agent. So, for example, if the hard goal "procure a computer" could be clear enough for a human agent, it might need to be translated within an organisation into a set of actions (tasks), necessary to procure a computer: "organise a competitive tender", "inform the bidders", etc. Our approach is quite informal and based on a combination of natural language and a semi-formal graphical notation, mainly derived from [6]. However, when preferred, or deemed as necessary, more formal approaches could easily be adopted, and integrated within the Framework, e.g. [18]. In particular, such an alternative could be suitable for critical parts of the process, or for activities that will not be enacted by humans.

2.3. Soft Goal Modelling

The *Soft Goal Modelling* aims at producing the operational definitions of the soft goals that emerged during the organisational modelling, sufficient to capture and make explicit the semantics that are usually assigned implicitly by the user [8,13] and to highlight the system quality issues from the start. A soft goal is refined in terms of subordinate soft goals, hard goals, tasks and constraints. Resulting soft goal, in turn, will have to be progressively refined until a set of hard goals, tasks and constraints is obtained (until all the "soft" aspects are dealt with). Constraints are associated with hard goals and tasks to specify the corresponding quality attributes. So, for example, the soft goal "procure a fast computer" will spawn the hard goal "procure a computer" and a set of associated constraints (e.g. CPU speed, memory size, cache characteristics, etc.) specifying the concept of fast computer. The resulting soft goal models are quality models, which play within the organisation a double role. In the case of the soft goal "buy a fast computer", for example, the emerging set of constrains can be seen as a way to characterise the hard goals (i.e. by constraining the kind of computer to be procured), but also as a model of the quality attribute *fast*. This model will represent the perception of the attribute fast at a given time, within a specific domain of the organisation, and according to a specific set of stakeholders.

In particular, soft goals may be decomposed and refined into attributes whose values/ranges can be specified as requirements and which are measurable. The values of the resulting IT system's attributes can thus be measured and compared to the initially specified values, for product validation purposes and for assuring that the user will get what he asked for, and therefore will be satisfied. For this decomposition, quality models like [9,10,11] or more advanced goal-oriented measurement paradigms like GQM [12] and its extensions [8,13] can be used. Such paradigms, in fact, are based on the idea that measurement models for quality attributes have to be defined starting out from the analysis of the goals that the involved actors have to or want to achieve. GQM, for example, for driving and supporting such an analysis, adopts a 5-facet goal structure: quality focus, object, purpose, point of view and context. Our framework can act as forerunner for GQM, by providing a clear identification of the stakeholders (agents), of their point of view, of the objects (IT system), of the quality foci (attributes), and of the specific context (application domain).

It is worth noting that it is possible to integrate within the framework other non-functional requirements modelling techniques, especially designed to better deal with and formalise the *softness* characteristics of quality attributes, which are themselves drawn from quality modelling approaches, such as the Non-Functional Requirements (NFR) Framework [19].

2.4. Using the Framework

As shown in Figure 1, the three discussed modelling activities do not exist in isolation, rather they interact in different ways. In Figure 1, the possible interactions between the three modelling efforts are represented as Development Flows, Verification Flows and Validation Flows. *Development Flows* show how information discovered in one model may feed the others, in a continuous loop. In other words, the resulting models, i.e. *organization models*, *soft goal models*, and *hard goal models*, will develop in an iterative and cyclic way. Through continuous interaction with the stakeholders, the analysts will deal first with the requirements at an organisational level, then at a process level, until the focus will be placed upon single agents and their roles within the application domain.

Verification Flows indicate activities that attempt to guarantee consistency between models, for example, to verify that all the hard goals emerging from the soft goal models are properly addressed by the hard goal models, whereas *Validation Flows* show where interaction with the stakeholders occurs. In other words, each type of model provides a specific knowledge representation vehicle that the analysts can use to interact with the stakeholders, in order to capture requirements, reason about them, negotiate potential conflicts and, eventually, reach an accepted formulation. For example, the soft goals models force the stakeholders to reason about their own concepts of quality, by reifying them into feasible and explicit sets of functions and constraints. Hard goal models allow each human agent to understand and validate the corresponding role he/she has to play within the organisation. Finally, the organisation models provide the organisation's management with a clear view of how the application domain will be changed, or affected, by the introduction of the new IT system.

3. An example application

The technology push and the legislative evolution, both at national and international level, have made information and communication technologies (ICT) the main enabling tool available to public sector organizations to improve their interactions with the citizens as well as their internal processes. ICT applications offer huge opportunities for improving the overall quality of administrative processes, by enabling radical ways for boosting *efficiency*, and by providing monitoring, flexible and cooperative mechanisms to increase *efficacy* [3].

An example of such ICT applications is described in [16], where a solution based on the integration of collaboration tools [15], Internet-based technologies, and digital documents management systems is proposed to support a decision making process of a public sector organization, for which a heavy flow of documentation among the involved actors is required. The process modelling framework proposed by us has been successfully applied within this project to deal with the first stages of the requirements engineering process. The framework was used to understand and formalise the real organizational needs, and to translate them into implementable requirements for the target IT system (simply referred in the following as *the workflow system*). Ensuring *high security*, improving *collaboration* between the decision makers, guaranteeing a *smooth transaction* to the new way of working (to increase chances of the new IT system being accepted), providing *high visibility*, and *adopting an open technology* (suitable to be integrated within the organisational IT infrastructure) turned out to be the most important issues to be addressed.

In this paper, for brevity, we limit our presentation to a few simplified extracts from this example application.

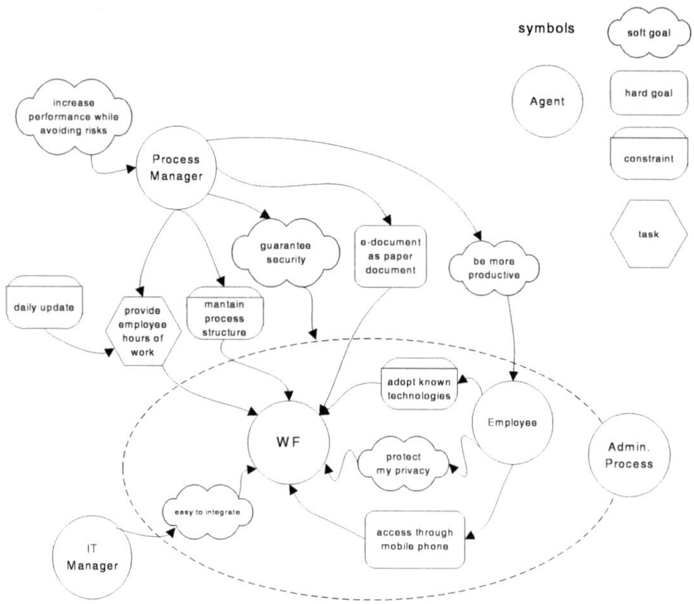

Figure 2. The Organisation Model

Figure 2 shows a simple organisation model, which employs the workflow system (WF). Circles represent *Agents*, and dotted lines are used to bound the internal structure of complex agents; that is, agents containing other agents. Consequently, the *Process Manager*, that is the responsible for the process, is a simple agent that interacts with the *Administrative Process* in order to monitor and manage its behaviour. The *Administrative Process* agent is a complex agent, encompassing the agents *WF* and several agents *Employee*.

Agents interact by exchanging goals and tasks. Clouds represent soft goals, rounded-rectangles represent hard goals, and hexagons represent tasks.

Thus, in Figure 2, the *Process Manager* receives, from the enclosing domain, the soft goal of "increase performance while avoiding risks" for the managed process. Goals, tasks and agents are connected by dependency-links, represented by arrowhead lines. An agent is linked to a goal when it needs that goal to be achieved; a goal is linked to an agent when it depends on that agent to be achieved. Similarly, an agent is linked to a task when it wants the task to be performed; a task is linked to an agent when the agent has to perform the task. By combining dependency-links, we can establish a dependency among two or more agents [7].

Each agent works as a goal transformer. Having received a goal, an agent will operate according to its own experience, knowledge or position within the organisation, in trying to achieve the goal. It will decide how to achieve the goal in terms of tasks and subordinate goals, and may choose to depend on other agents, by passing out some of these tasks and subordinate goals. For example, the soft goal model in Figure 3 explains the behaviour of the *Process Manager* to achieve the soft goal "increase performance while avoiding risks".

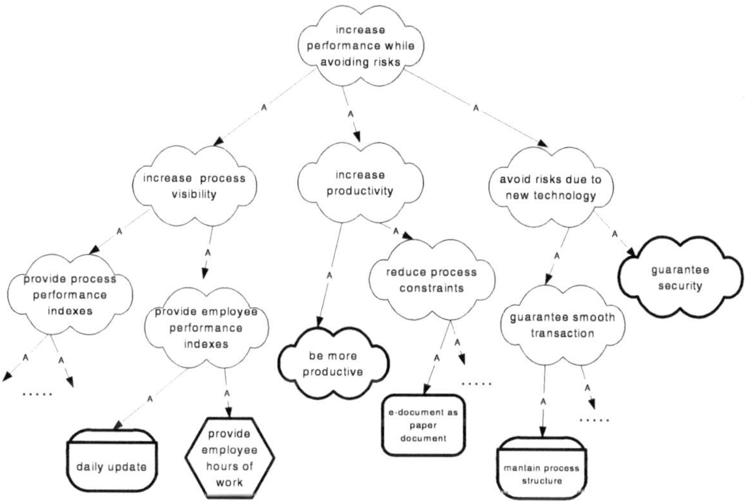

Figure 3. The Soft Goal Model "increase performance while avoiding risks"

In order to achieve the assigned goals, the *Process Manager* will need to "increase process visibility", to have better information upon which to steer the process, to "increase productivity", and to "avoid risks due to new technology". The first soft goal will spawn two subordinate soft goals, "provide process performance indexes" and "provide employee performance indexes", which will lead, after some refinement, to precise tasks (or functionality) that the *WF* agent has to provide. In this context, we are building the models of the attribute performance for the process and for the employee, from the *Process Manager* perspective. They will be expressed as a set of data that the WF agent will have to make visible, and a set of constraints characterising such data, e.g. precision, frequency of update, etc. As example, in Figure 3, it is shown the task "provide employee hours of work" and the associated constraint "daily update", which is represented by a rounded-rectangle with a horizontal line. The second soft goal "increase productivity" will spawn the soft goal "be more productive" for the *Employee* agent, and the soft goal "reduce process constraints" for the *WF* agent. From here, precise hard goals may be derived and placed upon the WF agent, for example the hard goals of "providing equivalence between electronic and paper document". Finally, the soft goal "avoid risks due to new technology" will spawn the soft goal "guarantee smooth transaction (to new technology)", from which the constraint "maintain (the original work) process structure" upon the *WF* agent, and the soft goal "guarantee security" upon the whole *Administrative Process* agent. This last soft goal, in particular, could lead to hard goals, tasks and constraints upon both the *WF* agent and the *Employee* agents. For example, an *Employee* could be required to use a smart card with biometric data to access the *WF*, and digital signature to deal with electronic documents. The *WF* will have to implement all these capabilities.

In Figure 3, the "A" annotation on each decomposition line indicates that all these goals must be satisfied ('AND' refinement), whereas the goals and tasks in bold outline are those that the *Process Manager* will pass out (see Figure 2), and they are not further refined.

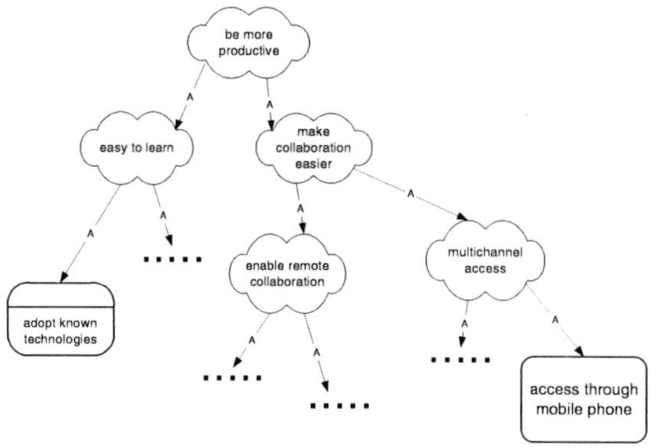

Figure 4. The Soft Goal Model "be more productive"

In order to "be more productive", that is to achieve the soft goal placed upon it by the *Process Manager*, the *Employee* will define its own strategy, eventually reaching an agreement with the *Process Manager*. Such a strategy is shown by the soft goal model in Figure 4, where we can see how in order to "be more productive" the *Employee* will ask that the system will be "easy to learn" and will "make collaboration easier" with the other employees. For sake of brevity, only a partial refinement of these soft goals is shown in Figure 4. The soft goal "easy to learn" will spawn the constraints "adopt known technologies" (i.e. technologies which the employees are used to), whereas the soft goal "make collaboration easier" will lead, through further refinement, to a series of hard goals implying specific *WF* capabilities (e.g. teleconference) and access channels (e.g. mobile phone, laptop, etc.). Of course, within the organisation, an agent may operate as goal generator, as well as a goal transformer. So, in Figure 2, for example, we can see that the agent *Employee* requires the *WF* to "protect my privacy", while the agent *IT Manager* requires the *WF* to be "easy to integrate (within the other internal IT systems)". By modelling the soft goals "protect my privacy", we can derive that the *Employee* wants to be sure that its own private area of work will not be accessible by others, and maybe to be able to increase this security level by adopting a cryptography tool to protect particular data. In addition, given that all its activity will be performed through the *WF*, it does not want someone to be able to monitor his actions, clashing with what was clearly required by the *Process Manager* (see the task "provide employee hours of work" in Figure 3). This last goal demonstrates an important issues, that different agents may have different opinions, and that soft goal models allow the analysts to detect conflicting requirements at the early stages of a new system development and, at the same time, provide a way to resolve them. A detailed analysis of the trade-offs between the options identified by the *Employee* and the *Process Manager* is outside the scope of this paper, and many approaches have been suggested to deal with conflicts [20,21]. However, we want to point out how the framework allows discovery and resolution of conflicts at a very early stage. In particular, differences will emerge during the modelling effort, and the models will act as vehicles to reason about problems and reconcile different points of view. It is a very informal approach, but we think it is suitable for the early stage of the requirements engineering process we are addressing.

The models of the soft goals and of the hard goals placed upon the new IT systems by the other agents operating within the organisation will lead to the system requirements. Although it is the whole set of the produced models which expresses the final requirements, it is interesting to note how each kind of model plays a specific role [1]. Hard goals models will translate into functional requirements (functionalities the system has to provide), while soft goals models will translate into non-functional requirements (actually into the combination of functional and non-functional requirements suitable to satisfy the stakeholders). On top of this, the organisation model will indicate how each agent within the organisation will interact with the new IT system, supporting system deployment and use.

4. Conclusions

The goal-oriented agent-based process modelling framework introduced in this paper combines requirements engineering methods with software quality modelling approaches. It provides an environment within which the stakeholders (the customer, the user, but also the business manager and the system developers) and the analysts can easily cooperate to discover, verify and validate the new IT system requirements, and also to design the *to-be* company that better integrates and exploits system's capabilities. It forces the stakeholders, and in particular the customer, to an early definition of the desired system functionality and attributes, improving the capability of achieving customer satisfaction. The framework results into a vehicle that effectively combines formal, semi-formal, and qualitative reasoning approaches, designed to deal with both functional and non-functional requirements. In particular, specialised goal-oriented measurement identification methods can be adopted to support reasoning about quality issues, and formalise non-functional requirements from the outset of a project.

The results of its applications [6,13], as briefly seen in Section 3, also suggest that the framework offers benefits both in the development and in the post-deployment phases. In particular, the clear links established between stakeholders' goals and system requirements, in addition to improving customer participation at the initial stage, allows the analysts to quickly identify the influence of environmental changes on the final system requirements, supporting *requirements management* during system development, and also *system maintenance* after deployment. Finally, since the goals are the most stable pieces of information within an organisation, the goal-requirements link is likely to facilitate and drive *system reuse*, or system's components reuse.

5. References

[1] Fickas, S., and Helm, B.R. "Knowledge Representation and Reasoning in the Design of Composite Systems", IEEE Transactions on Software Engineering, Vol. 18, N. 6, June 1992.

[2] Axel van Lamsweerde, "Requirements Engineering in the Year 00: A Research Perspective", International Conference Software Engineering (ICSE) 2000, Limerick, Ireland.

[3] Cantone, G. "Measure-driven processes and architecture for the empirical evaluation of software technologies", Journal of Software Maintenance: Research and Practice, N. 12, 2000.

[4] Boehm B., "Unifying Software Engineering and System Engineering", Computer, March 2000.

[5] Hammer, M., and Champy, J. "Reengineering the Corporation: A Manifesto for Business Revolution", Nicholas Brealey Publishing, London, 1995.
[6] Yu, E. "Why Agent-Oriented Requirements Engineering" Proceedings of 3rd Workshop on Requirements Engineering For Software Quality, Barcelona, Catalonia, June 1997.
[7] Donzelli, P., and Moulding M.R. "Developments in Application Domain Modelling for the Verification and Validation of Synthetic Environments: A Formal Requirements Engineering Framework", Proceedings of the Spring 99 Simulation Interoperability Workshop, Orlando, FL, March 1999.
[8] Cantone, G., and Donzelli P. "Production and Maintenance of Goal-oriented Software Measurement Models", International Journal of Software Engineering and Knowledge Engineering", (to appear, 2001).
[9] McCall, J., P. Richards, and G. Walters, "Factors in Software Quality", Technical Report 77CIS02, Rome Air Development Center, 1977.
[10] Boehm B., and Bose P., "Humans and Process Frameworks: Some Critical Process Elements", Technical Report USC-CSE-94-502, University of Southern California, 1994.
[11] IEEE Std 1061-1992, IEEE Standard for a Software Quality Metrics Methodology, 1992.
[12] Basili, V. R., Caldiera, G., and Rombach, H. D., "The Goal Question Metric Approach", Encyclopedia of Software Engineering, Wiley&Sons Inc., 1994.
[13] Cantone, G., Donzelli P. "Goal-oriented Software Measurement Models", European Software Control and Metrics Conference, Herstmonceux Castle, East Sussex, UK, April 1999.
[14] Cantone, G., Cantone L., and Donzelli P. "Models, Measures and Learning Organizations for Software technologies", Business Briefing: Global Semiconductor Manufacturing Technology, World Markets Research Centre, London, January 2001.
[15] C. Bussler, "Enterprise-Wide Workflow Management", IEEE Concurrency, July-September 1999.
[16] Antonelli, C., Donzelli P., Mastroianni, R. Setola, S. Vinti, S. Tucci A Web-based Workflow Solution to support the Italian Government Agenda Definition Process, Proceedings of the 2000 Conference of the Italian Automatic Computation Association, Taormina, Italy, 27-30 September 2000.
[17] D'Inverno M., and Luck, M. "Development and Application of an Agent Based Framework" Proceedings of the First IEEE International Conference on Formal Engineering Methods, Hiroshima, Japan, 1997.
[18] Dardenne, A., Van Lamsweerde, A., and Fickas, S. "Goal-Directed Requirements Acquisition" Science of Computer Programming, Vol. 20, North Holland, 1993.
[19] Mylopoulos J., Chung L., and Nixon B.A., "Representing and Using Non Functional Requirements: A Process-Oriented Approach", IEEE Transaction on SE, Vol. 18, N. 6, June 1992.
[20] B. Boehm, P. Bose, E. Horowitz and M. J. Lee, "Software Requirements As Negotiated Win Conditions," Proceedings of the First International Conference on Requirements Engineering(ICRE94), IEEE Computer SocietyPress, Colorado Springs Colorado, April 1994.
[21] Van Lamsweerde, A., Darimont, R., and Letier, E. "Managing Conflicts in Goal-Driven Requirements Engineering", IEEE Transactions on Software Engineering, Vol. 24, N. 11, November 1998.

The Holon Framework: A Software Project *Post-Mortem* Case Study

G.A. Bell, M.A. Cooper, J.O. Jenkins, A. Page, S. Qureshi, and J. Warwick

Abstract

This paper introduces the Holon Framework, which aims to improve and control the software development process. It is an interdisciplinary approach that is derived from the Systems Movement and Software Engineering, combining aspects of Soft Systems Thinking and Hard Systems Thinking. An overview of the soft and hard part of the Holon Framework is provided. The soft part of the framework, which is linked to improvement, is used to examine a completed software project. The research design of the case study is described and used to evaluate the findings of the investigation.

1. Introduction

We take as our starting point the systems movement, and the concepts of systemic wholeness and systematic analysis. We discuss the essence of Hard Systems Thinking and identify a key weakness which explains the development of Soft Systems Thinking and soft methodologies (*i.e.* Soft Systems Methodology). Again, a significant weakness is highlighted to explain our use of ideas from representational measurement theory.

A fundamental area of research in software engineering is software project management which subdivides into Software Process Control and Software Process Improvement, and are inextricably linked through the use of metrics. An overview of the Holon Framework is provided, but this paper is concerned with the soft part of the framework, which combines aspects of Soft Systems Methodology and the Goal/Question/Metrics methodology. This is associated with improvement for it addresses certain types of questions *i.e.* 'the what', 'the where', and 'the who'. The hard part of the framework is linked with control for it addresses different questions, *i.e.* 'the how', 'the why', 'the when', and uses the System Dynamics technique. It is contended that representational measurement theory will cement the soft and hard parts of the approach.

The soft part of the framework is used to investigate a completed project involving a software application developed for radiotherapy equipment. The aim of the study reported here is to highlight the problems ('the whats') during different phases ('the wheres') of the development process, from the point of view of the quality consultant ('the who'). We justify the selection of the case study approach given the exploratory nature of the investigation.

The study findings are outlined and evaluated both internally and externally through the research design. The internal evaluation requires confirmation of the different outputs of the work, *e.g.* identified problems, to the satisfaction of the stakeholders before commencing with the next stages of the framework. The external evaluation requires confirmation of the outputs with other research. Finally, we outline future research broadly based on the objectives of General Systems Theory.

2. Systems Movement

The systems movement contends that system concepts can provide a source of explanations for many kinds of observed phenomena, which are beyond the reach of reductionist science [1]. Checkland identifies Hard Systems Thinking (HST) and Soft

Systems Thinking (SST) as two fundamentally different ways of undertaking an inquiry in which systems ideas are applied.

Checkland considers both systems engineering and RAND systems analysis as hard systems methodologies, because both are systematic in the sense that they proceed in a rational and well-ordered manner. Moreover, he highlights the essence of their approach to real-world problem solving:

> *"there is a desired state S_1, and a present state, S_0, and alternative ways of getting from S_0 to S_1. 'Problem solving', according to this view, consists of defining S_1 and S_0 and selecting the best means of reducing the difference between them."*

It is argued that most hard methodologies are goal-centred or goal-orientated in that they assume the problem, *i.e.* 'the what', is given for the goal state S_1. For example, to build a product to meet certain requirements, the usual objective is to find the best way of building the product to meet the requirements *i.e.* 'the how'. Mathematical techniques such as regression analysis can investigate alternative ways to achieve state S_1. It is assumed that there is no ambiguity in the definitions of S_1 and S_0. The need to identify the problem, *i.e.* 'the what' is a significant weakness of HST.

When investigating social situations, systems theorists realised that the problem, *i.e.* 'the what', could not be assumed as given. Stakeholders may have different views of what are the most important problems to be solved in order to improve the situation. Over the last 20 years or so, 'soft' methodologies have emerged with the aim of attempting to assist in understanding the perspective of the stakeholder, leading, it is hoped, to relevant improvements in the area of concern. We argue that some soft methodologies use systems as mental constructs to help the stakeholder and the facilitator make sense of a situation. Note that the frame of reference of the modeller changes from 'observer' to 'facilitator' in order to understand stakeholders' points of view. Most soft methodologies can be associated with soft systems thinking. Bell *et al* [2,3] argue that the main aim of the soft systems thinker is to identify state S_0 problems, *i.e.* 'the whats', relevant to that social situation which require solving or controlling in order to produce a desired state S_1.

Soft Systems Methodology (SSM) [1] emerged from systems engineering. It is a systems-based general learning methodology for investigating, learning about and improving a problem situation. It has been argued that it should be combined with simulation and more specifically, System Dynamics. There are many accounts of successful applications of SSM in a variety of organisations. We would contend, however, that there are weaknesses in the method, and that one of these concerns the way in which system change is controlled. DeMarco [4] states that '*You cannot control what you cannot measure*". Bell *et al* [5] argue that the lack of use of metrics within SSM is a significant methodological limitation. Furthermore, they explain that the identification of relevant problems and their metrication will lead to more informed decision-making. In summary, the mix of SSM as a framework of enquiry and GQM [6] as a process for identifying goals and metrics results in a combined approach, the Holon Framework, in which each component enhances the other.

3. Software Engineering

The two fundamental research areas within software engineering are software technology and software project management; the latter is of interest here. As mentioned earlier, software project management subdivides into two important research areas, Software Process Control (SPC) and Software Process Improvement (SPI).

SPC research is underwritten by the notion that a disciplined approach to software production is needed in order to achieve sensible cost, schedule and quality targets. SPC focuses on the software development phases, *i.e.* product design, detailed design, programming/coding and system integration. SPC is attained through establishing a metrics programme, identifying project milestones, use of algorithmic cost models, monitoring differences between actuals and estimated milestones, explaining differences through the use of algorithmic cost models, and deriving strategies to enable milestones to be met. There are two fundamental and interrelated investigation areas associated with SPC research. These are: cost estimation (*e.g.* metrics and algorithmic cost models) and preparation methods (*e.g.* Work Breakdown Structures, Gantt and PERT Charts). SPI frameworks and methodologies are also used when establishing or updating a metrics programme to assist in deriving project goals.

SPI research is underpinned by the view that all issues of software quality revolve around improving the development process. Additionally, it aims to enhance quantitative understanding through numerical representation of identified problems in order to improve change management decision-making. SPI focuses on 'characterising', *e.g.* establishing and enhancing metric baselines, and 'improving', *e.g.* removing production "bottlenecks", and is underwritten by representational measurement theory [7]. Indeed, both SPC and SPI research are inextricably linked through the use of metrics.

Bell *et al* [5] find the GQM methodology a commendable approach to improving the quantitative visibility of the software development process. However, it does not in itself provide a structure for working with a client group; it does not give guidelines or methods for identifying the problems and goals as perceived by the stakeholders; and it does not encourage stakeholders to take action as part of the process improvement framework. It was felt that these problems could be rectified by the incorporation of GQM within the broader framework of Soft Systems Methodology, or broader system-based enquiry process. Moreover, the generation of software metrics enables the use of mathematical techniques such as system dynamics (SD).

The Holon Framework merges aspects of SSM and GQM methodology, which is associated with improvement. Furthermore, it integrates the use of the SD technique, which can be linked with control. Hence, we derive the conjecture *that the Holon Framework is the way ahead for SPI and SPC research*. To gain confidence in the emerging approach a study is undertaken using the soft part of the framework, which addresses 'the what, 'the where', and 'the who' type questions. Additionally, we have selected the case study approach, because of the nature of the research.

4. The Case Study Approach

Galliers [8] has produced a taxonomy of research approaches for Information Systems research highlighting their strengths and weaknesses. After examining Galliers' work, we have chosen the case study approach. Case studies attempt to describe relationships that exist within a single or organisational group. An important strength is that it captures 'reality' in greater detail and analyses more variables. Its weaknesses include difficulty in generalising for it can be restricted to a single organisation [8]. Our fundamental reason for selecting the approach is that a case study enables an investigation to retain the holistic and meaningful characteristics of a real-world situation.

Yin [9] contends that a good research design has five important components, which require enhancement with respect to the characteristics of our proposed case study. We next outline each component of our design. These components demand the development of a preliminary theory related to the topic of study. This is intended to improve the quality of the research design and become the main vehicle for generalising the results of the case study. An exploratory case study is undertaken to test our conjecture. The exploratory case study will serve to confirm, refine or refute our conjecture.

4.1. Component 1 – Research Question

The soft part of the Holon Framework attempts to examine the radiotherapy software project from the point of view of the stakeholder – quality consultant. We have derived two research questions.

- *Does the soft part of the Holon Framework capture relevant problems associated with a completed software project to the satisfaction of the stakeholder?*
- *Does the soft part of the Holon Framework identify metrics that could improve the quantitative visibility of completed software projects?*

4.2. Component 2 – Proposition

The exploratory study has two research hypotheses. These are related to the problem and metrication identification capabilities of the Holon Framework.

- Hypothesis 1 – *the soft part of the Holon Framework highlights the relevant problems associated with a completed software project.*
- Hypothesis 2 – *the soft part of the Holon Framework identifies metrics for a completed software project that could have improved its quantitative visibility.*

4.3. Component 3 – Unit(s) of Analysis

The soft nature of the investigation influences the unit of analysis. We believe that the stakeholder must confirm the outputs, *e.g.* Holons, problems, themes and metrics, from each stage of the framework before commencing with another.

4.4. Component 4 – Evaluation

We intend to internally and externally evaluate the capabilities of the soft part of the Holon Framework. The internal evaluation relies on the stakeholder to confirm the findings from the holon approach. Additionally, we compare the results of our work with an internal report on the radiotherapy software project undertaken by the organisation. The external evaluation uses a survey conduced by KPMG, which examines the primary causes of software runaways. We compare the case study and survey findings.

4.5. Component 5 – Interpretation of Findings

The evaluation of the problem and metric identification capabilities of the Holon Framework will allow us to test the two hypotheses. Additionally, we will attempt to answer the research questions through interpreting the study findings. Finally, this may lead to confirmation, refinement or refutation of the conjecture.

5. The Holon Framework

Checkland argues that researchers who apply systems concepts to investigate social situations face difficulties because these situations are never clearly defined. He prefers to use the word 'Holon' rather than 'system' as it highlights a distinctive approach to investigating such situations. Checkland indicates that the word 'Holon' was originally coined by Koestler to express the principle of hierarchical structure. We consider a Holon to be an abstract representation of a social situation that captures all problems. It is used as a framework to discover relevant issues from stakeholders' points of view; these are organised in a layered structure. In accordance with SSM, they are used to enquire into the problem domain by facilitating open dialogue. The Holon Framework (see figure 1.0) can be used for either *post-mortem* or visioning investigations.

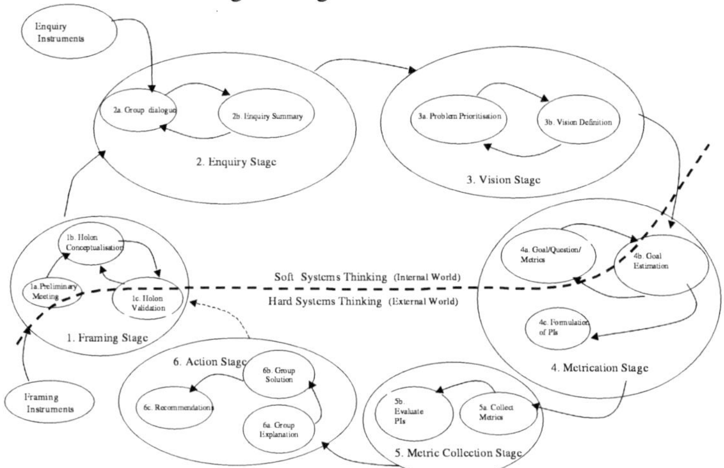

Figure 1.0: The Holon Framework Bell et a[2]

5.1. The Framing Stage

This stage has a number of objectives, among which are that the stakeholders are identified and familiarised with the framework being used, that the Framing Holon and environment holon are identified and labelled (including sub-holons where necessary) and that the investigators gain a broad understanding of the problem situation. Outputs from this stage will be the identified stakeholders ('the who') and an agreed Holon structure that can be used to guide the investigation and any modelling that takes place.

5.1.1. Illustration of Framing Stage through Radiotherapy Case Study

During the preliminary meeting we discussed the Holon Framework and agreed the aims of the study with the quality consultant. Additionally, we used a conceptual model that represented the software development process from a previous investigation to assist in the identification of the relevant holons. The software consultant suggested some changes that would be more representative of this particular project (see figure 2.0).

5.2. The Enquiry Stage

This stage aims to identify the problems as perceived by the stakeholders. The agreed conceptual model of the software development process provides a focus for dialogue. During group meetings with the stakeholders, information is placed in the relevant holons through the use of rich pictures and written notes. The output of this stage is a diagram (see figure 2) showing the problems in the situation of concern; this is verified by the stakeholders.

5.2.1. Illustration of Enquiry Stage through Radiotherapy Case Study

The enquiry stage comprised an informally structured interview to explore the perceptions of the software consultant in order to gain an understanding of the project. A large sheet of paper with the holons sketched on it was used to capture all of the relevant problems (see figure 2.0). The findings from the enquiry stage are now outlined.

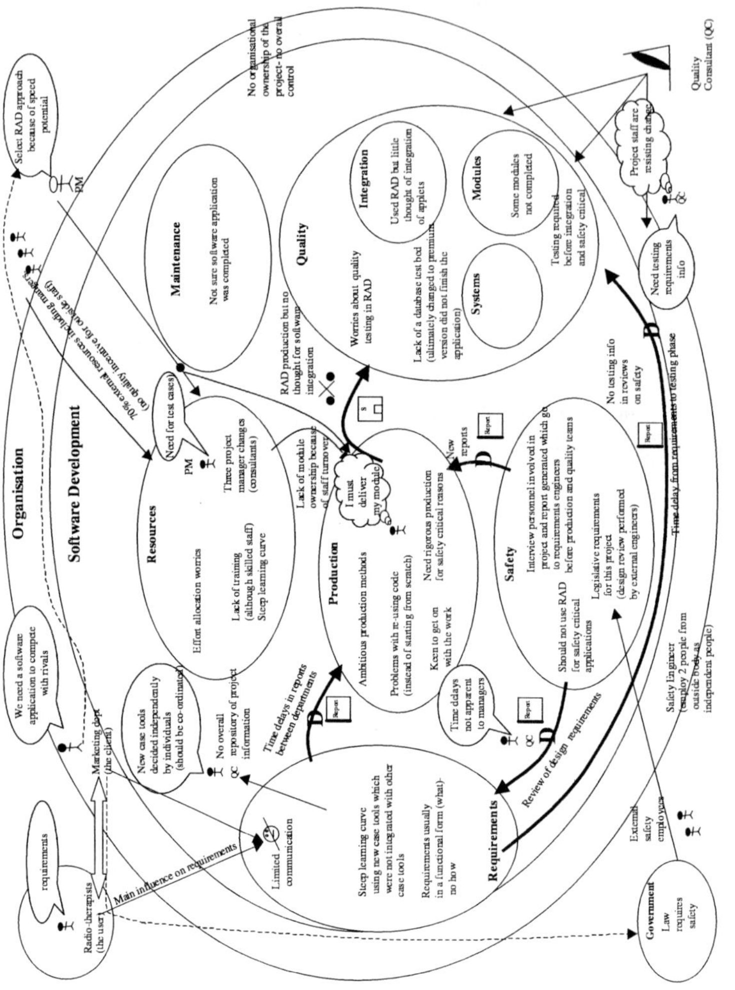

Rich Picture Dictionary

●✕●	Conflict	QC	Quality Consultant
D	Delay	Report	Report
	Poor Communication	S	Software
PM	Project Manager		Worldview of a stakeholder

Figure 2.0: Summary of Radiotherapy Software Project Rich Picture

Environmental Holon -- Organisation

The project involved changing an existing product, with the development of a Graphical User Interface (GUI) to replace the existing character-based version. The main concern of the client was the speed of product creation required to provide quick competition to a rival product; the standard product would be supplemented with a further improved premium version later. The project was initiated by the development manager and the system architect, who selected the Rapid Application Development (RAD) approach. This would permit the marketing department to compete quickly (and also to assess the use of a new type of methodology). As a safety critical project there was a requirement in law to employ independent safety engineers to ensure that the product fulfilled safety criteria and contingency plans were in place to provide a robust finished product.

Sub-Holon -- Resource

Resources were freely available, but problems arose concerning staff commitment to the project. The first manager left and after early indications of problems, the software development manager recruited an external project manager. He identified the need for a quality consultant to control quality issues. However, despite being contracted to complete the project, the external project manager left to be replaced by another. Lack of staff continuity at a senior level and use of resources external to the organisation resulted in problems with overall project control. Furthermore, large amounts of external resource (approximately 70% of the total) appeared to result in a lack of quality commitment to the product on the part of the 'temporary' employees. The developers were only interested in their particular part of the development and paid little heed to integration issues.

Sub-Holon -- Requirements

The requirements specifications for the interface were user-dominated and produced in the form of functional 'use cases'. However, these did not cover the internal behaviour of the software and so had to be translated into 'test cases' for quality testing to take place. This conversion process resulted in delays between requirements identification and quality testing.

Requirements specification was also affected by the use of a Computer-Aided Software Engineering (CASE) tool. The data produced from the CASE tool (although useful for requirements control) was not integrated with other CASE tools used in the project. Therefore, there was no overall database of information (repository) causing communication difficulties. In addition, the new RAD methodology and the new CASE tools (for which there was minimal training) involved a steep learning curve, which also caused delays.

Sub-Holon -- Production

A major influence on production was the RAD methodology employed. Using a RAD methodology meant that software production had to conform to stringent time periods, with each section responsible for a certain portion (or applet) of the system. This method relies on obtaining requirements quickly, but the requirements identification delays caused problems in achieving production schedules. The requirements and design issues that were identified were not dealt with at the time because of concerns in meeting the project milestones with resulting integration and quality issues. The new production methodology (RAD) also caused uncertainty in estimating the amount of time taken to produce the software.

Further problems occurred with the developers themselves who proved difficult to control, acting independently and often refusing to act on quality issues identified. This problem appears to be due to the transient nature of the largely external developers and to the changing project management identified in resources above. This control problem ultimately resulted in a lack of ownership of the software production.

In addition, an issue arose concerning the method of testing. Testing had to take place not on the finished product but on a simulation of the product, as the product was constructed in parts (following the RAD process). Testing proved difficult with simulation models.

Sub-Holon -- Safety

The RAD methodology used in the project had important safety implications. RAD is not considered robust enough for safety critical products. RAD increases flexibility, productivity and speed, at the expense of reliability and robustness. As this project concerned the interface for a radiotherapy desk top unit, it was considered by the development and system architect to be *not* safety critical. However, the interface could affect the dosages of radiation, and so had a safety sub-system and independent safety reviews. There was a difference in views as to whether the system was or was not safety critical; since the product as a whole is safety critical, its component parts should be treated in the same manner. Therefore, a RAD methodology should only have been employed with extreme caution.

As the software was safety critical, safety meetings were required involving the independent external safety advisors, the safety engineer and other project personnel. They produced a report containing a review of the design requirements. This report was requirements-orientated and went initially to the requirements engineer and the systems architect. However, it did not contain any test cases to prove that the contingencies to be built into the software actually worked. When it was seen by the quality consultant, he included quality personnel and the construction of test cases in the design requirements interviews and ensured that the reports reached the production and quality teams directly to minimise delay.

Sub-Holon -- Quality

Quality is imperative as the product is safety critical; however, it was constructed with little thought to quality. The test cases were initially omitted from the design requirements interview. There was also a lack of documentation of test plan cases with consequential uncertainties over what software tests had been made. These problems were subsequently addressed by the quality consultant, but his attempts to ensure production quality was adhered to was resisted by developers who appeared to be primarily interested in producing the software within given time-scales.

5.3. The Visioning Stage

This stage attempts to produce a vision for the situation of concern through solving some themes. Themes are a collection of related problems, which can be linked with a sub-holon hierarchical level. The stakeholders are asked to decide whether a theme is 'a must' or 'a want', *i.e.* a theme that must be solved or one which they would like to solve. The vision mode of the framework generates an attainable vision (based on Checkand's [1] root definition) which attempts to solve or control certain themes within the foreseeable future, *i.e.* 2 to 3 years. The outputs of this stage are identification of the themes and construction of an agreed vision for the situation of concern.

5.3.1. Illustration of Visioning Stage through Radiotherapy Case Study

We examined the information from the conceptual model and collated various related problems, which produced themes that could be linked to the sub-holon hierarchical level. A third meeting was arranged to confirm the themes and identify potential solutions (see table 1.0). It was found that some of the solutions to the themes required structural changes to the development process, *e.g.* construction of an information system, and others required metrication, *e.g.* monitor production effort allocation.

Project: Radiotherapy Software Application		**Where**: Resources	
What: Themes	**Who:**	**Must/Want**	**Solutions**
Concerns about the succession of managers leaving causing continuity problems and poor project control. **(Theme 5)**	Quality Consultant	M	Appoint a software project manager from within the organisation for stability and ownership purposes.
Concerns about effort allocation. **(Theme 6)**	Quality Consultant	M	Develop an effort allocation programme, that is linked to tasks to be completed.

Table 1.0: Key themes from Sub-Holon – Resources

5.4. The Metrication Stage

This stage analyses the themes and links the emergent problems with the appropriate hierarchical level. The GQM methodology is used to generate metrics that characterise the problems. The outputs of this stage are diagrams that highlight the hierarchical level of the problem and appropriate goal. Additionally, metrics tables are generated which highlight the theme ('what'), the appropriate holon ('where') the metrics should be collected, and the relevant stakeholder ('who').

5.4.1. Illustration of Metrication Stage through Radiotherapy Case Study

We produced a number of software metrics to some of the themes, which would improve the quantitative visibility of the project. Furthermore, numerous metrics tables were proposed, that could be placed in the metrics collection function of the Holon Metrics Tools.

Project: Radiotherapy Software Application			**Where**: Production			**Who**: Software developers	
What: (Theme)	Concern about Effort allocation.						
Goal:	Monitor production effort allocation						
Question	How much effort is required to produce modules?						
Metric	Production effort						
Dimension	Person hours						
Weeks	1	2	3	4	5	6	7
No of hours							
Comments							

Table 2.0: An Example of a Metrics Table

5.5. The Metrication Collection Stage

This stage (not applied in the radiotherapy *post mortem* case study) aims to collect software metrics over a period of time through the use of the Holon Metrics Tool, which is a web-based information system. Meetings are held regularly to enable the stakeholders to explain the dynamic behaviour patterns of the metrics. The outputs from this stage would be the refining of the Holon Metrics Tool and completion of the data collection process.

5.6. The Action Stage

This stage (not applied in the radiotherapy *post mortem* case study) aims to use the collected data to develop a SD model that explains the situation of concern, which is owned by the stakeholders. Model ownership is achieved as agreed verification and validation tests are passed to the satisfaction of the stakeholders. The SD model will enable the development of meaningful strategies to achieve the agreed vision through examination of various 'what if' scenarios. The outputs of this stage are the construction of a SD model to the satisfaction of the stakeholder and the development of strategies to achieve the agreed vision.

6. Case Study Evaluation

The soft part of the Holon Framework was internally and externally evaluated in order to test the hypotheses. The internal evaluation requires the outputs from the different stages of the framework, *i.e.* from framing to metrication, to be used as the units of analysis, which must be approved by the stakeholders. The holons ('the where') generated at the framing stage and the problems ('the whats') identified by the consultant ('the who') were confirmed.

Additionally, the metrics produced from the themes were verified to the satisfaction of the quality consultant.

The results of the exploratory case study were compared with an internal document that reviewed the radiotherapy project. This report (96 pages in length) systematically analysed the software development process, *i.e.* interviews with staff responsible for particular phases of the project, and took 2 months to complete. We found that the soft part of the Holon Framework identified most of the problems (see table 3.0), and only took 3 weeks to produce. Additionally, we identified various metrics that could enhance control of the software development process.

Example	Description of similarity
1	Software project planning concerns.
2	Introduction of new case tools decided independently by individuals.
3	High staff turnover causing software ownership problems.
4	Poor software quality control producing integration problems.

Table 3.0: Examples of Similarities between the Internal Report and Case Study

The external evaluation requires confirmation of the outputs with other research. A survey conducted by KPMG, which was enhanced by Glass [10] is selected. Table 4.0 highlights some of the case study and survey results. We believe the evaluation of the soft part of Holon Framework supports the two hypotheses.

Cause	Description of Cause (Glass)	Findings from Exploratory Case Study
1	Project objectives not fully specified	
2	Bad planning and estimating	Concerns about effort allocation.(Theme 6)
3	Technology new to the organisation	Concerns about introduction of new case tools creating steep learning curves for staff and causing project delays. (Theme 3)
4	Inadequate/no project management methodology	Concerns about poor project management of the development process. (Theme 2)
5	Insufficient senior staff on the team	
6	Poor performance by suppliers of hardware/software	

Table 4.0: Comparison between Primary Causes of Software Runaways (Glass [10]) and the findings from the Case Study

7. Conclusion

An outline of the soft and hard parts of the Holon Framework has been given. The soft part of the framework (*post mortem* mode) examined a radiotherapy software project. The strengths and weaknesses of the approach are shown through an exploratory case study. The study addresses two key research questions.

Does the soft part of the Holon Framework capture relevant problems associated with a completed software project to the satisfaction of the stakeholder? We believe the soft part of the framework highlights the relevant problems associated with the radiotherapy project. Furthermore, the units of analysis, *i.e.* the outputs, used for evaluation increased the quality consultants confidence in the framework. A strength of this systemic approach (underpinned by the systems thinking method) is that it can produce more comprehensive reviews of software projects, than a systematic approach (underpinned the analytic thinking method). A weakness of the exploratory case study was that only one stakeholder participated in the research.

Does the soft part of the Holon Framework identify metrics that could improve the quantitative visibility of completed software projects? We believe the identified metrics derived from relevant themes would increase the control of software project. Moreover, the quality consultant considered the metrics tables to be useful for they identified the problem and which part of the project the metrics should be collected and from whom. We contend that the exploratory case study confirms our conjecture and justifies further research.

Bell *et al* [2] are conducting a case study using the soft part of the Holon Framework (*visioning* mode) for higher education planning with several academics. The research to date suggests that the holon approach empowers stakeholders, because they identified the problems (at state S_0) which need controlling. Moreover, the study seems to confirm a principle of the Holon Framework –' *to be value-full rather than value-free'*. We contend that the units of analysis from the subjective case study can be used to find commonality between investigations. Finally, the two objectives of General Systems Theory guide our research: first, to identify common holons and problems which may constitute system dynamics archetype structures operating in different software development processes; and second, to base the maturing interdisciplinary framework on a spectrum of theories.

8. References

[1] Checkland, P.B. "Systems Thinking, Systems Practice", J. Wiley and Sons, Chichester, UK, 1981.

[2] Bell, G.A., Warwick, J., Cooper, M.A., and Kennedy, M. "Towards a General Holistic Framework for Improving and Controlling Human Activity Systems ", In Lehaney, Clarke and Nicholls (Eds) "Mixed Mode Modelling: Mixing Methodologies for Intervention", Kluwer Academic Publisher, Utrecht, Netherlands, (forthcoming).

[3] Bell, G.A., Cooper, M.A., Kennedy, M., and Warwick, J. "The Development of the Holon and Costing Framework for Higher Education Management", In Proceedings of the 18th International System Dynamics Conference, Bergen, Norway, 2000.

[4] DeMarco, T. "Controlling Software Projects", Prentice Hall, New York, USA, 1982.

[5] Bell, G.A., Cooper, M.A., Jenkins, J.O., Minocha, S. and Weetman, J. "SSM+ GQM = The Holon Methodology: A Case Study", In Proceedings of the10th European Software Control and Metrics Conference, Herstmonceux, England, 1999.

[6] Basili, V.R. and Rombach, H.D. " The Tame Project. Towards Improvement- Oriented Software Environments", IEEE Trans. on Software Engineering, 1988, pp. 758-773.

[7] Fenton, N.E. and Pfleeger, S.L." Software Metrics: A Rigorous and Practical Approach", International Thomson Computing Press, London, UK, 1996.

[8] Galliers, R.D. "Choosing Appropriate Information Systems Research Approaches", In Nissen, H.E., Klein, H.K., and Hirschheim, R. (Eds) "Information Systems Research: Contemporary Approaches and Emergent Traditions", North-Holland, Amsterdam, Netherlands, 1991.

[9] Yin, R.K. "Case Study Research: Design and Methods", Sage Publications, London, UK, 1984.

[10] Glass, R.L. "Software Runaways", Prentice Hall International Limited, London, UK, 1998.

Measuring the requirements management key process area

Annabella Loconsole

Abstract

The purpose of this paper is to provide software measurements for implementation of the goals of the Requirements Management Key Process Area (KPA) of the Capability Maturity Model (CMM), and to ease the adoption of the KPA. The paper also provides practical guidance for people trying to implement the Requirements Management KPA. The CMM, developed by the Software Engineering Institute (SEI) is not well supported by software measurement and it is somewhat complex. An application of the Goal/Question/Metric (GQM) paradigm to the Requirements Management KPA is therefore presented. The metrics obtained will help immature companies to satisfy the goals of the Requirements Management KPA.

1. Introduction

Software processes are considered to be the main area for quality improvement. There are two main streams within Software Process Improvement (SPI) [17]. One is based on assessments of organisations' capability, e.g. Capability Maturity Model for Software (SW-CMM) [12], Software Process Improvement Capability dEtermination (SPICE) [6], BOOTSTRAP [11], and the ISO9000 family. The other is based on measurements of software practices within an organisation, e.g. Goal/Question/Metric (GQM) [1], Quality Improvement Paradigm (QIP) [2], and Application of Metrics in Industry (AMI) [14]. These approaches complement each other because software measurement is inherent to the concept of improvement, but they are seldom applied together [17]. The assessment-based approaches should always include measurements, because it is necessary to estimate the state of the software process before action is taken to improve it and compare it with the state thereafter. The SW-CMM developed by the Software Engineering Institute is intended to help software organisations to improve the maturity of their software processes, but is weakly supported by a measurement-based approach. Therefore this paper proposes a set of measures for the Requirements Management Key Process Area (KPA) of the SW-CMM. This work has been done with the aim of joining the assessment and measurement based methodologies mentioned above. The underlying assumption in the paper is that it is easier to focus the measurement and improvement activities on a specific process area, rather than trying to measure and improve all the process areas at once. This is especially true for small-medium size enterprises, which do not have enough resources to train people on complex frameworks like the SW-CMM. The Requirements Management KPA has been chosen because it is important to control the continuing definition of requirements as they change throughout the software life cycle. Such control over the requirements helps in anticipating and responding to requests of change [16]. The aim has been addressed by analysing the Requirements Management KPA of the SW-CMM and its key practices [13], and applying the GQM paradigm to it.

The first contribution of this paper is to give a general and comprehensive set of software measures for the implementation of the goals of the Requirements Management KPA within the SW-CMM (see [7] for a definition of measure and measurement). This set of measures constitutes a "pick list" that can be tailored to the specific enterprise, offering small to medium size enterprises the freedom to choose suitable subsets of software measures. Another contribution of this paper is a simple method of improving the Requirements

Management activity and the presentation of basic software measures, which are easy to understand and to use. The paper presents a practical approach and a practical guidance for people trying to fulfil the goals of the KPA. The method can also be used to evaluate the state of the Requirements Management activity.

At the time of writing, the measures are being tested at Ericsson Erisoft AB in Umeå, Sweden, which is a medium size company. The results of this empirical study will help the author to demonstrate that a joint approach is more complete than an assessment or measurement based approach. The measures obtained can be used in quantifying the amount of changes to requirements and to predict the cost for a change, helping to control requirements and changes to requirements.

The measures will be grouped by maturity level. For instance an immature enterprise can start measuring the total number of requirements and the number of changes to requirements throughout the software life cycle. This would provide better control and visibility into the Requirements Management activity, improving the software process a small step towards the goal of having a repeatable process. For each measure proposed, improvement actions will be suggested to help decision makers in their job. After these actions are taken, an enterprise can follow the approach described in "Application of Metrics in Industry" [14], which suggests to cycle four steps (analyse, act, metricate, and improve) to continue with the improvement of the KPA.

The remainder of this paper is organised as follows: the section 1.1 describes related research in software measurement for the SW-CMM, sections 2 and 3 present an overview of the CMM and the GQM respectively, the application of the GQM to the CMM is described in section 4, section 5 contains initial results of the experiment started in the before-mentioned company, and concluding remarks and future directions are presented in section 6.

1.1. Related Work

Several studies on software measurement for the SW-CMM have been done prior to this work. One of the most relevant has been done by Baumert and McWhinney [3]. Their report provides a set of indicators (composite measures) that are compatible with the measurement practices of the SW-CMM. The indicators are categorised according to the quality attributes they fulfil and not by KPAs. Raynus [15] confirms the connection between software measurement and the SW-CMM. His work examines relationships between measurable process quantities, and reviews the SW-CMM demonstrating that software measurement can be used to improve the behaviour of a software development organisation. His book represents a quantitative approach to software management and SPI. He suggests some metrics for the SW-CMM and their use. In goal oriented software improvement, the measurements must be focused on specific goals, for example specific process areas, while the authors mentioned above, suggest indicators across all the maturity levels. Therefore, this paper presents a comprehensive collection of measures that are focused on a specific KPA namely the Requirements Management KPA of the SW-CMM.

2. The Requirements Management KPA of the Capability Maturity Model

As shown in figure 1, the CMM is composed of 5 distinct levels (Initial, Repeatable, Defined, Managed, Optimising) [12].

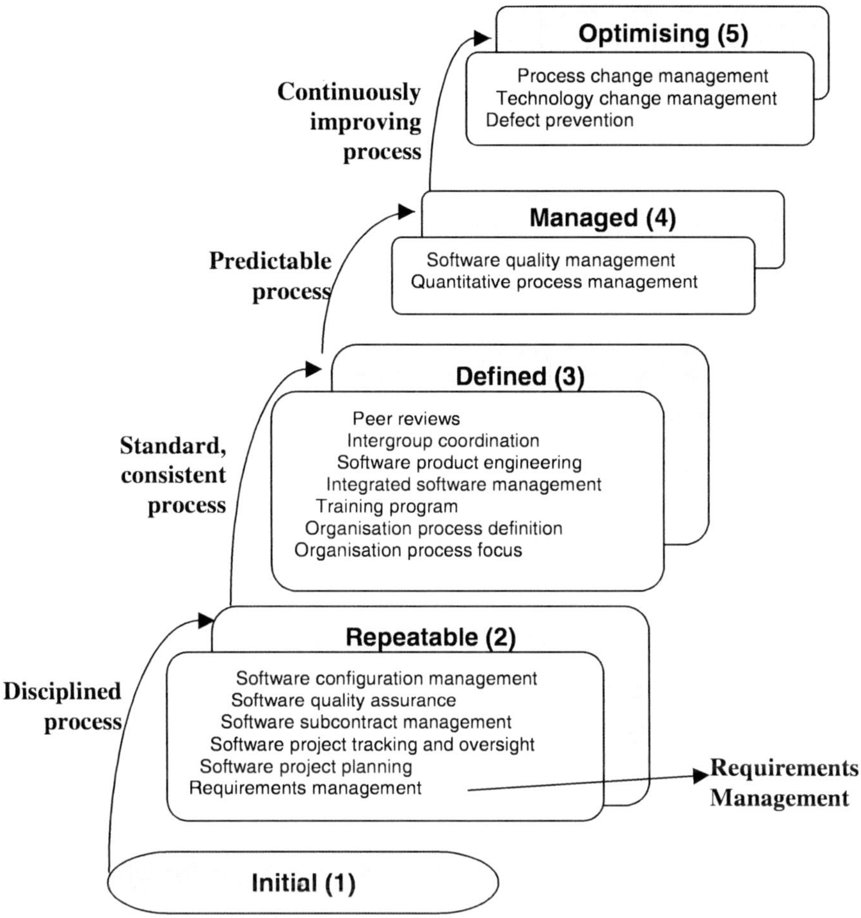

Figure 1: The Key Process Areas by Maturity Level [12].

Each CMM level, except the initial level, has several Key Process Areas (KPA). [12]. One level 2 KPA is Requirements Management. "*The purpose of Requirements Management is to establish a common understanding between the customer and the software project of the customer's requirements that will be addressed by the software project*" as defined in [13]. This means that the requirements of a software project should be complete, documented, unambiguous, controlled, etc., in order to design a software product, which satisfies the customer's needs. Very often, requirements change through the software development life cycle but the control of the change requests is poor. The activity of "Requirements Management" is focused on the control of the requirements gathering, establishing an agreement between the customer and the software team on the requirements, checking, reviewing and managing the changes on requirements. This activity is the process of ensuring that a software product produced from a set of requirements, will meet those requirements.

3. The Goal/Question/Metric Paradigm

The Goal/Question/Metric (GQM) paradigm is a method for helping an organisation to focus the measurement program on their goals. It states that an organisation should have specific goals in mind before data are collected [1]. GQM does not specify concrete goals. It is rather a structure for defining goals and refining them into a set of quantifiable questions These questions imply a specific set of metrics and data to be collected in order to achieve these goals. The GQM paradigm consists of three steps:

Purpose

Analyse some

(objects: processes, products, other experience models)

for the purpose of

(why: characterisation, evaluation, prediction, motivation, improvement)

Perspective:

with respect to

(focus: cost, correctness, defect removal, changes, reliability, user frien

from the point of view of

(who: user, customer, manager, developer, corporation,...)

Environment:

in the following context

(problem factors, people factors, resource factors, process factors,...)

Figure 2: Goal Template.

1. Specify a set of goals based on the needs of the organisation and its projects. Determine what should be improved or learned. The process of goal definition is supported by templates like the ones shown in figure 2 [1]. By using these templates it is possible to define the goals in terms of purpose, perspective, and environment. The identification of subgoals, entities, and attributes related to the subgoals is made in this step.
2. Generate a set of quantifiable questions. Business goals are translated into operational statements with a measurement focus. Basili and Rombach [1] provide different sets of guidelines to classify questions as product-related or process-related. The same questions can be defined to support data interpretation of multiple goals.
3. Define a set of metrics that provides the quantitative information needed to answer the quantifiable questions. In this step, the metrics suitable to provide information to answer the questions are identified and related to each question. Generally, each metric can supply information to answer several questions and sometimes a combination of metrics is needed to make up the answer of a question.

Once these steps are identified, data are collected and interpreted to produce an answer to the quantifiable questions defined to fulfil the goals of the organisation [1], [17].

4. Application of the Goal/Question/Metrics to the CMM

The CMM and the GQM can very easily be intertwined. The CMM defines one or more goals for each KPA as shown in figure 3. These goals can be used for the first step of the GQM. The CMM defines two distinct goals for the Requirements Management Key Process Area (KPA). The first ones states the following:

"System requirements allocated to software are controlled to establish a baseline for software engineering and management use" [13].

It focuses on the control of requirements to set up a baseline, that is a kind of standard by which things are measured or compared. If the requirements are not controlled, there will be no clear picture of the final product, because the final product is based on the requirements. The second goal of the Requirements Management KPA states the following:

"Software plans, products and activities are kept consistent with the system requirements allocated to software" [13].

The main focus of this goal is the consistency between the requirements and any software product created from those requirements. This consistency would result in the design of the product required by the customer. The goals presented can be redefined by applying the goal template in figure 2 as follows. To *Analyse* the system requirements allocated to software *for the purpose of* establishing a baseline *with respect to* the control of the requirements *from the point of view of* academy and the software manager, *in the context of* the company where the Requirements Management is implemented. The second goal can be redefined as follows: to *Analyse* software plans, work products and activities *for the purpose of* consistency with the system requirements allocated to software *from the point of view* of academy and the software manager, *in the context of* the company where the Requirements Management is implemented.

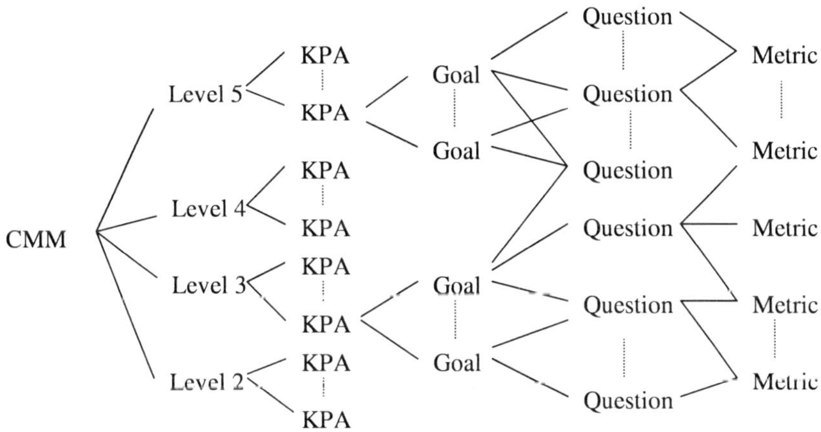

Figure 3: Relationship between CMM and GQM

The second step in the GQM paradigm is to generate a set of quantifiable questions. The questions have been produced by applying the guidelines for process related questions [1], analysing the goals of the Requirements Management KPA and the its Key Practices [13] word by word, reading papers [8], [3], discussing with colleagues, and browsing web pages. For some questions a rationale will be given to better understand the meaning and/or the utility of a certain question.

4.1. Questions for the First Goal of the Requirements Management KPA

By analysing the first goal, a question arisen is: how can the requirements be controlled? And why should we control them? We know that it is not possible to specify in the beginning exactly what the customer wants. Neither it is possible to dictate the frequency or desirability of changes. The changes can come at the worst moment and impede our ability to finish a project with the available resources. The only possibility is to control the continuing definition of requirements as they change throughout the life cycle [16].

Table 1: Questions and measures for the first goal of the Requirements Management KPA.

Questions	Measures
1 What is the current status of each requirement?	• Status of each requirement
2 What is the level of the stability of the requirements?	• # initial requirements • # final requirements • # changes per requirement
3 Why are the requirements changed?	• # initial requirements • # final requirements • # changes per requirement • # test cases per requirement • Type of change to requirements • Reason of change to requirements • Major source of request for a change to requirements • Phase where change was requested
4 What is the cost of changing the requirements?	• Cost of change to requirements • Size of a change to requirements
5 Is the number of changes to requirements manageable?	• Total # Requirements • # changes to requirements proposed • # changes to requirements open • # changes to requirements approved • # changes to requirements incorporated into base line • # changes to requirements rejected • The computer software configuration item(s) (CSCI) affected by a change to requirements • Major source of request for a change to requirements • Requirement type for each change to requirements • # requirements affected by a change
6 Does the number of changes to requirements decrease with time?	• # changes to requirements per unit of time
7 How are affected groups and individuals informed about the changes?	• Notification of Changes (NOC) shall be documented and distributed as a key communication document • # affected groups and individuals informed about NOC
8 How many other requirements are affected by a require ment change?	• # requirements affected by a change
9 In what way are the other requirements affected by a requirement change?	• Type of change to requirements • Reason of change to requirements • Phase where change was requested
10 Is the size of the requirements manageable?	• Size of requirements
11 How many incomplete, inconsistent and missing allocated requirements are identified?	• # incomplete requirements • # inconsistent requirements • # missing requirements
12 Does the number of "To Be Done" (TBD) decrease with time?	• # TBDs in requirements specifications • # TBDs per unit of time
13 How are the requirements defined and documented?	• Kind of documentation
14 Are the requirements scheduled for implementation into a particular release actually addressed as planned?	• # requirements scheduled for each software build or release
15 How many requirements are included in the baseline?	• # baselined requirements • phase when requirements are baselined

Any information on requirements can help to establish control. Especially important is to know the starting set and final set of requirements. To increase the control of the requirements, their status as well as their stability could be investigated (see questions 1 and 2 in table 1). The possible status of a requirement could be: new, analysed, approved, documented, rejected, incorporated into the baseline, designed, implemented, tested, etc. Requirements stability is concerned with the changes made in requirements, therefore a set of questions (see questions 3-9 in table 1) about requirements changes can be defined to refine the question 2. The level of requirements stability can be measured also by having information about the size of the requirements and by identifying problematic requirements (see questions 10-12 in table 1).

Once there is control over the requirements, a baseline must be established. Therefore some questions about how the requirements are documented, and how many of them are included in the baseline, are defined (see questions 13-15 in table 1).

Table 1 shows all the questions defined and the measures proposed to give information to answer questions. Please observe that some of these questions are also used for the second goal of the Requirements Management KPA, for instance, questions 13 and 14.

4.2. Questions for the Second Goal of the Requirements Management KPA

The purpose of the second goal is mainly to keep consistency between the requirements and the software project, therefore it is suggested to keep traceability among the software documents. Traceability between requirements and the software project facilitates the analysis of the effects of a software change and reduces the effort to locate the causes of a product failure. Tracking the requirements and changes made to requirements can help to maintain traceability (questions 1-7) among the requirement documents.

When the changes to requirements have been implemented, other documents are most probably affected by this change. Therefore it is suggested to check the status of software plans, work products, and activities, which could be "identified, evaluated, assessed, documented, planned, communicated to affected groups and individual, and tracked to completion".

Table 2: Questions and measures for the second goal of the Requirements Management KPA.

Questions		Measures
1	Does the software product satisfy the requirements?	• # initial requirements • # final requirements • # test cases per requirement • Type of change to requirements
2	What is the impact of the changes to requirements on the software project?	• Effort expended on Requirements Management activity • Time spent in upgrading • # documents affected by a change
3	What is the status of the changes to software plans, work products, and activities?	• Status of software plans, work products, and activities
4	Are the requirements scheduled for implementation into a particular release actually addressed as planned?	• # requirements scheduled for each software build or release
5	How are the requirements defined and documented?	• Kind of documentation
6	Does the number of TBDs prevent satisfactory completion of the product?	• # TBDs in requirements specifications
7	Are all development work products consistent with the requirements?	• # inconsistencies

5. Measures for the Goals of the Requirements Management KPA

The third step of the GQM is to define sets of metrics that provide the quantitative information necessary to answer the questions. In this paper, only a set of measures is presented, which is shown in tables 1 and 2. There are overlaps among the questions for the two goals and among the measures. The same measure can be used to give information to answer different questions. Some of the measures are suggested by the SW-CMM (status of allocated requirements, change activity, and cumulative number of changes to allocated requirements). Other possible measures are the number of test cases assigned to each requirement, by which it is possible to check how many requirements are verifiable; the size and the cost of a change request which could make it possible to predict the project cost and the schedule. Other measures on requirements are the ones recommended by [9] who measure attributes of requirements like ambiguity, modifiability, priority, etc. However, these are measures on the requirements and not on the requirements management process therefore these are out of the scope of this paper.

Once the three steps of the Goal Question Metric paradigm are defined, an organisation has to determine ranges for "good data" (for instance a company could accept no more then three change requests per week). Data must be collected and compared to the "good data", and eventually improvement actions are taken. A comparison of the data for the actual project with the once collected for previous projects will provide a baseline for the requirements and give meaning to the measures.

6. Testing the measures in a company

At the time of writing, the measures are being tested at Ericsson Erisoft AB in Umeå, Sweden, which is a medium-size company. People at the company used SW-CMM and improved their software process to level 2 but caused by a re-organisation they decreased their CMM maturity level. A previous study made in this company [4] shows that people at the company apply some basic measurements but they do not perform any significant evaluation of the data collected.

The test of the measures is conducted following the guidelines in [18] about how to conduct an experiment; the first step of the experiment process (definition of the experiment) has been done.

> *Object*: Requirements Management activity at Ericsson Erisoft AB in Umeå, Sweden
> *Purpose*: Evaluate the impact of the measures to improve the Requirements Management activity
> *Quality focus*: Control of the requirements
> *Perspective*: Academy
> *Context*: Medium-size company

While planning the study (which is the second step of the experiment process suggested in [18]), the author is learning the company's organisational structure, and the software processes used in the company. The software processes used are PROPS as management process and RUP (Rational Unified Process) [10] as software development process. The author is also going to map the terminology used by people in the company to the CMM terminology. Some data from studying one particular increment have been collected (a project can have many increments and each increment is a refinement of the software product). A preliminary conclusion of this study is that the domain analysis is not done very deeply and the requirements are added and changed during the software life cycle.

7. Concluding Remarks and Future Directions

An application of the GQM to the Requirements Management KPA has been reported. The result of the application of the GQM to the CMM, is a list of measures for each KPA.

The set of questions and measures presented should be tailored to the particular organisation. All level 1 companies interested in improving the Requirements Management activity are suggested to select a subset of these measures especially useful to start with. For instance, a level 1 organisation has most probably poorly defined requirements. The visibility of the process is very low at this level, and it is difficult to measure the process. Therefore, it is suggested that they count the number of requirements and changes to those requirements to establish a baseline. Other level 1 companies (like the ones referred in [5]) need to document the requirements before starting to measure. A company like Ericsson-Erisoft in Umeå (who has improved the process through the CMM in the past), can collect all the data regarding the change activity. This is possible because information about change requests is stored in reports and database.

The measures produced in this paper provide the organisation with improved visibility and better insight into the Requirements Management activity, improving the software process a small step towards the goal of having a repeatable process. The measures can be used in quantifying the amount of changes to requirements and to predict the cost for a change, helping to control requirements and changes to requirements. If the process is repeatable, more information on requirements can and should be collected, such as type of each requirement (database requirement, interface requirement, performance requirement, etc.) and change requests to each type. In general, the metrics collection will vary with the maturity of the process.

This work has been done with the aim of joining the assessment and measurement based methodologies mentioned above. The aim has been addressed by analysing the Requirements Management KPA of the SW-CMM and its key practices [13], and applying the GQM paradigm to it. The underlying assumption in the paper is that it is easier to focus the measurement and improvement activities on a specific process area, rather than trying to measure and improve all the process areas at once. The results are relevant to areas such as Requirements Management, Software Measurement, Software Process Improvement, Software Quality, etc.

The measures obtained, will be used for the elicitation of requirements information in the before-mentioned company. For each measure proposed, improvement actions will be suggested to help decision makers in their job. After these actions are taken, an enterprise can follow the approach described in "Application of Metrics in Industry" [14], which suggests to cycle four steps (analyse, act, metricate, and improve) to continue with the improvement of the KPA. Based on the data collected, suggestions for improvement of the Requirements Management activity will be given. The measurements will be automated as far as possible because personnel treat measurement as boring. Finally, application of the GQM to all the KPAs of the CMM levels will be considered.

8. Acknowledgements

Special thanks to my supervisor Jürgen Börstler for his suggestions and contribution to this paper and to all the people who have supported and contributed to the writing of this work.

9. References

[1] Basili, V.R. and Rombach, H.D., "The TAME project: Towards improvement-oriented software environments", in IEEE Transactions on Software Engineering 14(6), 1988, pp.758-773.

[2] Basili, V.R., Caldiera, C., and Rombach, H.D., "Experience Factory", Encyclopædia of Software Engineering Volume 1, (Marciniak, J.J., editor), John Wiley & Sons, 1994, pp. 469-476.

[3] Baumert, J.H. and McWhinney, M.S., "Software Measures and the Capability Maturity Model", Software Engineering Institute Technical Report, CMU/SEI-92-TR-25, ESC-TR-92-0, 1992.
[4] Bergström, C., "Process Metrics for Ericsson Erisoft AB- a proposal", Umeå University Report Umnad 292/2000, Umeå, Jan. 2000.
[5] Cline, A., "Overcoming Cultural barriers to the adoption of Object technology", in OOPSLA'97 conference proceeding, Atlanta, Oct. 1997.
[6] El Eman, K., Drouin, J.N., and Melo, W., "SPICE The Theory and Practice of Software Process Improvement and Capability Determination", IEEE Computer Society Press, Los Alamitos, California, 1997.
[7] Fenton, N.E. and Pfleeger, S.L., "Software Metrics - A Rigorous & Practical Approach", 2nd Edition, International Thomson Publishing, Boston, MA, 1996.
[8] Goodbrand, A.D. and Wang, Q., "Software Measurement Plan for the Requirements Management Key Process Area of the Capability Maturity Model for SENG623 Inc.", March 1997, http://www.cpsc.ucalgary.ca/~alang/SENG623/, (12 Feb. 2001).
[9] Hammer, T.F., Huffman, L.L. and Rosenberg, L.H., "Doing Requirements Right the First Time", CrossTalk, Dec 1998, pp. 20-25.
[10] Kruchten, P., "The Rational Unified Process- An Introduction", Addison Wesley Longman Ltd, Reading Massachusetts, May 1999.
[11] Kuvaja P. and Bicego, A., "BOOTSTRAP - Europe's Assessment Method", IEEE Software, May 1993, pp. 83-85.
[12] Paulk, M.C., Curtis, B., Chrissis, M.B. and Weber, C.V., "Capability Maturity Model for Software Version 1.1", Software Engineering Institute Technical Report, CMU/SEI-93-TR-24, ESC-TR-93-177, Pittsburgh, PA, 1993.
[13] Paulk, M. C., Weber, C.V., Garcia, S., Chrissis, M.B. and Bush, M., "Key Practices of the Capability Maturity Model Version 1.1", Software Engineering Institute Technical Report, CMU/SEI-93-TR-25 ESC-TR-93-178, Pittsburgh, PA, 1993.
[14] Pulford, K., Kunntzmann-Combelles, A., and Shirlaw, S., "The Ami Handbook: A Quantitative Approach to Software Management", Addison Wesley Longman Ltd. UK, 1996.
[15] Raynus, J., "Software Process Improvement with CMM", Artech House Publishers, Boston, 1999.
[16] Reifer, D.J., "Requirements Management: The search for Nirvana", IEEE Software, May/June 2000, pp. 45-47.
[17] van Solingen, R., and Berghout, E., "The Goal/Question/Metric Method - A practical Guide for Quality Improvement of Software development", McGRAW-Hill Companies, London, 1999.
[18] Wohlin, C., Runeson, P., Höst, M., Ohlsson, M.C., Regnell, B. and Wesslen, A., "Experimentation in Software Engineering An Introduction", Kluwer Academic Publishers, Boston/Dordrecht/London, 2000.

A framework for software project metrics

Terence L. Woodings, Gary A. Bundell

Abstract

Software Engineering is a discipline which is making exceptional progress in the development of new paradigms, methods, tools and techniques for the production of information systems. A weakness is that the academic development of the theory underlying these advances is often "out of synchronisation" with current usage. The use of metrics is a key factor in the establishment of a scientific basis for Software Engineering and the reduction of the gap between academics and practitioners. Systematic measurement is necessary for the formal modelling and evaluation of the new techniques and their optimal use within industry. A number of approaches (e.g. the Software Factory, CMM, Bootstrap, SPICE, GQM, Balanced Scorecard), have been advocated for the systematic design and introduction of software metrics for the purposes of process improvement and capability assessment in an organisation.

This paper defines a taxonomy of software metrics which is derived from the needs of users, developers and management. The properties of the classifications are discussed. Rules are then derived which generate a new set of metrics from an existing class. The rules complement standard approaches by focusing attention on user driven aspects of an organisation's measurement programme. They do this by directly linking product characteristics with organisational improvements. The method also has promise as an approach for validating process models and metrics.

Examples of the theoretical and pragmatic use of the taxonomy are provided. The paper concludes with a discussion of useful applications.

Keywords

Software Metrics, Software Engineering Management, Capability Assessment.

1. Background

Software Engineering is an immature discipline which has been making exceptional progress in the development of new paradigms, methods, tools and techniques for the production of information systems. Unlike other mature engineering disciplines, there is a demonstrable inability to estimate, plan and control projects. A hurdle to improving the respectability of the field is that the academic development of the theory underlying advances is often "out of synchronisation" with current usage. In some areas, such as formal verification methods, academia has had considerable trouble convincing industry to close the gap. In others, such as the human-computer interface, developers race ahead with new and practical concepts without waiting for theoretical justification.

This lack of synchronicity should be a cause for real concern. The use of metrics is now a key factor in the establishment of a scientific basis for Software Engineering. Systematic measurement is necessary for the formal modelling and evaluation of the new techniques and their optimal use within industry. Without metrics, it is difficult to convince industry of the advantages of adopting new academic advances such as proofs of program correctness. In medicine, new drugs are subject to rigidly controlled clinical trials. However, in information systems development, the selling of new techniques without prior assessment by an independent institution leaves it little better than a pseudo science.

The early, pioneering efforts to implement software metrics for process improvement [1, 2, 3] were often based on ad-hoc measurement programmes, which either concentrated on some key aspect of the system (such as defect counts) or came as a byproduct of other activities (such as counting lines of code during compilation). The concept of the Software Factory [4, 5, 6] was based, in part, on the philosophy of measuring every aspect of the development process in order to discover those factors of central importance.

Reaction to the limited success of these approaches and attempts to put the work on a more disciplined and scientific footing [7] led to top-down approaches [8, 9], with metrics programmes being derived from (and thus aligned with) organisational goals. This approach was further encouraged by such influential work as the Goal-Question-Measure (GQM) paradigm [10], the Capability Maturity Model (CMM) [11] and the Balanced Scorecard [12, 13].

The SPICE initiative, which led to the ISO 15504 [14] scales for organisation assessment, has provided a focus for work on software process metrics. It supplies a foundation for the measurement of an organisation's processes so that new assessments may be mapped to a standard (0 to 5) point scale.

However, there is still considerable concern regarding the potential for (and consequences of) misalignment of organisational strategy and project measurement [15]. In a recent paper, Boehm and Basili noted that "the primary difficulty in determining such metrics is that software projects are effectively unrepeatable in practice." They go on: "This changing nature means that most traditional measures of software productivity are increasingly irrelevant" [16].

However, there is a complementary bottom-up approach possible, where the measurements are driven by user needs and product characteristics. Quality Function Deployment [17], with its use of the 'Voice of the Customer', is an example of this - although measurements linked to QFD have been limited so far. In a similar vein, Gilb challenged: "We must stop messing with 'internal' software metrics such as complexity and function points and learn really powerful software metrics based on final-product, customer perceived results such as adaptability, availability, reliability, maintainability, security, portability and performance." [18]

Despite these difficulties with current metrics, it is essential that software engineering be placed on a sound basis through scientific measurement. Approaches to a formal theory for software metrics have been provided by a number of researchers [8, 9, 19, 20]]. A framework to facilitate understanding of the complementary uses of the various types of metrics and how they relate to each other is now necessary. In particular, this paper focuses on the dynamic performance of metrics - how their accuracy, precision and utility changes over the duration of a project, the life of a product or the strategic plan of an organisation.

2. Use of degrees of influence

One useful approach to the definition of a framework for the study of metrics is to examine the influence of classes of metrics upon each other. Distinguishing between Product and Process metrics has now become a well established practice (see for example Schulmeyer and McManus). Just as the properties of the product (the information system) are determined by the quality and effectiveness of the development process, so it is possible to extend this approach to other levels of the software industry. The attributes of the product and supporting services influence the mode of usage and degree of acceptance by the customer. Similarly the definition, extension of, and compliance to the process are determined by the management and staff of the software development organisation. In turn, there are a multitude of factors affecting the organisation (the economic situation, the marketplace, availability of resources, government policies and so on), but these drivers are generally external and outside the control of the software producer. A simple model of these hierarchical levels of influence is depicted in figure 1.

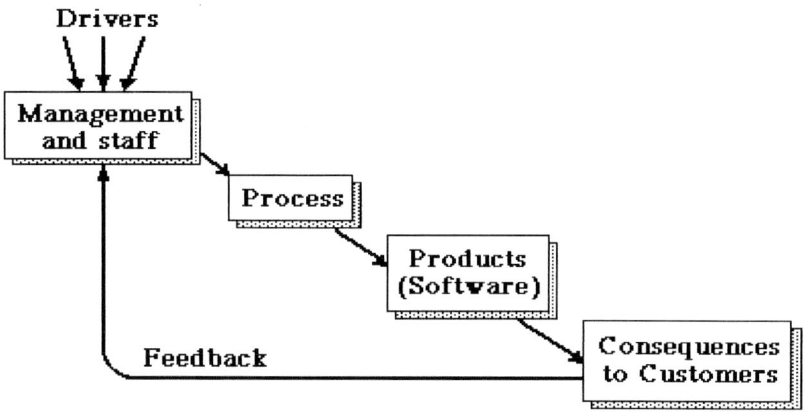

Figure 1 A hierarchy of levels of influence in software production

To state the obvious, in order to improve some aspect of software production and usage, it is necessary to modify the class of factors immediately above it in the hierarchy. As measurement is a prerequisite for an understanding of control and improvement, it is useful to attach a class of metrics to each level.

Returning to Gilb's previously quoted challenge, if there is to be an improvement in "The Only Thing That Matters" [21], the acceptance of information systems by the end-user, then it is necessary to trace and measure the cause and effect path of specific software usage attributes up through the hierarchy. This leads to a bottom-up approach to metric definition, which is complementary to the usual ISO, CMM or GQM top-down methods.

3. A taxonomy of software metrics

The class of metrics associated with each level of the hierarchy may be further divided according to usage (for example, internal versus external publication), degree of resolution (statements, objects, modules or systems) or scale. A simple taxonomy is given in table 1. This is taken from [22] which discusses and supplies references to the individual examples. Alternative discussions of the design and use of these (in some cases historical) metrics can be found in [7, 8].

This taxonomy has been found to be useful in focussing the attention of practitioners on the broad range of uses of metrics during software engineering courses.

Table 1 A simple taxonomy of metrics with examples

Measures of Customer satisfaction
- Proportion of Requirements met
- Amount of usage of new system
- Numbers of customers purchasing system
- Qualitative preference measures using Likert scales

Product Metrics
- System Size (e.g. Halstead's Volume, Function Points, KLOC)
- Complexity of design at various levels of resolution:
    - Code Statements (e.g. Halstead)
    - Control flow (e.g. McCabe's Cyclomatic metric)
    - Component (e.g. Troy & Zweben, Kafura)
    - Complete System (e.g. McCabe & Schulmeyer)
- Reliability - based on MTBF or statistical models
- Quality attributes - McCall's 'ilities' (based on ISO 9126 or COQUAMO templates)

Process Metrics
- Risk Assessment - given as probability x cost of impact
- Estimation accuracy
  (predicted versus actual delivery dates)
- Open question clearance rate
  (may be used to measure requirements creep)
- Defect occurrence rates and propagation
  (defect estimates versus historical data)
- Inspection and Test Efficiency
  (proportion of defects found by a set of tests)

Organisation Metrics
- Profitability (counting the dollars)
- Staff job satisfaction (shown by staff turnover, sick leave)
- Organisational Capability measured against:
    - Previous performance
      (e.g. process improvement over time)
    - Industry average performance
      (e.g. Capers Jones, ASMA)
    - An arbitrary and absolute standard
      (e.g. ISO 9001, CMM, SPICE, Baldrige)
    - Superior organisations
      (e.g. Benchmarking)
    - The theoretical state of best practice possible
      (e.g. Woodings [23])

Driver Metrics
- Management Commitment to improvement
- External pressures for change (e.g. % of competitors with better measurements)

4. The inter-relationship of classes of software metrics

As a quality improvement technique, software managers should be encouraged to explore the likely results (perhaps using Ishikawa cause & effect diagrams) of focussing staff attention on specific issues. For example, client satisfaction may be a function of 'Proportion of Requirements Met'. Over the life of a system, the ratio will depend on Change Requests received and implemented. One is outside the control of the software producer (although it may be predicted using patterns from previous projects), but the other is determined by productivity. This, in turn depends on resources, skills, tools, techniques, etc. These, in their turn, depend on the organisation's size, capability and management. Thus a trivial metric, 'Proportion of Requirements Met', which is simple to apply, can provide some useful insights into the performance of various levels of the organisation. (Note, the important pre-requisites for setting up successful metrics programmes are widely covered in the literature [e.g. 8] and will not be discussed here.)

Differences in a series of observations of a metric for a particular software property, over time or a number of project milestones, will provide the data for empirical prediction of future performance or the validation of theoretical models.

Clearly, in order to improve a software product by the application of some process, then *the rate of change of the product's characteristics is a measure of the effectiveness of the process.*

Similarly, an organisation's future competitiveness will be indicated by the rate of improvement of its processes.

In other words, modelling the differences between observations leads to a 'natural' evolution from product to project to organisation metrics. Most Software Engineering texts (see, for example, [24]), identify and discuss the use of specific metrics at various levels for software process improvement. Because they have quite different purposes, these levels have generally been studied in isolation. However, for measurements using a ratio scale, we postulate a simple and pragmatic mathematical relationship between the hierarchical levels of the taxonomy.

For any valid product metric, its derivative with respect to time is a valid process metric.

For any valid process metric, its derivative with respect to time is a valid metric for the organisation.

The authors have named these the Metrel (Metric Relationship) Rules. That is to say, when defining, modelling and validating a metric for a particular purpose, it is appropriate to also examine its rate of change, for the extra information it can provide.

Note that it is not necessary for the underlying mathematical model of the characteristic being measured to be continuously differentiable although this would be a preferred condition. These rules can provide useful insights and information using approximations based on discrete observations.

5. Use of the Metrel rules

To illustrate the use of the rules, their coverage of Moller's software measurements [25] is demonstrated. A practical example of their application is provided later in the paper.

Moller describes five of the most widely used measurements (System size, Test faults, Change requests, Departure from Schedule and Productivity), which are termed Global Metrics. Under Metrel, they may be covered in the following three linkages:

(i) The Size of a system (in thousands of lines of code (KLOC) or Function Points) is a valid and useful Product Metric.
Then the rate of production of code, (in KLOC/week), is a valid Process metric (assuming the project team is of constant size).
And the rate of change of productivity over time (in KLOC/week/week) is a valid Organisation metric.
This example is illustrated in figure 2.

(ii) The number of defects in a system is a useful and valid Product Metric.
Then the rate of insertion of defects into code per phase (the error proneness of the methodology) is a valid Process metric.
The rate of removal of defects per inspection (the test efficiency) is also a valid measure of the Process.
And the rate of improvement in test efficiency, over a series of projects, is a valid Organisation metric.

(iii) Lateness (slippage from schedule in days) is an important and valid attribute of the Product which is highly visible to the customer.
The variation in delivery date over a series of project milestones (the accuracy of estimates and schedule) within a project is a valid Process metric. This is usually measured by the Magnitude of the Relative Error (MRE), which is a ratio of times, a unitless number. (Note that this variation is also related to requirements creep which may be estimated by the number of change requests being logged. This leads to a set of complementary metrics.)
Then the rate of change of estimation accuracy over a number of projects (the decrease in MRE/project), is a valid measure of the Organisation's determination to improve.

6. The inverse of the Metrel rules

It should be noted that the rules have a natural (although seemingly not as useful), corollary based on integration, over time, of the higher level metrics. Thus it may be possible to gain some insights into measurements by starting with the organisation or process characteristic and then working down to the product. To add a further example:

(iv) The probability of schedule slippage for any given day of a project is a valid indicator of Process risk.
Thus, the integral over the project schedule gives the expected number of days delay in getting to market and represents the waste or cost associated with that system Product. This is related to a product's failure to meet customer delivery expectations.

7. Benefits of the Metrel rules

With the use of the Metrel rules, a number of advantages and useful techniques are apparent:

First, Metrel provides an efficient method for depicting on one graph the information needed for management, staff and customers to view the success or otherwise of process improvement efforts. There is a critical need for greater visibility of project activity in order to reveal the first signs of departures from plan [26]. Kitchenham in [27] notes: "A planning process in which full information about estimates is recorded and available to interested staff helps to avoid situations in which line managers are required to 'manage' schedule and budget risks resulting from 'political' estimates." Figure 2 uses the weekly graphing of productivity rates (perhaps corrected for team size) to portray three important measures for project progress meetings.

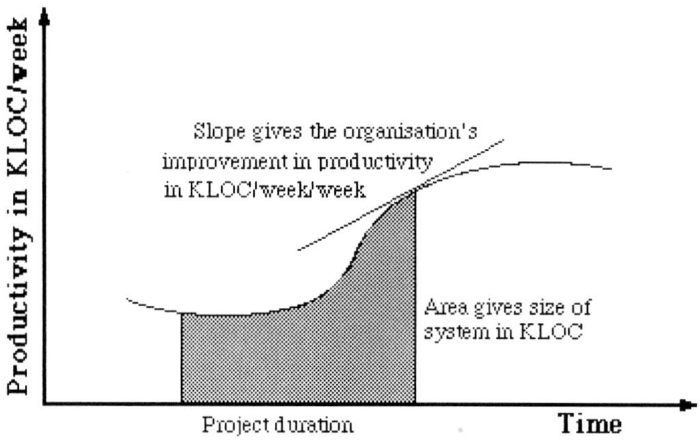

Figure 2 Three metrics portrayed as variation over time

Second, Metrel also provides a check into the way sets of software metrics are chosen. For example, stating a useful and valid unit of measurement for one level automatically determines the units for metrics above or below it. If clearly appropriate, then there is a partial confirmation of the choice.

Third, Metrel may be employed as a supplement to existing methods of metric definition and generation such as the GQM paradigm [10], the Constructive Quality Model (COQUAMO) [28] and Shepperd's Model-based approach [7]. As can be seen from the examples given above, the Metrel Rules lead naturally towards a refocussing of attention on 'impact on the customer'. From that basis, differentiation leads to succeeding higher levels of metrics being defined to improve the working methods (the quality culture) of the organisation. As customer satisfaction is the chief indicator of the future success of an organisation, this approach is a useful complement to the usual top-down methods of choosing properties to measure. It provides a direct mathematical link between product measurement and organisational improvement. Fenton and Pfleeger [8] note that "the GQM approach must be supplemented by one or more models that express the relationships among the metrics". The use of Metrel in this way is the subject of a separate paper, currently in preparation.

Fourth, Metrel is particularly important for the modelling of the software development process. It provides a mechanism for the expansion and transformation of models. The conversion of a mathematical statement for one level to represent activities at another, by means of differentiation or integration (over time or phases or projects), provides a simple but powerful extension for the analysis of the process.

8. Applications of the taxonomy and rules

The efficiency of a software test methodology may be measured by the proportion of defects removed from the product prior to installation. (Note, there are several ways of assessing the number of defects in a system - see, for example, [29].)

The model for improvement in test efficiency will be based on some research [30] into Post Implementation Reviews (PIRs). Figure 3 depicts the improvement in test efficiency from current capability c towards a desired benchmark b of 'best practice' over time t which is measured in units normalised to the average length of a project. The fraction g is the gain in efficiency per project PIR. The improvement in the process metric of Test Efficiency may be given by:

$$f(t) = b - (b - c)(1 - g)^t$$

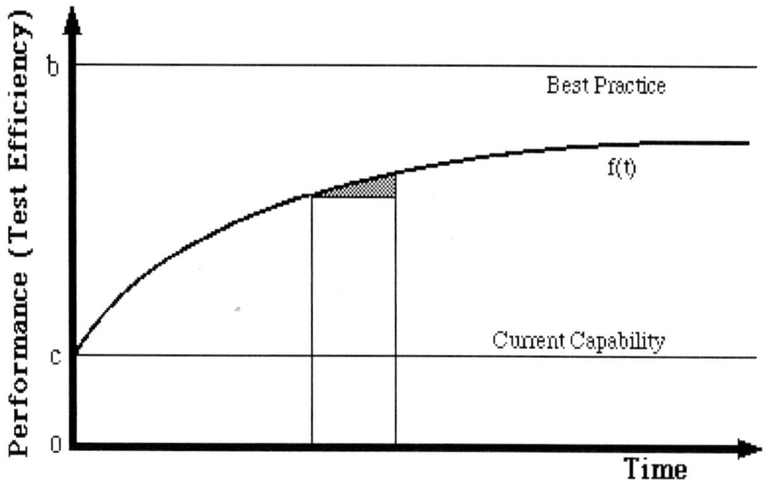

Figure 3 Improvement in capability over time, f(t)

In order to simplify the example, it is assumed that the benchmark and the existing baseline capability of the organisation are varying in much the same way and therefore the ratio c/b is considered a constant. The difference $f(t) - f(t-1)$ gives the improvement in testing due to better techniques identified from the PIR,

with $f(0) = c$ and $f(1) = c + (b - c)g$

Typical figures would be $c = 0.7$ with $b = 0.9$ as the target for test efficiency.

At the end of the first project, following a certain amount of effort expended on the initial PIR, the efficiency $f(1)$ is discovered to be 0.75 which gives

$$g = (0.75 - 0.7) / (0.9 - 0.7) = 0.25$$

This figure may be recomputed at the end of each project. The application of the Metrel Rules, states that the derivative of f with respect to time gives a valid indicator of the organisation's capacity to improve further.

$$f'(t) = -(b - c)(1 - g)^t \ln(1 - g)$$

Thus if the commitment of extra resources for improving test efficiency is held steady then

$$f'(t) = 0.06\,(0.75)^t$$

This figure would be useful for an annual benchmarking of the organisation Similarly, the integral of f with respect to time, over a given period, gives a measure of the defects found in projects in that interval.

$$\int f(t)\,dt = bt - (b - c)(1 - g)^t / \ln(1 - g)$$

To determine the expected number of defects d in the (n+1)st project, the integral from $t = n$ to $t = n+1$ is computed. This gives:

$$d(n+1) = (n+1)b - (b-c)(1-g)^{n+1} / ln(1-g) - bn + (b-c)(1-g)^n / ln(1-g)$$
$$= b + (b-c)\, g\, (1-g)^n / ln(1-g)$$

This is of pragmatic use in estimating the benefit of continuing with the process improvement. For this one project, the fraction of extra defects is indicated by the shaded area in figure 3 and is found to be

$$d(n+1) - f(n) \times (n+1-n) \quad = b + (b-c)\, g\, (1-g)^n / ln(1-g) - b + (b-c)(1-g)^n$$
$$= (b-c)(1-g)^n (1 + g / ln(1-g))$$

The project manager would be aware of the extra effort being expended on PIRs and the improved test techniques and this can be compared with the difference in cost of finding and fixing defect before rather than after installation of the system. In this example the fraction of extra defects to be found in the third project is expected to be

$$0.2 \times 0.75^2 \times (1 + 0.25 / \ln(0.75)) = 0.015$$

which appears quite small but when most new systems report defects in excess of 1000, then this is quite significant. More importantly, as many studies (for example, [31]), have suggested a cost ratio of at least five to one in not finding errors until after release, this suggests that the extra effort for PIRs and similar strategies up to 5 x 0.015 = 7.5% is well spent. That is to say, the average software house would benefit from investing ten days per person per year on improvements in testing.

It is worth noting that should the savings from better testing be reinvested to find yet further errors, thus keeping the length of the average project roughly constant, then this metric of test efficiency is similar to Hitachi's System Spoilage [32]. Over six project periods from 1976, the Hitachi metric had a gain rate of g approximately equal to 0.32, which was excellent.

To summarise, this example of the use of the Metrel Rules illustrates how managers can use this simple and pragmatic approach for quantifying process improvement.

9. Conclusion

The use of the Metrel Rules, and the corollary, leads to a number of insights into the derivation of software process models and the definition of appropriate metrics. In particular it leads to greater visibility of the many factors (and their relationships), in process improvement initiatives. Most importantly, it provides a direct linkage between the product characteristics, which impact on the end-user, and the measurements which are viewed by executives in managing a software organisation.

Current research is focused on the practical application of this rule in generating and validating useful metrics, particularly in the area of risk management. Further research will be needed on the use of this theory to optimise process improvement strategies.

With current software engineering practices exhibiting the symptoms of an immature discipline, the use of new approaches to promote measurement, modelling and optimisation of development processes is to be encouraged.

Acknowledgements

The authors appreciate the feedback of colleagues, particularly Peter Jones and Richard Thomas, in the preparation of this work. They would also like to express their thanks to the referees of a previous version of this paper.

References

[1] Conte, S D, Dunsmore, H E and Shen, V Y (1986) "Software Engineering Metrics and Models", Benjamin-Cummings.

[2] Gilb, T (1977) "Software Metrics", Winthrop.

[3] Watts, R A (1987) "Measuring Software Quality", NCC.
[4] Evans, M W (1989) "The Software Factory", John Wiley.
[5] Grady, R B and Caswell, D L (1987) "Software Metrics: Establishing a Company-Wide Program", Prentice-Hall.
[6] Johnson, J (1989) "The Software Factory", QED.
[7] Shepperd, M and Ince, D (1993) "Derivation and Validation of Software Metrics", Clarendon Press.
[8] Fenton, N E and Pfleeger, S L (1997) "Software Metrics - A Rigorous and Practical Approach" (2nd edition), International Thomson Publishing.
[9] Shepperd, M (1995) "Foundations of Software Measurement", Prentice Hall.
[10] Basili, V R and Rombach, H D (1988) "The TAME project: Towards improvement-oriented software environments", IEEE Transactions on Software Engineering, 14:6 pp758-773.
[11] Humphrey, W S (1989) "Managing the Software Process", Addison-Wesley.
[12] Ibanez, M and Reo, D (1998) "Measuring the Impact of Software Process Improvement on Business Objectives - ESI Balanced IT Scorecard", European Software Institute.
[13] Kaplan, R S and Norton, D P (1996) "The Balanced Scorecard", Harvard Business School.
[14] ISO (1998) "ISO/IEC TR 15504-1:1998 Information technology- Software process assessment. Part 1: Concepts and introductory guide", ISO.
[15] Becker, S A and Bostelman, M L (1999) "Aligning Strategic and Project Measurement Systems", IEEE Software, 16:3 pp46-51.
[16] Boehm, B W and Basili, V R (2000) "Gaining Intellectual Control of Software Development", IEEE Computer, 33:5 pp27-33.
[17] Zultner, R (1992) "Quality Function Deployment for Software Satisfying Customers", American Programmer, 5 pp28-41.
[18] Gilb, T (1996) "Level 6:Why we can't get there from here", IEEE Software. 13:1 pp97-98.
[19] Zuse, H (1997) "A Framework of Software Measurement", Walter de Gruyter.
[20] IEEE (1993) "Standard for a Software Quality Metrics Methodology P-1061", IEEE.
[21] Albrecht, K (1992) "The Only Thing That Matters". Harper Business.
[22] Woodings, T L (1995) "A Taxonomy of Software Metrics", Software Process Improvement Network (SPIN), available from Comast Consulting, Perth.
[23] Woodings, T L and Spencer, G J (1992) "Advances in Quality in the Information Technology Industry", Proceedings of Qualcon92, Australian Organisation for Quality, Perth.
[24] Vliet, J C van (1993) "Software Engineering - Principles and Practice", John Wiley.
[25] Moller, K H and Paulish, D J (1993) "Software Metrics - A Practitioner's Guide to Improved Product Development", Chapman & Hall.
[26] Youll, D P (1990) "Making Software Development Visible", John Wiley.
[27] Kitchenham, B A (1996) "Software Metrics - Measurement for Software Process Improvement", NCC/Blackwell.
[28] Kitchenham, B A (1987) "Towards a Constructive Quality Model - Part I: Software Quality Modelling, Measurement and Prediction", Software Engineering Journal, 2:4 pp105-113.
[29] Ebrahimi, N B (1997) "On the Statistical Analysis of the Number of Errors Remaining in a Software Design Document after Inspection", IEEE Transactions on Software Engineering, 23:8 pp529-532.
[30] Woodings, T L and Everett J E (1999) "A Methodology with Quality Tools to support Post Implementation Reviews", Proceedings of the 10th Australasian Conf on Inf Systems, Wellington.
[31] Boehm, B W (1981) "Software Engineering Economics", Prentice Hall.
[32] Tajima, D and Matsubara, T (1981) "The Computer Software Industry in Japan", Computer 14:5 pp89-96.

Risk-driven effort-estimation of tasks within the software performance engineering

Andreas Schmietendorf, Reiner Dumke, Erik Foltin

Abstract

The current methods of estimating costs frequently only indirectly take performance engineering (PE) tasks into account. Moreover, there are major differences in the propositions put forward by such methods. To create transparency and acceptance of these tasks, which are of great importance as part of the life cycles of IT systems, an approach is pursued which derives the costs from an appropriate risk analysis and, in the course of doing so, investigates the business process to be supported, the software development as well as active operations. The initial results of empirical analyses are presented by way of 6 industrial projects.

1. Introduction and motivation

To develop and introduce information systems which meet both functional and qualitative requirements, it is necessary to plan appropriate technical and human resources to implement the tasks involved. In general, it is easy to understand that a system with high quality requirements involves greater costs than one with lower quality requirements. However, if one examines the quality feature of spatial- and time-related efficiency (performance in general) as defined by the ISO 9126 quality standard, it then becomes more difficult to make an assessment. It is necessary to apply performance engineering methods during the entire software development process to guarantee this quality feature. Fig. 1 shows typical times when performance analysis methods are applied.

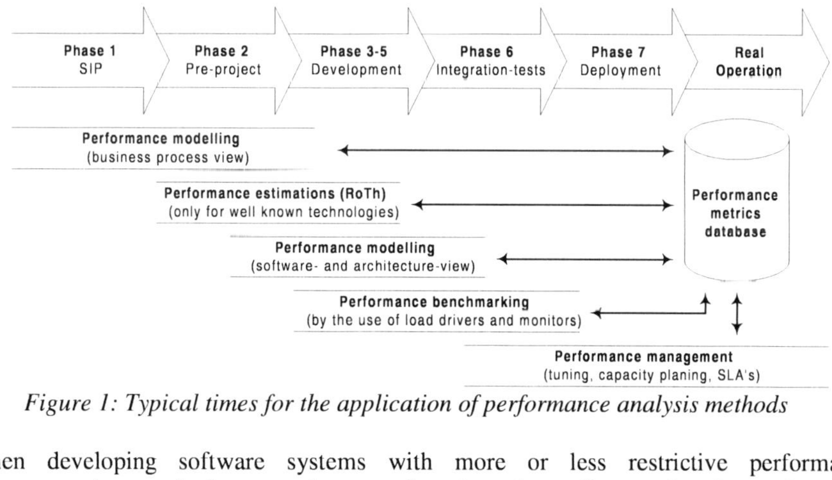

Figure 1: Typical times for the application of performance analysis methods

When developing software systems with more or less restrictive performance requirements, the standard approach currently adopted usually consists in performance features being examined towards the end of the development phase in the course of acceptance tests, or during pilot operation in the course of multistage introduction. The identification of performance shortcomings at the end of software development thus frequently leads to complex tuning measures, an expensive redesigning of the application, the utilisation of hardware with a higher capacity than originally planned or, in an extreme case, to the abandonment of the productive use of the entire information system. Apart from this expenditure which, in general, is not planned, costs especially arise due to the delay in the introduction of the information system and because of problems in the performance of actual functions during active operation, as the business process covered by the IT system is not being supported as planned.

There are various technical, methodical and economic reasons for this approach. One problem refers to the inadequate transparency of costs which makes it difficult for project management to understand which PE tasks are required. An appropriate approach to solving this problem will be presented in the course of this article.

2. Analysis of the current situation

2.1. Selected approach

The difficulty of determining the costs involved in performance engineering in monetary terms has already been expounded by [10]. In her view, these depend on the size of the project, its complexity as well as on several other influencing factors. Especially in the light of the constantly increasing cost pressure exercised on software development, it is only possible to apply performance engineering methods if, on the one hand, transparency is attained concerning the costs involved and, on the other, if the benefit can be quantified.

Cost evaluation procedures: An obvious approach is to analyse methods for the evaluation of costs concerning their consideration of appropriate costs. The first methods to estimate costs were developed and applied in the industry in the 1970s. While early versions of these methods disregarded qualitative aspects to a large extent, at least current versions consider quality to have an influence on the costs involved in development. Typical examples of this are the **function point method** and the **COCOMO** procedure.

Transparency of costs: In order to achieve transparency, it is necessary to know what costs are involved in the application of actual methods/tools of performance engineering. Apart from the performance analysis methods described in the introduction which generally give rise to most of the costs, other tasks must also be taken into account. For example, the analysis of performance requirements, the instrumentation of performance-critical functions of applications with respective measuring points or even the implementation of performance risk analyses. However, the costs involved in connection with such tasks will not be discussed any further in this article.

Quantification of the benefit: The benefit should be derived from a potential risk of non-performing functions of the software solution to be implemented, which means that the execution of concrete PE tasks may be considered similar to stating an insurance sum. [10], for example, states a costs ratio of 1:100, i.e. eliminating performance problems after implementation may be up to 100 times more expensive than their identification and elimination during the early phases of development (analysis/design).

2.2. Propositions of cost evaluation methods

Below, a brief description of procedures to evaluate costs is given concerning their mapping of performance-relevant aspects which may increase costs in this manner. However, a detailed description of the procedures and the approach during analysis is not given. Further details on the methods themselves or the analysis carried out can be obtained from the sources stated ([4]).

Function Point – This procedure which has been used for more than 20 years in different versions to determine development costs serves to estimate the functional scope of an information system. For this, the number of business transactions and their complexity is used, which basically provide unweighted function points **UFP**. Therefore, the function point method does not initially provide a starting point for performance-specific system aspects. These are not taken into consideration until the incorporation of a correction factor **VAF** which is composed of 14 system characteristics.

$$AFP = VAF * UFP \qquad \text{(Eq. 1)}$$

Two of these are especially relevant in connection with performance aspects. One is the influencing factor **C3** (user requirements for performance) and **C5** (the transaction rate to be expected). The weighted function point **AFP** resulting from the multiplication of the unweighted function points with the corrective factor may be increased by a maximum of 10% through performance-relevant influencing factors. [5]

Object Point – This method developed by [11] explicitly takes into account the object-oriented paradigm of software development. What are known as class points **CP** are determined as a measure for the cost involved in class development, message points **MP** as a measure for the cost involved in class integration and developer tests, and process points **PP** as a measure for the costs involved in system tests. Unadjusted object points UOP result from the addition of the individual points.

$$UOP = CP + MP + PP \qquad \text{(Eq. 2)}$$

Similar to the function point process, the UOP are weighted by an influencing factor as well as by a quality factor also which results in an adjusted object point AOP.

$$AOP = UOP * \text{influencing factor} * \text{quality factor} \qquad \text{(Eq. 3)}$$

Performance engineering aspects are considered within the quality factor consisting of 12 features through time and spatial efficiency features. The costs can therefore be increased by a maximum of 33% if maximum requirements exist for this area.

COCOMO - In this procedure, which evaluates costs (COCOMO II, cf. [1]), performance requirements influence the parameters of the model to evaluate costs and not the evaluation of the scope of the system to be created. Put simply, COCOMO uses evaluation formulas of the following kind:

$$PM - A * (SIZE)^{B} * EM \qquad \text{(Eq. 4)}$$

Whereby the value for **A** is a constant, **SIZE** is the scope of the system (to be assessed, in KDSI[1]), the exponent **B** comprises several scale factors which are mainly determined by the development environment. The actual performance requirements are to be found again in the cost multiplier **EM**. This (in the detailed Post Architecture Model) is the product of 17 influencing factors. Two of these influencing factors refer to "classic" aspects of performance engineering, i.e. the requirements for processing time **TIME** and the storage requirement **STOR**. Extremely high requirements in computing time and storage capacity can increase the cost to create a system by more than one-and-a-half fold (150%).

Test Point Analysis – The TPA® method serves to determine the costs involved in the tests and can be applied if an estimate of the costs is available according to function point. The established test costs include a high-level test exclusively and, in doing so, only identify the costs for a real-life or benchmark test taking place immediately after the actual

---

[1] KDSI – Kilo Delivered Source Instructions

development by using a load driver. This means that only one possible performance engineering method is considered. The test points **TP**, which are composed of dynamic and static test points, are determined by taking the size of the system to be tested into consideration and the parts of the system that must be tested. Only the dynamic test points $\mathbf{TP_f}$ for each function of an application to be tested, which are examined further below, are of interest with regard to performance engineering tasks. These are composed of figures resulting from the multiplication of the function point per application function $\mathbf{FP_f}$, with a valuation factor $\mathbf{A_f}$ and the dynamic quality influencing factor $\mathbf{Q_d}$. [7]

$$TP_f = FP_f * A_f * Q_d \qquad \text{(Eq. 5)}$$

4 quality attributes are explicitly recorded within the dynamic quality influencing factor. These attributes are the functionality, security, integration capacity and the performance within the scope of which performance aspects can be considered. In the event of maximum test requirements for the explicitly measurable quality feature of performance, the result is an approximately 10% influence on the number of dynamic test points per function.

2.3. Summarising comparison

The following table gives a summary of how different the evaluation methods examined take the costs put into SPE into account. Moreover, the table shows the propositions of renowned experts in the field of performance engineering and software metrics. It is possible to see that none of the methods can adequately reproduce the costs which must be invested for performance engineering, which underscores the need for a different approach.

Table 1: Comparison of different procedures for determination

	Method	Share of the project budget for SPE
Cost evaluation procedure	Function point	max. 10%
	TPA®	max. 10% of the test budget (black box)
	Object point	max. 33%
	Cocomo	max. 150%
Experts' propositions	Connie Smith	mostly under 1%
	Capers Jones	3% on average

The interrelation proven by Barry Boehm in connection with the development of the COCOMO procedure that an increase in product quality compared to the cost is not a linear relation is also reflected in the performance influencing criteria of the COCOMO Model and probably thus comes closest to reality.

Apart from the disadvantage of all the different procedures inaccurately and inconsistently mapping the costs involved in performance engineering, they also do not enable a direct identification to be made, which is the main reason why project management tends to disregard PE tasks.

2.4. The costs involved in concrete PE methods

The results from empirical studies of 30 performance analyses, which were carried out at Deutsche Telekom, flowed into the following overview. This was a case of 17 benchmarks carried out by using an appropriate load driver system, 4 performance modellings by means of an appropriate expert system and 9 performance analyses carried out on the basis of evaluation procedures. For the measurements/analyses, performance studies were carried out on the basis of prototypes by means of operating systems' and application systems' own means (e.g. measuring points) in the course of software development. The costs required for this were estimated on the basis of past experience.

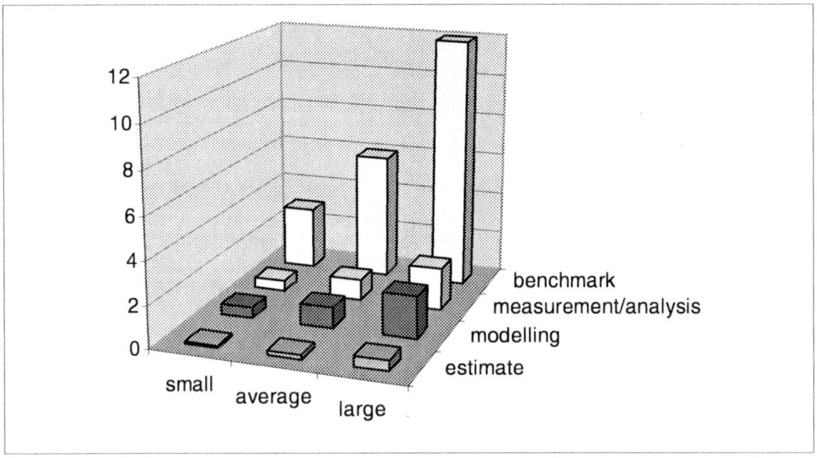

Figure 2: Average costs in PM when applying PE methods

The following criteria were applied to classify the project size:

- Large project – The application has a multistage client/server architecture which integrates a wide range of products. Appropriate test scenarios result from complex business transactions. More than 500 users work simultaneously with the application.
- Average-sized project – This is a case of a client/server architecture consisting at the most of 3 stages in which performance observations cover a maximum of 3 products. More than 500 users work simultaneously with the application.
- Small project – This is a case of a simple IT architecture with 1-2 protocol interfaces and simple test scenarios. Less than 500 users work simultaneously with the system. An appropriate test database exists.

Costs are also added to the personnel expenditure shown for the required hardware infrastructure (computer system and networks) and costs for appropriate SW licences.

3. Identification of risks involved in performance

3.1. Overview of the valuation model

To improve the situation, we propose a model for the classification of performance-related risks. In doing this, 3 "affected areas" can be identified, where losses will be incurred if a performance risk occurs. On the one hand, these are primary risks in connection with the business process and, on the other, secondary risks which can occur in the course of development and active operations. The valuation model depicted below is to serve to determine potential risks in the areas affected.

Ideally, it should be possible to back up this valuation model with objective statistical parameters. However, as the required objective measuring models are not available or the costs incurred in connection with their application are unreasonably high, we propose a questionnaire based on frequently used assessment procedures as an initial valuation model.

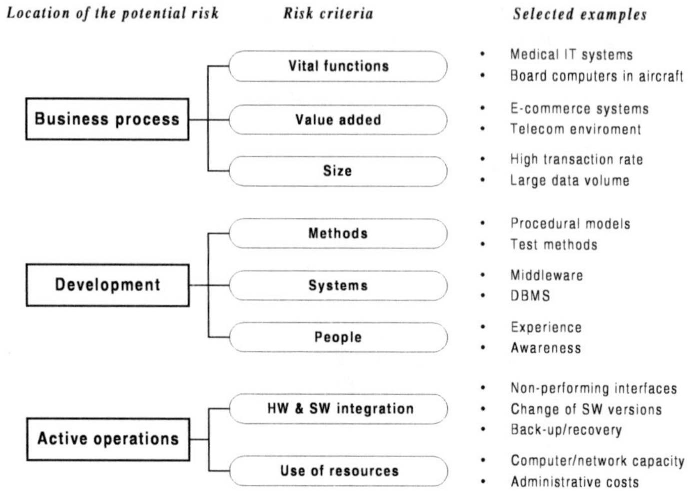

Figure 3: Valuation model for performance risks

3.2. Quantification of risks

To quantify the risks identified in the previous point, we intend to pursue two approaches. First of all, a methodology will be proposed which permits the costs of primary risks to be stated which have a direct effect on the business process supported by the IT system.

Table 2: Performance losses and effects on the business process

	Performance losses				
	Business case	X in %	....	Y in %	Breakdown
Response time	$t <= t_{Ref}$	$t > t_{Ref}$	...	$t >> t_{Ref}$	$t \rightarrow \infty$
Throughput	$B \geq B_{Ref}$	$B < B_{Ref}$	...	$B << B_{Ref}$	$B \rightarrow 0$

As a general rule, the development/introduction of a new software application requires proof of the benefit (business case) gained from it. If the business case of the application is to be fulfilled, the response time t must comply with user demands t_{Ref} or the throughput B must meet user requirements B_{Ref}. In the event of a breakdown (most extreme case of a loss of performance), the response time moves towards "infinite", the throughput towards "zero", i.e. the entire business case of the application is lost.[2]

To state the losses in monetary terms incurred due to an non-performing system, it is necessary to consult the purchaser of the application or the appropriate expert. Only these parties are able to assess the loss that will arise if, for example, due to insufficient throughput of the application, only 100 customers can be served per day instead of what would otherwise potentially be 300 customers. As shown in Table 2, it is meaningful to view the response time and throughput of graduated performance losses in relation to the functions of an application which are critical for performance. For example, an analysis would be possible for a performance loss of X=100% (double response time), of Y=200% (threefold response time) and the breakdown of the system. When considering these, not only the technical context of the application itself should be considered (direct additional costs) but also possible subsequent losses within the process chain. Moreover, potential contractual penalties

[2] Notations for the response time or rather the throughput were taken from ISO 14756

in the event of an non-performing system and damage to the company's image should also be taken into account.

We suggest a different approach to quantify the secondary risks which may arise at the time of software development or within active operations,. On the basis of general experience, measured objects (internal metrics) are considered which might have an influence on the performance features of an IT system (external metrics). To date, a direct statistical connection has been unable to be established due to a lack of empirical studies. However, the selected measured objects are frequently stated as being the reason for problems in connection with performance-relevant features. Table 3 shows an excerpt of the appropriate checklist.

Table 3: Monetary risk assessment (selected examples)

	Risk criteria	**Measured objects (internal metrics) *n***	**Empirical valuation (external metrics)**	**Basic risk in euros g_i**	**Probability of occurrence in percent p_i**	**Quantified effective risk in euros r_i**
Development	Methods	Approach model unrelated to PE	Extended project period Additional costs due to increased HW requirements Lower performance than expected ...			
		Test methods unrelated to PE				
		...				
	Techniques	Unknown performance behaviour of the middleware				
		....				
Active operation	HW & SW integration	Software updates	Lower productivity			
		...				
	Ressource requirements	...	...			
Total secondary risks r						

Calculation of the total secondary risk r:

$$r = \sum_{i=1}^{n} r_i = \sum_{i=1}^{n} g_i p_i [Euro]$$

(Eq. 6)

3.3. Application of the valuation model

The valuation model should be applied several times in the course of the life cycle of an IT solution, in the form of checklists to be filled in for each risk criterion. This enables risks involved in the business process to be recognised during an SIB (Strategic Information Planning, cf. Business Process Reengineering) for the first time. However, risks which refer to SW development and subsequent active operations are not recognised until the beginning or during the actual development project.

4. Empirical results

The practical application of the valuation model took place in the course of the PerfEng project [8]. This was carried out in the following stages:

1. Preparation of a representative checklist which includes potential risks entailed in the business process, development and active operations.
2. Conducting interviews with representatives of the specialist, developer and system provider side to incorporate performance risk metrics.
3. Statistical analysis of the gathered data and consideration of the scale features to verify and validate the valuation model.
4. Identification of the improvement potential of the valuation model and especially of the checklists used.

The following diagram summarises the results of the first application of the proposed valuation model in 6 projects in the field of telecommunications. An average of 6 man days (taking everyone involved into account) were required to implement a risk analysis in each of the projects.

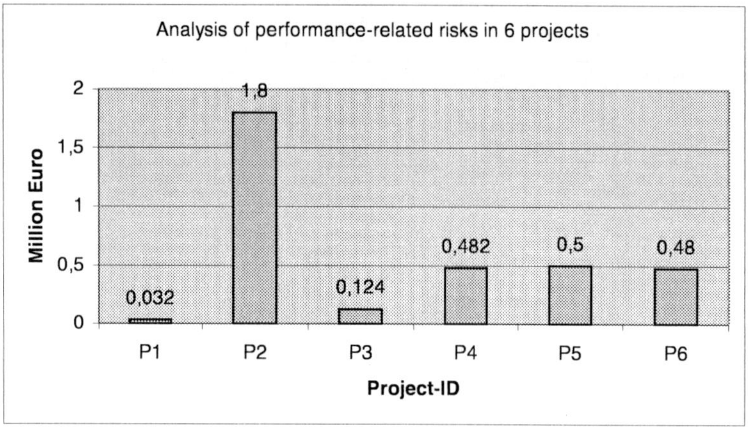

Figure 4: Results of the risk analysis

The monetary risks most frequently identified in connection with the performance features of a new system were as follows:

1. inadequate description and details of the business process to be supported
2. use of new technologies and techniques during development
3. lack of performance requirements (response time specifications)

During the interviews, it turned out to be very difficult to identify the business case of the applications. The information most frequently given related to the potential savings in personnel and less to statements which referred to the business process to be supported, e.g. the products sold per time unit. Moreover, the information was often gained from experience with subsequent efforts to improve the performance of an information system already in existence. For example, an extension of the project term by using new network and database technologies was a typical case.

A few potential improvements to the proposed valuation model are briefly listed below:

1. The analysis presented in this paper considered mainly projects with object-oriented development technologies. An attempt should be made to broaden the background of empirical experience and, if necessary, effect an appropriate clustering (e.g. SAP, Cobol projects, ...).
2. The contents of the checklists for the interviews should be left open so that suggestions can be included at any time. This procedure was already adopted in the interviews we carried out.

3. To collect performance risk metrics over the course of several projects and evaluate these on a statistical basis, a suitable basis of information must be developed which should best also include other performance-relevant metrics.
4. The valuation model should be applied several times within the software life cycle in order to successively gain more accurate results. Applying it two or three times appears to be worthwhile at the outset.

5. Summary and outlook

The idea proposed in this article of deriving the costs required to realise performance engineering tasks from potential risks has the advantage of enabling risks to be made transparent and of putting these into monetary terms as far as possible. On the basis of assessed risks it should be easier for project management to integrate PE tasks into the time schedules and costs of project plans and estimate their added value. Moreover, the selection of actual PE methods is supported by the definition of a costs framework.

It goes without saying that attempts should be made to generally determine qualitative risks in addition to performance-relevant risks and to integrate this methodology into standard cost evaluation procedures such as the function point procedure. However, it should continue to be possible to explicitly allocate the required costs to performance engineering so that the additional tasks of PE are not considered as additional costs under any circumstances.

Efficiently operating service providers who, on the one hand, are familiar with performance engineering methods and, on the other, also with those of software engineering are required to carry out performance engineering tasks. With regard to the costs, it has proved wise to make complex PE tasks, which require a high level of skill and extensive hardware and software equipment, available at a suitable centralised Competence Center. Smaller development companies should resort to the services offered by external providers.

6. Bibliography

[1] Boehm, B. W., "COCOMO II Model Definition Manual", University of Southern California, 1997

[2] Dumke, R., Foltin, E., Koeppe, R., Winkler, A., "Softwarequalität durch Meßtools", Vieweg-Verlag, Braunschweig/Wiesbaden, 1996

[3] Dumke, R., Foltin, E., Schmietendorf, A., "Kausalitätsprobleme bei der Aufwandsschätzung in der Softwareentwicklung und –wartung", Preprint Nr. 13, Otto-von-Guericke-Universität Magdeburg, August 1998

[4] Foltin, E., Schmietendorf, A., "Estimating the cost of carrying out tasks relating to performance engineering", in Dumke, R. et. al., "Software Measurement", Lecture Notes on Computer Science, Springer 2001

[5] IFPUG, "Function Point Counting Practices Manual", Atlanta, 1994

[6] Jones, D., "Software Quality – Analysis and Guidelines for success", International Thomson Computer Press, 1997

[7] Pol, M., Koomen, T., Spillner, A., "Management und Optimierung des Testprozesses", dpunkt.verlag, Heidelberg, 2000

[8] Schmietendorf, A., Herting, H., Wipprecht, M., "Erarbeitung und Vorschlag einer Performance-Risiko-Metrik – Fallstudie", unveröffentlichte Studie der T-Nova im Rahmen des Projektes PerfEng, Berlin, 2000

[9] Schmietendorf, A., Scholz, A., "A risk-driven Performance Engineering Process Approach and its Evaluation with a Performance Engineering Maturity Model", in proceedings of the 15th UKPEW, Bristol, 1999

[10] Smith, C.U., "Performance Engineering of Software Systems – The SEI series in software engineering", Addison-Wesley, Reading/Mass., 1990

[11] Sneed, H.M., "Schätzung der Entwicklungskosten von objektorientierter Software", SES Software-Engineering Services GmbH, Ottobrunn, München 1995

An investigation and analysis of risk models and the creation of a new framework for IT investment risks and model for risk management.

Jane Ferris

Abstract
The theme of this paper is the occurrence of risks within information technology and information systems investments. A taxonomy of the published classification frameworks of IT related risk is presented and a new comprehensive classification framework for IT investments (the TOPModel) is presented within the TRIP model of the risk factors and critical factors affecting IT investments. Risk management offers a pre-emptive method of managing IT investments, risk management is defined, explored and a new five-stage process; the MAPIT model of IT risk management is presented.

1. Introduction
Risks are inevitable in all investments, but why are investments in Information Technology (IT) and Information Systems (IS) perceived as a lottery of both returns and benefits (Beenstock, 1998; Wilcocks, 1992 and Schwartz, 1999)? Failure is a part of nature, it is still appropriate to ask why are IT investments failure statistics as high as 70% (Rosser, 1998)? Presented is the analysis of the current published literature relating to the risks occurring in IT/IS projects and several analytical devices for the management of these risks.

The current success of the IT industry is not indicative of IT investment projects. Methods used for developing and managing IT investments are floundering, this is illustrated by long development periods (Lester & Wilcocks, 1993 and Remenyi et al., 1997), high failure rates (Bacon, 1992; Wilcocks, 1994 and Wilcocks & Margetts, 1994) and the lack of realised benefits (Brynjolfsson, 1993 and Strassmann, 1996). For these reasons, IT projects and investments have been the consideration of a moderate amount of research which has sought to identify the reasons for the delays, overspends and failure of IT investments. The primary objective of such research is to identify and alert investment managers and IT professionals to the risks occurring within IT investments. This paper focuses on the published literature relating to IT investment risk frameworks and prescriptive management techniques currently available to develop practical management aids to reduce the occurrence of unsuccessful IT projects.

2. IT investment risks
The high degree of risk within IT has been a concern for many years, twenty-five years ago Mowshowitz, (1976) reported an 80% failure rate for IS development projects. Twenty years later a Standish Group survey reported that 73% of corporate America's IT projects were late, over budget or cancelled (Thorp, 1999). Studies from Europe concur. Wilcocks & Margetts (1994) reported a group study of two hundred organisation over a ten year period which concluded that 20% of IT investments were wasted and a further 30-40% realised no net benefit, however measured. A study by Bacon (1992) found that three years after installation, 60% of investments failed to deliver any expected benefits. The most conservative estimate of IT and IS investment failure is one in six (Wilcocks, 1994).

Current literature relating to risks and the IT investment environment has primarily focused on the classification and ranking of risks (Boehm, 1991 and Lyytinen & Hirsheim, 1987).

Classifications are made by authors and are based on a common likeness. Hence many bases and forms of classifications are present within the literature. Ultimately risks can be sorted into two forms of risks: controllable and uncontrollable. The author identified and investigated 12 risk classification frameworks, this is not a complete list but a list of those that are published within English language literature and obtainable by the author. The twelve IT risks classification frameworks are presented within a taxonomy (figure 1).

3. A taxonomy of IT investment risk frameworks

The taxonomy spans seventeen years of IT investments at the end of the twentieth century commencing with the work of McFarlan in 1981and ending with a 1998 study by Keil et al.. Following a discussion on the factors critical to the assessment and appreciation of the taxonomy, the importance of this taxonomy and the issues raised are discussed. A comparative analysis can only examine the issues identified within the published works. As the risks are those identified by IT professionals, the risks identified are pertinent and the combined works offer a comprehensive assessment of the risks occurring within IT investments.

3.1. Investment type

The majority of the risks identified and risk frameworks represent the risks in a general fashion, such that the risks are common to both the developments of hardware and software. There also exists those risks that are specific to software and hardware investments, these risks are however dependent on the nature of the investment. Classification of IT within the current literature corresponds to, the level of impact of the application, system or technology i.e. strategic or operational (McFarlan, 1981 and Ward, 1990). As there is no apt classification for the nature of IT investments, the investment type is distinguished within the taxonomy by reference to product type; software or hardware. A more specific classification of IT would be desired, but was neither available nor necessary.

3.2. Validation

Validation is one of the most important components of any piece of research. Validation is the evidence of the case, the foundations of the research. The research analysed stood on foundations of varying stability. Frameworks published within several texts offer no validation and it must be deduced that they are based solely on the experience of the authors (Davies, 1982; Parker et al., 1988; Corder, 1989; Keen, 1991 and Cash, 1992). The validation of the classification frameworks, based on the experience of the authors and referenced within the paper, are the works by McFarlan, (1981) Boehm, (1989) and Lyytinen et al., (1996).

The classification frameworks which offer solid validation are those based on empirical methods and surveys (Lyytinen et al., 1987; Boehm, 1989; Whiting et al., 1993 and Keil et al., 1998). Lyytinen et al., (1987) and Whiting et al., (1993), offer research that is based on a review of published literature and a questionnaire survey (respectively). The validation offered by these research publications is ideal. Boehm's paper is also based on a survey of experienced professionals, but not enough information is provided to completely validate the work. The paper presented by Keil et al., 1998 is a study based on the Delphi method. This method is a reputable form of analysis but it does present biased results, influenced by the opinions of the other participants of the survey.

Framework	Investment type	Validation	Risks identified
McFarlan (1981)	*IT*	*Experience*	*3*
Davies (1982)	*IT*	*None*	*4*
Lyytinen & Hirsheim (1987)	*IT*	*Literature review*	*12*
Parker, Benson & Trainor (1988)	*IT*	*None*	*5*
Earl (1989)	*IT*	*None*	*3*
Corder (1989)	*IT*	*None*	*15*
Boehm (1989)	*Software*	*Survey*	*10*
Keen (1991)	*IT*	*None*	*6*
Cash, McFarlan & McKenney (1992)	*IT*	*None*	*3*
Whiting, Knul & Davies (1993)	*IT*	*Survey*	*7*
Lyytinen, Mathiassen & Ropponnen (1996)	*Software*	*Literature review*	*4*
Keil, Cule, Lyytinen & Schmidt (1998)	*Software*	*Delphi study*	*4*

Figure 1. Taxonomy of published IT investment risk frameworks.

3.3. A review of the taxonomy

The majority of the frameworks neglect the risks exterior to the project environment. The identification of the risks 'internal' to the investment, is a result of the source of the information for the frameworks, the opinion of the project/risk manager. Therefore the managers of the investments are not aware of or concerned by the 'external' risks. But the over emphasis within the frameworks on the internal risks indicates an insular approach to the development of IT investments. By neglecting the 'real world' risks and developing the investment in isolation, the investment itself may reproduce existing results and the investments will waste valuable resources of both time and money. Improved communication, management and tracking of investment with perhaps the aid of project databases will help to reduce this risk.

4. A new comprehensive classification of IT investment risks

Analysis of the taxonomy concludes that risks within IT investments may be classified by four prime risk factors; organisational, project, technical and market risks. The four risk categorisations constitute the TOPModel.

Technical risks relate to the complexity and novelty of the technology. Organisational risks incorporate the ability of the organisation to support the investment with resources such as IT infrastructure, management structure, experience and the commitment of users and management. Project risks include risks concerning the stability of the project requirements such as definitional uncertainty and the problems inherent with size and structure. Market risks incorporate the economic, political and competitive environments surrounding the investment.

These risks are not of equal importance. These categorisations are inter-related with a lot of overlap existing between categorisations. For example, the risk of lack of experience of personnel with the technology involves three of the four classifications. The first organisation risk is the lack of experienced personnel, which illustrates the organisation's inability to support the investment. Second, a project risk, as the lack of experienced personnel or the contracting in of experienced individuals raises the risks inherent in projects. Finally, there is the technical risk associated with the use of a new technology relative to the organisation.

The critical factors surrounding IT investments identified by the author are illustrated in figure 2. The four risk factors identified from the taxonomy (organisational, project, technical and market) represent all risks occurring within the investment. Illustrated within the figure are the three prime contributing factors (user, analyst and management).

5. The changing issues of IT investment risks, 1989 to 1998

The taxonomy covers a spread of over fifteen years. Within this time, due to the ever dynamic and evolving nature of IT, many of the issues have understandably altered. The most significant changes have not only occurred with the technology, but also within the organisation. Comparisons and contrasts were drawn from two similar studies carried out a decade apart. These studies considered the assessment of risks by project managers in software development (Boehm, 1989 and Keil *et al.*, 1998). The significant issues identified by the comparative review are the management of investments, the availability of skilled personnel and the lack of adequate communication within investment projects.

5.1. Investment management

Uncontrollable events primarily relate to nature or 'acts of God,' for example, hurricanes and floods. Theoretically, all other events are controllable, if you possess sufficient time, money, information and energy. But, in reality other factors propel uncontrollable events such as governments and legislation, lack of resources and the will of other people.

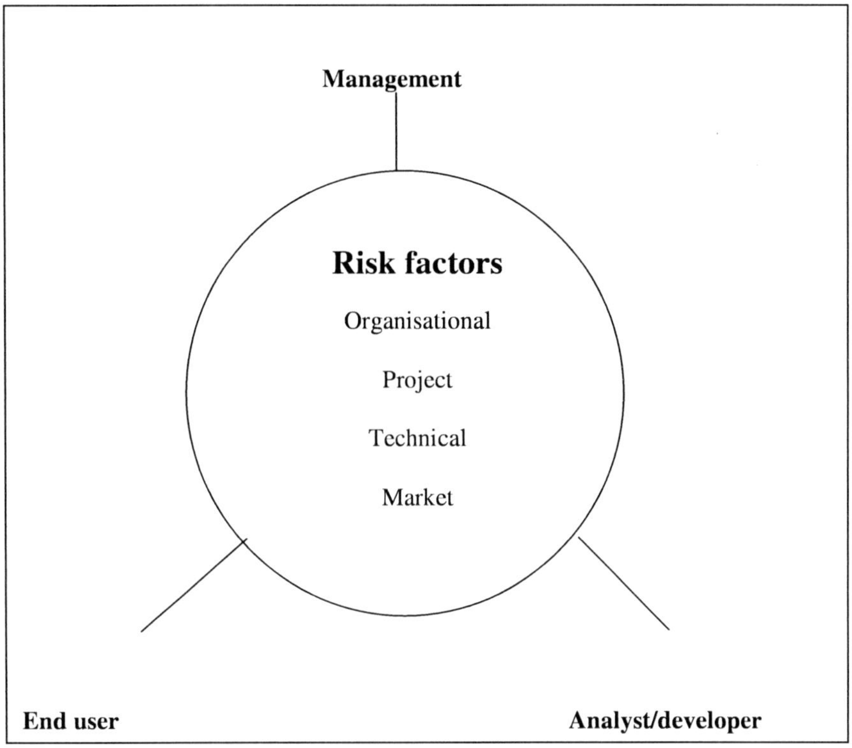

Figure 2. The TOPModel of critical factors affecting IT investments

At this new millennium, the most heartening point of interest from the comparative analysis, is the lessening of importance and omission of some project risks from the concerns of project managers. In 1989, project risks accounted for the first and second most important risks to the development of software (Boehm, 1989). The application of risk management techniques such as the Critical Path Method (CPM), to IT investment projects has reduced the occurrence of unrealistic schedules and eased the level of risk associated with inappropriate staffing levels. The effects of ineffectual management and planning of investment projects indicated by the risk of 'real time performance shortfalls' (due to lack of sufficient testing time), has also been, for the most part, eradicated from the concern of project managers.

5.2. Skilled personnel

Risks associated with shortfalls in staffing are a management of resources risk. Yet the 'personnel shortfall' of Boehm's work may also be interpreted as a lack of experienced personnel. The lack of sufficiently IT skilled and experienced individuals is a well-known lament of employers in Western Europe. The risk is lowered significantly when project/team members have experience of the technology or of similar projects. It appears that the lack of experienced IT professionals was a concern ten years ago and as indicated by the ranking of the risk, seventh in 1998 the lack of suitably experienced personnel will be a concern of the first decade of the millennium (Keil et al., 1998).

5.3. Communication skills

Another common thread between both the investment environments of 1989 and 1998, is the presence of the risk of definitional uncertainty. This risk has increased in significance over the past ten years. Within Keil et al.'s 1998 survey, managers identified the top six risks as being associated with projects definitional uncertainty. The risk of definitional uncertainty is a very important when we consider, that it is the failure in assessing the correct definition of the project's objectives and functions. This is what the investment product will and will not do. If the early feasibility phase of IT investments are managed correctly, then the risks of implementation and miscommunication are lessened. The increased initial and continued communication with and involvement of the end user in the definition and development of the project, gives the sense of 'ownership' to the end user and increases the commitment of management. Thereby diminishing the risk of failure or rejection. Effective communication between the organisation and the analyst also eliminates any misunderstanding of the requirement by the developers.

6. Risk management

It is reasonable to expect that IT investments benefit from the application of stringent evaluations and assessment procedures. The reality of IT management and the application of management aids is quite different. According to Farbey et al., (1992), only 25%, of organisations apply formal techniques to the financial evaluation of IT investments. Empirical evidence concurs, the majority of firms give little attention to risks other than quantifying risk as a cost in cost based analysis (Bacon, 1992; Wilcocks & Lester, 1994 and Galliers et al., 1996).

Risk management is

> "the science and art of recognising the existence of threats, determining their consequence on resources and applying modifying factors in a cost effective manner to keep adverse consequences within bounds."
>
> McGaughey et al., 1994)

The application of risk management techniques presumes that the problems associated with IT investments can be contained or lessened. Risk management applies the classical approach of management: planning, resourcing, controlling and monitoring to the risks occurring within the business and external to the business. Risk management is not only the assessment of risks. It also includes the development and implementation of strategies to address the risks. Risk strategies are the efforts made to reduce, remove or confront risks and to develop effective contingency plans for what can not be controlled (MacCrimmon & Wehrung, 1986 and Stringer, 1992).

All processes of risk management referred to within the literature are comparatively similar, all specify a 'simonian' model which consists of search procedures for information gathering, organisation and interpretation to simplify complex decisions (Simon, 1983). However each of the identified risk management processes (Boehm, 1991;Heemstra & Kusters, 1996 and Powell & Klein, 1996) all neglect an important risk planning phase. The evaluation of risks starts at the feasibility or appraisal stage of IT investments for the competent appreciation of the breadth and depth of the individual investment. If this critical step of the process is omitted, the process will not be managed effectively and the process may be disorganised and resources wasted. Often neglected and extremely important in IT development projects is the post completion evaluation or tracking of the projects and the experienced risks.

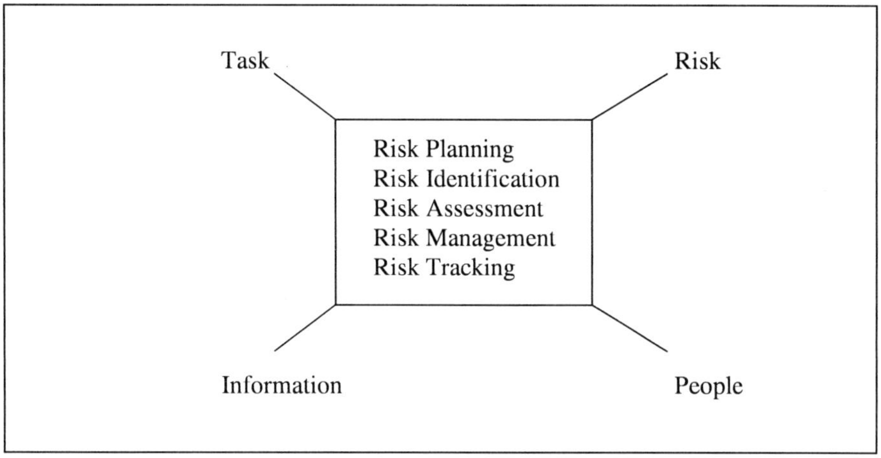

Figure 3. The TRIP model of risk management with the five stages of the MAPIT model of risk management at it's centre.

7. The MAPIT model of risk management

The author developed a new risk management process tailored for the management of IT investment projects; the MAPIT model of risk management that incorporates five distinct management phases. The TRIP model, which illustrates the MAPIT risk management process and the four prime factors that influence the process (the task, the risk, the information available and the participating people) is presented in figure 3. The MAPIT model introduces a new step to traditional risk management processes; the act of risk planning. Figure 4., illustrate the guidelines for successful adoption of a risk management for IT investment projects

Risk planning is a critical function of the process, the strength and quality of the management of the project starts at that point. The second and perhaps most crucial step of the MAPIT model of risk management is the identification of risks. If risks are not identified, they can not be assessed and managed. Within IT investments literature the most detrimental risk has been identified as the one 'unique' risk of the investment, that was new and unappreciated and of course not managed (Neo & Leong, 1994 and Tate & Verner, 1996). The third step of the process is the assessment of the identified risks. To obtain an assessment the probability of occurrence and size of the potential loss are estimated. The classification and ranking of risks is critical when the management of risks are considered. Risks do not act alone, often risks will combine and interplay developing into critical risks. If the structure and aggregation of the investment's risks are not appreciated the success of the investment is threatened.

The management of risk entails the development and implementation of strategies to control the risk factors. The generic strategies are risk avoidance, risk reduction, risk retention and risk sharing (Lauer, 1996; McGaughey et al., 1994 and Stringer, 1992). The choice of strategy is based on the risk profile and the resources available. Due to resource limitations the risks will never be managed as effectively as possible. The final step in the MAPIT risk management model is the tracking of the investment risks. Risks are tracked to understand how they develop and behave for the benefit of future similar investments. This tracking of risks necessitates an investment post-mortem to be executed and documented. This ensures that management identifies and learns from the mistakes of past investments. Such information increases the skill of the estimator or can be applied, by the use of databases for organisational use (Birch & McEvoy, 1995). The production of such information is extremely valuable and could lessen the high statistics of IT investment failure. The information gained from the tracking of the risks can also be used to update the risk management models and risk framework of the organisation.

Step 1. Define the nature and scope of the IT investment.
Step 2. Identify the stakeholders of the IT investment.
Step 3. Identify the criteria for success of the stakeholders.
Step 4. Define the objectives and list the criteria for success of the investment.
Step 5. Specify the limits of the investment and resource constraints.
Step 6. Review past similar investments and identify the risks evident within and the development of these risks.
Step 7. Specify the process of risk management and limits to be adhered to by personnel.
Step 8. Perform a preliminary review and assessment of the risks and identify potential risk strategies.
Step 9. Identify and specify the skills required by the investments' personnel
Step 10. Organise the place and time of weekly investment team reviews and client and end user updates.
Step 11. Plan and organise a periodical review and assessment of the risks.
Step 12. Organise an independent review of the investment at set time periods.

Figure 5. Guidelines for successful application of risk management to IT investment projects.

8. References

[1] Bacon, C., (1992), "The Use of Decision Criteria in Selecting Information Systems/Technology Investments." Management Information Systems Quarterly, September.
[2] Beenstock, S., (1998), "The calculation IT can't make." Management Today, June.
[3] Birch, D. & McEvoy, N., (1995), "Structured risk analysis for information systems." In Hard money, soft outcomes. Editors Farbey, Land & Targett, Alfred Waller Ltd 1st edition, 1995.
[4] Boehm, B., (1991), "Software risk management: principles and practices." IEEE Software, 8.
[5] Brynjolfsson, E., (1993), "The productivity paradox of information technology." Communications of the ACM, vol. 36, no. 12.
[6] Byrd, T. & Marshall, T., (1997), "Relating IT investment to organisation performance: A casual model analysis." Omega, vol.25, no. 1.
[7] Cash, J., McFarlan, F. & McKenney, J., (1992), "Corporate Information Systems." Irwin.
[8] Corder, C., (1989), "Taming Your Company Computer." McGraw Hill.
[9] Davies, G., (1982), "Strategies for information requirements determination." IBM Systems Journal, vol. 21, no. 1.
[10] Earl, M., (1989), "Management Strategies for Information Technology." Prentice Hall.
[11] Farbey, B., Targett, D. & Land, F., (1992), "Evaluating investments in IT." Journal of Information Technology, Issue 2.
[12] Heemstra, F. & Kusters, R., (1996), "Dealing with risk; a practical approach." Journal of Information Technology 11.
[13] Hochstrasser, B.& Griffith, C., (1990), "Regaining control of IT investments: A handbook for senior UK management." Kobler Unit.
[14] Keen, P., (1991), "Shaping the Future." Harvard Business Press.
[15] Keil, M., (1995), "Pulling the plug: Software project management and the problem of project esculation." Management Information Systems Quarterly, December.

[16] Keil, M., Cule, P., Lyytinen, K. & Schmidt, R., (1998), "A framework for identifying software project risks." Communications of the ACM, Vol. 41, no. 11.
[17] Kremer, C. & Sosa, G., (1991), "Systems development risks in strategic information systems." Information and Software, Vol.33, no.3.
[18] Lauer, T., (1996), "Software project managers' risk preferences." Journal of Information Technology, Vol. 11.
[19] Lester, S. & Wilcocks, L., (1993), "Evaluation and control of IS investments: Recent UK survey evidence." Oxford Institute of Information Management.
[20] Lyytinen, K. & Hirschheim, R., (1987), "Information systems failures- a survey and classification of the empirical literature." In Oxford Survey in Information Technology, Volume 4. (Editor Zorkoczy, P.I.) Oxford University Press.
[21] Lyytinen, K., Mathiassen, L. & Ropponnen, J., (1996), "A framework for software risk management." Journal of Information Technology vol. 11, no. 4.
[22] MacCrimmon, K. & Wehrung, D., (1986), "Taking Risks." The Free Press.
[23] McFarlan, F., (1981), "Portfolio approach to information systems." Harvard Business Review, 59 (5), September-October.
[24] McGaughey, R., Synder, C. & Carr, H., (1994), "Implementing IT for competitive advantage, risk management issues." Information Management, vol. 26, no. 5.
[25] Neo, B. & Leong, K., (1994), Managing Risks in Information Technology Projects: a casestudy of TradeNet. Journal of Information Technology Management, Vol. 5, no. 3.
[26] Parker, M., Benson, R. & Trainor, H., (1988), Information Economics. 1st edition, Prentice Hall.
[27] Powell, P. & Klein, J., (1996), Risk management for information systems development. Journal of Information Technology Vol. 11, no. 4.
[28] Remenyi, D., White, T. & Sherwood-Smith, M., (1997), Information systems management the need for a post modern approach. Working paper series, Henley Research Centre.
[29] Silk, D., (1990), Managing IS benefits for the 1990's Journal of Information Technology, issue 5.
[30] Simon, H., (1983), Theories of bounded rationality, behavioural economics and business organisations. 1st edition, MITT presses.
[31] Spinner, M., (1992), Elements of project management. 2nd edition, Prentice Hall.
[32] Strassmann, P., (1996), The Value of Computers, Information and Knowledge. Located at http://www.strassmann.com/pubs/cik/cik-value.shtml.
[33] Stringer, J., (1992), Risk in Large Projects. In Operational research tutorial papers, (Editor Mortimer, M.E.) 1st edition, Operational Research Society Publication.
[34] Tate, G. & Verner, J., (1996), Case study of risk management, development and evolutionary prototyping. Information and Software Technology, vol. 23, no. 3.
[35] Whiting, R., Davies, J. & Knul, M., (1993), Investment appraisal for IT systems. BT Technology Journal, vol. 11, no. 2.
[36] Wilcocks, L., (1992), IT Evaluation : Managing the catch 22. The European Management Journal, 10.
[37] Wilcocks, L. & Margetts, H., (1994), Risk assessment and Information Systems: developing the analysis. In Information Management: The evaluation of Information Systems Investments. (Editor Wilcocks, L.) 1st edition, Chapman & Hall.
[38] Wilcocks, L. editor (1994), Information Management: The evaluation of Information Systems Investments. 1st edition, Chapman & Hall.

Early risk factors for software development

Drew Procaccino and June Verner

Abstract

Factors such as poor requirements, lack of management support, and customers and users who do not make themselves available when required, are serious risks for software development success. The earlier in the development process problems arise, the more serious is the outcome. When there are limited resources, a project manager needs to know which factors are responsible for the greatest risks to the project. The earlier a project manager discovers that a project is going off course, the more effectively and efficiently adjustments be made. In order to investigate some of these early factors and their effect on project success we analyze 109 software development projects. The most serious risks were found to be different in each of the data sets. We investigate how our risk factors may be used to predict the success or failure of software development projects and the generalisability of the results.

1. Introduction

In 1994, 31% of all corporate software development projects resulted in cancellations [6] despite the extensive research into successful software development [e.g., 2, 7, 12, 9]. Clearly, systems development projects can present risks to an organization. Recent research that focuses on factors contributing to the failure of information systems projects takes a practitioner view (such as that of an IT manager, project manager or software developer) [5, 13, 7, 14]. Management, who is paying for the project, has a specific view of what constitutes a successful project. In some cases this view is different from that of the developers, while users may take a quite different view (Note: We will not be considering the user's view of project success here, as our research has a different focus). Major categories of factors contributing to the success or failure of software systems are: (1) management, (2) customers and users, (3) requirements, (4) estimation, and scheduling, (5) the project manager, (6) the software development process, and (7) development personnel.

The focus of the research described here is to provide insight into the most influential success factors that occur early in the development process. More insight will help project managers and other project stakeholders to predict the likelihood of project success. This will allow for corrective action to be taken early in the development process. This study is a first step to the establishment of guidelines for project risk prioritization in the early phases of software development. Because of the number of generic risks the project manager has to contend with, we would eventually like to provide a severity roadmap showing the consequences of early project actions (taken or imposed). In addition, we wish to determine if there are any differences between management and developer's perception of project success. To be successful, the project manager needs to be aware of success and failure factors from all stakeholder viewpoints, and be able to respond to these perceptions, either directly or indirectly [10], in a timely manner.

2. Background

The following factors emerge as reoccurring risks encountered early in software development projects:

Management support: Inadequate management practices have far reaching implications [1]. (When we refer to management, we are referring to corporate management. Where appropriate, we will explicitly refer to a project manager.) A project needs a committed sponsor throughout, who must encourage the same commitment from other stakeholders, as well as participation in the decision-making process. If no sponsor is available at the start of a project it is important to try to obtain one as soon as possible.

Customer/users: One of the most important contributors to successful project development is end-user involvement [8]. Further, involvement by all appropriate users should occur in <u>all</u> phases of system development [1]. Expectations of customers and users are also an important contributor towards the perceived success or failure of a software project. Realistic expectations can reduce conflict and this in turn supports the perception of project success, from both the developer and managerial standpoint [7].

Requirements: A clear understanding of the problem assists in well-defined requirements, and is essential to the development of a successful system [11, 15]. However, "we fail to use requirements management to surface (early) errors or problems" [4]. Poor requirements are involved in most project failures [5] and "requirements continue to be a huge problem for IS development" [11]. Unrealistic expectations that customers and users have regarding software projects often arise because projects start with incomplete requirements [9].

Given these software project problems, our investigation uses a number of software development efforts to shed some light, on the relative importance and severity of a number of risk factors, as they are perceived to impact project success.

3. Our investigation

In late 1999, we engaged in structured discussions with 21 IT professionals, from a large financial institution. We focussed on issues within their organization they identified as associated with software project success and failure. Based on these discussions, we developed a questionnaire that targeted software development practices, in an attempt to discover which development practices are most important for software project success (from both developer and management viewpoints). Our IT professionals each completed two questionnaires, one related to a successful project, the other to a less successful project. In early 2000, another group of software professionals, from several organizations, answered our questionnaire which is arranged under the following headings: (1) Requirements, (2) Management, (3) Customers and users, (4) Estimation, and scheduling, (5) Project manager, (6) Software development process, and (7) Development personnel. We also asked (a) Was the project pleasant to work on? (b) Did management consider the project a success (variable: MSUCCESS) and, (c) From the respondent's point of view, was the project a success (variable: RSUCCESS)? The research reported here is focused on management support, requirements, and customer and user involvement. The results of both our investigations are presented next. We follow this with a discussion section and conclusion.

4. Results

We received data from 42 software development projects, Data set 1, and 67 projects for Data set 2. All projects are development (rather than maintenance) projects. There were no significant differences between the numbers of staff and consultants/contractors employed in either data set. The average number of full-time developers was eleven and contractors (plus consultants) four. Questions in which where there are significant differences between the data sets are marked in Table 1 (which presents a summary of our results), with an '*'. We now list each question and comment on the results under the following headings: Management support, Customer/users, and Requirements. We follow this with sections on multivariate analysis, and management and developer's views of success. Our discussion is focused on those results that are important in the prediction of either MSUCCESS or RSUCCESS. Overall, while management thought 71% of the projects were successful (MSUCCESS), and there were no significant differences for this variable, we did find significant differences for RSUCCESS (0.0008); Overall RSUCCESS was 54%. For Data set 1 RSUCCESS was 43 %; for Data set 2, RSUCCESS was 61%.

4.1. Management support

We began with a number of assumptions regarding management support including: projects are more likely to succeed if (1) project managers are given full authority to manage their project; (2) the project has a committed sponsor(s); (3) the sponsor supports the project throughout the development process. Significant results are based on Chi-square tests between MSUCCESS, or RSUCCESS, and the various individual question responses ($\alpha = .05$). Based on these assumptions, we list our questions and the responses obtained:

Q1.1 Was the project manager given full authority to manage the project? This was not significant with MSUCCESS or RSUCCESS for any of the data sets.

Q1.2 Did the project start with a committed sponsor (or champion)? Although this variable was not significant with either MSUCCESS or RSUCCESS respondents overall considered 77% of the projects that began without a committed champion a failure, though only 41% of these projects were considered a failure by management.

Q1.3 Did this commitment last right through the project? Both management and respondents' perception of project success decreased when sponsor/management commitment did not last throughout the project. Not surprisingly, there is a significant correlation between Q1.2 and Q1.3. Overall, 67% of our projects had sponsor commitment from beginning to end (though 25% had no commitment at all and 4% began without a sponsor but managed to pick one up along the way).

Q1.4 Was the sponsor involved in project decisions? Both management and respondents' perceptions of success remained relatively constant whether or not the sponsor was involved in project decisions. We found no significant relationship with either MSUCCESS or RSUCCESS.

Q1.5 Were the other stakeholders committed and involved? Management's perception of success was relatively consistent whether or not the other stakeholders were committed and involved. However, the respondents' perception of success dropped by approximately one-half if there was a lack of commitment and involvement by the other stakeholders. We found no significant relationship with either MSUCCESS or RSUCCESS.

4.2. Customer/users

The assumptions behind our customer/user questions are: Projects will succeed if they have (1) customer/users who are highly involved and who stay involved throughout the project, (2) customer/users who contribute to project estimates, (3) customer/users with realistic expectations, and (4) a low level of customer/user turnover. With these points in mind, we asked the following questions:

Q2.1 What was the level of involvement of customer/users? As customer/user involvement increases, so do the chances of a project being viewed as a success by managers and developers. Across all levels of customer/user involvement, management categorized a higher percentage of projects as successful than did respondents. This variable was significant with both MSUCCESS and RSUCCESS for Data set 1. For the combined Data set, we found evidence of a relationship with RSUCCESS, not with MSUCCESS. For this combined group, 37 % of the projects had high customer/user involvement, 28% had a reasonable level, 15% had some involvement, 16% had little involvement and only 6% had no customer/user involvement. Both groups' perceptions of success increased as customer/user involvement reached "reasonable" and "high" levels.

Q.2.2 Did the involved customer/users stay right through the project? Both developers and management are more likely to view the project as a success if customers/and users stay involved right through a project. Both developer's and management's perception of success decreased noticeably when this did not occur. We found evidence of a relationship with both MSUCCESS and RSUCCESS for all data sets.

Q2.3. What level of confidence did the customer/user have in the project manager/team members? The higher the level of confidence that customers/users have in the project manager and development team, the more likely developers are to consider the project a success. For the combined data set Chi-square tests were significant with both MSUCCESS and RSUCCESS, and for Data set 1 was significant with RSUCCESS

Q2.4 Were the customer/users involved in making schedule estimates? Both management and respondents' perception of success increases when customer/users are involved in making schedule estimates.

Q2.5 What level of customer/users staff turnover did you have to contend with? The respondents' perception of project success decreased as customer/user staff turnover increased. Management categorized a higher percentage of projects as successes than did developers across all levels of staff turnover.

Q2.6 Did the customer/users have realistic expectations? Developers are more likely to consider the project a success if the customers/users have realistic expectations. For the combined data sets, we found evidence of relationship with both MSUCCESS and RSUCCESS. However the answers to this question were significantly different for Data set 1 and Data set 2. The Data set 2 respondents did not feel their projects were so heavily impacted by customers/users with unrealistic expectations.

Q2.7 Did you run into problems due to the large number of customer/users involved? Although it could be expected that success would decrease with a large number of customer/users, the statistical evidence did not support this, as a Chi-square test was not significant with either MSUCCESS or RSUCCESS.

4.3. Requirements

We expected that those projects viewed as successful would (1) begin with complete and accurate requirements that were (2) gathered using a specific methodology, together with (3) a well defined scope that (4) remained consistent throughout the project. With these points in mind, we asked the following requirements-related questions.

Q3.1 Were requirements gathered by using a particular method? We found no significant relationship with either MSUCCESS or RSUCCESS.

Q3.2a Were the requirements complete and accurate at the start of the project? Both management's and developers' views of success decreased when the requirements were not complete and accurate at the start of the project. From management's perspective 23% of these projects failed while 48% failed from the respondents' point of view. We found no evidence of a significant difference between the two samples for the answers to this question.

Q3.2b If requirements were not complete and accurate at the start, were they completed adequately? Both managers and developer's perception of success decreased markedly when requirements are not completed adequately. For the Combined data set, 40% of the projects that had incomplete requirements failed from management's viewpoint and 75% from the respondent point of view. There were significant differences for both MSUCCESS and RSUCCESS across all data sets.

Q3.3 Was the scope of the project well defined? Both management's and respondent's perception of success dropped if the project scope was not well defined. However, management's perception of success dropped more severely (75% to 35%). For the combined data set, we found evidence of a relationship with both MSUCCESS and RSUCCESS.

Q3.4 Did the scope change during the project? Both management's and developer's perception of success remained relatively constant whether or not the scope changed during a project. Some scope changes may of course have a positive effect on a project.

Q3.5 Did the customer/users make adequate time available for requirements gathering? Management's perception of success went from down from 86% to 65% when customer/users did not make adequate time available for requirements gathering, while developers' perception of success decreased substantially for such projects (75% to 27%). For the Combined data set, we found evidence of a relationship with both MSUCCESS, and RSUCCESS.

Q3.6 Was there a single central repository for the requirements? Management obviously had no interest in whether or not there was a central repository for requirements, as their perception of success remained relatively constant for this factor. However, developer's perception of success decreased dramatically (70% to 39%) if the project was without a central requirements repository. With the Combined data set, we found evidence of a relationship with RSUCCESS, but not with MSUCCESS.

Q3.7 Did the requirements result in well-defined software deliverables? Management's perception of success increased slightly if the requirements resulted in well-defined software deliverables. However, developer's perception of success decreased by more than half for projects lacking well defined software deliverables (76% to 33%). With the Combined data set, we found evidence of a relationship with RSUCCESS, but not with MSUCCESS. Sixty percent of our projects had requirements that resulted in well-defined software deliverables, and 83% of these projects were considered a success by management, while 76% were considered a success by developers. Based on Chi-square tests, there is a significant difference between data sets for this question. Data set 1 has a greater percentage of successful projects without well-defined software deliverables (85%) than Data set 2 (59%).

Q3.8 Did the size of project negatively affect requirements elicitation? Both developer's and management's perception of success decreased with large projects whose size negatively affected requirements elicitation. However, developer's perception of success decreased notably

(71% to 38%). We found evidence of a relationship with RSUCCESS, but not with MSUCCESS. Overall, 37% of our projects were large enough in size to negatively impact requirements elicitation. Based on Chi-square tests, there is a significant difference between samples for the answers to this question. Data set 1 had 50% projects whose size affected requirements elicitation while Data set 2 had only 29% of such projects.

	Data set 1		Data set 2		Combined Data set	
	MSUCCESS	RSUCCESS	MSUCCESS	RSUCCESS	MSUCCESS	RSUCCESS
Q1.3	0.005	0.004		0.025	0.002	0.000
Q2.1	0.015	0.000				0.000
Q2.2	0.008	0.007	0.007	0.020	0.013	0.000
Q2.3		0.001			0.047	0.000
Q2.4	0.006					
Q2.5				0.022		
Q2.6*		0.018			0.050	0.001
Q3.2a*						0.002
Q3.2b	0.034	0.006	0.003	0.008	0.000	0.000
Q3.3*			0.004	0.004	0.001	0.000
Q3.5		0.004	0.012	0.001	0.020	0.000
Q3.6						0.008
Q3.7*			0.011	0.000		0.000
Q3.8*		0.004		0.001		0.002

Table 1 Significant Chi Square results with MSUCCESS and RSUCCESS

4.4. Multivariate analysis

Next, we conducted a multivariate analysis to explore the impact that the variables generated have on developer and management perceptions of project success (RSUCCESS and MSUCCESS, respectively). Since the success variables are coded as zero for "unsuccessful" and one for "successful," we were unable to use ordinary least squares regression. Instead, we conducted a logistics regression analysis. We also recoded variable 2.1 to a two-point scale to avoid using dummy variables.

(1) Prediction of success from the developer viewpoint

Data set 1: Three variables entered our logistics regression equation ($R^2 = 0.68$; see Table 2). Parameter estimates for project success are all significant at the 5% level. Our logistic equation correctly predicts 85% of projects overall (86% of the unsuccessful projects and 82% of the successful projects).

Variable	Parameter Estimate	Standard Error	Probability
Q1.3.Level of confidence customer has in team	2.0978	1.1396	0.0657
Q2.1 Level of involvement of customer/users?	3.0422	1.2630	0.0160
Q3.5 Customer made time available for requirements	2.5087	1.1206	0.0252
Constant	-5.461	1.7356	0.0017

Table 2 Logistic Equation for Prediction of RSUCCESS Data set 1

Data set 2: Two variables entered our logistics regression equation (R^2 = 0.51; see Table 3). The parameter estimates for project success are all significant at the 1% level. Our logistic equation correctly predicts 85% of projects overall (50% of the unsuccessful projects and 100% of the successful projects). We have 8 failed projects predicted to be successes.

Variable	Parameter Estimate	Standard Error	Probability
Q3.7 Requirements resulted in well-defined deliverables	2.493	0.8101	0.0021
Q3.8 The size of project negatively affected requirements	-2.193	0.8255	0.0079
Constant	0.717	0.6436	0.9113

Table 3 Logistic Equation for Prediction of RSUCCESS Data set 2

Combined Data set: Three variables entered our logistics regression equation (R^2 = 0.48; see Table 4). The parameter estimates for project success are all significant at the 5% level. Our logistic equation correctly predicts 86% of projects overall (69% of the unsuccessful projects and 98% of the successful projects). With a single variable in our prediction equation (either Q1.3, Q2.1 or Q3.8) our prediction of project success is 75%.

Variable	Parameter Estimate	Standard Error	Probability
Q1.3.Level of confidence customer has in team	1.696	0.612	0.0142
Q2.1 Level of involvement of customer/users?	2.126	0.6834	0.0019
Q3.8 The size of project negatively affected requirements	-1.7307	0.6755	0.0104
Constant	-1.4942	0.6429	0.0201

Table 4 Logistic Equation for Prediction of RSUCCESS Combined Data set

(2) Prediction of success from management viewpoint

Data set 1: A single variable entered our regression equation (R^2 = 0.28; see Table 5). The parameter estimates for project success are all significant at the 10% level. Our logistic equation correctly predicts 79% of projects overall (67% of the unsuccessful projects and 83% of the successful projects are predicted correctly).

Variable	Parameter estimate	Standard error	Probability
Q3.3 Was the scope of the project well defined?	2.2865	0.7688	0.0029
constant	-0.1823	0.6055	0.7633

Table 5 Logistic Equation for Prediction of MSUCCESS Data set 1

Data set 2: A single variable enters the regression equation (R^2 =0.24; see Table 6). This equation successfully predicts 82% of the time. It predicts 55% of the failed projects and 89% of the successful projects. There are 5 failed projects predicted as successful and five successful projects are predicted as failures.

Variable	Parameter Estimate	Standard Error	Probability
Q2.2 Involved customer/users stay right through	2.303	0.8602	0.074
Constant	-0.180	0.6055	0.7633

Table 6 Logistic Equation for Prediction of MSUCCESS Data set 2

All data: Two variables entered our logistics regression equation ($R^2 = 0.39$; see Table 7). The parameter estimates for project success, all of which are significant at the 5% level, are shown in Table 7 below. Our equation predicts correctly 84% of projects (82% of the unsuccessful projects and 86% of the successful projects). Only three of the unsuccessful projects are erroneously predicted as successful, and two successful projects are erroneously predicted as unsuccessful.

Variable	Parameter estimate	Standard error	Probability
Q2.2 Involved customer/users stay right through	1.684	0.8421	0.0455
Q3.2b Requirements completed adequately	2.543	1.1299	0.0244
Constant	-0.476	0.6540	0.4669

Table 7 Logistic Equation for Prediction of MSUCCESS Combined Data set

The above results will help project managers to predict the likely success of their projects, and to be able to do so with reasonable accuracy early in the project. From developers and management's perspective, the level of involvement of the customers and users is the most critical factor for project success. It is somewhat surprising that we are able to predict the success, or otherwise, of software development projects with this degree of accuracy from so few project variables.

To investigate the reliability of our approach we used results from one data set to predict success for another data set. We obtained the following results:

Using Data set 1 to predict Data set 2 RSUCCESS 80% MSUCCESS 57%

Using Data set 2 to predict Data set 1 RSUCCESS 73% MSUCCESS 88%

These results are not statistically different from our results when we used logistic regression with each of the data sets. Using data from one's own organization might possibly give better results but if the data is not available, then using someone else's results should provide a good indication of a project's likely success.

5. Discussion and conclusions

Of our 109 projects, 71% were considered a success by management (MSUCCESS), and 54% were considered a success by developers (RSUCCESS). A Chi-square test indicated a significant difference between MSUCCESS and RSUCCESS ($\alpha < .05$). We believe that the difference in viewpoint is attributable to the different perspectives typically associated with the roles of management and developers. For example, considering Q2.4, while management may view customer input into schedule estimates as politically important (or expedient), developers might view this input as intrusive. Another example is reflected in Q2.1, where the developers are concerned with the level of customer and user involvement, while managers are not. Since requirements gathering is the responsibility of the developers, it is no surprise that they consider the level of customer involvement as key. Management is concerned with the final product, and considers requirements a deliverable from the developers, not from the customer. In the final analysis, it appears that most of the differences in success factors can be attributed to respective project responsibilities with developers concerned primarily with things affecting their job performance, and management concerned only with the final products.

It is possible to predict project success and failure reasonably early using only a few variables. Our data shows that customers and users are probably the most important influence on project success, for without their cooperation projects will be difficult. To ensure a successful project, we found that the most important factors are:

- Customers and users must have confidence in the team, have a high involvement with the project, make adequate time available for requirements gathering and stay right through the project.
- The project manager must make sure that the requirements result in well-defined software deliverables and, if the project is large, that its size does not affect the project.

One of the most compelling reasons to investigate the views of those involved with software development is that perceptions of project success, whether or not they are consistent with reality, can dramatically affect the health of the project's manager, team, and thus the health of the project. As our results show, there are differences between developers' perception of project success factors, and their perceptions of how management personnel view project success and failure. Developers take a mainly inward-looking view of project success, concentrating on the things that affect them and their ability to do their job properly. The management viewpoint appears to be more politically orientated to keeping customers and users, rather than developers, happy. With the current level of IT shortages, management needs to be more aware of what keeps developers happy in order to avoid staff turnover and loss of motivation.

Because all the questions we asked deal with factors generally acknowledged to be essential to successful project development, the most interesting results from our research are identification of those factors that are <u>not</u> significant in predicting success. Our results suggest that we can still have a successful project, from both management's and developer's points of view, even if we do none of the following:

- give the project manager full authority to manage the project.
- start a project with a committed sponsor (or champion)
- have our sponsor involved in project decisions
- have other stakeholders committed and involved.
- gather requirements by using a particular method
- and keep the scope of the project unchanged

We found that nine of our projects did not have any of the above factors, and, without even considering any other factors (or factor interactions) seven of the nine projects were successful from management's point of view, and four from the developer's viewpoint.

It is surprising that we can predict successful software projects so well (at a reasonably early stage of the development) with just one or two variables,. Some of the factors such as: "involved customers and users stayed right through the project" and "the requirements resulted in well defined software deliverables", may on their own, predict up to 80% of successful projects. These results will certainly cause the thinking project manager to concentrate his or her efforts on factors which are more likely to ensure success from both management and developer points of view.

Further questions that have emerged from this analysis include:

- How consistent are management's perceptions of project success and developer's views of those perceptions?
- Are customer's perceptions of project success consistent with both management's and developer's perceptions?
- How influential are specific perceptual variables in predicting or changing the course of unsuccessful projects? What are the critical success factors? What are the interactions of these variables? Additional data and path analysis techniques should help to provide some answers to these questions.

6. References

[1] Amoako-Gyampah, K. and White, K. B., "When Is User Involvement Not User Involvement", Information Strategy: The Executive's Journal, Vol. 13, Issue 4 (Summer 1997) p.40-45.

[2] Boehm B. W., Software Engineering Economics, Prentice Hall, Englewood Cliffs, NJ (1981).

[3] Brooke, C. and McGuire, S., "Systems Development: A Restrictive Practice?", International Journal of Information Management, Vol. 18, Issue 3 (1998) p.165-180.

[4] Clavadetscher, C. "User Involvement: Key To Success", IEEE Software. Vol. 15, Issue 2 (Mar/Apr 1998) p. 30, 32.

[5] Glass, R. L. Software Runaways, Prentice-Hall, Upper Saddle River, New Jersey, 1998.

[6] Linberg, K. R. "Software Developer Perceptions About Software Project Failure: A Study", The Journal of Systems and Software, Vol. 49, Issue 2/3 (December 30, 1999) p. 177-192.

[7] McConnell, Steve, Rapid Development, Microsoft Press, Redmond, Washington, 1996.

[8] Nolan, A. J. "Learning From Success", IEEE Software, Vol. 16, Issue 1 (Jan/Feb 1999) p. 97-105.

[9] Pressman, R. Software Engineering: A Practitioners Approach, McGraw Hill (1996).

[10] Rockwell, C. "Customer connection creates a winning product: building success with contextual techniques", Interactions, Vol 6, Issue 1 (Jan. 1999), p. 50 - 57.

[11] Schenk, K.D and Vitalari, N. P., et al. "Differences Between Novice and Expert Systems Analysts: What Do We Know and What Do We Do?", Journal of Management Information Systems, Vol. 15, Issue 1 (Summer 1998) p.9-51.

[12] Paulk, M., Curtis B., Chrissis M., and Webster C., Capability Maturity Model for Software, Technical Report, CMU/SEI-93-TR-024, Software Engineering Institute, Carnegie Mellon (1993).

[13] Glass, R. L. "How Not To Prepare For A Consulting Assignment And Other Ugly Consultancy Truths", CACM. Volume 41, Issue 12 (December 1998) p.11-13.

[14] Reel, J.S., "Critical Success Factors In Software Projects", IEEE Software, Vol. 16, Issue 3 (May/June1999), p. 18-23.

[15] Verner, J. M, Overmyer, S. P. and McCain, K.W. "In The 25 Years Since The Mythical Man-Month What Have We Learned About Project Management?", Information and Software Technology, 41 (1999), p. 1021-1026.

Revisiting Optimal Software Components

William M. Evanco, June Verner

Abstract

In this study, we revisit the question of identifying the characteristics of "optimum" software components. Specifically, we focus on those characteristics that are expected to minimize defect densities uncovered during the testing phases of software development. Although a number of such models have been examined in the past, these models have embodied some methodological difficulties that we attempt to remedy. Using data from C subprograms, we examine the optimum relationship between the internal and external complexities of subprograms. Internal complexity is related to the workload of a subprogram; because workload is difficult to measure we use the number of unique operands in a subprogram as its proxy. External complexity is related to the call structure among the subprograms. Our results show that the optimum number of calls for a subprogram depends on the number of unique operands in that subprogram. For example, a subprogram with forty-seven operands and corresponding to about eighty source lines of code should make about fourteen calls to other subprograms.

1. Introduction

In this study, we are interested in identifying the values of software characteristics that lead to high reliability. For example, software modules that are either too small or too large may have defect densities greater than a module of some intermediate size and there has been some research into this topic. It may then be possible to identify the ideal size for a module that minimizes the defect density. Similarly, accounting for tradeoffs between internal and external complexities, there may be an ideal call structure that minimizes architectural complexity and hence defect density. Software components with such characteristics we call optimal software components.

Numerous studies have been conducted to analyse the relationship between software quality outcomes and the internal characteristics of software. The models resulting from these studies generally focus on the quality attributes of reliability, as measured by faults, defect counts and defect densities [1,2,3], and maintainability, as measured by the efforts to repair or change software [4,5].

As a general rule, the specific functional forms for these models cannot be specified based on *a priori* theoretical grounds. Instead, we assume that there exists a functional dependency between quality and software, the exact form of the function being unknown. This functional relationship is then expressed as a Taylor series expansion of the software characteristics or their logarithms, and only the first order terms of this expansion are kept, thus generating parametric linear models. Multivariate regression techniques are then used to determine the values of the parameters associated with each of the linear terms. Once we have these models, they can be used to predict the quality factors associated with a new project based on its software characteristics. The advantage of such models is that the software characteristics are generally known long before the software quality factors.

As a general rule, these predictive models do not lend themselves to an analysis of optimal software characteristics. Linear models are monotonic in their behaviors with respect to the explanatory variables and these variables are not linked in any way that would allow for an examination of tradeoffs. Greater values of some software characteristic, such as cyclomatic complexity for example, leads to a greater expected number of defects [2]. In none of these linear models is cyclomatic complexity coupled to nesting depth or to the call structure, for example, so that tradeoffs cannot be examined among these independent variables with regard to their impacts on defects.

We propose some models that are non-linear in their explanatory variables. Specifically, in the next section, we examine structural issues by analysing the tradeoffs between internal and external complexities of components to identify the optimal subprogram coupling in a call tree structure. In Section 3, we discuss our defect density model and, in Section 4 present the results of an empirical analysis. Our conclusions are discussed in Section 5.

2. Overview of Problem

The strong focus on design methodologies in the development of software systems attests to the importance system architecture plays in various development outcomes. These outcomes, which we mentioned earlier, include a variety of software quality factors such as reliability and maintainability.

Card and Agresti [6] analysed local vs. structural complexity tradeoffs in the framework of a univariate model with a focus on reliability. Although they developed two variables—one for local complexity and the other for structural complexity—they did not conduct a multivariate analysis because of a paucity of data. Instead they added the two variables and then proceeded with an analysis showing, for example, that the optimum number of calls for a subprogram with 100-200 input/output variables is three, while for 35 to 100 input/output parameters, the optimum number of calls is two.

These results appear to be an intuitively unappealing. The input/output lists in subprograms for a variety of systems that we have examined tend to have substantially fewer than 35-200 elements (a vector or array is counted as one element). The results appear to tell us that very little use of subprogram calls is warranted with typical subprograms having fewer than ten input/outputs.

The approach of Card and Agresti is flawed because a more general linear combination, $y = ax_1 + bx_2$, is warranted (where x_1 and x_2 represent the local and structural complexities, and a and b are parameters to be estimated) rather than the $y = x_1 + x_2$ variable that they chose. One simply cannot combine two disparate metrics as a sum without accounting for the scale differences between them.

In addition, Shepperd [7] pointed out that using the number of inputs plus outputs might fail to capture work that is completely internal to a module, which may be related to size. He, consequently, proposed a measure for workload based on the number of primitive functional requirements supported by the module. The problem with this measure is that it is somewhat subjective since the definition of a primitive functional requirement may vary from analyst to analyst.

3. Defect Density Model

The objective of the following analysis is to identify an optimum relationship between subprogram size and the delegation of work within that subprogram to other subprograms via the call tree. The internal complexity of a subprogram is a function of the amount of work that it must perform. We relate the work performed by a subprogram to the number of unique operands in the subprogram as defined by Halstead [8]. In contrast to this approach, Card and Agresti [6] related the workload to a subset of these operands, namely, the set of input/output variables of the subprogram. By relating the workload to all of the unique operands, we address the issues raised by Shepperd [7] regarding component size. Based on our sample of subprograms, which will be further discussed below, the correlation between size, as measured by source lines of code (SLOC), and the number of unique operands is .82.

If the workload is deferred to lower levels through the use of subprogram calls, then the internal complexity is correspondingly reduced. Given a subsystem consisting of subprograms, we compute the internal complexity (denoted by IC) as the total number of unique operands in the subsystem (denoted by Tn_2) divided by the total number of subprogram calls within that subsystem (denoted by TC) :

$$IC = (Tn_2/TC) \qquad (1)$$

This internal complexity represents the mean number of unique operands supported by each call statement. Alternatively, we can view the internal complexity as the mean number of unique operands per subprogram divided by the mean number of calls per subprogram:

$$IC = ((Tn_2/NS)/(TC/NS)) \qquad (2)$$

where NS is the number of subprograms in a subsystem.

In the spirit of Card and Agresti [6], the structural complexity (denoted by SC) associated with a subsystem is taken to be the square of the average number of calls per subprogram[1]:

$$SC = (TC/NS)^2 \qquad (3)$$

This definition of structural complexity is not identical to that of Card and Agresti, since they take the square of the number of calls for each subprogram, sum over all subprograms, and then divide by the number of subprograms. Using this definition would not allow us (or them) to apply the results of the analysis at the subprogram level in a mathematically rigorous manner.

Lastly, we relate the internal and structural complexities to the defect density of a subsystem as follows:

$$DD = a_0 + a_1*IC + a_2*SC \qquad (4)$$

where a_0, a_1, and a_2 are parameters to be estimated. In addition to the model in equation (4), we also calibrate a model accounting for reused code as follows:

$$DD = a_0 + a_1*IC + a_2*SC + a_3*FREU \qquad (5)$$

---

[1] A question may arise in the reader's mind as to why we take the square of the average number of calls per subprogram. To test the reasonableness of this assumption, we conducted a non-linear regression analysis as opposed to the ordinary least squares regression discussed below treating the exponent as a parameter. We found the exponent to be equal to 2.33 with a standard error of .6. Thus, based on this standard error value, we can reject the hypothesis that this exponent is significantly different from 2.0. We did not report the details of this non-linear analysis in this paper, since the introduction of an additional parameter made the estimates of one of the other parameters unstable due to the small number of observations.

where FREU is the fraction of source lines of code that is reused in a subsystem and a_3 is an additional parameter to be estimated. The defect density in this case is computed as the defects divided by the number of new source lines of code.

In contrast to the formulation above, Card and Agresti defined a composite complexity variable CC=IC+SC which would be equivalent to setting $a_1=a_2$ in equation (4). Since the dimensions of IC and SC are totally different, defining the composite complexity variable in this way could lead to counter-intuitive results as we have seen.

4. Analysis and Results

Our empirical sample consisted of a single software project programmed in C of 2221 subprograms contained in fourteen subsystems. These subprograms were analysed using UX-Metric, a commercially available software analyser developed by Set Laboratories, Inc. The analyser provided us with a variety of metrics for each subprogram including size measures, such as lines of code, various Halstead measures, nesting depth, and cyclomatic complexity. The defect data were available only at the subsystem level, so we aggregated the metrics obtained from the analyser to derive the internal and structural complexity measures as described in the previous section.

For this software system the total number of source lines of code was 77,081 with 15,925 lines reused; the reused lines of code were concentrated in two subsystems. A total of 249 defects were uncovered during system testing. The mean number of lines of code per subprogram was about 35 with a standard deviation of 43 and a maximum of 450. The mean number of unique operands was 19 with a standard deviation of 20 and a maximum of 205.

Based on this empirical data, we estimated two models, one with twelve observations (involving no reuse) using equation (8) and the other with fourteen observations (involving reuse) using equation (9). Ordinary least squares was employed to estimate the model parameters, the results for the twelve observations being

$$DD = -12.03 + .036*IC + 4.66*SC \qquad R^2=.78 \qquad (6)$$
$$\quad (3.84) \quad (.006) \quad (1.42)$$

while for the fourteen observations

$$DD = -11.31 + .035*IC + 4.43*SC + 35.59*FREU \qquad R^2=.98 \qquad (7)$$
$$\quad (3.19) \quad (.005) \quad (1.22) \quad (1.86)$$

The equation estimates have high coefficient of determinations (R^2). The standard errors associated with the parameter estimates are shown in parentheses below the parameter values. The parameter estimates are significant to within the 1% level. Also, based on the above results, the parameter estimates for the internal and structural complexities are not significantly different from each other in equations (6) (.036 and 4.66, respectively) and (7) (.035 and 4.43, respectively).

Since the coefficients of equations (6) and (7) are comparable, we used equation (6) and the definitions of IC and SC given in equations (2) and (3) above, to calculate the optimum number of calls per subprogram as a function of the number of unique operands. To do so, we take the derivative of equation (10) with respect to TC/NS, set the derivative equal to zero and solve for TC/NS getting:

$$TC/NS = 4*(Tn_2/NS)^{1/3} \qquad (8)$$

The value of TC/NS as indicated in equation (8) yields the minimum defect density since the second derivative of (6) with respect to TC/NS is positive.

Given that the average C subprogram in our system has 19 unique operands, the optimum number of calls would be about eleven from equation (8). However, the mean number of calls per subprogram, derived from the data is 9.7, with a standard deviation of 18.6. Thus, for this system, the mean number of calls is not substantially different from the optimum number of calls derived from equation (8).

Using the 2221 subprograms, we establish the relationship between source lines of code and the number of unique operands, n_2, based on an ordinary least squares analysis. We get:

$$SLOC = \underset{(.87)}{4.24} + \underset{(.05)}{1.48} * n_2 + \underset{(.0004)}{.003} * (n_2)^2 \qquad R=.68 \qquad (9)$$

We tabulated equation (8) to relate the optimum number of calls for various numbers of unique operands and then used equation (9) to relate the optimum number of calls to source lines of code. Thus, 47 unique operands correspond to about eighty source lines of code from equation (9). Using equation (8), the optimum number of calls for such a subprogram would be about fourteen. Since the variables in equation (8) are continuous while the number of calls and the number of source lines of code are discrete (count) variables, we truncated our results to the nearest integers. Figure 1 shows the overall relationship between subprogram source lines of code and the corresponding optimum number of calls.

5. Discussion and Conclusions

We calibrated two models relating the structural characteristics of a system as characterized by the call tree to the internal characteristics of subprograms. The models could be used to estimate the optimum number of calls in a subprogram based on its workload as represented by its number of unique operands. Results from the structural analysis were expressed in source lines of code rather than the number of unique. We found, for example, that the optimum number of calls is around fourteen for a subprogram having eighty SOURCE LINES OF CODE corresponding to forty-seven unique operands.

The questions that we have answered in this study and posed above are important for both procedural languages and object-oriented languages. In object-oriented languages, objects or classes encapsulate subprograms (or methods). Nevertheless, subprograms do much of the calculational work in these languages and contain between 70-80% of the defects found in object-oriented programs [9]. For object-oriented languages, functional and data abstraction are generally employed in parallel. The functional abstraction leads to a set of layered subprogram calls that support a hierarchy of layered virtual machines [10]. A virtual machine consists of a set of instructions organized to solve a given problem. Instructions consist of operations on objects and lower level virtual machines in the form of subprogram calls. Consequently, the idea of a call tree is relevant even for object-oriented systems and studies such as this can contribute toward improving software development practice.

The approach discussed in this study needs to be further tested across a variety of programming languages and for larger amounts of data than we used. Notable questions to be answered are: How much variation will there be in the optimal call estimates for subprograms (methods) in objected-oriented languages? To what extent will the object-oriented features such as inheritance, affect the value of the optimal calls as a function of source lines of code for methods?

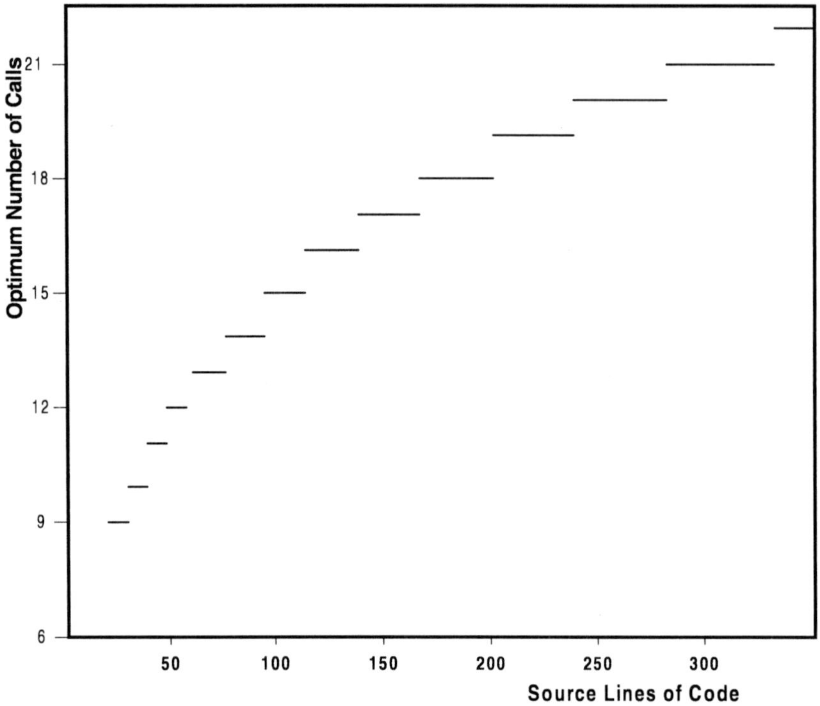

Figure 1: Optimum Calls vs. Source Lines of Code

6. References

[1] Munson, J. and T. Khoshgoftaar (1992), The Detection of Fault-Prone Programs, IEEE Transactions on Software Engineering, 18 (5), pp. 423-433.

[2] Briand, L.; Basili, V.; Thomas, W. (1992), A Pattern Recognition Approach for Software Engineering Data Analysis, IEEE Transactions on Software Engineering, 18 (11), pp. 931-942.

[3] Agresti, W., and W. Evanco (1992), "Projecting Software Defects from Analyzing Ada Designs," IEEE Transactions on Software Engineering, Volume 18, Number 11, pp. 988-997.

[4] Evanco, W. M. (1995), Modeling the Effort to Correct Faults, Journal of Systems and Software, Volume 29, pp. 75-84.

[5] Rombach, D. (1987), A Controlled Experiment on the Impact of Software Structure on Maintainability, IEEE Transaction on Software Engineering, 13, pp. 344-354.

[6] Card, D. and Agresti, W. (1988), Measuring Software Design Complexity, J. Syst. Softw., 8, pp. 185-197.

[7] Shepperd, M. and Ince, D. (1990), Multi-Dimensional Modelling and Measurement of Software Designs, Proceedings of the 1990 ACM Annual Conference on Cooperation, pp. 76-81.

[8] Halstead, M. (1977), Elements of Software Science, Elsevier Science Publishing, New York, New York.

[9] Tang, M; Kao, M; Chen, M. (1999), An Empirical Study on Object-Oriented Metrics, Proceedings of the 6th International Software Metrics Symposium, Boca Raton, FL, pp. 242-249.

[10] Nielsen, K. and Shumate, K. (1988), Designing Large Real-Time Systems with Ada, McGraw-Hill: New York.

Empirical Study Evaluating Component Reuse Metrics

Pentti Virtanen

Abstract

A new method for estimating the software development effort, Component Reuse Metrics, CRM, combines the best means of component technology and the analysis of human behaviour into simple calculation rules. This study presents the results of the survey of the tenets of CRM and the field experiments about its use. The survey was sent to all of the project managers who were members of the Finnish Information Processing Association. These experts, who had a long experience of the effort estimation, assessed the importance of the project and the human factors of software development establishing the default values of the quantitative parameters of CRM.

1. Introduction

Component Reuse Metrics, CRM, is a new effort estimation method, which considers software development as a series of tasks of assembling software components [1]. CRM adds assessments of project and human effects of the development project to the component-based effort estimates. The approach of this study is empirical. The main result of this paper is an evaluation of the CRM method by a survey and by case studies.

Chapter 2 gives an overview of CRM and its calculation rules. CRM uses a questionnaire to assess the project and human effects of the project, which it is estimating. The main part of the survey of this study is to assess the importance of the questions of the CRM questionnaires. The numerical value describing the importance of a question gives the default weight of the factor of the effect for CRM calculations. Chapter 3 describes the realisation of the survey. The results of the survey are in the following chapters and in the appendixes, which contain the survey data in table form. The case studies, which are described in chapter 7, focus on the practical issues of the usage of CRM. The main question is the existence of a component structure in different kinds of software.

2. Overview of CRM

A software component is a unit of composition with contractually specified interfaces and explicit context dependencies only. It can be deployed independently and it is subject to composition by third parties [2]. Component Reuse Metrics is based on the counts of the components of the product of the project. There are several kinds of components and the granularity of these components can vary [10]. In practical component-based development user interface components are best known. In CRM historical data about tasks of reusing components is collected. In addition to effort information this data contains assessments of the influence of project and human effects to the effort. The estimation process of CRM resembles the estimation process of PROBE because it uses components as proxies of effort [3]. The first step is to define the component structure of the product to be developed. The history data gives the effort of the tasks in the baseline situation. In the baseline case a highly skilled and motivated person without a need for teamwork or any risk accomplishes the task without additional features or process changes. Finally the project will be manned and project and human effects will be assessed and added to the calculations. In project tracking these effects will be reassessed before the data is stored in the history database.

The estimated effort of a project is

(1) $\mathbf{P = \sum I}$, where

- P = estimated effort of the new project, where the efforts of all tasks of all of the persons of the project have been summed and
- I= personal share of a person of the effort of a task of the project.

The personal share of the effort of a task is

(2) $\mathbf{I= cc*ci*s*m*f*t*r*\sum_i(nc_i *p*Ec_i)}$, where

- I= personal share of a person of the effort of the task,
- cc= the share of the task of the total effort of the component,
- ci= personal share of the person of the total effort of the task,
- s= personal skill effect coefficient of the person in the task,
- m= personal motivation effect coefficient of the person in the task,
- f= project change effect coefficient of the task,
- t= team effect coefficient of the task,
- r= risk effect coefficient of the task,
- nc_i= number of components of type i in the task,
- p= coefficient for process effect and
- Ec_i= effort of the component of type i from the project history.

The value range of the shares cc and ci is from 0 to 1 and they are normally expressed in percentages. The value of the effect coefficients s, m, f, t, r and p is 1.00 if the baseline effort can be used.

CRM does not have a unique size metric because software products are composed of non-unique parts and the proportions of different kinds of parts vary widely. It counts the components and calculates the effort of each type of component separately. The productivity can be assessed in a component type level, which is an improvement compared to task based estimation. Productivity in producing an average component is useful if the composition of the products remains the same. By the analogy with function-points, the average component could be called component-point.

Each effect coefficient is estimated by a questionnaire, which analyses a group of affecting factors (appendix A). The answers are scaled to a small number (1 to 5) and weighted by a number, which corresponds to the importance of the factor. The importance of the effect is

(3) $\mathbf{imp = (\sum ans*w) /(\sum w)}$, where

- imp = importance of the effect,
- ans = answer of the question (scaled from 1 to 5) and
- w= weight of the question given by the results of this study.

The initial values of the weights are calculated from the results of the survey by scaling the assessment of importance from 1 (very small) to 5 (very large) and counting the average (appendix A). The least squares method can calculate the coefficients for each effect when histories of actual efforts and weighted averages of the answers of the questionnaires are available. In equation form

(4) **corr = a * imp + b,** where

- corr= any of the effect coefficients (s, m, f, t, r or p),
- imp = importance of the effect and
- a and b = coefficients of the equation.

3. Survey

The addressees of all 955 project managers and system managers were picked from the member database of Finnish Information Processing Association. In May 2000 516 letters were sent and in June 434 letters. 5 foreign addresses were ignored. Totally 70 replies were received, three of which were empty. The percentage of the replies was 7,1 % (67 replies out of 950), which was a little better than expected. Because the number of replies was larger than 50, the results of individual questions are statistically significant. However, comparisons of the answers of different questions must be omitted and conclusions must be careful. The questions that could not pass the Chi-square test with at least 98% of confidence have been omitted, because the answers were distributed so evenly that the zero-hypothesis of randomness could be true.

A phone survey was done in June in order to evaluate the differences between the actual replies and the replies of people who did not respond. 30 randomly selected people were called. One of them had changed his job and had not received the survey, 14 of them would have responded like the actual respondents and 15 did not reply because estimation of software development projects does not (currently) belong to their job. The phone survey confirms that the results are representative of the population of the project managers.

The experience of estimation of software development projects of the 67 respondents was on average 14,6 years (confidence interval 1,5 years). Eight of them were interested in taking part in a small case study and the results of 6 case studies are presented in this paper and two of them gave up due to schedule reasons.

4. Background information of the respondents

In order to obtain some background information from the respondents, a few questions were asked about the current practices of software development and estimation.

Analysis, design, testing and delivery were often done in more than one phase. 55% of the respondents used iterative models always or mostly and correspondingly 41% of them used waterfall models. This result shows that it is important that estimation methods are suitable for iterative processes. 40 % of the respondents used prototyping for finding the customer requirements always or mostly and 31% similarly for technical reasons. The usage of design methods is low. 29% of the respondents used data flow analysis always or mostly and only 19% used object-oriented methods always or mostly.

The usage of component technologies is low. Only 7 % of the respondents used ActiveX always or mostly. The corresponding figures for DCOM and CORBA were 3% and 5%. Self-made module (37% always or mostly) and class libraries (34% always or mostly) are the most important reuse methods.

Task based estimation is the most common method and numbers of windows, reports and database tables are the most common metrics (appendix C). Function-point method (10% mostly or always) and COCOMO are not used generally. Estimation was seen important and it is often used in adapting the scope of the project to the available budget. Project history was seen useful but its use is not robust.

5. Results of the survey

The survey was used to assess whether the effort of assembling a component is really constant. In the example of the survey a business graphics component (like Microsoft Chart Control) was assessed. The distribution of the effort due to the reuse case was estimated to be less than 10% in 17% of cases, 10%-25% in 26% of the cases, 25%-50% in 30% of the cases, 50%-100% in 17% of the cases and more than 100% in 9% of the cases.

The respondents of the survey saw that the distribution of the effort of a typical software development project was: planning and implementation of the components 35 %, added features 21 %, training for the task 11 %, added effort due to low motivation 10 %, team work 13 % and risks 11%. The default values of the coefficients s, m, f, t and r of the equation (2) can be calculated from this result (1.30, 1.29, 1.60, 1.38 and 1.32 respectively).

The process effect in CRM is used to calculate the influence of the process changes to the effort. In the easiest form methods and tools are the same in the new project as in projects in the history database. Table 1 shows the factors of the process effect. The result implies that there is no single tool or process change, which could dramatically improve the productivity of software development, which requires many co-ordinated methods and tools. Testing, development environment and quality were seen the most influential parts of the development process.

The survey about the amounts of added and removed features showed that adding new features is common. The amount of added effort (answered as always or mostly) is less than 10% in 33% of the cases, 10-20% in 43% of the cases, 20-50% in 22% of the cases and more than 50% in 1% of the cases. The amount of cancelled effort (answered as always or mostly) is less than 10% in 46% of the cases, 10-20% in 15% of the cases, and more than 20% in 0% of the cases.

Table 2 shows the factors of project change effect. The most significant factors are requirement errors, inaccurate analysis and end-users' views. The case studies confirmed that the estimator has a view of possible areas of new features, because the scope of the project is not unambiguous at the beginning of the project. The end user organisation normally pays for these features and that can often be done without renegotiating the contract.

Teamwork introduces communication to the project. It includes meetings, project management and continuous interpersonal communication. Because software development cannot be partitioned into even approximately separate independent tasks, a large amount of communication is needed [9].

Table 3 shows the factors needed for estimating the team effect coefficient. Relative importance of the factors depends on the project. The numbers of the developers and users and the organisation add another view to the factors of the team effect. One of the case studies revealed that travel time is significant in international projects though it is a minor factor on the average. The case study number 3 noticed the effect of synergy, which would decrease the effort because it increases the productivity in teamwork.

Risks are a major part of software development. Table 4 shows the factors needed for estimating the risk effect coefficient. The respondents thought that personnel risks are the most significant in their projects. The risk analysis and common risk factors are well known [6], but their relative importance depends on the project.

In order to be able to produce the desired software, the developers must understand the problem and its solution and express the solutions using the available programming environment. Software development requires many types of skill [5]. The assessment of learning time is in principle task and developer specific. There are two kinds of learning time: the time used to participate in training and time used within the productive work. Learning within work is a good method to learn and we need to estimate the effort used to it. Table 5 shows the survey results about skill factors. In addition to personality, the matching of the experience with the tasks, was seen important.

The respondents estimated that the additional effort of an expert for learning during the assembly of the example component is less than 10% in 42% of the cases (answered always or mostly), 10%-25% in 39% of the cases, 25%-50% in 13% of the cases and more than 50% in 4% of the cases. The same effort for a normal developer is less than 25% in 16% of the cases, 25%-50% in 34% of the cases, 50%-100% in 39% of the cases and more than 100% in 9% of the cases. The additional effort for a novice is much larger: less than 50% in 9% of the cases, 50%-100% in 33% of the cases, 100%-200% in 43% of the cases and more than 200% in 16% of the cases.

There are many references to motivation of the software developers. The most important motivation factors of programmers and analysts are achievement, possibility of growth, work itself, personal life and technical supervision opportunity [6],[7]. Management practices are also important. A wide survey is given by Humphrey [8].

Table 6 shows the results of the survey about the motivation factors of the team members. The Pearson correlation between these replies and replies concerning the motivation of the respondents themselves is from 0,79 to 1,0 excluding the questions of possibility for initiative and independence (0,61) and responsibility (0,67) showing that it is acceptable to use only one set of motivation factor weights in the calculations.

6. Practical issues

In its most accurate form CRM estimation process requires a considerable amount of calculations. There exists a Microsoft Excel-sheet for CRM calculations. Summary level assessments will decrease the effort needed for assessments.

The lack of historical data can be compensated by manual estimates. However, collecting classified data is necessary for increasing the quality of the estimates. Table 7 shows that the respondents of the survey trusted in the possibility to estimate the effects needed in CRM calculations especially after the project (appendix B). The respondents of the survey considered the amount of estimation work to be reasonable if these estimates are made on (sub)project and on personal level and more exactly only when necessary. The case studies confirmed that assessment.

It is possible to create useful project histories because estimating and tracking the effects of CRM separately after the project is feasible. Tracking of the co-ordination work has been found successful also in another study [4]. The case studies showed that the assessment of the project manager is needed in addition to the questionnaires.

7. Case studies

This paper reports six case studies, which contained a half-day interview and a trial of CRM in selected corporations.

The problem of component structure was studied further in the case studies. These revealed that it is difficult to define the components of software, which is not component-based. It was easy to estimate a small application, which contains clear user interface components. Component counting was also feasible in a large application, where the parts of the application can be handled as components. The boundaries of the components in traditional applications and HTML-applications were obscure and there were no reused components, which could be used as proxies of the development effort.

In case 1 the effort of a small mobile application was estimated in two hours. Components were easy to find because they were common user interface components included in the development environment. The effort of a component was easy to assess because the project manager had experience of similar components in PC environment. The assessment of project and human effects looked easy, but their actual influence was surprising. The first implementation of the project was discarded after 585 hours. The programmer was seen incompetent for the task. The estimate was 184 hours and the actual effort of the second, successful, implementation was 204 hours.

In case 2 the effort of a large mostly traditional application was recalculated successfully within the session. The parts of the application were seen as components, because they are logically identical and they have been good proxies of the effort in previous projects.

In case 3 the effort of a HTML application was seen difficult to estimate using CRM, because the structure of the software was unclear. There were large differences in the effort of using a same user interface component in various places because large amount of hand coding was needed in each case.

In cases 4,5 and 6 there were no on-going projects to assess within the session. The problems of component definition were addressed and the project managers thought that the problems could be solved in each of the cases.

8. Conclusions

Task based estimation is the most commonly used effort estimation method. The most important metric is the numbers of windows and database tables. CRM can be seen as an extension to that method.

The case studies confirmed that component-based development creates an acceptable component structure for CRM calculations. This is also true in selected traditional applications. The weights of factors of the project and human effects were estimated and there was a confidence of the possibility to assess these effects. The case study, where an actual project was estimated and accomplished showed that CRM is quite accurate if these assessments are accurate. However, the assessment of project and human effects proved to be difficult at least without experience and any historical data.

Because of the importance of the productivity part of the effort estimates, there is a need to focus on more thorough analysis about the factors of productivity. CRM creates a framework for that.

9. References

[1] Virtanen P.: Component Reuse Metrics - Assessing Human Effects in Katarina Maxwell, Rob Kusters, Erik van Veenendaal, Adrian Cowderoy (eds), Proceedings of the combined 11th European Software Control and Metrics Conference and the 3rd SCOPE Conference on Software Product Quality, page(s) 171-179, Shaker Publishing, April 2000.

[2] Szyperski, C., "Component Software - Beyond Object-Oriented Programming", ACM Press, New York, 1998.

[3] Humphrey W. S., A discipline for Software Engineering, Addison-Wesley Publishing, 1995.

[4] Toffolon, C., Dakhli, S.: The Cost of Co-ordination in Software Engineering in Katarina Maxwell, Rob Kusters, Erik van Veenendaal, Adrian Cowderoy (eds), Proceedings of the combined 11th European Software Control and Metrics Conference and the 3rd SCOPE Conference on Software Product Quality, page(s) 171-179, Shaker Publishing, April 2000.

[5] Hohmann L.: Journey of the Software Professional, Prentice-Hall, 1997.

[6] McConnell S.: Rapid Development, Microsoft Press 1996.

[7] Boehm B. W.: Software Engineering Economics, Prentice-Hall, Englewood Cliffs NJ, 1981.

[8] Humphrey W. S., Managing Technical People, Addison-Wesley Publishing, 1997.

[9] Brooks F. P. Jr.: The Mythical Man-Month, Anniversary Edition, Addison-Wesley Publishing Company, 1995.
[10] Herzum,P., Sims,O.: Business Component Factory, Wiley Computer Publishing, 2000.

Appendix A. Questionnaire.

Table 1. The factors of process effect.

Estimate the effect of the following methods and tools to the development effort (%)	Very large	Large	Medium	Small	Very small	Don't know	I don't use	Weight
Programming language	7	31	34	22	3	0	1	4.13
Development environment	10	31	37	10	1	0	9	4.45
Database management tools	9	18	43	22	3	0	4	4.06
Tools for analysis and design	4	28	37	22	4	0	3	4.03
Project management tools	1	13	33	37	10	3	1	3.55
Configuration management tools	3	25	27	25	4	4	10	4.07
Documentation tools	4	16	37	34	7	0	0	3.71
Tools for testing	7	36	28	19	4	1	3	4.22
The method of quality assurance	10	24	43	16	3	0	3	4.20
Special quality requirements	15	36	30	13	3	0	3	4.44
Project management methods	9	30	36	21	3	1	0	4.16
Testing methods	10	45	34	9	1	0	0	4.47
Documentation standards	3	21	37	36	3	0	0	3.79
Partitioning of the project	7	40	27	24	1	0	0	4.22
Finding and assessing components	3	12	34	30	4	6	10	3.88
Assuring of generality	7	27	34	18	3	3	7	4.25

Table 2. The factors of project change effect.

Factors influencing new unexpected features during a project (%)	Always	Mostly	Often	Rarely	Never	Don't know	Weight
Error in requirement specification	6	42	33	15	3	1	3.33
Inaccuracy of analysis	7	43	42	7	0	0	3.51
Inaccuracy of design	3	22	57	16	0	1	3.12
Partition of the project	0	6	31	54	6	3	2.38
Views of the customer's management	0	16	42	34	6	1	2.70
Views of the IT-management	0	6	27	58	6	3	2.34
End user views	9	46	36	4	4	0	3.51
Programmers' views	4	12	43	36	4	0	2.76
Views of the project manager	4	15	40	40	0	0	2.84
Good idea invented during the project	3	24	55	16	0	1	3.14
Technological surprises	3	19	40	34	3	0	2.85
Change control	6	19	24	45	4	1	2.77
Commercial factors	3	12	22	49	10	3	2.46
Inaccurate contract	0	25	33	24	12	6	2.76
Invoicing method (by hours, contract price)	1	7	24	30	30	7	2.15

Table 3. The factors of team effect.

What is the influence of the following factors of team work in your projects(%)?	Very large	Large	Medium	Small	Very small	Don't know	Weight
Meetings included in the project plan	18	36	27	13	3	3	3.54
Ad hoc meetings	21	52	21	3	0	3	3.94
Unnecessary meetings	4	9	25	36	15	10	2.47
Meeting practice (being punctual, preparation, ...)	7	46	30	13	0	3	3.49
Travel time	0	1	36	42	16	4	2.23
Slack time due to travelling	0	4	24	46	19	6	2.14
Phone calls and faxes	3	19	30	33	10	4	2.70
Writing email	12	27	34	19	4	3	3.23
Reading email	12	31	36	13	4	3	3.34
Personal supervision of work	18	37	33	7	1	3	3.65
Discussions with the users	28	46	13	7	0	4	4.00
Discussions with customer's management	27	40	24	6	0	3	3.91
Writing minutes and other documents	10	25	42	16	3	3	3.25
Reading minutes and other documents	7	34	33	21	1	3	3.26
Unanimity about the objectives	24	43	18	10	0	4	3.84
Unanimity about the working methods	22	39	22	12	0	4	3.75
Interruptions of work	19	37	27	12	1	3	3.63
Disturbances in the information flow	34	37	16	7	0	4	4.03

Table 4. The factors of risk effect.

A risk is an incident, which has a probability of influencing a project. If a following risk comes true, how large is its expected influence (%)?	Very large	Large	Medium	Small	Very small	Don't know	Weight
Changes in personnel	34	48	16	0	0	1	4.18
Sickness	12	37	34	13	1	1	3.45
Technical disturbances (black outs, equipment failures ...)	4	12	30	34	18	1	2.50
Failures in technology	24	39	16	16	3	1	3.65
Unexpectedly difficult software bugs	10	49	24	12	3	1	3.53
Errors due to carelessness	7	25	46	13	4	3	3.18
Sabotage (viruses, hacking ...)	13	9	13	24	31	9	2.44
Unpunctuality of the contractor, subcontractor or customer	24	43	22	9	0	1	3.83
Organisational changes	1	30	43	19	4	1	3.05
Failures in subcontracting and purchasing	15	43	18	13	4	6	3.54
Disputes	10	25	25	33	4	1	3.05
Estimation errors	19	46	27	6	0	1	3.80
Economic risks	3	27	39	30	0	1	3.03
Juridical risks	3	6	21	43	21	6	2.22

Table 5. The factors of skill effect.

What is the influence of the following factors of the skill of software development (%)?	Very large	Large	Medium	Small	Very small	Don't know	Weight
Education	12	21	42	21	4	0	3.15
Courses	7	16	52	22	1	0	3.06
Length of experience	15	42	43	0	0	0	3.72
Quality of experience	46	39	15	0	0	0	4.31
Familiarity of the applications area	39	45	16	0	0	0	4.22
Experience of team work	4	27	46	18	3	1	3.12
Familiarity with the program (to be maintained)	43	33	21	1	0	1	4.20
Knowledge of methods and tools	27	51	16	4	0	1	4.02
Personality (intelligence, emotional intelligence, sense of responsibility, diligence)	42	34	21	1	1	0	4.13

Table 6. The factors of motivation effect.

Estimate the influence of the following motivation factors on increasing or decreasing the productivity of software development. Assess the motivation factors of your team(%)	Very large	Large	Medium	Small	Very small	Don't know	Weight
Challenge or lack of it	16	55	22	3	0	3	3.88
Ambition	9	36	40	12	0	3	3.43
Possibility to accomplish something, achieve results	9	43	40	4	0	3	3.58
Possibility for initiative and independence	9	31	48	9	0	3	3.42
Good/bad leadership	33	37	24	1	1	3	4.02
Too large, appropriate, too small pressure	12	43	33	7	0	4	3.63
Possibility for career	12	24	40	19	1	3	3.26
Good/bad relationships especially within the team	27	42	24	1	1	4	3.95
Appreciation, respect	22	37	31	6	0	3	3.78
Salary and benefits	13	31	40	12	0	3	3.48
Responsibility	9	27	46	13	1	3	3.29
Being noticed or lack of it	19	42	30	4	1	3	3.75
Possibility to develop oneself, to learn new things	21	46	27	3	0	3	3.88
Working conditions	10	34	36	15	0	4	3.42
Interesting work, the work itself	18	55	16	4	0	6	3.92

10. Appendix B. Practical issues of CRM

Table 7. The capability of the project manager to estimate the effects.

The project manager can estimate the influence of the effect in a software development project (%)?	Always	Mostly	Often	Rarely	Never	Don't know
Process when new methods and tools have not been tested?	4	24	31	24	6	10
Process when new methods and tools have been tested	4	34	39	15	0	7
Process when also new methods and tools have been used in actual projects	16	40	24	12	0	7
Project change after the project	24	61	10	3	0	1
Teamwork before the start of the project	3	27	49	13	3	4
Teamwork after the end of the project	13	54	22	3	1	6
Risk before the start of the project	3	33	43	15	4	1
Risk after the end of the project	12	61	21	3	0	3
Skill before the start of the project	6	43	37	10	3	0
Skill after the end of the project	24	58	16	0	1	0
Motivation before the start of the project	4	31	42	15	1	6
Motivation after the end of the project	18	51	22	1	1	6
Is the effort needed for estimating reasonable?	7	63	18	9	0	3
When must human effects be estimated for each component separately?	4	16	36	28	1	13

11. Appendix C. Background information

Table 8. Estimation methods and metrics.

I use the following methods and metrics estimating software development effort(%)	Always	Mostly	Often	Rarely	Never	Don't know
No estimate before the project start	1	1	10	19	66	1
Project is adapted to the budget	12	27	22	33	6	0
Task based estimation	25	63	12	0	0	0
Comparison with similar projects	13	49	31	6	0	0
COCOMO	0	0	3	4	46	46
Function-point Analysis	4	6	28	18	33	10
Comparison with project tracking history	6	22	37	27	6	1
Number of subsystems	4	30	22	19	15	9
Number of windows, reports and database tables etc.	12	58	18	7	1	3
Number of classes	4	13	13	27	31	10
Lines of code	0	0	27	19	49	4
Number of customers of the component	1	1	6	18	57	16

A Functional Sizing Meta Model

Ton Dekkers, John Kammelar

Abstract

"Not everything that can be counted counts, not everything that counts can be counted". This quote from A. Einstein in another setting illustrates the dilemma that confuses all the discussions about size estimation. Supporters and opponents of function points analysis are both addressed by this quote. This paper introduces a meta model for functional sizing that provides a framework for ISO 14143 compliance and illustrates that size is relative with respect to the context and scope.

1. Introduction

Facing many non-conventional emerging development environments with even so much different types of specifications the need is felt for a generic scalable model to which sizing elements could easily be mapped in their own context. Elaborating sizing approaches for Object Oriented (OO) environments and Component Based Development (CBD) environments a meta model for functional sizing was developed.

Starting point for the meta model was Function Point Analysis (FPA). FPA is a standard 'Functional Sizing Method' (FSM) that complies with a certain degree to the ISO standards for a FSM [1]. FPA puts heavy emphasis on "functionality visible to the user" and as a result measures the functional size from the user perspective. CBD is of special interest because development has to be considered from two different perspectives: the business view resulting in the business application requirements specifications and the architectural view resulting in the component requirements specifications. Both views are projections on functional specifications in a different context and with a different scope. The meta model offers a generic structure to accommodate estimation elements for both perspectives in their own context and with their own proportion. The estimation elements can be expressed in a chosen unit of measure that can be gauged with productivity figures pertinent to the context.

2. The principles of the meta model

2.1. The start of Function Point Analysis

At this time FPA is the mostly and widely accepted sizing method. To get to the meta model it's necessary to look at the history and the development of this sizing method.

Once upon a time in software development there was a need for comparison of software projects. A very obvious solution was to investigate the effort in relation to the size of the product, the application. Figure 1 shows the view on the product that was used to define FPA.

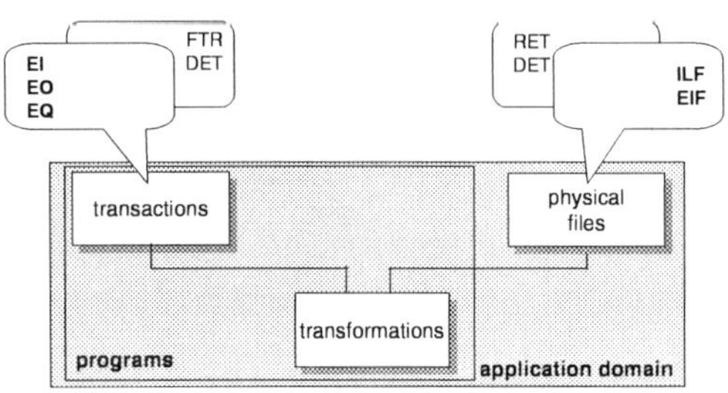

Figure 1 - original FPA view

Mainly two elements determine the effort: data (in physical files) and programs (the implementation of the transactions and transformations). FPA introduced a unit of measure that expresses the correlation of size and effort: the function point.

In FPA the files were differentiated in the types: Internal Files (ILF) and External Interface Files (EIF). The size is defined as a variable of the number of fields and the number of record types in relation to the type. The transactions have other variables. FPA defines 3 types of transactions: External Input (EI), External Output (EO) and External Inquiry (EQ). For each type, size is determined by the number of (physical) files types referenced (FTR) and the number of fields involved in the transactions (DET).

2.2. User perspective

The results of the first function point analyses made clear that although it was useful comparing delivered applications insight in size (and costs) was needed on beforehand and not only when the project was finished.

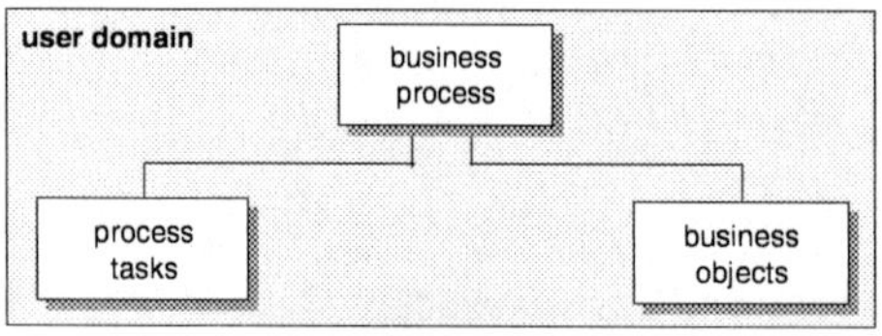

Figure 2 - user view

Looking from the user perspective a similar model can be defined in the user domain. This model comprises the elements by which the requirements of a process can be described fully independent of the development / implementation context. The elements in the user domain are expressed as FUR's (Functional User Requirements) [1] and define the system in implementation context independent terms. With respect to figure 1, business objects relate to files and subsequently process tasks relate to transactions.

2.3. A Functional Sizing Model

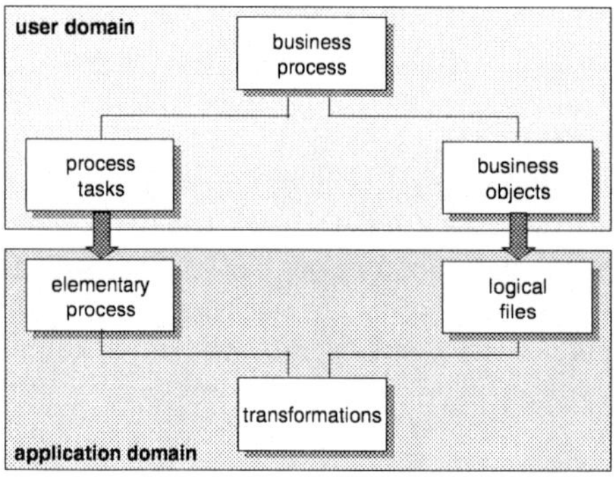

Figure 3 - Conceptual Sizing Model

Bringing together the user domain (showing "what" the application should do, reflected in FUR's) and the application domain ("how" it is realised, which application element implement which user requirement) the functional sizing model arises.

The application domain comprises functional specifications of elements that implement the FUR's. These functional specifications are described by ISO [1] as Base Functional Components (BFC's). Logical files implement the FUR's defined as business objects, elementary processes implement the FUR's defined by process tasks. The way elements are implemented may vary according to the chosen implementation context.

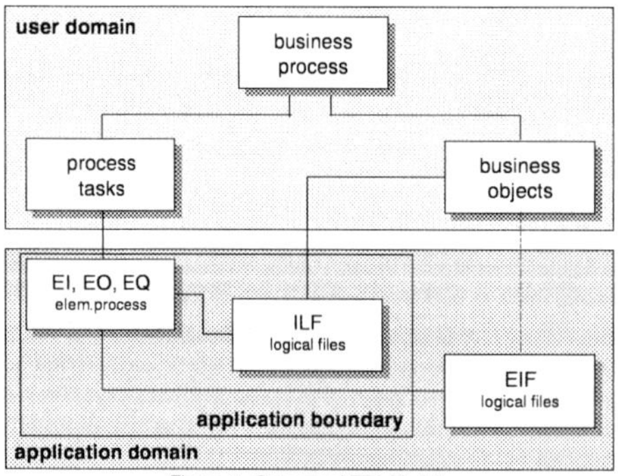

Figure 4 - Conceptual FPA Model

A projection of the actual FPA approach [2] on the application domain is depicted in the following figure. FUR's describing process tasks are implemented by EI, EO and ER functions, which are in fact BFC's, representing elementary processes. FUR's describing data (business objects) are implemented by ILF's within the application boundary and EIF's belonging to other applications. ILF and EIF are in fact BFC's representing data groups.

2.4. Broadening the scope of sizing

In a project environment the user domain of figure 3 produces documents like Functional User Requirements Specifications (FUR's) whereas in the application domain documents like Functional System Design (FSD) are produced. The FSD is actually the specification of the solution for the FUR's and are recognised as (functional) Product Specifications (BFC's). In order to establish a correlation between functional size and development effort, the focus is on BFC's. Actually the relation between FUR's and effort is via BFC's because these are the sizable elements to which a value is assigned.

In figure 3 the lower part of the sizing model is called *application domain.* This applies to a scope called *application development.* Replacing the application domain by a different domain, the model accommodates a different scope. In this way the lower part of the sizing model can be instantiated with different sets of (functional) product specifications, which makes the model applicable to various contexts. This is illustrated in figure 5. From left to right three different scopes / domains are shown: *build, test, and maintenance.* Each of them is providing a solution for a different type of requirement, using a different set of specifications pertinent to the domain.

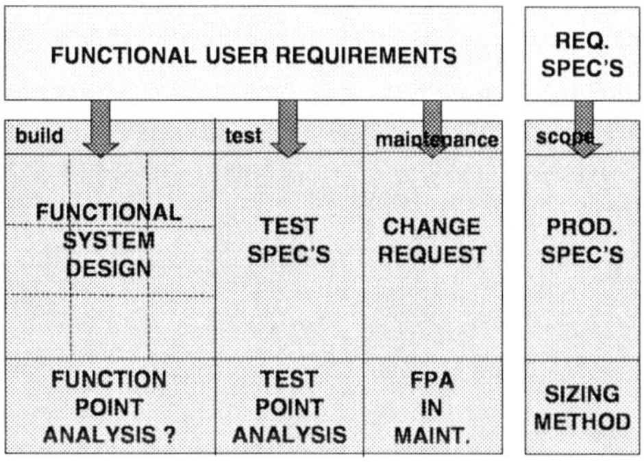

Figure 5 - Multi scope

The *build* scope illustrates that a solution specified by a functional system design may consist of a complex product composed from components. This product structure is illustrated in figure 5 by means of partitioning the FSD area.

To measure the implication of the test strategy you will find in Tmap® [4] another variant based on Function Point Analysis: Test Point Analysis. TPA introduces additional variables to enhance function points in a way so that it expresses the size and complexity of the test activities in the unit of measure test points. Another workgroup of the NESMA "Function Point Analysis in Maintenance Situation" introduced the impact factor as a counting variable to handle various effects of maintenance. So each discipline creates a specific scope on functional sizing to be able to find a unit of measure to be helpful on effort estimation.

3. A Functional Sizing Meta Model

Struggling with many non-conventional environments and even so much different types of specifications the need was felt for a generic scalable model to which the sizing elements could easily be mapped in their own context. The meta model is developed by Ton Dekkers (IQUIP Software Control) and John Kammelar (ECsoft). A rudimentary form of the meta model was already implemented in method and tool Integrated Function Point Analysis [5]. The discussions in the NESMA Workgroup New Technology about the model made clear that this model was fit for purpose. The first experiences in practice are very promising and encouraging.

The idea behind the meta model is the generic structure of the subject of the sizing considered in it's own context, the scope. Through this starting point the model is scalable from its design principle. The model assumes that a subject of sizing comprises many (scope) elements that in turn may be elementary or compound. A scope element is a sizeable unit. Basically the estimation elements are the elements of the subject to which size can be

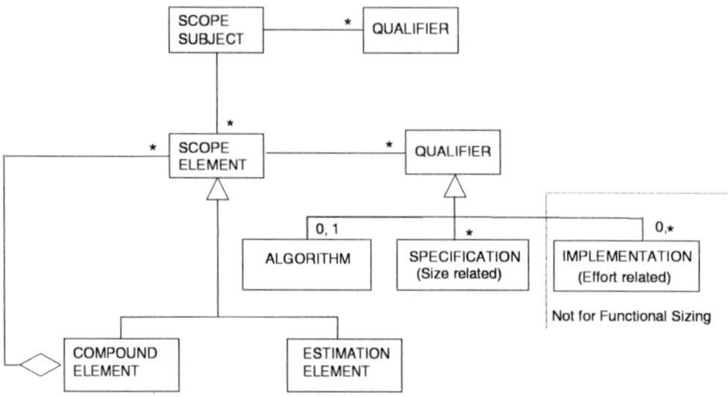

Figure 6 - Meta model Functional Sizing

assigned. Scope elements are specified through qualifiers. For instance a qualifier can define the type of element, or the way the element can be obtained. Having a closer look at the qualifiers and trying to classify them by type we distinguish three types: *algorithm, specification* and *implementation*. A qualifier that relates to specification of the element describes "what the element is for". A qualifier that relates to implementation specifies "how it is realised". The algorithm type qualifier is a special one. It specifies the formula to transform the size-related qualifiers into a quantifiable sizing result.

In the meta model both types of scope elements can have qualifiers. However qualifiers at different levels are of different order. So qualifiers that describe a compound element distinguish from qualifiers, which specify an estimation element. Qualifiers at the level of the scope subject describe the subject of sizing as a whole. These qualifiers are understood as general system characteristics (GSC's).

The terminology used in the meta model is adopted from the estimation approach of the Object Factory [7,8].

4. The Meta Model applied to FPA

Table 1 shows how the meta model is instantiated for FPA.

Table 1 - Meta Model / FPA

Elements		*Qualifiers*	
	Scope Subject	*Type*	*Description*
	Application	S A	• value adjustment factor - 14 general system characteristics • Formula for VAF calculation.
Level	*Scope Element*	*Type*	*Description*
Level	*Estimation Element*	*Type*	*Description*
1.1	Internal logical files External interface files	S A	• # record element types • # data element types • valuation table ILF • valuation table EIF
1.2	External inputs External outputs External inquires	S A	• # file type referenced • # data element types • valuation tables for EI, EO, EQ

A detailed description of the FPA sizing method can be found in [2].

5. The meta model applied to CBD

5.1. Components, a new phenomenon

With respect to functional sizing components are really a new phenomenon. Many definitions can be found in recent literature [6, 9-11] but all refer to the following.

A component is a unit of:

- functionality;
- development;
- distribution;
- composition;
- deployment.

Essential in the definition of Szyperski [6] which was first formulated at the European Conference on Object-Oriented Programming (ECOOP) 1996 is the recognition that *components are subject to composition by third parties*. In other words the designers and manufacturers of components and the consumer of components have a supplier / consumer relation and reside obviously in different organizations. Some properties of a component conflict with FPA principles:

- fragmented visible to the user;
- not necessarily related to one and only one application (preferably to many);
- boundary cannot be determined from the user's perspective, but rather from an architectural perspective.

A CBD-application is a framework of services controlled by business rules implemented by well-defined interfaces of components in a defined interoperation context.

5.2. The CBD process

In order to be able to establish a sizing approach for CBD it is necessary to have a clear understanding of the development process. The measuring of the FUR's to be realized and the development effort derived from the measurement have to fit into the development process. For this purpose the development process described hereafter is considered a model development scenario for CBD.

The CBD process consists of two parallel sub-processes, one from the business view and one from the (functional) architectural view. Both views are projections from different perspectives on the same business activities. The following stages can be recognized.

- Domain modelling;
- Role- / Component modelling;
- Provisioning (make: design, build, test or buy)
- Assembly (transaction management, glue logic) & Implementation

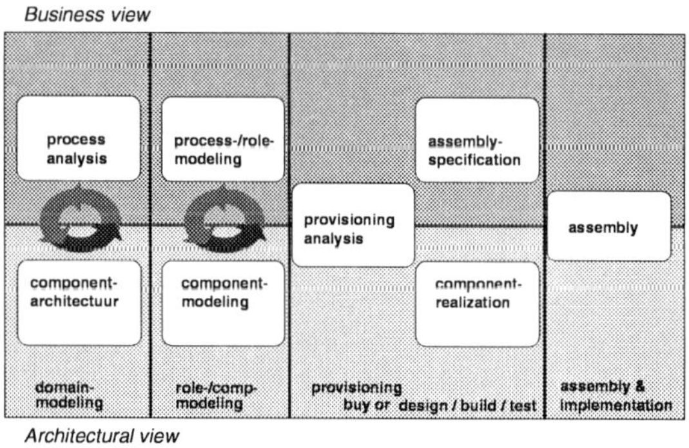

Figure 7 - The CBD Process

The CBD process and the stages of development are shown in figure 7.

Domain modelling encompasses two activities. From the business view process analysis is carried out which results in a specification of the business processes within the scope of the project in terms of workflows, and business objects. From the architectural perspective the business processes are structured into a component architecture comprising candidate component frameworks with the best possible outlook on encapsulation and integrity assurance.

Role and component modelling are detailed analyses of the business processes and domain models respectively. From the business view role modelling results in descriptions of use cases and subsequent transactions. From the architectural view component modelling results in collaborations of business objects (and their behaviour) that implement a use case.

The provisioning process involves the activities to obtain components that implement the functionality defined and structured in the previous stages of the CBD process. Provisioning may imply a search for "commercial of the shelve" software components or components that are to be developed by the using organization itself. The essence of the provisioning process is that the relations between the transactions of the business process and the services to be provided by the components are explicitly specified. The component realization is considered an optional activity that may be subcontracted or may not be carried out at all.

The last stage of the CBD process is the assembly or implementation stage. During this stage the transaction managing "glue logic" is coded and the actual implementation of the persistent data portions of the business objects are realized.

5.3. Specifications during the CBD process

Specifications with a sufficient degree of detail for purpose of functional size measurement come into existence during role- / component modelling. From the business view the process- and role modelling results in specifications of a domain model: *use case descriptions, transaction descriptions and business object specifications*. From the architectural view the component modelling results in *specification models* of components. Specification models describe the functional characteristics of the component, i.e. what the component does, not how it does it. A specification model comprises (at least) *interface(s), specification types (views), and operations.*

5.4. Staging and sizing

In figure 8 the measurement points during the development process are indicated. When the meta model is applied to the CBD process, the business view and architectural view are considered different *scopes*. From the business view it is assumed that FPA can be applied, provided that the boundary of the planned application can be determined and whether business objects are within or outside that boundary. The unit of measure in which the size of the measured subjects will be expressed is *function point*. The moments of size measurement are shown in the figure in the upper part labelled as 1b, 2b, 3b and 4b, indicating measurement from the business perspective.

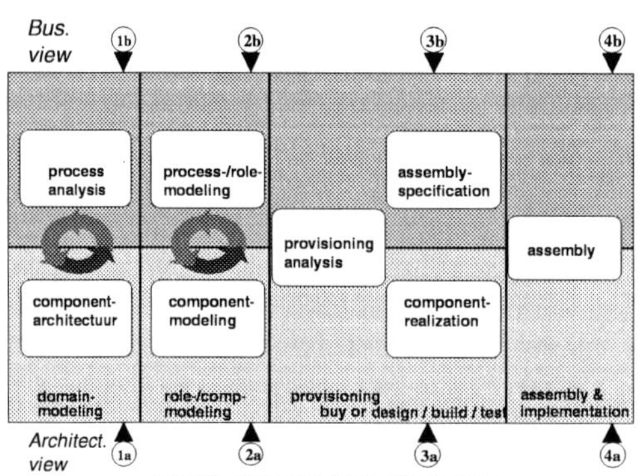

Figure 8 - Measurement during development

In the lower part of the figure the moments of size measurement are labelled as 1a, 2a, 3a and 4a, indicating measurement from the architectural perspective. The unit of measure to be used will be different from the function point. For functional size measurement of components a new unit of measure is introduced: the *service point*. This unit of measure expresses the nature of the measurement, which is from a functional requirements point of view in a CBD architectural environment, independent from implementation or development technique.

5.5. Count types from business view

As described before FPA is applicable for count types 1b through 4b. It is assumed that during the development process FUR's come available in a way that they can be recognized as counting elements for FPA. A detailed description of the FPA method can be found in [2].

5.6. Count types from architectural view

During the development process our sizing approach for CBD distinguishes three types of estimation with an increasing degree of accuracy. The following count types are recognised.

5.6.1. *Domain Model Count (1a)*

This early type of count has not been elaborated yet. This part of the approach is still subject of study of the NESMA Workgroup New Technology.

5.6.2. Analysis Component Count (2a)

The objective of the Analysis Component Count is to measure the amount of functionality to be provided by planned components or component frameworks. The functional size will be expressed in *service points (SP)* and will be based on the results of component modelling.

<u>Counting elements</u>

Aggregated per *interface*:

- Specification types;
- Services

The Analysis Component Count results in a list of components, with every interface of a component consisting of one or more services with their respective size expressed in SP's.

Applying the meta model to the Analysis Component Count will result in the following table.

Table 2 - Meta Model / Analysis Component Count

Elements		*Qualifiers*	
	Scope Subject	*Type*	*Description*
	Component	S I	• design - published pattern - specific • ORB standard
Level	*Scope Element*	*Type*	*Description*
1	Interface (set of services)	S	• # parameters • # specification types (views)
Level	*Estimation Element*	*Type*	*Description*
1.1	Specification types (views)	S A	• media type • data retention • Algorithm to obtain a size (t.b.d.)
1.2	Service	S A	• collaborators y/n • # specification types (views) • compound / elementary • conditions y/n (invariants, constraints) • Algorithm to obtain a size (t.b.d.)

5.6.3. Design Component Count (3a)

The objective of the Design Component Count is to provide an accurate measurement of the amount of functionality to be provided by (interfaces of) components or component frame works, based on the results of the first (logical) design iteration.

<u>Counting elements</u>

Aggregated per *interface*:

- Specification types

- Services specified by
  - operations

It is assumed that a service is a recognisable unit of functionality and that the functional requirements are expressed in such units. The design count results in an accurate component size calculated from the size of the counting elements.

According to Einstein's quote in the introduction. It is clear that the number of qualifiers assigned to the estimation elements have to be limited to a small number with the highest relevancy. FPA for example uses only two qualifiers for valuating transactional function types: # file types referenced and # of data elements processed.

During a pilot period of nearly two years at a governmental organisation in the Netherlands, the engineering and realisation of components was monitored and the relevancy of size qualifiers was discussed and reviewed by several iterations. Trying to find a correlation between development effort and component properties (qualifiers) a size model was derived that gave fairly good predicable and reproducible results with respect to the development effort. From this pilot project the following sizing rules were derived.

5.6.4. Counting Algorithms

Valuation matrix for specification types:

#Attributes	<3	3 – 6	>6
# SP's	2	5	7

Valuation matrix for operations:

Properties	N	Y
> 3 Specification Types	-	1
Compound UI	-	1
Collaborators	-	1
Minimum value	1+	Σ

The number of properties may vary from 1 (minimum value) to 4. The number of SP's is calculated by the formula: SP's = 2^P , which result in a range of values for an operation of 2, 4, 8, 16. During the pilot project mentioned before this formula has been derived.

Applying the meta model to the Analysis Component Count results in the following table.

Table 3 - Meta Model / Design Component Count

Elements		*Qualifiers*	
	Scope Subject	*Type*	*Description*
	Component	S I	• design - published pattern - specific • ORB standard
Level	*Scope Element*	*Type*	*Description*
1	Interface (set of services)	S	• # parameters
1.1	Service		
Level	*Estimation Element*	*Type*	*Description*
1.2	Specification type	S A	• # attributes (flat data) • data retention - indefinite • valuation table for specification types

1.1.1	Operation	S A	• # views of BO's • UI-type - non - single - compound • collaborators y/n • valuation matrix and formula for operations

5.6.5. Component Product Count (4a)

This type of count is currently beyond the scope of this document.

6. Conclusions

The development of the meta model together with experiments to prove the fitness for use lead to the following conclusions.

- The meta model provides a framework to functional sizing approaches for compliance with ISO 14143.
- The meta model provides a uniform structure for a sizing approach that can be applied to various purpose and scope. Yet the analogy remains the same.
- Using the same pattern for different scope and proportion, a common basis for exchange of ideas comes within reach.
- Instantiation of the meta model with FPA-elements as well as with completely new sizing elements originating from contemporary environments the value of the meta model has already been proven in practice.

7. Glossary of terms

BFC Base Functional Component; a BFC is a defined category of elementary units recognised in FUR's defined and used by a FSM for measurement purposes.

Business Object Some thing a business needs to keep track of, which is a participant in line-of-business processes. Business models describe the type of BO's that an enterprise uses, and their associated business operations.

CBD Component Based Development: development process of building applications by combining and integrating pre-engineered, pre-tested components (provided by third parties).

CBD-application A framework of services controlled by business rules implemented by well-defined interfaces of components in a defined interoperation context.

Collaborator Component invoked by the component under study. A set of components can be structured as a framework.

Component A component is a piece of software that is a unit of functionality, development, distribution, composition, and deployment. Components are subject to composition by third parties.

FSM Functional Sizing Method; a FSM produces a functional size of a product by counting and weighting (or assigning numeric values to) BFC's recognised in FUR's.

FUR Functional User Requirement; FUR's describe the purpose of the application in terms of "what the user can do with the application".

GSC General System Characteristic; a property that is "intrinsic" to the application. The 14 influence factors in FPA are considered GCS's.

Interface A set of operation specifications for a semantically related set of operations together with a specification type model.
A component may support one or several interfaces. The same interface might be supported by several components. A consumer's requirement may be expressed as a requirement for one or more interfaces.

Operation A discrete unit of functionality defined by an interface.

ORB Object Request Broker: technical middleware interoperation standard for (language independent) component deployment.

Pattern A structure that occurs repeatedly in similar form. Pattern specifications describe the similarity and the variations.

Process task A sequence of activities (usually determined by unity of time, place and action) that is carried out under the responsibility of one user (actor). Use cases are supported by the computer application by performing one or more services.

Service Services are the implementation of a transaction (i.e. a computer supported activity of a process task). A service is recognised by the user as an indivisible unit of functionality that yields a discrete goal. Services are implemented by one or more operations provided through component interfaces.

Specification (component) model The functional specification of a component, defined in terms of one or more interfaces, where each interface is a collection of related operations related to the interface's specification type model.

Specification type A transient entity type that will not be implemented in the data structure design and has no persistent views. Transient entities may have attributes, relationships, operations and identifiers. Also term (transient) view will be used in this document.

Specification type model The set of specification types and component constraints of an interface (or component) that together define the domain concepts necessary for understanding and using the operations of that interface or component.

8. References

[1] ISO (International Organization for Standardization),"Information Technology - Software Measurement - Functional size measurement: ISO/IEC 14143-1", 1998.

[2] IFPUG (International Function Point User Group), "Function Point Counting Practices, release 4.0", IFPUG, January 1994.

[3] NESMA (Netherlands Software Metric Association), "Function Point Counting Practices, release 2.0", NESMA, April 1996.

[4] Tmap®, Pol, Martin, Veenendaal, Erik van, "Structured Testing of Information Systems", Kluwer, ISBN 90-267-2910-3, 1998.

[5] Dekkers, Ton, "Functional System Design Integrated FPA tool", IQUIP Informatica B.V., Diemen, 1997.

[6] Szypersky, Clemens "Component Software, Beyond Object-Oriented Programming", Addison Wesley, 1998.

[7] "Estimating Web-Based Application Development", The Object Factory, February 2000.

[8] "Estimating Software Projects Using ObjectMetrix", The Object Factory, April 1999

[9] Short, Keith, "Component Based Development and Object Modelling, version 1.0", Sterling Software, 1997.

[10] Allen, Paul, Frost, Stuart, "Component Based Development for Enterprise Systems", Cambridge University Press, 1999

The CBD96 Standard, version 2.1, Standards for Specifying & Delivering Software Components Using COOL:Gen, July 1998, Sterling Software, Application Management

Mastering rapid delivery and change with the SAIV process model

Barry Boehm, A. Winsor Brown

Abstract

Ensuring on time, within-budget delivery is increasingly difficult in the information technology (IT) field because of the increasingly rapid rate of requirements volatility of IT systems under development. This paper describes the Model-Based (System) Architecting and Software Engineering (MBASE)'s Schedule as Independent Variable (SAIV) approach to this problem, and illustrates the nature of the solution with examples.

1. Introduction

Future software developers will be increasingly challenged to develop on time, within-budget, on-target IT systems because of several complicating trends. These especially include increasing complexity (systems of systems, networks of networks, agents of agents), rapid change (of technology, organizations, and market conditions), and decreased control of content (via unavoidable dependence on commercial-off-the shelf (COTS) solutions). Current software development processes have serious difficulties in coping with these trends, particularly for rapid-delivery systems undergoing significant in-process change.

We have encountered these challenges in developing and evolving our MBASE approach over several years of experience in applying it to an annual series of digital library projects [1, 2]. These projects are largely web-based services developed by 5-person MS-student teams, using the MBASE Guidelines [3] and the MBASE Electronic Process Guide [4].

The teams' main challenges are to develop a Life Cycle Architecture (LCA) package, described below, for a USC Libraries client's application in 12 weeks during the fall semester; and to develop and transition an Initial Operational Capability (IOC) in 12 weeks during the spring semester. These are extreme examples of schedule being the independent variable, since the USC semester schedule is fixed and the students disappear (to graduation or summer jobs) at the end of the spring semester.

E-commerce companies have had similar challenges in delivering to short fixed schedules in a climate of rapid change. We have also had the opportunity to refine MBASE in collaboration with some of our USC-CSE E-commerce Affiliates, particularly Rational, C-Bridge, and MediaConnex.

These experiences have led to the SAIV approach described below. We begin with a short summary of the MBASE process framework. We next describe the SAIV process strategy and process elements, in the context of USC digital library examples. We conclude by summarising our SAIV experience across 19 delivered applications, and by discussing the critical success factors involved in the approach.

2. The MBASE Process Framework

Software projects are guided by models that they adopt (knowingly or unknowingly) to help their participants make decisions affecting the project. These models include <u>Product models</u> such as object models, architectures, and traditional requirements models; <u>Process models</u> such as lifecycle and risk management models; <u>Property models</u> such as cost, schedule, and performance models; and <u>Success models</u> such as contractual agreements, correctness, business-case analysis, and stakeholder win-win. Many of the most serious difficulties encountered by software projects can be traced to clashes among the models they have adopted [2.5].

MBASE uses a process framework in which stakeholders express their initial desired success models, and proceed to adjust these and their associated product, process, and property models to achieve a consistent and feasible set of models to guide the project and its stakeholders. The actual process, as illustrated in Figure 1, generally takes several iterations, and requires some common intermediate checkpoints. MBASE also uses an extension of the original spiral model [6] to include stakeholder win-win model negotiation and a set of common anchor point milestones [7]: key life-cycle decision points at which a project verifies that it has feasible objectives (LCO); a feasible life-cycle architecture and plan (LCA); and a product ready for operational use (IOC).

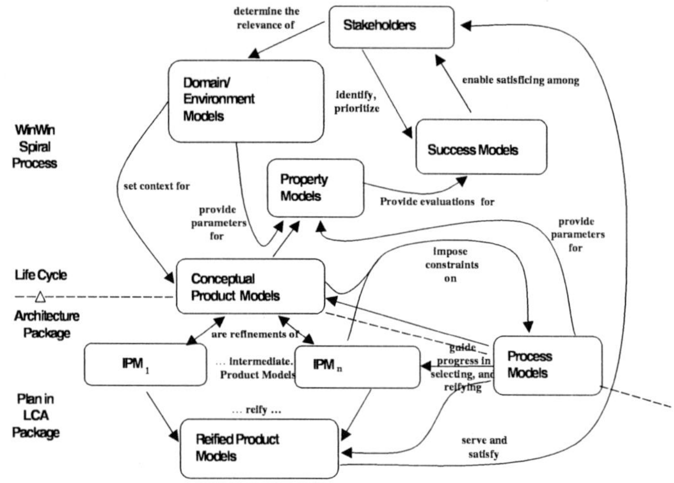

Figure 1: MBASE Process Framework

Thus, if the overriding top-priority success model is to "Demonstrate a competitive agent-based data mining system on the floor of COMDEX in 9 months," this constrains the ambition level of other success models (provably correct code, fully documented). It also determines many aspects of the product model (architected to easily shed lower-priority features if necessary to meet schedule), the process model (SAIV), and various property models (only portable and reliable enough to achieve a successful demonstration).

The achievability of the success model needs to be verified with respect to the other models. In the 9-month demonstration example, a cost-schedule estimation model would use various product characteristics (sizing of components, reuse, product complexity), process characteristics (staff capabilities and experience, tool support, process maturity), and property characteristics (required reliability, cost constraints) to determine whether the product capabilities achievable in 9 months would be sufficiently competitive for the success models. Thus, as shown within Figure 1, a cost and schedule property model would be used for the evaluation and analysis of the consistency of the system's product, process, and success models. If they are shown to be consistent, the project passes its LCA milestone and follows the process plan in the LCA package to refine the architecture into an operational product.

In other cases, the success model would make a process model or a product model the primary driver for model integration. An IKIWISI (I'll know it when I see it) success model for a small application would initially establish a prototyping and evolutionary development process model, with most of the product features and property levels left to be determined in the process. A success model focused on developing a product line of similar products would initially focus on product models (domain models, product line architectures), with process models and property models subsequently explored to perform a business-case analysis of the most appropriate breadth of the product line and the timing for introducing individual products.

MBASE differs from Model-Based Systems Engineering (MBSE) [8], in that MBSE concentrates almost exclusively on product models (and their associated property models). This is also the case for the Software Engineering Institute's Model-Based Software Engineering [9] and Honeywell's Model-Based Software Development [10] approaches.

MBASE is most compatible with the Rational Unified Process [11,12,13], which has adopted the MBASE anchor point milestones. MBASE has adopted Rational's Inception/Elaboration/Construction/Transition phase definitions for the activities between the milestones.

3. The SAIV Process Model

The SAIV Process model provides a general version of the process described for the fixed-schedule e-commerce project above. It consists of six major steps:

1. Shared vision and expectations management
2. Feature prioritisation
3. Schedule range estimation
4. Architecture and core capabilities determination
5. Incremental development
6. Change and progress monitoring and control

3.1. Shared Vision and Expectations Management

As graphically described in Death March [14], many software projects lose the opportunity to assure a rapid, on-time delivery by inflating client expectations and overpromising on delivered capabilities. The first step in the SAIV process model is to avoid this by obtaining stakeholder agreement that meeting a fixed schedule for delivering the system's Initial Operational Capability (IOC) is the most critical objective, and that the other objectives such as the IOC feature content can be variable, subject to meeting acceptable levels of quality and post-IOC scalability.

Often, the librarians and computer science students have unrealistic expectations about what is easy or hard for each other to do. We have found that providing them with lists of developer and client "simplifiers and complicators" improves their ability to converge on a realistic set of expectations for the delivered system [15]. The resulting shared vision enables the stakeholders to rapidly renegotiate the requirements as they encounter changing conditions.

3.2. Feature Prioritisation

With MBASE at USC, stakeholders use the USC/GroupSystems.com EasyWinWin requirements negotiation tool to converge on a mutually satisfactory (win-win) set of project requirements. One step in this process involves the stakeholders prioritising the requirements by assessing their relative importance and difficulty, each on a scale of 0 to 10. This process is carried out in parallel with initial system prototyping, which helps ensure that the priority assessments are realistic.

3.3. Schedule Range Estimation

The developers then use a mix of expert judgement and parametric cost modelling to determine how many of the top-priority features can be developed in 24 weeks under optimistic and pessimistic assumptions. For the parametric model, we use COCOMO II, which estimates 90% confidence limits on both cost and schedule [16]. Other models such as SLIM [17], SEER [18], and Knowledge PLAN [19] provide similar capabilities.

3.4. Architecture and Core Capability Determination

The most serious mistake a project can make at this point is just to pick the topmost-priority features with 90% confidence of being developed in 24 weeks. This can cause two main problems: producing an IOC with an incoherent and incompatible set of features; and delivering these without an underlying architecture supporting easy scalability up to the full feature set and workload.

First, the core capability must be selected so that its features add up to a coherent and workable end-to-end operational capability. Second, the remainder of the lower-priority IOC requirements and subsequent evolution requirements must be used in determining a system architecture facilitating evolution to full operational capability. Still the best approach for achieving this to encapsulate the foreseeable sources of change within modules [20].

3.5. Incremental Development

Since the core capability has only a 90% assurance of being completed in 24 weeks, this means that about 10% of the time, the project will just be able to deliver the core capabilities in 24 weeks, perhaps with some extra effort or occasionally by further reducing the top-priority feature set. In the most likely case, however, the project will achieve its core capability with about 20-30% of the schedule remaining. This time can then be used to add the next-highest priority features into the IOC (again, assuming that the system has been architected to facilitate this).

An important step at this point is to provide the operational stakeholders (users, operators, maintainers) with a Core Capability Demonstration. Often, this is the first point at which the realities of actually taking delivery of and living with the new system hit home, and their priorities for the remaining capabilities may change.

Also, this is an excellent point for the stakeholders to reconfirm the likely final IOC content, and to synchronize plans for conversion, training, installation and cutover from current operations to the new IOC.

3.6. Change and Progress Monitoring and Control

As progress is being monitored with respect to plans, there are three major sources of change, which may require revaluation and modification of the project's plans:

1. Schedule slips. Traditionally, these can happen because of unforeseen technical difficulties, staffing difficulties, customer or supplier delays, etc.

2. Requirements changes. These may include changes in priorities, changes in current requirements, or needs for new high-priority requirements.

3. Project changes. These may include staffing changes, COTS changes, or new marketing-related tasks (e.g., interim sponsor demos).

In some cases, these changes can be accommodated within the existing plans. If not, there is a need to rapidly renegotiate and restructure the plans. If this involves the addition of new tasks on the project's critical path, some other tasks on the critical path must be reduced or eliminated. There are several options for doing this, including dropping or deferring lower-priority features, reusing existing software, or adding expert personnel. In no cases should new critical-path tasks be added without adjustments in the delivery schedule.

3.7. SAIV and Time-Boxing

The SAIV process model differs from classic time-boxing, in which small fixed increments of capability are assigned to fixed-length time boxes. This works fine in the nominal case in which no unforeseen difficulties or significant changes are encountered. But it has no flexibility built into its stakeholder expectations, its feature prioritisation, or its product architecture to enable it to adapt to difficulties which break one of the time boxes. The more adaptive form of time boxing used in Adaptive Software Development [21] comes closer to the SAIV approach, but is considerably more informal. The SAIV approach described here tries to steer the project toward a balance of flexibility and discipline with a low risk of failure.

4. SAIV Experience

4.1. USC Digital Library Projects

The USC digital library projects [1,22] use the MBASE approach. To elaborate on its top-level description in Figure 1, it involves the concurrent development of several initial artefacts: an Operational Concept Description, a Requirements Definition, an Architecture Description, a Life Cycle Plan, a Feasibility Rationale, and one or more prototypes. These are evaluated at two major pass/fail points, the Life Cycle Objectives (LCO) and the Life Cycle Architecture (LCA) milestones. Both milestones use the same primary pass-fail criterion:

- If we build the system to the given architecture, it will satisfy the requirements, support the operational concept, be faithful to the prototypes, and be buildable within the processes, budgets, and schedules in the plan.

For the LCO milestone, this criterion must be satisfied for at least one choice of architecture, along with demonstration of a viable business case for the system and the expressed concurrence of all the success-critical stakeholders. For the LCA milestone, the pass-fail criterion must be satisfied for the specific choice of architecture and COTS components to be used for the system, along with continued business case viability and stakeholder concurrence, plus elimination of all major project risks or coverage of the risks in a risk management plan.

One of our primary goals in the project course is to give the students experience in risk management [23]. Our risk management lectures and homework exercises emphasize a list of the ten most serious risk items: personnel risks are number 1, and budget-schedule risks are number 2. The student projects' risk management plans must show how their team will avoid the risks of delivering an unsatisfactory Life Cycle Architecture package in the first 12 weeks (fall semester), and of unsatisfactorily delivering and transitioning an Initial Operational Capability (IOC) in the second 12 weeks (spring semester). The MBASE Guidelines recommend that they adopt the SAIV model described in Section 3; so far, all the projects have done this.

Also, we work in advance with the USC Library clients to sensitise them to the risks of overspecifying their set of desired IOC features, and to emphasize the importance of prioritising their desired capabilities. This generally leads to a highly collaborative win-win negotiation of prioritised capabilities, and subsequently to a mutually satisfactory core capability to be developed as a low-risk minimal IOC.

The projects' monitoring and control activities include:

- Development of a top-N project risk item list which is reviewed and updated weekly to track progress in managing risks (N is usually between 5 and 10).
- Inclusion of the top-N risk item list in the project's weekly status report.
- Management and technical reviews at several key milestones
- Client reviews at other client-critical milestones such as the Core Capability Demonstration.

The use of SAIV and these monitoring and control practices have led to on-time, client-satisfactory delivery and transition of 17 of the 19 products developed to date. One of the two failures was in our first year, when we tried to satisfy three clients by merging their image archive applications into a single project, and underestimated the complexity of the merge. As a result, "merging multiple applications" has become one of the major sources of project risk that we consider.

The second failure happened recently when a project which appeared to be on track at its Transition Readiness Review, simply did not implement its transition plan when its client suddenly had to go out of town. We were not aware of this until the client returned after the semester was over and the students had disappeared to graduation and summer jobs. We have since revised our system of closeout reviews to eliminate this "blind spot" and related problem sources.

On the other 17 projects, client evaluations have been uniformly quite positive, averaging about 4.4 on a scale of 1 to 5. A particularly frequent client evaluation comment has been their pleasure in being able to synchronise product transition on a specific fixed date with their other transition activities. The digital library artefacts can be reviewed on the class web page, http://sunset.usc.edu/classes.

4.2. E-Commerce Projects

One of our industrial affiliates, C-Bridge, Inc., uses a very similar SAIV process model, which enables them to consistently deliver e-commerce systems on fixed schedules between 16 and 26 weeks. Their Rapid Value™ approach uses milestones very similar to MBASE's LCO, LCA, and IOC milestones; their counterpart phases are named Define, Design, Develop, and Deploy. They use similar approaches in working in advance with their clients to ensure a workable SAIV scope and schedule, and in anticipating and pre-working potential transition problems to client-based operations and maintenance [24].

5. SAIV Limitations and Extensions

5.1 SAIV Limitations

The primary limitation of the SAIV approach can be visualised in terms of the canonical software production function shown in Figure 2. It is slightly modified and updated from [25, p. 193]. As with most production functions, it is an S-shaped curve with three segments:

- An <u>investment segment</u>, in which necessary infrastructure capabilities are developed, but very little value-generating applications capability is developed.

- A high-payoff segment, in which incremental investments in applications capability produce significant added value to the organisation.
- A diminishing returns segment, in which incremental investments in applications capability produce decreasingly small added value to the organisation.

For any given project duration T, and for any given set of project parameters such as the COCOMO II cost drivers, there is a smaller set of capabilities that can be developed with 90% confidence of completion, and a larger set of capabilities that can be developed with 50% confidence of completion. These are shown in Figure 2 with respect to two example project durations, T = 12 months and T = 6 months.

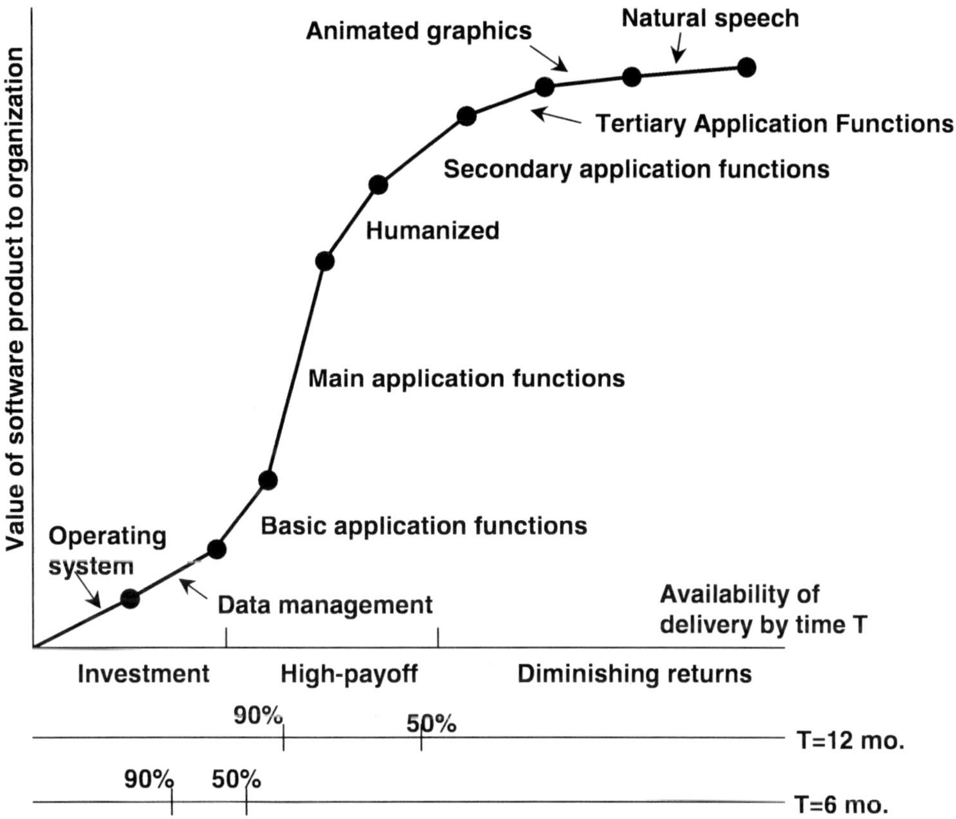

Figure 2. Canonical production for software product features

For the 12-month project duration, the value profile is compatible with a SAIV approach, since even at a conservative 90% completion confidence level, enough applications software is achievable within 12 months to produce appreciable value, and the value goes up significantly at the 50% confidence level. Thus, one could plan for an increment 1 core capability that (sometimes with some extra effort or descoping) would produce acceptable value even in the worst case.

However, for the 6-month project duration, even the 50% confidence level feature set does not reach an adequate value to be worth the investment, and the 90% core capability does even worse. Thus, we see that Step 3 of the SAIV approach, Schedule Range Estimation, actually includes a decision branch that terminates the process if an inadequate core capability results from the analysis. With both the USC digital library projects and the C-Bridge e-commerce applications, an exploratory effort with the clients determines whether a project is worth pursuing within a desired time period.

5.2 SAIV Extensions

In some cases, particularly if the infrastructure development is considered strategically important and the specific applications choices are unclear, an organisation may still consider the options furnished by the infrastructure to be of sufficient value to invest. Providing a decision framework for such options is one of the attractive prospective extensions of the SAIV approach [26].

Another attractive prospective extension discussed in [26] is the concept of using realised value as the basis of the project monitoring and control feedback cycle. In this case, not only is project progress monitored, but also the counterpart initiatives and assumptions linking the developed software applications to the realised benefits. These benefits are quantified in the business case for the application; the relation of the business case to counterpart initiatives and assumptions can be developed using the Results Chain in the DMR Benefits Realisation Approach [27]. This would enable projects to use earned-value systems related to real value for project monitoring and control, as compared to current "earned value" systems, which actually monitor and control budgeted cost and schedule rather than realised business value.

6. Conclusions

The six-step SAIV process model presented here has been used successfully on 17 of 19 digital library applications at USC, and on a similar percentage of e-commerce applications at C-Bridge, to deliver highly client-satisfactory applications on a fixed schedule in a climate of rapid change. Its critical success factors are:

- Working with stakeholders in advance to achieve a shared product vision and realistic expectations;
- Getting clients to develop and maintain prioritised requirements;
- Scoping the core capability to fit within the high-payoff segment of the application's production function for the given schedule;
- Architecting the system for ease of adding and dropping features;
- Disciplined progress monitoring and corrective action to counter schedule threats.

The approach can also be applied to its counterpart Cost As Independent Variable (CAIV) process model. It can also provide a way to transform the current dilemma, "Cost, Schedule, Quality: Pick Any Two," to "Cost, Schedule, Quality: Pick All Three." Attractive future extensions include options-based software design and development and realised-value based monitoring and control.

7. References

[1] Boehm, B., Egyed, A., Kwan, J., Port, D., Shah, A. and Madachy, R., "Using the WinWin Spiral Model: A Case Study", IEEE Computer, July 1998, pp. 33-44.

[2] Boehm, B. and Port, D., "Escaping the Software Tar Pit: Model Clashes and How to Avoid Them," ACM Software Engineering Notes, January 1999, pp. 36-48.

[3] Boehm, B., Port, D., Abi-Antoun, M. and Egyed, A., "Guidelines for Model-Based Architecting and Software Engineering (MBASE)" version 2.2, USC-CSE, (Feb.2001), http://sunset.usc.edu/Research/MBASE

[4] Mehta, N., "MBASE Electronic Process Guide," USC-CSE, September 1999, http://sunset.usc.edu/Research/MBASE

[5] Boehm, B., Port, D. and Al-Said, M., "Avoiding the Software Model-Clash Spiderweb," IEEE Computer, November 2000, pp. 120-122.

[6] Boehm, B., "A Spiral Model of Software Development and Enhancement," IEEE Computer, May 1998, pp. 61-72.

[7] Boehm, B., "Anchoring the Software Process," IEEE Software, July 1996, pp. 73-82.

[8] Fisher, J. et al., "Model-Based Systems Engineering: A New Paradigm," INCOSE INSIGHT, October 1998, pp. 3-16.

[9] Gargaro, A. and Peterson, A.S., "Transitioning a Model-Based Software Engineering Architectural Style to Ada 95," SEI Technical Report CMU/SEI-96-TR-016, 1996.

[10] Honeywell Technology Center, "Model-Based Software Development," Course Announcement, Minneapolis, MN, 1998.

[11] Jacobson, I., Booch, G. and Rumbaugh, J., The Unified Software Development Process, Addison-Wesley, 1999.

[12] Kruchten, P., The Rational Unified Process, Addison-Wesley, 1998.

[13] Royce, W.E., Software Project Management: A Unified Framework, Addison-Wesley, 1998.

[14] Yourdon, E., "Death March," Prentice Hall, 1997.

[15] Boehm, B., Abi-Antoun, M., Kwan, J., Lynch, A. and Port, D., "Requirements Engineering, Expectations Management, and the Two Cultures," Proceedings, 1999 International Conference on Requirements Engineering, June 1999.

[16] Boehm, B., Abts, C., Brown, A.W., Chulani, S., Clark, B., Horowitz, E., Madachy, R., Reifer, D. and Steece, B., Software Cost Estimation with COCOMO II, Prentice Hall, 2000.

[17] Putnam, L. "Software Life Cycle Model (SLIM)," QSM, 2001, http://www.qsm.com

[18] Galorath, D., "SEER-SEM," Galorath, Inc., 2001, http://www.galorath.com

[19] Jones, C., "Knowledge PLAN," Artemis/SPR, 2001, http://www.spr.com

[20] Parnas, D., "Designing Software for Ease of Extension and Contraction," IEEE Trans. Software Engr., March 1979, pp. 128-137.

[21] Highsmith, J., "Adaptive Software Development," Dorset House, 1999.

[22] Boehm, B., Egyed, A., Port, D., Shah, A., Kwan, J. and Madachy, R., "A Stakeholder Win-Win Approach to Software Engineering Education", Annals of Software Engineering, April 1999.

[23] Port, D. and Boehm, B. "Educating Software Engineering Students to Manage Risk," Proceedings, ICSE 2001, May 2001.

[24] Madachy, R., Pan, A. and Arboleda, A., "Processes for Rapid Development of Internet Applications," LA SPIN Presentation, January 24, 2001.

[25] Boehm, B., "Software Engineering Economics," Prentice Hall, 1981.

[26] Boehm, B., and Sullivan, K., "Software Economics: A Roadmap," in A. Finkelstein (ed.), "Software Engineering Futures," Proceedings, ICSE 2000, June 2000.

[27] Thorp, J., "The Information Paradox," McGraw Hill, 1998.

MRE and Heteroscedasticity: An Empirical Validation of the Assumption of Homoscedasticity of the Magnitude of Relative Error

Tron Foss, Ingunn Myrtveit, Erik Stensrud

Abstract

The Magnitude of Relative Error, MRE, is probably the most widely used basic metric in common evaluation criteria, e.g. MMRE and PRED, to assess the performance of software prediction models. The implicit rationale of using a relative error measure, rather than an absolute one, is to have a measure that is independent of scale. In this paper, we investigate if this implicit claim holds true using a data set of 81 ERP projects. The results suggest that MRE is not independent of scale. Rather, MRE is larger for small projects than for large projects. A practical consequence is that a project manager predicting a small ERP project will falsely believe in a too high accuracy in terms of MMRE. Vice versa when predicting a large ERP project.

1. Introduction

The Magnitude of Relative Error, MRE, is probably the most widely used evaluation criterion to assess the performance of models for predicting the effort of software projects. MRE is used as the basic metric in MMRE (Mean MRE), MdMRE (Median MRE) and in PRED(k)=n (where n is the percentage of projects with MRE<=k). MRE is defined as follows.

$$MRE = \frac{|y - z|}{z}$$

where z is the actual effort and y is the predicted effort.

The concept of *relative* errors makes intuitive sense to software researchers and practitioners alike. It seems reasonable that we should be able to predict the effort of small and large systems with the same relative accuracy. That is, it seems the ambition of MRE is to provide us with a measure that is independent of scale. It is well known that software project data sets are heteroscedastic, in general. This means that the error term increases with project size. The larger the project, the larger the expected absolute inaccuracy. Thus, by measuring the relative error, i.e. MRE, rather than the actual absolute error, i.e. the residual, one assumes that one counteracts this heteroscedasticity and obtains a measure that is independent of scale. That is, one assumes that the variance of the relative error, MRE, is homoscedastic.

To our knowledge, however, the assumption of homoscedasticity of MRE has never been empirically validated on large industrial data sets. Specifically, we are not aware of any empirical justification for ERP (Enterprise Resource Planning) data sets. In this paper we investigate if the homoscedasticity assumption of MRE can be justified for ERP projects. The results suggest that the homoscedasticity assumption of MRE cannot be justified. Rather, the results suggest that MRE is heteroscedastic, decreasing with project effort. We therefore recommend exercising care when evaluating data sets with MRE if the data span over a wide project size range or if one compares data sets of small and large projects, respectively.

2. Related work

Evaluation of the evaluation metrics themselves seems to have received little attention since Conte, Dunsmore and Chen [1] publicised MMRE and PRED. The only related work we are aware of is Miazaki et al. [3] and Kitchenham et al. [2]. Both of them discuss issues related to the use of MMRE and PRED, but none of them have investigated the homoscedasticity assumption of MRE.

3. Data

The data set used for the MRE analysis consists of 81 ERP projects, four predictor variables (users, sites, interfaces, modules) and one response variable (effort). The projects span from 320 to 111420 workdays. There are no missing values. Descriptive statistics for the cleaned and complete data set is provided in Table 1. This data set was derived from a larger data set consisting of 178 ERP projects and ten predictor variables. It is beyond the scope of this paper to detail how the data set was reduced in number of projects as well as in the number of predictor variables. Nevertheless, the next section, Initial data and data analysis, briefly describes the initial data cleaning procedure. It may be read as a side bar for those who are interested.

Variable	N	Mean	Median	StDev	Min	Max
Users	81	999	300	2430	6	17000
Sites	81	29	5	75	1	500
Interfaces	81	29	15	50	0	270
Modules	81	5	5	2.7	1	13
Effort	81	11526	7300	15170	320	111420

Table 1. Descriptive statistics for ERP data set

4. Initial data and data analysis

The original data set consists of 178 ongoing and completed ERP projects. All the ERP projects in the sample implement ERP systems from one single ERP vendor, SAP. 176 projects have implemented the client-server version (R/3) of SAP. Two projects have implemented the mainframe version (R/2). Therefore, it is a homogeneous data set. The original data set includes 10 continuous predictor variables, and effort is reported for three phases and total.

The data were gathered from 1990 to 1998 in a multinational consultant organisation with 70,000 employees. The projects span many industries and countries in all regions of the world. The predictor variables that are used define the intra-organisational standard "size" measure for ERP projects. It is beyond the scope of this paper to explain them. Interested readers are referred to [6] for a definition of the variables.

The data have been reported by project managers who themselves use the database to plan and estimate future projects. The company has a standard ERP methodology. Therefore, the data presumably have been reported in a consistent manner. See also [4] and [5] for an evaluation of the data quality.

The initial cleaning basically consisted of removing active, ongoing projects (for which effort actuals do not yet exist, naturally) and projects with large measurement errors. Large measurement errors, or wild values, were identified by a combination of regression analysis, scatter plots and expert judgement. (One of the authors is an ERP project manager).

Likewise, to determine which predictor variables were the most important, we applied a combination of OLS regression analysis, best subset regression, scatter plots and expert judgement.

Thereafter, six projects with large residuals were identified and removed by applying residual analysis resulting in the final model presented in table format in Table 2.

We used a log-linear OLS regression since the data are heteroscedastic. The log-linear model conformed reasonably well to the homoscedasticity assumption of OLS regression (not reported). Residual analysis suggested that the distribution of residuals of the log-linear model was normally distributed. (See Normal Plot of Residuals and Histogram of Residuals in Figure 1.) This was also confirmed by applying the Anderson-Darling test of normality (p=0.493). The residual analysis did not reveal any non-linearity either (Residuals vs. Fits, Figure 2.) All the coefficients are significant. (See Table 2, T and P columns.) There is no significant multicollinearity (VIF<5).

Predictor	Coef	SE Coef	T	P	VIF
Constant	4.8504	0.2972	16.32	0.000	
LN(Users)	0.27452	0.06306	4.35	0.000	2.0
LN(Sites)	0.15303	0.05515	2.77	0.007	1.3
LN(Interfaces)	0.28894	0.05849	4.94	0.000	1.3
LN(Modules)	0.7316	0.1639	4.46	0.000	1.4
S = 0.5806	R-Sq = 73.5%		R-Sq(adj)= 72.1%		

Table 2. OLS regression model

5. Data Analysis of MRE

The analysis of MRE required that we back-transform the residuals and fits since OLS regression was applied to a log-linear model. To calculate the original residuals and fits we applied the following formulas.

$$originalresidual = \left(1 - e^{-residual}\right) * actual\_effort$$

$$originalfit = actual\_effort - originalresidual$$

The original residuals vs. original fits clearly will exhibit heteroscedasticity, as is suggested by the scatter plot in Figure 2 where we have shown only projects smaller than 25000 workdays and residuals within plus or minus 20000 workdays.

6. Results

The scatter plots of MRE vs. Actual Effort in Figures 3 and 4, suggest that MRE decreases with project effort, thus casting doubt about MRE's *raison d'être*. We investigated this further by dividing the projects into two groups of large and small projects. Small projects are less than 5001 workdays whereas large projects are greater than 9999 workdays. The initial results in Table 3 also suggest that MRE decreases with project effort.

We finally applied two tests, a two-tailed Mann-Whitney 2-sample rank test to test the hypothesis that MdMRE of small and large projects is different and a two-tailed 2-sample t-test to test that MMRE of small and large projects are different. From Table 4, the Mann-Whitney test did not reveal any significant difference (p=0.22) whereas the 2-sample t-test did suggest that the MMRE of small and large projects differ (p=0.04). The scatter plot of the residuals (Figures 3 and 4) suggests that MRE decreases with project effort, and the t-tests of difference suggest there is a difference in MMRE and MdMRE between the two groups.

Thus, the Mann-Whitney rank test suggests that we cannot reject the assumption of homoscedasticity of MRE whereas the second test says we can reject the assumption of homoscedasticity of MRE at the 5% significance level. The latter test is more efficient than a rank test. Overall, therefore, the results suggest that MRE probably is not independent of scale, and that it rather decreases with project size.

Effort range	N	MdMRE (%)	MMRE (%)
<=5000	31	45	70
>=10,000	31	38	39
All	81	36	48

Table 3. Median/Mean MRE of small vs. large projects

MdMREsmall<>MdMRElarge	MMREsmall<>MMRElarge
0.22	0.04

Table 4. Results of hypothesis tests (p-values)

7. Discussion

In this section we discuss two issues. The first issue is whether the 2-sample t-test is appropriate or not. The second issue concerns an apparent conflict between the homoscedasticity assumption of regression analysis and our result that MRE is heteroscedastic.

The 2-sample t-test requires that the distribution of the sample mean is normal. That is, if we draw infinitely many samples of MRE_small (or MRE_large) and calculate the mean each time, the distribution of all these sample means should be normal for MRE_small (or MRE_large). The distribution of the sample mean will be normal if the population is normal. We do not know if the population of MRE_small should be expected to be normal or skewed. If it is skewed, however, the central limit theorem comes to our rescue. It states that the sample mean will be normally distributed even if the population is not completely normally distributed provided n is large. As a rule of thumb, "n=large" means n>30. We have n=31. Therefore, the 2-sample t-test should be valid.

Concerning the heteroscedasticity finding of MRE vs. homoscedasticity requirement of regression, the result that MRE is dependent on scale apparently is in conflict with the assumptions of regression analysis. This apparent conflict becomes evident by observing the following.

$$Originalresidual = (1 - e^{-residual})actual\_effort$$

Then we have that

$$MRE = \frac{|Originalresidual|}{actual\_effort} = \left|1 - e^{-residual}\right|$$

That is, if the residual is constant, MRE should be constant, too. In other words, if the residual is homoscedastic, MRE should be independent of scale. Now, we have found that MRE is not independent of scale, implying that the residual cannot be homoscedastic. It therefore seems we have committed an error somewhere.

By closely inspecting the log-log plots of the response variable against each of the predictor variables, we observe that the variance is almost constant for three out of the four predictor variables. For the fourth, Modules, it seems that the variance increases somewhat with size. Thus, we comply reasonably well, but not perfectly, with the homoscedasticity requirement of regression analysis. Since the residual is reasonably homoscedastic, we should expect MRE, too, not to vary much with size.

Nevertheless, the results clearly suggest that MRE decreases with actual effort, especially for small values of actual effort. The explanation may be that MRE is not symmetric. A negative residual of a given magnitude will not have the same MRE as a positive residual of equal magnitude since MRE divides the residual by actual effort rather than by predicted effort. Thus, if we have a majority of negative residuals, MMRE will be different than if we have a majority of positive residuals. In our case, 26 out of the 31 cases with Effort<=5000 ("small projects") have negative residuals whereas in the group of projects with Effort>=10,000 ("large projects") only 11 out of the 31 cases have negative residuals.

8. Conclusion

The rationale for using a *relative* error measure such as MRE rather than using a non-relative error measure must be to compensate for the heteroscedastic nature of software project data sets and obtaining a homoscedastic error measure, i.e. an error term that is independent of scale.

Using a data set of 81 ERP projects we found empirical evidence suggesting that MRE is heteroscedastic rather than homoscedastic, decreasing with project effort. Thus, from the perspective of *scale independence*, one should exercise caution when using MRE as an evaluation criterion for data sets spanning from very small to very large projects. In particular, one should be careful when using MRE to compare two different data sets if the data sets span different ranges of project size.

From a practitioner's point of view, this result has a serious implication. Since MRE decreases with size, MMRE is not a good indicator of the accuracy to expect. Predicting a small project, MMRE will falsely lead us to believe in a too high accuracy, and vice versa when predicting a large project. Therefore, risk-averse project managers and customers should be particularly careful when predicting a small project.

Finally, this result casts some doubt on whether one gains anything by using the mean of the *relative* error, MRE, rather than the mean of, say, the residual as a measure of prediction accuracy. The *raison d'être* of MRE therefore seems questionable.

Acknowledgements

This work was partly financed by Accenture's (formerly Andersen Consulting) Research Fund in Norway. Thank you Accenture!

References

[1] Conte SD, HE Dunsmore, and VY Shen, "Software Engineering Metrics and Models", Benjamin/Cummings, Menlo Park CA, 1986.

[2] Kitchenham BA, SG MacDonell, LM Pickard, and MJ Shepperd (Unpublished paper), "What Accuracy Statistics Really Measure", (Available upon request from the first author, barbara.kitchenham@cs.keele.ac.uk.)

[3] Miyazaki Y, M Terakado, K Ozaki, and H Nozaki, "Robust Regression for Developing Software Estimation Models", Journal of Systems and Software, Vol. 27, 1994, pp. 3-16.

[4] Myrtveit I, and E Stensrud, "A Controlled Experiment to Assess the Benefits of Estimating with Analogy and Regression Models", IEEE Trans. Software Eng. 25, 4, 1999, pp. 510-525.

[5] Stensrud E, and I Myrtveit, "Human Performance Estimating with Analogy and Regression Models: An Empirical Validation", Proc. METRICS'98, IEEE Computer Society Press, 1998, pp. 205-213.

[6] Stensrud E, "Estimating with enhanced object points vs. function points", Proc. COCOMO'13, B. Boehm and R. Madachy (Eds.), USC Center for Software Engineering, Los Angeles CA, 1998.

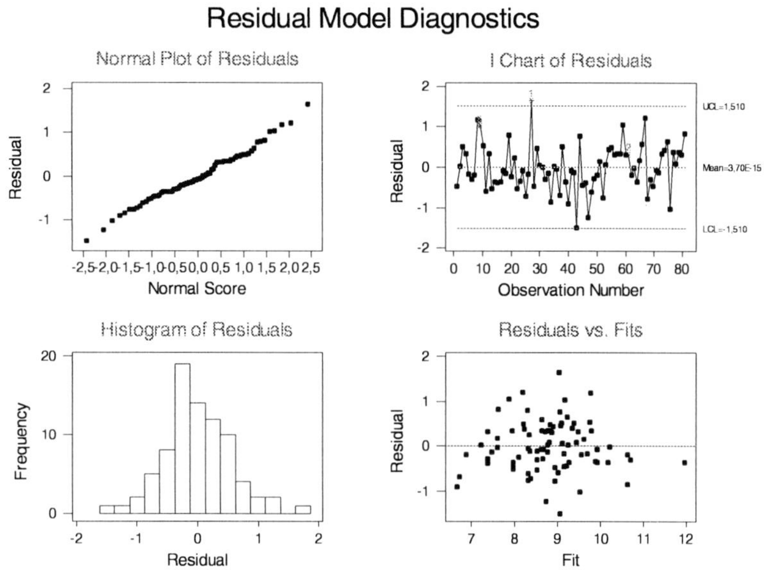

Figure 1. Residual model diagnostics

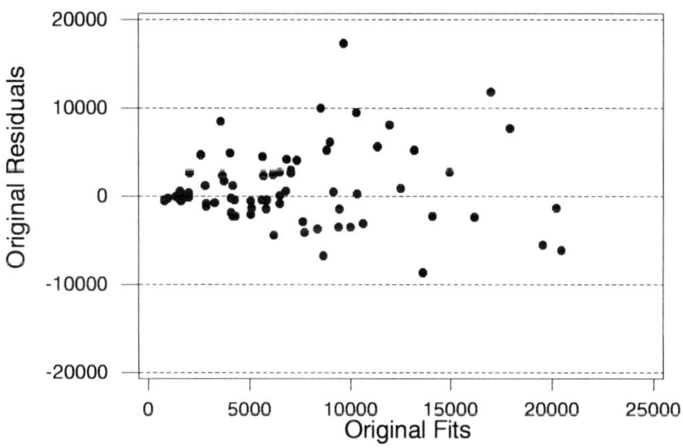

Figure 2. Original Residuals vs. Original Fits (zoomed in).

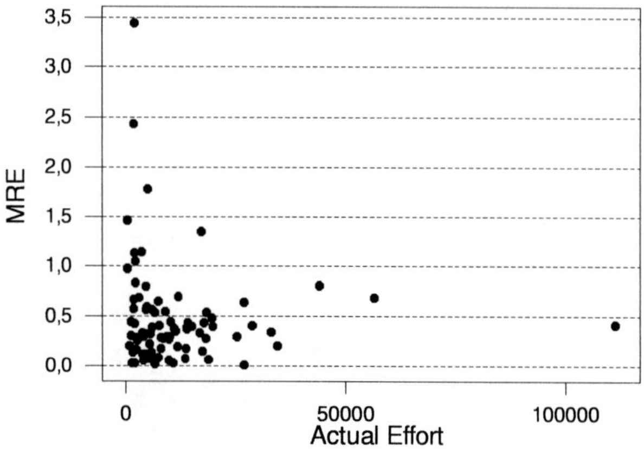

Figure 3. MRE vs. Actual Effort.

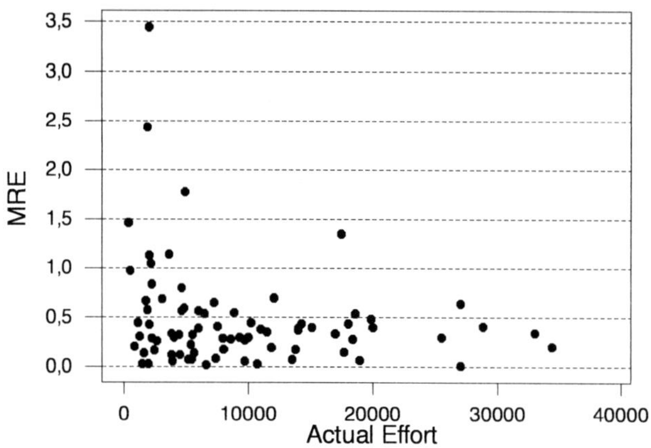

Figure 4. MRE vs. Actual Effort (zoomed in).

Measurement and the software development process

Colin Kirsopp

Abstract

This paper argues that software measurement and the software development process are mutually dependent. Firstly, a high-level view of the relationship between measurement and the development process is taken. This view shows where the various activities within software measurement are positioned within the context of the high-level project stages. The topic of process modelling is introduced, and is used to develop a lower-level view of measurement integration with process. This shows that process models for measurement integration should be sufficiently fine-grained to show when measurements should be collected, how they should be collected, who should collect then, and how the results will be used (the usual lifecycle models are too coarse-grain to achieve this). It is also shown that measurement can be most easily integrated within an automated environment, as measurement collection should itself be automated.

The initial work on the integration of measurement with process shows that there are elements of measurement, such as measurement definition and empirical validation, that must be considered outside of an individual project. To facilitate these cross-project measurement activities, the organisational structure within which the individual projects run is examined. To illustrate this, the authors discuss the use of measurement within the organisational model provided by the TAME project [1-3].

1. Introduction

Software measurement is often considered in isolation from the software development process within which the measurements are taken. Metrologists discuss the details of measurement definition and validation. Process modellers discuss the ordering and organisation of development activities. These groups rarely meet, except perhaps in the field of software process improvement. It is the contention of this paper that software measurement and the software development process are (or should be) mutually dependent activities. The paper sets out to show these dependencies and examine their implications for organisations involved in software development.

Section 2 of this paper discusses the relationship between software measurement and the software development process. It first establishes the dependencies between measurement and the development process and then considers how the activities of the measurement process fit within the high-level stages of the development process.

One way of integrating measurement and process is through process modelling. An overview of process modelling is given in section 3. The uses of measurement within process models are also considered, as are the forms of process models suitable for measurement integration.

Software measurement is sometimes used for process improvement. The position of measurement within an improvement oriented organisational structure is also considered. This consideration is based around work done as part of the TAME project outlining an organisational structure for process improvement combining support for model building, project guidance and measurement [1-3].

2. The relationship between measurement and process

The famous quote from DeMarco that "you can't control what you can't measure" [4] shows the dependency of development process control on software measurement. What may perhaps be less apparent, though equally true, is the dependency of measures on process. The needs of the process dictate what should be measured. The process defines when measurements should be taken and how the results of measurement will be interpreted (and perhaps feedback). For these reasons measurement should be considered as an integral part of the development process and not merely an adjunct to it. Figure 1 outlines the way that measurement process activities may be positioned within the high-level stages of a development project.

Figure 1: The position of measurement elements within project performance

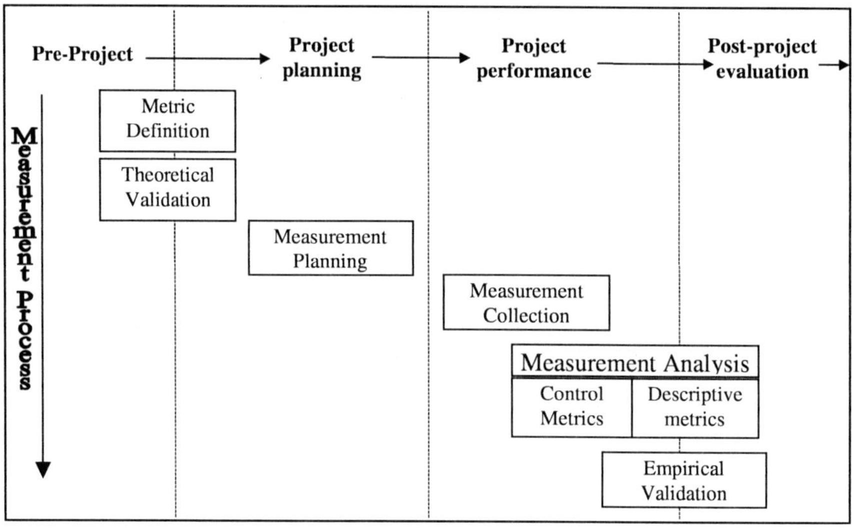

When considering the integration of measurement into process, the first thing to consider is which elements of the measurement process require integration. At a basic level measurement programmes may be considered to consist of planning, collection, analysis and validation [5].

The first activities of the measurement process are metric definition and theoretical validation. Although these are necessary activities in an overall measurement *process*, they will usually have already been completed before the project process begins and so are not considered part of a measurement *programme*. They are included here mainly for reasons of completeness. However, it is possible that if a project has requirement for a new measure that these activities will be done during the project planning stage.

Deciding which measurements to make, and when to make them, ought to be done during the planning stages of the project and will be an integral part of the design/selection of the development process. It need not therefore be integrated into the development process model.

The collection and analysis of measures intended for project control must be integrated within the development process. Their use for process control can be integrated into the process model by using the results of measurement as event guards/triggers. This prevents activities from occurring unless particular measurement values (or ranges) have been achieved, or force activities to occur that would otherwise be bypassed. Within quantitative process models measurement values may also be used to select between alternative courses of action. Among other things, this provides a means of quantifying the exit criteria for iterative cycles within processes. However, care must be taken when using quantitative process models to ensure that they are not too prescriptive. The measures on which decisions are taken are often only indirect measures (or predictions) of the data which would ideally be used to make the decisions. Decisions based on such approximations should be made with a sensible degree of flexibility.

As well as control measures, descriptive measures may be collected. These are measures that do not directly affect the control of the project on which they are collected. Their use may be to help empirically validate metrics which are being considered for the control of future projects or to gain a quantitative understanding of what is happening within the project to help suggest process improvements. Adding this type of measurement produces what is termed an instrumented model. It is quite possible for such measures to be collected during a project but not analysed or applied until after the project's completion.

Empirical validation is an on going process, where each successful use of a metric increases confidence in its utility. The empirical validity of metrics may either, be reassessed as soon as the data becomes available (during the project), or may be left until after the project's completion.

3. Software process modelling

One obvious approach to integrating (or describing the integration) of measurement with the development process is with the use of process models.

3.1. What is Software Process Modelling?

Software process modelling is the formation of, and reasoning about, abstract representations of the processes and people concerned with the development and maintenance of software systems. The purpose of a process model will dictate the elements of the process that are included in the model. Curtis lists five possible purposes of process modelling: understanding and communication; process improvement; enhanced process status visibility; automated process guidance; process enactment [6]. Shepperd adds a sixth, the reuse of successful processes [5].

The particular aspects of a process that are modelled will depend on the detail of how it will be used. There are many aspects that may form part of a model. These aspects include:

1 the tasks to be carried out;
2 the order in which the tasks should be carried out;
3 the inputs and outputs to each task;
4 when and where a task will be performed;
5 how and why a task is done;
6 the roles and agents involved in performing the various tasks;
7 the iterative, interleaved and concurrent nature of tasks/sub-processes;
8 the conditions under which branches in process control are made;

9 the artefacts produced by or used in the process;
10 the resources used during a task;
11 the roles or activities which are dependent upon a task being completed.

3.2. Process Modelling Techniques

Shepperd divides the methods used in process modelling into five main categories [5]: lifecycle models; executable models; formal models; psychological models and graphical models.

3.2.1. Lifecycle Models

Lifecycle models are probably the best-known representations of software development processes. They are generally very coarse-grained models. Lifecycles can be split into two major types those derived for traditional structured development and those more recently proposed to allow for the differences in approach of object-oriented development.

3.2.2. Executable Models

Executable models are those which are written in computer enactable form. They tend to be much finer grained than lifecycle models. The advantage of an executable model is that they can be used to support automated software engineering environments. Several types of executable model have been used. These range from variations on standard procedural programming languages, such as the use of the Ada in the REBUS tool [7, 8] to functional languages and AI approaches.

This type of executable process model has been compared to software itself [9] . This has some interesting implications. If we can treat processes as software then the techniques and principles that can be applied to software production should also be applicable to process modelling. This includes: desirable properties like reversibility [10] and seamlessness [11]; constructing process models from reused components; and using process patterns for common types of modelling problems.

The above implications may only be considered useful or valid if we can model processes in the same way as software. As Curtis points out process modelling is different from other modelling in software engineering because some of the roles it models must be performed by people [6]. The introduction of people into the models adds a level of non-determinism which does not exist in software modelling [5]. Some might consider this to be sufficient grounds for treating software design and process modelling separately. However, software design techniques and notations are commonly used for representing process models.

3.2.3. Formal Models

Formal models involve the production of a mathematical description of the process. This type of process modelling has been done using both algebraic (OBJ) and model based (VDM) methods. Their strict formalism allows mathematical reasoning to be applied to process descriptions. However, formal method's determinism raises doubts as to whether they can properly describe human behaviour.

3.2.4. Psychological Models

Psychological modelling results in a very different type of model. They have their primary focus on modelling how people actually perform activities and make decisions. A model has been developed by Guindon and Curtis of designer behaviour using JSD [12]. This model shows that designer jumps between levels of abstraction and between design and requirements whilst producing a solution. This shows a possible advantage of this type of modelling. Most process models of design would have assumed a textbook top-down or bottom-up approach. Without studying how people perform processes any process script may not be very precise.

3.2.5. Graphical models

Most process modelling methods fall into the graphical modelling type. This includes: general modelling methods such as flowcharts; notations borrowed from management planning like PERT charts or critical path analysis; software design notations from both structured methods (DFD, ERD, STD) and object-oriented methods (OMT, UML); and notations designed specifically for process modelling such as role activity diagrams (RADs).

3.3. Process modelling considerations

Deciding on the notation for a process model requires a clear purpose. There are a number of aspects of this purpose that may be considered to help make a choice of modelling notation.

3.3.1. Granularity

The granularity is the level of detail with which the process is described, or alternatively the size of the basic elements of the model. The purpose of a model will require certain information to be represented at a particular level of detail. If a notation is used which not capable of sufficient detail the purpose may not be achieved. If a notation is used which prescribes a finer granularity than necessary then the model will be cluttered with unnecessary information and consequently more difficult to use than it might be.

A related consideration in the choice of notation is the precision required of the model. The precision is the degree to which the model represents *all* steps to be carried-out to produce desired results. This is in effect the fidelity of the model.

If our purpose in modelling is to enable measurement to be integrated with the development process, then the granularity and precision of the method chosen must be commensurate with this purpose. Although lifecycles do provide a representation of the software development process, they have too coarse a grain to show how measurements would affect project control flow, or what measurements should be taken when. This leads to the conclusion that a more detailed description of software processes is required. Methods from within each of the other categories appear capable of representing processes at a sufficiently fine-grained manner to enable measurement integration.

3.3.2. Formality

The level of formality of modelling methods varies greatly from the strict formalism of VDM and OBJ to the more human centred psychological modelling. Process models intended for machine enactment are generally termed process programs. These models require a high degree of formality to give precise execution semantics. Process programs have the advantage that they are amenable to static checking (completeness, consistency and correctness) and dynamic checking (reachability, deadlocks and race conditions).

Process models that are intended for human enactment are usually termed process scripts. The non-determinism inherent in human action requires that process scripts have a substantial degree of flexibility within them. In general, for process descriptions intended for humans, expressiveness and comprehensibility are more important than strict formality.

If we again consider the various methods' suitability for measurement integration there are problems with the strictly formal methods like VDM and OBJ. The first problem is scalability. Although formal methods can be effectively used to represent fairly simple systems they may have difficulty with a fully formed industrial process. A second problem is the limited use and understanding of formal methods in industry and the associated reluctance to use them. These problems may mean that strict formal models are unsuitable for measurement integration on anything other than small academic examples.

On the other extreme, psychologically derived models may lack sufficient formalism to allow any useful computer enactment. It is generally agreed that industrial scale measurement will require automation. Possible difficulties in combining a manual process enactment with automated metrics collection may also rule-out psychological models for use in measurement integration.

3.3.3. Modelling style

Modelling styles can be divided into three perspectives, prescriptive, descriptive and proscriptive. Prescriptive models specify how the process must be performed. This detailed description of exactly what must be done can clash with human agents who tend to do things in a less regimented way. In such circumstances the process which is actually followed may often not be that which is prescribed. Descriptive modelling is used to determine the process that is actually being used. The third perspective on process modelling, proscriptive modelling, describes behaviour which is not allowed in the process. It is impossible in practice to describe the complete set of things which should not be done in the performance of a particular process (the list would be virtually endless). For this reason proscriptive modelling is usually used as an adjunct to prescriptive and descriptive models. In this situation they can be used as constraints on activities or events.

Since measurement may be used to describe processes or the control them via prescriptive or proscriptive means, any of these styles could be use for measurement integration.

4. Measurement and organisational structure

As was discussed in section 2, some aspects of software measurement involve inter-project activity that cannot be done within a single project's process model. Also, an individual project's process doesn't exist in isolation, it is designed and applied within the wider company structure and operates within an historical context of previous projects and the experience gleaned from them. To consider these inter-project questions an organisational structure will be examined that has been designed with these issues in mind.

4.1. The TAME model

The diagram below shows the improvement oriented organisational structure developed by the TAME project [1-3]. The model is made up of individual project organisations which use (or reuse) elements supplied from an experience factory. The results from, and lessons learned whilst performing, each individual project are used to populate the experience base.

An individual project has its own characteristics and goals. These are used to choose appropriate models and metrics from the experience factory to be used during the project performance. The models may include product models, process models, resource models, and quality models. The project is then planned, performed and monitored using the models and metrics. Records of the project performance and any lessons learned during the project are fed back into the experience factory. This new experience is then packaged for future use, or used in the repackaging of existing models and metrics.

Figure 2: Organisational structure tailored for measurement

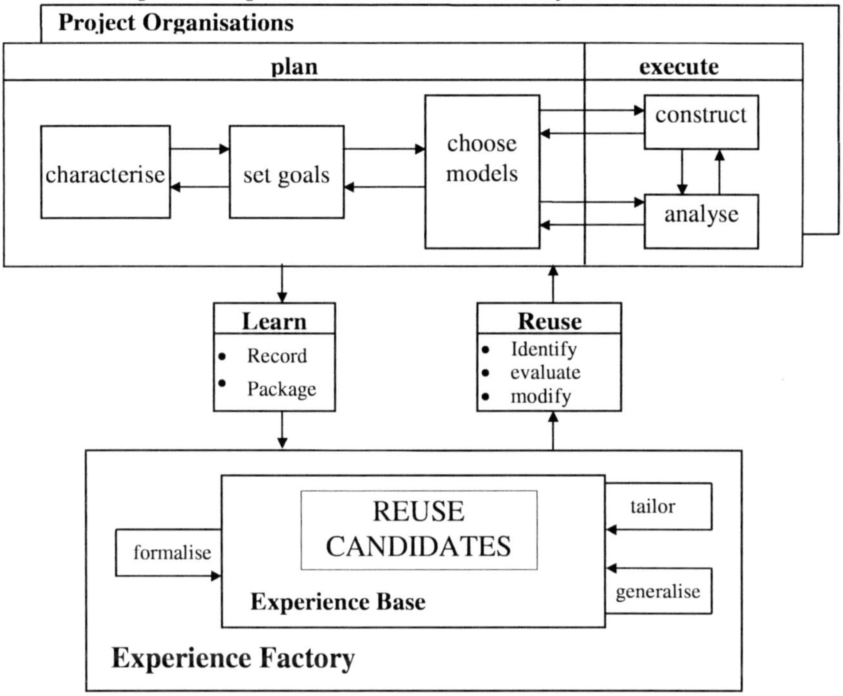

4.1.1. Project organisations

A project organisation deals with the performance of a single project. Within each project there are a set of standard activities, i.e., characterisation, goal setting, model selection, construction, and analysis.

Characterisation takes place during a project's planning stage. It involves assessing various project attributes in order to aid model selection. In order to be useful there must be a record of the characterisations of previous projects, the various models they used and the degree to which those models were considered to fit that project after-the-fact.

Goal setting is the selection, and operational definition, of goals for the construction and review (analysis) of the system being built. The team who produced the TAME model were also central in producing the goal question metric paradigm (GQM) [13] and they suggest relating the setting of project goals to measurable outcomes using GQM.

Model selection uses the analogies drawn from the characterisation to chose models to be used in the performance of the current project. As has been previously mentioned, it may be that there is no sufficiently close model to use and a new model may need to be constructed.

Construction is the process of actually producing the end product of the project. The construction is done according to the chosen development process model and the selected methods and tools.

The analysis and packaging of data from a project organisation must be done with reference to the existing data in the experience factory. Using knowledge of the existing models and metrics it must be decided what form of analysis would produce results suitable for packaging, storage and reuse.

4.1.2. Experience factory

The experience base holds the complete body of experience that is available for use by the project organisations. The experience factory contains the experience base and also associated processes for working with stored experience. These process include: tailoring existing experience to be reused in new contexts; generalising specific experiences to make then more widely applicable (and hence more reusable) and formalising experience into models that may also be reused more easily.

In general, the experience-base may contain any product or process entities that a company feels may be usefully reused. If a more specific view is taken, relevant to integrating measurement with process, the set of entities of direct interest can be listed and discussed. These entities may include entity models such as attribute models, process models, resource models, quality models and process models. They may also include the goals and questions used to select measures, the measures themselves, measurement results and the heuristics or thresholds used for the interpretation of measurement results.

4.2. TAME and the measurement process

4.2.1. How is measurement used in the TAME model?

There are several places within the organisational structure where measurement is used. Measures may be used to characterise projects. Project goals should be set in measurable terms (often via GQM). The models used in the construction and analysis phases of a project, e.g., quality models, are often measurement-based. As Basili states, 'analysis (including measurement) cannot be an add-on but must be part of the execution process and drive the construction' [1]. This means putting then actual construction of the product under measurement control.

4.2.2. How does the TAME model facilitate measurement?

A major advantage to measurement of using the TAME model would be in planning a measurement programme. Measurement planning requires the selection of which measures to collect as well as how and when to collect them. An experience base can help with this is several ways. It can provide process models (or model sections) already packaged with the necessary control measures, including when and how they should be collected and how the results will be used. Storing historical GQM hierarchies can help to associate a new project's goals with relevant measures. Pre-packaged quality, resource or product models may also be defined in terms of measures. All of this stored experience can be used to reduce the effort in measurement planning.

As mentioned previously, empirical validation is an on going process, where each successful use of a metric increases confidence in its utility. This means that the validity of measures must be constantly reassessed each time new data becomes available from a project.

The database of measurement results must be maintained outside of any individual project, as it will contain the results from many projects.

The storage of historical measurement data would also be useful in the tuning of measurement thresholds or ranges used in process control or quality evaluation. Again this data is collected across a number of projects and so must be stored outside of any individual project organisation.

5. Summary

Software measurement and the software development process are (should be) mutually dependent. The most promising means for integrating measurement and process seems to be process modelling. Process models intended for measurement integration should be sufficiently fine grained to show when, and how measurements should be taken, who should take then, and how they will be used. The necessity for this level of granularity excludes the use of the standard lifecycle models.

Measurement can be most easily integrated within an automated environment as the measurement collection must also be automated. This may lead to a preference for executable process models for measurement integration. These executable models may, however, have problems representing non-deterministic human behaviour. This problem of ease of automation versus ease of understandability and precise representation of human behaviour doesn't appear a particularly tractable one. It seems likely that trade-off and compromise are required here rather than attempting to find an 'ideal' solution.

A measurement programme may be split into its constituent parts of planning, collection, analysis and validation [5]. Of these parts the measurement planning must be done during the project planning stage before the development process model can be enacted. Validation may be split into theoretical validation and empirical validation. Of these theoretical validation may be done during project planning. Measurement collection must be integrated with the development process and taken into consideration when choosing/designing the process. The analysis of any measures that can effect the control of the process must also be integrated with the process. The analysis of descriptive measures that do not impact process control may be done during the process or may be left until after the development is complete. Empirical validation may be done as soon as the results are available, but may often be left until after the completion of the development.

Empirical measurement validation and measurement reuse are mutually dependent activities. Unless a measure is reused the necessary corroborative evidence cannot be gathered for validation and assessment of generality. Unless a measure is validated it will not be reused. Both of these aspects of software measurement involve inter-project activity that cannot be done within individual project organisations. To consider these inter-project questions we need to define the organisational structure within which individual projects take place.

One model for an organisational structure is that produced by the TAME project. This structure is used as an example to demonstrate the interaction of measurement and process and show the facilities that need to be in place, at an organisational level, to aid measurement integration with process. It also shows how these facilities interact with individual projects.

6. Conclusions

If measurement and process are mutually dependent they should be planned, stored and reused together. Measurement programmes require cross-project structures for data storage, analysis, threshold tuning and validation. The TAME model provides the mechanism for achieving these goals.

Would the author recommend every software development company to drop their existing organisational structure and adopt TAME? In reality, no. No one would seriously consider swapping their organisational structure in a revolutionary way. So you might say, what's the point of the work? The TAME model provides an example of an organisational structure with facilities to support measurement and for development to be supported by measurement. It isn't necessary that the TAME model be adopted. However, it is desirable is that those in software development gain an understanding of the inter-dependencies of measurement and process, and understand the facilities that need to be put in place in order to take advantage of them.

7. References

[1] Basili, V.R. and Rombach, H.D., "The TAME project: Towards Improvement-oriented software environments", IEEE Transactions on Software Engineering, 1988. 14(6), p. 758-771.

[2] Lott, C.M. and Rombach, H.D., "Measurement-based guidance of software projects using project plans. Information and software technology", 1993. 35(6/7), p. 407-419.

[3] Basili, V.R. and Rombach, H.D., "Support for comprehensive reuse", report No. CS-TR-2606, 1991, University of Maryland.

[4] DeMarco, T., "Controlling software projects", Yourdon Press, New York, 1982.

[5] Shepperd, M., "Foundations of software measurement", Prentice Hall, 1995.

[6] Curtis, B., Kellner,M.I. and Over, J., "Process modeling", Communications of the ACM, 1992. 35(9), p. 75-90.

[7] Sutton, S.M., Heimbigner, D. and Osterweil, L.J., "Language constructs for managing change in process-centered environments", ACM SIGSOFT Sofware Engineering Notes, 1990. 15(6), p. 206-217.

[8] Sutton, S.M., et al. "Programming a software requirements specification process", in 1st IEEE International Conference on the Software Process, Redondo Beach CA, 1991.

[9] Osterweil, L.J., "Software Processes are Software Too", in 9th International Software Engineering Conference, IEEE Computer Society Press, 1987.

[10] Shepperd, M.J. and Ince, D.C., "Derivation and validation of software metrics", Open University Press, 1993.

[11] Avotins, J. "Towards an object-oriented metric modeling method", in OOPSLA'96 - workshop: OO product metrics, 1996.

[12] Guindon, R. and Curtis, B., "Control of Cognitive Processes during Design : What tools would support software designers?", in Proceedings of CHI'88, New York: ACM, 1988.

[13] Basili, V., Caldiera, G. and Rombach, H.D., "The goal question metric approach", in Encyclopedia of software engineering, Wiley, 1994.

Distributing Human Resources among Software Development Projects[1]

Macario Polo, María Dolores Mateos, Mario Piattini and Francisco Ruiz

Summary

This paper presents a method for estimating the distribution of human resources to be assigned to development projects. The estimation calculates the optimal distribution from the economical point of view (i.e.: that which less costs). To accomplish this, we built an economical model to distribute human resources among projects in one organisation. The equations and algorithms used to do this are presented in the paper. We also briefly present a tool which does these estimations.

1. Introduction

In the last few years, an increasing demand for personnel qualified in Information Technologies has been observed, which greatly exceeds the offer: in 1998 there was in Europe 500,000 free positions in IT, with an expected increase of up to 2.4 million people for the year 2004 [1]. Some reports from the European Commission also confirm this tendency [2][3], which is reviewed by daily newspapers almost every month. The situation in the U.S.A. is quite similar: the yearly number of visas for foreigners qualified in Information Technologies has been increased to the point of 300,000 ones, although big software organizations have solicited a greater number of licenses.

With this situation, software organizations must do an adequate planning of their human resources among the different projects that they are carrying out. An additional difficulty is to fix the number of development projects to be accepted by a software organization, when many times it is known that the organization has not (and will not have) people enough to execute all the projects in time and budget. However, the rejection of a software project will cause probably the loss of that customer for the organization, and maybe a negative impact on other potential customers.

Therefore, it is important to accept projects, but it is also a basic activity to distribute the human resources in an adequate way among all of them, and this one is the main goal of this paper.

We propose to make an economical model of the portfolio of software development projects, in order to estimate the optimal quantity of human resources to be devoted to each project, during every day of the considered period. We have successfully tested the method with several projects which use different life cycle models, although we have reasons to believe that it can be easily adaptable to still-non-studied life cycles. This method is a very advanced evolution of the work presented last year in this same forum [4].

The paper is organized as follows: Section 2 explains the model we use to represent a portfolio of development projects from an economical point of view, which includes several equations. In Section 3, an algorithm to calculate the distribution is presented, as well as

[1] This work is part of the MPM and MANTIS projects. MPM is developed with Atos ODS, S.A. and partially supported by the Ministerio de Ciencia y Tecnología, Programa de Tecnologías de la Información y las Comunicaciones (FIT-070000-2000-307); MANTIS is partially supported by the European Union and CICYT (1FD197-1608TIC).

CRED, a tool we have developed to do estimations. Section 4 exposes our conclusions and future and immediate work lines.

2. Economical model of a portfolio of development projects

One of the primary goals of the software organization is to obtain economical benefits from the developments. Independently of the life cycle selected for a given project, this one can be considered as the union of several subprojects. Sometimes, the consecution of a subproject will be a must to start another one (in the waterfall life cycle model, the requirement analysis comes before the design phase), but other times, the life cycle selected allows to develop in parallel different parts of the system. Depending on the contract between the customer and the supplier organizations, maybe some of those subprojects must be delivered according to a previously signed scheduling. For example, a system developed using the Unified Process can be delivered in several releases, each one with some increment of functionality with respect to the previous one. These successive releases constitute partial results whose date of deliver, prize and possible sanctions by delay may be covenanted in the development contract.

2.1. Maximization equation

The software organization must take into account all these factors to do an adequate resource assignment to each project and subproject, with the primary goal of maximize its economical benefits. This can be represented by the following equation:

$$Max\ B = I - C = \sum_{i=1}^{N}(Ii - Ci) \quad \textbf{Eq. 1}$$

In Eq. 1., B represents the benefits produced by the N development projects in the portfolio; I and C respectively are the total incomes and costs, whereas Ii and Ci represent the incomes and costs of the *i-th* project.

As every project is an aggregation of subprojects, Eq. 1 can be rewritten in this way:

$$Max\ B = \sum_{i=1}^{N}\sum_{j=1}^{Ni}(Iij - Cij) \qquad \textbf{Eq. 2}$$

In Eq. 2, Ni is the number of subprojects if the *i-th* project, and Iij and Cij are, respectively, the incomes and costs of the *j-th* subproject of the *i-th* project (thereinafter, the *ij* subproject). Depending so on the contract as on the selected life cycle, sometimes Iij will be zero, since not all subprojects will be delivered to the customer and they will not produce any income. In the other side, Iij is typically covenanted in the development contract, since the customer organization needs to know the project budget before its assignment to the development organization.

Costs of each subproject are different: each one takes more or less time than another one, and the people in charge of them have different levels and salaries (analysts, programmers, tests engineers...). Another influencing factor on the costs of a subproject (and, therefore, on the costs of the complete project) is the existence of delays in the date of delivering and of sanctions by delays. With this assumption, costs of the *ij* project can be represented in this manner:

$$Cij = Rij + Qij \quad \textbf{Eq. 3}$$

Rij are the costs of the resources devoted to the subproject, whereas Qij is the quantity to be paid by sanctions due to delays in the ij subproject. We suppose that a subproject needs only one type of resource (analysts, for example): otherwise, it could be divided into more subprojects. With this consideration, Rij can be expressed in this way:

$$Rij = \sum_{t=1}^{F} (Tijt \cdot ht) \qquad \textbf{Eq. 4}$$

In Eq. 4, $Tijt$ is the number of hours of the t-th resource needed to execute the ij subproject; F is the number of different resources (analysts, programmers, test engineers, etc.); ht represents the cost of one hour of resource of the t type.

The second variable of Eq. 3, Qij, depends on the scheduled date of delivering (or scheduled duration) for the ij project and on the real date (or real duration). At a first sight, Qij can be expressed in this way:

$$Qij = Sij \cdot (Eij - Pij) \qquad \textbf{Eq. 5}$$

In Eq. 5, Sij is the covenanted sanction for the ij subproject (obviously, if such subproject will not be delivered, it will not have any sanction, although it could have some influence on next subprojects). Eij is the real number of days used to finish the ij project, whereas Pij is the scheduled duration, also in days, which depends on the total number of hours of effort required by the ij project ($\sum_{t=1}^{F} Tijt$).

Pij was estimated by the software organization using some estimation method and is covenanted in the contract. The value of Eij depends on the number of hours devoted to the subproject. In a given subproject, we will reach the value of Eij when the sum of the hours devoted each day to the ij project will be equal to the number of required hours of the t-th resource, $Tijt$. In other words:

$$Eij = m \;\; / \sum_{k=1}^{m} \sum_{t=1}^{F} e_{ijk}^{t} = \sum_{t=1}^{F} Tijt \qquad \textbf{Eq. 6}$$

In Eq. 6, e^{t}_{ijk} is the number of hours of the t th resource devoted to the ij project in the k-th day.

At his point, we have characterized all the variables we need to rewrite Eq. 1:

$$Max\, B - I - C = \sum_{i=1}^{N} (Ii - Ci) = \sum_{i=1}^{N} \sum_{j=1}^{Ni} (Iij - Cij) = \sum_{i=1}^{N} \sum_{j=1}^{Ni} [Iij - Rij - Qij] =$$
$$= \sum_{i=1}^{N} \sum_{j=1}^{Ni} \left[Iij - \left(\sum_{t=1}^{F} (Tijt \cdot ht) \right) - Sij \cdot (Eij - Pij) \right] \qquad \textbf{Eq. 7}$$

In Eq. 7, the only unknown quantity is Eij, since the rest have previously assigned values.

2.2. Constraints

To estimate the optimal distribution of resources, we must identify now the possible constraints to be applied to Eq. 7.

The first constraint represents the fact that the sum of the hours of a given resource devoted during a concrete day to all subprojects cannot be greater than the available number of hours of that kind of resource in that day ($A_1, A_2\ldots$):

$$\begin{cases} e^t_{1j1} + e^t_{2j1} + \ldots + e^t_{Nj1} \leq A_{t1} & \forall t \in [1, F], \forall j \\ e^t_{1j2} + e^t_{2j2} + \ldots + e^t_{Nj2} \leq A_{t2} & \forall t \in [1, F], \forall j \\ \ldots \end{cases}$$

The t subindex is used to group resources by its type (i.e.: analysts, programmers...). Eq. 8 summarizes the previous equations:

$$\sum_{i=1}^{N} e^t_{ijk} \leq A_{tK}, \; \forall t, k \qquad \textbf{Eq. 8}$$

The next constraint means that the time devoted to a subproject must be equal to the time required by it:

$$\sum_{j=1}^{Ni} e^t_{ijk} = Tijt, \; \forall i, k, t \qquad \textbf{Eq. 9}$$

The following simple constraints determine the minimal values of the variables that intervene in Eq. 7:

$$\begin{aligned} &Iij \geq 0 \quad \forall \text{i}, \text{j} \\ &hij \geq 0 \quad \forall \text{i}, \text{j} \\ &Sij \geq 0 \quad \forall \text{i}, \text{j} \\ &T^t_{ij} \geq 0 \quad \forall \text{i}, \text{j}, \text{t} \\ &e_{ijk} \geq 0 \quad \forall \text{i}, \text{j}, \text{k} \\ &A_{tK} \geq 0 \quad \forall \text{j}, \text{k} \end{aligned} \qquad \textbf{Eq. 10 to 15}$$

2.3. Complete model (for reference)

With all the equations stated in the previous subsections, the portfolio of projects can be modelled with the following equation:

$$\begin{cases} \text{Max } B = \sum_{i=1}^{N}\sum_{j=1}^{Ni}\left[Iij - \left(\sum_{t=1}^{F} (Tijt \cdot ht) \right) - Sij \cdot (Eij - Pij) \right] \\ \text{subject to:} \\ \sum_{i=1}^{N} e_{ijk}^{t} \le A_{tK}, \ \forall t,k \\ \sum_{j=1}^{N} e_{ijk}^{t} = Tijt, \ \forall i,k,t \\ Iij \ge 0 \quad \forall \text{i, j} \\ ht \ge 0 \quad \forall \text{i, j} \\ Sij \ge 0 \quad \forall \text{i, j} \\ Tijt \ge 0 \quad \forall \text{i, j, t} \\ e_{ijk}^{t} \ge 0 \quad \forall \text{i, j, k} \\ A_{tK} \ge 0 \quad \forall \text{j, k} \end{cases}$$

The meaning of each variable in the left side is the following:

- N = number of projects in the portfolio
- Ni = number of subprojects in the *i-th* project
- Iij = incomes by the *ij* subproject
- F = number of different types of resources
- $Tijt$ = number of hours required of resource type *t* by the *ij* subproject
- ht = cost of each hour of resource devoted to the *ij* subproject
- Sij = sanction to be paid by each day of delay in the deliver of the *ij* subproject
- Eij = real number of days used to finish the *ij* project
- Pij is the scheduled duration (in days) of the *ij* subproject
- e_{ij}^{t} = resources devoted the *k-th* day to the *ij* subproject
- A_{tK} = available resources of the type *t* in the *k-th* day

It is important to remember the following definition of *Eij* (Eq. 6): $Eij = m \ / \sum_{k=1}^{m}\sum_{t=1}^{F} e_{ijk}^{t} = \sum_{t=1}^{F} Tijt$. This equation is the basis to estimate the optimal distribution of resources.

3. Resources estimation

All we need to estimate the resources to be assigned to every development project in the portfolio is to resolve the equation shown in Section 2.3. As not all the constraints are lineal (see Eq. 6), the simplex method cannot be used. Some of the candidate methods to resolve this kind of equations are Genetic algorithms or Simulated annealing. However, as the number of unknown values is very little, we can find a very good approximation to the optimal solution testing all the possible combinations.

3.1. Algorythm

A "coarse" version of the algorithm could be the following:

```
max =-MAXDOUBLE
for k=0 to maxDuration
        for i=1 to N do
                for j=1 to F
                        for e=0 to A[t,k]
                                e[i,j,k,t]=e
                                if Benefit()>max then
                                        max=Benefit()
                                        saveParameters(i,j,k,e)
                                endif
                        end
                end
        end
end
```

Figure 1. First version of the algorythm.

Obviously, the code in Figure 1 can be very optimized through the application of the constraints and some other rules. For example:

- We will assign resources (assignment of values to the *e* array in Figure 1) when:
  - The *ij* project needs them
  - In the *k-th* day, there are available resources of the type which is being tested.
- We will calculate the benefit (Eq. 7) when the current combination which is being tested implies the finalization of all the projects in the portfolio.
- The *e* array can be a vector (with the consequent memory saving): only some transformation rules are required.

3.2. CRED: a tool for estimating resources distribution

In order to do the automatic estimation of resources, we have developed CRED, a tool which helps in the calculus of the resources distribution. It implements an optimised version of the algorithm previous. Figure 2 shows one the CRED's screens, in the moment of doing an estimation.

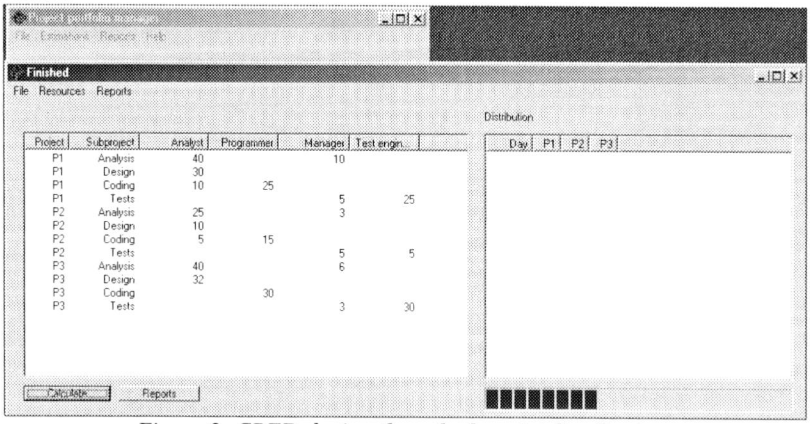

Figure 2. CRED during the calculus of a distribution.

CRED allows the tracking of the projects, to change the assignation, etc. In this manner, several kind of reports, statistics and graphics can be obtained, in order to analyze efforts, resources, etc., and compare them against a baseline. Figure 3 shows the screen used to change the temporary availability of resources.

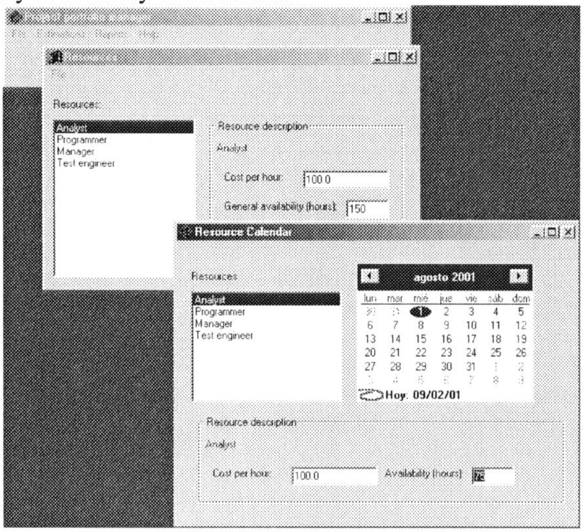

Figure 3. Changing resources availability.

Figure 4 shows a view of the class diagrams used to build the tool: resources needed by a subproject are determined by the association with the "ResourceNecessity" class.

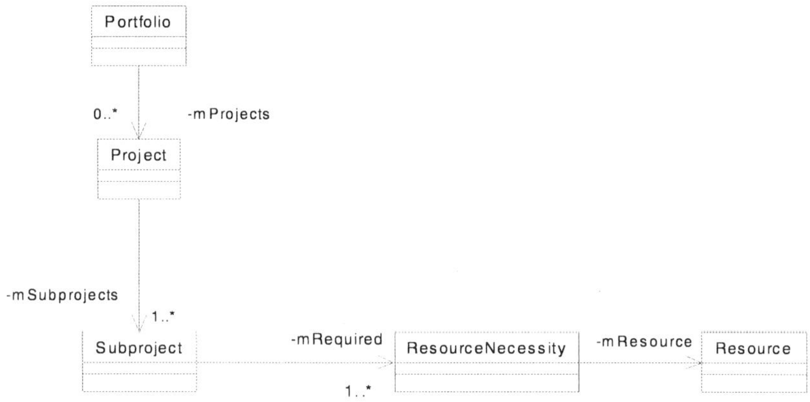

Figure 4. Conceptual diagram.

3.3. Context of CRED

CRED is now being adapted to allow its full integration in MANTIS [5], an integral environment for managing maintenance projects. MANTIS uses XMI to exchange information among the tools that compose it. In this context, CRED should be capable of sending its information to MANTIS in a standardized format based on XML, which is one of our current works.

4. Conclusions and future work

This paper has presented a method and a tool to estimate the distribution of resources to be assigned to development projects. The estimation attempts to assure an optimal distribution from the economical point of view.

Both the method and the tool must be modified in order to take into account:

- Dependencies (i.e.: a subproject cannot begin before the end of another one)
- Indirect costs (i.e.: the organization cannot accept a project because it will not have available resources)

5. References

[1] Bourke, T.M. (1999). Seven major ICT companies join the European Commission to work towards closing the skills gap in Europe (Press Release). Available also at (Nov., 7, 2000): http://www.career-space.com/whats_new/press_rel.doc

[2] European Commission (1999). *The competitiveness of European enterprises in the face of globalisation.* Available at (Nov, 7, 2000): http://europa.eu.int/comm/research/pdf/com98-718en.pdf

[3] European Commission (2000). *Employment in Europe 2000.* Available at (Nov., 7, 2000): http://europa.eu.int/comm/employment_social/empl&esf/docs/empleurope2000_en.pdf

[4] Polo, M., Piattini, M. and Ruiz, F. (2000). *Planning the non-planneable maintenance.* Project Control, The Human Factor: Proceedings of the ESCOM-SCOPE 2000 Combined Conference. Munich, Germany.

[5] Ruiz, F., Piattini, F. and Polo, M. (2001). An Integrated Environment for Managing Software Maintenance Projects. In van Bon (Ed.): World Class IT Service Management Guide, 2nd edition. Addison Wesley.

SouthernSCOPE – A Method for Acquiring Custom Built Software or Let the Customer Manage Software Acquisition

Anthony L Rollo, Terry Wright

Abstract

The current size of the global industry developing custom built software is estimated to be in excess of $US200bn annually. The performance of the software industry in developing successful projects is poor with an estimated 32% of projects terminating before delivering anything to business and only 11% completing within budget. Of the remainder that do complete, the average budget overrun is 87% [2]. A Recent survey of the International Software Benchmarking Group data repository has shown that the costs paid by business for comparable software can vary 7 fold [3]. This litany of software failure makes the development of techniques to allow business to retain control of software acquisition compelling and ever more urgent.

*Southern*SCOPE *is a framework strategy for software acquisition, which is designed to allow project business sponsors the ability to control and manage acquisition projects. The method allows the business sponsor to retain control of project scope and expenditure in terms that business can understand. The risk of budget overrun is considerably reduced as the sponsor is always in control of the scope; this ensures good value for money. The potential for bidding low and then loading the price of changes is largely eliminated.*

*The State Government of Victoria, Australia introduced the initial ideas in 1996 and has since developed several projects refining the method in the light of experience. This has resulted in the development and introduction of the Southern*SCOPE *method as the standard purchasing policy of the state. This paper will explore the underlying ideas behind the method and the experience of the State government of Victoria in developing this unique approach to software acquisition. The paper will also review a case study of a software acquisition project.*

1. Introduction

The State Government of Victoria Australia has an annual software budget of around $50 Million (AUD), (29 Million Euro). The state government is a leader in the use of IT in the provision of services to its citizens. The UK government has based a large part of its e-government initiative on ideas originated by the state government. Yet despite a good record of achievement in the field of government on-line the state government was faced with the problem of acquiring software within budgets and of suitable quality. These are problems that any organisation faces when acquiring software. The difficulty is well categorised by a recent report. An estimated 32% of projects terminate before delivering anything to business and only 11% complete within budget. For projects that complete the average budget overspend is reported by the CHAOS report [2] as being some 87%. This report also stated that the situation was no better than the previous survey some years earlier. "There is no evidence that budget performance of software projects has changed"[2]. These figures are depressingly familiar to IT managers and stand as an indictment of the global software industry. A survey by the International Software Benchmarking Standards Group reveals that the cost differential between companies purchasing similar software can be seven to one [3].

A more recent synopsis of a survey has been released by SPC [4] they summarise the top project planning weaknesses as:

- Poor contingency preparation
- Overestimating team productivity
- Inability to scope the project
- To meet schedule constraints
- Resource and skill availability
- Lack of continuous planning in response to scope changes

"Being unprepared for any of these threatens projects with derailment or delay [4]."

Faced with the responsibility of spending public tax dollars the IT management of the State Government of Victoria Australia decided to try and remedy the situation, at least as far as possible.

2. The Problem

Prior to its current practice the State Government in common with many other organisations insisted on fixed price contracts. Software suppliers' reaction to this policy was to adopt the practice of bidding a low price to win the contract, in the expectation that the users will propose a considerable number of changes during the development of the software. They then charge a high rate to incorporate these inevitable changes. Thus the aims of requiring fixed price bids – that of allowing line management to have confidence in its predicted costs and timescales – was defeated. The problem remains that whether using fixed price or cost and materials approaches to software acquisition, software costs have a tendency to rise rapidly as changes to the original specification cause the project scope to creep ever wider.

Line managers are managing departments whose business is not software development. Such Managers will generally lack a thorough understanding of the software development process. The consequence of this is that they have little control over these projects. The manager is seldom provided any certainty as to *what* will be delivered or *when* it will be delivered or the final *cost* of the delivered software. Additionally at the end of the project they have no real way of determining whether they received value-for-money, nor are they able to make realistic comparisons with similar projects.

Additionally when a software project is put out to tender the users prepare a document that contains the requirement of the system as they see it. All the companies bidding for the contract then respond with a proposal document that reflects the users stated requirements and incorporates suggestions that they contend will improve the end product. Once the contract is let the developers start the requirements gathering phase and essentially the users' specification of requirements is rewritten. This has therefore involved both the users and the bidding companies in often-considerable effort in writing the original tender and proposal documents and then redoing the whole thing again during the requirements gathering phase.

An analysis of the situation outlined above reveals that unlike projects in other disciplines such as small scale construction there is no objective measurement of Software. A general manager can look at and make sense of construction plans for say an office or workshop. The size and features of such a building are expressed in terms that can be understood. The building will have dimensions and a number of rooms, the rooms, will have power points and other facilities that can be easily understood. No such system exists with software; the terminology is confusing and developers often offer several options which the manager cannot envisage. Thus it is difficult for line managers to discriminate between proposals on grounds other than price. Most Governments and many organisations have a system of approved suppliers in order to attempt to ensure that the bidders will be high quality software developers. However these approved suppliers and reliance on fixed price alone rarely result in the development of software that meets the users needs in terms of either cost or functionality. It is perhaps appropriate to repeat the advice given by Capers Jones [6] when he warns that entering into a fixed price contracts without having determined the size of the work to be done (or at least allowing for that to happen in the contract) is a very hazardous undertaking. Indeed so hazardous is it that many large software companies expend a considerable amount of effort in client relationship management in order to prepare the client for any shortfall of expectation in the completed software, whether in terms of cost, quality or timescale. This practice of managing expectations is major diversion of project management activity, which might be better expended keeping the project under control.

3. The Solution

The solution that was adopted by the state government is the apparently simple idea of determining the size of the software solution in terms of function points. They encouraged managers to think – somewhat simplistically perhaps – of function points as being the equivalent to square metres in a construction project. Would you contract to build a house without knowing how many square metres it will contain? "Neither clients nor contractors should enter into development agreements without formal sizing of the work to be performed"[6]. They propose that when a contract is let the users publish a brief description of the software: what type it was, what the expected size would be and so on. Software companies then bid for the contract in terms of price per function point ($/FP).

The immediate advantage for both supplier and customer is that there is now no effort being wasted in the preparation of tender and proposal documents. There is of course a need for the software supplier to understand their own productivity and the factors that impinge upon it. A further benefit for both supplier and client is that *Southern*SCOPE is an effective method of highlighting requirements change. Scope creep is a major cause of projects overrunning budgets and failing to achieve the required quality or timescales. A typical rate of requirements change in a government project is given as 2.5% per month [6]. A rate of change of this order will soon result in an uncontrollable degree of expansion of the software that must be built. For commercial software the rate is given as 3.5% per month!

At first glance it is difficult to see how the use of function points benefits the manager – who has only a simple understanding of function points. At this point it is worth introducing the scope manager who is an integral and essential part of the *Southern*SCOPE method. The scope manager is a function point specialist and is responsible for determining the size of software at various stages in development. The scope manager has a powerful tool available from the International Software Benchmarking Standards Group (ISBSG). The ISBSG maintains a repository of project data, which may be consulted to determine typical price per function point. This is available on floppy disk and is reasonably simple to use. Thus the manager with advice from the scope manager can see if the proposals received are in a typical range, well above or well below. This allows a sensible decision to be made from the range of proposals. Once the requirements have been determined the software can be resized and the cost determined. The manager can now assess this and if it exceeds the available budget then it is possible to reduce the requirements until the system comes into budget. The manager needs the input of a scope manager so that the relative cost of competing requirements can be determined and prioritised in terms of the cost and utility to the users.

4. *Southern*SCOPE

The method proposed above has been developed over a number of years in the light of experience. And the method as it now stands is outlined below. The essential steps are:

- The project sponsor identifies that a need exists to acquire application software and prepares a Project Requirements document to define the project.
- The project sponsor engages an independent scope manager to perform a preliminary function point count (PFPC), and from this provide early estimates of cost and duration.
- The project sponsor invites proposals to satisfy the identified need, with the payment for the software based upon dollars per function point delivered.
- The project sponsor selects the best proposal and engages the successful developer.
- The development commences with a phase of analysis that produces a System Requirements Specification.
- The scope manager conducts a function point count on the System Requirements Specification. With adjustments to balance budget with requirements, this determines the baseline functionality for the software, and thus the remaining project budget.
- During the project, the project sponsor makes payment to the developer on the basis of software, or other measurable products, actually delivered. During this period, the scope manager helps determine the price impact of changes raised after the Requirements Specification.

The key difference between the *Southern*SCOPE method and the older fixed-price approach is the direct linking of the price to the unit of delivery [5]. Though the emphasis of the method is on the development of new software, it can also apply to projects that involve major additions of functionality (enhancements) to existing software.

However the role of the scope manager requires some explanation and is key to the successful operation of the *Southern*SCOPE method. The scope manager is an independent person with expertise in functional size measurement (function point analysis,) who also has experience in software project management. The scope manager conducts the preliminary function point count (PFPC) performed during project initiation, and then the baseline function point count (BFPC) of the requirements specification that sets the precise project budget. Throughout the project, the scope manager monitors any significant changes raised, evaluating their impact against the BFPC and advising each party of the implications of the changes.

The success of a ***Southern*SCOPE** project for **both** parties depends upon the independence of the scope manager. Though the project sponsor typically pays the scope manager's fees, it is important that the scope manager act independently to protect the interests of both project sponsor and developer.

5. Appropriate projects for the method

Does *Southern*SCOPE suit all software projects? The answer unfortunately is probably not, at the moment, though developments in Functional Size Measures [3] suggest that the situation is likely to change soon.

5.1. Software products used by government agencies

Typically the software that is used by government agencies falls into one of three categories. These categories are:

- Personal productivity (software that improves the productivity of individuals in their work e.g. word processors, spreadsheets, e-mail, drawing).

- Information infrastructure (software that supports information management needs fundamental to all organisations e.g. accounting and financial management, human resources and payroll, document management).
- Core agency operation (software that supports the core operations of the agency e.g. court case management, hazardous waste transport certificate management, training organisation funding application and disbursement).

The ***Southern*SCOPE** method most suits the acquisition of software for *information infrastructure* and *core agency operation*. It can work with both package customisation and custom development approaches to the provision of software.

5.2. Typical Software projects

Software projects in industry in general will themselves typically fall into one of five categories:

- Development of a new software product for business needs that did not previously exist, or were not previously met with software, e.g., the creation of software to support electricity trading when the UK government created a wholesale electricity market.
- Redevelopment of an existing software product using new technology, and probably also to meet new business needs, e.g., the creation of a web-based product ordering system to replace a mainframe-based ordering system.
- Purchase of a software package and subsequent development work to customise it to the specific business needs of the customer, e.g., the purchase of an enterprise resource-planning package such as PeopleSoft, SAP.
- Enhancement of an existing system to meet new and additional business needs through additional functionality. For example, the enhancement of a payroll system to track superannuation payments.
- Adaptation of existing functionality to fit it to a changing business environment, without adding significant new functionality. For example changing a product ordering system to handle the introduction of General Sales Tax (Recently introduced into Australia equivalent to VAT).

The ***Southern*SCOPE** method works well for the first four of the five categories of software project listed.

Taking an alternative perspective, the ***Southern*SCOPE** method works well on software projects with the following characteristics:

- There exists a well-accepted technique for measuring the functionality of the delivered software.
- The project is able to limit the number of changes to functionality occurring between completion of the requirements specification and delivery of fully functional software. *Note* that all software project management methodologies have difficulty keeping within fixed budgets when there are high numbers of changes during software construction.
- Completing the project within a controlled budget is of primary importance.
- The requirements of the project can be documented with sufficient precision for functional size measurement.

All information infrastructure support software has these characteristics, and most software for core business operations also has them.

At present IFPUG function points have the highest level of acceptance across the Australian software industry; MKII Function Points have a large following in the United Kingdom and IFPUG is acceptable in most European Union Countries. However, these FSM's do not measure with acceptable accuracy the functionality of all types of software.

The new FSM, COSMIC-FFP has started to be used and is providing a good sizing method for use with real-time, scientific, process control, infrastructure and telecommunications software. This new method will, for the first time allow the consistent measurement of size across a wider range of software application types. If this new method is allied to the *Southern*SCOPE technique then the days of software development becoming out of control may be limited.

6. Case Study – Business Licence Information Service

In 2000, the Business Licence Information Service (BLIS) was a finalist in the National Awards for Excellence in Information Technology. BLIS also took out the Victorian Gold Award in the Government Technology Productivity Awards. Contributing to the success of the BLIS Internet and call-centre service was the use of the *Southern*SCOPE method in its development.

6.1. What is BLIS all about?

Business Victoria (part of the Department of State and Regional Development) commissioned the redevelopment of BLIS to operate the site as a one-stop shop licence inquiry facility that provides information to business on all Commonwealth, Victorian and local licences required. When you use the BLIS service you can nominate any business activity and find out which licences, permits and regulations are required to operate in Victoria. Accessible via the Internet, BLIS provides you with information on starting a business and on specific business activities. A call centre also supports the BLIS website.

6.2. How was BLIS developed?

The BLIS website was built using Lotus Notes technology which enables one database to hold information from all levels of government. Because keeping up-to-date information is so important, BLIS includes Internet-based distributed authoring. This feature allows more than 150 Victorian agency representatives and approximately 80 local government representatives to maintain their own licence information. However in order to maintain data quality, there is a Content Quality Manager coordinating the efforts of agency staff in maintaining their licence data. BLIS is a second-generation software system (the first system was installed in 1988), which began, in its current form in July 1999. Redevelopment of BLIS started in 1998 with the preparation of a Request for Tender. At this time, the project engaged a scope manager, who measured the first system at 250 function points. The additional functionality for the new BLIS was measured at an additional 200 function points. This information was included in the request for tender, which stated that BLIS would be built on Lotus Notes, with no more than 500 function points, and requested tenderers were to provide a `dollar per function point' price.

Work started on the BLIS website with 10 weeks set aside to analyse the requirements. The scope manager measured the signed-off Requirements Specification at 452 function points. As Dr. Grahame Jackson, Director of Electronic Service Delivery and project sponsor commented, "function points gave me an element of control I don't think many people commissioning software have." This project size resulted in an acceptable total budget. At the beginning of the design and construction phase, Dr Jackson made a commitment not to vary anything on the requirements specification. The developers would build to the specification, and the delivered software would be the foundation for future enhancements. "We saw some changes that we might make", reported Dr Jackson, "but we decided to add them later rather than muck around with change processes." On completion of the project, the scope manager measured the delivered software at 475 function points. This was less than a 5% increase on the project budget. The resulting website and project budget performance combined to result in a successful project.

6.3. Why did it work?

Setting a limit at project initiation of 500 function points worth of functionality ensured that, despite not having a precise specification and variations to the functional size during the project development, the forecasted budget was met. This is highly unusual, as most budgets set at project initiation are unreasonably optimistic. The *Southern*SCOPE method gave the project sponsor a mechanism to control the budget, but still obtain the functionality required in the project. Helen Robinson, the BLIS Content Quality Manager, noted that the *Southern*SCOPE method allowed Business Victoria to meet their business objectives in a creative way, but also within a controlled budget.

7. Case Study – Student Management System

In November 1998, several Victorian TAFEs implemented a new Student Management System. The system had 5000 function points and a $2 million budget. Despite its size, the project was completed on schedule and on budget. This is an impressive achievement (only 9% of large software projects achieve this and almost 60% of large software project do not complete at all [1]. The Student Management System was completed in less than 13 months and project managers strictly observed the 'dollar per function point' principle to ensure it was completed on budget.

7.1. Student management system in a nutshell

The Student Management System is an integrated approach to managing student information. The system handles information such as:

- Applications to enrol;
- Collection of fees;
- Student satisfaction;
- Class scheduling;
- Student and lecturer allocation;
- Calculation of performance measures;

Student information is core to the operation of TAFEs, so a key role for the system is holding a consolidated view of all student information. The system reduces the duplication of student information maintained by staff.

7.2. The student management system project

With the assistance of a Scope manager, the Office of Post-compulsory Education, Training and Employment (PETE) prepared a Request for Tender. The Scope manager measured the preliminary system specification at 4300 function points. With large projects often going significantly over budget and over-time, the Request for Tender document issued asked for tenders on a 'dollar per function point' basis. It also stated requirements that would influence the price, such as the use of client/server architecture operating on UNIX or Microsoft Windows™ NT Server. Several companies submitted tenders, with a three to one range between the lowest and highest '$/FP' tendered. PETE chose the company that offered a solution based on an existing software package at a price of $390 per function point.

While the chosen package solution provided 50% of the required functionality, the project still required an analysis phase. The analysts together with the users reviewed the package documentation and analysed the necessary requirements for a new function point count. The Function Point Count came in at 5000 FP, which kept the project under its budget of $2 million. Subsequent function point measurements helped PETE prioritise the functionality, identifying high-cost functionality that had low value to the users. PETE's project manager, commented that "Function points helped tightly monitor scope creep, making sure that we kept the project under budget, but still delivering the most important functionality".

On the advice of the Scope Manager, it was decided not to use function point analysis to measure changes. Instead, the project used the normal change management process of raising changes with the developer, receiving quotes and deciding whether to proceed.

7.3. Lessons learned

PETE project managers learned several lessons about the '$/FP' method:

- Using the method provided more for the budget dollar, as it provided a clear productivity benchmark to evaluate suppliers. More importantly, it allowed PETE to prioritise budget expenditure to high-value functionality and drop low-value functionality from the budget.
- There was less difficulty for the client and supplier because function points provide an objective measure to control the main factors influencing budget - the amount of functionality the developer was to provide.
- They suggested that package customisation projects would benefit from refining the single dollar per function point figure into several figures based on a classification of the function points. This would make the budget changes that result from scope changes fairer, and make it easier to apply the 'dollar per function point' method to change management.

8. Review of Software Charged by Unit of Delivery (SCUD)

The State Government of Victoria has commissioned an independent survey, conducted by Sage Technology, an Australian consultancy. The review is generally favourable.

However some difficulty was recorded in the area of costing changes. This conflict resulted because all developers and scope managers questioned the ability of IFPUG function points to measure changes with sufficient accuracy for a fair application of the $/FP price to changes. Function points were useful in pricing new functionality added after requirements specification, but had little value in pricing changes to functionality already specified. This is because the IFPUG technique is very effective at providing a macro-view of software functionality (and thus effort), but doesn't apply well at the micro-view of typical software changes. This difficulty would be obviated by the use of the NEFPUG enhancement measurement method or by using either MKII FPA or the new COSMIC-FFP method.

Another problem with the SCUD method's ability to manage change is how changes may impact on the validity of the agreed $/FP price. The method's ability to manage change depends upon how well the function point measurement of a subset of the functionality correlates to the cost of delivering that subset. Scope managers and developers have stated that when the functionality of a software product is divided into subsets, the one $/FP price cannot apply to all subsets. In effect, software products typically comprise cheap-to-construct function points and expensive-to-construct function points.[1] The project's $/FP price depends upon the ratio of this functionality in the complete software product.

Developers quickly become aware of this problem, and it contributes to their resistance to the method. The causes of this problem are several, including the technology necessary to construct the specific subsets of functionality, the complexity existing in software artifacts

[1] This two-category distinction is totally arbitrary; some scope managers are exploring four and five categories.

that function points don't measure, and other factors that influence the \$/FP price, such as the team size and the client organisation type.

As a consequence, the application of a single \$/FP price to all the function points in a software product depends upon the following constraints There is:

- No major change to the ratio between cheap and expensive functionality during the project.[2]
- No change to the technology used to construct the software in the course of the project.
- No major change in the productivity factors that influence the \$/FP point price.

9. Conclusions

9.1. Benefits

The *Southern*SCOPE method appears to provide software projects with the following benefits:

- They are highly likely to finish within a controlled budget, which is a budget based on a high-quality requirements specification plus a 10% contingency for changes.
- They are more likely than typical software projects to meet their objectives and achieve all of the important requirements.
- Customers received good value. They received \$/FP point prices 23% better than current industry best practice. In turn, industry best practice prices are generally half those of typical industry practice.
- The method will not stop either the customer or the developer trying to exploit the other party, but when applied well, will make it harder for them to do so.

9.2. Issues

The method in its current form appears to have the following issues:

- A low level of usage probably the result of a lack of awareness of the benefits of the method compared to the typical software project.
- It doesn't appear to result in better schedule estimates or shorter delivery times.
- Developers are reluctant to use of the method, probably because of a lack of knowledge and a loss of control. They will use it if customers require them to.
- Scope managers and developers must stay alert to the constraints on the validity of the \$/FP point price if developers' interests are to be protected.
- For managing the changes to requirements and project scope that occur during design and construction, the SCUD method doesn't provide major advantages over current best practice.

However of particular note is that:

Customers who used the SCUD method valued its benefits highly, and most would use the method again on an appropriate project.

The method may be a new best practice for software project management. The performance of the software industry would probably improve significantly if this approach to purchasing custom software was used whenever appropriate.

Using the estimate of \$50 million software expenditure within Victorian government and setting a target of 80% of Victorian government projects using the SCUD method, the potential savings on the purchase of custom-built software is at least \$9 million per year.

---

[2] An alternative approach to resolve this problem is to have multiple \$ per function point prices in the project based upon categorization of the functionality.

Alternatively, the government could receive 30% more functionality for the current level of expenditure.

10. For more information

For more information on the BLIS Channel http://www.business.channel.vic.gov.au/

For more information on the *Southern*SCOPE method and to find out how to manage your custom built software development project on time and within budget visit the Multimedia Victoria website at http://www.mmv.vic.gov.au/southernscope

11. References

[1] Jones, C. *Conflict and Litigation Between Software Clients and Developers,* SPR Technical Paper, WWW.spr.com

[2] SPC, *A Survey of 1000 Projects*, Software Productivity Centre, http://www.spc.ca/prrp

[3] Computer Weekly, Wide Disparity in Bespoke Software costs, Computer Weekly, 05 Oct. 2000 London

[4] Standish Group, *The CHAOS Report*, The Standish Group, www.standishgroup.com/visitor/chaos

[5] Wright T. *Acquisition of Software Charged by Unit of Delivery*, Technical Report, Multimedia Victoria, Victorian Department of State and Regional Development, terry.wright@mmv.vic.gov.au

Project screening: How to say "No" without hurting your career or your company

Eduardo Miranda

Abstract

Despite the large number of failed projects due to unrealistic schedules, their sponsors continue to push for development times that bear no relation to the productivity of their organisations, in the hope that next time things will be different. This paper postulates, that is possible to discriminate a challenging project from a death march one by comparing its footprint or profile to the constraints imposed on it.

1. Introduction

Could you succeed at a project that would require you to:

- Bring together a team of 50 people in a month and a half?
- Integrate 100 interfaces in 40 days? and
- Complete more than 30 tasks, all of them on-time?

Although nobody benefits from failed projects, their sponsors continue to push for development times that bear no relation to the productivity of their organisations, in the hope that next time things will be different. In the meantime, developers, out of inexperience or fear, continue to agree and sometimes even foster unforgivable timetables. Reasonable schedules can only be attained if there is an equal understanding among all project stakeholders about the magnitude and complexity of the work to be done.

The three questions above focus on essential and highly visible attributes understandable to all project stakeholders: Can a project team be put together, can all the pieces be made to work in concert, and can a large number of tasks be consistently finished on-time? If a developing organisation is not able or willing to fully staff a project, if the number of people is just too big for the team to jell on the time available, if there is no room to recover from a couple of late tasks, or if the are too many interfaces to integrate and keep under control, the project is not a *"challenge"*, it's a *"Death March project"*[1].

The idea behind project screening, is to compare the characteristics of project you are about to take on, to the profiles of several idealised projects whose staff requirements, interface complexity and on-time probability can be calculated using few data and common sense expressions, and to use these profiles to decide whether you have a reasonable chance of success or not. The comparison between the requirements of an idealised and a real project is a valid one, since the distance that separates a *challenging* project from a *death march* project, is not 1 or 2 people or whether the probability of being on-time is 74% versus 75.5%, it is rather in the order of 25 to 40% of whatever a plausible estimate is.

The need for a method to supplement the expert judgement with some estimators of the true project complexity, has its root in the inability of the human mind to deal with non-linear phenomena[2], which as will see, result from just breaking down the system into one more subsystem to do more in parallel or from adding a couple of people to speed-up the development process.

The present article explains how these profiles can be constructed and gives an example of how they could be used.

2. The Project Mechanics

Process improvement is a win-win strategy, but usually it does not happen overnight. Neither does it yield the quantum-leap productivity increases many projects require to bridge the gap between what is wanted and what can be afforded. Therefore, other things being equal, the bigger the product or the shorter the time, the more people are needed.

Once the methods, tools and technical approach have been decided, there are only three basic trade-off a project manager can resort to:

- Time-Resources
- Time-Functionality
- Resources-Functionality

By extending the development time, the headcount requirement is reduced. Conversely, by adding more resources the development time is shortened. But as shown by Figure 1, the number of communication channels grows in geometric proportion to the team size, so as people are added to the project, the communication and co-ordination needs of the team increase, taking away part of the productivity contributed by each individual. This law of diminishing returns prevents the unconditional swap of months by people[3].

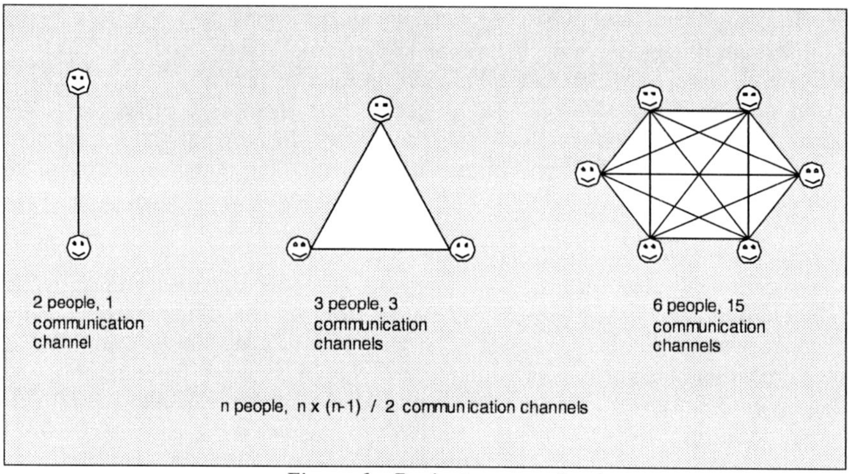

Figure 1 - Project communication

In reality, not everybody in a project communicates with everybody else. As illustrated by Figure 2, there are clusters of people where practically everyone communicates with everyone else and there are "gatekeepers" which communicates across clusters. It is not difficult to conclude, that these clusters correspond to people working closely together, for example into common subsystems. Therefore, a more realistic approximation of the number of channels in a project is given by the mixture of intra- and inter-team interactions as shown by Figure 3.

As we will see, the increase in communications overhead is not the only undesirable side effect of an increase in team size. It also affects the integration effort and the project's on-time probability.

3. Project Profiling

A project profile is an abstraction or idealisation of the characteristics of a project. As the purpose here, is to quickly evaluate the feasibility and the risk of a project, I chose to profile a project in terms of the approximate number of people that will be involved, the number of interfaces it will need to handle and its probability of being completed on-time. Obviously, other profiles are possible, but one that includes these three variables is certainly appropriate for our stated purpose.

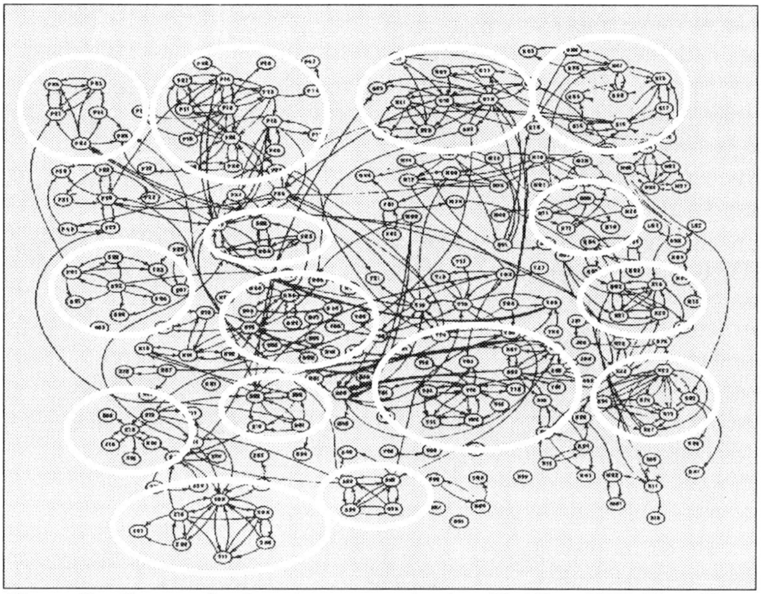

Figure 2 – Communications in an organisation, T. Allen, MIT, Class Notes

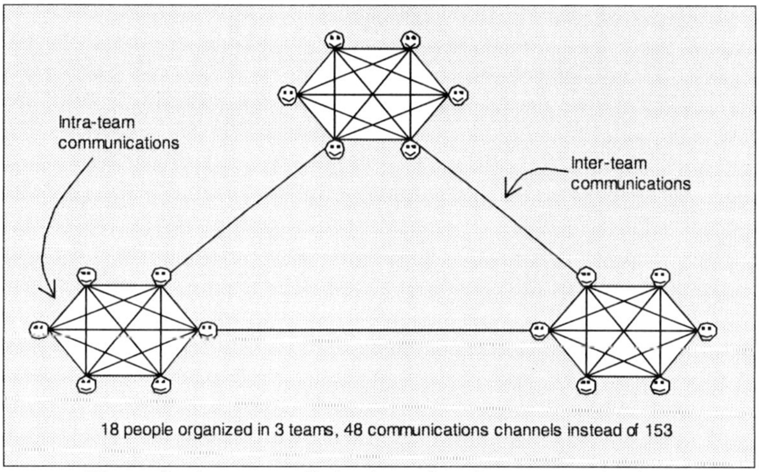

Figure 3 - A more realistic view of project communications

Paraphrasing J. Forrester[4], the impossibility of not knowing the exact values or relationships between all variables, should not preclude as from building useful models which could help us better understand complex problems and make better decisions. A project profile does not need to be exact to be useful, it will not be used for planning or tendering, it suffices that it answers the questions we post to it more precisely and accurately than alternatives methods and that is equally understandable to practitioners and laymen.

The following paragraphs define the calculations I chose to build the project profile. Three parameters: Uncertainty Assessment, Number of Subsystems and Communication Overhead are used to capture project-specific information.

The **UncertaintyAssessment**, express the variability that could be expected in the completion of a task, based on common risk factors. See Table 1 for a definition of common risks. A low value of this parameter means that the task is likely to be completed on time. The value should be jointly estimated by the project sponsor, the project manager and the system architect.

The **NoSubsystems** is a technical parameter, which reflects the breakdown of the system into cohesive parts as decided by the system architect.

The **CommOverhead** parameter captures the effort lost per interaction among members of the same or different teams. For example, if one engineer spends on average 30 minutes every time he communicates with one of his colleagues, the communication overhead parameter will be about 6%.

When looking at the specific calculations, please bear in mind that these expressions do not pretend to define, the probably un-calculable "true" value of the attribute, but rather to express meaningful relations between: project size, project schedule, staffing levels, integration complexity and on-time probabilities.

Table 1 - Uncertainty Assessment Table

	Risk Factor		**Prob. of not completing the task on-time (%)**
	Initial uncertainty value[1]		5
If applicable	New product development	+	[2.5, 5]
If applicable	New technology / process being used	+	[2.5, 5]
If applicable	People capability / experience	+	[2.5, 5]
If applicable	Multiple organisations involved	+	[2.5, 5]
If applicable	Own risk factors	+	[2.5, 5]
	Uncertainty Assessment (%)	=	Σ risk factors

3.1. Project Staff

Using a simple productivity number as a starting point, the approximate number of people needed by a project could be calculated using the equations shown in Figure 4.

3.2. Internal Interfaces

The number of Internal Interfaces is used as a surrogate for the integration and configuration management needed to put the system together. Its calculation is shown in Figure 5. As illustrated in Figure 6, for every combination of system size and development schedule, there is an optimal **NoSubsystems** that minimises the number of internal interfaces.

[1] These values could be used as guidelines, but they have no other meaning.

$$ProjectStaff = NominalHeadcount + IntraTeamAdj + InterTeamAdj$$
$$NominalHeadcount = \frac{ApplicationSize}{Productivity * Schedule}$$
$$TeamSize = \frac{NominalHeadCount}{NoSubsystems}$$
$$IntraTeamAdj = \frac{TeamSize * (TeamSize - 1)}{2} * CommOverhead$$
$$InterTeamAdj = \frac{TeamSize * NoSubsystems * (NoSubsystems - 1)}{2} * CommOverhead$$

Figure 4 - Team size calculations

$$InternalInterfaces = NoSubsystems * ModuleInterfaces + SubsystemInterfaces$$
$$ModuleInterfaces = \frac{TeamSize * (TeamSize - 1)}{2}$$
$$SubsystemInterfaces = \frac{NoSubsystems * (NoSubsystems - 1)}{2}$$

Figure 5 – Interface calculations

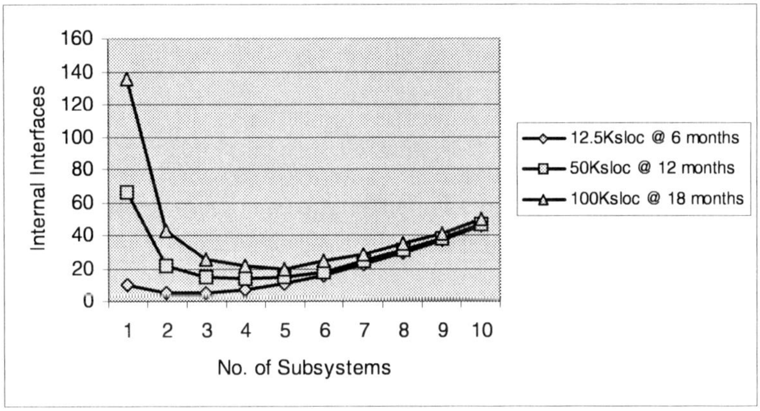

Figure 6 - Impact of system partitioning on the number of internal interfaces

3.3. On-time Probability

The On-time Probability, is a subjective probability reflecting the likelihood of completing the project in a time not exceeding, by more than 10% the scheduled development time, that is for a project scheduled to be 12 months long, to finish on or before 13.2 months. Figure 7 explain the meaning of the **OnTimeProbability** attribute. As with the other attributes, the **OnTimeProbability** should not be taken literally, but as an indication of the level of uncertainty to be expected in a project as the result of estimation errors, productivity assumptions, technology instability, etc.

The asymmetry of the triangular distribution chosen, reflects the existence of a minimum time beyond which it is almost impossible to complete the project, and the fact that there are very few things which could be done to shorten the schedule which are not discounted for at the outset of the project, while many that could go wrong are usually not accounted for[5]. The triangular distribution also captures the fact, that in a software development project most

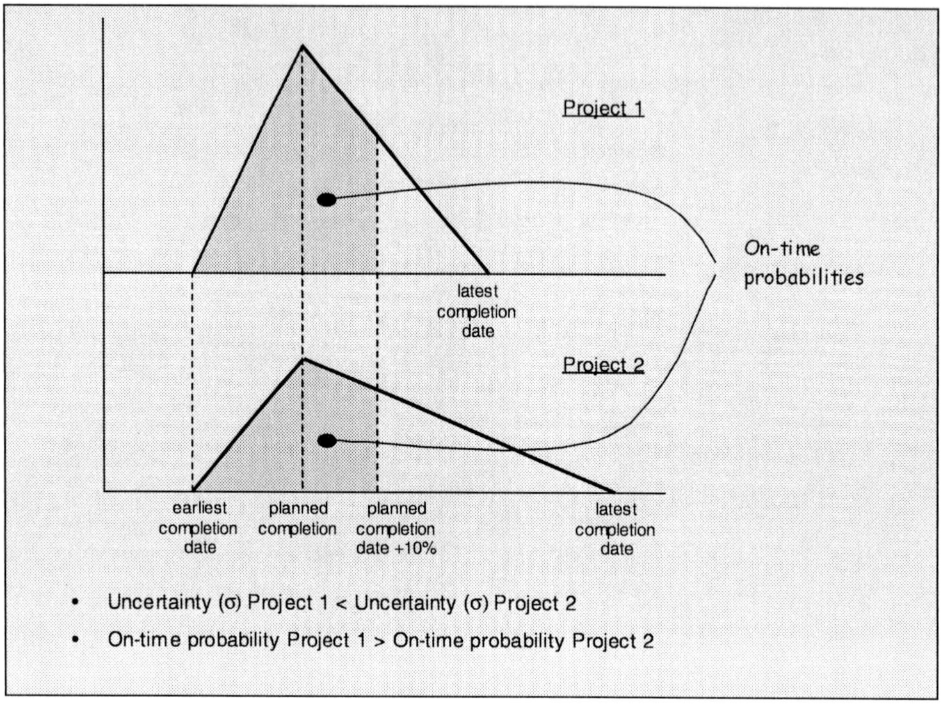

Figure 7 – The meaning of the OnTimeProbability

tasks' duration are not independent, but rather correlated through factors like complexity and team capability, so adding-up tasks' duration, does not result in a nice bell-shaped curve but rather on some skewed distribution that mimics Murphy's law!

Figure 8 depicts the work organisation selected for the calculation of the project's **OnTimeProbability**, and Figure 9 the calculations themselves.

The standard deviation[2] of the tasks is assumed proportional to the following factors:

- Task's duration;
- UncertaintyAssessment;
- NoSubsystems in the case of the design activity;
- ProjectStaff in the case of the development; and
- InternalInterfaces in the case of the Integration

Each of the last three driving factors contributes 1%[3] of the task duration, times the magnitude of the factor, to its variability. For example, a 10 person project, lasting 12 months and having 3 subsystems will have an intrinsic variability of 2.7 days in design, 14.6 days in development and 19.1 in integration. Please notice that variability does not mean adding days to the tasks' duration, but rather that the duration of the task is a random variable whose actual value has a high probability, around 97%, of being comprised in the four σ interval existing between the earliest completion date and the latest completion date[4] of the task or project.

---

[2] σ Is the Greek letter used to denote the standard deviation of a random variable.

[3] This is a magic number. On its own it looks quite harmless, but when multiplied by the number of internal interfaces or the number of people in the project, it produces amazing results.

[4] Chebyshev's Theorem states that $P(|X-\mu| \geq k\sigma) \leq 1/k^2$. Although this might not be a tight bound in all cases, it is surprising that such a bound can be found to hold for all possible discrete and continuous distributions.

4. The Project Profiles Table

The Project Profiles Table (PPT), tabulates a number of project profiles for common combinations of project size, productivity and schedule, see Table 2. The PPT also includes references to previous developments carried out by the organisation to be used as size and productivity clues. For example, Project "Y" size was 25 KSLOC[5] while Project "Z" was 75 KSLOC with productivity in the order of 500 and 250 KSLOC/MM respectively.

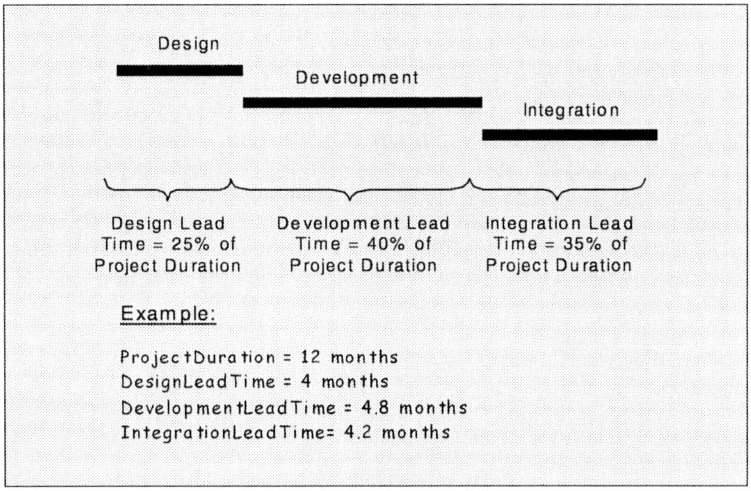

Figure 8 - Project model

$$OntimeProbability = 1 - \frac{(LatestCompletion - PlannedCompletion + 10\%)^2}{(LatestCompletion - EarliestCompletion) * (LatestCompletion - PlannedCompletion)}$$

$$EarliestCompletion = PlannedCompletion - \sigma_{Project}$$

$$LatestCompletion = PlannedCompletion + 3 * \sigma_{Project}$$

$$\sigma_{Project} = \sqrt{\sigma^2_{Design} + \sigma^2_{Development} + \sigma^2_{Integration}}$$

$$\sigma_{Design} = DesignLeadTime * (UncertaintyAssessment + NoSubsystems * .01)$$

$$\sigma_{Development} = DevelopmentLeadTime * (UncertaintyAssessment + ProjectStaff * .01)$$

$$\sigma_{Integration} = IntegrationLeadTime * (UncertaintyAssessment + InternalInterfaces * .01)$$

Figure 9 - Probability calculations

The PPT provides project stakeholders the means to screen-out death march projects and produce ballpark estimates by just looking at the attributes tabulated in it. The PPT is not an estimation tool, it is designed to be a negotiation tool and help you give an answer to your boss, when he or she request a "quick estimate" for this new hot project, that the Director of Finance or the marketing guys have just requested

5. Using the Project Profile Table

To illustrate the use of the PPT, a hypothetical dialogue between John, a Product Manager, and Caroline, a Project Manager in charge of developing a new product, will be used.

[5] The size units should reflect whatever is used by the organisation, be it: SLOC, Function Points or Object Points. The key is understandability.

John – *"We need to have the new software ready by the end of the year"*

Caroline – *"That leaves us with only 6 months to complete the project"*

John – *"That's our market window"*

Caroline – *"Judging from the product spec, the new software is going to be bigger than Application Y and smaller than Z, let's say around 50 KSLOC, so if we want to have it in six months, with the resources available, we will have to perform at least as good as we did in Project Y."*

John – *"What about putting more people into it? We need to get the new release ready for December 23rd."*

Caroline (looking at Table 1) – *"We'll need around 22 people. We could steal some of them from another project, but we still have to test and integrate roughly 47 internal interfaces, and our overall probability of success will be about 43%, less than 50/50 chance. Do you want to bet our bonus and, probably our careers on that?"*

John – " *What is the basis of your estimate?"*

Caroline – *"I am assuming we break the system down into 5 or 6 subsystems that we can develop in parallel, and that there is not a lot of unknowns, let's say around 15% due to problems with the new midleware and some changes in marketing."*

John – *"So, what do you propose?"*

Caroline – *"Well, we either perform twice as better as Project Y by putting our best people into it, I think we could do somehow better, but I doubt we can double it, or we can cut the software size down to the 25-30 KSLOC range. In both cases we' ll need around 11 people and our overall probability of success will be about 53%"*

John – *"It doesn't look good, does it? ...."*

Caroline – *"If we could trim some gold-plated features, and put our best people, I would feel much more confident."*

John – *"OK, will do. But we better get started, you go do the detailed planning, while I go to talk to the marketing guys, we are already one hour late!"*

Table 2 - Project Profile Table, Uncertainty Assessment = 15%, No. of Subsystems = 5, Communication Overhead =10%, the highlighted values are used on the example bellow.

	Schedule & Productivity	Size **25**	Project "Y"		Size **50**			Size **75**	Project "Z"	
	6 months	Proj. Staff	Internal Interfaces	On time probability	Proj. Staff	Internal Interfaces	On time probability	Proj. Staff	Internal Interfaces	On time probability
	250	**22**	47	43%	**50**	235	30%	**83**	657	27%
Proj. Y	500	**11**	17	53%	**22**	47	43%	**35**	115	35%
	1000	**6**	11	58%	**11**	17	53%	**16**	28	48%
	2000	**3**	11	59%	**6**	11	58%	**8**	12	56%
	12 months									
	250	**11**	17	53%	**22**	47	43%	**35**	115	35%
	500	**6**	11	58%	**11**	17	53%	**16**	28	48%
	1000	**3**	11	59%	**6**	11	58%	**8**	12	56%
	2000	**2**	11	60%	**3**	11	59%	**4**	11	59%
	18 months									
Proj. Z	250	**7**	11	57%	**15**	25	49%	**22**	47	43%
	500	**4**	11	59%	**7**	11	57%	**11**	17	53%
	1000	**2**	11	60%	**4**	11	59%	**6**	11	58%
	2000	**1**	11	60%	**2**	11	60%	**3**	11	59%

The use of the PPT could be complemented with that of two other tables (Table 1 and 3), which add objectivity to the process:

- The "Uncertainty Assessment Table" and
- The "Go-ahead Decision Table".

These two tables provide simple heuristics about how to quantify risk factors and action guidelines for those deciding the birth of a project.

The numbers on the Uncertainty Assessment Table express the probability of not completing individual tasks on-time due to common risk factors. The use of very small probabilities makes it difficult for anyone to disagree with them in isolation. The surprise usually comes when they are combined and compounded throughout a large number of tasks.

The Go-ahead Decision Table is read from left to right along the grey scales until a conclusion is reached, i.e. "Go-ahead" or "Renegotiate the project". The conditions contained in each column under the headings "People", "Internal Interfaces" and "On-time Probability" should be asked and answered using the values provided by the PPT for the project being screened. For example, if the PPT specifies a staff of 35 people, the questions are: Do I have 35 people available to work on this project? Can I make them work as a team in six months?, etc.

Table 3 - Go-ahead guidelines

People	Internal Interfaces	On-time Probability	Criticality of delivery date	Action
Have resources Able to build team Able to manage team Enough leaders to co-ordinate	Able to manage Able to test Able to integrate	> 50%		Go-ahead
		35 < p <=50%	High	Renegotiate Schedule Reduce Functionality Establish contingency plans Improve productivity
			Low	Go-ahead
		p <=35 %		Renegotiate Schedule Reduce Functionality Improve productivity
	No to any of the above			Renegotiate Schedule Reduce Functionality Improve productivity
No to any of the above				Renegotiate Schedule Reduce Functionality Improve productivity

6. Summary

The John and Caroline story has a happy ending, but it's not always like that. Too many careers, personal lives, and businesses have been hurt because of unrealistic expectations. By promoting a mutual understanding between project stakeholders about the complexity and magnitude of the job to be done, the PPT helps project managers and sponsors avoid committing to impossible schedules.

In putting together a PPT for your organisation, privilege simplicity and visibility over unnecessary and unattainable accuracy. Remember that the miscalculations at the root of a Death March project are those off by more than 25 percent.

Taking into consideration all the simplifications made in calculating team sizes, number of internal interfaces and on-time probabilities, the PPT could be regarded as a very favourable scenario. Therefore, if you do not feel comfortable with the numbers shown in it, reality will not make the job any easier. Good luck with your next project.

7. Acknowledgements

Thanks to Sylvain Lemire, Sylvain Loranger, Gaetano Lombardi and Tamara Keating for their comments and insight.

8. References

[1] Yourdon, E., Death March, The Complete Software Developer's Guide to Surviving "Mission Impossible" Projects, Prentice-Hall, 1997
[2] Doner, D., The Logic of Failure, Addison-Wesley, 1996
[3] Brooks, F., The Mythical Man-Month, Addison–Wesley, 1975
[4] Forrester, J.W., Industrial Dynamics, The MIT Press, 1961
[5] Grey, S., Practical Risk Assessment for Project Management, S. Grey, John Willey & Sons, 1995

Software project measurement using Function Point: a continuous improvement

Stefano Fabrizi[1]

Abstract

Banca d'Italia has been one of the early users of the Function Points Analysis (FPA) in Italy and one of the promoters of the Gruppo Utenti Fuction Points Italia (GUFPI) that is the Italian User Group on Function Points. The FPA key success factor has been an uninterrupted monitoring and maintenance of the "Banca d'Italia FP counting guide lines". This paper describes the Banca d'Italia experience during the last ten years and provides a descriptions of the actual works related to the use of the new software development methodologies and the new technologies.

1. Introduction

The Banca d'Italia is the Italian central bank. The powers invested in the central bank enable it to exercise a controlling and guiding influence over banking activities in the field of payment services.

The Information and Communication Technology in the Banca d'Italia is a fundamental instrumental asset since the early '60s. In the late '80s, a massive outsourcing of software product development activities was decided to satisfy a growing ICT demand. In order to manage and control the production process a wide metric system was adopted and the Function Point Analysis (FPA) was one of the critical success factor [1].

2. The past

2.1. The software development methodology

In the initial step, the outsourcing process was supported by the classic "waterfall" methodology, using the DeMarco [2] approach (see fig. 1).

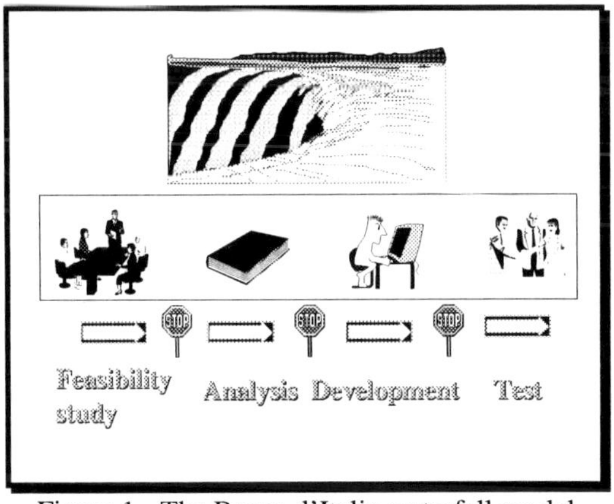

Figure 1 - The Banca d'Italia waterfall model

[1] The views expressed in the article are those of the author and do not involve the responsibility of the Bank.

This was a good starting point to standardise the dialogue between the Banca d'Italia personnel and the software houses.

But also the problems were soon evident. The time pressure involved an overlap between the analysis, development and testing phases. In other words, is impossible to put "start-to-end" relations between the life cycle activities.

Furthermore, the methodology was applied the same way to every project (see fig. 2). For simple applications the cost related to the methodology use wasn't acceptable.

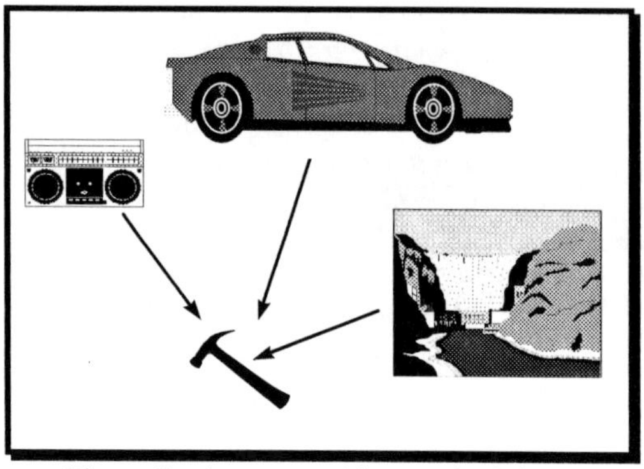

Figure 2 - A non sensitive methodology

2.2. The outsourcing approach

During the past Banca d'Italia used to draw up single contract for every project. So, the partnership with the supplier finished at the end of the software development cycle.

Considering that Banca d'Italia isn't a private company and that normally it calls 4/5 suppliers for every tenders, a single applications was developed and enhanced by different software houses.

2.3. The Banca d'Italia way to the FPA

We started using Function Point (FP) only for new software development project, referring to the 3.2 version of the IFPUG Counting Practice Manual.

Banca d'Italia also defined specific "guide lines" that allow project managers to recognise the single Function Type in the software development life cycle milestones (see fig. 3).

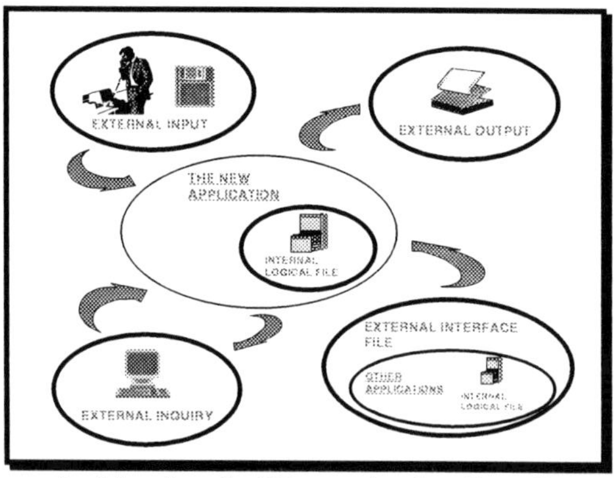

Figure 3 - Mapping the FP onto the data flow diagrams

This solution worked well with new software projects but gave some problems during enhancement activities.

3. The present

3.1. The software development methodology

The actual software development methodology always refers to the "waterfall model" but has high degrees of parallelism.

Banca d'Italia adopts a kind of incremental model that is also the way to allows time pressure. The methodology provides mechanisms to manage the different priorities between the user functions [3].

Finally, we have specific standards for ERP and Data Warehouse projects.

3.2. The outsourcing approach

Today Banca d'Italia has three year development and enhancement contracts.

Every single contract is related to an application domain and provides a maximum number of FP for new development activities and a maximum number of FP for maintenance activities.

Every activity is estimated in terms of FP and its cost is "a priori" established.

3.3. The Banca d'Italia way to the FPA

We use the 4.0 IFPUG Counting Practice Manual (instead of the 4.1) [4], because there is an official Italian version.

We have also some guide lines to estimate:

- enhancement projects;
- ERP development activities;
- distributed applications.

The last problem was hard to solve. The only way to consider the complexity of a distributed application with FPA is the maximum evaluation of a single "General System Characteristic (GSC)". But its tribute to the FP number is +/- 2,5% and sometimes this isn't sufficient.

So, the Banca d'Italia guide-lines provide a standard to "adjust" the "Value Adjustment Factor (VAF)" for distributed applications.

4. The future

4.1. The software development methodology

The Banca d'Italia is now working to a "back bone with traffic-lights" methodology.

Some software development life cycle phases are destined to remain (e.g. User Requirements), because they are technologically independent.

Vice versa the use of specific technology will insert a "proprietary paths" in the "back bone" (see fig. 4).

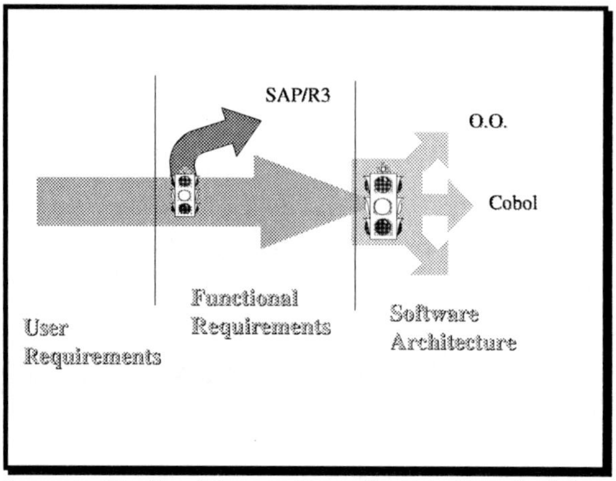

Figure 4 - The "back bone with traffic-lights" methodology

4.2. The outsourcing approach

The actual three years contracts satisfy the Banca d'Italia demands in terms of:

- flexibility;
- dead lines;
- economy.

Banca d'Italia is now testing a full outsourcing service for non-critical applications. In this context we will probably have to consider other metrics to place side by side to the FP [5].

4.3. The Banca d'Italia way to the FPA

Actually the complexity is located in the system architecture instead of in the applications.

Logical and physical tiers of hardware, communication software and system software (generally, "technical software") are growing up.

But these elements are difficult (or impossible ?) to consider with Function Point Analysis, and the GSC are not sufficient to evaluate their weight

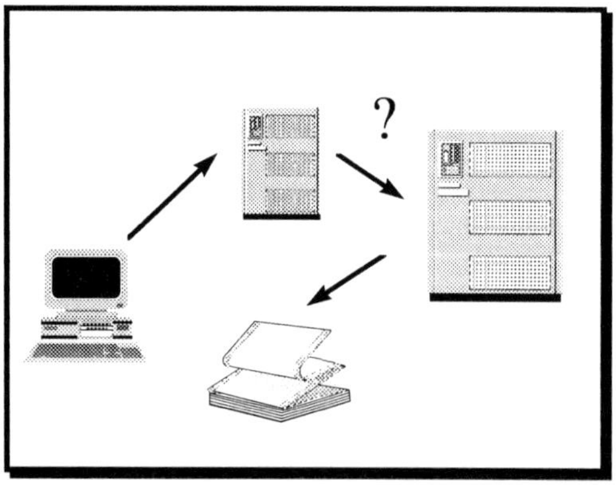

Figure 5 - The measure of non-functional software

The appearance on the market of a new functional measurement method denoted as Cosmic Full Function Point, will potentially reconcile the two parties (functional and technical features) [6].

5. References

[1] Fabrizi S., Minnucci C., Russo D.,"Software Metrics: Banca d'Italia Experience", Proceedings of 6th “European Software Cost Modelling Conference (ESCOM 95), Rolduc (The Netherlands), 1995.

[2] DeMarco, T.,“Controlling Software Projects”,Prentice-Hall 1982.

[3] Royce W., “Software Project Management - A Unified Process”, Addison-Wesley, 1998.

[4] IFPUG, “Counting Practices Manual rel. 4.1”, International Function Point Users Group, 1999

[5] Fabrizi S., Russo, D.,“Function Points (and other metrics) and the outsourcing management process: Banca d’Italia experience”, Proceedings of the “7th European Software Control and Metrics Conference, Wilmslow (United Kingdom), 1996.

[6] Abran, A., “FFP Release 2,0: An Implementation of COSMIC Functional Size Measurement Concepts”, Presented at FESMA 99, Amsterdam, October 4-7, 1999.

Estimating ERP developments

Robert Ward

Abstract

This paper addresses the issues raised in the measurement of ERP projects and examines some of the issues experienced when estimating ERP projects. It is not meant as a complete solution, more a description of the model that QSM are using to help our clients improve their ERP estimating process. One of the biggest challenges is sizing an ERP system. This paper suggests a sizing method and then uses this as a base to estimate future implementations. The conclusion indicates the next steps in our research and describes how the model is applied to benefit our customers.

1. Introduction

QSM have been measuring software development projects for the last 22 years. Our success has been notable, working with over 200 top companies across the world. The QSM model of software development has been applied to a wide range of software types and methods. However, those software development projects are, in many cases, only part of the whole picture. Many companies are now using off the shelf ERP software packages to run their back office and to provide the backbone for integration with e-applications.

These off the shelf products involve some "traditional" software development, but they involve considerable set-up and configuration, processes that have been persistently hard to measure and quantify. Even more than traditional developments, ERP project are associated with the words 'over-budget', 'bad resourcing' and the inevitable 'extension of go-live dates'.

2. What makes ERP different?

The ERP project process starts with package selection. The structure of the project may be very different, depending on the package selected. This complication leads to the necessity for a different approach to estimating and a different set of specialised skills. The methodology followed to implement the chosen package differs from that of more 'traditional' projects, and traditional estimating models must be adapted to cope.

However, our research has shown that ERP packages have the same relationships between cost, effort, schedule, reliability and cost as more 'traditional' software developments. This enables us to use the QSM model and tool-set with a modified approach. The particular difficulty with ERP projects has been the accurate high-level measurement of the system size and the formulation of a model that can be consistently used to predict cost, effort, schedule and reliability.

3. The difference between project and software size

Project size and software size are not the same thing; the size of the project is measured in terms of the size of the project team. The size of the system however is a quantification of the software being built and configured. Two teams of different ability would require different size projects to build the same system.

System size in the case of ERP is the measurement of how many business processes are being configured, how many modules of the base system will be utilised and how many modules of the base system will be modified or affected by interface development and software changes.

When estimating a "traditional" software development project we measure size in terms of lines of code, function points, or any other measure consistently applied across the project. The key to the whole process, and QSM's software measurement principles is the consistent application of a sizing unit.

. QSM use a top down approach to estimating software projects. The first step is to know the size and reliability of the system that was built, how many people were used, and for how long. Calibrating this enables us to derive a 'productivity factor', and to benchmark performance across multiple projects. This productivity factor is the horsepower of the development environment; it is this that provides the key to estimating future projects and performing trade-offs between cost, schedule and effort.

4. Sizing ERP

The size of an ERP system depends on broad factors. Namely, the scope of the business functions being implemented, and how well the chosen system fits the client's business processes. In a nutshell, how much initial configuration and subsequent development of the software is required to make it fit the organisation.

From this it is obvious that the unit used to measure ERP projects will not be comparable with traditional measures such as counting lines of code or function points. ERP demands a different measurement approach.

4.1. ERP sizing unit

From a high level, all ERP systems can be measured by counting the numbers of functional areas, departments and high-level business processes that are being implemented.

Figure 1

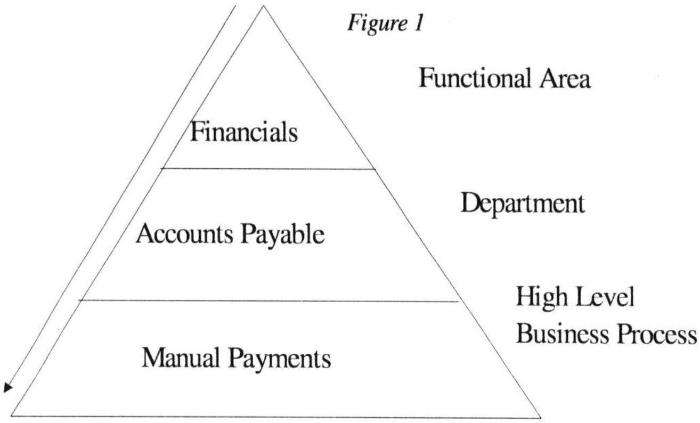

Underneath these three levels of functional decomposition the measures become package-dependant. Particular ERP vendors have their own unique architecture. We use different sizing units for different packages.

4.2. The base size

In SAP the number of lines of IMG that need to be configured provide the basic measurement of size. In Oracle the number of tables that need to be set-up will provide the size. In JDE how many objects are going to be used provide the unit for the size. The resulting count of each of these will therefore form an objective, top-down measure of the size and scope of the implementation (although the units will not be comparable between different packages). This count of tables, object, etc is called the "base size". This base size is not intended to accurately measure the work load required to implement a system; it is intended as a first estimate of the extent of the system implementation.

4.3. The adjusted base size

Even in ERP projects, not all the development relates directly to the functionality provided by the package. Some effort is spent in a more traditional development role using a high level language to write and test code. The amount of code written does not necessarily depend on the number of IMG lines, objects or tables. Therefore it is important to add the amount of code written to the base unit to report the total size size. The amount of code written includes an allowance for reused code but, unlike traditional coding, we do not normally give equal weighting to new lines of code and adjusted lines.

- Numbers of base units + Lines of code adjusted for reuse = Adjusted Base size

4.4. Specific ERP complications

Many "environmental" factors (relating to technical and people issues) are known to influence development projects. In the case of ERP developments, our research has shown that some of these factors not only affect the level of productivity but also increase the size of the system being built.

- An ERP implementation can be affected by the technical complexity of the installation process. Questions such as how many servers, over what link, replication etc will have a direct impact on the size of the system, the amount of configuration code and so on.
- Software product stability will drive the size of the system. If the implementation is using a new release that has not been implemented at many sites then there will be software bugs and quite possibly major areas of functionality that need re-work and testing due to the immaturity of the software
- Geographical spread is a direct driver of size, the more geographically spread the implementation the more set-up will be required. Each of the packages has localizations that need to be applied to each country along with additional configuration requirements.
- The complexity of data conversion and the numbers and complexity of any interfaces will both have an obvious impact on the software size

These factors can impact both the amount of software to be written (system size) and the productivity of the development process itself. In terms of size, we need to increase the adjusted base size arrived at earlier. We do this using a weighting scale, where a zero value implies no impact, and a value of ten implies maximum impact. Indeed our research shows that a relatively small system in terms of adjusted base size can become considerably larger if two or more of the above factors score highly.

4.5. The ERP unit

Our measure of the software size of an ERP system is therefore based on the scope of functionality (base size), adjusted for the extent to which the package must be modifed to meet functional requirements (adjusted base size), plus the additional elements described above as "complications". For SAP, one variable (IMG Lines) is added to another variable (ABAP) lines and then adjusted for further compexities. At the end of this process we arrive at an 'ERP Unit'. We have implemented weightings behind these figures to adust all three measures to a common unit of relative effort to complete a task, and we are refining these weightings as we gather more data.

It is accepted that this ERP unit is not an absolute figure and that the units are not the same across different ERP packages (SAP, JDE, etc). However, it provides a base line for both estimating future project size and calibrating past productivity.

5. Data collection and calculating productivity

In addition to software size, we are, of course, concerned with the size of the development project itself. This model will not be concerned with any business reorganisation or change procedures that accompany the implementation of an ERP package, as there is no evidence that this effort follows the same behaviour patterns as a 'software build' project

Our approach requires a high level view of projects – "how many people for how long?" For example fifty people working for 24 months is 1200 man months of effort (we ignore adjustments such as holidays, overtime, etc). The data should is relatively easy to obtain.

We need to know project duration, at least for the Implementation Phase which starts with the planning of the software implementation and finishes when the system goes live. We include all the full time project staff involved with analysis, design, configuration, development, and testing during this period. We include the activities usually referred to in ERP projects as "applications", "development" and "technical infrastructure". We exclude business process re-engineering because it is unrelated to the system development.

Given the software size and the project time and effort, we can use the same equations used in QSM's proven model to calibrate development performance – the Productivity Index. This is well inderstood in the industry – see the references at the end of this paper. Suffice it to say that the PI is a measure of the capability of the development process and is not simply "loc per day" or "FP per manmonth".

When we calibrate productivity in completed projects or make assumptions about future productivity, we expect it to be influenced by many factors – technical, personnel, environmental, etc. For instance, we expect the four environmental factors (in 4.4 above) to also affect the productivity of the process as well as the software size. In our data analysis to date, we have specifically included just one additional environmental factor, – the experience/skill level of the implementation team, again on a 1-10 scale.

6. Project estimation

The above data collection provides historic data from completed projects; this enables trend analysis and benchmarking. Perhaps the real value in this data is through the baseline this provides for future estimates. There is no better indicator of future results than that of previous performance. This data enables us to calibrate the productivity of the process, which we can then extrapolate to a new project.

We estimate the size of the project that we wish to build and then apply the productivity index. This provides estimates of effort and schedule.

When we estimate a new project, our assumptions (which are the inputs to the estimating process) are always uncertain. By default, we normally think along the lines of the most likely values but realistically we can specify a range of possible values. This applies to all the factors in the equation, the software size, the assumed productivity and the other influences.

The size of this range will depend on many factors, have we done a system similar to this before, in this country with this same team, or are all these factors unknown? For example, we may expect a system to be 1000 ERP units, if we are confident then we may set the upper limit at 1100 and the lower limit at 900. If this was the first time that we had estimated an ERP project then we may set the range between 500 and 1500.

Using the expected value and the range of likely values we perform Monte Carlo Simulation to generate a spread of different results. The result is an expected estimate based on the midpoint of this spread and a range of other values that are bigger or smaller than this expected value. We refer to this midpoint as the "50% estimate", meaning that there is a 50% chance of the project being smaller and a 50% chance of the project turning out larger.

To have the good chance of meeting our targets, say a deadline date, we may choose an ***expected*** schedule, which is less than the deadline in order to give higher probability finishing within time. We can generate a faster schedule by adjusting some of the assumptions – the system size, the number of staff used or even (very risky!) the productivity.

Of course, in making such adjustments, other results will change (e.g. cost, quality etc). This reflects what normally happens in reality. From this position we are able to answer questions, such as 'What if we were to put another two people on the project, what would this do to the schedule and cost'? Or 'What if we absolutely have to go-live by a certain date, how many people do we need to be 75% sure of attaining this goal and what will this do to our cost'?

6.1. Reliability

So far we have ignored reliability. QSM's model for software development estimates and measures the mean time to defect. There is of course a relationship between schedule and reliability. If we are to double the size of our project team then the numbers of defects will increase as team communication decreases. With the ERP model we are collecting defect data, however this is not yet readily available. If periodic information on the numbers of defects found starting at testing through to post go-live the QSM model encourages the use of this information as part of the estimating process.

7. Conclusion and next steps

Any measurement method consistently applied has value. The principles of collecting good, ordered high-level metrics are as applicable to ERP projects as any other. We have shown that not only do ERP projects behave in the same way as more traditional software projects, but also that they can be measured and therefore predicted in the same way.

We are confident that our work is providing valuable information to business managers, and we are currently working with a number of large ERP implementation partners. As with any metrics related project, the value of this model will increase as we collect and collate more data. If collected consistently then it will be possible to benchmark ERP projects and improve the calibration of our model. Our aim is to reduce the uncertainty in costing and planning ERP implementations to the benefit of both the customers and the implementation consultancies who have to commit to deadlines and budgets.

QSM is therefore seeking cooperation from organisations with experience of multiple ERP projects to collect and analyse data and improve on the work done so far. If your organisation would like to help QSM develop this model please contact Rob Ward on +44207 252 2325 or 'rob.ward@qsm-consulting.com'

8. References

[1] Putnam, L, Myers. "Measure For Excellence"; Yourdon Press ISBN 0-13-567694-0
[2] Putnam L, Myers "Controlling Software Development", IEEE Computer Society

Software estimating at the task level - the SPECTRE approach

David Victor, Kevin Daily

Abstract

The SPECTRE approach to task estimation has been developed from accumulated observation and examination of patterns of behaviour conducted over many years in application software construction, at companies including Coutts Bank, Samuel Montagu, IBM and Swiss Bank Corporation. The result is a reasoned strategy for predicting task development time and module size which is sensitive to local factors such as task content and complexity as well as individual knowledge and experience. Its reliability has been verified by using test cases derived from real software projects, so that the approach can be calibrated to most development languages and situations. It can be applied not just to new coding but to design re-use and software adaptation.

1. The SPECTRE approach

Failures of software development projects on the grand scale are newsworthy, but their problems are not restricted to the project level. Estimating for the software development tasks performed by individuals is fraught with its own special difficulties; formal methods may be generally little more than systematised guesswork, estimators may be swayed by what they believe management is expecting to hear or they may lack the confidence or experience to defend their figures.

This realization prompted the author, David Victor, to start taking serious notice of how his fellow professionals worked. Trends and patterns which have emerged from these observations over the years have crystallized his views on how development time and task size are sensitive to functional content, complexity, knowledge and experience.

In 1985 the author decided to produce a method and tool based on a set of algorithms that could estimate task size in Lines of Code (LOC) and effort in days. However, owing to the exigencies of 'normal' work, the first prototype was not produced until the mid-1990s. The name SPECTRE™ was given to this prototype, which has now evolved into a task estimating method and commercially usable tool.

The author was fortunate to be working for a major software house who were interested enough to offer facilities and, very significantly, to provide a variety of test cases. This led to a broadening of SPECTRE's scope and a refinement of its internal tuning to the point where it consistently attained a high degree of reliability and precision.

2. Construction Points™

Construction Point Evaluation™ (CPE) is a task-based metrics method which the author developed for the SPECTRE Task Estimator tool. There are similarities to Function Point Analysis (FPA) in the way both metrics are applied, but their respective target entities and their chronological points of application in the development process are very different - and, most importantly, their fundamental objectives.

FPA is used "*as a sizing measure to readily determine rate of delivery, cost per unit, and quality rates...the size measure is **based on the user's view of the functions required** and provided by the application. This is done without regard to the technology, design, tools or language used*" (Linda Smith, Predicate Logic, Inc.).

"*The value to be gained from utilizing a functional sizing technique, such as Function Points, is primarily in the capability to* ***estimate a project early in the development process***" (Herron & Garmus, The David Consulting Group).

"*Function Points give software engineering researchers a way of sizing software through the analysis of the implemented functionality of a system* ***from the user's point of view***" (Capers Jones, chairman of Software Productivity Research).

What CPE and FPA have in common is that a points score is assigned to selected entities in a specification and that this score is adjusted in the light of perceived complexity. There are, however, fundamental differences between the CPE and the FPA approaches (as the above citations show). These differences reflect the fact that Function Points Analysis is a project-oriented metric while Construction Points Estimation is a task-oriented one.

Thus, the specification whose Function Point Count is measured will be that of a project (or at the very least a discrete business application); whereas Construction Point Evaluation encompasses a single development task. FPA is applicable from project inception onward but has no direct relevance to individual tasks; CPE is relevant to individual tasks only and its target entities reflect this deliberately chosen and precisely limited focus.

To illustrate the operational areas of CPE and FPA, a simplified description of FPA is given below. (Note: the fact that FPA Mark II is covered does not imply a recommendation for Mark II vis-a-vis Mark I but simply acknowledges that Mark II is the successor version and has more points of measurement.)

3. Function Points

A Value Adjustment Factor (VAF) is determined, based on a number of General System Characteristics (GSCs). In Mark II there are 14 of these, as listed in Table 1.

Table 1. General System Characteristics in Mark II Function Points

• Data Communications	• On-Line Update
• Distributed Data Processing	• Application Complexity
• Application Performance	• Reusability
• Degree of use of Hardware Platform	• Ease of Installation
• Transaction Rate	• Operational Ease
• On-Line Data Entry	• Multiple Sites
• End-User Efficiency	• Ability to Undergo Change

Each GSC is influence-rated in the range 0 to 5, based on an assessment of five Function Point Components, namely:

- External Inputs
- External Outputs
- External Inquiries
- Internal Logical Files
- External Interface Files

The total of the complexity-rated values of each occurrence of these Components is calculated and then multiplied by the VAF to give Total Adjusted Function Points. (Details of how the VAF is derived and how complexity rating is performed are outside the scope of this paper; the interested reader is referred to the International Function Point Users Group).

4. The SPECTRE task estimating technique

SPECTRE task estimating consists of three phases:

1. Construction Evaluation
2. Development Effort Calculation
3. Results Display

(In the SPECTRE tool, each phase is supplemented by comprehensive Help Text, some examples of which are given below - SPECTRE is a practical technique which also is intended to help the user to understand the task estimation process.)

4.1 Phase 1 – Construction Evaluation

Construction Evaluation recognises two classes of function: Input/Output and Processing.

4.1.1 Input/Output

Information about the task specification is analysed to identify its input/output operations, as listed in Table 2.

Table 2. Input/Output Operations for Tasks

• read from a file • write to a file • delete from a file • update a file • select from a table • insert into a table	• delete from a table • update a table • interface with another program • generate a report • generate a display

Each Input/Output operation in the task carries its own Construction Point cost. These costs are accumulated, with repeated occurrences of a feature shaded down in value to take account of the probability of shared code being used (e.g. for error and exception handling). This gives a total for the task.

Figure 1 shows the relative Construction Point cost of Input/Output operations; the higher the position in the graph, the greater the number of Construction Points needed. (The preliminary count calculated for the task is later adjusted in the light of the task's complexity.)

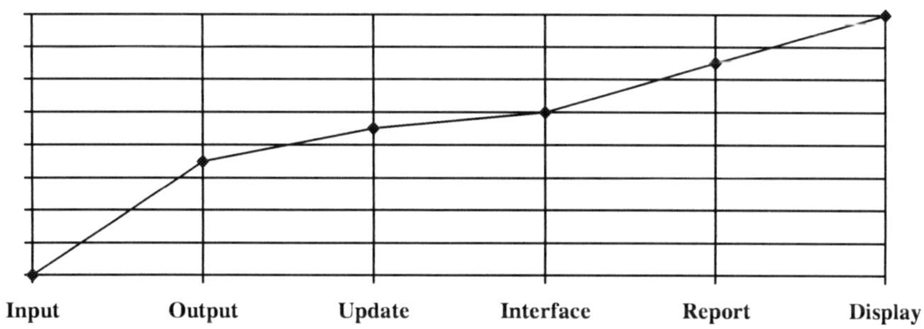

Fig. 1 Construction Point Cost of I/O Operations

4.1.2 Processing

Analysing the task specification also identifies the features of the processing logic listed in Table 3.

Table 3. Processing Logic Features

• data restructuring	• sorting
• conditions	• data presentation
• linkages with other programs	• testing considerations
• data retrieval	• performance considerations
• calculations	

Each applicable feature is given a weighting which represents its degree of complexity, from which a Complexity Coefficient is derived for the task.

(The author freely acknowledges the pioneering work of others in the evolution of estimating techniques, in particular the research into the relative power of different programming languages as exemplified by the Programming Languages Table published by Software Productivity Research, Inc. This prompted the realisation that such a relationship should also be capable of derivation for Construction Point assessment, which has indeed proved to be the case. SPECTRE is therefore able to determine the number of lines of code (LOC) required to implement a 'quantum' of Construction in the languages currently in its repertoire. These figures are of course smaller than those for Function Points.)

Table 4 shows the LOC-per-Construction Point for a selection of languages.

Table 4. LOC–per-Construction Point

VS COBOLII:	45
PL/I:	40
C++:	25
Delphi:	15
VB6:	12

LOC is calculated as the Construction Point Total times the LOC for one point's-worth of Construction in the programming language to be used. The Complexity Coefficient is then applied to arrive at the final LOC value.

4.1.3 Languages

When the requirement arises for SPECTRE to handle a new programming language, it is researched by pragmatic reference to its structure and character, by means of the author's personal contacts within the IT industry, and by investigation of public domain sources such as web sites, the press and available literature. Feedback from SPECTRE users is expected to become more significant as its usage grows.

4.1.4 Notes on Complexity

The degree of complexity of is an important characteristic of all aspects of processing logic and therefore requires precise categorisation. Table 5 shows extracts from the SPECTRE tool's Help Text which illustrate the classification of complexity as Simple, Average or Complex.

Table 5. Complexity ratings for Task Conditions and Calculations

CONDITIONS	
Simple:	Straight-through control flow; low proportion of branching logic.
Average:	Some non-linear logic consisting mainly of IF/THEN/ELSE or CASE constructs.
Complex:	Processing heavily conditional; logic affected by timing and/or resource-usage constraints; several logical levels.
CALCULATIONS	
Simple:	Mostly addition and subtraction (e.g. spreadsheet type with column and/or row totals); simple multiplication, e.g. compound interest computation.
Average:	As above but requiring use of IF/THEN/ELSE or equivalent; straightforward iterative or statistical operations.
Complex:	Computation-heavy; includes recursion, non-linear calculations, fuzzy logic, calculus etc.

Figure 2 shows the relative complexity weighting of each of the above features; the higher the position in the table, the greater the weighting.

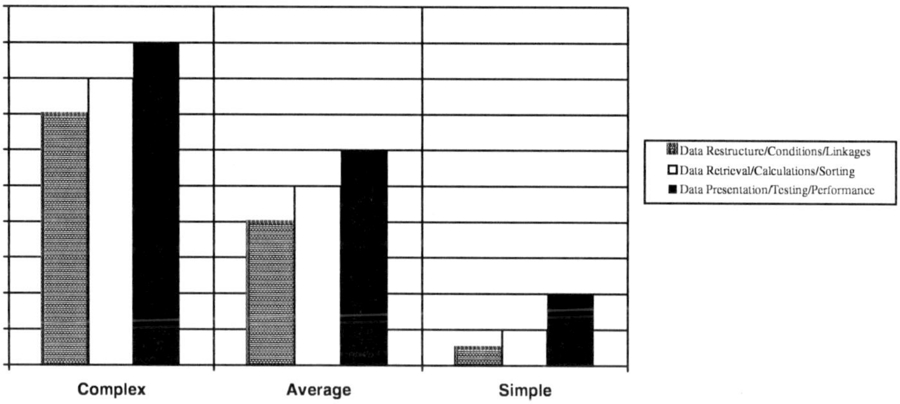

Fig. 2. Relative Complexity of Processing Features

Phase 2 - Development Effort Calculation

This phase of SPECTRE takes into account the grade and experience of the programmer assigned to the task (the assignee). Allowance is made for the possible re-use of existing code and program design. The result is an estimate of the number of days' effort required from receipt of specification to completion of unit testing (or equivalent acceptance point).

Table 6 shows the parameters that Development Effort Calculation requires.

Table 6. Parameters for Development Effort Calculation

• LOC	• Assignee's Knowledge
• Basic Lines Per Day	• Knowledge Required
• Assignee's Grade	• Percentage of Design and Code that could be adapted from existing source
• Assignee's Experience	

LOC has already been estimated (see above).

Basic Lines Per Day is the LOC per day that the installation would expect to achieve for code-and-unit-test as an average for all development staff.

Grade is not necessarily a function of job-title; it is an indication of where a neutral observer would place the assignee on a scale ranging from Expert downwards.

Experience is weighted by reference to a scale ranging from High downwards. The weightings are grade-specific, e.g. a high-experience senior programmer is rated at slightly less than a low-experience expert. Grade and Experience are combined to give an **Experience Coefficient**.

Guidelines from SPECTRE's Help Text for quantifying these two factors are shown in Table 7.

Table 7. Guidelines for Grade and Experience

GRADE	
Junior:	Up to 2 years experience; not expected to function unaided.
Average:	Between 2 and 4 years experience; lacks expertise and likely to require guidance.
Senior:	More than 4 years mostly relevant experience; may lack some detailed technical refinement but likely to be comfortable with the assignment; solutions may sometimes seem unnecessarily complex.
Expert:	Probably at least 6 years relevant experience; a strong degree of technical competence and highly regarded; depending on breadth of experience may not always find the 'best' approach but can recognise and appreciate it; produces solutions that look simpler than the problems they address; generates design and code that demonstrate a high degree of maintainability; a significant contributor to installation standards.
EXPERIENCE	
Low:	Recently arrived at this grade and likely to remain there for at least another year.
Average:	Well-established at this level but not yet ready to advance.
High:	Functions very well at this level.

Figure 3 illustrates the relative weightings given to Grade and Experience.

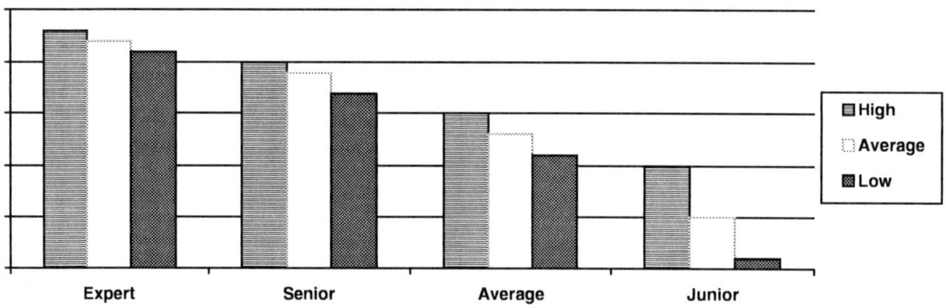

Fig. 3. Relative ability by grade and experience

Assignee's Knowledge is an assessment of how much the assignee knows; not only of the task in question but also of relevant related subjects. It is broken down into a number of descriptors ranging from detailed knowledge of the task and related subjects, to no knowledge of the task and little or no general knowledge of related subjects. The subjects covered are:

- The current task
- Installation Standards
- Operating System
- Operating Hardware

Knowledge Required is an assessment of the relevance of the Assignee's Knowledge. This weighting is applied to the Assignee's Knowledge to give a **Knowledge Coefficient**.

Figure 4 illustrates the relative weightings given to the shortfall between Assignee's Knowledge and Knowledge Required (the higher the position in the table, the higher the Knowledge Coefficient):

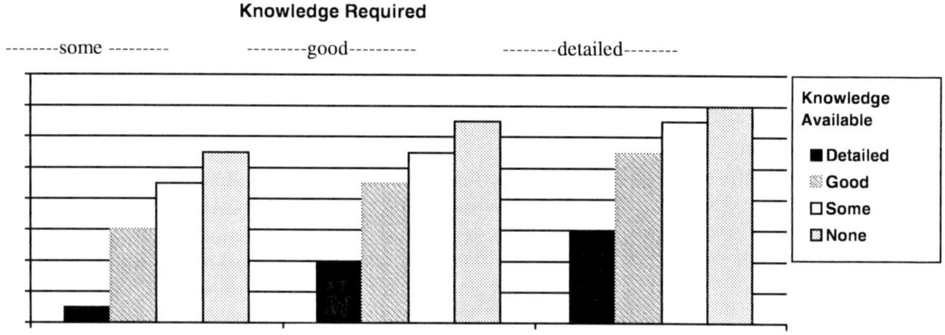

Fig. 4. Relative Knowledge Shortfall

Many applications contain tried-and-tested pieces of design and code (for exception handling, processing transactions against a master-file, etc.). The percentages of design and code that could be adapted from other sources permit the economies of re-use to be taken into account (with an allowance for customisation).

The LOC estimate is divided by the basic lines per day to give an initial number of days, and then the Experience and Knowledge Coefficients are applied to give the final estimated development effort in days for this assignee.

4.3 Phase 3 - Results Display

The SPECTRE tool displays the results of a task estimate in two sections:

4.3.1 Results - Section 1

This section gives the actual estimate and consists of the following items:

- LOC
- Lines per day
- Development effort in days

4.3.2 Results - Section 2

This section shows a number of additional items which may be of value or interest.

- Time saving through code/design adaptation
- Complexity rating
- Experience rating

- Knowledge rating
- Construction Point score

SPECTRE evaluates all the above in terms of size, range or scope as appropriate, and appends a comment - in particular, any factor considered to be significantly outside 'normal' expectation is highlighted. (Help Text in the SPECTRE tool clarifies all the items shown above.)

5. Accuracy

5.1 Author's background

It is relevant here to describe the author's background, since this is a significant factor in the development of SPECTRE. David Victor has been involved in software development since 1968, when he joined British European Airways as a programmer. He has worked for many major organisations (some of which were noted earlier) where he gained extensive experience of low and high-level languages including ALGOL, various Assembler and COBOL implementations, PL/I and SQL. In 1977 he was elected a Fellow of the Institute of Data Processing.

His interest in task estimation dates back to the mid-80s when he started to record the observations that were to form the basis of SPECTRE. From November 1993 to the end of 1997, while was working full-time with IBM, SPECTRE was brought from prototype status to a full working version. IBM's management was kind enough to provide a series of test-cases which allowed the accuracy of the method's internal calibrations to be refined to the point where it was consistently out-performing its author's predictions, both in LOC and effort estimation! As a result of the experience gained during this period, SPECTRE's range of Processing Features was expanded to its current set.

5.2 Test case performance

Table 8 shows how SPECTRE performed with the final set of test cases. The 7th and 8th programs in the table were specifically selected to test its ability to handle tasks at both ends of the size spectrum. The 9th and 10th were also used to test development effort estimation, where 22 days were predicted for both against actual values of 23 and 25 days - this is a good illustration of how SPECTRE's time estimates are conditioned by far more than raw LOC.

Table 8. SPECTRE test cases

Test Case programs	LOC Estimated	LOC Actual	Deviation %
1	1287	1338	-3.9
2	4715	4848	-2.8
3	5684	5695	-4.7
4	1560	1551	+0.6
5	11280	10776	+4.6
6	5520	5963	-7.5
7	540	634	-14.8
8	11424	12590	-10.0
9	2277	2342	-2.8
10	4175	4080	+2.3

Test data reproduced with permission of IBM United Kingdom Ltd.

6. Conclusion

The SPECTRE approach to task estimation is based on accumulated observations over many years of experience in software construction. The result is a rational and realistic approach to task development, with known and verified accuracy. It is sensitive to all the parameters that the author's experience has shown contribute to success or failure, including functional content, component complexity, and the knowledge and experience of the task assignee. SPECTRE also takes account of opportunities for the re-use and adaptation of designs and code. Its accuracy has been verified by using test cases from real projects.

The following are some of the questions which can be answered by timely, soundly-based - and politically neutral - task estimating:

"*How much time should be allowed for this task*?"
"*What level of skill and experience will it require*?"
"*Am I trying to put too much functionality into a single task*?"
"*How can I convince my staff that these estimates are fair and attainable*?"
"*How can I convince my management*?"
"*How can I convince myself*?"

SPECTRE is at its most effective when applied to a task specification that is complete and confirmed. Nevertheless, it can be used to advantage throughout the whole process of developing the task specification; for example, to give an early feel for notional best, average and worst cases. If a task threatens to exceed reasonable limits of size, complexity or effort, or looks as if it will require very specific skills, then the earlier these possibilities are flagged and resolved, the better.

The arguments for using the SPECTRE method can perhaps be best summarised by two favourite quotes, both from "The Mythical Man Month" by Fred Brooks Jr (Addison-Wesley) who states memorably that "*adding manpower to a late software project makes it later*." In answer to his own question: "*How does a project get to be a year late?*" his telling answer is, simply, "*one day at a time*."

Deriving a Software Quality View from Customer Satisfaction and Service Data

Sunita Chulani, P. Santhanam, Darrell Moore, Bob Leszkowicz, Gary Davidson

Abstract

Most quality and cost models use defect density to represent software quality. Customer's quality expectations are not typically based on size and complexity of the product they buy and their satisfaction can be influenced substantially by other product attributes that are not typically mapped to defects (e.g. Ease of installation and use, timely support, etc.). Consequently, new ways to measure customer view of quality are needed. In this paper, we provide analyses of customer service and survey data from eight products and discuss some key insights to lay the foundation for a better understanding of customer view of software quality. We believe that this approach[1] can help us identify actions in software development and support that will address the concerns of our customers and improve their satisfaction with our products.

1. Introduction

Software economics and measurement research work in recent years has focused on building models for software cost, schedule and quality prediction (for example, USC's COCOMO II suite [1], Putnam's SLIM [2], Jones' KnowledgePlan [3], etc.). The extent of the quality prediction is in determining the defect density of the product when its fully operational in the field in terms of defects/KSLOC (Thousands of Lines of Code) or defects/FP (Function Point), where a defect is viewed as problem resulting in some change of code distributed to the customer. While this metric may represent quality adequately from the development point of view, a typical 'customer' for software does not take into account the size or complexity of the product in judging the quality of the product. In addition, defect density does not really capture the overall customer satisfaction experienced by the users of the software product. For example, when a customer has difficulty with product installation, he calls in for service and this user problem is not necessarily coded as a defect as it may not need a change in the code base. Thus, even though the customer may not be satisfied, the currently available quality/cost models don't incorporate this dissatisfaction in any way.

There has been some prior work (e.g. [4]) establishing some link between service and customer satisfaction metrics. Yet, more effort is needed to define meaningful and practical ways to measure the impact of the entire software development life-cycle, including the service phase, on overall customer satisfaction when the product is fully-operational in the field. This paper attempts at building this bridge between development, service and in-field customer satisfaction. It presents analyses that can be used to help determine quantitative answers (not just inclinations or expert opinion) to questions such as:

---

1 Note: This paper that does not capture all the processes/analyses done in a large organization. The field of customer satisfaction and software quality is a broad and complex field and this paper makes an attempt to uncover some useful insights that may help us manage our products in a more beneficial way.

(i) What are the top 3 attributes customers care about the most?

(ii) What is the relationship between kinds of customer problems (e.g. Duplicate problem report, problem affecting a data record, etc.) and product attributes, i.e. Performance, Reliability, Usability, etc.?

(iii) Does the defect density or the time to resolution have a higher impact on overall customer satisfaction?

(iv) Does customer satisfaction improve if time to resolve severity 1 field defects is reduced?

Section 2 provides some background for the reader; section 3 details some analysis examples that help the reader understand techniques that help answer questions of the sort raised above. Section 4 provides the conclusions and future research.

2. Background

Over the past year, we have commissioned a study with participants from different groups within our organization encompassing most of the entities of the software product life-cycle, in particular, product development teams, service teams and customer satisfaction analysts. The product development teams are the primary producers of the product; the service teams work with the customers once the product is generally available and helps the customer if the customer experiences any problems with the product; the customer satisfaction analysts capture and analyze several different marketing aspects of the organization and products such as brand name satisfaction, trends in the marketplace with respect to product customer satisfaction and its relationship with competitor products' customer satisfaction, etc. Often times, these different groups are separate entities with different focus areas. The theme of this study is to recognize and exploit the benefits of using data and information across these teams together to make better decisions to improve customer satisfaction. The reader should note that this paper presents a subset of activities/analyses done in a large organization.

Customer satisfaction that is addressed in this paper is related to product attributes that manifest as defects in software. Other aspects of customer satisfaction, such as functionality provided vs. customer expectations, price considerations, vendor relationships, etc. are not directly addressed in this study. Thus it is really from the point of view of the IT professional in the customer organization developing and supporting applications or servers using IBM software. They do not typically make the decision to buy the software and they are also not the end user of the software that is being deployed.

2.1. Data sources

Quality is viewed from three chronological views as shown in Figure 1 [see 5 for an overview of quality views, metrics and models]. Two of the views are formed by the data that were available for this study i.e. (i) data from field defects from our service teams and (ii) customer satisfaction data from our marketing teams.

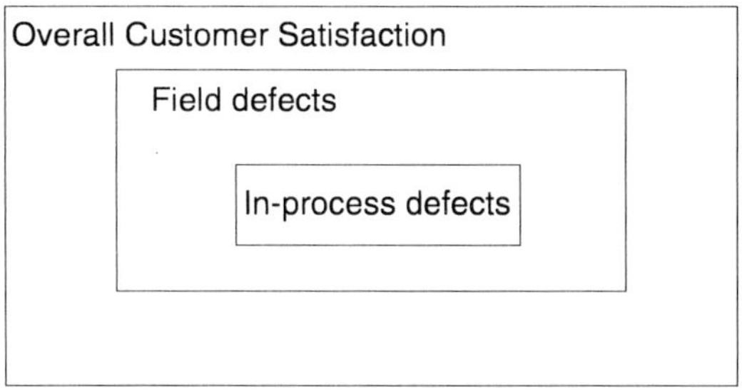

Figure 1: Quality Views

When the product is being developed, several defect detection/prevention/removal activities are employed which detect in-process defects [6]. Once the product is ready and shipped, customers encounter problems and call in to the product service centers for help. These problems that cause a change in the product are recorded as field defects by the service personnel. When the product is in the field, marketing teams do surveys to capture overall customer satisfaction of the product. The timeline of when what data is collected is shown in Figure 2. All these different pieces of data are used to monitor progress and identify areas of improvement.

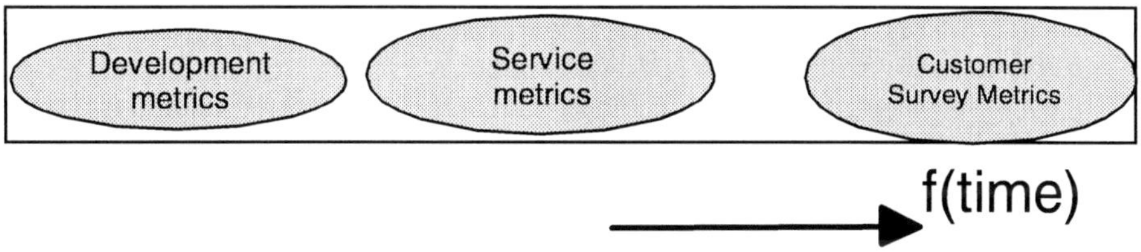

Figure 2: Timeline of quality-related measures

The next few paragraphs describe in detail the two sources of data available for this study. It is also important to note that the processes and the associated data collection do not necessarily apply to all of IBM's business units thus limiting the scope of this work.

2.1.1. Service data

Once an IBM product is generally available, customers who have problems with the product contact our call management center and are connected to the appropriate technical support staff that helps them resolve the issue either in a preventive or a corrective way. During this process, a lot of data gets recorded in IBM's defect databases. This data is used as a means of communication between the teams and also for analysis to improve the overall service process.

For example, when a customer calls in with a problem, the service representative opens a 'Problem Management Report' or more commonly known as a PMR at IBM. The service representative then works with the customer and/or the development team to resolve the problem. The resolution of the problem may or may not cause a change in the product. If a change is made, the problem is termed as a 'Defect Oriented Problem' and is coded as an 'Authorized Program Analysis Report' or an APAR. The change is a PTF or a 'Program temporary Fix' until it is incorporated in the next release. If a change is not made, the problem is a 'Non-Defect Oriented Problem'. The process is illustrated in figure 3. For this study, we had service data for 8 products.

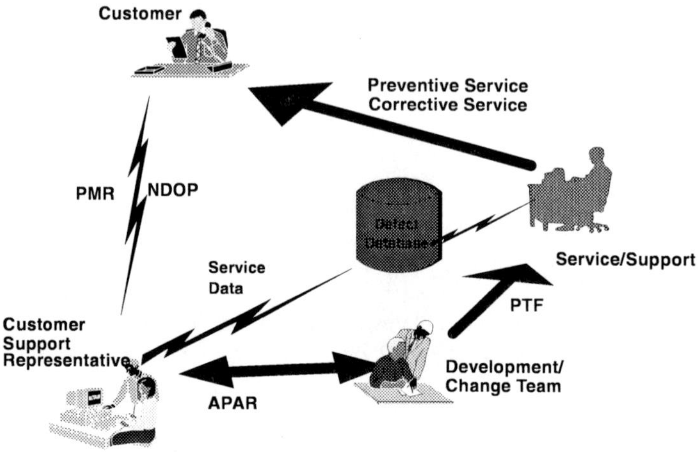

Figure 3: Service Process - High Level View

2.1.2. Customer Satisfaction Survey Data

Customer satisfaction is measured by marketing groups that survey the customer base and capture overall customer satisfaction in several dimensions. The key dimensions used at IBM are popularly known as CUPRIMDSO (C: Capability, U: Ease of Use, P: Performance, R: Reliability, I: Ease of Installation, M: Maintainability, D: Documentation, S: Service/Support, O: Overall Satisfaction). In addition to these, other dimensions such as Price, Availability, etc. are also used.

For each of the dimensions, a qualitative scale is often times used which has ratings such as (i) Very Dissatisfied (ii) Dissatisfied (iii) Neutral (iv) Satisfied (v) Very Satisfied. Net Satisfaction Index is computed using the responses on the rating scale as a weighted satisfaction index.

For the purposes of this study, we had customer satisfaction data for 8 products. A lot of marketing research has been done to study customer satisfaction data [7, 8, 9]. But most of these efforts are limited just to the marketing data source and do not establish links between other quality views to exploit all the information to complete the picture.

3. Analysis Results

As described above, for the purposes of this study, we had marketing data for 8 products that are very often used together. Detailed analysis on the data gave some interesting insights in the customer satisfaction of this set of products. Some of the highlights of the analysis are presented in the next few paragraphs.

3.1 What are the top 3 attributes customers care about the most? What are we doing to address these attributes?

One question on the customer satisfaction surveys that we ask is: "What quality characteristics come to mind when considering a high quality software product on this operating system?" Answers to this question are in the form of free text and customers can say as much as they wish. Sometimes they have a long list of characteristics and sometimes just a single attribute. This data gives us the most direct response from our customers to improve customer satisfaction. Using our data and text mining on the free text answers we can understand what quality characteristics are important to our customer and what we should focus our efforts on. Such analysis may reveal that in addition to CUPRIMDS, other attributes such as Speed, Compatibility, Price, etc., may also be relevant.

Using this knowledge that we can extract from our data and by doing some additional mining using our marketing data, we can further analyze if we are indeed satisfying our customers in terms of the top attributes that are revealed as relevant when analyzing this data. For example, for each of the CUPRIMDS attributes we ask our customers two questions: (i) How satisfied are you with the attribute for this product and (ii) how important is this attribute. This data can help us do gap analysis to understand if we are meeting our customers expectations.

For the set of 8 products, lets say attribute A is the most relevant characteristic our customers care about. Gap analysis on attribute A can help us answer the question: "Are we meeting our customer's expectation for attribute A?" Figure 4 illustrates the Satisfaction v/s Importance ratings for attribute A.

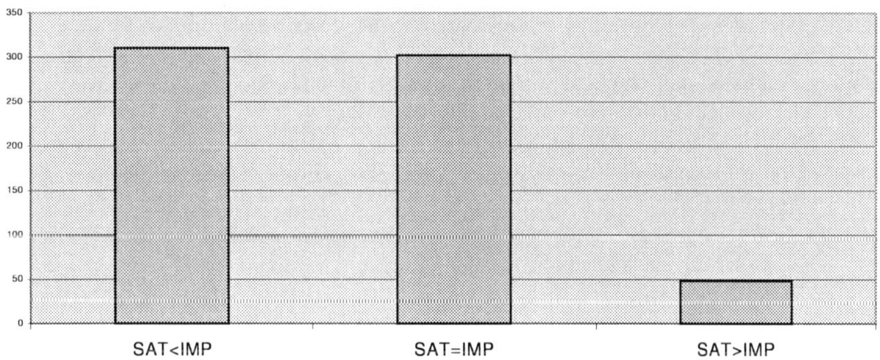

Figure 4: Satisfaction v/s Importance for Attribute A

From the above chart, we can clearly see that for attribute A, our data distribution indicates that our customers are not getting the same level of Satisfaction as they think is Important. Hence, we really need to focus our efforts, in reducing the height of the SAT<IMP bar on attribute A and other high impact attributes. What actions can we take earlier in the life of the product? For example, using our service data to improve overall customer satisfaction? We will discuss this in the next section.

On the other hand, consider a different scenario: say the gap analysis results showed the distribution depicted in figure 5. In such a scenario, we are meeting our customer's

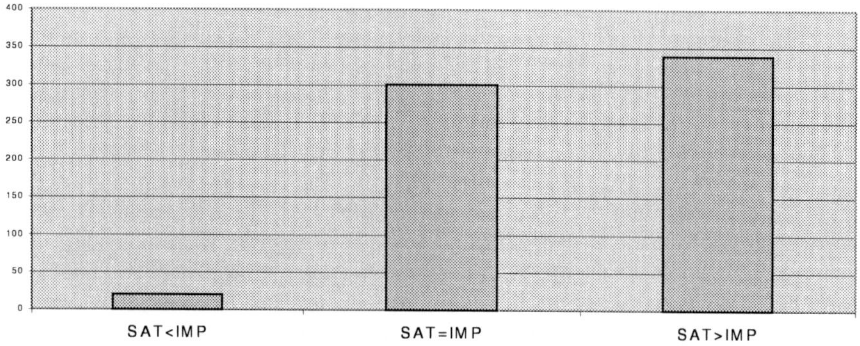

expectations as the frequency of SAT<IMP is much lower than that of SAT>IMP.

Figure 5: Satisfaction v/s Importance for Attribute A (A different scenario)

3.2. What is the Relationship between Customer Problems and Product Attributes?

Let's look at an example and see how we can use our Marketing data and Service data to improve the Satisfaction on some product characteristic, say Reliability. This example can be used to do analysis to answer the question: What is the relationship between kinds of customer problems (e.g. Duplicate problem report, problem affecting a data record, etc.) and product attributes i.e. Performance, Reliability, Usability, etc.?

As explained in section 2, when a customer has a problem they contact our service teams. The service team help resolve our customers problems and in the process they record a lot of detailed information about the problems encountered in-field. If we can analyze the defects to understand which types are highly correlated to Reliability and resolve these defects more efficiently then we have a chance of improving the Satisfaction on Reliability.

Doing a correlation study on our data, we find that Reliability is most highly correlated to defects which are classified as "Records closed as they are duplicates of open records". Similarly, Reliability is less correlated to records which are classified as "Change team could either not reproduce the problems and the problems had already been resolved". Based on this information, we know that as soon as we have a customer-reported defect that is a duplicate, we focus our efforts on resolving it soon, if we want to focus our efforts in improving satisfaction with Reliability. Similarly, our data shows that our customers are usually quite satisfied in terms of Reliability when they call in with a problem and our teams respond with a fix (the problem has been fixed). Hence, this process helps us focus our service efforts in the right direction to improve a customer satisfaction attribute (such as Reliability) based on actual information that is gathered by our service teams.

3.3. Does defect density or time to resolution have an impact on Customer Satisfaction? Does Customer Satisfaction improve if time to resolve severity 1 field defects is reduced?

The next few paragraphs present ways for the reader to look at different data that is available in any large organization to facilitate better decision-making. Lets try to answer the question: Does the defect density have an impact on overall customer satisfaction?

Table 1 shows the Overall Satisfaction and # of APARs for the 8 products for 2 years. The table is sorted in the order of satisfaction index of 'O' i.e. Overall Satisfaction with the product. This table shows no relationship between the # of APARs and O. Common sense would say that as the # of APARs increases, Overall Satisfaction should decrease but this is clearly not true for all the products. Further analysis of this trend shows that some of the products have been in the market longer than others and the extent of usage explains the higher number of APARs in some products that have high Overall Satisfaction (for example, product G). The metrics "# of APARs/Thousand Lines of Code" or "# of APARs/Function Point" may be better to use for such an analysis but this information wasn't available for all the products in this sample set.

*Table 1: Trend of Overall Satisfaction and Total # of APARs**

Product #	O	Total # of APARs
Prod A	69	17
Prod B	69.4	15
Prod C	70.9	167
Prod D	75	38
Prod E	75.6	455
Prod F	77.5	100
Prod G	80.8	5125
Prod H	82.6	278

Now, lets determine if the time to resolution of defects has an impact on satisfaction? Lets consider 3 of the 8 products which have steadily increasing Overall Satisfaction ratings. For example, lets consider products D (O = 75), F (O=77.5) and G (O=80.8). Product F's O is about 3.3% higher than Product D's O and Product G's O is about 4% higher than Product F's O. Now, lets see if the time to resolution of a subset of field-reported defects, say Severity 1 APARs, has any impact on the steadily increasing O for these three products. Table 2 illustrates the # of Severity 1 APARs, the percentage of Severity 1 APARs, average time to resolve a Severity 1 APAR and Overall Satisfaction for products D, F and G.

*Table 2: Trend of APAR severity, density, time to resolution**

Product #	# of Sev 1 APARs	% of Sev 1 APARs	Average Time to Resolution	Overall Satisfaction
Prod D	3	8	129	75
Prod F	15	15	111	77.5
Prod G	943	18	69	80.8

* *Please note that the defect data in tables 1 and 2 has the trends of the original data but the numbers have been multiplied by a constant to assure confidentiality.*

Table 2 clearly shows that even though the number (and percentage) of Severity 1 APARs increases, the decreasing time to resolution of these APARs results in the Overall Satisfaction to steadily increase. This helps our teams focus efforts on reducing the time to resolution of defects if our goal is to increase Overall Satisfaction.

Several other analyses have been done using the service/marketing data to improve quality and customer satisfaction of our products in ways similar to the ones shown in the above paragraphs. Such analysis helps us answer the questions posed in the abstract. The aim of this paper was to show some of the ways analysis can be done to improve our products. We strongly believe that analyzing historic data is a very good way to better manage our products.

4. Conclusions and Future Research

This paper presented examples of analysis that illustrate the relationship between development and service metrics (number of defects discovered, time to resolve a defect, severity of defects, etc.) and customer satisfaction survey metrics (overall customer satisfaction, top attributes customers look for in a product, etc.). Data from 8 different products is analyzed using several analytical techniques in a systematic way to help answer many important questions related to improving overall customer satisfaction.

A lot of research needs to be done in this broad and complex area of understanding our customers and their level of satisfaction with our products. We are continuing to do more work in this area to further improve our product quality and customer satisfaction. Some of the areas that we are actively working on include: understanding satisfaction with the service process once the customer problem has been resolved, determining a solution-based versus product-based view of customer satisfaction, etc.

5. References

[1] Boehm, B.W., Abts, C., Brown, A.W., Chulani, S., Clark, B.K., Horowitz, E., Madachy, R., Reifer, D. and Steece, B., "Software Cost Estimation with COCOMO II", Prentice-Hall, 2000.

[2] Putnam, L.H. and Myers, W., "Measures for Excellence", Yourdon Press Computing Series, 1992.

[3] Jones, C., "Applied Software Measurement", McGraw Hill, 1997.

[4] Buckley, M. and Chillarege, R., "Discovering relationships between service and customer satisfaction", Proceedings of the International Conference on Software Maintenance, Opio (Nice), France, October 16-20, 1995.

[5] Kan, S., "Metrics and Models in Software Quality Engineering", Addison-Wesley, 1996.

[6] Chulani, S., "COQUALMO (COnstructive QUALity MOdel): A Software Defect Density Prediction Model," in European Software Conferences On Metrics (ESCOM) proceedings, April 1999.

[7] Mendonca, M, "An Approach to Improving Existing Measurement Frameworks in Software Development Organizations", Ph.D. Dissertation, University of Maryland, Computer Science Department, 1997.

[8] Shaw, J., "Customer Inspired Quality: Looking Backward through the Telescope", Jossey Bass Inc., August 1996.

[9] Chakrapani, C., "How to Measure Service Quality and Customer Satisfaction", American Marketing Association, 1997.

Cost drivers of annual maintenance: One commercial bank's experience

Katrina D. Maxwell and Pekka Forselius

Abstract

Over an application's life cycle, more money is spent on software maintenance than software development; however, not much is known about the factors which influence annual software maintenance cost. In this article, the authors present the results of an analysis performed on one commercial bank's software maintenance database to determine their key cost drivers.

1. Introduction

If you don't measure and control maintenance effort, it will grow more than necessary. One great risk is that work not allocated during more strictly controlled new development projects will be hidden in maintenance endeavours. That is why one of the biggest commercial banks in Finland began to collect development and maintenance effort data as early as 1985. Every employee, including managers and secretaries, reported time spent on all types of projects into an effort accounting system every week.

The bank's knowledge of new software development projects was already very good because of systematic project portfolio management. Between 1987 and 1995, 250 new IBM applications were developed during a big migration project to move applications from a Bull mainframe environment to 3-tier architecture system constructed of PC's, local servers and IBM mainframes. Running and maintaining two separate mainframe environments was very expensive. Migration projects could not be cancelled and all available resources needed to be allocated to them to finish the migration program as soon as possible. In addition, the amount of maintenance effort was growing and becoming more important each year. This, combined with a pressing need to minimize personnel costs due to a recession and banking crisis in Finland, made controlling maintenance costs a priority.

In order to improve the annual budgeting of maintenance effort, both for the in-house maintenance suppliers and the owners of the applications, Pekka Forselius and his team collected a large amount of data including actual effort, size, age, defects, classification variables and risk factors to help them to better understand the qualitative differences among applications. This data was simply used to help organise maintenance and manage risks, it was not statistically analyzed at the time.

What could the bank have learned through the statistical analysis of this rich data set? Statistical analysis would have been useful to determine which of the factors collected had a real impact on maintenance cost. In addition, other interesting relationships could have been studied, for example: What effect did the application's age have on maintenance effort? Did any development tools prove to be more productive than others? For example, did applications built with Telon require less maintenance than traditional Cobol applications? What impact did the number of design defects have? In this paper we present the results of our statistical analysis of this dataset to answer these questions. We conclude with Pekka's response to a very important question: Would he have recommended that anything be done differently had he had this knowledge at the time?

Although this study looks in detail at the software maintenance database of one bank, it should be of interest to a wider audience because nearly all of the applications were programmed with the most widely used maintenance language, Cobol. Cobol applications and mainframe computing dominate a large segment of the business community in which conventional data- and transaction processing requirements drive major applications [1]. Cobol mainframes process more than 83% of transactions world-wide [2]. The maintenance of Cobol applications is especially critical in the banking sector where large customer databases (1-2 million customers), large account databases, and advanced online services typify banking projects. In a recent merger of two banks, the Cobol-based assets of one bank were cited as one of the key reasons for the merger [2].

Table 1 – List of Variables

Variable Name	Type	Values (or levels)	Definition
			Classification Variables
BORG	nominal	5	Business Organization Type (retail, company, big corporation...)
MORG	nominal	17	Internal Business Unit (deposit, treasury, accounting, payment, securities trading…)
APPTYPE	nominal	4	Application Type (information service/decision support, operative back office, operative core banking, interconnection service)
DBMS	nominal	2	Database Management System (DB2, IDSN)
TPMS	nominal	5	Transaction Processing Management System (IMS, batch,…)
CRITIC	nominal	5	Longest acceptable break in operations
T	nominal	4	Capability to recover application after crash
			Quantitative Project Data
OBLEFF	ratio	25 - 3031	Annual obligatory maintenance effort in hours
TOTALFP	ratio	18 - 2328	Total number of function points
PCOBOL	ratio	0 – 100	Percentage of Cobol code
PTELON	ratio	0 - 87	Percentage of Telon code
PEASY	ratio	0 - 52	Percentage of Easytrieve+ code
PJCL	ratio	0 - 96	Percentage of JCL code
AGEE93	interval	8 - 85	Total number of months maintained at the end of 1993
AVETRAN	ratio	0.1 - 345	Average no. thousands of transactions per 24 hours
DISKSP	ratio	0.1 - 39012	MB disk space
CPU	ratio	0.1 - 2197	seconds/24 hours
DDY93	ratio	0 - 163	Number of design defects found during year
			Risk Factors
R1	ordinal	1-5	number of users
R2	ordinal	1-5	flexibility of configuration management
R3	ordinal	1-5	flexibility of change management
R4	ordinal	1-5	structural flexibility / maintainability
R5	ordinal	1-5	quality of documentation
R6	ordinal	1-5	dependence on people
R7	ordinal	1-5	shutdown time constraints
R8	ordinal	1-5	integration of online transaction processing
R9	ordinal	1-5	integration of batch processing
R10	ordinal	1-5	capacity flexibility

2. Presentation of Data

250 applications in one business environment is a large number; unfortunately, not all of them were controlled equally. Data was collected with varying accuracy and completeness by the different departments responsible for the application's maintenance. Based on Pekka's knowledge, we used only applications that had the most complete and valid data for our study. Thus of the 250 IBM mainframe applications, a subset of 67 applications which were being maintained during 1993 and which had effort, size, and defect data were analysed. Risk factor data was available for 56 of these applications. All applications studied were developed in-house and all but 2 used the DB2 database management system. The applications used combinations of 4 different programming languages. All but 5 used Cobol. Most also used JCL, a language for programming and controlling batch processing in an IBM mainframe environment. In addition, some applications used Easytrieve+, a language for generating reports and/or Telon, which is a higher level tool for generating Cobol code. Table 1 presents the 28 variables used in our analysis. These are broken down into 3 groups: classification variables, quantitative project data, and risk factors. Additional background about how the data was used to manage risks and definitions of the 10 risk factors can be found at: http://www.datamax-france.com/riskhtml.

Size was initially measured in source statements of code. The number of source statements of Cobol, Telon, Easytrieve+ and JCL were counted individually. The equivalent number of function points was backfired for each language using Capers Jones' table [3]. The number of function points for each language was then combined to give the total number of function points. The size of the application was determined in the summer each year and was thus an indicator of the average size of the application during the year.

Obligatory effort was defined as changes that were necessary in order to keep the application running. This included fixing bugs, making very easy technical improvements such as implementing and testing improved features of new versions of development tools to improve lay-outs, and testing the application when the environment changed. For example, if the system level software, source libraries, DBMS version or operating system version changed, some parameters or interfaces may require modification. Obligatory effort did **not** include the day-to-day effort needed to run the application (parameter changes, repairing inputs, controlling data transfer interfaces), or the effort needed to enhance or redo the application for the customer. Obligatory effort was aggregated on an annual basis in January for the previous year.

Defect statistics were collected very carefully in the bank. All defects in the IBM environment were classified into 11 types (application design, parameter data, operator, data communication, device, and so on) and 5 categories (tiny to very serious) and recorded. Data collection was as automatic as possible. All run-time defects were logged by a defect tracing system and all logical errors detected by end-users were entered by their representatives or by help desk staff. The classification was made by project managers. In our study, we concentrated on total design defects because they are an important indicator of application quality. We did not use the category breakdown because of the small total number of defects and applicable applications. 8% of all registered defects were design defects. Design defects were defined as defects which originated during the requirements specification phase. Either someone had misunderstood the requirements, or a requirement was missing, with the result that during the maintenance phase it became evident that the application was working in a different way than the customer intended. Design defect data was compiled on an annual basis in January for the previous year. According to the users, the quality of the applications was "satisfying". 21 applications had zero design defects, 10 had one defect, and 6 had two defects. Only 7 applications had more than 21 design defects.

3. Results of Analysis

The data was statistically analysed using a stepwise analysis of variance method in order to determine which combination of variables explained the most variance in annual obligatory maintenance effort. All the steps of the statistical analysis and the raw data will be published in 2002 [4]. The analysis was first performed on the entire dataset. In addition, in order to evaluate the strategic decision to use the Telon development tool, the same analysis was undertaken for the 11 applications which used Telon.

3.1. Annual Obligatory Maintenance Effort

Each autumn, representatives from the independent business unit of software development and maintenance staff, and the banking business units (morg) who owned the application, met to negotiate next year's costs. The amount of maintenance effort was one of the most important cost drivers. It is widely believed that maintenance costs represent as much as 50-80% of the total software lifecycle costs [5,6,7]. Maintenance effort was divided into two main categories: obligatory maintenance and independent enhancements. Our study looks in detail at obligatory maintenance because it is more related to design defects, and because it is a more sensible value to compare among applications.

The obligatory effort model is presented in Table 2. Five variables explained 61.5% of the variance in annual obligatory maintenance effort. The variables are listed in order of importance. The single most important variable was the size of the application. Size alone explained 27% of the variation in effort. Annual obligatory maintenance effort was found to increase with increasing application size. Once size had been taken into consideration, the next most important variable was the integration of batch processing. Annual obligatory maintenance effort was found to increase with a higher integration of batch processing. The next variable to enter the model was morg – i.e. which organisational team planned the maintenance. This variable also represents the internal business sectors of the bank.

Table 2: Annual obligatory maintenance effort model

DEPENDANT VARIABLE	SIGNIFICANT VARIABLES	EFFECT ON DEPENDANT VARIABLE	TOTAL VARIANCE EXPLAINED
Obligatory Effort 56 observations	Size in Function Points Batch Processing Integration Internal Business Sector Change Management Dependence Number of months maintained	positive positive depends on type negative negative	61.5%

Figure 1 shows the annual obligatory maintenance delivery rate by internal business sector for the sectors that had 4 or more observations. After adjustment for application size, securities trading systems and deposit applications required the most annual obligatory effort; accounting, payment, treasury and common banking service applications had lower obligatory efforts.

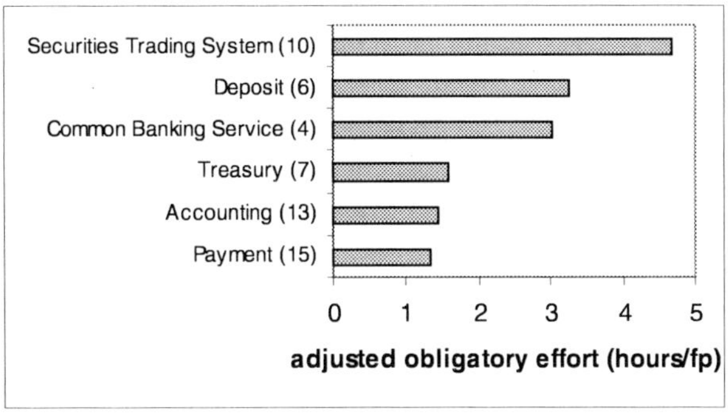

Figure 1: Annual maintenance delivery rate (hours/fp) by internal business sector

Some differences in effort among sectors can be attributed to application structures, for example, the deposit applications were all very big and independent. Also there were remarkable differences by user interface architecture. Most of deposit applications were actually server parts of cooperational client/server systems. Banking products: payment, accounting, and common banking service systems, were probably less complex than the others. Common banking services included common services that other applications use: customer management services, customer database services (over 2 million customers), product management system, product management database and an organisation management system (who is responsible for each customer and contract). Some of these used online processing and some used batch processing. The amount of effort required by treasury applications was actually greater in practice than appears in this dataset. The treasury market in Finland and resulting business instruments were changing so fast that the most complex applications were not in the mainframe environment we studied. They were lighter PC-applications and we don't have any reliable effort data for them. Although very important in banking, loan applications do not appear in this analysis because they did not have enough detailed data.

Securities trading systems required the highest annual obligatory maintenance effort per function point. These systems were very integrated, big batch processing applications. The rules for securities instruments were different with numbers of exceptions. They changed frequently as there were often new series of shares and new types of issues. Hence, lots of testing was needed. Standardisation was very low as companies were always inventing new ways of getting funding. It was difficult for software staff to predict and plan for the next financial innovation.

Although the actual levels of average effort by sector would be different in other banks, what is important here is that we have found significant differences in effort and productivity for "internal business sectors" within the bank. In this bank for example, payment systems required the lowest annual obligatory maintenance effort per function point. This is because payment system maintenance was very well standardised. In the 1990s in Finland, there was a very high level of automation between companies and banks, and between banking groups. Everything was processed electronically. In the UK, however, all banks sent material to a clearing centre. These differences have a strong influence on the way payment system applications are developed in various countries, and their resulting maintenance needs.

The 4th most important variable was dependency of change management. Less obligatory effort was required by applications that were dependent on other applications, had more owners, and for which no quick decisions could be made. Meetings between several parties were required before deciding on modifications to these types of applications, and it is likely that only very necessary modifications would be agreed on.

Finally, the number of months the application had been maintained had an impact on annual obligatory maintenance effort; less obligatory effort was required for older applications. Figure 2 shows the relationship between annual obligatory maintenance effort and the age of the application. If we hold the other 4 variables (size, batch processing integration, internal business sector and change management dependence) constant (represented by k in Equation 1), effort equals a constant multiplied by an "age multiplier" – i.e. an exponential function dependent on age. The age multiplier is 1 when the application enters the maintenance phase and decreases thereafter.

$$effort = ke^{-0.0157 \times age} \qquad (1)$$

It is of interest to note that we found that age had an exponential effect on effort in our analysis. Exponential functions are commonly used in business, economics and the sciences to express rates of growth and decay. Interest compounding is generally expressed in terms of exponential functions dependent on time. In this case, the relationship we have found between age and effort bears a close resemblance to equations used to calculate the decay rate of elements, such as Carbon 14. Similarly, we can think of our age multiplier as a "Software Maintenance Decay Rate".

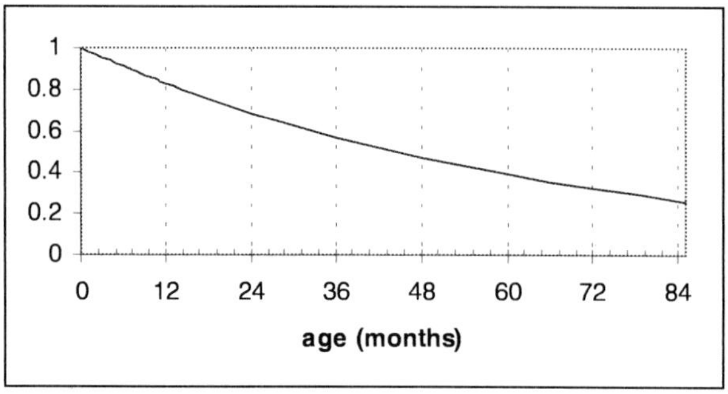

Figure 2: Software maintenance decay rate as a function of age

In this bank, annual obligatory maintenance effort was found to decrease at the rate of approximately 17.2% per year. Thus we would expect that an application which required 100 hours of annual maintenance effort for its first entire year of maintenance, would require 82.8 hours for the following year, and 68.6 hours for the next year - if nothing else about the application changed.

No other variable explained any additional variance of annual obligatory maintenance effort. It is of interest that the variable design defects does not appear in the multi-variable model. This is because design defects was strongly correlated with the size of the application. The bigger the application, the more design defects. Thus once the effect of size had been added to the annual obligatory maintenance effort model, the number of design defects was no longer significant. Design defects alone explained 3.5% of the variance in effort while size alone explained 27% of the variation. Size was a more important indicator of effort than the number of design defects.

3.2. The Choice of Development Tools

"The Telon salesman said that it would be more productive both in the development project and especially in maintenance."

If you are going to develop 250 integrated software applications that you plan to maintain for 20 years on average, it is very important to select the right strategic tools - the earlier the better. It is very expensive and in most real-world cases almost impossible to change tools later. Not enough is known about the real impact on effort until you have trained many people to use the tools and implemented approximately 50% of the applications. The most important reason Telon was selected as a tool was that it was purported to be more productive in the development project and especially in maintenance, compared to Cobol. Was the decision to select Telon a good one?

Of the 56 applications in the dataset, 11 were developed mainly by Telon. We found that less obligatory maintenance hours per function point were required for Telon applications; 1.19 hours/fp compared with 2.47 hours/fp for applications which were not developed by Telon. However, this result is not statistically significant. Thus, we decided to study the 11 Telon applications in more detail.

The Telon models are presented in Table 3. We found a very strong relationship between the percentage of Telon code and the annual obligatory maintenance effort. Using more Telon decreased obligatory maintenance effort (see Figure 3). The relationship when obligatory effort is adjusted for size is also very strong.

We were also interested to know if the use of Telon decreased the quality of the applications. We found that a weaker, although significant, relationship exists between the number of design defects and the percentage of Telon code used. The linear model implies that the more Telon is used the less defects there are. However, Figure 4 shows that the relationship is not linear but U-shaped, and suggests that the number of design defects decreases with the % of Telon used up to about 50%, is the lowest between 50-70%, and increases again after 70%.

Table 3 – Results for applications using Telon

DEPENDANT VARIABLE	SIGNIFICANT VARIABLE	EFFECT ON DEPENDANT VARIABLE	TOTAL VARIANCE EXPLAINED
Obligatory Effort 11 observations	Percentage of Telon code	negative	72%
Obligatory Effort per function point 11 observations	Percentage of Telon code	negative	64%
Design Defects 11 observations	Percentage of Telon code*	negative	22%

All variables significant at the 5% level except those marked with an asterisk which are significant at the 10% level

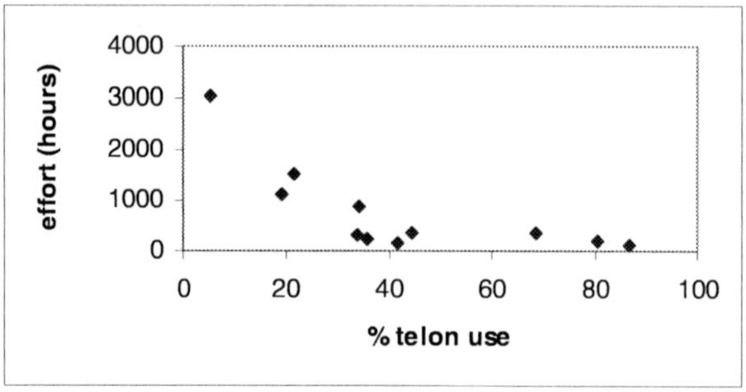

Figure 3 – Obligatory Effort vs. % Telon Use

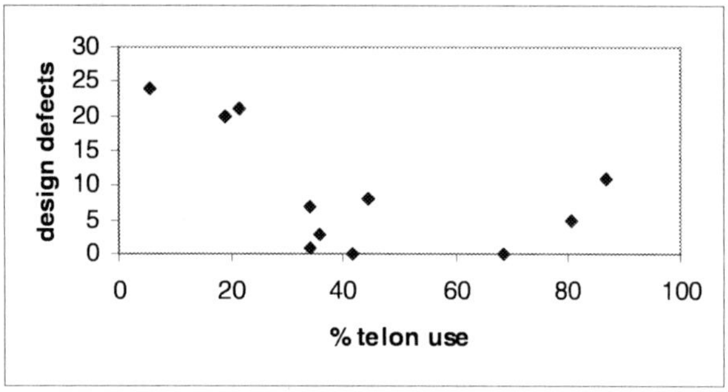

Figure 4 – Number of Design Defects vs. % Telon Use

4. Conclusions – Lessons Learned

Software managers often find it difficult to plan for maintenance work, and there is little quantitative empirical research devoted to improving their performance. [8]. Through the statistical analysis of one commercial bank's data, we have determined which factors had a real impact on the bank's annual obligatory maintenance effort. While it is interesting to know which factors are important, it is even more valuable for software managers to be able to reduce future software maintenance cost by changing their practices. Which of these factors are within the manager's control, and what would Pekka have done differently?

The percentage of Telon use (ptelon) can be modified. For applications which used Telon, using more Telon appeared to decrease annual maintenance effort. Pekka would prefer to use Telon in all new development projects but not for all kinds of functionality. He would increase the % to within the optimal range. Although we only studied 11 projects, this was enough evidence for him, as it confirmed his intuition based on experience with 19 other Telon projects that did not collect detailed data and were not included in the analysis. In addition, Kemerer and Slaughter [8] found in their study that modules generated by a backend case tool that generated Cobol code were significantly less likely to be repaired. There is also evidence that using Telon (compared with traditional Cobol coding) improves development productivity. The ISBSG database shows a median delivery rate of 8.6 hours/fp for Telon as opposed to 11.8 hours/fp for Cobol [9] for mainframe platforms. Thus it appears that the salesman was right, and that using Telon can improve the productivity of the software life-cycle.

Obligatory maintenance effort increased with a higher integration of batch processing (r9). This factor can be controlled to some extent. If all possible interconnections are not implemented, the application itself will be simpler but will need much more manual effort from the user organisation and much more human control too. The more you automate the process, the smaller the total effort, although the obligatory maintenance effort may increase slightly. Batch processing also causes more problems compared to online transaction processing. It is usually done at night when the online processing system is off. 50% of the applications were integrated in online processing. 80% of the applications had a high batch integration. Because batch processing integration is important in the model, and integration of online transaction processing (r8) is not a significant factor, Pekka would recommend moving some interfaces from batch processing to online processing.

The risk factor, dependence of change management (r3), can be partially controlled. Pekka was surprised to learn that less obligatory effort was required by applications that were dependent on other applications, had more owners and for which no quick decisions could be made. He wondered if it had anything to do with the number of defects. Did the ability to do things quickly result in more defects? Close inspection of the data revealed that this was not the case. He can't see why more dependent applications would be more productive to maintain, so believes that this result must be due to the change management process. He can't change the applications dependency, he can't change the number of owners, but he can change the decision making process. He would not allow quick decisions. He would recommend a more formal controlled change management process. He believes this would lead to better reasoning for change requests which would be analysed and formulated better. Part of the problem with interpreting this variable is that the definition is complicated and includes 3 different factors: dependence of changes, number of owners, and quickness of decisions. We would recommend splitting this variable into 3 different variables in the future.

The business sector classification (morg) cannot be changed but it is useful to know that different productivities can be expected for the various internal business sectors. This could help in the negotiations between the maintenance staff and the application owners.

We also found that maintenance effort adjusted for size (hours/fp) decreases with increasing size. This was an interesting result, as Pekka was concerned that developing big applications would have a bad impact on maintenance productivity. We have now found economies of scale both in the development productivity [10] and maintenance productivity of Cobol applications in banks.

Since age is important, Pekka would start recording actual efforts and number of defects every month during the first years of maintenance. Although we have no empirical evidence, he believes that the first months are critical. Some of the most design defects were found in old applications, which had caused problems from the start, and he believes that if they had been better controlled in the beginning their lifetime maintenance costs would be much lower.

He also found it interesting that the status of documentation (r5) did not come out as being important. This is probably because there were no applications for which there were no documents and for which even understanding the code was difficult. Another probable explanation is the very low volatility of staff in the early 1990s. Something that is clear and understandable to the original developer could be very difficult to understand for any new maintainer.

Unfortunately, the lessons learned will not be able to be put into practice for this bank. Although the bank had developed a very good understanding of its software development and maintenance activities, and one could even say that they were ahead of their time as far as software measurement goes, strategic decisions high up in the bank were soon to change everything. In early 1995, near the end of the banking crisis in Finland, and just a couple of months before the large migration project was successfully completed, the bank merged with another bank. A major motive for the merger was to benefit from economies of scale by eliminating overlapping operations. This resulted in the adoption of nearly all of the other bank's Information Systems. Thus only a few of the applications studied still exist today. It is for this reason that we are able to make these results public.

5. Acknowledgements

We would like to thank Chris Kemerer for his comments on an earlier version of this paper.

6. References

[1] Carr, D. and R.J. Kizior, "The Case for Continued Cobol Education", IEEE Software, Volume 17, Number 2, March/April 2000, pp. 33-36.
[2] Arranga, E., "In Cobol's Defense", IEEE Software, Volume 17, Number 2, March/April 2000, pp. 70-75.
[3] Jones, C., "A new look at languages", Computerworld, November 7, 1988, pp.97-103.
[4] Maxwell, K., "Software Manager's Statistics", Upper Saddle River, New Jersey, Prentice Hall, forthcoming 2002.
[5] Ramaswamy, R., "How to Staff Business-Critical Maintenance Projects", IEEE Software, May/June 2000, pp.90-94.
[6] Kemerer, C.F. and S. Slaughter, "Methodologies for Performing Empirical Studies: Report from the International Workshop on Empirical Studies of Software Maintenance", Empirical Software Engineering, Vol.2, 1997, pp.109-118.
[7] Kemerer, C.F. and S. Slaughter, "An Empirical Approach to Studying Software Evolution", IEEE Transactions on Software Engineering, Vol. 25, No. 4, July/August 1999, pp. 493-509.
[8] Kemerer, C.F. and S. Slaughter, "Determinants of Software Maintenance Profiles: An Empirical Investigation", Software Maintenance Research and Practice, Vol. 9, 1997, pp.235-251.
[9] ISBSG, The Benchmark Release 6, International Software Benchmarking Standards Group Limited, Australia, 2000, p.55.
[10] Maxwell, K. and P. Forselius, "Benchmarking Software Development Productivity", IEEE Software, Volume 17, Number 1, January/February 2000, pp. 80-88.

Validation of measures to assess the maintainability of SQL programs

Martínez A., Piattini M.

Abstract

Due to the expansion of Fourth Generation Languages (4GL), it has become increasingly interesting to have a set of metrics through which the quality of the systemas developed using this kind of environment can be assessed. And especially their maintainability, since maintenance constitutes the main problem of software development, involving 60 to 80 percent of the life cycle costs.

Some types of measures have been defined for fourth generation environments, up to now, these works have focused on the assessment of development effort and its correlation with the size of a 4GL program, but not on 4GL program maintainability.

When it comes down to defining metrics for 4GL programs, we face the problem of the great heterogeneity of sentence types that may be contained in this kind program. We have identified different sub-languages in order to cope with that heterogeneity: procedure, visual, exception-handling, database definition, database manupulation, security and transaction manage sub-languages.

In this paper we propose a set of measures to control the maintainability of programs developed in a fourth generation environment, focusing on the database manipulation sub-language. We present an empirical validation that includes a study case in a Public organization (the Country Council of Ciudad Real) and an experiment applying Taguchi's Method. Finally, we outline the conclusions and subsequent work.

1. Introduction

Experimentation in software engineering is necessary. Common wisdom, intuition, speculation, and proofs of concepts are not reliable sources of credible knowledge [1].

The technique of defining and investigating all possible conditions in an experiment involving multiple factors is known as the design of experiments. In the literature this technique is also referred to as factorial design. The concepts of design of experiments have been in use since Fisher's work in agricultural experimentation, approximately half a century ago. Fisher successfully designed experiments to determining optimum treatments for land to achieve maximum yield. Numerous applications of this approach, especially in the chemical and pharmaceutical industries, are cited in the literature [2]. A thorough coverage of this subject is beyond the scope of this study, but the method and its advantages and disadvantages from an engineering point of view.

For a full factorial design the number of possible designs N is

$$N = L^m \qquad (1)$$

where L = Number of levels for each factor.
and m = Number of factors

Thus, if the qualities of a given product depends on three factors. A, B, and C and each factor is to be tested at two levels then, Eq. (1) indicates 2^3 (8) possible design configurations.

1.1. Taguchi

Taguchi contributed discipline and structure to the design of experiments. The result is a standardized design methodology that can easily be applied by investigators. Furthermore, designs for the same experiment by two different investigators will yield similar data and will lead to similar conclusions. Taguchi overcame the limitations of factorial and fractional factorial experiments.

Taguchi espoused an excellent philosophy for quality control in the manufacturing industries.

Taguchi constructed a special set of orthogonal arrays (OAs) to lay out his experiments. The use of latin squares orthogonal arrays for experiment designs dates back to the time of World War II. By combining the orthogonal latin squares in a unique manner, Taguchi prepared a new set of standard OAs to be used for a number of experimental situations. A common OA for 2 level factors is shown in table 1. This array, designated by the symbol L_8, is used to design experiments involving up to seven 2 level factors. The array has 8 rows and 7 columns. Each row represents a trial condition with factor levels indicated by the numbers in the row. The vertical columns correspond to the factors specified in the study.

Table 1. Orthogonal Array L_8 (2^7)

TRIAL NUMBER	FACTORS A	B	C	D	E	F	G
1	1	1	1	1	1	1	1
2	1	1	1	2	2	2	2
3	1	2	2	1	1	2	2
4	1	2	2	2	2	1	1
5	2	1	2	1	2	1	2
6	2	1	2	2	1	2	1
7	2	2	1	1	2	2	1
8	2	2	1	2	1	1	2

Each column contains four level 1 and four level 2 conditions for the factor assigned to the column. Two 2 level factors combine in four possible ways, such as (1,1), (1,2), (2,1), and (2,2). When two columns of an array form these combinations the same number of times, the columns are said to be balanced or orthogonal. Note that any two columns of an L_8 (2^7) have the same number of combinations of (1,1), 1,2), (2,1), and (2,2). Thus, all seven columns of an L are orthogonal to each other.

The OA facilitates the experiment design process. To design an experiment is to select the most suitable orthogonal array, assign the factors to the appropriate columns, and finally, describe the combinations of the individual experiments called "trial conditions ". Let us assume that there are at most seven 2 level factors is the study. Call these factors A, B, C, D,

E, F, and G assign them to columns 1, 2, 3, 4, 5, 6 and 7 respectively of L_8. The table identifies the eight trials needed to complete the experiment and the level of each factor for each trial run. The experiment descriptions are determined by reading numerals 1 and 2 appearing in the rows of the trial runs. A factorial experiment would require 2^7 or 128 runs, but would not provide appreciably more information.

The array forces all experimenters to design almost identical experiments. Experimenters may select different designations for the columns but the eight trial runs will include all combinations independent of column definition. Thus the OA assures consistency of design by different experimenters.

1.2. Analysis of results

In the Taguchi method the results of the experiments are analyzed to achieve one or more of the following three objectives:

1.To establish the best or the optimum condition for a product or a process.
2.To estimate the contribution of individual factors.
3.To estimate the response under the optimum conditions.

The optimum condition is identified by studying the main effects of each of the factors. The process involves minor arithmetic manipulation of the numerical results and usually can be done with the help of a simple calculator. The main effects indicate the general trend of the influence of the factors. Knowing the characteristic, i.e., whether a higher or lower, value produces the preferred result, the levels of the factors which are expected to produce the best results can be predicted.

The knowledge of the contribution of individual factors is a key to deciding the nature of the control to be established on a production process. The analysis of variance (ANOVA) is the statistical treatment most commonly applied to the results of the experiment to determine the percent contribution of each factor. Study of the ANOVA table for a given analysis helps to determine which of the factors need control and which do not.

Once the optimum condition is determined, it is usually a good practice to run a confirmation experiment. It is, however, possible to estimate performance at the optimum condition from the results of experiments conducted at a non-optimum condition. It should be noted that the optimum condition may not necessarily be among the many experiments already carried out , as the OA represents only a small fraction of all the possibilities.

Taguchi suggests two different routes to carry out the complete analysis. First, the standard approach, where the result of a single run, or the average of repetitive uns, are processed through main effect and ANOVA analyses as identified above. The second approach, which he strongly recommends for multiple runs, is to use signal to noise ratio (S/N) for the same steps in the analysis. S/N analysis determines the most robust set of operating conditions from variations within the results.

2. PROPOSED MEASURES FOR ASSESSING SQL PROGRAMS

When it comes down to defining metrics for 4GL programs, we face the problem of the great heterogeneity of sentence types that may be contained in this kind of program. We have identified different sub-languages in order to cope with that heterogeneity: procedure control, visual control, exception-handling, database definition, database manipulation, security control, and transaction control sub-languages [3].

SQL language is composed of different kinds of statements: definition statements (e.g. CREATE TABLE), manipulation statements (e.g. INSERT) and control statements (e.g.

COMMIT). Four different manipulation statement can be found: SELECT, INSERT, DELETE and UPDATE. We focus our work on manipulation statements.

We propose the following four measures:

- **NS**
  The total number of SELECT statement.
- **NI**
  The total number of INSERT statement.
- **ND**
  The total number of DELETE statement.
- **NU**
  The total number of UPDATE statement.

3. Empirical validation

We must bear in mind that the application of the experimental paradigm in software engineering is still very recent, and that we are still learning how to design experiments and how to draw useful knowledge from them [4].

Experimentation helps determine the effectiveness of proposed theories and methods. But computer science has not developed a concise taxonomy of methods for demonstrating the validity of new techniques [5].

The empirical validation of the proposed measures is to be carried out on a real case as well as an experimental one. The real case is an application written in a fourth generation environment (CA-OpenIngres/4GL). The experimental case consists in eight questions that combine SQL sentences according to Taguchi's Method. As far as we know, it is the first time that Taguchi's Method is applied to the empirical validation of software metrics.

3.1. STUDY CASE

3.1.1. General system characteristics

The system is composed of 141 programs developed over a period of one year at the Data Processing Center of the Ciudad Real County Council. The system is a transaction processing system for data maintenance.

More importantly, the system developed was functionally sound, providing an actual working solution to an actual organizational problem.

3.1.2. Data collection

The maintenance process includes adding functionality to the software (adaptive maintenance) and correcting defects discovered in the systems (corrective maintenance).

Our study examined data from a maintenance period beginning with the original installation of the product and ending the product's second release. The required changes varied in magnitude from a simple command line option change to a more complex one. During the maintenance period the programmer recorded daily effort maintenance product, descriptions of the faults encountered as a consequence of enhancement activities, time spent correcting these faults and the functions to which the time and faults could be attributed. This tool is implemented in CA-OpenIngres.

3.1.3. Data analysis and results

For the correlation test we use Spearman´s non-parametric correlation. We do this in order identify potential relationships between the variable time of maintenance effort (expressed in minutes) and the measures defined, as well as the relationships that could exist between the same variables. The results are shown in table 2.

Table 2. Spearman's correlation coefficients

		NS	NI	ND	NU	TIME
Spearman	NS	1,000	0,409	0,127	0,137	0,803
	NI	0,409	1,000	0,207	0,094	0,407
	ND	0,127	0,207	1,000	0,234	0,156
	NU	0,137	0,094	0234	1,000	0,089
	TIME	0,803	0,407	0,156	0,089	1,000
Sig	NS		0,000	0,129	0,102	0,000
	NI	0,000		0,013	0,266	0,000
	ND	0,129	0,013		0,005	0,063
	NU	0,102	0,266	0.005		0,289
	TIME	0,000	0,000	0,063	0,289	
N	NS	141	141	141	141	141
	NI	141	141	141	141	141
	ND	141	141	141	141	141
	NU	141	141	141	141	141
	TIME	141	141	141	141	141

The statistics show strong significant relationships between the variable time of maintenance and the defined measurement NS. We can observe that the relationships between the specification of the measured NS, NI, ND and NU not are significant.

3.2. Experiment

In this section we summarize an experiment done in order to validate NS, NI, ND, and NU measures. This empirical validation has been carried out following the experimental method applied to software engineering [6], [7], because not have correlation between the defined measuremen (NS, NI, ND, NU).

Our the experimenter wants to determine the optimun combination of the levels of these factors and to know the contribution of each measures can be used for measuring the understandability of the SQL statements which influences its maintainability.

The Taguchi method does not specify any general guidelines for predicting interactions.

3.2.1. The Design

There are four factors, each at two levels, thus and L_8 will be suitable. An L_8 OA with spaces for the factors and their levels is shown in table 3. This configuration is a convenient way to lay out a design. Since an L_8 has eigth columns, the four factors can be assigned to these columns in any order. Having assigned the factors, their levels can also be indicated in the corresponding column.

There are eight independent experimental conditions in an L_8.These conditions are described by the numbers in the rows. For an experienced user of the technique, an array with factors assigned as shown in table 3, contains all the necessary information. But for others, a descriptive arrangement of the factors constituting different conditions of the experiment may be helpful.

Table 3. The factors and their levels

TRIAL NUMBER	FACTORS/MEASURES NS	NI	ND	NU	E	F	G
1	1	1	1	1	0	0	0
2	1	1	1	2	0	0	0
3	1	2	2	1	0	0	0
4	1	2	2	2	0	0	0
5	2	1	2	1	0	0	0
6	2	1	2	2	0	0	0
7	2	2	1	1	0	0	0
8	2	2	1	2	0	0	0

3.2.2. Order of Running the Experiments

Whenever possible, the trial conditions (the individual combinations in a designed experiment) should be run in a random order to avoid the influence of experiment setup. If only one run for each of the above conditions is planned, they could be run as experiment number 2,5,7,4,3,1,8 and 6, or any other random order.

3.2.3. Subjects

The participants of the field test were Computer Science students at the University of Castilla-La Mancha (Spain), who were enrolled in a database course lasting two semesters. Until the day of the experiment, the students did not known that they were to do it. The experiment was developed by 34 students, but only 19 test cases were selected, because it answered right full the questions.

We have tried to minimize variability among participants by choosing people of the same degree, in particular from the third year.

3.2.4. Experimental materials

Eight separate SQL statements were required to the experiment. In each one values of the four measures were different. There were two possible values for NS (one or three), two for NI (one or three), two for ND (one or three) and two for NU (one or three). The documentation accompanying each design was approximately twelve pages long including the tables and the queries. In appendix A the tables and the SQL statements are shown.

The same table was used to reduce semantic variability in all the eight cases. In order to avoid learning errors, the eight cases were in different order for each subject, and the subjects were forced to follow the order in which cases appeared in the experimental material.

The subjects were asked to write down the initial and the final time, and the result for each query. We only counted the time employed in giving correct answers.

To increase the power of the test, α has been set to 0.1 instead of 0.05 level which is more common [8].

3.2.5. Analysis of Results

Taguchi replaces the full factorial experiment with a lean, less expensive, faster, partial factorial experiment. Taguchi's design for the partial factorial is based on specially developed OA. Since the partial experiment is only a sample of the full experiment, the analysis of the partial experiment must include an analysis of the confidence that can be placed in the results. Fortunately, there is a standard statistical technique called Analysis of Variance (ANOVA) which is routinely used to provide a measure of confidence. The technique does not directly analyze the data, but rether determines the variability (variance) of the data. Confidence es measured from the variance.

Analysis provides the variance of controllable and noise factors. By understanding the source and magnitude of variance, robust operating conditions can be predicted. This is a second of the methodology.

	Sum of Squares	DF	Mean Square	F	Percent contribution
TIME	613,50	4	153,38	29,93	
NS	528,13	1	528,13	103,05	83,98
NI	28,13	1	28,13	5,49	4,47
ND	36,13	1	36,13	7,05	5,74
NU	21,13	1	21,13	4,12	3,36
Explained	613,50	4	153,38	29,93	
Residual	15,38	3	5,13		2,45
Total	628,88	7	89,84		100

Table 4. Results of the experiment

If we compare the values of table 4 with $F_{.05}(1,3) = 10,128$, we can be certain that:

Since 103,05 > 10,128, we can say that NS does affect maintenance time.
Since 5,49 < 10,128, we can say NI does not.
Since 7,049 < 10,128, we can say ND does not.
Since 4,122 < 10,128, we can say NU does not.

If we take into account the percentage of contribution (table 4) for each measure, we see that the NS measure is significantly high, unlike NI, ND, and NU.

We can conclude that the number of SELECT sentences of an SQL program is a solid indicator of the comprehensibility and therefore influences the maintainability of the programs. We can assert that NI, ND, and NU measures have no significant influence on the maintainability of SQL programs.

NS can be classified a dominant measure, whereas NI, ND, and NU can be regarded redundant measures, according to [8] terminology.

Therefore, the SELECT sentence is the most complex to understand and maintain in the SQL programmes.

4. CONCLUSIONS AND FUTURE WORKS

There is a great need to measure the quality of applications using SQL programs. The measures can help us characterize certain software quality attributes which can then be used to construct better software products.

We have proposed and validated different metrics for the measure of the maintainability of data-intensive 4GL applications. With the results we have obtained, we conclude that the number of SELECT sentences (NS) affects the maintainability of SQL programs.

Furthermore, measures of the data sublanguage are not sufficient to assess the quality of the products developed with fourth-generation languages, so they should be complemented with many others in order to characterise the different sub-languages included in fourth generation environments: visual, procedural, etc.

5. REFERENCES

[1] Basili, V.R., Shull, F. y Lanubille, F., "Building Knowledge through families of experiments", IEEE Transactions on Software Engineering, 1999, pp. 456-473.

[2] Fisher R.A. "Design of Experiments"., Oliver y Boyd, Edimburgo, 1951.

[3] Martínez, A. and Piattini, M., "Validation of 4GL metrics", Proc. of the Software Measurement in Practice, 10th Anniversary Conference, United Kingdom Software Metrics Association, Londres, 1998, pp. 1-19.

[4] Briand, L., Bunse, D., Daly, J. and Differding, C., "An experimental comparison of the Maintainability of Object-Oriented and Structured Design Documents", Proc. Int. Conference on Software Maintenance, Harold, M.J. Visaggio, G. (eds), Bari, 1997, pp.130-138.

[5] Zelkowitz, M.V. y Wallace, D., "Experimental validation in software engineering", Information and software technology, 1997, pp.735-743.

[6] Ranjit, R., "A primer on the Taguchi method". Society of Manufacturing Engineers, 1990

[7] Ross, P.J.," Taguchi Techniques for Quality Engineering". McGraw-Hill, 1996.

[8] Schneidewind N.F. Software metrics for quality control. Proceedings of the fourth international software metrics symposium. *IEEE Computer Society Technical Council on Software Engineering*, 1997, pp.127-136.

6. APPENDIX A

TABLE FIELD DESCRIPTION

TABLE DESCRIPTION: employee

```
Name:               employee
Owner:              ingres
Created:            24/03/1999 14:08:38
Type:               user table
Version:            OPING1.2
```

Column Information:

Column Name	Type	Length	Nulls	Defaults	Key Seq
id_emp	varchar	9	no	no	1
namef_emp	varchar	40	no	no	
name_emp	varchar	30	no	no	
direction	varchar	40	no	no	
post_office	varchar	5	no	no	
town	varchar	2	no	no	
village	varchar	3	no	no	
phone	varchar	9	yes	null	
sex	varchar	1	no	no	
status	varchar	1	no	no	
children	varchar	2	no	no	
birth	date		no	no	
birth_town	varchar	2	no	no	
birth_village	varchar	3	no	no	
birth_country	varchar	3	no	no	
number_social_sec	varchar	14	no	no	
number_social_sec1	varchar	6	yes	null	

The table "employee" has 4 rows.

TABLE DESCRIPTION: h employee

Name:	h_employee
Owner:	ingres
Created:	20/11/1998 18:05:17
Type:	user table
Version:	OPING1.2

Column Information:

Column Name	Type	Length	Nulls	Defaults	Key Seq
code_service	varchar	3	no	no	
code_subs_service	varchar	2	no	no	
id_emp	varchar	9	no	no	
number_fic	varchar	4	no	no	
remainder1	float	8	no	no	
remainder2	float	8	no	no	
remainder3	float	8	no	no	
remainder4	float	8	no	no	
remaindert	float	8	no	no	
remainderf	float	8	no	no	
period	integer	1	no	no	
year	integer	1	no	no	
tipe_hour	integer	2	yes	null	
subtipe	integer	2	yes	null	
key_emp	varchar	15	yes	null	
date_certificate	varchar	6	yes	null	
situation	varchar	1	yes	null	
remainderf	date		yes	null	

The table "h_employee" has 3 rows.

TABLE DESCRIPTION: control employee

Name:	control_employee
Owner:	ingres
Created:	04/03/1999 13:46:31
Type:	user table
Version:	OPING1.2

Column Information:

Column Name	Type	Length	Nulls	Defaults	Key Seq
id_emp	varchar	9	no	no	
number_fic	varchar	4	no	no	
date	varchar	6	no	no	
hour	varchar	4	no	no	
code_incidence	varchar	2	yes	null	
control	varchar	2	yes	null	
status	varchar	1	yes	null	
code_center	varchar	2	yes	null	
tipe	varchar	2	no	no	

The table "control_employee" has 72 rows.

Practical uses for a corporate process database

Lori Vaughan

Abstract

This paper discusses TRW's approach for capturing and using project performance data. The Project Comparative DataBase (PCDB) is TRW's central repository for historical data, including work descriptions, labor, subcontractor, and other direct cost data. TRW's streamlined historical data collection process will be highlighted. The project descriptive and accounting data is collected, then mapped against a standardized WBS enabling generation of accounting reports. Once the reports are validated with the project staff, software productivity can be calculated and a validation of the effort can be modeled with a software parametric cost model. The calibrated cost models form a basis for estimating, analyzing and predicting process performance. Utilizing this process for our corporate project database serves as a foundation for ISO9001 and SEI/CMM process improvement objectives.

1. Introduction

TRW Space and Defense business center has a legacy of software data collection dating back to Dr. Barry Boehm's research in the field of Software Engineering Economics [1]. TRW's Systems Integration and Technology Group has been collecting project historical data and storing that data in an organizational central repository since 1980. Currently, this central repository is called the Project Comparative DataBase (PCDB) established in 1989 and is maintained by the Office of Cost Estimation (OCE). As our organization's software methodologies and processes evolve, our historical database proves to be the foundation for our process improvements. This paper will highlight our project historical data collection process, the type of data we collect, and some of our practical uses for that data.

2. Project historical data collection process

Once a TRW project is completed, or when a significant milestone in a project is achieved, the Office of Cost Estimation will contact the project manager to request assistance in collecting data for the PCDB. As part of our senior management's commitment to collecting project historical data and as an incentive to project managers, we have linked submitting project data to their management performance goals. The project staff in co-operation with the OCE staff maps the project Job Numbers (JNs) into the PCDB standard Work Breakdown Structure (WBS). The PCDB standard WBS contains the broadest possible cross section of WBS elements used on TRW projects. This mapping into a consistent WBS permits comparisons to be made between projects. Project actuals (labor hours and costs) are then collected from TRW's accounting systems and related to the PCDB standard WBS. A report is generated and verified with the project team to determine if all intended data has been collected and properly categorized. This particular step may require a few iterations. Selected projects then undergo a parametric modeling analysis or validation. These validated parametric historical baselines are then used for similar domain estimating exercises. The following section outlines the type of data that is collected.

TRW's streamlined historical data collection process depicted in Figure 1 is a well established parametric cost model validation and calibration process that uses data which has been collected and analyzed during the past 11 years.

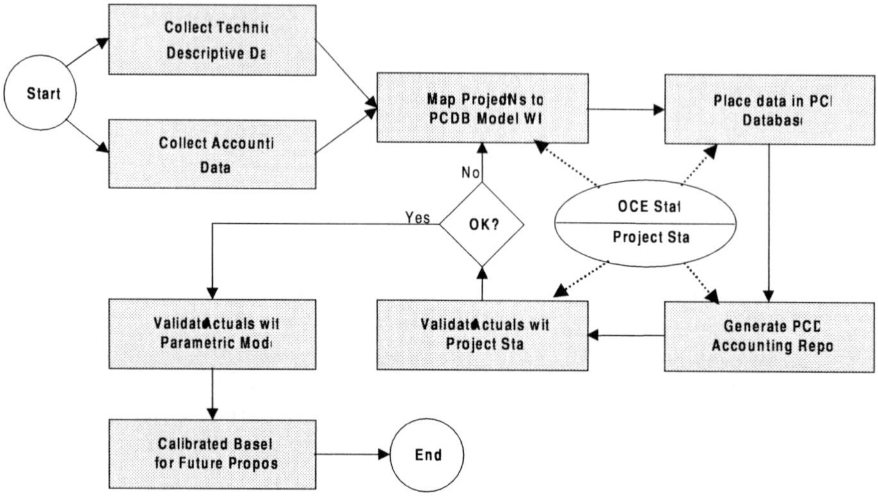

Figure 1. TRW's streamlined historical data collection process.

3. Project historical data description

This section will describe the type of data contained in the PCDB as well as the sources of that data and any important aspects to consider when collecting and analyzing that data. The PCDB contains cost data from certified accounting systems, project descriptive data and derived data from these two types of data. The PCDB relates the cost data to the PCDB standard WBS work elements as well as the technical characteristics of work performed. The term cost data refers to effort and dollar data.

Descriptive data includes such items as: project name, project manager, project duration, staffing profile, software program or subsystem name(s), program software source lines of code, size and language of source software components, hardware and software program problem reports and project hardware and site environment. Accounting data is any cost data associated with a WBS element. Derived data is any data that is calculated as a result of any relation of the descriptive data to the accounting data. An example of derived data would be the average productivity for a particular software program. This productivity (derived type of data) is a result of the software size (descriptive type of data) divided by the amount of software development effort or dollars spent to produce a program (accounting type of data).

The PCDB standard WBS contains the following major elements: Project Management, Systems Engineering, Hardware Development, Software Development, System Integration and Test, Site Activation, Integrated Logistics, Product Assurance, Configuration Management, Data Management and Operations and Maintenance.

Typically, a project business manager is responsible for mapping the project WBS to the PCDB standard WBS. In order to capture certain project metrics without subjectivity it is necessary for the project business and project control personnel to follow OCE guidance with regards to establishing their project WBS and introducing Job Numbers. A few examples of helpful project control practices for collecting accounting metrics are:

- establishing a new set of job numbers at the beginning of a new build or increment of development
- defining an appropriate level of granularity of job numbers for different PCDB WBS elements and sub-elements.

An appropriate level of JN granularity must be balanced with the performer's ability to correctly identify the correct JN to charge against. The ability to recognize the difference of the tasks being performed needs to be obvious enough for a performer to clearly distinguish the work being performed and thus capturing the intended data.

When collecting historical data, it is necessary to co-ordinate with the project manager and project business manager to identify a scope of work or product produced and the respective time frame of the accounting data. The sources of accounting data need to be considered as well. If a teaming partner or subcontractor effort is integral to the product being developed, it will be necessary to collect their cost data at a JN level or take a representative percentage of the work performed to calculate the derived data.

The descriptive data is usually obtained by interviewing the various integrated product team (IPT) leads. We have found it beneficial to perform software lines of code counts prior to meeting with IPT leads. This way the various types of code written, nature of the code and rework percentages can be discussed and recorded. Size is the underlying basis for parametric modelling and estimating equations. The more refined your understanding of the type and amount of code that has been developed, the more accurate your project validations will become and therefore a more representative baseline for future proposals and planning.

4. Process database uses

Now that we reviewed the type of data that is collected and stored in TRW's PCDB, a few of the practical uses of this historical data are illustrated in Figure 2.

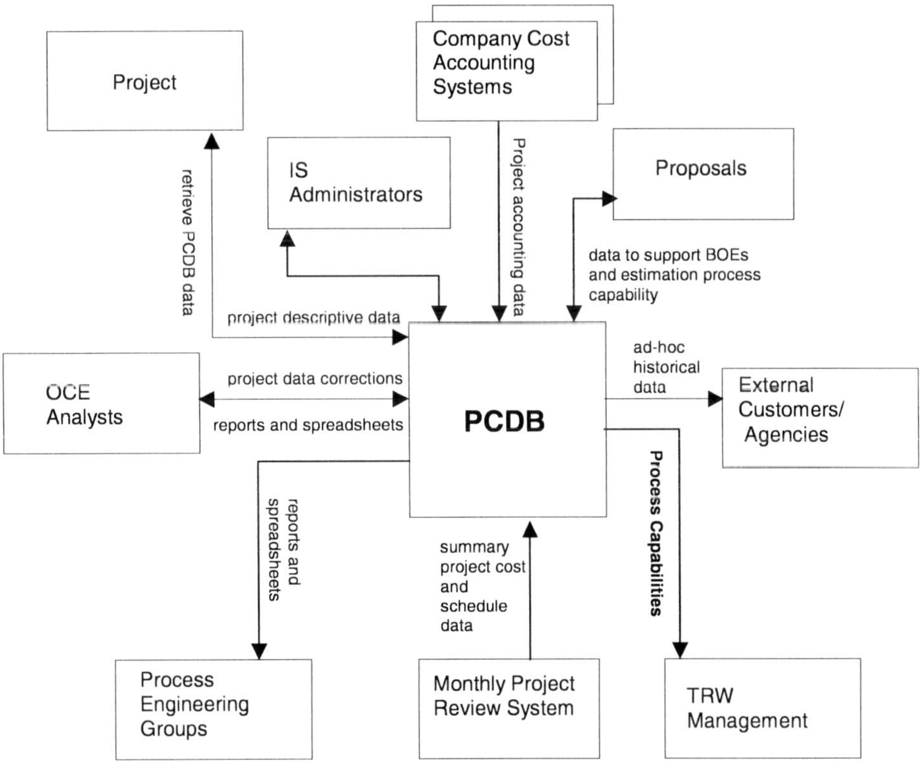

Figure 2. TRW's PCDB interfaces with multiple logical sources and users. [2]

The arrowheads pointing away from the PCDB represent users of the PCDB and the incoming arrowheads represent logical sources. As a framework to highlight some of our practical uses of the PCDB, selected SEI Capability Maturity Model [3] organizational maturity levels, key process areas and the activities are cited Table I. The PCDB is part of the organizational process asset library and is used to perform these key activities. This framework underlies the criticality of the historical database as a foundation for any process capability assessment and growth. Capability Maturity Model level 5 can only be obtained from a strong quantitative foundation and a stable process.

Table I. Selected Capability Maturity Model: level, key process area and activity

- **Level 2: Repeatable**
  - Software Project Planning
    - **Activity 9**: Estimates for the size of the software work products are derived according to a documented procedure.
    - **Activity 10**: Estimates for the software project's effort and costs are derived according to a documented procedure.
- **Level 3: Defined**
  - Organization Process Focus
    - **Activity 4**: The use of the organization's software process database is co-ordinated at the organizational level.
  - Organization Process Definition
    - **Activity 5**: The organization's software process database is established and maintained.
  - Integrated Software Management
    - **Activity 5**: The organization's software process database is used for software planning and estimating.
- **Level 4: Managed**
  - Quantitative Process Management
    - **Activity 4**: The measurement data used to control the project's defined software process quantitatively are collected according to a documented procedure.
    - **Activity 7**: The process capability baseline for the organization's standard software process is established and maintained according to a documented procedure.

TRW's Office of Cost Estimation utilizes historical data on completed efforts to:

- populate the database
- calibrate the parametric models, such as COCOMO II [4]
- derive cost estimating relationships
- provide historical data for proposals, project planning, re-planning and level 3 compliance
- define risk affordability and analysis
- conduct historical studies

PCDB will serve as the foundation for Capability Maturity Model level 4 quantitative metrics and will be expanded to allow use in levels 4 and 5 metrics analysis.

5. Summary

Once an organization has historical, representative, regularly collected data, that organization has the ability to measure the capability and better predict how they will perform on a given effort and make better decisions which are in line with their corporate business goals. To date the PCDB has been an acronym for the Project Comparative DataBase, yet as our organizational processes stabilize and mature; possibly a more appropriate name to attach to the PCDB acronym will be the TRW **P**rocess **C**apability **D**ata**B**ase.

Our corporate process database not only supports numerous practical tactical business decisions, yet also is essential to our strategic goals as a corporation. As in the words of Dave Cote, TRW President-CEO, "People are more willing to make decisions if they can trust that they're getting all the data and that they're supported in the system....That decisiveness, that ability to get the facts, make a decision, and act will drive decisiveness. That sense of urgency, that ability to get those facts, and make something happen are essential to TRW."[5]

6. References

[1] Boehm, B.W., "Software Engineering Economics", Prentice-Hall, Inc., Englewood Cliffs, N.J. 07632, 1981.

[2] Rowe, G., "PCDB Re-architecture CONOPS", TRW internal document, March, 2001.

[3] Paulk, M.C., Curtis, B., Chrissis, M.B., Weber, C.V., "Capability Maturity Model for Software, Version 1.1", Software Engineering Institute Carnegie Mellon University, Pittsburgh, Pennsylvania 15213, February 1993.

[4] Boehm, B.W., Abts, C., Brown, A.W., Chulani, S., Clark, B.K., Horowitz, E., Madachy, R., Reifer, D.J., and Steece, B., "Software Cost Estimation with COCOMO II ", Prentice Hall PTR, Upper Saddle River, New Jersey 07458, 2000.

[5] Cote, D., TRW President and CEO, "TRW Intranet Webcast Transcript", February 1, 2001

Measuring Integrated Product Teams

Richard D. Stutzke

Abstract

Many of today's software development projects use Integrated Product Teams (IPTs) to develop software products. Such teams are composed of individuals from several organizations. This presents challenges for defining a standardized production process and standard metrics, and for collecting the measurements.

This paper describes the challenges we encountered in establishing a metrics program for a large (300 people) organization that uses IPTs for software development and maintenance projects for a wide range of product types. The IPT includes U.S. Government employees and contractor employees from multiple contractors. We defined a set of standard metrics applicable for all the product types and project types (new development versus maintenance), and we devised a way to collect metrics from organizations with different reporting and accounting systems. Our metrics process has been in operation for over four years, and our organization was rated Level 4 on the Software Engineering Institute's Software Capability Maturity Model [1] scale in April 2000. We also present summaries of metrics characterizing our projects and our metrics database. Lastly, we describe some lessons we learned in developing and implementing our metrics program.

1. Introduction

For the past eight years our company has been working with a U.S. government organization and other contractors and subcontractors in an Integrated Product Team (IPT) environment. The organization develops and maintains software for tactical missiles, air vehicles (manned and unmanned), command and control systems, test measurement and diagnostic equipment, and various engineering simulations used for feasibility studies and performance analyses.

In 1991, the organization began a software process improvement program based upon the Software Engineering Institute's Software Capability Maturity Model (SEI SW-CMM) described in [1] and [2]. A key part of the SW-CMM requirements is metrics to characterize software products and the projects that produce these products. The SEI SW-CMM defines the following types of metrics:

- Product size
- Development effort
- Development schedule (or duration)
- Product quality
- Product performance

Several SEI technical reports describe these metrics in detail [3], [4], [5], and [6]. The exception is product performance, which has no descriptive report. (John Baumert's report, reference [3], does provide some references to other sources.)

Our organization's Software Engineering Process Group (SEPG) established a metrics program that met the SEI criteria for the first four items listed above. Product performance metrics include CPU resource utilization, accuracy, and response time. These measures depend on the type of product and the customer's particular requirements. Due to the wide range of products that we develop and maintain, we did not attempt to define standardized product performance measures as part of our metrics program.

In this paper we first describe two challenges that we faced. Next, we describe our process for developing and maintaining software. Then we focus on our process to collect metrics for products, processes, and projects. We conclude by presenting lessons learned about the metrics program over the past eight years. The main achievements of our process improvement program are:

September 1991	-	First assessment
May 1994	-	Organization rated CMM level 2
November 1996	-	Organization rated CMM level 3
April 2000	-	Organization rated CMM level 4

2. Software Production Process

Achieving a SW-CMM Level 4 rating was not easy for two reasons. First, the organization has a wide diversity of products and project types. Second, the projects use Integrated Product Teams. Each of these presents particular challenges.

2.1. A Process to Handle Diversity

The organization develops products in several domains (command and control, trainers, fire control, aviation, etc.) These products utilize over 11 different high order languages. At any one time, the organization has approximately 50 active projects. These include new development, transition, and maintenance ("sustainment"). New development projects start with specifications and develop the necessary product. Transition projects establish a capability (tools, techniques, and trained people) to sustain a software product and its associated documentation that were developed outside of the organization. (We say that the product is "transitioned" into the organization from the external developer.) Sustainment projects maintain existing software and add enhancements. (We prefer to use the word "sustainment" because too many people the word "maintenance" connotes merely correcting errors. A large part of our work is adding new features requested by the users.)

To cope with the wide range of product and project types, we defined an integrated project management flow, which is shown in Figure 1. The key feature of the process flow is that it uses the *same* management process for all types of projects. The only differences between new development, transition, and sustainment projects are the engineering activities performed by the project team. Different versions of the engineering activities accommodate these project types, as well as various life cycles, product types, etc. In this way we handle the diversity of project and product types.

We now explain the flow shown in Figure 1 in detail. The columns in this figure represent the primary roles involved in the production process: customer, project leader, project team, and the organization's management. Each box in the figure represents a process activity. The boxes are positioned in particular columns to indicate which role has the primary responsibility for performing that activity. (The boxes have an identifier in the lower right corner that indicates their type. For example, PM-1 means "project management activity number 1". These identifiers are used to index the activity to descriptive text contained in a set of process documentation.) The activities generally flow in time sequence from the upper left to the lower right of the figure. We divide the activities into four zones. In Zone 1, a project begins when a customer initiates a request. The project team analyzes the request, defines an approach, generates an offer (i.e., a proposal or a tender), and delivers the offer to the customer. This completes the activities in Zone 1. After negotiation (which may involve some iteration), the project is authorized to proceed and we begin Zone 2. At this point, the project team obtains resources, prepares detailed plans needed to perform the negotiated work, and receives approval of these plans. Once the plans are approved, Zone 3 begins, and the project team develops and tests the products. This zone also includes activities such as monitoring and controlling the project, and reviewing status at various levels. This zone ends with the customer's acceptance of the product. Zone 4 captures lessons learned and metrics in a "project closeout report". Zone 4 may also involve fielding products. (Often, fielding is done by other organizations. If, however, our organization does fielding, this is often treated as a separate project. Fielding may take several months. We capture the project closeout data at the end of product development, instead of waiting until product fielding is completed. Otherwise, the team tends to forget lessons learned during development.

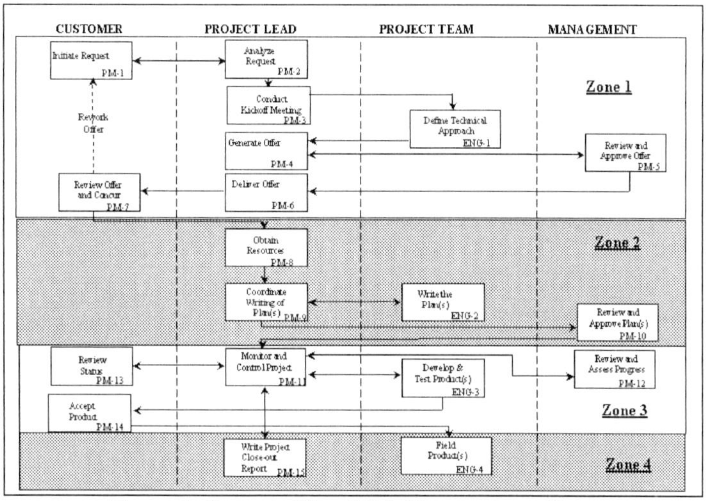

Figure 1: Process Flow With Measurement Zones

Our projects are typically small, with product sizes ranging from 3 to 25 people. The project duration (build cycle) ranges from 3 to 18 calendar months. A particular project team maintains a body of code ranging from 5 to 800 thousand source lines of code (KSLOC). (Most of our projects are sustainment projects, not new development projects.)

2.2. A Process to Collect Metrics from Multiple Organizations

The second challenge we faced arose from the use of Integrated Product Teams. The projects in the organization are staffed with a mix of personal drawn from four sources: government employees, SAIC contractor employees, SAIC's subcontractors, and other competitive contractors and their associated subcontractors. The challenge was to capture effort and cost data for each project in a consistent way.

Figure 2 illustrates the basic problem. Each organization has its own accounting system for labour and costs. Government employees report the effort they expend on *project tasks* to the Government Business Office using biweekly time cards. Employees of each of the various contractors (and their associated subcontractors) report their effort via biweekly time cards (not synchronized with the government's biweekly intervals) to their company. Each contractor's accounting department then consolidates the data, and reports effort, cost, and schedule information to the Government Procurement Office. This information is reported by *contract task*, often decomposed into labour categories. The Government Procurement Organization provides this information to the organization's upper management. Upper management uses information from the government employees, the contractors, and effort and schedule information obtained directly from the project (as described below) to assess overall program status. They report this data to the customer, which is a Project Management Office. (The Government Procurement Organization also provides cost information to the Project Management Office.) The problem is that effort and cost are reported based on organization type, illustrated by the *horizontal* layers shown in the figure, while a project slices *vertically* through the three horizontal layers. We need to measure the effort and schedule for a project in terms of its phases and activities. This is required to track project progress, to prepare estimates, and to comply with the SEI SW-CMM. For these reasons, we had to define a way to collect data in the vertical slice.

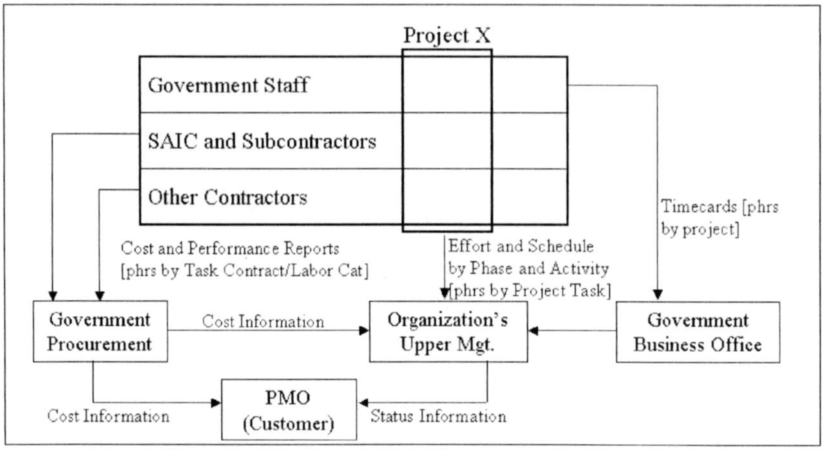

Figure 2: Challenge: Multiple Accounting Systems

The solution was to collect effort data by having every employee fill out a special biweekly "effort collection worksheet" shown in Figure 3. These worksheets are tied to the standard management process with the zones previously shown in Figure 1.

BI-WEEKLY EFFORT COLLECTION FORM (SUSTAINMENT)

PROJECT: ______________________ BUILD: _____ PERIOD ENDING ______________

ROLES	ZONE 1	ZONE 2	ZONE 3					ZONE 4	Customer Support	Training
			Analyze Rqmts.	Design Product	Perform Code & Unit Test	Conduct Product Tests	Baseline Products			
S/W Eng.										
Proj. Lead/ Tech. Lead										
QA										
CM										
H/W Eng.										
V & V										
Interop.										
Other										

Figure 3: Standardized Effort Collection Worksheet

Figure 4 shows all the types of data that we collect and how it reaches our centralized metrics database. We collect the effort for project tasks using the biweekly effort collection worksheets. We collect data on defects using peer review results forms. The duration of project activities comes from a schedule that the Project Leads provide to the organization's director on a monthly basis. We collect additional information on defects, as well as component size, from the automated status accounting system operated by the Configuration Management (CM) organization. (These defects are discovered and recorded during integration testing and product acceptance testing.) The CM organization also collects information on change requests submitted by customers for the products that we maintain. Skipping to the bottom right side of Figure 3, the project closeout report captures actual information on product sizes, effort, duration, and defects. In the center of Figure 3 at the bottom we have the Project Profile form. This is an important document because it captures characteristics of the project and product that we used to group data for analysis. For example, these characteristics allow us to separately analyze data on new development projects for trainers from new development projects for command and control systems.

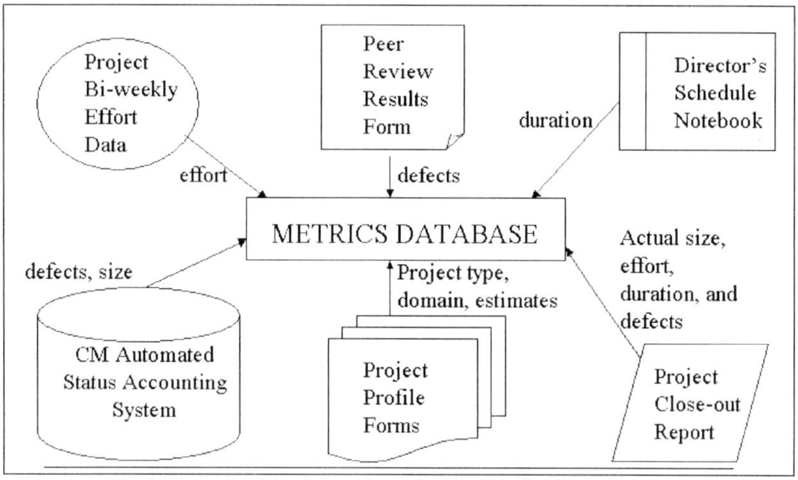

Figure 4: How Data Gets to the Metrics Database

Table 1 shows the types of information that we capture using the Project Profile form. The first two items (customer and funding type) are for business analysis. The next several items deal with the type of product, type of project, build type, and the lifecycle model. The build type distinguishes normal builds, emergency builds, and engineering builds. A normal build is the usual case. In some cases, an extremely urgent modification must be made and this is done with a streamlined process called an emergency build. To support development and testing of other systems, we sometimes produce an engineering build of a product that may contain additional instrumentation for data collection, customized interfaces to new versions of external systems, etc. The next set of items on the form captures high-level size, effort, and duration information for the project. (Note that we collect both the original estimated values, and the actual values. The actual values are obtained from the project closeout report and stored in the project profile record.) Lastly, we provide a narrative field to allow the Project Lead to document any exceptional features of the project. These might include additional documents that must be delivered, prototyping activities that might increase the costs, etc.

Table 1: Project Profile Data

• **Customer** • **Funding Type** • **Product type (tactical system, trainer, C3, etc.)** • **Project type (ND, TR, SU)** • **Build type (normal, emergency, engineering)** • **Life cycle model (waterfall, incremental, ...)** • **Exceptional features (narrative)** • **Estimated/Actual size (equivalent new PSLOC by language)** • **Estimated/Actual effort** • **Estimated/Actual duration**

We began collecting data in 1995. To establish our organization's baseline performance we analyzed historical data for projects completed as early as 1990. (We called this "forensic accounting". The quality of the data was not good, but at least it gave us a place to start. In some cases, we had to convert old data to new units of measure.) At the present time (February 2001) we have data on 196 completed projects ("builds") and 290 peer reviews. In total, these builds delivered over 400,000 source lines of code (SLOC) and expended over 228,000 person-hours of labor. On the average, a project delivered only 2000 SLOC and expended only 1200 person-hours. These values are smaller than one might expect because many projects only modify existing code.

Table 2 shows the allocation of effort by role for new development and sustainment projects. Project Management (PM), Quality Assurance (QA), and Software Engineering Environment (SEE) operations are essentially the same. QA is slightly higher for sustainment because our QA engineers also participate in regression testing. CM is much larger for sustainment because there is more information to be controlled when the project starts. Software Engineering (SWE) is less for sustainment because the engineers do the requirements analysis and high-level design work when they analyze problem reports in order to estimate the cost to correct. (This effort is funded separately from the project and so is not included in the values shown.)

Table 2: Allocation of Effort by Role (in %)

	Role				
Project Type	**PM**	**SWE**	**QA**	**CM**	**SEE**
New Development	18	70	9	1	2
Sustainment	22	49	12	14	3

2.3. Using Statistical Process Control

One area of special interest is statistical process control (SPC) of our product quality and process performance. William Florac and Anita Carleton describe SPC as applied to software in their book [7]. (An earlier version of this material appeared as an SEI technical report [8].) Like many other organizations, we have chosen to apply SPC to peer review data. The reason is that this is our richest source of statistically useful data, and it provides immediate feedback to ongoing projects. The goal of SPC, after all, is to provide information so that the project team can correct their performance before a defective product is delivered to the customer. Initially, we lacked a large amount of data so we decided to aggregate the information from our projects simply in terms of new development versus sustainment, and code versus documentation. This means that we separated the data into four categories for analysis. We did not initially analyse data based upon product type or other characteristics.

Figure 5 shows our process for analysing peer review data. We have four columns corresponding to the roles of the various participants. The peer review team, which consists of engineers, testers and possibly other individuals, performs the review of the product. The peer review moderator (who leads the peer review meeting) collects the results and then calculates certain quantities (described in the next paragraph). Then the moderator obtains control limits for these quantities from the organization's "infocenter". The peer review moderator determines whether the values calculated for the peer review are within the control limits. If not, the peer review moderator must identify the "special causes" of the observed deviation from the expected performance, and must also describe and execute any necessary corrective actions. If the metrics are within the control limits, no additional analysis or explanation is required. In either case, the peer review moderator delivers the peer review results to the Software Engineering Process Group (SEPG). The SEPG reviews the data for validity, consistency and completeness, and places it in the organization's metrics database. The SEPG then periodically analyses the data to calculate updated control limits. In some cases, the SEPG also uses this information to revise the organization's standard process itself in order to reduce the amount of variation in product quality and process performance.

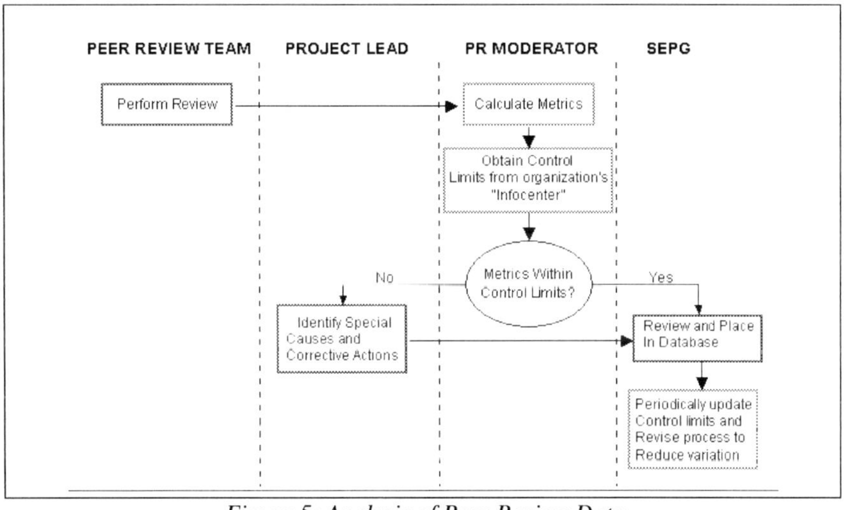

Figure 5: Analysis of Peer Review Data

Our organization collects and analyses three metrics for every peer review. Two of these are process metrics. One is a product quality metric. The first process metric is the review rate, defined as the amount of product reviewed divided by the sum of the preparation time and the meeting time. The amount of product reviewed is expressed either in pages (for documents) or source lines of code (for software). The preparation time is the number of labour hours expended by the reviewers to analyse the product prior to the review meeting. The meeting time is the time expended by all of these individuals in the meeting where they discuss their findings and consolidate their comments. The second process metric is the time ratio, defined as the sum of the preparation time divided by the sum of the meeting time. This metric was chosen to indicate whether the teams were preparing adequately for a review. We typically expect that the time ratio will be greater than one. If not, we believe that the team has not prepared adequately for the review. The product quality metric is defect density, defined as the sum of the defects found divided by the size of the product. We basically define a "defect" as anything that the review team decides should be fixed. We do collect information on the severity of the defect (critical or significant) and where the defect was injected. We are not currently using this information to control our process. Once we have collected enough data, however, we hope to use it. (We are currently trying to improve our definition of defect. See Lessons Learned below.) The size of a product is measured as either the number of pages or the number of lines of code in the product. For sustainment, however, the size only includes the pages or lines of code that were added, changed, and deleted from the product. The size does *not* include the total amount of pages or lines of code in the product. To do otherwise would distort the defect density of the product. Often, we only modify small portions of a product, leaving the rest unchanged.

Table 3 shows some sample data for document peer reviews. Specifically, we show the control limits for the three quantities we have just defined for both new development and sustainment projects. New development projects provided 60 data points for our sample. Sustainment projects provided 92 data points. (This data is as of 29 December 2000). The values for both types of projects are similar. We will continue to collect and analyse this data in the future. We may be able to observe some conclusive differences then.

Table 3: Document Peer Review Data (29dec00)

New Development (60 data points)

Metric	Average	Lower Control Limit	Upper Control Limit
Review Rate (pages/hour)	4.6	0.0	13.6
Time Ratio (Preparation Time/Meeting Time)	1.6	0.0	3.8
Defect Density (defects/100 pages)	14.3	0.0	44.7

Sustainment (92 data points)

Metric	Average	Lower Control Limit	Upper Control Limit
Review Rate (pages/hour)	3.2	0.0	8.9
Time Ratio (Preparation Time/Meeting Time)	2.0	0.0	4.8
Defect Density (defects/100 pages)	23.5	0.0	82.3

2.4. Continuous Improvement

We have continued to improve our metrics collection process over the years. This section summarizes our progress. The oldest data in our database dates from fiscal year 1990. Prior to fiscal year 1995 (which ended 30 September 1995), Project Leads collected metrics data for their individual projects. They collected whatever data they felt was appropriate for their projects. This led to an inconsistency in the data collected. Consequently, the SEPG defined the metrics program and began collecting data in fiscal year 1995 through interviews with the Project Leads. The members of the metric team used templates to collect information in a structured and consistent way. In fiscal year 1996, the SEPG initiated biweekly collection of project metrics. (This was when the biweekly effort collection form was first introduced.) In fiscal year 1998, the SEPG updated the metrics process, including associated standards and procedures. The SEPG also added the requirement for projects to define process performance and product quality goals. In fiscal year 1999, the SEPG initiated the automated collection of effort by providing simple tools (Excel spreadsheets and access databases). The SEPG also added statistical process control procedures for peer review data that were described above.

3. Lessons Learned

We have learned the following important lessons over the last eight years:

- Provide operational definitions
- Train the staff
- Expect the definitions to change
- Process the data promptly
- Automation is essential

The following paragraphs describe each lesson.

The first lesson is that we need better definitions for our metrics. As an example, we originally did not specify a precise format for the project schedules that were delivered to the organization's director every month. The director received schedules ranging in size from a single page to 38 pages. To correct this problem we want to define a precise "operational definition" for each metric. The operational definition means that we define how the metric is to be collected in a precise way. This ensures that the person collecting the metric and the person analysing the collected data agreeing on exactly what the data represents. For details on this concept see the book by Florac and Carleton, as well as the SEI measurement books, referenced in Section 1.

One area that we continue to find difficult is defining "size" for sustainment projects. The basic issue is whether to use the total size of the product (document or code) or the size of the portion of the product that is touched (added, changed, or deleted).[1] Another problem with size measurements for sustainment is that peer reviews often combine the review of code and documents. The reason is that it is more cost effective to review these products together when the modifications are minor. (This also helps ensure consistency between the code and the documents.) We have not yet found a good way to calculate productivity numbers and defect densities for combined reviews because the size combines pages and SLOC, and we have only the total effort.

Our second lesson is that the staff must know the definitions in order to apply them correctly. We provide paper-based forms with the definitions of the fields in the template defined on the back of the page. This means that the definition is available simply by turning the page over. For online systems we provide online help. Lastly, we provide training to the staff on metrics so that they all use the forms correctly.

The third lesson is that whatever definitions you choose, they will surely change. Before April 1996 we only collected the total effort for each project. (We have found effort is the hardest metric to collect.) From April 1996 through August 1998, we collected effort for 15 different engineering activities. (This seems to be too many for the engineers to consistently distinguish.) From September 1998 to the present time we use the effort collection worksheet shown previously. The effort is divided into four zones, with a variable number of activities

[1] Function point counting makes this distinction. Counts provide the functionality perceived by the user and functionality perceived by the developer. User-oriented size reflects asset value of the product. Developer-oriented size reflects the amount of effort expended by the developer or maintainer.

depending upon the person's role. The partitioning in this particular worksheet is chosen because the engineers expend most of the effort on the project. Thus, we want to divide their effort more finely. We do this by providing them with separate fields on the template for analysis, design, coding, and testing. The other roles (project management, configuration management, and quality assurance) consume only a small part of the total project's effort. Thus they provide data in a more aggregated fashion.

The fourth lesson is that we must process the data promptly. At one point we had accumulated data on 67 peer reviews. We then began analyzing the data. We found we had to discard data on 20 of these peer reviews because the forms had been incorrectly filled out and were incomplete. Since the peer reviews had occurred months before, it was impossible to go back and collect the missing information.

The fifth lesson is that we believe that automation is essential for a successful metrics program. It reduces the collection effort and promotes the completeness and consistency of the data that is collected. Initially, we used Excel spreadsheets. The project leaders would complete data on the spreadsheets and submit them to the metrics team either on diskette or via electronic mail. Currently, we have an online system that is implemented with a custom Visual Basic program, supported by an Access database.

4. Acknowledgements

The author would like to thank Dr. Terry Palmer for providing the latest data values from the metrics database. He would also like to thank the members of the Software Engineering Process Group who worked together to define the process described in this paper.

5. References

[1] Paulk, M.C., Curtis, B., Chrissis, M.B., et at., "Capability Maturity Model for Software", SEI Technical Reports CMU/SEI-91-TR-24, August 1991.

[2] Paulk, M.C., Curtis, B., Chrissis, M.B., and Weber, C. V., "Capability Maturity Model for Software, Version 1.1", SEI Technical Report CMU/SEI-93-TR-24, February 1993.

[3] Baumert, John H. and McWhinney, Mark S., "Software Measures and the Capability Maturity Model", SEI Technical Report CMU/SEI-92-TR-25, September 1992.

[4] Park, Robert E., "Software Size Measurement: A Framework for Counting Source Statements", SEI Technical Report CMU/SEI-92-TR-20, September 1992.

[5] Goethert, William B., Bailey, Elizabeth K., Busby, Mary B., "Software Effort and Schedule Measurement: A Framework for Counting Staff-Hours and Reporting Schedule Information", SEI Technical Report CMU/SEI-92-TR-21, September 1992.

[6] Florac, William A. "Software Quality Measurement: A Framework for Counting Problems and Defects" (SEI-92-TR-022), Research Access Inc., 1992, ISBN 999-544045-8.

[7] Florac, William A. and Carleton, A., "Measuring the Software Process: Statistical Process Control for Software Process Improvement" (The SEI Series in Software Engineering), Addison-Wesley, 1999, ISBN 0-201-160444-2.

[8] Florac, William A., Park, R., Carleton, A., "Practical Software Measurement: Measuring for Process Management and Improvement", SEI Guidebook CMU/SEI-97-HB-003, April 1997.

Experimental Evaluation of Pair Programming[1]

Jerzy Nawrocki, Adam Wojciechowski

Abstract

Pair programming is a kind of collaborative programming where two people are working simultaneously on the same programming task. It is one of the key practices of eXtreme Programming. In the paper we compare it with two variants of individual programming: one of them is based on Personal Software Process that has been proposed by W. Humphrey, and the other is a variant of eXtreme Programming tailored to individuals. Four experiments are described that has been performed at the Poznan University of Technology. During those experiments 21 students wrote 4 C/C++ programs ranging from 150 to 400 LOC. The obtained results are compared with the results of similar experiments described by J.T. Nosek and L. Williams et al.

1. Introduction

Pair programming is programming done by a pair of programmers. While one of them is creating a software artefact (e.g. a UML diagram or C++ code) the other is continuously assuring quality, i.e. he/she is watching, trying to understand, asking questions, looking for alternative approaches, helping to avoid defects. Two programmers are given one computer and they have to share it. After some time they are switching the roles: creator becomes quality assurer and vice versa. Since 1995 pair programming is gaining more and more popularity. It is one of the twelve practices of eXtreme Programming (XP for short) [1].

Despite its growing popularity, we still know very little about pair programming in sense of reliable experimental data. We know of only two experiments concerning pair programming. The first one was reported by John Nosek [5]. He describes an experiment in which 15 full-time system programmers from a program trading firm were asked to write a script that performs a database consistency check. The programmers were split into 5 pairs and a control group consisted of 5 individuals. Five measures have been considered. Four of them were subjective grades: two of them given by programmers (confidence about the solution and enjoyment of the process) and two other given by two independent graders (readability and functionality). The fifth measure was an objective one: it was time spent on writing the script. The average time for completion was 42 minutes for individuals and 30 minutes for pairs. So, pairs needed only 71% of the completion time necessary in case of individuals. However, in total, they consumed 43% more time than individuals. Unfortunately, that experiment concerned only one very short programming assignment (the allotted time was 45 minutes). This is in contrast with programming practice. For instance Beck suggests the following: '*if several tasks each take an hour, combine them to form a larger task*' [1, page 92]. So, tasks taking a few hours each would be much more representative.

The second experiment we know of has been conducted at the University of Utah [6]. Forty-two senior software engineering students have been split into 14 pairs and 14 individuals. They were asked to write 4 programming assignments in 6 weeks. The results of that experiment are even more optimistic than those received by Nosek. They report that '*the pairs completed their assignments 40% to 50% faster*' and total programmer hours to

[1] This work has been financially supported by KBN grant 8T11A01618.

complete an assignment '*after the adjustment period (..) decreased dramatically to a minimum of 15%*' [6]. Unfortunately, they do not say what were the assignments about, what was the process used by the students, what were the sizes of solutions, how many hours the students spent on writing the programs, and last but not least, what was deviation in time, test cases passed, and size. Moreover, for one of the programs '*data entry problems prevented accurate recording of the completion times*'. This shows that further experiments are needed to investigate efficiency of pair programming.

In the paper four experiments are described that have been conducted in winter semester 1999/2000 at the Poznan University of Technology. The aim was to evaluate efficiency of pair programming. We decided to compare pair programming, which is a practice of XP [1], with individual programming in its rigorous version proposed by Humphrey and known as Personal Software Process (PSP) [3].

In the following sections we shortly describe PSP with focus on elements used in our experiments, and then we proceed to eXtreme Programming practices and pair programming. Next we present organization of the experiment and its results. The paper ends with conclusions and remarks concerning future research in the area.

2. Personal Software Process

Personal Software Process (PSP) and Capability Maturity Model (CMM) have been developed at the Software Engineering Institute, Carnegie-Mellon University. The aim of CMM and PSP is to improve software processes. While CMM aims at software organizations, PSP tries to help individual programmers. Both CMM and PSP define a few levels of maturity. For PSP there are the following levels of maturity (from the least to the most advanced):

PSP0: Development time and defects are recorded. Defects are categorized according to a defect type standard.

PSP0.1: Coding standard and size measurement are in use. Observed opportunities for improvement are put in a form of process improvement proposal.

PSP1: Software size is estimated and test reports are written.

PSP1.1: Task and schedule planning are in place.

PSP2: Code and design reviews are performed.

PSP2.1: Design templates are in use.

PSP3: Incremental approach is applied to software development.

Levels PSP0 and PSP0.1 are called Baseline Personal Process, BPP. In our experiments the programmers worked at the level of BPP.

In PSP an important role is assigned to strict software process definition which is a description of "*sequence of steps required to develop or maintain software*" [3]. A process can be split into a number of smaller processes called phases. Each process/phase is described by a script, which specifies not only the steps but also the entry criteria and exit ones. In his book Humphrey proposed to focus on three phases: design, code and testing. The reason for that choice is that according to Boehm those phases consume form 59 to 68 percent of development cost in most software organizations [2] as well as the fact that these are the parts of the process where a running product is created. Moreover, he introduced to the process so called 'postmortem' phase during which the programmer has to complete process logs and summary report. A typical process suggested by Humphrey for the BPP level is depicted in Figure 1 (that process has been used in our experiments).

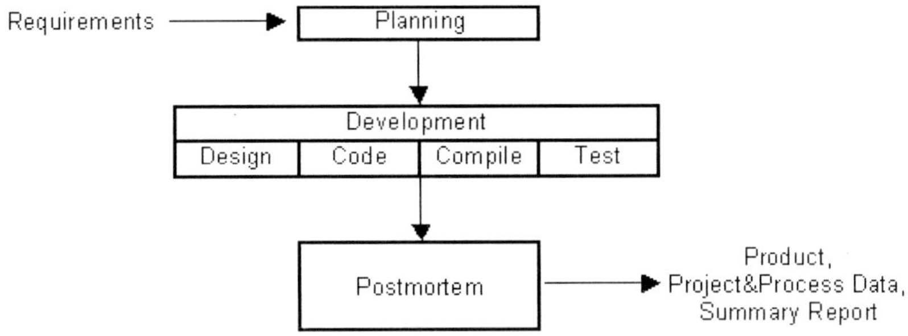

Figure 1. The PSP0 process

Specific to this approach is its reflective character, since the programmer does not use a compiler until the whole program is coded. Compilation starts from the moment when a compiler is used for the first time and it lasts till the first successful compilation. The testing phase comprises all the activities from the first successful compilation till the moment when acceptance criteria are met (in practice the program should pass all the tests – unfortunately, the scripts for BPP do not specify when the test cases should be created).

3. eXtreme Programming

eXtreme Programming [1, 4], XP for short, is a relatively new methodology of software development. It was proposed in response to problems concerning changing (dynamic) requirements and new technologies. Here are the practices of XP that have been used during our experiments:

- *Pair programming*. Pairs of programmers instead of individuals do coding. Each pair member is expected to feel an author and to fully understand the piece of code that is developed.
- *Experimentation and test-centred quality assurance*. Writing a piece of code should be preceded by preparing a set of test cases. If a defect is detected the programmer should write test cases that are able to detect the defect whenever it reappears. Each code must pass all the unit tests.
- *Simple solution*. Design should be as simple as possible and no functionality should be added early. Any optimisation that is not put in the requirements should be avoided.
- *Risk minimisation*. Spike solutions are recommended to reduce risk.
- *Keep moving*. Members of the programming teams should be moved around (we moved them before starting work on a new assignment).

Since the chosen programming assignments were small (150-400 LOC) and the requirements were stable

- we have not used user stories,
- there was no on-site customer and planning game,
- integration was very simplified,
- there was only one very short iteration lasting not longer than one day, and
- the students participating in the experiment did not use CRC cards.

4. Description of the experiment

The aim of the experiment was to compare pair programming along with other practices of the XP (see Sec. 3) with the PSP approach described by Watts Humphrey (see Sec. 2). We have decided to use a set of programming assignments proposed by Humphrey [3] and measure both the development time and the number of defects. Experiment took place at the Poznan University of Technology, during laboratory classes at 4th year of studies (computer science major). The students have had similar experience in programming. They knew that the aim of the experiment was to evaluate the methodologies, not their skills.

XP-like pair programming and PSP are very different. They differ with regard to number of programmers and type of processes. Because of this we have decided to introduce XP-like software process that was targeted at individual programmers. All in all we had three software processes:

- Baseline Personal Process as introduced by Humphrey - referred to as **PSP**;
- XP-like pair programming – referred to as **XP2**;
- A version of XP for single programmers (the practices listed in Sec. 3 have been reduced to *Experimentation and test-centred quality assurance*, *Simple solution*, and *Risk minimisation*) – it will be named **XP1**.

A group of 21 students was divided into three sub-groups:

- PSP: 6 programmers,
- XP1: 5 programmers,
- XP2: 5 pairs of programmers (10 students; each pair was equipped this one computer).

We have assigned the students to the groups (PSP, XP1, and XP2) in such a way that for each group the average value of GPA (Grade Point Average) was almost the same. The students did all the work at the university when one of the authors was present, so we can trust their time records.

The students might choose their programming language between Pascal, C or C++. All of them used C or C++. Programs for the experiment were taken from [3] to make it easier to compare collected results to records presented in Humphrey's book, and to be sure that those programs suite well the methodology proposed in the PSP approach. The assignments were the following (this is a rough description – for details see [3]):

- **Program 1**. *Write a program to estimate the mean and standard deviation of a sample of n real numbers* [3, Program 1A].
- **Program 2**. *Write a program to calculate the linear regression parameters* [3, Program 4A].
- **Program 3**. *Write a program to count the logical lines in a program, omitting comments and blank lines* [3, Program 2A].
- **Program 4**. *Write a program to count the total program LOC, the total LOC in each object the program contains, and the number of methods in each object* [3, Program 3A].

Students using PSP approach were asked first to write their program on a sheet of paper, then to use a computer. Because they complained on loosing time while rewriting code, we allowed them, from the second program on, to use text editors, but we asked them to run a compiler not before the code is complete (such a strict approach is suggested by Humphrey).

The XP paradigm assumes that each of the two programmers working on a program is equally involved in the program creation. Thus, we had to prevent a danger that only one student would develop entire code while his partner might remain passive. To make sure that this will not happen we decided that once a program is finished and accepted we will inject three errors by performing the following modifications:

- Adding an assignment instruction.

- Removing an assignment instruction.
- Changing an instruction (not more than two lexical units could be changed).

After acceptance of a program the students were given a modified program and rough information about location of each injected error (an area of 20 lines of code was indicated). By comparing the fix time data for XP2 with that for PSP and XP1 we were able to check if the XP2 students have had the same knowledge about theirs programs as the PSP and XP1 students had.

During entire process of code development students had to tract time and defects using special logs (time recording log, and defect recording log) [7], similar to those proposed by Humphrey. Information collected there includes time of starting and finishing of each phase as well as notes on all errors encountered in code, tests etc. We also wanted students to keep track how long they spent on uncovering and correcting their own errors as well as those injected by us after the program was accepted. Duration of each break in program development was subtracted from the time spend in particular phase of software process.

5. Results

Each of the experiment sessions gave us 16 logs concerning development time and 16 logs containing data about programming defects. Those records have been taken together for statistical analysis. The results are presented below.

First let us compare average value of total development time gained in XP1, XP2 and PSP groups (see Figure 2). From Figure 2 it follows that for the first three programs there is **almost no difference in development time between XP2 and XP1**. This suggests that **pair programming is rather expensive technology.** It is surprising, especially when you take into account results obtained by J.T. Nosek [5] and L. Williams et al. 7[6].

For Program 4 there is a significant difference between XP1 and XP2. This can be attributed to assignment interpretation problems one of the XP1 programmers have had (if we removed his data from the set, the average development time for XP1 would amount to 3 hours 40 minutes and this is just slightly above the average time for XP2).

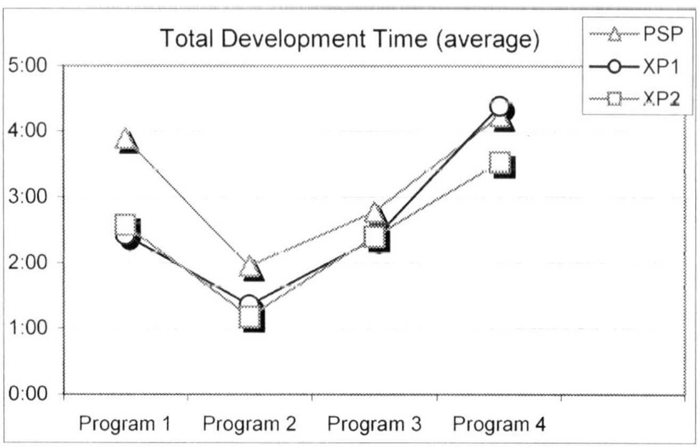

Figure 2. Comparison of average values of total development time.

Notice that the distance between average development time for PSP and XP2 is maximal for Program 1. It can be attributed to our early requirement that a program should be first written on a sheet of paper, then entered to the computer – that requirement was not in force for the remaining programs. Since average program size was 150 LOC for Program 1, one should subtract about 30 minutes from the average time for Program 1 and PSP. Nevertheless PSP takes longer than XP2 and XP1. Especially important is the difference between PSP and XP1. It suggests that **experimentation and test-centered thinking reduces development time**, at least in case of small programs. In this context the strict waterfall approach presented in [3] (design – coding – testing) seems less efficient.

We have also analysed standard deviation of development times and program sizes in each of the groups (see Figure 3). From this analysis it follows that deviation both in development time and in program size for XP2 is smaller than for XP1 and PSP (the only exception is the development time for the first program). It indicates that **pair programming is more predictable than individual one**.

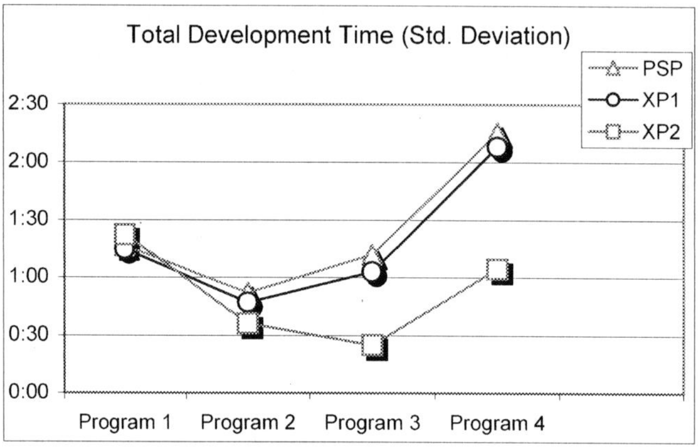

Figure 3. Standard deviation in development time.

Another interesting attribute of a software process is programming efficiency measured in lines of code (LOC) per hour per person. From Figure 4 it follows that **XP1 is the most efficient programming technology, while PSP and XP2 are more or less the same**. This can be attributed rather flexible process used by XP1 programmers and the requirement to write test cases before coding.

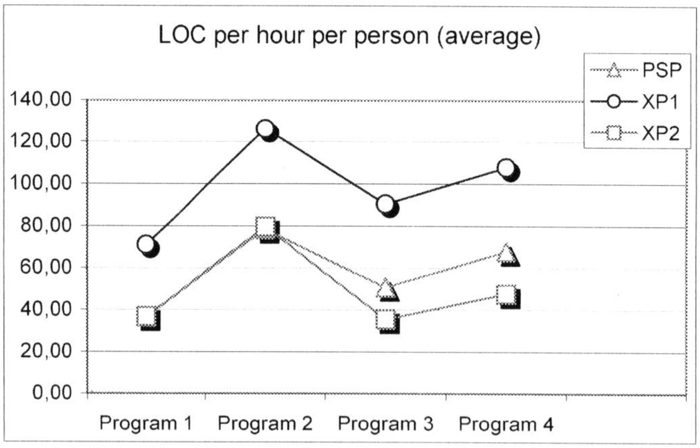

Figure 4. Programming efficiency (LOC per hour per person).

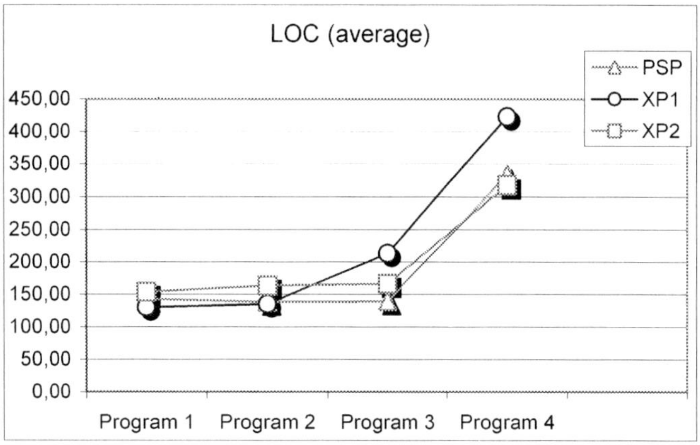

Figure 5. Average program size (LOC).

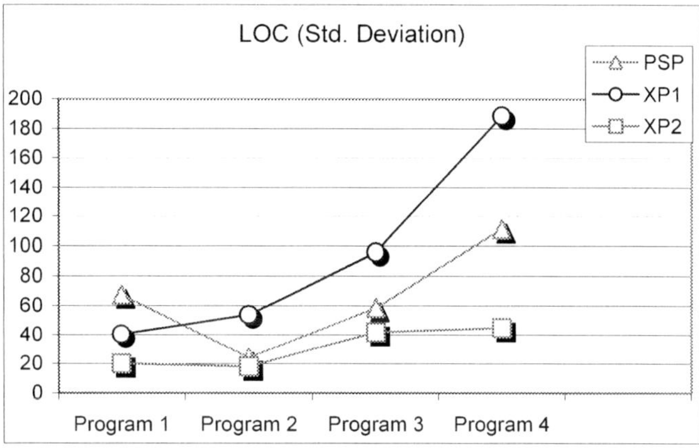

Figure 6. Standard deviation in code size.

Data concerning program size for each program are presented in Figure 5. For the first two programs the average program size was almost the same for each of the approaches, but for Programs 3 and 4 XP1 provided longer programs (on average) than PSP and XP2. From Figure 6 it follows that standard deviation of program size for XP2 was the smallest one. It means that pair programming leads to more stable solutions. Notice that XP1 is (except Program 1) least predictable in sense of program size.

Another interesting indicator of software process efficiency is the number of errors uncovered during acceptance testing. In Figure 7 the number of re-submissions of corrected programs is depicted. In ideal case that number should be equal to zero. From the figure it follows that all the groups have had similar level of acceptance errors and XP2 is slightly better.

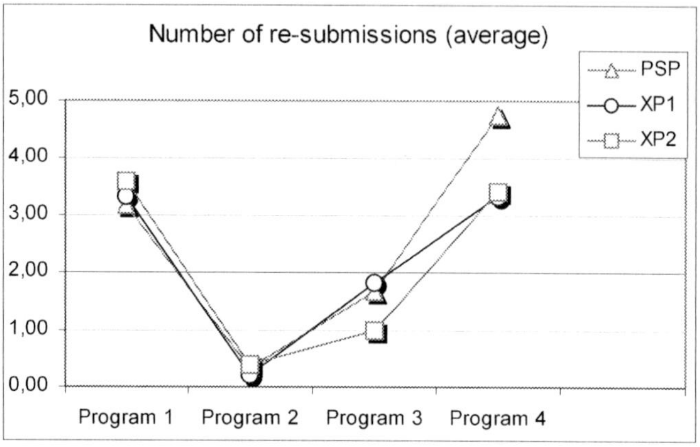

Figure 7. The number of re-submissions of corrected programs.

6. Conclusions

In the paper we have compared XP-like pair programming with individual programming based on PSP and XP practices. From our research it follows that:

- XP-like pair programming appears less efficient than it is reported by J.T. Nosek [5] and L. Williams et al. [6]. Only in one case (Program 4) reduction of average development time for XP2 (to 77% of the time needed by XP1) was similar to that reported by J. T. Nosek (reduction to 71%) but still it is far from the level of 50% mentioned by L. Williams et al. Moreover, in case of Program 4 one of the students misunderstood the assignment and this distorted the results.
- PSP seems less efficient than XP1 (see Fig. 2). Maybe it is too restrictive? However, its average code size for programs 3 and 4 was considerably smaller than in case of XP1 (see Fig. 5).
- Pair programming is more predictable than individual one with regard to development time and program size (i.e. standard deviation is the lowest one – see Fig. 3 and Fig. 6).
- Experimentation and test-oriented thinking reduces development time.
- The number of re-submissions indicates that the amount of rework for XP2 is slightly smaller than for XP1 or PSP.

However, one should take into account that the research was restricted to relatively small programs (150 – 400 LOC). Although our assignments were a few times longer than one used by J.T. Nosek, we think that further experiments are needed oriented towards larger programs.

7. References

[1] K. Beck, *Extreme Programming Explained: Embrace Change*, Addison-Wesley, Boston, 2000.

[2] B.W. Boehm, *Software Engineering Economics*, Prentice-Hall, Englewood Cliffs, 1981.

[3] W.S. Humphrey, *A Discipline for Software Engineering*, Addison-Wesley, Reading, 1995.

[4] http://www.extremeprogramming.org, January 2000.

[5] J.T. Nosek, The cast for collaborative programming, *Communications of the ACM*, vol. 41 (1998), No. 3, 105-108.

[6] L. Williams et al., Strengthening the case for pair programming, *IEEE Software*, vol. 17 (2000), No. 4, 19-25.

[7] http://www.cs.put.poznan.pl/awojciechowski/research/pair_programming/, February 2001.

An overview of COSMIC-FFP field trial results

Abran A., Symons C., Oligny S.

Abstract

The Common Software Measurement International Consortium (COSMIC) was formed in 1998 to design and bring to market a new generation of software measurement methods. The COSMIC group reviewed existing functional size measurement methods, studied their commonalities, and proposed the basic principles on which a new generation of software functional size measurement methods could be based. In November of 1999, the group published version 2.0 of COSMIC-FFP, a measurement method implementing these principles, and put its measurement manual on the Web for public access. Over the past year, industrial organizations have contributed data in the context of COSMIC field trials. This report present an overview of the field trial results, including an analysis of the relationship of effort with respect to the software functional size, measured in COSMIC-FFP size units. The data set is described, as well as the constraints for the interpretation of the results.

1. Context

Quantifying the size of software is generally recognized as one of the keys to adequate estimation of effort, cost and schedule of software projects. Source lines of code was the first generally accepted measure for this purpose and is still used extensively, as demonstrated by the many estimation models that include this measure as a key parameter [1, 2]. As a measure of software size though, the source code measure carries some inherent limitations, and this has been recognized by software engineering practitioners and researchers alike [3]. Among the practitioners, Allan Albrecht was the first to propose, over 20 years ago, a new way of quantifying software size based on the user's view of the software [4]. Albrecht's 1979 method, now referred to as the IFPUG method, is still used today and provides useful results in many organizations, but it also has some limitations and these have been well documented over the past 15 years. One of these limitations is the difficulty of applying such a method outside the MIS domain, as documented by [3, 5, 6, 7, 9, 10, 11, 12, 13, 14]. In 1996, the industry sponsored the development of an IFPUG extension for real-time and embedded software, which was put into the public domain under the name of Full Function Points [8, 15, 16].

Building on the strengths of this work and with the support of the industry, the Common Software Measurement International Consortium (COSMIC) was formed in 1998 to design and bring to market a new generation of software measurement methods. The first functional sizing method should be designed to work equally well for 'data-rich' business/MIS software and for 'control-rich' or 'real-time' software, that is software which is to be found in telecoms, avionics, process control, embedded and operating systems. The method should be able to size such software in any layer or peer-item of a multi-layer and/or multi-tier architecture. It is not designed to measure functionality of software which is 'algorithm-rich', that is software which is dominated by complex mathematics.

The COSMIC group reviewed existing methods (IFPUG, MarkII [17], NESMA [18] and version 1.0 of the Full Function Point methods [8]), studied their commonalties, and proposed the basic principles on which a new generation of software functional size measurement method could be based [19, 20, 21]. In November of 1999, the group published version 2.0 of COSMIC-FFP [23], a measurement method implementing these principles, and put its measurement manual on the Web for public access. Overall, close to 40 people from 8 countries participated in the design of this measurement method. The Measurement Manual, describing the method, is available in English, French, Japanese and Spanish. The purpose of this paper is to introduce the COSMIC-FFP functional size measurement method and to present some results of the field trials, gathered over the past year.

2. The measurement method

2.1. COSMIC-FFP measurement systems

The COSMIC-FFP measurement method explicitly defines a measurement system which includes a measurement principle, base functional components, a standard unit of measure and an aggregation function.

- *Measurement principle*: based on the COSMIC-FFP generic software model (Figure 1), the method, through a defined set of rules and procedures, produces a numerical figure to represent the functional size of this model. These rules implement the principle that the functional size of a piece of software is directly proportional to the number of its data-moving sub-processes. By convention, this numerical figure is then extended to represent the COSMIC-FFP functional size of the software itself.

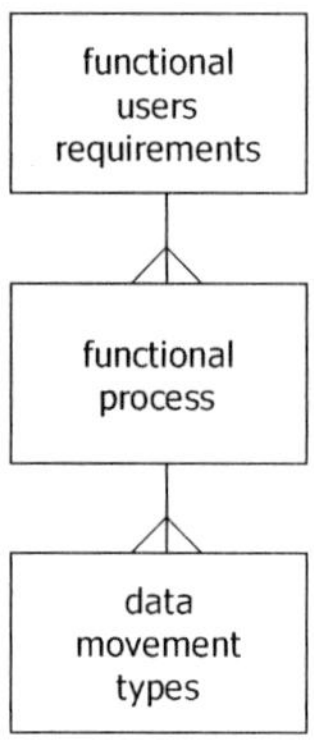

Figure 1: COSMIC-FFP generic software model

- *Base functional components*: version 2.0 of the COSMIC-FFP measurement method uses only four types of data-moving sub-processes, referred to as base functional components in ISO/IEC 14143-1 [22]: entry, exit, read and write; each one is defined in [23].
- *Standard unit of measurement*: the standard unit of measurement, that is, 1 *Cfsu*, is defined by convention as equivalent to one single data movement type at the sub-process level.
- *Aggregation function*: The functional size of the data movement base functional components can be combined to obtain the size of any higher-level functional structures such as that of functional processes, components within layers or whole applications. This is performed by arithmetically adding together the functional sizes of the constituent functional structures according to the purpose of the measurement.

The measurement system proposed by the COSMIC-FFP measurement method offers a scalable result, which means that the functional size figure can be constructed at the desired level of abstraction. Furthermore, as demonstrated by Fetcke in [24], the COSMIC-FFP measurement system meets the dominance and the monotonicity properties; two distinctive and desirable measurement properties, violated by some other functional size measurement methods, and contributing theoretically to a) better predictability of effort estimates (in the case of dominance) [24, pp.150] and b) better predictability of functional size itself (in the case of monotonicity) [24, pp. 152].

2.2. COSMIC-FFP field trials

The field trials of the COSMIC-FFP method were organised:

- to test that the COSMIC FFP V.2 documentation is understandable and interpretable in a common and repeatable way across software developers working in different domains, with different methods of expressing requirements and with different development technologies, and can be applied with acceptable effort;
- to test that the functional size measures obtained properly reflect the functionality of the related software requirements as perceived by experts in the requirements and/or that the functional size measures correlate with development effort;
- to enable a full transfer of the COSMIC FFP method to the organisations participating in the field trials, such that they regard it as 'implemented';
- to establish initial benchmark performance levels according to the COSMIC FFP method, against which the participating organisations can compare their own performance.

A protocol was documented to collect specific and standardized data from each participating industrial partner. This protocol included the subset of compulsory data attributes specified in the data collection protocol of the International Software Benchmarking Standards Group (ISBSG) [25].

Specific reports have been prepared for each of the participating field trials organizations addressing how each of the above field trials aims has been met for their own organization; in addition, specific benchmarking of organizational performance against the full trial data set was delivered to each participant. This report presents an overview of the field trial results, including an analysis of the relationship of effort with respect to the software functional size, measured in COSMIC-FFP size units (Cfsu). The data set is described, as well as the constraints for the interpretation of the results. Further specific reports discussing each of the other field trials aims will be prepared and published over the next few months.

3. General acceptance of the method in the field trials

During the field trials, the COSMIC FFP method was applied to software in different layers and peer items of multi-layer, multi-tier architectures from the application areas of telecommunications (switches and mobile devices), avionics and other defence control software, process control, and banking software. The projects were either new developments, or enhancements to existing systems. As with any measurement process carried out in any field of sciences and engineering, each organisation has to specify its measurement procedure for the application of a measurement method in their specific context. This is necessary to implement the generic functional size measurement rules in the context of the specific organisational means of documenting requirements or functional specifications such as UML Use Cases or SADT diagrams. In all cases, measurement procedures were developed to implement the general COSMIC FFP principle and rules and which satisfied the local need for unambiguous and repeatable interpretation.

Two specific trials were conducted to test repeatability of sizing of the same specifications by different measuring engineers. In the first trial, the documentation of some avionics software was available to a very high standard and the five engineers who each sized two sets of specifications were all familiar with the domain. Near-perfect repeatability was obtained.

In the second trial on specifications of process control software, engineers who were familiar with the domain obtained results of reasonable repeatability. However, junior engineers with limited experience of the domain showed poor repeatability.

Our conclusion is that experience of both the COSMIC FFP sizing method and of the domain are essential to ensure repeatability of sizing. Specific measurement procedures for implementing the method in the context of local documentation standards are also necessary.

The general consensus of those participating in the trials was that the COSMIC FFP functional size method is 'easy' or 'reasonably easy' to apply. The measurement effort is similar to that needed for established functional sizing methods.

Comments from individual organisations participating in the trials include the following:

- 'Project Teams were able to grasp the elements of the method easily and were enthusiastic about the method'
- 'Documentation and effort needed is similar to that for applying the IFPUG method, though there is an extra step to identify layers'
- 'The Z-unit has now also continued COSMIC FFP measurements with new starting projects and decided to implement this measurement technique as a standard procedure in their development process '

Finally, organisations that have tried the COSMIC FFP method have realised the value of producing requirements which are *measurable*, (as well understandable, traceable, testable, etc.) In two cases, errors were discovered in the documentation of software during the field trials as a result of the rigour of applying the COSMIC FFP sizing method.

4. Relationship with project effort

Field trial data were received from a variety of sources. The data analysed here have been selected because they belong to the same functional domain: they are all for projects developed for the domain of highly-constrained real-time software.

4.1. Presentation of the data sample

The data used in the analysis below are the 12 software projects from the real time domain; these projects were developed and measured by three different organizations from three countries. Training on the COSMIC-FFP method was organized at these three organizations using the same training material. All projects were completed either in 1999 or early 2000. The total size of the 12 software is 13 961 *Cfsu*; there were therefore 13 961 elementary data movements identified at the functional level. The data sample is presented in Table 1 below. Of the 12 projects, ten projects were for the development of new software applications while the other two were projects implementing functional enhancements to existing software applications. In terms of functional size, four projects delivered under 100 *Cfsu*, six between 142 and 810 *Cfsu* and two projects were much larger, delivering 3004 and 8251 *Cfsu* respectively.

While these organizations measured the functional size using the same measurement standard, that is COSMIC-FFP 2,0, it can be observed from Table 1 that these organizations had different time recording systems, some with details for three project phases (Specify,

Build, Test) while others had information only for one or two of these project phases. Effort is reported in hours, as specified in the data collection protocol defined by the International Software Benchmarking Standards Group (ISBSG) [25].

Table 1 – COSMIC-FFP data sample for selected field trial results

Project	Type	Size (Cfsu)	Specify effort (person-hours)	Build effort (person-hours)	Test effort (person-hours)
A	Development	32	n.a.	252	n.a.
B	Development	76	381	1457	401
C	Development	56	68	487	335
D	Development	142	136	643	n.a.
E	Development	8	115	116	n.a.
F	Enhancement	142	2 060	1 487	5 055
G	Development	332	468	11 382	254
H	Enhancement	624	n.a.	15 815	1 372
I	Development	810	1 304	10 903	4 548
J	Development	484	n.a.	20 808	6 772
K	Development	8251	49 000	66 000	93 000
L	Development	3004	32 000	27 000	20 000
TOTAL		13961			

4.2. Relationship between software functional size and effort

The analysis of the data for the sample represented some difficulties for the following reasons:

- Size of the data sample: even though 12 data points is within the usual size of samples in publications (e.g. of the 21 empirical duration models analysed in [8], 12 of them are derived from samples containing 20 data points or fewer), it is still a small sample for statistical analysis; care must thus be exercised in the interpretations of the results.
- Non-homogeneity of the development processes. Data was received from three different organisations each with their own development processes. Even though their processes could have some similarities within the respective organisations due to the implementation of internal organisational standards, such a level of standardisation cannot be expected across organisations.
- Non-homogeneity in the range of some of the key variables: for example, in this sample, the two larger projects have a functional size of an order of magnitude greater than the other ten projects. In this context, a simple regression model cannot be used since one of its key requirements is not met, that is that the variables must have a gaussian distribution (e.g. a normal distribution). A mathematical transformation is then required: in this specific instance, a log transformation was used to normalise the data set. This allowed then for a proper use of the regression models, while making data interpretation more difficult for practitioners not familiar with interpretation of figures with logarithmic scales. These comments also apply to the other key variable, the project effort (and for the same two projects with the largest effort).
- Non-homogeneity in the standards across organisations for data collection of the effort variable: this is directly illustrated in the data set by the different abilities of the organisation of recording effort by project phases (Specify, Build and Test phases), and indirectly since each organisation had their own practices in defining project phases, even though the reporting was based in their best effort to match the ISBSG definition of project phase.

4.2.1. *Effort to specify*

The effort variable is available for the Specify phase for nine projects. The log-log representation of this subset is presented in Figure 2. The coefficient of regression R^2 is 0,7824 for the linear regression model:

$$\text{Specify Effort} = 4{,}0342 \times (\text{Size})^{0{,}9903}$$

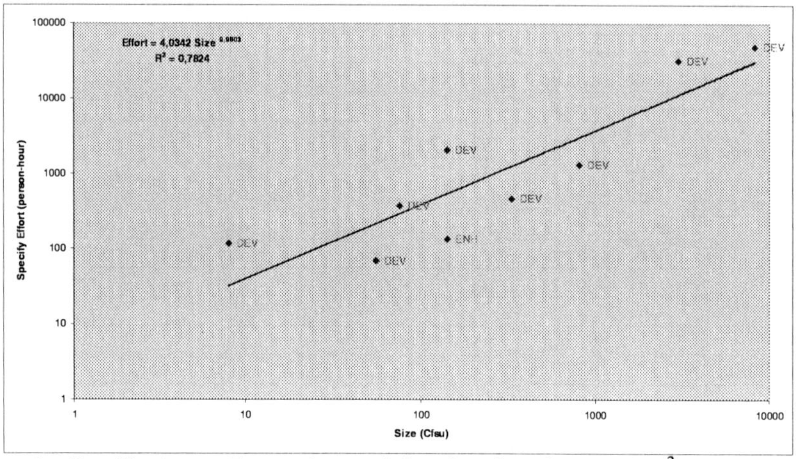

Figure 2 – Specify phase – Regression model on Log-log plot (n = 9, R^2 = 0,7824)

4.2.2. *Effort to build*

The effort variable is available for the Build phase of the full set of 12 projects. The regression model for these 12 is presented in Figure 3. The coefficient of regression R^2 is 0,8971 for the linear regression model:

$$\text{Build Effort} = 12{,}313 \times (\text{Size})^{1{,}015}$$

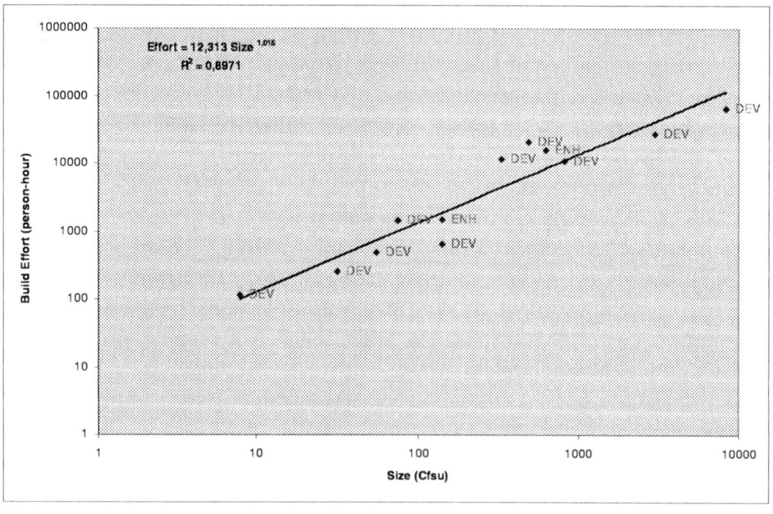

Figure 3 – Build phase regression model on Log-log scale (n = 12, R^2 = 0,8971)

4.2.3. Effort to test

The effort variable is available for the Test phase for 9 projects. The regression model for these 9 projects is presented in Figure 4. The coefficient of regression R^2 is 0,7019 for the linear regression model:

$$\text{Test Effort} = 5{,}2124 \times (\text{Size})^{1{,}024}$$

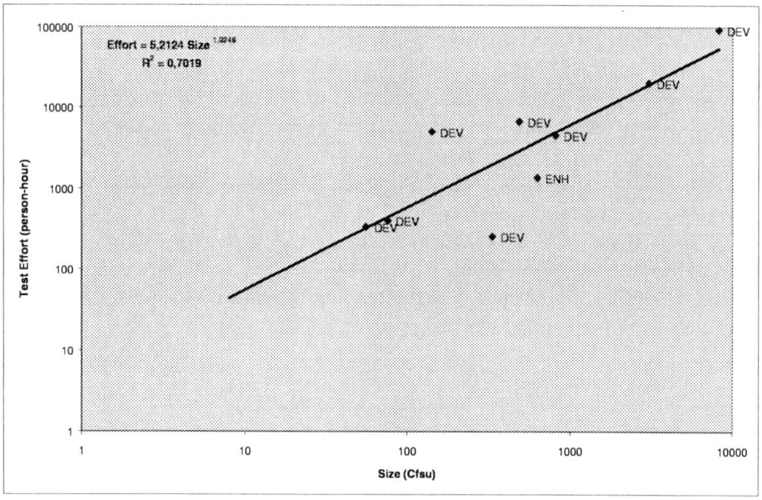

Figure 4 – Test phase regression model on Log-log scale
(n = 9, R^2 = 0,7019)

5. Concluding remarks.

This paper has presented the highlights of the analysis of the relationships of project effort with respect to the functional size variable as measured with COSMIC-FFP. Taking into account the significant non-homogeneity of the origin of the data sample (three organisations from three different countries with different development methodologies and platforms), we would have expected much less consistency on the relationship across both variables. For all of the three project phases for which data was available, the coefficients of determination between size and effort, on a log scale, varied between 0,7019 and 0,8971 depending on the project phase. These results are of course of a preliminary nature, and should be considered only as indicative due to the nature of the data set.

On the other hand, such results have been highly valued within the organisation which provided the largest number of projects within this sample. Using the measurements from the projects contributed to the COSMIC field trials, they have built their own productivity and estimation models, using COSMIC-FFP as the standard for functional size measurement and adding other in-house variable to take into account such productivity factors as programming platform and levels of reuse. Of course such in-house estimation models can be expected to perform much better than models built from non homogeneous multi-organisational data sets.

The COSMIC FFP method is the first Functional Sizing method to

- be designed by an international group of experts on a sound theoretical basis
- draw on the practical experience of all the main existing FP methods
- be designed to conform to the ISO standard on 'Functional Size Measurement' (ISO/IEC 14143-1)

- be designed to work across MIS and real-time domains, for software in any layer or peer item
- be tested in field trials before being finalised

6. Acknowledgements

The authors of this paper wish to acknowledge the data collection contributions of the field trials organizations who for competitive reasons have selected to remain anonymous.

7. Bibliography

[1] B.W. Boehm, R.W. Wolverton, "Software cost modelling: some lessons learned", Journal of System and Software, 1:195-201, 1980.

[2] V. Côté, P. Bourque, S. Oligny, N. Rivard, "Software metrics: an overview of recent results", Journal of System and Software, 8:121-131, 1988.

[3] C. Jones, Applied software measurement - Assuring productivity and quality, 2nd Edition. New York, NY: McGraw-Hill Inc., 1996.

[4] A.J. Albrecht, "Measuring Application Development Productivity," presented at IBM Applications Development Symposium, Monterey, CA, 1979.

[5] S.A. Whitmire, "3D Function Points: Scientific and Real-Time Extensions to Function Points," presented at Pacific Northwest Software Quality Conference, 1992.

[6] D.J. Reifer, "Asset-R: A Function Point Sizing Tool for Scientific and Real-Time Systems," Journal of Systems Software, Vol. 11, p. 159-171, 1990.

[7] T. Mukhopadhyay and S. Kekre, "Software effort models for early estimation of process control applications," IEEE Transactions on Software Engineering, Vol. 18, p. 915-24, 1992.

[8] A. Abran, J.M. Desharnais, M. Maya, D. St-Pierre, P. Bourque, "Design of a functional size measurement for real-time software", Research report no. 13, Software Engineering Management Research Laboratory, Université du Québec à Montréal, Montreal, Canada, November 1998.

[9] S.D. Conte, H. E. Dunsmore, V. Y. Shen, Software engineering metrics and models. Menlo Park: The Benjamin/Cummings Publishing Company, Inc., 1986.

[10] R.B. Grady, Practical software metrics for project management and process improvement. Englewood Cliffs, New Jersey: Prentice-Hall Inc., 1992.

[11] B. Hetzel, Making Software Measurement Work - Building an Effective Measurement Program. Boston: QED Software Evaluation Series, 1993.

[12] S.H. Kan, Metrics and models in software quality engineering. Readings, Massachusetts: Addison-Wesley Publishing Company, 1995.

[13] D.C. Ince, "History and industrial application", in N.E. Fenton, Software metrics: a rigorous approach, Chapman & Hall, UK, 337 pages, 1991.

[14] S. Galea, "The Boeing Company: 3D function point extensions, v. 2.0, release 1.0", Boeing Information and Support Services, Research and Technology Software Engineering, June 1995.

[15] A. Abran, M. Maya, J.M. Desharnais, D. St-Pierre, "Adapting Function Points to real-time software", American Programmer, Vol. 10, no. 11, p. 32-43, November 1997.

[16] D. St-Pierre, M. Maya, A. Abran, J.M. Desharnais, P. Bourque, "Full Function Points: Function Points Extension for Real-Time Software - Counting Practices Manual", Technical Report no. 1997-04, Software Engineering Management Research Laboratory, Université du Québec à Montréal, Montreal, Canada, September 1997. Downloadable at http://www.lrgl.uqam.ca/ffp.html.

[17] C.R. Symons, Software sizing and estimating – MkII FPA (function point analysis), John Wiley & sons, Chichester, UK, 1991.

[18] The Netherlands Software Metrics Users Association (NESMA), "Definitions and counting guidelines for the application of function point analysis, version 2.0", 1997.

[19] C.R. Symons, P. G. Rule, "One size fits all – COSMIC aims, design principles and progress", Proceedings of ESCOM '99, p. 197-207, April 1999.

[20] A. Abran, "FFP Release 2.0: An Implementation of COSMIC Functional Size Measurement Concepts", Proceedings of FESMA '99, Amsterdam, Oct. 1999.
[21] C.R. Symons, " COSMIC aims, design principles and progress", Proceedings of IWSM '99, pp. 161-172, September 1999. Proceedings are downloadable at http://www.lrgl.uqam.ca/iwsm99/index2.html.
[22] International Organization for Standardization (ISO), "ISO/IEC 14143-1:1997 – Information technology – Software measurement – Functional size measurement – Definition of concepts", October 1997.
[23] A. Abran, J.-M. Desharnais, S. Oligny, D. St-Pierre, C. Symons, "COSMIC-FFP Measurement Manual, version 2.0", Ed. S. Oligny, Software Engineering Management Research Laboratory, Université du Québec à Montréal, Montreal, Canada, Oct. 1999. Downloadable at http://www.lrgl.uqam.ca/ffp.html
[24] T. Fetcke, "A Generalized Structure for Function Point Analysis", Proc. of the International Workshop on Software Measurement (IWSM '99), Lac Supérieur, Canada, Sept. 1999, Downloadable at http://www.lrgl.uqam.ca/ffp.html.
[25] International Software Benchmarking Standards Group (ISBSG), ISBSG. Worldwide Software Development - The Benchmark. Victoria, Australia International Software Benchmarking Standards Group, 1997. http://www.bs.monash.edu.au/asmavic/isbsg.htm.
[26] B.A.Kitchenham. Empirical studies of assumptions that underlie software cost-estimation models. Information and Software Technology 34(4):211-218 1992.

The Strengths and Weaknesses of Functional Measure as a Good Negotiation Tool for New Development Projects

Jean-Marc Desharnais, Peter Westwood and Tony Rollo

Abstract

The user/contractor negotiations when constructing a software application are not easy. Many factors need to be considered (cost, product deliver, technical issues, competition, risk, etc.). In this article our focus is on the delivery of the product through the different phases of a project, using functional measure. To follow a product though different phases, a measure that can cope with preliminary requirements must be used. So, functional measure is preferable to lines of code (1). But lines of code are not totally eliminated. Some have used FPA (Function Point Analysis) to predict lines of code (1,2) or to predict FPA from lines of code (backfire) (3). However there has been very little study, to our knowledge, that analyses the performance of FPA as a predictor, from the user requirements through to the implementation of the software (2).

The following article relates our experiences measuring, at different project phases (early, intermediary and final), two software development projects using different methodologies for counting and validating function points. We found that it was necessary to consider different types of users when counting software, not only the end user. What one user could see as technical could be seen as a functional requirement by another. This challenges the common view about what functional measure is measuring. In both projects a report generator was seen as the solution for the many reports identified in the requirements. This resulted in a lower number of function points. Other less obvious infrastructure processes were constructed to improve the quality of the product. We were not able to do the count of those processes based on FPA actual rules. Those processes are considered as technical.

The final result for one project had no more than 6% difference in the number of function points between early, intermediary and final report. What was surprising for the supplier was the fact that the number of function points went down. There were many disagreements between the client and the supplier about the extension of the requirements caused by the construction of infrastructure processes not considered by FPA.

The intermediary result of the second project showed minus 16% difference between the requirements and the second count when considering only the number of function points. For this particular project, it was decided to look more closely at the infrastructure processes considering different types of users. We used a measurement methodology that takes in account the different type of users (COSMIC-FFP[1]). As a result, at the intermediary stage, the difference between the requirements count and the second count was 2%. Our conclusion is that, in order to control the cost of a software development project, the measurement methodology must consider the different types of users

1. Main Steps for the Measurement

To improve user/developer negotiations, the Government of Canada suggested Function Point Analysis (FPA) for new development projects. In 1998, we were asked to measure, at the preliminary requirements phase, the size of two different project products, before the suppliers were selected. A second measure was done later for the two projects after the

---

[1] COSMIC-FFP Measurement Manual, Field trials version 2.0, October 1999. The document is available at s: www.lrgl.uqam.ca.

suppliers were chosen and had documented their own solutions, based on the requirements. Finally, one of the two projects was measured when finished. The final measurement phase for the second project is due Fall 2001.

The first step of the measure was at the preliminary **requirements phase**. The information was at a high level, from the user point of view. For example, for one project, the security was described in 12 statements like this one:

- "The solution must provide the facilities to be able to control the functions that any user can access".

For the audit there was only 10 statements like this one:

- "The solution must record the user, date and time, location information, and specific transactions attempted for all activities on the system".

The requirements were clearly stated form the point of view of different users. There was no reference about the way to implement a specific function. This respects "l'esprit et la lettre" of the functional measure. The documents, with all the preliminary requirements, were part of the contracts between the contractor (for a public bid) and the client (a specific Governmental Agency).

The result of the measure was an estimate of the project product size based mainly on a hypothesis about what the users really wanted at the end of the project. In order to measure the product size a specialist in software measure was helped by the client2 to interpret the requirements.

The next step was to measure the contractor's functional specifications. At this phase the architecture was well described along with some technical solutions. There was a complete entity-relationship model available, together with descriptions of the different functionalities based on the requirements describing the manipulation of the data within different processes (read, write, entry and exit).

The result of this measure was a more precise estimate of the size based on how the architects and analysts saw the requirements. This phase helped to determine if the specialist in measurement, who was helped by the client, had the same understanding of the requirements as the developer.. This helped to clarify the requirements and their interpretation. The requirements were an important reference through the development as they were the basis of the contractual agreement.

The final step was to measure **the software as delivered** (or almost delivered) when the code was tested and the user has at least almost finished the system test. If a system is delivered on time within the budget and within 20% of the predicted size, most will consider it to be a success. (It is also necessary to consider the quality of the deliverables - function points do not measure this.)

2. Methodologies Used

Two methodologies were used: Function Point Analysis and COSMIC-FFP. The following explains the different steps of their use, and why and how a second measure was used.

2.1. Methodologies

We used Function Point Analysis version 4.1 for our count for the two projects. We used COSMIC-FFP for a partial count in one of the projects.

The International Function Point User Group (IFPUG) released version 4.1 in January 1999 (7). Interpretations of the rules are based on industry rules jointly used by Australians

---

[2] The client is a Government Manager who knows the requirements for the software very well.

and Canadians in the past few years (5) incorporating some recent interpretation from the IFPUG Counting Practice Committee (e.g.: how to differentiate a query from an output).

For one project we also used COSMIC-FFP methodology (6) developed by the University of Quebec in Montreal (UQAM) and industry partners. You can find the Guide explaining this methodology at www.lrgl.uqam.ca/.

At the end of each count with FPA, we used the validation process from Desharnais and Morris to ensure the quality of the count. This method is described in (8) and (9).

For the counting, we followed the different steps, which are a part of the IFPUG Counting Practice Manual (7), except the ones in bold referring to the adjustment factor. Scientific papers (12) already suggested the limits of the adjustment factors. For this reason we did not use them.

- Purpose of the count
- Scope and Boundary
- Data functions count
- Transactional functions count
- FPA unadjusted
- **Adjustment factor**
- **FPA adjusted**

The boundary of the software is linked to the purpose of the measure[3]. In these cases the purpose was to measure what need to be developed by the contractor, excluding the packages used by the contractor, to implement the solution. This is an important consideration. For example, if the contractor used a report generator already on the market, instead of developing it, there are no function points to measure except the functionality developed to adapt the package. The package is then outside the boundary. We also measured what was developed to convert the data from one application (the old one) to the new application. This corresponds to the definition of measurement of a development project with FPA (IFPUG 4.1, Chapter 4).

2.2. Why use COSMIC-FFP

Considering that we need to measure all of the software, not just a part of it, FPA rules are not complete (10) when identifying only one level of software to be measured. The FPA rules do not consider more than one layer of software and clearly reject all other layers seen as "technical" software because it is part of the solution, not of the product[4]. This paper challenges this view considering that a solution for one user is a product for another. Within COSMIC-FFP version 2, it is possible to take into account different parts of the software using the concept of "layer"(6). Our definition of layer is based on the concept described in version 2 of COSMIC-FFP[5].

There are 10 principles to determine if there is more than one layer within a software product. The main principle is that from one layer to another, the data is seen from a different perspective. An example of two different layers is the report generator versus the reports. The developer using a report generator is interested in the parameters used to construct a report, while the end user is interested in the different attributes showed in the report. Another example is the functionality of the language used to develop a software or macro (in this perspective MS Excel is a language) versus the functionalities delivered by the software to the

[3] IFPUG Counting Practice Manual uses the word "count" while ISO 14143 uses the word measure instead.

[4] "Measure software development and maintenance independently of technology used for implementation" IFPUG 4.1, page 3-2, January 1999.

[5] (6) pages 23-24.

end user. By analogy, to a manager, the accounting report provides information on expenditures against a budget, but to an archivist the same physical document is a piece of paper to place on the shelve in the right place.

One of the reasons why FPA does not deal with infrastructure processes is because the FPA rules do not apply within infrastructure processes:
• FPA makes a distinction between different types of transactional functions (INPUT, OUTPUT and INQUIRY). An infrastructure process often deals with more than one transactional function, which mean that an INPUT could be just a part of the elementary process. The definition of the INPUT is then in contradiction with the intent of measuring a transactional function and the definition of an elementary process[6]. • An infrastructure transactional function can be very simple or extremely complex. The actual IFPUG rules do not provide more than 7 points for a transactional function. This leads to some problems with infrastructure software and real-time software (10) • Adding the data functions to the transactional functions dilutes the relationship between what is perceived as being done for the user and the size.

From this perspective, we found for both projects that different pieces of the software product were developed not only at the end user level but also for different types of users. Within an organization there is more then one type of user. Some users are technical relative to other users. For example, if an organization has the need to maintain a security system, this is definitively not a task for the end user, but another type of (technical) user. Also, the maintenance of the parameters for the report generator is relatively technical, even if it is functionality delivered by the contractor. The audit trail is also relatively technical for the end user. We classified each piece of software by layers (10).

Those considerations could be also very important for the cost per function point. At a lower level of layer (e.g.: constructing a report generator) we suspect that the cost per function point is higher. At a higher level or end-user level (e.g.: producing the report) the expected cost per function point is lower. As long as the number of FPs for the lower level is relatively low, the margin of error for the price is low enough to permit an average cost for the entire project. However contractors would probably like to see more refinements to the price structure. Those considerations are linked to the concept of functional reuse and the role of infrastructure to improve the value of software. The concept was already presented at the ESCOM-SCOPE conference April 2000 in Munich (11).

3. Results and Comments on Results

3.1. Project 1

Project 1	FPA from Requirements	Diff	FPA Contractor first solution	Diff	FPA Final count
With no Report Generator	**1037**	3%	**1073**	2%	1060
With Report Generator	951	4%	987	2%	**974**

The difference is less than 5% in all cases. Every measure was produced from a non-adjusted base. The measures in **bold** were the ones presented to management at different phases of the project. We did not count the Report Generator as a solution at the

6 An *elementary process* is the smallest unit of activity that is meaningful to the user(s).

Requirements phase, neither did the contractor, which explains the differences. As already mentioned, the final measure (974) is lower than the two earlier measures (1037 and 1073) mainly because of new agreements between the contractor and the user to use a report generator tool instead of programming directly the 30 different reports. The number of function points for the reports at the requirement phase was 150 FPA. The number of points to adapt the report generator was 64 points even though the report generator (an infrastructure project) gave more opportunities for additional functionality for the end user. In fact, instead of having just 30 reports, the possibilities are for many more. This shows that just adding the Report Generator functionality (or any infrastructure functionality) could be misleading and lead to misunderstanding between the user and the contractor. The second project shows more clearly this problem.

3.2. Project 2

Project 2	From Requirements	Diff	Contractor's first solution	Diff	Final count
First count with contractor's first solution	1189	-16%	993	NA	NA
Second count (including COSMIC FFP)	1189	2%	1210	NA	**NA**
Second count including additional user functionality	**1468**	2%	1489	NA	**NA**

The final measure has not been done yet. For reasons that will be explained below, two intermediary measures were performed ("first count with contractor's first solution", "second count".)

From the preliminary requirements we measured 1189 function points. It was already clear the software required was multi-layered. We performed the Contractor's first solution measure when the contractor's solution was specified. When we finished the Contractor's first solution measure of the original preliminary requirements with 993 points (counting only the end-user level or client layer) there were a lot of discussions between the client and the contractor. The contractor believed that his solution was giving more functionality and quality than the one strictly counted at the end-user level. . The client conceded that that this was probably so, but he needed some objective method of measuring the additional functionality. So it was decided to measure not only the functionality provided to the end user, but also the functionality provided to different (technical) users. COSMIC-FFP was used to measure the layered software defined by the contractor in a second measure. It resulted in 217 points being added, without any extra user defined functionality being added.

In addition there was clearly some additional user functionality that had been requested by the client. This was measured at 279 points.

Those who are interested in the equivalence between an FPA measure and a COSMIC-FFP measure should refer to an article already published by Morris and Desharnais (10). At the client level for an MIS system the result is roughly the same. For a real-time system and an infrastructure project with complex processes there is a difference.

Without measuring the impact of the layered software, and ignoring the added user functionality, there was a 16% difference between the function point measure at the preliminary requirements stage and that at the contractor's first solution stage. By taking into account the impact of the layered software, and accounting for the added user functionality the 16% difference reduced to a 2% difference. Once that 2% difference conclusion had been made then the client and the contractor could conclude their agreement.

3.3. Comparison between the requirements and the components at different phases

The exercise showed that the function point method is generally good at predicting the size of new software development at the end-user level. The margin of error between the different measures from Requirements to the Functional Analysis was between 2% and 16%. Even if the margin suggested by the literature is 20% the contractor and the client did not consider that precise enough.

3.4. Considerations regarding the experience of the users, the contractor and the counter

The following conditions, combined together, helped the success of the count:

- The client had a good idea of the system he wanted.
- The client and the contractor were experienced in the software domain.
- The requirements were relatively clear to understand at the functional level.
- The contractor agreed to follow the process and give the information to the expert in functional measure. The expert in functional measure had then the opportunity to talk directly to people who knew the requirements and the client needs.
- The expert in functional measure counter is experienced at measuring FPA.
- The expert in functional measures counting was the same from the beginning of the process.
- The expert in functional measures counting had many years of experience in data processing.
- The client and the contractor respected the functional measure counting expertise of the expert.

3.5. Measuring Effort

Considering a development between 2 to 5 person years, the 5 person weeks taken for the measurement of each project, is relatively low. Base on our experience, measuring 250 points per day is the average in a normal measurement environment (this assumes: the availability of quality documentation, and the availability of the subject matter expert). When the task must be auditable and needs multiple verifications and validations before delivering the results, the number of function points per day will be lower. The approval of the contractor and the client at each step takes additional time, and needs to be considered.

4. Conclusion

From this experience, our conclusion about the strengths and weaknesses of using only FPA are the following.

<u>Strengths:</u>

- It is possible to compare the requirements with the results at different steps of the exercise.
- FPA gives good results globally when comparing the number of function points by phase.
- The counting is relatively reliable when using a validation method.
- FPA gives to the user a way to know if what will be delivered is what they asked for in the requirements.

- FPA can be used as a tool to discuss the final cost of the contract.
- FPA can be used as a tool to give more insight for some requirements.
- FPA can be used as a tool to check the "scope creep" of the project during the different phases of the development.

Weaknesses

Using FPA:

- It is not possible to determine the impact of a particular change in a defined process to the global project.
- There is no direct relation between a specific number of points (e.g.: adding a new report) and the effort to realize the task. This drives to a certain misunderstanding between the developer and the FPA measurer. The measure does not take into account the extreme complexity of some processes.
- We cannot measure the quality of software when delivered. The choice of some tools could accelerate the development of the software, however slowing down drastically the use of the software. (Quality criteria need to be included in a contract, they are independent of functionality and Function Point counts.)
- It is not possible to determine the impact of one layer on another (10).
- There is no explanation on how to deal with different of levels of software such as: report generators, drivers developed for a specific user, using macros to derive reports instead of constructing different reports, constructing generic functionality usable by different parts of the software, etc.

COSMIC-FFP concept of layers is a direct answers to the last two points. COSMIC-FFP measures the data movement of the processes instead of using tables, and adding transactional functions and data functions is a direct answer to the first four points (10). The size of a functional process is not limited by a number in a table, but by the number of data movements. Taking account the different layers helps to understand quality – for example: providing a generalized report generator instead of a certain number of individually programmed reports - but it is not sufficient

5. Future Research

Some more research is needed in order to make functional measure more efficient:

- An evaluation should contain some quality measure, not just functional measure. The main quality measures that could be considered are: speed of the software considering a specific environment (equipment, network, etc.); the volume of transactions that should be managed by the system; the number of defects in the delivered software, the quality of the documentation for the user. Each criterion should be documented in the requirements.
- The functional measure should be more related to the size of each process, instead of having a global count. This will give more insight into the impact of a particular change in a process.
- There is a need to improve the interpretation of the rules.

6. References

[1] Betteridge, R, "Function Points vs. Lines of Code", System Development, p. 4-6, 1990

[2] Betteridge, R, Successful experience of using function points to estimate project costs early in the life-cycle, Information and Software Technology, Vol. 34, no 10, p. 655-658, 1992

[3] Henderson, G.S., "The application of function points to predict source lines of code for software development", Faculty of the School and Logistics of the Air Force Institute of Technology, Air University, 190 pages, 1992.

[4] Jones, C., "Backfiring: Converting Lines of Code to Function Points", IEEE Computer, Vol. 28, no 11, p. 87-88, November 1995.

[5] Resolving FPA Count Issues Resolution Guidelines conformant with IFPUG 4.1 – Counting Practices Manual, Copyright Total Metrics, Version 1.7, Australia

[6] COSMIC-FFP Measurement Manual, Field trials version 2.0, October 1999.

[7] IFPUG, Counting Practice Manual, Version 4.1, 1999.

[8] Morris P., Desharnais J-M, "Validation of Function Points – An Experimental Perspective", IFPUG, 1996, pp. 167-184.

[9] Desharnais J.,M., Morris P., "Post Measurement Validation Procedure for Function Point Counts", Position Paper Forum on Software Engineering Standards Issues, October, 1996.

[10] Morris P., Desharnais J-M, "New Methods for Measuring Function Points in Outsourcing Contracts", IFPUG, Orlando 1998.

[11] Ho, V.T., Abran A., Oligny S., "Using COSMIC-FFP to Quantify Functional Reuse in Software Development", ESCOM-SCOPE 2000, April 18-20, 2000.

[12] Kemerer C.F., Reliability of Function Points Measurement: A Field Experiment, MIT, December 1990.

A framework managing requirements volatility using function points as currency

Frank Armour, Bill Catherwood and Craig Beyers

Abstract

Requirements volatility often results in significant growth in size from the time of initial requirements specification to final system deployment. The idea of controlling the overall system size while still meeting the customer's critical business needs is not just about limiting the scope of requirements growth due to volatility. To address these challenges, a Life Cycle Estimation Framework consisting of a number of estimating methods is applied to key spots in the lifecycle. The customer and developer agree after an initial round of early estimating to a specific amount of functionality for a specific cost and time frame. The "proxy" for representing the functional size is function points, reflected as set of initial high level requirements. Then, as development proceeds and new requirements are discovered, the framework is used to assign function point count to each new and/updated requirement. These requirements are then analyzed and reviewed to determine their impact on the project. Appropriate resizing of the system can then take place.

1. Introduction

Volatility and growth ultimately result in missed deadlines, cost overruns, overworked development teams, unhappy customers, and missed business opportunities. The idea of controlling the overall system size while still meeting the customer's critical business needs is not just about limiting the scope of requirements growth due to volatility. There is a need to ensure that the correct requirements are identified, sized, and prioritized based on both their criticality to business needs and their feasibility and impact on the project resources. AMS has developed a Life Cycle Estimation Framework (LCEF) to manage and control requirements volatility.

In the Framework, the customer and developer agree after an initial round of early estimating, to a specific amount of functionality for a specific cost and time frame. The "proxy" for representing the functional size is function points, associated with a set of initial high-level requirements.

To alert the project management to functional growth, function point counts (FPCs) are performed on a regular basis throughout the development life cycle. As development proceeds and new requirements growth is discovered, the framework assigns function point count to each new and/updated requirements set. These requirements are then analyzed and reviewed to determine their impact on the project. Given the fixed cap size, if the new requirements materially impact the project, AMS developers, working with the customer, will "trade off" existing requirements of equal size (based primarily on function points) for the new requirements. When the count exceeds the amount agreed upon, the customer must select whether to:

- Accept the new functionality and thereby relax the schedule and resource constraints,
- Tradeoff already accepted requirements for the new requirements or
- Give up the new requirements.

This approach helps enable the stakeholders to address the issue of requirements volatility to deliver the high priority pieces of an IT system within the customer's timeframe and budget.

2. The requirements volatility problem

As an initial set of requirements are elicited, analyzed and documented, there is a high probability that the effort to develop and implement a system based on these requirements will exceed the customer's time and budget constraints. In addition, some subsets of the requirements are more critical and of higher priority than others in addressing the customer's objectives and goals for the system, see Figure 1 below. Typically, the implementation of the entire requirements set would involve an effort exceeding the customer's budget and time constraints.

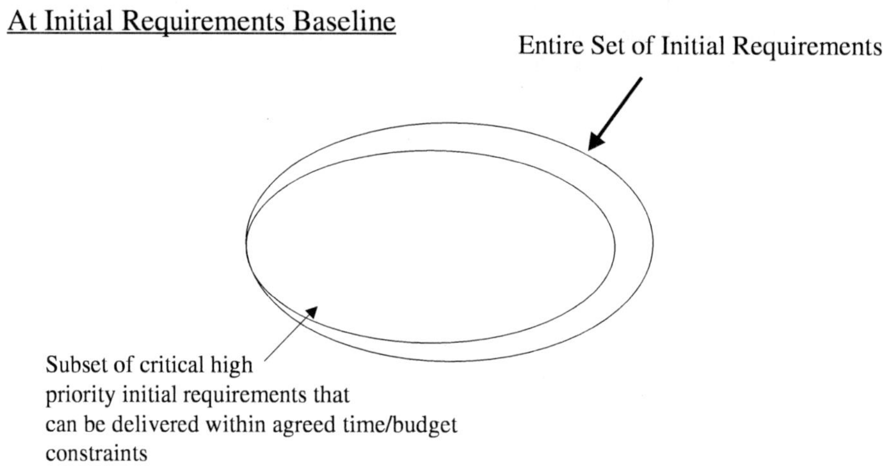

Figure 1. High Priority Requirements are a Subset of Overall Requirements

Given this combination of constraints, a "give and take" occurs where the developer works with the customer to identify the most critical, high priority requirements from the larger requirements set. The size of this subset of requirements is selected based primarily on the customer's budget and time constraints. The non-critical requirements will either be discarded or slated for a later development effort. The critical high priority requirements are then baselined, along with associated function point counts.

However, as system development progresses, almost invariably new requirements will be discovered and/or existing requirements will need to be modified or changed. In today's world of rapidly changing business and technology requirement, this is something that is inherent in the software development process and cannot be ignored. If a project wishes to be successful, it must factor in that requirements will change and that these changes need to be managed, so that the impacts on the client's resource and time requirements are addressed as well. As requirements evolve and change, the project must continue to reprioritize and resized.

As new requirements are discovered, just as in the initial requirements set, some will be of higher priority than others. In addition, some the new requirements will be of higher priority than requirements in the existing baseline, see figure 2.

When new requirements are discovered, but before they are accepted for development, the set of baselined requirements will have to be adjusted to reflect both the new prioritized requirements set. This new requirements set is bounded by factors such as budget and cost. We have developed a function point-driven life cycle requirements control framework to manage the impact of requirements volatility.

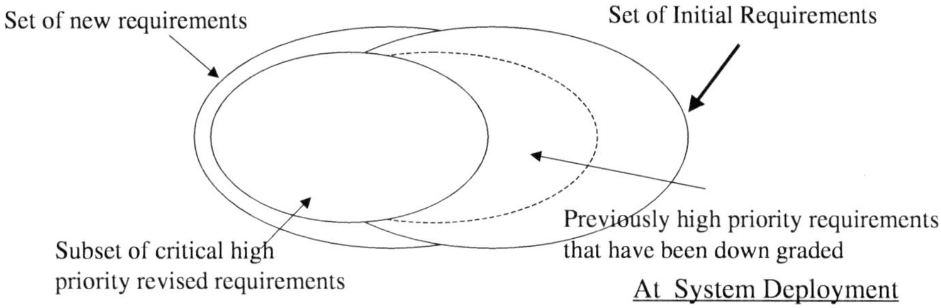

Figure 2. Requirements at System Deployment

3. The life-cycle estimation framework

In this section we introduce and discuss the life-cycle estimation framework. The framework stresses the use of function points as a proxy for system size. The framework utilizes:

- Feasibility Estimating, which includes:
  - Early requirements definition along with associated function point analysis
  - Initial estimates of schedule/duration, level of effort, cost, and quality

- Operational Estimating, which includes:
  - Continuous function point recounts
  - Incremental and iterative development
  - Re-validation of initial estimates or re-estimating based on scope changes in planned increments

When attempting to estimate final systems size during a large system effort, it's obviously difficult or impossible to accurately define the complete requirements set up front. As the development progresses, new/updated requirements will be discovered, adding to the overall functional size of system. As the system development effort progresses, a system initially sized at 8,000 function point can easily turn into 12,000 function point or more, with resulting deployment delays and increased costs. However, customers typically have fixed budgets and/or firm deadlines for the system deployment. On-time deployment is particularly critical in newer e-Business systems development, where time to market is critical.

To help address these challenges we employ the concept of "Function Point Currency" to size the requirement set and then trade-off requirements as the system development progresses. Based on an initial function point count we agree to a fix amount of functional size to deliver. The requirements are then baselined and partitioned into manageable groups for iterative development. Each requirements group has a function point count associated with it. The project development lifecycle is divided into a series of development increments, which are developed in an iterative fashion. Once a Function point "Cap" size has been agreed to, the development progresses. As are new requirements are discovered, their size is determined by a function point count. During development, if the client wishes to add additional or modified requirements, the client must tradeoff existing undeveloped requirement for the new ones. Undeveloped is a critical qualifier here, as once we start the detailed design activity, effort has already been expended on the old requirements. An iterative/incremental lifecycle approach is assists in this regard.

In this sense, we use the function point count as currency. A project could use any size measure as currency, but function points are independent of implementation, credible, known, standard, accepted within the community, and the International Function Point Users Group (IFPUG) [1] provides certification accepted around the world. The key steps in the Estimation Framework are presented in Figure 3 and discussed next two sections.

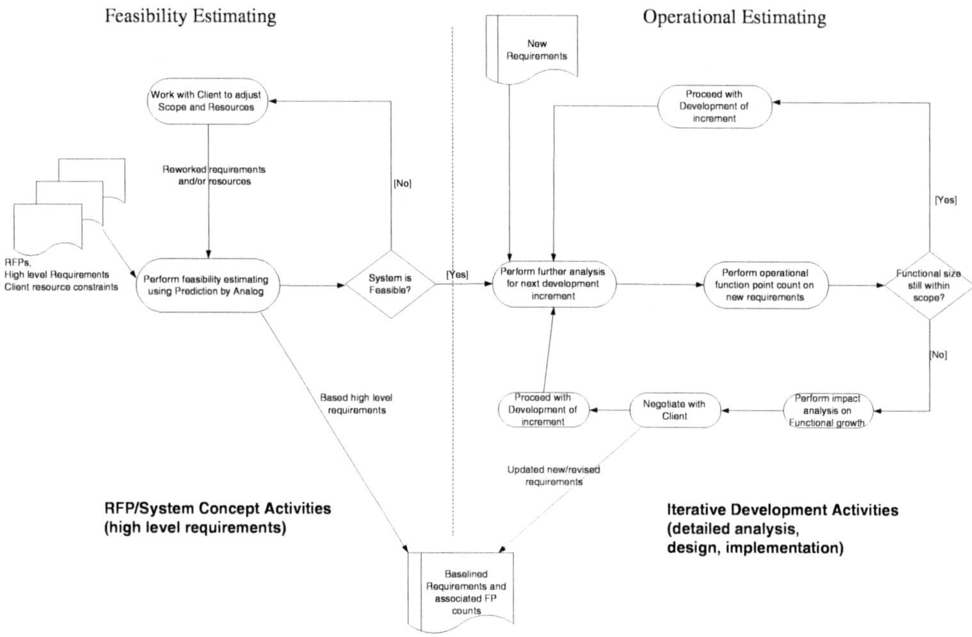

Figure 3. Life-Cycle Control Currency Framework Estimation Framework

3.1. Request for proposal/System Concept – Feasibility estimating

When reviewing a RFP or a high level set of requirements, we attempt to determine the feasibility of the ensuring development effort by comparing estimated size of the system to existing systems. Within vertical business domains, where AMS focuses its efforts, such as telecommunication, financial systems etc, it is often possible to compare the size of existing system to a planned system to initially scope its size by performing an initial feasibility estimate, see Figure 4.

We use a technique, referred to as "Prediction by Analogy" [2]. This approach is useful when responding to an RFP or evaluating a project where only requirements are available. This technique compares the new system requirements to already developed systems that provide similar functionality. This technique maps function point counts from previous, similar efforts to the high level representation of functionality defined for the proposed effort developed. Figure 5 is a conceptual picture of this functional mapping.

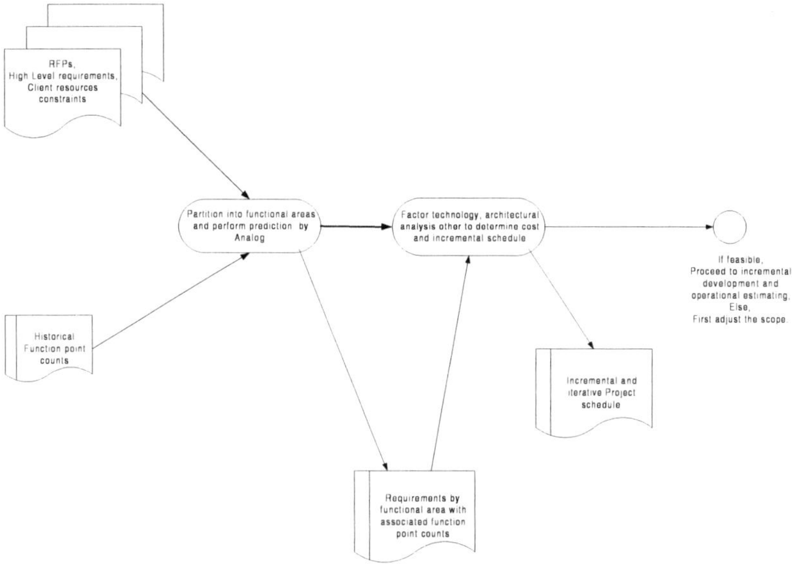

Figure 4: Key Activities in Feasibility Estimating

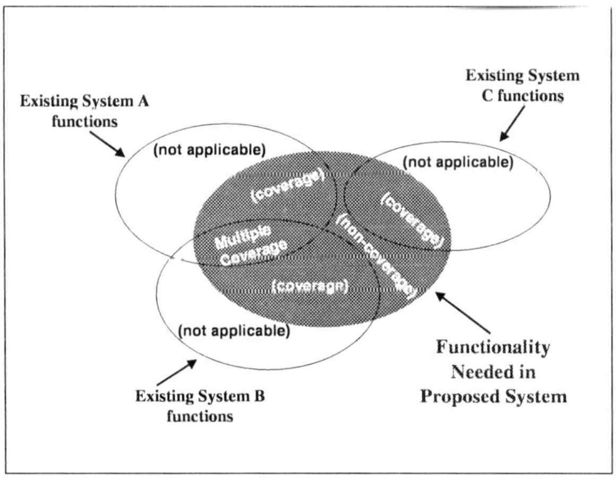

Figure 5. Estimation by Analogy - Functional Sizing

The requirements are grouped and compared to functional groupings from previous efforts. An initial estimate is made and the requirements are partitioned by functional groupings and associated with their function point sizes. For example, see Table 1.

Table 1. Estimation by Analogy Size Example

Requirements subset	**Associated function point counts**
Customer Care	2,300
Service Activation	1,200
Service Request/Order	1,200
Rating and Pricing	4,600
Billing	2,900
Product Catalog	2,400
Total	**14,600**

We use these function point counts as input to develop early estimates of size, cost and time. Historical data guides rough orders of magnitude for Function Point size--compare with size of prior applications for similar systems. We have collected empirical data on how results of how early function point counts map to final implemented function counts, [3] [4]. We then factor technology, architecture, resources etc., to determine a cost and the incremental development schedule. If this is acceptable to the client, we move forward with development. If it is not acceptable, we work with the client to assign priorities to requirements (critical to negotiating and agreeing on size), adjust scope (i.e. revise requirements) or adjust schedule/cost constraints until an agreement on system size represented by a function point cap size and associated baselined requirements. We will use the above information to discover unanticipated functional growth as the system development effort progresses and to address requests for new or updated requirements

Please note that we prefer to complete at least a full system concept [5] before bidding on a fix price contract, however, in many cases the client wants a formal bid based on an in-depth RFP. In these cases, if after performing feasibility estimating, we feel confidence in our estimate, we move foreword with a system concept, and start operational estimating at this point.

3.2. Operational Estimating: Development and Control Approach

As the system development proceeds, requirements volatility will result in new and/or updated requirements being identified. We continue to re-estimate to ensure that the any new requirements are within functional scope. The impact on project (e.g. schedule, staff, dependency, cost etc) of these new requirements will need to be quickly assessed. In order to address the impact, tradeoffs in terms of what functionality will be determined and proactive adjustments to the project plan will need to be made. An iterative management and control approach is used, which utilizes the function points as a "proxy" for system size

The development effort that follows uses an incremental and iterative development cycle, where subsets of the baselined requirements are selected and detailed requirements analysis is then conducted. After each detailed analysis, an operational function point count is performed to determine and ensure that the project requirements are still within the functional size previously agreed to. For example, if a subset of requirements are selected for development which have been sized at 600 function points and the new function point counts show a new size of 800 function points, a impact analysis needs to be performed to bring the count back down to 600 function point. For example, analysts could consider reducing the number of reports developed, partial implementation of some features (while deferring full implementation for later increments), or changing the scope of the increment to include development of the 800 function points. This final option is usually not recommended as it tends to extend development time, increasing dependency risk for later increments.

A closer look at the iterative and incremental estimating cycles is shown in Figure 6. The high-level requirements analysis feed more detailed analysis. Recommended points for operational FPA include at the end of high-level requirements analysis and at the end of detailed analysis within each increment. During detailed analysis, a refined set of requirements functional size and system characteristics needed for project planning and expectation setting is developed. During this activity, estimating via function point count on detailed use case descriptions and object models is used to forecast size growth in the requirements and track development progress.

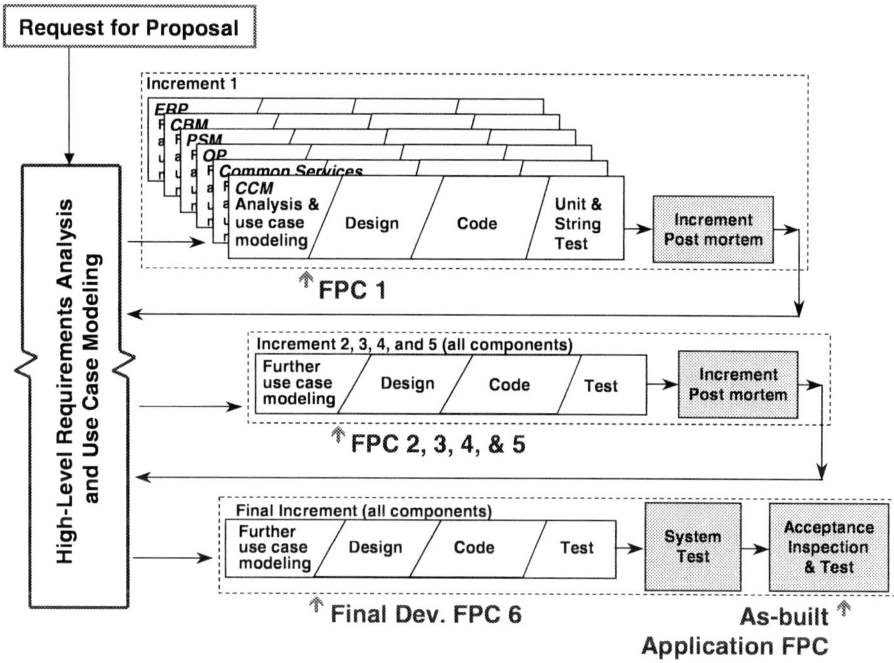

Figure 6. Operational Estimating: Development and Control Approach

During incremental design, again, a further refined set of functional size and characteristics are needed for project re-planning. During this activity, estimating via function point count on detailed designs (e.g., user interface screens and detailed object models) is used to forecast size growth in the requirements and track development progress. When an operational function point count identifies unanticipated system growth, project management executes the following steps:

<u>Document the new requirements</u>
Formally document newly discovered requirement and associate a function point count with the requirements. New requirements are typically injected from either formal change requests, or more insidiously from misinterpretation of the initial baselined requirements.

Prioritise the new set of requirements

The newly discovered requirements are prioritized against each other and against the existing baselined requirements

Determine impact of new requirements on project

Based on the size of the new requirements in function points as well as other factors such as code dependencies, legal deadlines, resource constraints etc, the impact of the new requirement is determined and factored into a revised cost and time estimate.

Reviewed schedule and estimates and re-plan with the client

If estimate is still within the function point cap size and delivery capacity, include the new requirements and proceed. However, if the new function point count exceeds the cap size, project management has several options, including:

- Tradeoff existing requirements, for new higher priority ones, using the associated function points as currency, to remain within the cap size
- Postpone the development of the new requirements until a future release.
- Add the new requirements to the existing baseline, with the client and developers accepting the increased cost and effort and delaying increment completion.

This re-planning involves negotiations with customers to make requirements trade-offs, additions, and rejections. Developers could limit the number of reports to be developed, for example. They could also negotiate to only build limited functionality, deferring full functionality into later increments. Developers and customers could also choose to slightly extend or reduce the length of the increment. Factored into this re-planning is the importance of this set of the requirements and their dependency on other requirements. Rework of software that implements existing requirements will cost more, based on this new requirements. Increments must be kept to a manageable size--based on function point-so that meaningful functional increases result from each increment. But extending increment schedules must be minimized so that later increments aren't held captive by functional dependencies. The incremental nature of the framework helps to alleviate these concerns, since new requirements are normally contained within the scope of the requirements selected for this increment. Requirements already developed in previous increments are off limits and subtracted from the total size that can be traded off. The iterative nature of the framework, with function point counts early in each increment assists in address changes to functionality.

Once we have negotiated a new prioritized set of requirements with the client (assuming that schedule/cost cannot be relaxed, we baseline the new requirements and associated FP counts and then proceed with the development of the increment. A key success factor in this approach is to perform detailed analysis occurs before actual coding within this increment, since this allows the team to trade off the requirements before significant design and coding effort has be expended on the new requirements

Finally, at Post-Implementation an application function point count is performed to determine as-built functional size and system characteristics needed to compute process capability measures. These counts provide feedback both to how well the process works as well as feeding into a historical database for use by future projects.

4. Challenges and Lessons Learned

Function points do work as a control currency, as the approach helps to control overall scope, and manage the overall schedule. However, key challenges to address when using this approach include[6]:

- Must Gain customer management and staff buy-in. The credibility of framework and currency is important, if not critical, to buy-in and continued use; everyone must believe the functional size is correct and understand the estimating process

- Make sure that function points are consistently counted; using the IFPUG Counting Practices Manual and IFPUG-certified function point counters ensures repeatability, consistency, and credibility.

- Beware of function point "tricks". Several that we ran into include: A client representative suggested deleting some needed batch functionality--to reduce FP size--to get more GUI functionality; the individual didn't realize--or conveniently "forgot"--that some GUI functionality depended on the results of batch job processing!

Someone suggested not including the conversion functionality in the FP count, since it didn't represent "functionality" in the new system--essentially ignoring the real need to build conversion software to move to the new system (it was part of *our* assumptions!)

- Validate and communicate. Communicate: not just internal, but keep clients involved in the process; don't just provide the development results

- Use an incremental development life-cycle. An incremental development helps support the continuing monitoring and adoption based new and changing requirements

5. Conclusions

Our project could not have succeeded without this approach Advantages to this approach include controlling overall scope and helping to manage overall schedule, since the cap size, determined in function points managing the uncontrolled addition of new requirements. Also, Because requirements are prioritized based on customer needs, the correct requirements are developed, given the limited resources. Next steps include: more research is needed to validate on large projects and to test the framework on *e*Business projects.

6. References

[1] International Function Point User Group (IFPUG), "Function Point Counting Practices Manual", Release 4.1, 1999.

[2] Catherwood, Bill, Monica Sood, and F. J. Armour,. "Life-Cycle Estimation for Object-Oriented Systems: Prediction by Analogy," Proceeding of FESMA '98 Conference, May 1998, Antwerp, Belgium.

[3] Armour, F.J., Bill Catherwood and Sean Furey, "Experiences measuring object oriented system size with use cases", Proceeding of 1996 European Conference on Software Control and Measurement, May 1996, Manchester, UK.

[4] Armour, F.J., Bill Catherwood and Monica Sood, "Continued Experiences measuring object oriented system size with use cases", Proceeding of 1997 European Conference on Software Control and Measurement, May 1997, Berlin, Germany.

[5] IEEE Guide for Information Technology – System Definition – Concept of Operations Documents, IEEE Std 1362-1998, IEEE Press
[6] Beyers, Craig P., Bill Catherwood, and F.J. Armour, "Using Function Points for Size-Boxing Engagements", International Function Point Users Group Annual Conference, September 2000, San Diego, California, U.S.A.

Individual Software Process Improvement Does Europe Need It?

Rory O'Connor and Gerry Coleman

Abstract

Every so often, a new methodology is launched onto the software engineering landscape with all the force of a religious crusade. From its humble beginnings, Software Process Improvement (SPI), which includes initiatives such as CMM and ISO 9000, has spread its wings into virtually every sector of the software engineering community and in the process has transformed itself from a bag of tools and techniques, into a serious set of methodologies for enhancing organisational effectiveness and competitive success. In the latter half of the 1990's, individual SPI methodologies such as PSP [1] and PIPSI [2] were promulgated as approaches to make the individual a better software engineer. Essentially they are a bottom-up approach where individual software engineers manage and assess their own work, as opposed to the delegated practices of large, organisation-wide SPI models.

Many surveys of European software organisations have shown support for SPI. For example, the SPIRE project [3] showed that: 83% of companies believe that SPI is essential for future success and 87% of companies believe that SPI can significantly improve software quality. However, time, cost and lack of knowledge are seen as the main barriers to SPI usage. In Europe to date, process improvement programmes have been concentrated at the organisational level but there has been less adoption of SPI at the level of the individual.

This paper explores the use of individual SPI methodologies such as the PSP and PIPSI in a European context and poses the question – Does Europe Need Them?

1. Introduction

Software engineering is a discipline whose aim is the production of fault-free software that satisfies the users needs and that is delivered on time and within budget. Sounds nice, but in order to achieve these goals, appropriate software engineering techniques have to be used in all phases of software production, and maintenance. In order for these techniques to be employed, they have to first be taught. Once in use, they may then be integrated as part of the corporate culture and improved upon.

The training provided should enable the definition of a software process that supports sound software engineering principles. Individuals should be trained in the necessary techniques, which facilitate process maturity. The training should be geared toward the perspective of the individuals being trained for it to have the most effect. For example, it does no good to train an entire set of developers in the nuances of Software Quality Assurance (SQA), it is enough that they understand the role of SQA.

All members of the team should be provided training in the applicable life cycle model. This should include the various phases of the software process, from requirements to retirement, paying special attention to problems associated with each phase. This type of training provides all members of the team with a common understanding and clear indication of the road to completion. These individuals should also be provided training in any applicable new technology areas. For example, training in object-oriented design and/or software reuse.

Technology can help to tackle many of the problems associated with software development, but ultimately people and organisations produce software. This straightforward observation has led to focus improvement on the software process. From this point of view, we can recognise two intertwined trends: Firstly, software process improvement at the organisation level, such as CMM, the ISO 9000 series and SPICE (now ISO 15504). And secondly, software process improvement at the level of the individual of small teams, such as PSP, PIPSI and TSP [5].

Process improvement at the organisational level suffers from some drawbacks. It is usually a very top-down approach, that gives little support to individuals and risks not addressing their day to day problems; and it is cumbersome and especially ill-adapted to SME's. The bottom line is that people develop software. Establishing, a software engineering process, and improvement upon that process, depends on the individuals working in an organisation. If the individuals are disciplined, and adequately trained in the principles of software engineering, the chances are good that the software process will be successfully defined, implemented, and improved. This, in-turn, increases the probability of achieving the aim of an on time, within budget, error-free software product.

In the following two sections we introduce two SPI methodologies aimed at the level of the individual software engineer, the PSP and PIPSI, in order to get a better perspective of individual software engineer's SPI needs. We will then compare the results of these two methodologies and assess both their usefulness and relevance in the context of the European software engineering business.

2. PSP

The PSP (Personal Software Process) was developed at the Software Engineering Institute (SEI) by Watts Humphrey. It is designed to bring discipline to the practices of individual software engineers. The PSP provides students and practising software engineers with a framework for measuring and analysing their development work so that they produce programs of higher quality and in a more predictable manner. More specifically the objectives of the PSP are as follows:

- To introduce students and engineers to a process-based approach to developing software
- To show students and engineers how to measure, estimate, schedule, and track their work
- To show students and engineers how to improve the quality of their programs

The concepts, structure, and activities of the PSP are described in detail in the textbook , "Discipline for Software Engineering" [1], in which Humphrey characterises the purpose and scope of the PSP: *"The PSP's sole purpose is to help you be a better engineer. ... It can help you plan, better track your performance precisely, and measure the quality of your products. Whether you design programs, develop requirements, write documentation, or maintain existing software, the PSP can help you do better work. ... The PSP is not a magic answer to all your software problems. Although it can suggest where and how you can improve, you must make the improvements yourself."*

Humphrey's books (along with the instructor support materials) is used as the basis for many courses taught in industry and in academia. While PSP training includes learning a specific personal process, the point of the training is to teach process improvement concepts and to give the engineer an appreciation of the value of a defined process. PSP-trained engineers are expected to evolve their own processes from what was taught in class - to make them truly personal processes. This places control of the process squarely in the hands of the individual who is in the best position to optimise it.

Although the components of the PSP are not complicated and they are based on sound engineering principles, both teachers, students, and engineers have found that learning PSP is a demanding and challenging activity. PSP training is a significant investment (about 150 hours per engineer to complete the course). This is because the course is more than just a class; it is a boot camp. It goes beyond telling the engineers what to do, by having them use the principles while writing ten programs and collecting and analysing data about their performance. In the PSP training, the engineers convince themselves of what works for them and what doesn't so that they can take control of their personal software process.

The PSP provides an incremental approach. It includes seven PSP processes can be grouped into four process levels (figure 1) that have following focus:

- PSP0 - establish a measured performance baseline
- PSP1 - make size, resource, and schedule plans
- PSP2 - learn defect and quality management
- PSP3 - scale up PSP methods to larger projects

The processes are said to be "defined" since that include precise and unambiguous procedures for carrying out the process. Each process is structured into a set of processes phases; each phase has a script that gives a step-by-step description of the tasks to be completed; and there are forms and documented standards that are used in carrying out the process tasks. There is also additional guidance and advice on how to analyse and improve one's process.

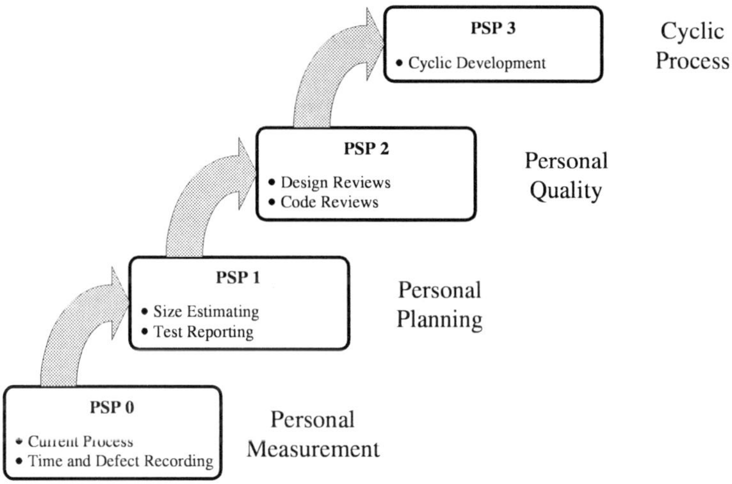

Figure 1 - The PSP Structure

Reporting of actual industrial use data about the effects of the PSP has been limited by several factors:

- Many companies are reluctant to release specific data that competitors or customers could use to identify actual cost and defect levels.
- Most companies have little or no historical data to compare PSP data against, so it is difficult to quantify the effects that PSP had on their costs and schedule.
- PSP has not been widely adopted, so there are fewer cases available to draw from.

One of the first organisations to report their results after using both PSP and TSP was Teradyne. Their return on investment (ROI) analysis indicates that by using PSP and TSP on 2 projects totalling 112 KLOC, they have benefited by approximately $5.3 million to date in saved engineering time. With code developed using TSP/PSP, they are saving approximately 120 hours/KLOC in integration, system, and field testing. Quality levels improved 20 times over prior projects and actual effort and schedule were within 8% of plan (early). Below are specific details about one of Teradyne's projects. Teradyne estimates the cost of PSP training to be one month per engineer. Boeing, AIS, and Hill Air Force Base have also reported receiving significant benefits from PSP and TSP use [7]. However, the results from applying the PSP are contradictory. In classroom setting [6] developers reduce the number of defects they leave in their programs while not changing their productivity. In industrial setting [7] [8] estimate accuracy improves and the same happens to the quality of the product.

However, problems are reported too. El Emam [9] reports a high rate of recidivism where following PSP training many workers do not persist with the disciplines and return to their original pre-PSP development practices. Morisio [10] reports that the duration of training is often unsustainable for SME's, tool support is essential, human factors (such as privacy of data) are key, and finally that the PSP cannot be applied to individuals in isolation when they work in cohesive groups.

Feedback from PSP training programmes in Ireland [11] has suggested that the absence of a support tool, to simplify the recording and analysis of the data produced is one of the major barriers to continued usage of the methods. Developers tire of recording data on paper forms and eventually usage of the disciplines peters out. There is also corroborating evidence from the USA. For example, [12] and [13] report on experiences of a two year PSP study which questioned the quality of the data recorded. They found that there was significant data quality issues with manual PSP, for example, not all defects were recorded because the overhead in recording was too expensive.

Based on findings from literature and on the direct experience of the IPSSI consortium partners [14], it was clear that the PSP needed a number of modifications to become more suitable to industrial applications, especially in a European context. These modifications included:

- Reduce the duration of training to make it more affordable.
- In general, simplify the contents of the PSP, although keeping the original contents.
- Provide tool support for collection of data, computation and analysis of measures.
- Address human factors, build data privacy in the supporting tools.
- Don't overlook the transition phase from training to day to day usage in industry.

The following section describes a European-developed individual SPI framework "PIPSI" (Process for Improving Programming Skills in Industry), which was developed based on the above premise.

3. PIPSI

The IPSSI (Improving Professional Software Skills in Europe) project [14] is an ESSI funded project which aims to provide a process improvement framework for use by individual software engineers working in European SMEs. The focus of the project is on improving individual software engineering skills thus generating bottom-up improvement. At the heart of the IPSSI initiative is the PIPSI (Process for Improving Programming Skills in Industry) approach, whose aim is to present the techniques in a way that makes them more attractive and more easily used in small and medium-sized organisations and development teams. The projects three main deliverables are

- A personal process improvement methodology
- A set of configurable training materials
- A Personal project tool to support data gathering

The focus of the PIPSI is on bottom-up process improvement as illustrated in figure 2, which shows the three main elements of PIPSI personal software engineering:

- defining a personal process
- personal project management
- personal quality management.

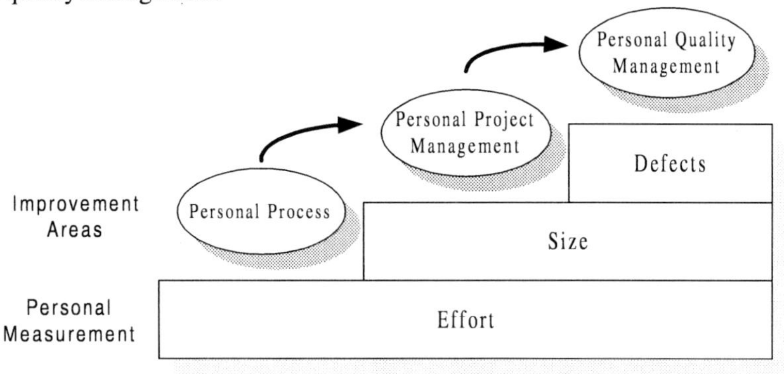

Figure 2 - The PIPSI Structure

The entire model is buttressed and controlled through the use of measurement. By collecting data on their own performance, software engineers learn about how they develop software. The measures help them understand the fundamental relationship between size and effort and, through this understanding, enable them to improve their estimating abilities. Furthermore, by gathering data on their defect rates they witness how employing practices such as personal code reviews and the use of checklists will allow them to produce higher-quality software products. The measures provide information on performance, information can then lead to process improvement and process improvement can lead to the production of better quality software on time. Finally collecting performance data on an ongoing basis moves developers from defining their own development process, through managing it to optimising it.

Through PIPSI training, developers complete programming tasks on which they collect increasing quantities of data. Early exercises capture effort measures. Subsequent exercises gather size data whilst the concluding exercises capture defect and quality measures. This is hugely empowering for both the programmer and the organisation as a whole. Programmers are now in a position where they can provide the project manager with achievable deadlines and the project manager can develop more accurate and predictable delivery schedules. The final element of PIPSI is that of personal quality management. As developers complete PIPSI program exercises, they collect data on the defects injected into those programs.

This process illustrates in which development phases they inject and remove defects. Furthermore, the defects are categorised by type thus allowing a causal analysis to be performed which can then lead to defect prevention. PIPSI focuses on proven quality control mechanisms such as design and code reviews which enable developers to remove defects earlier in the development process. This achieves the twin objectives of removing defects at the front end of the development cycle where they are cheaper and easier to fix and, as a corollary, means testing time is more focused as fewer defects are escaping into test.

Feedback from similar training programmes has suggested that the absence of a support tool, to simplify the recording and analysis of the data produced is one of the major barriers to continued usage of the methods [11]. Developers tire of recording data on paper forms and eventually usage of the disciplines peters out. As part of the PIPSI project, a tool set, which consists of data gathering and data analysis tools for use in a web-based environment, has been developed. The PIPSI support tool enables the measures to be collected as a simple complement to the development process. The tool also analyses the data collected to provide the developer with important process feedback.

4. Marketing PIPSI in Europe

During the early stages of the IPSSI project (1998-1999) the consortium partners conducted a series of awareness activities across a number of Europe countries (specifically, Ireland, Italy, Spain, France, Sweden, and Denmark). Typically they consisted of seminars or contributions to seminars, addresses to professional and industry associations, and short courses for managers. A technical briefing on PIPSI was developed, and used in mail-outs to promote PIPSI training. As well as promoting awareness of PIPSI in industry, some attention has been given to the academic community, with a series of talks and papers presented to groups interested in software engineering and process improvement throughout Europe.

The PSP has been promoted by the Software Engineering Institute (SEI) and its accredited training partners through training courses aimed at software developers, and has had some success in large (primarily USA-based) companies and in University training. It has not found any significant success among European SMEs.

At the start of the IPSSI project, a series of surveys was conducted in partners countries to assess both the level of awareness and usage of PSP (and the general level of SPI at the individual level). A summary of the main consortium partner regions at that time is as follows:

- Ireland - as a result of training run by the Centre for Software Engineering, a small number of individuals had been trained, but only one company have adopted PSP as its company process [11].
- Spain - although the ESI is a licensed PSP trainer, no Spanish SMEs have adopted the PSP.
- Italy - one Italian company has adopted some elements of the PSP, in a project partnered by the Politecnico di Torino [10].
- Sweden - no Swedish SME's were using the PSP.

PIPSI was marketed as a public course in Ireland, Italy, Spain and Sweden, and in France it was incorporated into the industrial training delivered as part of their normal business by AFTI. The most successful take-up was in Spain, where a full public course with participants from industry was run. In Sweden, the course was run in-house in a software company in Gothenburg. In Italy and Ireland, the response from industry was insufficient to make a public course viable. In each of these countries the course was run for third-level students of software engineering. In Spain PIPSI training was taken up by practitioners from several different software companies, representing the industry, banking and manufacturing sectors.

The success in marketing the course in Spain is the more marked because previous attempts to run PSP courses there have failed, despite the ESI being an accredited PSP trainer. In contrast, the take-up in Ireland and Italy was low, although in both countries PSP courses have been successfully run. While there is interest in PIPSI in both countries, the consortium felt that the indications are that the perceptions of the PSP as being rigorous and expensive have carried over onto PIPSI, and made it more difficult to sell.

Also, in an Irish context, because of the relatively high awareness of PSP, organisations had already made a decision as to whether individual software processes were of any value to them. As such, despite the focused nature of PIPSI, organisations had already made their decision in this regard. In Ireland much of the interest in PIPSI was from organisations previously unaware of PSP or those who had not pursued training or time investment in this regard.

Throughout the project much interest was expressed in PIPSI by project managers as witnessed by the success in staging the PIPSI for Managers course which culminated in a successful tutorial presentation at EuroSPI 2000 [15]. However, whilst very supportive of the ideas contained within PIPSI managers decided against investing in practitioner training. Qualitative feedback and empirical comment in this regard, suggested that they were more likely to invest in what they perceived as skill-base enhancement such as training in new development languages or tools.

5. PIPSI Case Studies

This section will provide an overview of the results of a series of selected case studies [16] based on PIPSI training as follows:

- Ireland – undergraduate students, Dundalk Institute of Technology
- Italy – undergraduate students, Politecnico di Torino
- Spain – industrial training, European Software Institute
- Sweden – postgraduate students, Chalmers University

In all cases PIPSI was tailored to the specific needs of the group being trained. However, all groups completed a series of 5 PIPSI exercises. During each of the 5 programming exercises participants are required to collect successively more detailed data as shown in Table 1. By following this approach, participants adhere to the PIPSI model by commencing with effort measures, then progressing to personal project management by relating effort to task size and finally focusing on quality management through understanding defects.

Table 1 - PIPSI Data Gathering Requirement

Exercise	1	2	3	4	5
Activity	Estimate of time required	Estimate of time required	Estimate of size (LOC)	Estimate of size (LOC)	Estimate of size (LOC)
	Measure Total Time	Measure time by phase	Calculate productivity from programs 1 & 2	Calculate Productivity from Programs 1, 2 and 3	Calculate productivity from programs 1, 2, 3 and 4
		Measure of size on completion (LOC)	Estimate of time based on size estimate and productivity	Estimate of Time based on size estimate and productivity	Estimate of Time based on size estimate and productivity
			Measure time by phase	Measure time by phase	Measure time by phase
			Measure of size on completion (LOC)	Measure defect data by phase	Estimate defects by phase
				Measure of size on completion (LOC)	Measure defect data by phase
					Carry out a code review
					Measure of size on completion (LOC)

From the point of view of the PIPSI instructors, PIPSI was deemed very useful to give to the students an introduction to software engineering concepts and methods. The course was especially suitable for students without any notion of software engineering. On the other hand, the course would not be suitable for students with a deep knowledge of software engineering. The structure of the course, with theory and exercises to apply it in practice, was deemed very useful.

From the point of view of the students, the main comments were:

- Interest for the exposition to new concepts
- Appreciation for the practical application of concepts, with a nearly one to one correspondence between theory and practice
- Difficulty in agreeing on the interest of estimation. This depends both on the small time required for exercises, and in the lack of industrial experience. In fact, students with some form of experience of work in real settings were more interested in estimation.
- Difficulty in agreeing on the lifecycle and the three phases (pre build, build, post build). Again, this was due to the small time required by exercises. However, the students agreed that the problem was a problem of scale, and not conceptual.

Overall PIPSI training was found to be very effective in introducing the concepts of Software Process Improvement, and in making plain the benefits of the personal SPI techniques. The student responses to the course also indicated that they understood the need to collect metrics on their work.

Whilst the data collected [15] does not provide conclusive proof of the benefits of using PIPSI there are many encouraging signs. Though time estimation has not improved during this instance of PIPSI training the practice of estimating time does possess particular difficulties. For example, the short exercises can generate quite large estimating errors, as participants tend to overcompensate for previous errors. Also, small tasks will always produce significant percentage errors, e.g. a 2-minute underestimate in a 20-minute task is a 10% error. It is expected that when applied to larger tasks and when size and productivity data are introduced that time estimates will be reduced.

The data does however, show improvements in size estimating and particularly in defect management. Again, the number of data points is insufficient to supply any definitive proof but the signs are encouraging. Indeed, the data should act as a momentum to participants to continue to use and monitor the PIPSI approaches to determine how they work for them in the longer-term.

There were also some qualitative benefits from the study. Many of the students commented on how they had not thought about programming in this way. A number expressed how previously, they were unaware of the proportions of time they were spending in the various development phases and furthermore had not taken product size into account.

For those who followed them most assiduously, code reviews provided the major benefit and, after the course, several developed a working checklist of potential defect causes to assist with their reviews.

The benefits, to the developer, of using IPSSI are ultimately self-convincing. The results above require supplementary exercises to allow more data to be collected and subsequently a clearer pattern of the developer's process. As IPSSI is aimed at industrial practitioners, these exercises could be real world projects. Ultimately, it is through applying IPSSI disciplines in their own daily work that developers can become convinced of its benefits.

Improving the quality of software products is a very important goal for both companies and developers. The trials show that if all of the exercises as currently designed are not completed then there is very little data on defects and the potential advantages of code reviews. It may be necessary either, to increase the number of exercises or introduce code reviews into earlier exercises. Either way this would provide more defect data and more feedback on the application of the reviews.

At present, within the exercises participants are asked in the later exercises to estimate the time required to complete an exercise based on the their estimate of the size of the program and their historical productivity. Whilst this is useful in highlighting the relationship between size, productivity and effort, no allowance is made for the complexity of the task.

6. Conclusions

The experience of the IPSSI consortium in investigating industry requirements and defining an appropriate method has been worth while and rewarding. While the response from industry to the method developed has been slower than anticipated, the reaction has been positive, and it seems clear that there is a potential market for such methods. For example, there has been considerable interest from managers and academics who have heard about these methods, but little practical follow up.

In view of this, the consortium has decided that the best future for methodologies such as PIPSI lies in making they more widely and easily available. We have therefore decided to make PIPSI available as 'freeware', accessible from the IPSSI web page [14]. In this way, it is anticipated that a wider recognition of the method will grow, and individuals and companies will be encouraged to experiment with it.

The Consortium also notes that the companies (such as AIS, Motorola, Teradyne) that have had most success with PSP have previously invested heavily in CMM or other corporate SPI initiatives. Our experiment leads us to believe that PIPSI has a brighter future as a complement to corporate process improvement rather than as a stand-alone methodology.

7. Where Next?

Based on results to date [17], using a defined, planned, and measured personal process appears to offer many benefits. Assuming that further experience confirms these early results, one would expect methodologies such as PSP and PIPSI top be widely adopted and used. However, from experiments reported in this paper and elsewhere, it is also clear that industrial introduction is not easy.

Some SPI researchers [10] believe that the future of such individual-level SPI methodologies is not as an as-is process for industrial contexts. Rather, researchers, can use it as-is in academic teaching, where they can change context variables. Engineers can use it as a process template to inspire team or group process improvement.

Presuming the demand for skilled software engineers continues to increase, the most appropriate way to introduce SPI may be through the educational system. Rather than having students first learn undisciplined practices and then unlearn them, we should introduce disciplined methods at the beginning of the curriculum.

One avenue which may offer possibilities to PIPSI, is as a complement to SPICE (ISO 15504), where following PIPSI disciplines will support accreditation efforts. As SPICE is designed to be more easily tailorable for SME's in comparison to the bureaucratically-heavy CMM, there may be potential gains and acceptance in this approach.

On a positive note ESSI PIE's such as PIOJAVA [18] have demonstrated that acquiring new technological expertise and process improvement can go hand in hand, and indeed that the latter can boost the effectiveness of technology acquisition. This is still a message that needs to be put across to hard-pressed European software development organisations, difficult through it may be to change attitudes in today's skill hungry and fast changing technology market, and to explain the need to change a sceptic, questioning European culture.

8. Acknowledgements

This research is partially supported by the European Commission as ESSI project 27453. The authors gratefully acknowledge the value gained from discussions regarding this work with their research partners: Dublin City University, European Software Institute, IVF - The Swedish Institute for Production Engineering Research, Politecnico di Torino and AFTI (formally Universite Thomson).

9. References

[1] Humphrey, W.,"A Discipline for Software Engineering", Addison Wesley, 1995.
[2] Coleman, G. & R.O'Connor, "Power to the Programmer - Using measurement to optimise the software process at the individual level", In Proceedings of 11th European Software Control and Metrics conference, Munich, Germany, April 2000.
[3] "The SPIRE Handbook", Centre for Software Engineering, 1998
[4] Taylor, A., "IT Projects: Sink or Swim", The Computer Bulletin, January 2000.
[5] Humphrey, W., "Introduction to the Team Software Process", Addison Wesley, 2000.
[6] Hayes, W. and J.Over, "The Personal Software Process (PSP): An Empirical Study of the Impact of the PSP on Individual Engineers", Technical Report SEI-97-001, Software Engineering Institute, December 1997.
[7] Humphrey, W.,"Using a Defined and Measured Personal Software Process", IEEE Software, May 1996.
[8] Ferguson, P., W.Humphrey, S.Khajenoori, S.Macke and A.Matvya, "Results of Applying the Personal Software Process in Industry", IEEE Computer, May 1997.
[9] El Emam, K., B.Shostak, N.Madhavji, "Implementing Concepts from the Personal Software Process in an Industrial Setting", Proceedings of Software Process 986, IEEE Computer Society Press, Brighton, 1996.
[10] Morisio, M., "Applying the PSP in Industry", IEEE Software, December 2000.
[11] O'Beirne, P. and J.Sanders, "Personal Software Process: Does the PSP Deliver its promise?", Proceedings of Inspire '97, Gothenburg, Sweden, 1997.
[12] Disney, A., and P.Johnson, "Investigating data quality problems in the PSP", Proceedings of the ACM SIGSOFT Sixth International Symposium on the Foundations of Software Engineering, Florida, USA, 1998.
[13] Moore, C., "Personal Process Improvement for the Differently Disciplined", Proceedings of the International Conference on Software Engineering, Los Angeles, USA, 1999.
[14] IPSSI (Improving Professional Software Skills in Industry), ESSI Project number 27453, http://www.compapp.dcu.ie/ipssi/
[15] "PIPSI", Tutorial presented at EuroSPI'2000, Copenhagen, Denmark , November 2000.
[16] O'Connor, R., H.Duncan, G.Coleman, M.Morisio, C.McGowan, C.Mercier & Y.Wang "Improving Professional Software Skills in Industry - A Training Experiment", Technical Report CA-0201, Dublin City University, 2001.
[17] Humphrey, W., "The Personal Software Process: Status and Trends", IEEE Software, December 2000.
[18] Chappell, C., "Does Europe have the right attitude to process improvement?", Software in Focus, Issue 14, October 2000.

QMIM : Quality through Managed Improvement and Measurement
Towards a phased development and implementation of a quality management system for a software company

Katalin Balla, Theo Bemelmans, Rob Kusters, Jos Trienekens

Abstract

The paper describes results of a longitudinal study of developments in the area of software product and process quality improvement within a Hungarian software company, IQSOFT Ltd. Over the last 8 years 5 phases could be distinguished. Each phase is described shortly, following the same structure, namely: basic starting points, key problem areas, literature consulted, activities and design executed, reflections on what happened and why. The lessons resulting from the analysis of this case have been formulated in terms of guidelines. These guidelines are developed around a framework containing the basic issues of software production (project management, technical processes and products).

1. The case study

1.1. IQSOFT Ltd., the environment of the case study

IQSOFT Ltd. (IQSOFT Intelligent Software. Ltd.) is one of the main representatives of the software industry in Hungary. The company was formed in early 1990 from part of a large state organisation, the Theoretical Laboratory within the Computer Technology Co-ordination Institute (SZKI). The company is a medium-sized one, having at present 74 employees. IQSOFT Ltd. has three main software activity types: software development (mainly in a database environment, using 4GL development tools), software integration, and software implementation. The projects are generally small to medium size and can differ widely in their characteristics. Research and training are also important activities in the company's activity profile.

The case study can be distinguished into 5 phases:

- The enthusiastic start, dealing with quality (1993-1994)
- Seeking new ways and means (1995)
- The successful recommence (late 1995-mid 1997)
- The new ISO 9001 project (mid 1997 – April 1998)
- Process improvement (May 1998 – 2000)

In the following sections we will describe these phases into more detail.

1.2. Phase 1: The enthusiastic start, dealing with quality

Since 1993, efforts have been made at IQSOFT to develop and introduce an internal QMS. The basic reason of the IQSOFT's management decision was - by that time - the emerging request to be ISO-certified, formulated by a (potential) foreign customer. At that time , no Hungarian software company was registered according to ISO 9001 [1], so it would have been a strategic advantage to be the first registered Hungarian software company.

In 1994 the overall company and two concrete projects were assessed according to the Bootstrap methodology. The results of this assessment pointed out that the whole organisation was situated on level 1.25 in the CMM model, while some of the activities (such as detailed planning, project management and usage of development model) raised above level 2. Due to an insufficient understanding of the interconnections between CMM and ISO 9000, we were unable to use the assessment results in an appropriate way. We had to accept that the efforts made in building up and introducing a QMS at IQSOFT [2, 3] did not produce the desired results. By the beginning of 1994 all basic quality documentation had been finalised, but, as the management did not make their usage mandatory, remained almost unused. Though the documentation set was ISO 9001- conform, there was a huge gap between ISO 9001 prescriptions used in the documentation and the real life practices. We believed at that time that the main reasons for this slow adaptation of new procedures were both the diversity of projects (IQSOFT's projects were difficult to standardise) and the human factors dimension (software developers were resistant to accept standard prescriptions).

1.3. Phase 2: Seeking new ways and means

Experiencing the "failure" of the quality-exercise, the management and the employees became sceptic about the possibility to improve daily practices. The customer enforcing ISO – certification disappeared, and during 1995 there was no concrete idea about what the next step in quality management should be. Quality activities were not stopped, but became a kind of background activities, thus limiting to research in the domain.

We *felt that* some important elements were lacking. It became obvious, that a QMS, even a structured system-development or project management methodology can not be introduced at once at IQSOFT. It also became obvious that first of all organisational and working-style changes were required at the company, as a first step towards quality management.

We came to the idea that a software QMS will not be really operational and useful if we would take into account the ISO 9000-prescriptions only.

Research done in parallel confirmed our ideas. We learned about Fenton's basic entities ([4]): products, processes and resources. Before these entities would be understood, precise definitions would be needed (which seldom exist). Next to that we began to understand the relationships with the several software quality attributes. We placed all these elements into a matrix, representing our "chosen quality framework" (see figure 1). The word "chosen" indicated in fact, that we wanted to look to quality through this framework: we wanted to deal with the quality of all objects. Yet, it was not clear *how* it would be possible to do this.

Figure 1: The chosen quality framework

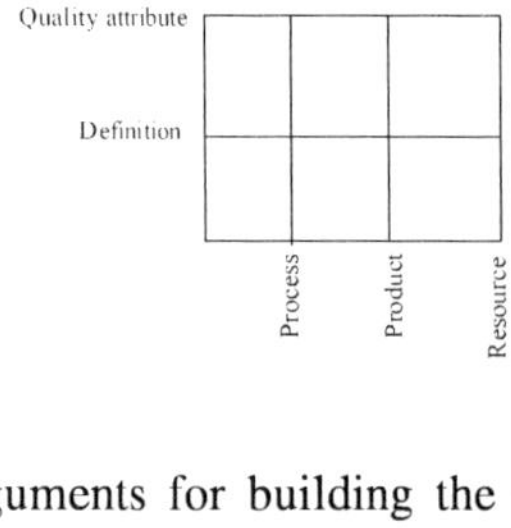

We remarked the existence of many other approaches on software quality. Process oriented approaches - completing ISO 9000 -, CMM ([5], [6]), Bootstrap ([7]), and SPICE ([8]) have been studied. We learned about approaching software quality by the several product characteristics (Boehm and McCall models ([9], [10]), ISO 9126 ([11])). In many articles, e.g. [12], [13] we found arguments for building the quality systems in a customised way, taking into account the company's own needs. And still it wasn't clear what to do, which approach to choose from the many existing ones, and how to combine them to have a complete picture about quality.

1.4. Phase 3: The successful recommence

This phase had its origin when in 1995 IQSOFT won an EU PHARE tender "Technology Development and Quality Management (TD&QM)", thus gaining support for quality – oriented activities. That was the beginning of the so called $IQPM^2$ project.

IQSOFT management was now aware of the fact that it was impossible to introduce a QMS at once. So, also taking into account the results of the Bootstrap assessment, they decided to use the opportunity to introduce a project management methodology. Taking into account the former co-operation with Lucas Management Systems, the PM^2 methodology of this company, distributed by Metier Plancon (NL) had been chosen for supporting the project.

The project started in February 1996 and finished in May 1997. The basic phases were: awareness and requirements gathering, development of project management standards and procedures, solution definition and implementation of a software tool, testing the developed standards and procedures, measuring and evaluating the results, improving the standards and procedures according to the results obtained in the baseline projects.

We can state that the $IQPM^2$ project was successful: it reached its goal within the planned time and budget limits. A key factor in the success was the very strong support of the management, which attached a high priority to the project. The employees were kept informed during the whole project about its evolution. Working together with many employees in defining the needs, in putting things on paper, in trying out the newly written prescriptions in real projects contributed to the diminishment of the previously hostile or passive attitude towards all quality-issues at the company. People saw that it was possible to work out a set of prescriptions that were really helpful for their work [14, 15].

During this phase 3 it became obvious that there were serious communication problems within the company (e.g. employees were not aware of the management's requirements regarding their work). Therefore, the management decided to develop a handbook containing the description of the IQSOFT organisation, the possible positions, functions, roles and responsibilities. During the analysis made before developing this handbook, it was decided to start with a formal quality department.

According to a Bootstrap assessment carried out in 1997, the overall organisation had the maturity level 2, while the pilot projects reached 2.50 in CMM. Issues related to organisation were situated on level 3, life cycle independent functions and process related functions reached level 2.75. Compared to the assessment made in 1994, this Bootstrap assessment showed an increase especially on those fields related to the $IQPM^2$ project goals: organisation, description of standards and procedures, project management practices. This increase supported management's belief that we were moving in the right direction.

Besides the planned ones, the $IQPM^2$ project produced a series of side results, which, from the company's long-term perspective, were even more important than the planned ones.

We understood that the processes of a software company could be - in our case: should be - divided into at least two distinct activity types: *project management processes* and *technical processes*. Project management processes are those concerned with the successful management of the project, regardless to what technical activities (e.g. system development, system integration, support etc.) are being done in the project. Technical processes are concerned with the technical work done in the project.

Projects can be modelled according to both activity types, so project management models and project type models can be situational configured. We noticed that project management activities in our company were more stable than the technical ones, which justified again their separation. With the standardisation of project management activities –building the (*single*!) project management model of the company - we made the first important step towards bringing order in IQSOFT. At that moment we consciously left the technical activities undefined, just grouping them into several "project types", which would be worked out later. The finding that there were just a few, well definable project types (development project, system integration project, implementation project, research project) strengthened again the belief that it was possible to structure the company's activities.

Following this argumentation, *we regrouped Fenton's entities into the following objects: Project Management (PM), Technical Process (TP)*, and *Product. (P).* Basic reason for this regrouping was the fact that the objects we were talking about were not Fenton's "narrow" objects, but were more business objects. Fenton's "resources" were incorporated into project management, because we considered that all resource-related subjects were addressed within the project management issues.

We called the horizontal dimension of the matrix presented in figure 1 the "object" dimension. It changed, now having the elements: *Project Management (PM), Technical Process (TP)* and *Product (P)* (See figure 2). The vertical dimension remained unchanged. We called it the "*quality- specification*" dimension.

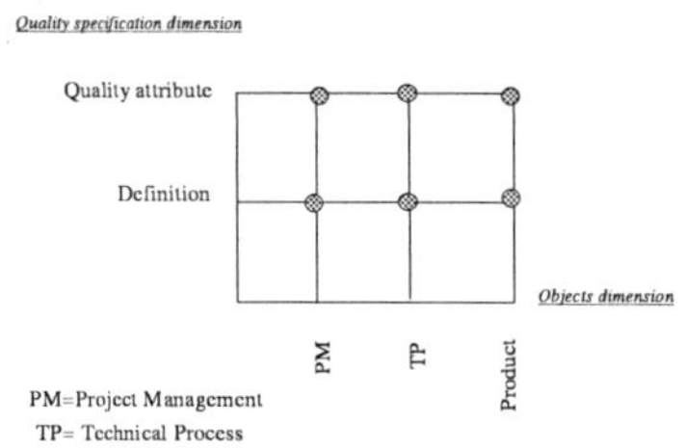

Figure 2: The changed quality framework

1.5. Phase 4: The new ISO 9001 project

With the positive experiences of phase 3, IQSOFT's management decided to go again for ISO 9001 registration. This decision was a logic consequence of the results obtained in the previous phase. On the one hand, the CMM level close to 3 is said by literature to be more or less an ISO 9001-conform level. On the other hand, it was clear what had to be done: the project model developed in phase 3 had to be completed with the type models, the non-project- related activities had to be standardised as well. A very important fact was that the employees were accepting the need for an organised way of working.

The situation on the software market had also changed since IQSOFT's fist attempt to register: by November 1997 a number of 6 Hungarian software companies had been registered according to ISO 9001. Being registered was not a novelty any more, while not being registered started to be a serious handicap.

On this basis a project was started to obtain registration. It can be called a "new approach" project because it had the scope of obtaining ISO 9001 certification using all former experience of IQSOFT in building a *customised QMS. The project was declared a top-priority one*. The project team was formed by a project owner - the technical director-, one of the authors was declared project leader, and 10 project members - one representative for each of IQSOFT's departments - spent part of their time working on the *type-models of their departments*. The estimated internal effort was 250 man-days. Official start date of the project was preceded by two training sessions: an internal auditor course was organised for all project members, and a course attended by the top management and the leaders of the different departments.

The quality management system was fully operational beginning with February 1998. The final audit for the registration took place in April 1998, and it was successful. It is important to show the structure of IQSOFT's internal QMS: it follows the recommendations of the ISO standards, but it is built to fit the specific needs of the company itself. The basic idea underlying the QMS was *that project- related activity and non project- related activities exist at IQSOFT*. We grouped these into "*project- related processes*" and "*non project- related processes*". Describing the "non project - related processes" was easier: the processes related to sales, training, computer system administration and secretariat were relatively well defined already in 1993. Having the experience of the IQPM² project, *we separated the project management activities from the technical ones.* This way, a company-wide standardisation became possible: the project management standards - which were worked out earlier, within the IQPM² project - were valid for all projects. The differences were described in the so-called "project type models".

The ISO 9001 project has been evaluated to be a successful one. It reached its goals within the planned time and cost limits, and it produced the planned results. We can state that the success of the project was strongly influenced by the strong support of the top management. The employees accepted to work in a standardised way. There was no evident opposition from any departments; passive opposition (characterised mainly by the absence of co-operation) was rarely observed.

1.6. Phase 5: Process improvement at IQSOFT Ltd.

The QMS built in phase 4 is being used actively ever since. This fact is shown by the relatively high number of requests for changes in the prescriptions, templates, employees' propositions and problems raised in connection with the QMS. The procedures are updated to fit the modified practice, and, as new practice is being observed, new ideas are introduced to make things work better. Some figures about usage of the quality management system in 1998 and 1999 are shown in table 1. According to the evaluations, working in conformance with the prescriptions of the quality management system causes about 30% of extra effort in small projects, and about 10-20% in the bigger projects.

Table 1: Some figures about usage of the quality management system (QMS) in 1998 – 1999

Activities / events / data related to the QMS	In 1998	In 1999
New issue of the prescriptions	65 times	16 times
New issue of the templates and models	37 times	6 times
Employees' propositions and problems raised in connection with the QMS	72	87
Quality - oriented training	± 30 days	± 30 days
All effort connected to quality management	319 days	121 days

IQSOFT did not want to stop quality-related activities on ISO 9001 level. Therefore, new ways of improving quality have been searched. Having in mind the framework presented in figure 3, we decided to concentrate on elements not taken into account so far. Literature (theory of measurement ([4], [16], [17], [18]), the Quality Improvement Paradigm (GQM, Experience Factory Organisation [19], [20]) shows that *measurement* has to be done to assure that quality of each object of software production is of the requested level. The framework can be completed with the "metric" element, an important item "telling something" about the quality of the objects.

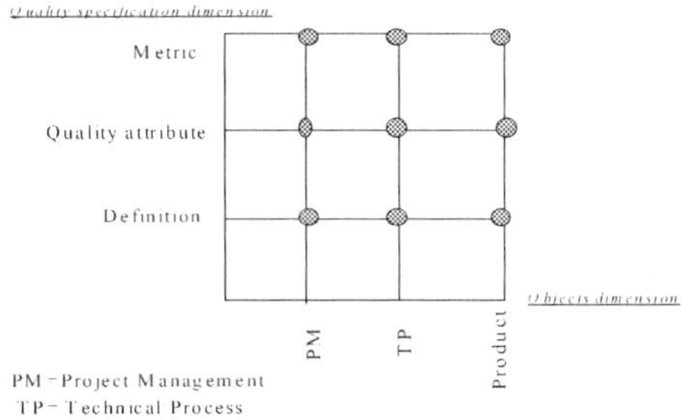

Figure 3: The QMIM framework

This way, the quality framework changed to the one presented in figure 3, called the QMIM framework (Quality through Managed Improvement and Measurement). The QMIM framework shows all the elements to be taken into account when dealing with software quality. The level requested by ISO 9001 does not address at all products and metrics, while the grade of detail of the elements "definition" and "quality attribute" vary according to the company's level of understanding. According to the framework, IQSOFT had two possibilities to develop its QMS: either start using metrics or concentrate on product quality. Knowing QMIM, the technical director decided in 1999 that metrics should be introduced. After an analysis of the actual situation (including a study of possible metrics) the decision to improve software estimation and productivity at IQSOFT was taken. Two metric programs were carried out using basically the GQM paradigm. The selected projects were medium sized. The analysis of the obtained data showed that in three cases the effort needed has been underestimated and the projects did not finish in time. The technical director considered the data obtained interesting, although no general conclusions could have been drawn. This fact shows probably that IQSOFT was not yet ready to carry out efficiently and effectively metrics programs.

The management of the company decided in the summer 2000 to establish a testing team. Working with the most modern testing tools, this activity seems to give good results. Therefore the next step for IQSOFT will probably be a better understanding of products and their quality characteristics.

2. The QMIM reference framework and model

While running the case study described in chapter 1, a series of lessons was learned. Here we review and structure these findings, as we feel they are applicable in other low-level maturity software organisations, too.

One basic issue in the case study was the construction of the QMIM framework, presented in figure 4. The basic elements of this framework are: project management, technical processes and products. Any organisation starting to do quality improvement will have to take these elements into account. The definitions of the elements have to be set. Understanding that the quality of the elements is characterised by their quality attributes, which have to be measured using appropriate metrics, is extremely important. Using QMIM framework does not enforce having all its elements in place from the beginning: it only gives its user the understanding of the important elements of software quality management. This understanding also provides a structured view on the approaches existing in literature. The user will be able to place the models, standards, approaches found in books into the QMIM framework, being able to see the issues addressed by each approach, and thus selecting more easily the one which best fits the own needs.

The way that QMIM is used in an organisation is important. The elements defined, the degree of detail of the definitions, the interconnections observed, the literature approaches or their elements chosen at a certain moment of time by an organisation can differ according to the specificity of the organisation using the model, according to the level of the organisation's maturity, according to the degree of change accepted by the management, etc. Therefore we consider it appropriate to describe *guidelines* of applying the framework. The guidelines are, in fact, about building the *QMIM reference process model*, which will help every company using QMIM in building its own process model.

First of all, QMIM helps in identifying the actual state of a company's quality management system compared to a reference model.

While using QMIM, it is important to understand that the framework should be kept in mind *at any moment of time, on whatever maturity level the company is situated on, may its business goals be as they are.* In a low maturity level organisation few elements of the suggested framework will be in place at the beginning. However, in the QMIM framework even the situation where no quality management system is in place, can also be regarded as a certain "level".

The degree of detail in which a concept can be defined at a certain moment in time depends on the maturity level of the company. But *it is very important to think of all concepts on any maturity level.* As the company grows in maturity, the *focus will shift from the one concept to another.*

We suggest that software companies situated between levels 1 and 4 of CMM should think about the following basic activities in order to deal with quality management issues: *define project management, define technical processes, define products, define supporting metrics.*

Notice that we *did not* give sequence numbers to the four basic activities mentioned before, suggesting by this fact *that the activities can be performed in any order.* However, our experience has shown that performing them in the sequence: *(defining project management → defining technical processes → defining products → defining metrics)* works well in a low maturity level software company. Looking to the reference framework suggested by QMIM, *the organisation is able to understand the place and the interconnection of all elements that are important to deal with quality in a complete, unified and balanced way.* Using this framework, *the company can choose its own direction of development, depending on its maturity, on specific business goals at a certain moment in time, on business policy, etc..*

Some possible approaches of using QMIM could be to define *all objects* of the framework in the specific organisation (start completing the matrix horizontally) (see figure 4, approach 1.) or to define all aspects of an object, e.g. definition, quality attributes and metrics of *project management* (complete vertically the PM aspects in the matrix) (see figure 4, approach 2.)

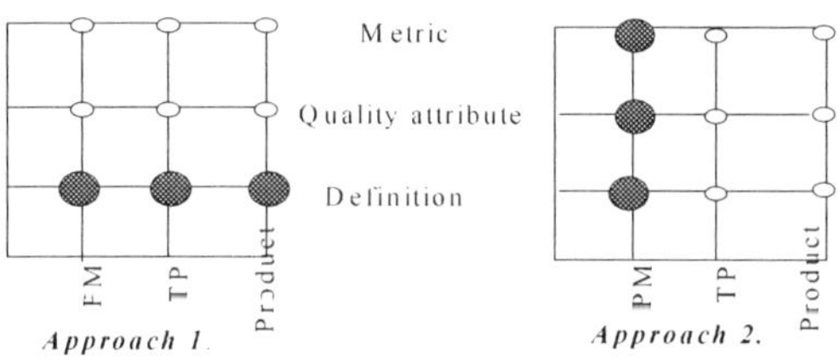

Figure 4: Two possible approaches to start dealing with quality

Summarising, the QMIM reference framework can be used in the following way:

Step 1:

Identify the actual state of the company's QMS regarding concepts, definitions, procedures, support (templates, tools etc.). The result of this identification step will be a company's version 0 of QMS. Its degree of completeness will reflect the company's actual level of maturity.

Step 2:

The QMS version 0 can be compared with the *QMIM framework, a high level reference* This comparison will show the strengths and weaknesses of the actual situation and will result in identification of missing elements. This can trigger an additional *analysis* for a next improvement step. Type, ambition level and direction of the proposed change will need to take into account the maturity level of the company and the ability and readiness of staff as well as the body of knowledge, described in literature. The own company's framework will be completed gradually. For the existing elements quality attributes can be defined, and their quality can be judged (maybe using metrics). The result will be a quality system version 1.

It is important to notice that QMIM suggests several possible directions of growth / improvement. After *a certain direction of improvement has been chosen*, QMIM offers the possibility to choose among existing approaches in order to achieve that improvement. (E.g. ISO 9000 can be chosen if the organisation wants to define its processes, ISO 9126 can be chosen if the organisation wants to understand its products etc.).

Step 3:

QMS version 1 will be compared again to the reference provided by QMIM. Step 2 is repeated, resulting in a quality system that is more and more close to the reference ideal.

Figure 5 represents these guidelines as a continuous process of quality improvement.

To support these guidelines a suggestion for a sequence of activities is given below. The QMIM guidelines are founded on the basic idea that all QMIM concepts should be kept in mind on any maturity level. Therefore no strict sequence of the activities to perform is given. However, based on our experience with a low maturity-level software company and on the experience of working with QMIM, we give a possible best sequence of the different activities. It facilitates a company's own methodology to deal with software quality in a unified, balanced way.

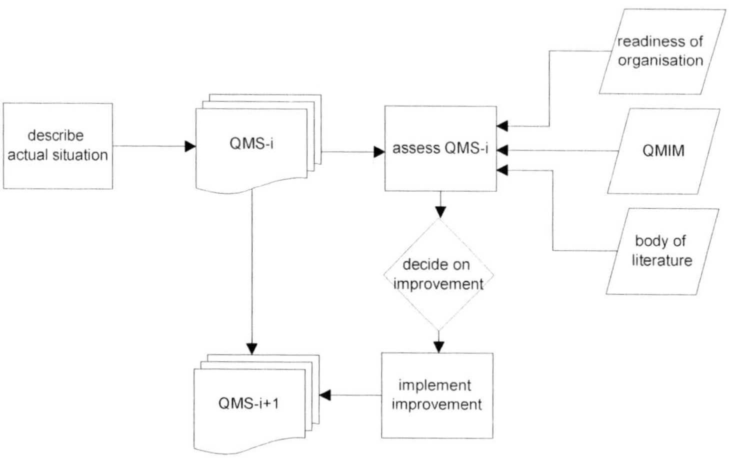

Figure 5: The way of using QMIM in different organizations

Taking into account the above mentioned ideas, the following appeared to be helpful:

1. Understand the CMM model. Place your company on the CMM maturity hierarchy. An assessment method, e.g. a Bootstrap assessment can be used for this purpose. Following guidelines refer mainly to low maturity level companies.
2. Separate the project management activities from the technical ones. The project management activities are more stable than the technical ones, and can provide a common framework for all projects within the company.
3. Understand the concept of generic project modelling and build such a generic project model for the company.
4. Investigate the existing project management methods, procedures, standards, way(s) of working at the company. Make use of the viable project management elements.
5. Identify the needs existing at the company in terms of project management improvements. For the identification a structured methodology can be used (e.g. Pm^2 methodology of Artemis International).

6. Understand the basic concepts of a project management model and build the own project management model for the company.
7. On the basis of the needs defined in 5., develop and document the project management system at the company. For the development a structured methodology can be used (e.g. Pm^2 methodology of Artemis International).
8. Assess the maturity of your company again (e.g. with a Bootstrap assessment). Draw consequences to the results of the assessment compared to the results of the assessment done in 1. Maturity should increase most probably to level 2.
9. Define quality characteristics of the project management processes.
10. Define and start using metrics to measure project management characteristics.
11. Use measurement results as a feedback for improving the project management system.
12. Investigate the existing methods, procedures, and standards referring to the technical activities at the company. In the following make use of the viable elements identified.
13. Identify the needs existing at the company in terms of technical processes. Use interview techniques for the identification.
14. Understand the concept of project type models and build own project type models for the company.
15. On the basis of the needs identified in 13., develop and document the quality management system referring to all processes at the company. When developing the quality management system, understand and apply ISO 9001 requirements for such a system. The quality management system will refer both to project management and technical processes.
16. Assess the maturity of your company (e.g. with a Bootstrap assessment). Draw consequences to the results of the assessment compared to the results of the assessment done in 1 and 8. Maturity should increase most probably to level 3.
17. If results of the assessment made in 16. are close to CMM level 3, you can think of an ISO 9001 registration.
18. Define quality attributes of the technical processes.
19. Define and start using metrics to measure technical process characteristics. Continue using project management metrics.
20. Use measurement results as a feedback for improving the quality management system.
21. Understand the product types existing at the company.
22. Define and describe the existing product types. This description will complete the existing quality management system.
23. Define quality attributes for the products existing. Make use of ISO 9126 standard to identify product quality attributes.
24. Define and start using metrics to measure product quality characteristics. Make use of ISO 9126 standard to identify product metrics. Continue using project management and technical process metrics.
25. Use measurement results as a feedback for improving the quality management system.
26. Assess the maturity of your company (e.g. with a Bootstrap assessment). Draw consequences to the results of the assessment compared to the results of the assessment done in 1, 8 and 16. Maturity should increase most probably to level 4.
27. Continue using all QMIM concepts to refine your models and quality system.
28. Data referring to the objects, concepts and interactions can be recorded in a data - base. Recorded data can be used in drawing conclusions and making estimations and predictions. We remark that this step can be started anywhere in the for mentioned list of guidelines.

Notice that we emphasised the importance of starting measurement already on low maturity levels. It is up to the company to decide about the complexity of these measurements. We do not have a precise solution how to continue after step 20: it is possible to start dealing with product quality (as it happened at IQSOFT, see 1.6), or it is possible to concentrate on metrics, conducting wider measurement programs. The choice will depend on the company's way of thinking, its priorities, its business goals etc.

3. Final remarks

In this paper we described a longitudinal case study regarding quality management issues in a specific Hungarian company, IQSOFT. As we have shown, the way towards a complete and consistent Quality Management System for a software company is a long lasting and difficult journey. Those people, who believe that such a QMS can be in place within a short period of time, are wishful thinkers. Introducing a QMS can only be done step by step, consolidating each time the achieved results and continuously enforcing the people involved. As we have demonstrated the commitment of all people within a company is of the utmost importance, ranging from top management till all employees of the "working floor". Introducing a QMS is in that sense a matter of changing the way of thinking and the way of doing. This is not a pure rational process but mainly an organisational learning process.

As a result from our longitudinal study we believe that there are a number of useful guidelines for those organisations which are just in the beginning of this type of exercise. In the last chapter we were presenting these guidelines in short in the hope that these guidelines may be helpful for companies, striving at a higher quality level in software activities.

4. References:

[1] ISO 9001: Quality systems, 1987; ISO 9000-3: Quality management and quality assurance standards, 1991

[2] Balla, K.: Attempts to introduce software quality management. In: Austrian-Hungarian Workshop on Software Engineering, pg. 6.1.-6.10, Klagenfurt, 8-9 April 1994.

[3] Balla, K.: Software quality management : ISO 9000- but not only. Research Report. Technical University Eindhoven, March 1995. (EUT/BDK/68, ISBN 90-386-0055-0, ISSN 0929-8479)

[4] Fenton, N.E.: Software metrics - a rigorous approach. Chapman&Hall, 1992.

[5] Humphrey, Watts: Managing the Software process. Addison-Wesley, 1989.

[6] Paulk, Mark C.: The Evolution of the SEI's Capability Maturity Model for Software. In: Software process - Improvement and Practice, Pilot Issue, August 1995, pp.:3-15

[7] Kuvaja,P., Simila, J., Kranik, L., Bicego, A., Saukkonen, S., Koch., G.: Software Process Assessment & Improvement. The Bootstrap approach. ISBN O-631-19663-3, Blackwell, 1994

[8] Rout, T. P.: SPICE A framework for software process assessment. In: Software Process - Improvement and Practice 1(1), pp. 57-66, August 1995.

[9] Boehm B.W. Characteristics of software quality, North Holland, 1978

[10] McCall J. A.: The utility of software metrics in large scale software systems development, IEEE Second software life cycle management workshop, August 1978

[11] ISO/IEC 9126. Information technology - Software product evaluation- Quality characteristics and guidelines for their use. 1991.

[12] Kusters, R., Heemstra, F., Trienekens, J.: Defining systems quality: involving end-users, in: Proceedings of the Profiting from Software Measurement Conference, European Function Point User Group, 25-26 March 1993, Bristol, England, pg. 1-12.

[13] Trienekens, J.J.M., Thoma, P.: Customer oriented design of quality management systems (QMS): learning from industrial management, in: Building quality into software M. Ross, C.A. Brebbia, G. Staples,..et al, eds., Software Quality Management II, vol.2, 1994, pg. 17-32.

[14] Balla, K., Langer, T.: Beneficial effects of IQpm² on the quality oriented work. In: Proceedings of the Annual Meeting of European Artemis Users Association, T2, pp.1-10, Oslo, Norway, 1997. Sept. 18-19.
[15] Balla K., Langer T.: Process Improvement for Better Software Quality. Proceedings of the "ESI & ISCN" International Conference. Budapest, 1997. November 11-12.
[16] Gillies, A.: Software Quality - Theory and management. Chapman & Hall Computing, 1992.
[17] Software Quality Assurance and Measurement - A Worldwide Perspective. Edited by N. Fenton, R. Whitty, Y. Iizuka. International Thomson Computer Press, 1995.
[18] Fenton, N.E., Pfleeger, Sh. L.: Software Metrics: a Rigorous & Practical Approach. International Thomson Computer Press, 1997.
[19] Basili, V.: SEL's Software Process Improvement Program, IEEE Software, Nov. 1995.
[20] Basili, V.: Applying the Goal/Question/Metric paradigm in the experience factory. In [17], pp. 21-43.

Using measures to understand requirements

P. Grant Rule

Abstract

Many approaches fashionable with technically-oriented practitioners clearly fail to satisfy the need for clarity of requirements. Some even trade short-term acceleration for long-term maintenance & support costs. What is missing? What can be done to ensure that new technologies help rather than hinder? This paper suggests some simple process improvements that might have made all the difference in a number of cases including:

- *A bespoke client/server development using Use Cases to drive OOA/D, cancelled at a cost of £5m GBP due to poorly understood requirements.*
- *A global, multi-release development where the customer/supplier relationship broke down due to misunderstood tradeoffs between speed and productivity.*
- *The case of an organisation driven by marketing & competition that has struggled to understand and control requirements and costs.*
- *A case where the 'flow of requirements' to an outsourced supplier is controlled using measures agreed at a contractual level.*

1. Introduction

Business organisations need, above all else, huge predictability.

In order to manage their budgets and the commitments to their stakeholders, business organisations rely on software projects completing on-schedule, for predictable costs. If they fail in this, the organisation may be absorbed or destroyed altogether.

However, the business and technical environment in which commercial organisations operate is forever changing. Organisations are subject to pressures from customers, competitors, legislators, predators, shareholders and staff... and the pace of change seems to be increasing. Hence, there is contention between the need for predictability and the dynamic nature of the environment.

Some fashionable approaches to software development have been derived to resolve this conflict.

Arguably, structured and object-oriented methods, including the Unified Modeling Language (UML), have been produced to reduce the variability of the technical processes of software development and maintenance. Similarly, project management methods, from the 'waterfall' and 'spiral' models, through Rapid and Joint Application Development and now eXtreme Programming, have 'evolved' in reaction to changing requirements.

Through all this, the ability to understand and to be able to communicate about, the requirements allocated to software remains a necessity. Without a clear understanding of the requirements, and the changes to the requirements, it must remain difficult to deliver a predictable software process.

2. Improving the use of use cases

- *Case: A bespoke client/server development using Use Cases to drive OOA/D, cancelled at a cost of £5m GBP due to poorly understood requirements.*

2.1. It is important to understand the granularity of the requirements

The Use Case technique is one of the most popular modern methods of documenting requirements. However, in practice there seems to be much disparity in how different people understand use cases. Various practitioners, including IBM, report finding up to 32 different interpretations [1]. As different individuals apply different rules, even within one project, the results can be ambiguous.

Over the past few years, SMS consultants have observed a number of projects using the use case technique, in a variety of application domains, and have identified a number of common issues.

The main concern is that there is a tendency for developers to define the 'easy' use cases first and in great detail, while documenting more 'difficult' use cases very briefly, putting them aside 'until later'. At the extreme, we have found use cases that say the equivalent of 'do stuff' or 'browse content', wholly failing to describe the required interaction between the actor and the application.

The result in a number of projects is that around 80% of the project budget and schedule is expended on 'easy' use cases (which may represent only 20% of the functionality). Then, as the project deadline approaches, the project team realises that the 20% of uses cases that remain, the ones that are 'difficult' or 'complex', represent maybe 80% of the functional size (see Figure 1). By the time this realisation dawns, there is insufficient budget and time remaining to complete the required work. Hence the project is late, over budget, the customer is dissatisfied and someone has to find the unbudgeted funds or make-do with inadequate functionality.

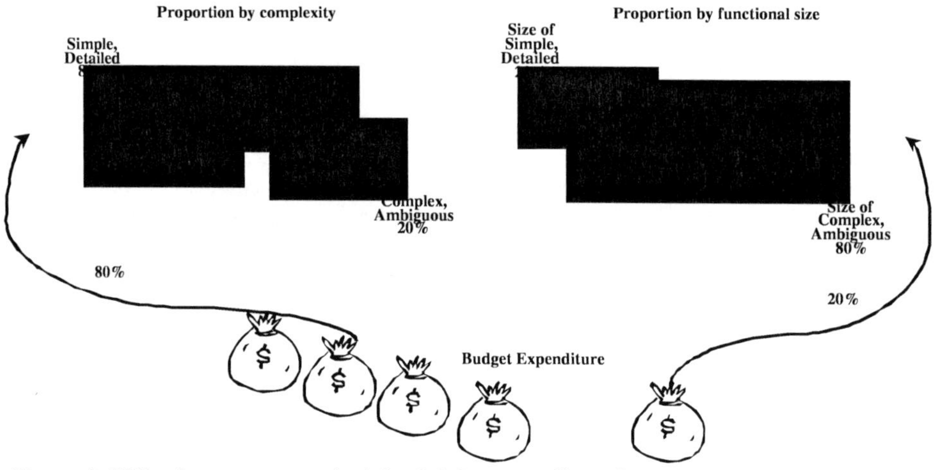

Figure 1: 80% of use cases may be 'simple', but a small number of 'complex' use cases may account for 80% of the functional size

2.2. It is important to analyse the problem, rather than someone's interpretation

Another factor affecting the productivity of some projects is a result of the way the elicitation and description of requirements is organised. Often the customer has a specialist group, let's call it 'Business Planning', that is deemed to be 'responsible for defining the customer's business requirements'. This group interacts with the end users and managers to determine the customer organisation's needs. They also have the responsibility to convey the customer requirements to the supplier. On the supply side, there may be a 'systems analysis' group, responsible for 'determining the customer requirements'. However, in practice they communicate to and through the customer's Business Planning group. They are not permitted to talk directly to the end users (that would 'interfere with the normal business processes and production'). All communication between the supplier's systems analysts and the end users is filtered through Business Planning. This is a recipe for much misunderstanding.

We have seen several projects that involve a chain of activity (see Figure 2) where...

...Business Planning documents 'business requirements' in textual form – they then pass the resulting documents to the supplier's Systems Analysts. The Systems Analysts take the textual requirements and document a set of 'high level use cases', often cutting & pasting the text directly from one document into another. The added value, if any, is limited to a use case diagram of doubtful worth. Subsequently, there is a further activity by a 'system designer' to analyse the 'high level use case' and to produce one or more 'detailed use cases'. Again, often the text is directly copied and little value is added, although the format may change.

This process wastes much time, effort and budget, adds little value and fails to describe requirements such that they can be understood unambiguously and implemented efficiently. The last two steps are self-referential and cannot possibly improve on the initial statements, because they only refer to an ***interpretation*** of the problem, rather than to the problem itself.

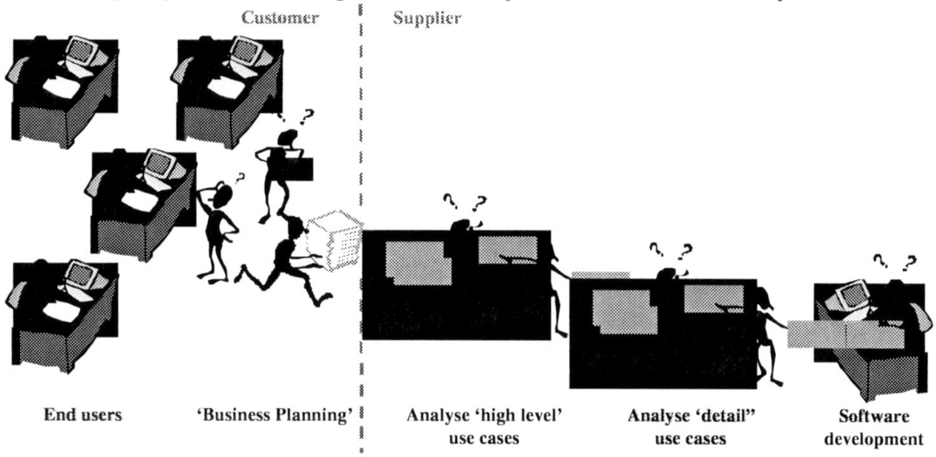

Figure 2: A wasteful chain of requirements 'engineering' activity

In order to derive additional detail and remove ambiguity, the supplier's systems analysts ***must*** be given access to the end users and managers and allowed to analyse the requirements themselves. The customer's 'business planning' group may help, establish the scope, determine the feasibility and benefits from the customer's viewpoint, but they must not be allowed to filter (ie. 'act as a barrier to') communication between the supplier and the owners of the requirements.

2.3. Measuring requirements enforces rigour and highlights ambiguity early

Software measurement techniques help engineers to produce software requirements that are unambiguous and can be sized. They improve the rigour with which requirements are documented. Thus they can be used as the basis for agreement between customer and supplier.

During 2000, SMS performed a Functional Sizing & Estimating Study for one supplier that had been working on Phase-1 of a multi-phase project for some 12 months. Phase-1 had already overrun by several months, making the management wonder about the commitment represented by subsequent phases. The study showed that the project was some ***five times larger*** than the supplier had originally understood. After protracted discussions with the customer, the supplier withdrew from the project at a cost to them of £5m GBP ($7.5m USD), leaving the customer with nothing to show for nearly 18 months of work.

An example of the use case template used by this project is presented in *Table 1*.

Field	Field Contents
Use Case Name:	Unique identifier for the use case
Primary Actor:	Name of the main actor
Supporting Actors:	Names of associated actors assisting the Primary Actor
Description:	Text description of the interaction between Actor and Application
Assumptions:	Conditions that are assumed to be TRUE
Pre-Conditions:	Entry Conditions that must be TRUE before the use case can commence
Primary Course:	A description of the most common set of steps in the use case. In practice, this usually means a list of the stimulus/response pairs that make up the use case, where the Actor provides the stimulus and the application provides the response.
Post Conditions:	Exit Conditions that must be TRUE at the end of the use case
Alternate Courses:	A description of other steps and results that may occur instead of the Primary (most likely) Course. This includes all possible error conditions.
Activity Diagram:	An illustration intended to clarify the text of the Primary and Alternate Courses.
Used By:	Identification of any other Use Cases that (re)use the functionality of this Use Case.
Uses:	Identification of any other Use Cases that this Use Case (re)uses.
Issues:	Description of any unresolved queries regarding the requirements described by this Use Case
Version Number:	The version number of this version of the Use Case document
Last Date Changed:	The date this document was last modified
Last Changed By:	The name of the author who made the last modification

Table 1: Example of a use case template (adapted from a real project)Illustrations of the way this template was used is given in Figure 3 & Table 2.

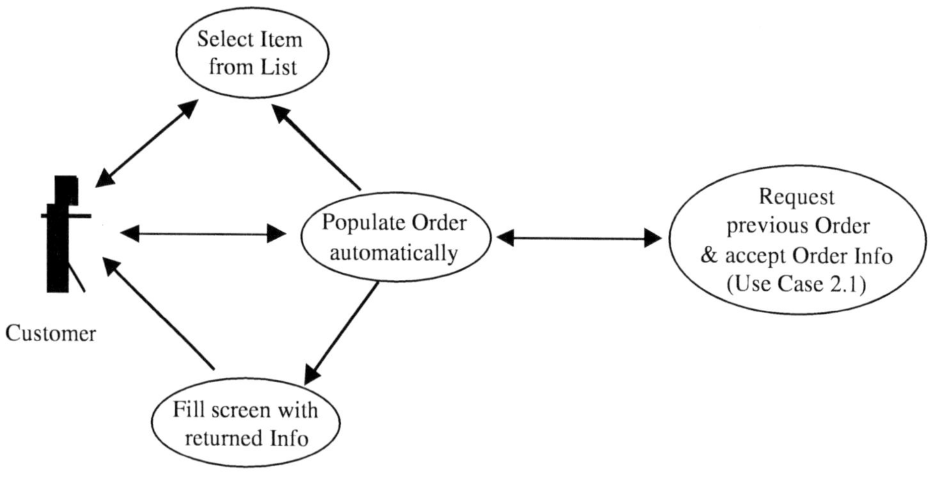

Figure 3: Example of a 'typical' use case diagram (adapted from a real project)

Early measurement of the requirements would have exposed the real size of the product and enabled better cost estimation and decision making by both customer and supplier. Simply applying measurement to the requirements identified various issues of ambiguity and highlighted the amount of uncontrolled scope-creep that was being experienced.

Table 2: Example of a 'detailed use case' (adapted from a real project)

Use Case Name	**UC1.1.1 Display Previous Order List**
Primary Actor	Order System
Supporting Actors	none
Description	The Order System shall be able to retrieve previous Orders as a list from which a selection may be made. The list shall be in descending sequence of Order Number for the current Customer only. The System shall mark Orders in the list as "Completed" or "Partial". The displayed list shall be ten items long. Only Orders created within the last thirty days will be displayed, it shall be possible to request the next ten Orders in descending Order Number order. It shall also be possible to select a particular Order by Order Number, previous Orders will be displayed with sufficient information to enable the Customer to make a choice.
Assumptions	none
Pre-Conditions	Customer has requested a list of previous Orders
Primary Course	Order System requests an Order collection using enter Customer criteria from Order Information Order Information System returns a collection of Orders Order System displays list of Orders with information to enable a choice to be made
Post Conditions	List of Orders satisfying selection is displayed on Web Page
Alternate Courses	none
Activity Diagram	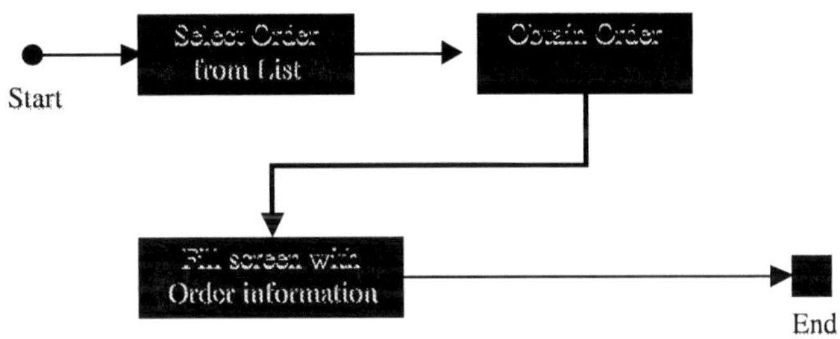
Used By:	none
Uses:	The Use Case uses Request Previous Order from Order database (UC1.3.1) and Send Previous Order from Order database (UC1.3.2)
Issues	none
Version Number	1.0000.
Last Date Changed	2/2/2000
Last Changed By	A. N. Other

In practice, as a means of describing the requirements allocated to software, use case descriptions seem to suffer from the following problems:

- lack of rigour in the application of the technique
- lack of a consistent level of granularity – hence, although a developer may know the ***number*** of use cases, this tells them little about the ***size*** of the application to be developed and hence the effort required

- UML practitioners freely apply the concept of abstract use cases ('uses/used by' and 'extends') that are more concerned with identifying opportunities for reuse than with analysing the problem and describing the requirements
- too early 'optimisation' of the solution and a tendency to jump into 'the first solution that is thought of' rather than do a considered evaluation of a number of solution options

These faults can be counter-balanced by incorporating the MkII Function Point Analysis (FPA) concept of the 'logical transaction' into the use case description.

In fact, the functionality described by the use case in consisted of that shown in Table 3.

Table 3: Actual functionality expressed as Stimulus/Response Pairs

Stimulus/Response 1	An Actor selects the Display Customer Details function from the application menu and the application responds by displaying the Select Customer screen.
Stimulus/Response 2	The Actor enters a value for the Customer_Id and the application responds by retrieving the Customer Record with a matching Customer_Id and displaying the Customer Details screen – if no match is found, the Select Customer screen is displayed with an error message 'No match found for that Customer_Id' – the Actor may then repeat the operation.
Stimulus/Response 3	The Actor selects the List Orders function from a drop-down menu and the application responds by listing all Orders in descending sequence whose Ordered_By field contains a value equal to the previously entered Customer_Id and whose Order_Date is not more than the Current_Date less 30 days.
	If there are more than 10 Orders, the most recent 10 Orders are displayed (ie. the Orders with the 10 latest Order_Numbers). A scroll bar is provided to enable the Actor to scroll up and down the list of orders for this customer. If there are zero Orders, the screen is displayed with a message 'No orders made within last 30 days'.
	Each Order is listed on one row, including an Order_Status field, indicating whether this order is Partial or Completed.
Stimulus/Response 4	The Actor highlights one of the Orders from the list and selects the Display Order Details function from a drop-down menu and the application responds by retrieving the details of the highlighted Order and displaying them.

This maps very well to the MkII FPA logical transaction [2], which is defined as…

…the lowest level business process supported by a software application. It comprises three elements: input across an application boundary, some related processing, and output across the application boundary. Each logical transaction is triggered by a unique event of interest in the external world, or a request for information and, when wholly complete, leaves the application in a self-consistent state in relation to the unique event.

Hence, the Primary Course and Alternate Course parts of the use case template can be replaced (or at least supplemented) by a table (see Table 4) that decomposes the Actor/Application interaction into logical transactions. This can be done very early in the product lifecycle, can be refined later as necessary, enforces a consistent level of granularity, highlights ambiguity where it exists and is inherently measurable.

Table 4: Expressing the example use case as measurable logical transactions

Id	Stimulus	Input fields	Object Class Referenced	Response	Response fields
1	Select function from menu	None **0**	None **0**	Display empty screen <Select Customer>	None **0**
2	Query Customer Details	Customer_Id **1**	Customer **1**	Primary Route Display screen <Customer Details> Alternate Route Display screen <Select Customer>	Primary Route First_Name Last_Name Organisation Address Phone Fax Alternate Route Error Message **7**
3	Select List Orders	Customer_Id **1**	Customer Order **2**	Display screen <Orders List>	Primary Route Order_Id Order_Date Product Quantity Order_Status Alternate Route Info Message **6**
4	Select Specified Order	Order_Id **1**	Order Product **2**	Display screen <Order Details>	Order_Id Order_Date Product Quantity Order_Status Product_Description Product_Price Order_Value **8**
Sub-Totals:		**3**	**5**		**21**
MkII Weights:		**0.58**	**1.66**		**0.26**
Contributions:		**1.74**	**8.3**		**5.46**
Functional Size		**= 1.74 + 8.3 + 5.46 =**	**15.5 fp (MkII r1.3.1)**		

3. Trading speed and productivity

- *Case: A global, multi-release development where the customer/supplier relationship broke down due to misunderstood tradeoffs between speed and productivity.*

Late in 1999, a supplier organisation performing a bespoke project in Denmark called upon SMS to assist with sizing and estimating requirements. The supplier had just made delivery of Phase-1 of the project and completed User Acceptance Testing of the product with their customer. However, this success was only achieved at the expense of many late nights and the provision of additional resources to the project team. Furthermore, the supplier was being castigated by the customer because of their apparent 'inflexibility' and 'poor productivity', which was 'lower than that previously achieved by the customer's in-house software staff'.

The project used use cases to document requirements. These requirements were initially documented by a 'business planning' group which handled all interactions with the suppliers' systems analysts. The end-users were located at over 200 different sites. The architecture was three-tier client/server.

The results of SMS' initial study of Phase-1 indicated that the supplier was being asked to deliver in some 7 months, functionality that had previously taken between 18 and 24 months to deliver. That is, about 3 times faster than previous projects of similar size performed by the in-house staff.

Both the supplier and customer organisations recognised from their experience of this first phase that better understanding and control of the requirements were needed. Subsequent phases applied a systematic estimation process and the plans and commitments were based on those requirements.

4. Requirements in a telecoms organisation driven by marketing

- *Case: The case of an organisation driven by marketing & competition that has struggled to understand and control requirements and costs.*

Many organisations already have a wealth of software. Their concern is not so much the development of new applications, but the maintenance and support of their existing software portfolio. This is especially a problem when the market in which the organisation operates is highly volatile and competitive, the size of the software applications is large, the volume of data that must be processed is high and the quality of the service provided to customers must be 'best in class'. All the above criteria apply to the world of mobile telephony.

Telecommunications software bridges the exceedingly vague borders between highly constrained signal-routing software operating close to real-time and the less constrained information processing applications used for customer billing, management information, etc. However, as the tariff to be applied to a mobile telephone call, and indeed whether there is sufficient credit available to make the call, has to be calculated before the call is connected, even the 'less constrained' applications have to perform well.

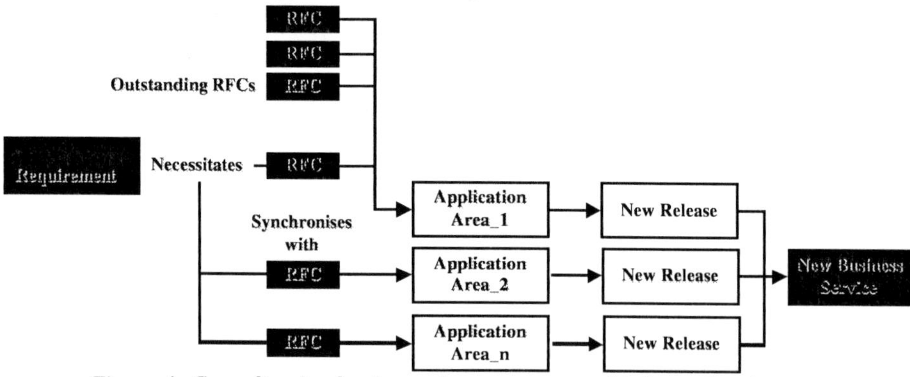

Figure 4: Co-ordinating business change across multiple application areas

Telephony also is a highly competitive business. Organisations must rapidly take advantage of each new technological advance in order to present new services to their customers, or risk losing market share to competing companies. Consumer-oriented business is cyclical in nature, driven by seasonal sales peaks, such as the Christmas period, that dominate annual sales of, for example, 'pay as you go' mobile phones. Due to the lead-time necessary to prepare marketing and sales campaigns, it is often necessary for organisations to prepare and run advertising campaigns for new services before the software capability to support those services is available. In such an environment, the software enhancement strategy is based around many relatively small, monthly releases.

The management task is complicated even further when business critical applications are outsourced to specialist suppliers over whose staff the organisation has no direct control.

In the case in question, the Programme Office has identified the application areas that absorb around 80% of the maintenance & support budget. Each of these areas is supported by a dedicated team that handles many Requests-For-Change (RFC) during each year. Each RFC is prioritised from the business perspective and the impact of that change is assessed from the perspective of the software engineers, both in the application area immediately concerned and across other application areas that may be impacted (see Figure 4). Often there is a need to co-ordinate and synchronise multiple RFC's in more than one application area in order to deliver a new business requirement.

The RFCs scheduled for completion each period are sized using MkII FPA and this information, along with records of effort expended, duration and cost are reported to senior management quarterly. This information is used to help inform decisions about the estimates and feasibility of future work and also to evaluate the productivity and performance and in-house groups and external suppliers.

An external agency, SMS, is used to collect functional size figures for each period, while effort figures are collected via an purpose built Time Recording System, supplemented by project management records made by individual project managers. Data relating to operational failures originated from software defects are collected via the help desk systems and an independent testing group. This measurement regime currently is exercised to varying degrees by the different application areas. It is a continual struggle to improve the quality of the project management data when so much effort is focused on delivering new services on time. The improvements likely to make most impact in the short term are:

- Making the measurement information more readily available to individual project teams.
- A more rigorous approach to configuration management, including version control of requirements documents and specifications
- Moving the measurement activity to the stage when business requirements are specified as well as when each RFC is completed – this will enable measurement and subsequent prediction of the scope creep experienced and enable the functional analysis and measures to feed into test case design
- Change to using the COSMIC-FFP [3] functional sizing technique to better capture the functional size of the multi-layered software architectures involved in telephony applications. Recent trials with this have shown great promise
- Management commitment to improve the completeness and accuracy of work time records
- Better recording and investigation of software defects, both during testing and operation

5. Controlling requirements outsourced to a supplier

- *Case: An outsourced organisation where the 'flow of requirements' to an external supplier is controlled using measures agreed at a contractual level.*

For the past three years SMS has provided a Functional Size Audit service to a large UK retail bank. This client has outsourced all its software development and maintenance activities to a supplier via a contract valid for seven years. Each year, the supplier is obliged by the contract to measure and report the functional size of all software requirements fulfilled during the year, whether new requirements or enhancements (additions, changes and deletions) made to existing requirements.

The supplier has several hundred software engineers involved in this contract, with one or two specialist staff dedicated to managing the collection, quality assurance, analysis and reporting of the data across the entire outsourced organisation. Around 30 staff have been trained to use the functional sizing technique (in this case, MkII Function Point Analysis) and the functional size measurements are made by trained staff from one project being seconded for short periods to the project for which measurements are needed.

The supplier is very conscientious and the measurement staff use, as well as the standard public domain references, local counting practices supported by 'case histories' for unusual situations. They operate well-defined documentation and quality control procedures to ensure that the measurements are consistent and repeatable by different individuals. The supplier's Quality Assurance group performs reviews of the practices, procedures and results, reporting issues and tracking them to resolution.

None-the-less, regardless of all these efforts by the supplier, because the measurement data is used to determine the price of the services supplied to the customer, it is of such importance that the customer needs assurance that the procedures and results are reasonable and truthful. Hence, the customer employs SMS as an independent third party 'auditor' to verify and validate the suppliers practices.

The results over three years have shown that there is a mean size error between the un-audited and the audited results of between +/–2% and +/–2.5% for each individual project. Over the entire annual workload, this reduces to an error of less than +/–1% (due to the 'swings and roundabouts' effect).

Clearly this gives very good confidence to both customer and supplier that these measurements form a stable basis for the contractual arrangements.

6. Conclusion

These cases show that organisations are using measurement techniques to improve the correctness, completeness, consistency, testability and traceability of functional requirements. Very simple techniques can be used easily to improve the quality of common requirements approaches. These techniques enable the requirements to be quantified and the measurement procedures employed and the results produced can be subject to audit and quality assurance. Hence they can form a solid foundation for pricing software, negotiating contracts and controlling scope creep.

Understanding the product size is crucial to understanding the software process and for managing project constraints such as duration, time-to-market and productivity, along with other factors that affect customer satisfaction.

Measurement techniques such as these are a necessary first step in implementing process improvements in a systematic way.

7. References

[1] C. R. Symons & G. Jensen: "Collaborative Study of Object Oriented Software Developments", IBM Global Information Services & Software Measurement Services, limited circulation to study participants, 1998/99

[2] UKSMA Metrics Practices Committee: "MkII Function Point Analysis Counting Practices Manual v1.3.1", UK Software Metrics Association, September 1998

[3] Common Software Measurement International Consortium: "COSMIC-FFP Measurement Manual Version 2.0", October 1999.

SquaRE The next generation of the ISO/IEC 9126 and 14598 international standards series on software product quality

Motoei AZUMA

Abstract

In this presentation, overview of current 9126 and 14598 series are introduced followed by some problems to be solved. Then the concept and architecture of SQuaRE are discussed. Finally, new parts, i.e., Quality in Use, Quality Requirements, and Elementally Metrics are explained.

1. Introduction

Software product quality has been increasingly important in the computerized society. Quite a few efforts have been made and contributed for improving the quality. A software product, which simply does not contain any defect and therefore is reliable, satisfies only the necessary condition. It can claim to be sufficient quality only when it satisfies requirements for other quality characteristics, such as functionality and usability.

ISO/IEC 9126-1991 [1] defined six quality characteristics. Since then, ISO/IEC JTC1/SC7/WG6 has contributed to develop two series of international standards on software product quality, i.e., ISO/IEC 9126 and ISO/IEC 14598 series. Five parts of ISO/IEC 14598 (Part 1 through Part 5) have been already published [2], [3], [4], [5]. [6]. ISO/IEC 9126-1 and ISO/IEC 14598-6 will be published soon. Remaining Parts, i.e. ISO/IEC 9126-2, -3 and –4, will be finished soon as they are at the final letter ballot stage.

While working on the two series of standards, SC7/WG6 identified additional problems and issues in the series for the further improvement. However, in order to avoid unnecessary delay in the project, WG6 decided to solve these problems and issues in the next generation of the series. It means that WG6 finishes the existing task first and then start editing new documents. The plan for the next generation of 9126 and 14598 series has been discussed in parallel with the work on the current series.

Initial idea of the SQuaRE as well as the name was introduced in the WG6 Kanazawa meeting in November 1999 and refined in the Madrid meeting in May 2000. The plan was introduced at the SC7 Madrid plenary meeting and approved by the SC7. This paper introduces the concept and outline of the SQuaRE. The SQuaRE plan will be realized after the formal procedure of both JTC1 and JTC1/SC7. Therefore, the plan, contents and document numbers may be modified by discussion in SC7 and SC7/WG6.

2. History and achievements of ISO/IEC 9126 and 14598 series

The project 7.13, which was originally responsible for "Software product quality evaluation", was started in 1985, by nominating a list of quality characteristics and their definitions. The WG members initially referred to Boehm model [7] and McCall model [8]. It also decided that quality evaluation process be included in the standard.

However, membership in the WG was not stable, which made the work not so productive. The 1st-DP (Draft Proposal) was submitted in 1986. The international standard was published in 1991 as "ISO/IEC 9126: Information technology-Software product evaluation-Quality characteristics and the guidelines for their use".

Based on the needs for more information on the software product quality, the project 07.13, which was started as a single standard project, was divided into three sub-projects; 07.13.01 Quality Characteristics, 07.13.02 Quality subcharacteristics, and 07.13.03 Measurement and Rating, at the SC7 Budapest meeting in November 1989.

Based on the growth in technologies and advance in the work, the project 07.13 was re-arranged as five sub-projects in June 1992, and as eight sub-projects at the SC7 Tokyo meeting in May 1993. Then the project 07.13 was divided into 07.13.01 and 07.13.02, which are responsible for ISO/IEC 9126 and series respectively, at the SC7 Ottawa meeting in May 1994. Next May in 1995, the titles of the ISO/IEC 14598 series were modified. WG6 further decided to modify the name of ISO/IEC 9126 series and 9126-1, and proposed to add new part 9126-4 Quality in use metrics [9]. As the result, current ISO/IEC 9126 and 14598 series are as follows [10].

- **ISO/IEC 9126**: Software engineering - Product quality – (Part 1: Quality model, Part 2: External metrics, Part 3: Internal metrics, Part 4: Quality in use metrics).
- **ISO/IEC 14598**: Software Engineering - Product evaluation – (Part 1: General overview, Part 2: Planning and management, Part 3: Process for developers, Part 4: Process for acquirers, Part 5: Process for evaluators, Part 6: Evaluation module).

3. Problems of ISO/IEC 9126 and 14598 series

ISO/IEC 9126-1991 has been and widely referred and used and is considered as a successful standard. Some countries including Japan national body (JISC) have adopted it as a national standard. However, though the last part (ISO/IEC 9126-1: Part 4 Quality in use metrics) was added fairly recently in 1998, while standardization work was under way, WG6 identified new problems and issues for further improvement. They are caused mainly by changes in environment and advances in the information technologies.

Needs for unique new architecture and umbrella guide

There are two international standard series, i.e. ISO/IEC 9126 and 14598, which are closely related to each other. It is difficult to remember those meaningless numbers. WG6 considered that these facts might be a factor that makes difficult to be more popular.

Good architecture is always important not only for a software system but also for a series of standards, because a series of standard is also a kind of software system. Needs for a good guide is identified. It is also important that the series of standard has the identification name of the series, which is easy to identify and remember.

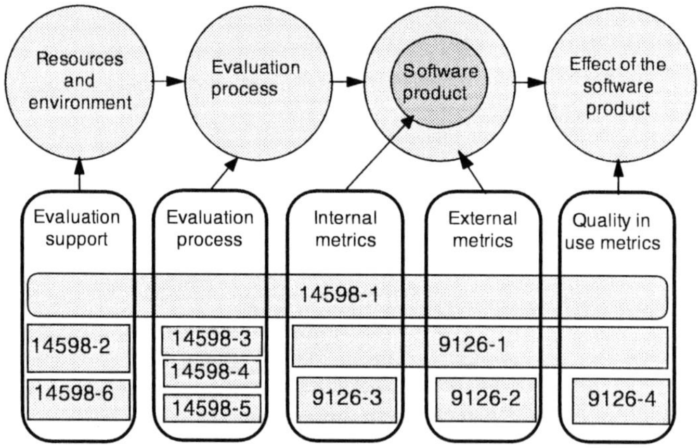

Figure 1: Current architecture of ISO/IEC 9126 and 14598 series

New issues on metrics

While discussing metrics standards, some new issues were raised.

- There are those metrics that are commonly used for composing different kinds of metrics, such as internal metrics and external metrics.
- Some metrics, which is necessary for evaluating the product quality, are used for measuring not an attribute of the software product. Examples are compilation times, and total man-hour for reviewing. Such metrics are mainly used for normalization, for example, the number of fault divided by testing man-hour. Therefore, this kind of metrics should be listed in the series.
- There are such metrics that have no verified direct co-relation with quality characteristics, but generally recognized as related with product quality. Examples are Cyclomatic Complexity, Cohesion (of a module), and fan-in. WG6 tentatively calls this class of metrics as Pure Internal Metrics.
- Some important information on metrics is distributed in several parts of the series, making difficult to find and understand all related necessary information for an in-depth understanding. For example, general *requirements* for metrics are listed in ISO/IEC 9126-1 as normative reference, while the common section that explains metrics in general are in each of 9126 Part 2, Part 3, and Part 4.

  (Note: Two kinds of the term "requirement" are used in this paper. Italic "*requirements*" means the "requirement" by the standard, which the user of the standard must conform. Normal "requirements" means as that is used commonly in the software engineering.)

Lack of quality requirement standard

As stated before, the original ISO/IEC 9126 series was separated into 9126 and 14598 series, because the quality model and metrics are useful not only for product evaluation but also for other purpose including quality requirements specification. Quality evaluation is possible and meaningful only when quality requirements are clearly specified. However, if the quality requirement standard be proposed not as a part on the series but as an independent standard, then it will cause another confusion to the users• Therefore WG6 decided that the quality requirement be proposed as a part of the next major update of the standard series.

4. SQuaRE overview

4.1. Concept

Taking the above issues and other technical issues for improving the series, SC7/WG6 decided to redesign the architecture of the series and named it SQuaRE (Software Quality Requirements and Evaluation).

There are two important aspects, product aspect and process aspect in the field of software quality assurance. SQuaRE focuses on the product side. SQuaRE recommends the use of a quality model, which refines the required quality into characteristics and subcharacteristics and clarifies the relationship among them

A software product, which only contains few defects or faults and therefore behaves correctly, cannot be regarded as a high quality product. It is very important that the product meets the users needs. In other words, the product must fit the intended users' characteristics, such as experience of keyboard operation and knowledge of the graphical user interface, and purpose of use as well as the target task.

The basic concept is that in order to achieve product quality, quality requirements be defined for all the quality characteristics based on the quality model and associated metrics. During development, test and use/operation process, measurement and evaluation are carried by using quality model and associated metrics again. Some important concepts of SQuaRE are as follows.

Lifecycle View

In order to develop, acquire or use a software product of satisfactory quality, it is necessary that the quality be identified, planned, measured and evaluated through its lifecycle using quality metrics based on the quality model.

At first, needs should be identified from the users' view, by identifying the purpose of use, target task, users' profile or characteristics, and effects of use as well as the expected results. These identified needs are transformed into requirement specifications as quantitatively as possible using external metrics. The specified requirements are useful as the evaluation criteria. Then the specified requirements are transformed into the design. Design strategies and goals are to be clarified at the beginning of the design stage. SQuaRE and lifecycle are explained more in detail in clause 6.

Quality model

In order to acquire the suitable quality product, various quality characteristics and subcharacteristics, such as usability and efficiency, should be. Quality model is the set of characteristics and sub-characteristics and the relationships among them. In general, a quality model depends on the category of target product. For example, a car and a television need different quality model. However, if a new quality model is developed for every time when a product in a same category is developed or acquired, it is waste of human resource. Therefore, standard quality model is useful.

ISO/IEC 9126 was developed for this reason. It recommends it be used as a default model, and make change on it when it is necessary. ISO/IEC 9126-1 improved the original model by defining subcharacteristics, separating internal and external characteristics and adding quality in use characteristics. SQuaRE will inherit the model. However, the issue of clarifying the relation between the model and pure internal attributes remains unsolved.

Metrics and measurement

A software product is an entity that has various properties, which makes it difficult to measure the entity itself directly. That is why quality characteristics are used. In order to define quality requirements and to evaluate the product quality, each quality characteristic and subcharacteristic should be measurable.

However, quality characteristics and subcharacteristics are not measurable directly by their nature. For example, many attributes, such as an icon, a pull down menu, and an error message contribute usability. Therefore, it is suggested that those attributes be measured using base metrics. Then the measured values are transformed into the higher level of value that indicate a characteristic or subcharacteristic, using a formula, which compose a quality metric.

Therefore, most of the metrics provides a formula. A variable that compose the formula is not always obtained by measuring an attribute of the target entity. For example, a measure that indicates security of a software product (target) is obtained by measuring the number of the failed attempts (users' behaviour) and the number of tried attempts to unauthorized access. Depending on the stage of the lifecycle, different attributes should be measured, because different materials, such as specification, source code, executable codes are available for measurement.

In the case of software measurement, it is widely known that the value for the same measure, for example LOC (Lines Of Code), may be quite different, if measurement is carried by using different measurement method (or counting rule). Therefore, the "Metric" is defined as "the defined measurement method and measurement scale"

Management

SQuaRE encourages the users to establish supporting function, which may be independent organization, department or a person in charge of it. The *requirements* for the supporting function and guides are in the "Part 11: Planning and management". Their role is to acquire the new standards, technique and tools, as well as to carry out technology assessment, technology transfer and technology management.

Because information technologies are changing and evolving very rapidly, it is very important for the organization that develop and/or acquire a software product to watch and trace the advance and evolution in the related technology, assess them and transfer them to the relevant projects.

Provision of html documents

Different from, for example, hard disc specification standards, SQuaRE is aiming at a large number of and wide variety of audiences. Therefore, it is necessary that sufficient information be provided before they purchase the standards.

SQuaRE is the Multi-parts standard, which consists of total 14 Parts. Most of them are closely related to each other. Therefore, SC7/WG6 is investigating the possibility of publishing the SQuaRE as a set of hyper-media documents. It is also planning to provide headline information of each part by WWW (World Wide Web).

4.2. Architecture

Based on the above concept, the SQuaRE architecture was defined.

SQuaRE consists of five divisions, such as software quality general division, quality model division, quality metrics division, quality requirement division, and quality evaluation division, which are shown in figure 2.

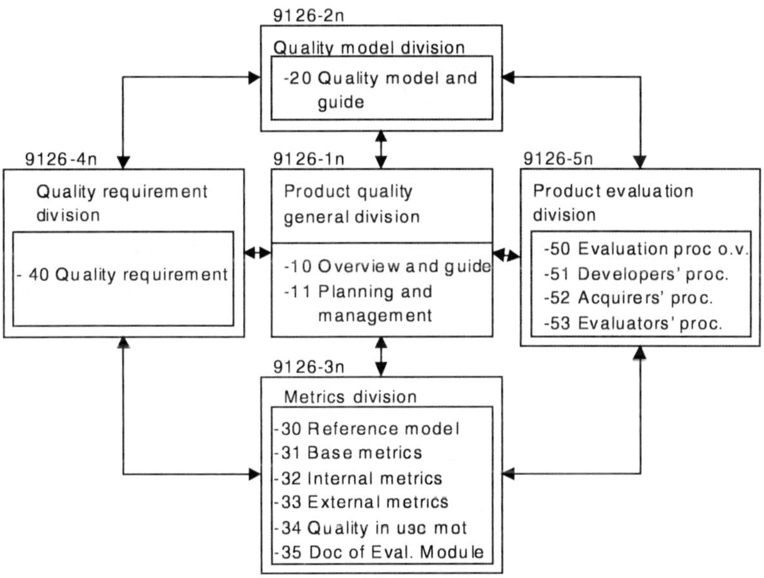

Figure 2: Architecture of the SQuaRE

5. Outline of each division and part

The first division of SQuaRE is located in the middle of the "square", which the remaining four divisions compose. This first division states the general *requirements* for a software product quality, and explains the overview of the SQuaRE and how to manage technologies necessary for improving software product quality by using the SQuaRE.

5.1. Software product quality general division

This division states the general *requirements*, overview of the SQuaRE and how to manage the technologies necessary for the use of SQuaRE. This division consists of two parts, Part 10: General overview and guide, and Part 11: Planning and management.

Part 10: General overview and guide to the SQuaRE (new)

The purpose of the Part 10 is to states general *requirements* for the software product quality and to provide guidance for the use of the series of documents that compounds the SQuaRE model. It introduces the SQuaRE model, explaining its architecture, the planned evolution, the other parts and possible usage. It also provides a general overview of the evaluation process, as well as of the quality model, becoming an important document for the comprehension of the complete series.

Part 11: Planning and management (revision of 14598-2)

Purpose of the Part 11 is to provide explanation about the planning and management for use of quality model and metrics for quality requirements specification and evaluation. It includes *requirements*, recommendations and guidelines for a supporting function, which is responsible for acquiring, standardizing transfering and managing technologies in the area of SQuaRE. It also gives guideline for assessment of the organization for supporting function and product evaluation.

5.2. Quality model division

"Quality model" is the set of characteristics and the relationships between them, which provide the basis for specifying quality requirements and evaluating quality. This division states the general *requirements* for a quality model, recommended model, and guides to customize and use the model. It consists of the following single part.

Part 20: Quality model and guide (revision of 9126-1)

Purpose of the part includes describing a model for software product quality, which consists of two parts, i.e., internal and external quality model part and quality in use model part, and guiding users to apply the model to a specific product. It includes characteristics and sub-characteristics for internal and external quality, characteristics for quality in use, and guide to use the model.

5.3. Quality metrics division

"Metric" is the defined measurement method and the measurement scale. This division consists of general *requirements* for quality metrics, the lists of recommended metrics, and guide for use the metrics. It consists of the following six parts.

Part 30: Metrics reference model and guide (new)

This part gives general information about the quality metrics as an umbrella document of the metrics division. It provides introductory information, the reference model and the definitions that are common to a set of base metrics, internal metrics, external metrics, and quality in use metrics. It includes the general *requirements* (shall) for use of metrics, which is currently stated in the 9126-1 normative annex. It also includes the guidance to users for selecting or developing, and applying metrics from the Part 31, Part 32, Part 33 and Part 34.

Part 31: Base metrics (new)

This new part will define and specify a set of recommended base metrics, which can be used during the whole software development lifecycle. Base metrics are specific by their nature and form the common denominator for several software quality characteristics or sub-characteristics within the SQuaRE. This set of metrics can be used not for the quality evaluation only, but also for the prediction of other software engineering characteristics (e.g. development effort, minimal coding and testing time).

This part will contain; a set of base metrics, guides to use base metrics, methods of the base metrics data gathering, a set of data (measured values) recommended to be recorded during the lifecycle, and an example of use of base metrics.

Part 32: Internal metrics (revision of 9126-3)

This Part defines internal metrics for quantitatively measuring internal software quality in terms of characteristics and sub-characteristics defined in ISO/IEC 9126-20. It includes a basic set of internal metrics for each sub-characteristic, and guides and examples of how to use internal metrics during the software product life cycle.

Part 33: External metrics (revision of 9126-2)

This Part defines external metrics for quantitatively measuring external software quality in terms of characteristics and sub-characteristics defined in ISO/IEC 9126-20. It includes a basic set of external metrics for each sub-characteristic, and guides and examples of how to use metrics during the software product life cycle.

Part 34: Quality in use metrics (revision of 9126-4)

This Part defines quality in use metrics for the quality in use characteristics defined in ISO/IEC 9126-20. It includes a basic set of quality in use metrics for each quality in use characteristic, and guides and examples of how to use metrics during the software product life cycle.

9126-35: Documentation of evaluation module (revision of 14598-6)

An evaluation module is a package of evaluation technology for measuring software quality characteristics, sub-characteristics or attributes. Currently this part is a part of 14598 product evaluation series. However, as it defines how to specify a metric and how to use it, it is more reasonable that it be a sub-part of new metrics part. This part defines the structure and content of the documentation to be used to describe an Evaluation Module.

5.4. Quality requirement division

This division consists of single part that includes quality requirements and guide for use of it.

Part 40: Quality requirements (new)

This Part enables software product quality to be specified as quality requirement. The requirement to be tracked, validated and managed with evaluation from different perspectives by those associated with acquisition, requirements analysis, development, use, evaluation, support, maintenance, quality assurance and audit of software. It also includes guide to use the model and metrics for requirement definition.

5.5. Quality evaluation division

This division consists of the following four parts.

Part 50: Evaluation process overview (revision of 14598-1)

This part succeeds 14598-1, but inherits only general part for product evaluation. It introduces the other parts of this division. It contains general *requirements* for specification and evaluation of software quality and clarifies the general concepts. This part provides a framework for evaluating the quality of all types of software product and states the *requirements* for methods of software product measurement and evaluation.

Part 51: Developers process (revision of 14598-3)

This part provides *requirements* and recommendations for the practical implementation of software product evaluation when the evaluation is conducted in parallel with the development and carried out by the developer.

Part 52: Acquirers process (revision of 14598-4)

This part contains *requirements*, recommendations and guidelines for the systematic measurement, assessment and evaluation of software product quality during acquisition of "off-the-shelf" software products, custom software products, or modifications to existing software products.

Part 53: Evaluators process (revision of 14598-5)

This part provides *requirements* and recommendations for the practical implementation of software product evaluation, when several parties need to understand, accept and trust evaluation results. In particular, it may be used to apply the concepts described in ISO/IEC 9126-1n.

6. Guides to use the SQuaRE

SQuaRE can be used by various users, for various purposes and, to various products. Examples of SQuaRE are software product developers, users and acquirers, as well as quality assurance staff and managers. Guides for using 9126 and 14598 series are scattered in the current version, which make the use of the series difficult. Therefore, all the necessary information to use SQuaRE at the beginning is contained in the ISO/IEC 9126-10. ISO/IEC 9126-10 explains the relation among QIU (Quality In Use) characteristics, external characteristics, internal characteristics, and software lifecycle (Figure 3).

At the beginning of software product development, it is necessary that needs be clearly identified. The needs can be specified using QIU metrics. Then requirements are specified as the external specification in order to satisfy the needs. The requirements and their criteria can be specified using external metrics. The requirements are converted into the internal design specifications. Internal metrics can be used for specifying the criteria of the design. Typical use of SQuaRE is as follows.

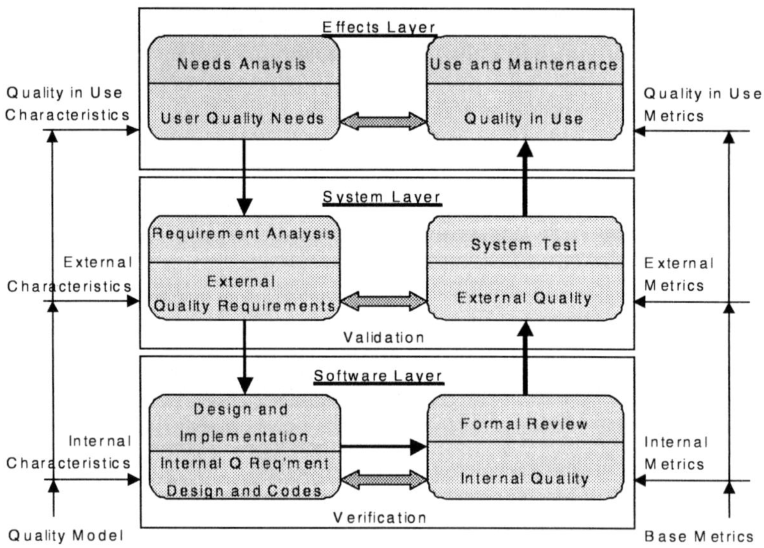

Figure 3: ISO/IEC 9126-1 U-Model

6.1. Needs analysis stage

Needs is the expectation for the effects of the product when it is used. As requirements do not always reflect real users' needs, needs analysis is the most important process of the software lifecycle. By the definition of QIU, it varies depending on the context of use.

Quality in use scenario or use case scenario may be useful for identifying the context of use. Then the listed scenarios must be classified, selected and transformed into the context of use. The next step is to categorize each selected context of use, using such criteria as target task, method of usage, environment, and frequency of use. Finally, identified needs can be specified for each QIU characteristics. The level of satisfaction should be defined for each context of use, using the indicator. In order to define level of satisfaction, at least one indicator should be defined for each QIU characteristic.

6.2. Requirement analysis stage

The next activity is to specify external quality requirements based on the defined user quality needs. There is no automated procedure for the conversion from identified needs to the requirement specification. Each context of use and associated level of satisfaction for each QIU characteristic must be examined when the conversion is done. Quality requirements shall be defined for every external quality characteristics, possibly using external quality metrics that is defined in part 33.

6.3. Design and implementation stage

In order to design and develop the software product that satisfies requirements, the designer should develop a design strategy, which includes selecting appropriate design method and tools as well as defining architecture, at the beginning of the stage. For example, good and solid architecture can improve maintainability, and object oriented technique can improve usability. For the purpose, 9126-10, -11, -20, and –30, -31, 32 may be helpful. However, as SQuaRE focuses on product side, it may not help the work directly, while designing and implementing the product.

6.4. Formal review stage

Though this stage may vary depending on the lifecycle model and process design, the software product evaluation should be done iteratively depending on the previous design and implementation stage. The review can be categorized into design review and code review. The former uses the design documents as the target, and the latter uses source code for review. None of them is usually executable. Therefore, internal metrics in 9126-32 are useful in this stage.

However, when such lifecycle model as prototyping or incremental development is applied, external metrics and, some times, quality in use metrics are also useful.

6.5. System test stage

The target software is executable, in this stage. The target attributes of measurement are behaviours of the system. In most of the case, external metrics are used. The measured values are compared with those criteria that are defined in the requirement specifications. As developers, acquirers, and third party evaluators may be involved in the evaluation process, they can be possible users of SQuaRE. Therefore, 9126-33 as well as 9126-51, 52, and –53 are main parts of SQuaRE in this stage.

6.6. Use and maintenance stage

After the users begin to use the software product, it is important that real contexts of use be collected with measured values, that data be analysed and to use the information for the next version. For this reason, QIU characteristics are measured at the users' site. Measured values are transformed into the higher level of measures or indicators, and the results are to be compared with the evaluation criteria. Finally, the results are to be interpreted and reported.

7. Conclusion

The work for developing SQuaRE has been recently just initiated. The plan of SQuaRE, as summarized in this paper, is the initial input to the project. SC7/WG6 invites more contributions to improve SQuaRE. It may be modified and should be continuously improved because, both technologies for the SQuaRE and the target software are changing very rapidly, and usually, the work for developing standard is time consuming because of the necessary formal balloting procedure.

8. references

[1] ISO/IEC 9126: Information technology-Software product evaluation-Quality characteristics and the guidelines for their use
[2] ISO/IEC 14598-1: Software Engineering - Product evaluation – Part 1: General
[3] ISO/IEC14598-2: Software Engineering - Product evaluation – Part 2: Planning and management
[4] ISO/IEC 14598-3: Software Engineering - Product evaluation – Part 3: Process for developers
[5] ISO/IEC 14598-4: Software Engineering - Product evaluation – Part 4: Process for acquirers
[6] ISO/IEC 14598-5: Software Engineering - Product evaluation – Part 5: Process for evaluators
[7] B. W. Boehm, et al., Qualitative evaluation of software quality, Proc. 2nd ICSE, 1976, pp 592-605
[8] J. A. McCall, et al., Factors in software quality, Rome Air Develop Centre Report TR-77-369, 1977
[9] M. Azuma, QUALITY IN USE; Its Concept, Metrics and Methodology, Proceedings 2nd WCSQ 2000
[10] M. Azuma, Software Products Evaluation System: Quality Model, Metrics and Process - International Standards and Japanese Practice, Inf. & Software Tech., Elsevier, Vol.38, No. 3, 1996

9. Acknowledgement

The author expresses his sincere appreciation to WG6 members, especially editors, co-editors and WG6 secretariat for their continuous efforts and contributions. They are Nigel Bevan, Jorgen Boegh, Gilbert Le Gall, Michael Gayle, Vipula Godamunne, John Harautz, Tom Ipoly, Antonia Jeanrenaud, Ota Novotony, Danilo Scalet, Renate Sitte, Witold Suryn, Yukio Tanitsu, Jiri Vanicek, Atsushi Yamada, and Toshihiro Komiyama as the secretariat.

Quantitative and qualitative methods in process improvement and product quality assessment.

Anna Bobkowska

Abstract

Successful improvement of the development process and product quality assurance should take advantages of complementary use of both quantitative and qualitative methods. In the paper, experience of such integrated activities during students quality lab is presented.

1. Introduction

One of the recommendations of the TQM (Total Quality Management) says: "Measure your success!" [4] However things defined by business case or external problems such as cancelled projects, late deliveries, exceeded budget, and useless software are just a tip of the iceberg containing issues of the complex project reality. In order to make improvements effectively good understanding of those subtitles is needed. One can argue that quantitative methods are not sufficient for the purpose of successful software quality assurance. Intentional and systematic use of qualitative methods can provide missing part of the solution.

2. Complementary applications of quantitative and qualitative methods

Quantitative and qualitative issues are strictly related, but in software engineering qualitative methods are treated rather informally. Comparison of both approaches in aspects of techniques and applications is presented in the figure 1.

Quantitative methods	**Qualitative methods**
Measurement	Comments, notes and schemas
Quantification	Discussions and observations,
Computations	Questionnaires, interviews
	Analysis, reasoning
Applications	**Applications**
Statistical results	Problem identification and removal
Control and management	Theory generation and improvement
Comparison of similar products	Understanding of project reality
Integration with other indicators	Enhancement of the measurement structure
	Cross-case analysis
	Focus on details, complexity
	Non-technical aspects

Figure 1. Comparison of quantitative and qualitative methods in aspects of techniques and applications.

2.1. Quantitative methods

Quantitative methods use numbers. Measures are easy to take when there are countable objects e.g. number of persons, number of elements of given type on the diagram, or there are standard devices or agreements for objective measuring a given feature, e.g. time, cost. In the case when those conditions are not satisfied but a number that represents a state according to the defined goal is needed, it is necessary to quantify that feature. Examples include: ease of use, understandability, and cover all the cases when it is very difficult to find objective metrics. Quantification is concerned with assigning numbers to the states of reality with appropriate rules of representation [3]. During quantification there is a problem of subjectivity and imprecision of the achieved data although they are represented by numbers.

Quantitative methods are necessary for comparison of similar products, control and management. Quantitative data easily deliver statistical results and can be processed automatically. Another advantage of their use is ease of integration with systems covering other indicators. It is important to define goals of measurement and prepare an appropriate measurement plan. This can be done with GQM (Goal-Question-Metric) [2] approach or FCM (Factor-Criteria-Metrics) structure [3] or Goal-Subgoal-Metrics structure [6].

In application of software quality defect density metric is used. Although defects are countable ideas, it is not fully objective metric since defect classifications are made by humans. Apart from the problem of "not discovered defects", importance of the defect can differ in cases when it has occurred a serious defect, a mistake or just a misunderstanding.

Another approach is concerned with FCM structure and making computation in order to achieve numbers that represent higher level quality indicators. This is usually more total approach which allows to involve non-technical (e.g. human) aspects of quality. This approach is used and extended in the presented research.

2.2. Qualitative methods

Qualitative methods use objects different then numbers e.g. words, pictures. The techniques include interviews, discussions, observations, comments, notes, questionnaires, and schemas. Usually the results are more subjective and more difficult to process, and thus require more work during analysis. But they give richer and more informative results.

Quantitative methods can be applied to theory generation and improvement, problem identification and removal, and cross-case analysis [8]. They are necessary in the situations when better reality or system understanding is required, and complexity, not reductions and quick processing are a value. Searching for reasons of things and non-technical aspects are good fields for them. Although they seem to be intuitive their application also requires infrastructure preparation and special methods of results analysis.

Qualitative methods can be helpful in optimising a structure of measurements. On the other hand, metrics can provide assessments or problem indication to focus on with qualitative methods. After identification of the reasons of problems and their removal quantitative methods can be used again to track the project.

3. Development process improvement

There is a relationship between development process parameters and software quality. While attempting to achieve high quality products one should provide also optimal development process. Optimal process being goal of this research is characterised by:

- An appropriate schedule, in which deadlines are set to avoid late deliveries, and there is unified weekly workload during all the semester.
- Infrastructure for efficient co-operation between participant with different roles in the project is provided, and there are some facilitators for internal organisation in the group, e.g. task sequencing and work distribution.
- Product templates for each phase are defined to fit the type of the system and avoid over-documenting.

Before the changes, OMT [7] method without measurements and reviews was used. There were problems with late deliveries, poor quality products, and student's complaining about workload. But there was no base to verify the workload and find reasons of problems. So, the development process was exchanged to a more controlled process described in brief in section 3.1, and then it was optimised with use of combination of quantitative and qualitative methods in the three following years.

3.1. Making a difference

Any set of improvement activities must be based on the development process definition. Software development process, in this case, was tailored for Internet applications and covered the phases of requirements specification, object-oriented analysis, design, implementation and testing. The products of the analysis and design were documented with UML [5] and structured text. Implementation technology was a design decision. Additionally the method of playing roles by the groups of project participants [1] was introduced. There were the following roles:

- Developer - responsible for the project and the delivery of products,
- Customer – responsible for the problem domain, and
- Quality expert - responsible for quality assurance.

It was assumed that groups playing the roles co-operate in partnership. The process included reviews after each phase, and technical meeting of all participants after requirements specification review phase.

Measurement plan was established. Collected data contained information about: time of work spent on project activities by the participants, late deliveries and evaluation of products quality delivered by the developer (self-evaluation), the quality expert, and teacher. Apart from that, participants described way of work distribution, internal communication, and main problems concerned with the phase. Those comments as well as observations and discussions were used to find problems and look for solutions.

Introduction of the measurements and comments revealed author from relaying on opinions and beliefs, and allowed to rely on facts. Metrics easily verified concepts, for example, real time of work, quality of products, and scale of late deliveries (if those were problems of all groups or just an exception!). On the other hand, descriptions gave an understanding of activities made by students and their problems. A lot of problems were concerned with poor organisation, misunderstanding, and had simple solutions. But there were also serious problems that needed more advanced activities. In the task of searching for suggestions that facilitate organisation or explanations that allow to better understand project issues, metrics and descriptions made complementary work.

3.2. Process optimisation

Optimisation activity aimed to change process parameters in these places where problems occurred. Collected data enabled tracking results of the new development process. Number of weeks set for the development tasks, average time of work per group and deviation that indicates how the results differ among groups are presented in the table 1. Symbols of '*' indicate different development tasks made during the same period of time, e.g. in the first iteration there was phase of design that covered system design and component design. Data are taken from four best projects for each iteration.

Table 1. Number of weeks for a development task (#weeks), average time of work (ATW) and deviation (d) in the iterations.

Development tasks	#weeks in iter.1	ATW	d	#weeks in iter.2	ATW	d	#weeks in iter.3	ATW	d
Vision							1	10.3	2.1
Requirements specification	1	15.6	4.7	1	15.8	6.3	2 *3	28.5	14.7
Review	1	6.7	1.45						
Analysis	3	23.8	6.3	2	32.6	10.4	2 *3		
Review	1	12	2	1	8.3	1.4	1	11	3.5
System design	3 *1	24.9	14.5	2 *2	24.5	8.8	2 *4	17	7
User interface prototype				2 *2			2 *4		
Review				1	6.6	1.4	1	7.7	2
Component design	3 *1			2	37.5	14.3	2 **	27.3	8.8
Review	1	10.3	3.1	1	4.2	1.1	1	5.6	1.2
Implementation	3	52.3	19	3	119.4	33.9	3 **	22.2	8.8
Tests	1	8.2	4	1	6	1.6	1	7.9	1.6
Total	14	161.8	29.9	14	251.8	55.1	14	133.7	24.3

Time for review was not limited. Quality expert's task was to find as many defects as possible and then make evaluations and quality predictions. Just looking through documentation one could find it was more precise and reader friendly then before the change. Also late deliveries (except from design phase) did not happen in the scale of the students group. However some problems appeared. Results of the revision of the first iteration and improvement activities undertaken to avoid the problems in the next iteration are presented in the table 2.

Table 2. Problems collected in the first iteration and improvements in the second iteration

Problems	Improvement activities
Large time of work, especially in the implementation phase (it is co-related with the measured time of work)	Establish groups of 3 persons instead of 2. Support internal organisation of the group by delivering suggestions of sequence of task and work distribution. Simplify questionnaires.
Late deliveries in the design phase (each group was late 1 or 2 weeks)	Split design (as one task lasting a long time) into two: system design and component design.
Medium level of the customer satisfaction at the end of project.	Introduce prototyping user interface task with review made by the customer.

The improvements gave satisfactory results. In the second iteration the customer's satisfaction level was higher, there was no late deliveries of system design, but there were still problems with component design. It was possible to decrease the time of work (see large deviation in the second iteration), but average results are so large because of a very good group that worked a lot, but also delivered excellent products. The list of problems found in the second iteration and improvement activities for the next iteration are presented in table 3.

Table 3. Problems collected in the second iteration and improvements in the third iteration

Problems	Improvement activities
Is there possibility to make the process more efficient? Still large time of work was reported.	Simplify of Requirements Specification document: Vision of the system is made during the first week and non-functional requirements selected to fit best this type of system are delivered together with the analysis phase.
Late deliveries in component design phase	Introduce two phases of component design together with component prototyping, implementation and writing technical documentation (the second one includes also system integration) instead of the component design phase and implementation phase.
Different understanding of the system by the quality expert, the customer and the developer after system design review and user interface prototype review.	Introduce meeting of all participants after system design review and user interface prototype review to make compromise for the design and implementation.

After those improvements there were no late deliveries, time of work decreased, and level of customer's satisfaction was good. This optimal process enabled to make observations on human factors, e.g. adequacy of assigning persons with certain competencies and personality to the development tasks.

Presented work describes activities taken to achieve the optimal process with no late deliveries, unified time of work during all the semester, good infrastructure supporting development process and optimal product templates. Each iteration allowed to remove more detailed problems. Removal of the most visible problems resulted in appearance of more hidden ones, e.g. different views of an expert and customer would not be possible to find without review of user interface prototype, or without split for system and component design it would be difficult to locate the problem in component design. It is also interesting that problems indicated by measurements usually have their explanations, e.g. late deliveries in component design are caused by poor knowledge of implementation environment and difficulty to imagine how the system works.

4. Product quality assessment

Inspections and tests are main techniques of quality assurance with focus on product. Inspections can be applied to the documentation in early phases to avoid defect propagation and thus minimise time and cost of improvements. In the final version of this work, reviews of analysis and requirements specification, system design, and detailed design with component implementation were made by the quality experts, and user interface prototype was verified by the customer. Questionnaire templates with metrics and comments collection as well as reasoning about quality were designed in order to support reviews. Tests were made by both the quality experts and the customers at the end of the project.

4.1. Questionnaires for reviews

First activity in product quality assurance, and especially review design, is quality definition. The FCM structure was used for this purpose, and for this type of application desired quality was defined with the following factors:

- Functionality – with criteria of completeness, adequacy and coherency,
- Satisfaction – which was verified by checking ease of use, productivity and general aesthetics,
- Maintainability – which was decomposed to documentation quality, portability and modifiability,
- Dependability – in aspects of security and error-tolerance.

It was assumed that quality metrics assigned to criteria and factors were in scale [1..5], where 1 meant very low quality, and 5 – very high.

In order to achieve those quality metrics data collection according to the following elements were used:

- Diagram metrics - they covered counting of elements on the diagrams, and allowed to compare those numbers with expected values, which could be derived from historical data about similar projects. Those expected values were not given in all projects, and thus intuitive estimation of them had to be made. Diagram metrics were also a basis for local size calculation which was used for defect metrics calculation. There was possibility to comment on those values. This is a potential place for automation, but in the author's opinion these kind of calculations bring very uncertain information. Diagram metrics are objective, but quite a lot of subjectivity is associated with the expected values application.
- Evaluations with comments - evaluations are numbers that represent subjective feelings about some aspects of the work, e.g. ease of understanding, aesthetics, precision, etc. Sometimes they are more efficient then metrics, e.g. instead of counting all the attributes and compare it with fuzzy expected values, one can evaluate that (always, usually, ..., never) attributes are complete and adequate and thus description is detailed enough (or not). They could be given in the scale [1..5] described above or described as comments.
- Defect collection according to the defect classification - those defects can be then counted and combined with the diagram metrics. Such metrics are good quality indicators.

The templates were prepared to integrate quality issues with documentation fragments in order to focus attention of the reviewer on limited fragment of documentation, e.g. one type of diagram with descriptions, with their relevant metrics, evaluation and potential defects. Then those elements were integrated into quality metrics that represented factors and recommendations of improvement were generated. During the lab, intuitive reasoning supported with questionnaires was used, but in this part quantitative calculations with formulas that model quality relationships mathematically can be applied to partially automate the process.

To summarise use of qualitative and quantitative methods: comments had application during the project to data collection, reasoning about quality factors and criteria, and generation of recommendations for improvement by the quality experts. Also questionnaire analysis and optimisation over the iterations was possible thanks to those comments. Metrics of diagrams and number of defects were used for calculation of the defect metrics. Quantified values of criteria and factors allowed to compare products and gave an idea about the time needed to make corrections.

4.2. Results

One of the constraints of this research is that participants are students, and not real customers, developers and quality experts. In order to achieve possibly the most reliable results ten best projects are analysed.

In the table 4 metrics of diagrams and defects are presented. Then average value (AV) and deviation (d) are calculated. Since analysis consists of the use case model, class diagram and sequence diagrams with descriptions, the metrics and defects are concerned with them. For the use case diagram, there are the following metrics:

- number of use cases (# use cases),
- number of actors (# actors),
- number of elements including use cases, actors and relationships (# elements),
- number of elements incoherent with Software Requirements Specification (# incoherent),
- number of inadequate elements (# inadequate), which includes missing, wrong scope elements, and not needed elements,
- number of elements difficult to understand (# dif. to understand), which includes ambiguous and surprising elements and statements.

Table 4. Metrics of diagrams and defects of the analysis phase for ten projects (P1-P10)

Description	P1	P2	P3	P4	P5	P6	P7	P8	P9	P10	AV	d
# use cases	8	11	13	5	6	14	14	12	17	9	10.9	3.12
# actors	2	2	3	4	1	4	2	3	2	3	2.60	0.80
# elements	20	30	37	16	17	38	36	31	36	34	29.5	7.10
# incoherent	2	7	7	6	3	8	1	3	2	2	4.10	2.32
# inadequate	3	8	4	1	2	9	3	2	2	6	4.00	2.20
# dif. To understand	2	7	3	2	3	4	1	3	3	0	2.80	1.24
% inadequate	15%	27%	11%	6%	12%	24%	8%	6%	6%	18%	13%	6%
% dif. to understand	10%	23%	8%	13%	18%	11%	3%	10%	8%	0%	10%	5%
# classes	13	11	4	14	10	24	16	13	9	9	12.3	3.70
Size of the class diagr.	30	24	8	35	19	48	41	24	19	17	26.5	9.60
# imprecision	3	8	4	3	4	4	1	4	3	1	3.50	1.30
Precision evaluation	3	3	3,5	5	4	4	3,5	4	3,5	3	3.65	0.48
# inadequate	2	6	5	2	2	6	4	1	2	3	3.30	1.56
# dif. to understand	2	4	2	0	2	2	1	1	0	2	1.60	0.88
% imprecision	10%	33%	50%	9%	21%	8%	2%	17%	16%	6%	17%	11%
% inadequate	7%	25%	63%	6%	11%	13%	10%	4%	11%	18%	17%	11%
% dif. to understand	7%	17%	25%	0%	11%	4%	2%	4%	0%	12%	8%	6%
# sequence diagr.	8	11	8	5	2	14	10	11	11	1	8.10	3.30
Size (# interactions)	48	49	134	36	6	84	37	20	33	17	46.4	25.9
# incorrect interactions	4	3	3	0	2	3	3	2	2	2	2.40	0.80
# m_exceptions	x	3	5	1	4	4	2	x	x	x	x	x
%incorrect interactions	8%	6%	2%	0%	33%	4%	8%	10%	6%	12%	9%	6%
# inco A-SRS	3	4	3	0	2	1	0	2	0	0	1.50	1.30
# inco CD-UCD	0	3	5	0	1	0	0	0	2	3	1.40	1.48
# inco CD-SD	0	3	3	1	0	0	2	1	0	1	1.10	0.94
# inco UCD-SD	2	6	6	1	4	1	3	2	6	5	3.60	1.80

Defect metrics are calculated by division of the number of inadequate elements by the number of elements (% inadequate), and the number of elements difficult to understand by the number of elements (% dif. to understand). The number of elements stand here for the size of use case diagram. Similar metrics are collected for the class diagram, but in this case precision is also important and it is difficult to be captured by metrics, so apart from discovering imprecise elements (# imprecise) there is precision evaluation in the scale of [1..5]. The size of the class diagram is here defined as a sum of classes and relationships. And for sequence diagrams there are the following metrics:

- number of sequence diagrams (# sequence diagr.),
- size counted as a number of interactions,
- missing exceptions (# m_exceptions) - "x" is used when there is a lot of exceptions missing.

And finally coherency between the diagrams is checked:

- incoherence between analysis diagrams and requirements specification (#inco A-SRS),
- incoherence between class diagram and use case diagram (# inco CD-UCD),
- incoherence between class diagram and sequence diagrams (# inco CD-SD), and
- incoherence between use case diagram and sequence diagrams (# inco UCD-SD).

In the table 5, quality metrics for the same projects being result of the reasoning on the basis of the metrics described above together with evaluations and comments are presented.

Table 5. Quality metrics for the criteria in ten projects.

Description	P1	P2	P3	P4	P5	P6	P7	P8	P9	P10	AV
Completeness	3	3	3	3	5	4	5	4	5	4	3,9
Adequacy	3,5	2	4	4	4	3	4,5	3	3	3	3,4
Precision	3,5	3	3	5	4	4	3,5	4,5	4	2	3,7
Functionality	4	3	4	5	4	5	4	4	4	3	4,0

The questionnaires support finding defects and help to integrate information taken from different sources. For more precise reasoning it would be useful to introduce some standard rules. Concrete defects are closely connected with the domain of application and they are used during the project to improve quality, so other considerations then classified defect metrics have no sense in this analysis. Statistics of the diagram metrics can be applied for gathering expected values. Let us assume that average value is an expected value, and deviation sets the range of accepted values. In this case, range of expected values for the number of classes is [8..16], and it is possible to find automatically anomalies in project P3 with too little classes (4), and project P6 with too many (24).

5. Conclusions

In the paper, experience of process improvement and product quality assessment in early phases of software development with use of quantitative and qualitative methods is presented.

Defined process and collected data plan were the basis for making improvements. They enabled to rely on facts, not opinions during revisions. Quantitative methods were used to verify concepts, and qualitative ones for problem identification and removal, and deeper analysis of project issues. After the change concerned with introduction of the new method with reviews and measurements, the development process was optimised over three iterations. Every iteration allowed to identify and remove more and more detailed problems.

In product quality assessment qualitative and quantitative methods were used by the quality experts to data collection, reasoning about quality factors and criteria, and generation of recommendations for improvement. They were also used in questionnaire optimisation.

6. References

[1] Bobkowska A., "Training on High Quality Software Development with the 3RolesPlaying method", in SCI'98/ISAS'98 conference proceedings, Orlando, USA, July 1998.

[2] Briand, L. C., Differding C. M., Rombach D. H., "Practical Guidelines for Measurement - Based Process Improvement", Technical Report of the International Software Engineering Network (ISERN-96-05), 1996.

[3] Fenton N.E., "Software Metrics. A Rigorous Approach", Chapman&Hall, 1993.

[4] Grudowski P., Kolman R., Meller A., Preihs J., "Zarządzanie jakością" (Quality Management), Wydawnictwo Politechniki Gdańskiej, Gdańsk, 1996.

[5] Rational Software Corporation, "UML Notation Guide", www.rational.com

[6] Rational Software Corporation, "Rational Unified Process", www.rational.com

[7] Rumbaugh J., Blaha M., Premerliani W., Eddy F., Lorensen W., "Object-oriented modelling and design", Prentice-Hall, 1991.

[8] Seaman C. B., "Qualitative methods in Empirical Studies of Software Engineering.", Transactions on Software Engineering volume 25, 1999, pages 557-572.

Measuring design diagrams for product quality evaluation

A. Inkeri Verkamo, Juha Gustafsson, Lilli Nenonen, Jukka Paakki

Abstract

Many important product quality characteristics, such as performance and maintainability, cannot be added on late in the development, and hence early warnings of poor quality expectation would be very useful to allow early corrective measures. To produce such information, we base product quality prediction on measurements and calculations of the UML design diagrams of the software. Some design metrics may be used as direct predictors of quality; as an example, cohesion and coupling metrics are generally considered good predictors of the maintainability of the product. On the other hand, certain quality characteristics, e.g., performance, require more complex analysis of the design by computing predictions of the execution time of a typical use case with user provided information of the input size and attributes.

Another way of taking advantage of the design diagrams is by detecting design patterns and anti-patterns in the design, and using these as predictors of the final product quality. While using design patterns is considered to have a positive effect on the quality and productivity of the development process, their effect in product quality is more complex and may in fact be positive or negative, depending on the context. We suggest using the pattern library to store information of the previous uses of the patterns and the quality of the corresponding systems, to predict the quality effects of the design patterns.

In our paper, we present a tool for measuring UML diagrams of the product to predict three central product quality characteristics, size, understandability, and performance. The tool also detects all occurrences of a previously defined set of design patterns and anti-patterns from the diagrams. Our paper reports industrial experience in using the tool to detect patterns and measure quality of design diagrams.

1. Introduction

While software development has long been mostly focused on improving product time to market, recently a growing interest has also been taken in quality issues. But there is a fundamental difference in the way that product quality concerns affect the software development process, as opposed to improving development efficiency. Development time may often be decreased by means of corrective actions in a single phase of the lifecycle, e.g., by using improved methods or better tools in code generation or testing. But if we aim at improving product quality this goal must be kept in mind throughout the development process, as it is likely to require changes in several phases of the lifecycle.

A typical example of a quality characteristic that cannot be added on in a late phase is performance [21]. Contrary to what many textbooks claim (see, e.g., [4]), tuning of the fully implemented system is not the winning strategy to ensure adequate performance, but rather performance requirements must be taken into account in early stages of software development. Similarly, maintainability requires much more than producing documentation in a late phase of software development, and satisfactory usability cannot be guaranteed simply by including a package of GUI routines to the software distribution.

The development of a new software product seldom starts from scratch. In particular with the object-oriented approach to software development, the idea of reusing parts of old products has gained wider acceptance. The reused parts may be anything from chunks of actual code to design ideas or design solutions to well defined problems. But this way of producing software may also affect the quality of the final product. To take full advantage of the reuse based approach, previous experience of the quality characteristics of the reused parts should be made available and used to predict the quality of the new product.

In this paper we address the problem of product quality prediction during an object-oriented software process. In Section 2 we take a look at measuring and predicting quality of the software product, and in Section 3 we study some quality measures that can be obtained during the design phase. In Section 4 we discuss design patterns, which have been suggested as a means of improving the quality of the design phase, and address the connection between design patterns and product quality. In Section 5 we describe our approach of including product quality prediction as part of the design phase, and in Section 6 we give some examples of using our tool for quality predictions in industry level software development. Finally Section 7 is a short conclusion.

2. Quality measurement and prediction

Various sources describe important aspects of software quality and attempt to define metrics for product quality evaluation. Several software quality models have been defined (some of the early references are [3, 15]), and while the structure and other details of such models differ, there is wide agreement that certain factors, e.g., usability, efficiency (or performance), maintainability, and reliability, should be included in our notion of product quality. As the emphasis of the various quality characteristics may differ widely from one product to another, part of the requirement analysis phase should be an explicit definition of the quality factors that are relevant to the product [8]. To evaluate the existence or lack of quality in our product, we then need to find suitable metrics for the given quality factors; a useful aid for this purpose is the GQM approach [2].

Finding an appropriate set of metrics for measuring a certain quality factor of the product is often a difficult task. Usability is certainly very tightly coupled with the needs of the intended users, and thus can hardly be evaluated without a set of usability tests taken by a representative group of users. Similarly, running performance tests requires that we have a clear understanding of the typical workload of the system, descriptions of the use cases and their portion in the job mix, and a set of typical inputs for each case. Reliability testing again requires extensive runs or simulations of the software to ensure that failure density remains below the acceptable level.

The problem with this type of quality measurement is the need for test runs on the final product, which is very intensive on the final testing phases of the development lifecycle. However, if product quality is found unacceptable, improvement often requires changes in the design of the system and thus may result in extensive rework. It would be very helpful to find predictive metrics of product quality that could be applied earlier in the development lifecycle, so that corrective actions could be taken immediately if the predicted quality does not meet the requirements. The design phase is particularly important in this respect, since many of the crucial decisions stem from the product design. To diminish the amount of unnecessary rework, our purpose is to define design metrics that can be used especially to predict the quality of the final product.

3. Measuring in the design phase

To obtain useful quality information early enough for improvement purposes, we base our quality predictions on measurements and calculations of the high-level design diagrams of the software. In defining a software architecture, various views on its different aspects are used, such as the four views and the set of scenarios suggested by the "4+1 model" [11]. A widely used presentation for describing these views is the Unified Modeling Language (UML) [5], which is fast developing into a de facto standard of the field.

Depending on the quality factors that we are interested in, we may need to study various types of UML diagrams. For predicting software size or run time space requirement we use class diagrams and object diagrams. For performance prediction we need more process-oriented diagrams such as activity diagrams and sequence diagrams. Some of the parameter data may be obtained from diagrams presenting the physical view of the software, such as deployment diagrams. Scenarios typically presented as use case diagrams are necessary to track the behavior of the system during a typical or particularly interesting use case.

Some design metrics may be directly useful as predictors of a certain quality characteristic. For instance coupling, as measured by the CBO (coupling between objects) metric of Chidamber and Kemerer [7], is considered a good predictor of the changeability of the product [10], while the DIT (depth of the inheritance tree) metric has been shown to be a good indicator of fault-proneness [1]. On the other hand, predicting certain quality characteristics requires more elaborate analysis of the design. For performance prediction we need a fairly detailed description of the execution structure and also user provided information of the input size and characteristics, to be able to compute best case and worst case execution times, or the average execution time of a particular use case. Suitable forms of presentation for the execution structure are extended sequence diagrams, activity diagrams or execution graphs [19].

4. Design patterns

Predicting quality characteristics is radically improved by taking advantage of the experience gained in previous projects. It is particularly useful to recognize the reuse of earlier design solutions and take into account their observed quality effects. In the object-oriented field the wide acceptance of UML makes it easy to reuse the work done by others, and active collection of reusable design solutions has already emerged. High quality design solutions to frequently occurring software problems, generally known as *design patterns*, have been described and stored in pattern libraries using a standard format [9]. Correspondingly, bad solutions, or *anti-patterns*, have been detected and they can likewise be stored together with a description of their disadvantages [6].

Using patterns has been advocated because of their positive effect on the software structure, and their potential to speed up the design process and to improve its quality. So far, little is known about the effect of patterns (and anti-patterns) on product quality, although recently some interesting observations on performance anti-patterns have been published [20]. In fact, from the point of view of product quality, some of the commonly used design patterns are not necessarily good or bad per se, as their quality effects may depend heavily on the situation where they are used. Therefore the pattern library should be augmented by recording user experience on previous uses of the patterns and related quality information, to improve the common understanding of their applicability.

Let us take an example from the area of performance concerns. Here it is quite possible that a certain design pattern may have either positive or negative effects on product quality depending on the characteristics of the application area and the intended workload [22]. For example the scalability of the solutions may be different and a design pattern suitable in one environment may be quite inappropriate in another one. Hence the difference between a "good" pattern and a "bad" one may be in the parameters of the system, and storing this type of dependency information in the pattern library can aid the designer in predicting the quality of the software.

As an example, let us look at the *Mediator* design pattern in Figure 1, where all communication between the partners is handled by the DialogDirector [9]. This may be very efficient if the communication is infrequent and the messages are complex, but it turns out to be disastrous if the number of communicating partners is large and each of them frequently sends short messages to the others. Evaluating the actual performance effects of this pattern requires knowledge of the hardware environment and the projected workload, and maybe even some prediction of how the workload may change during the lifetime of the software.

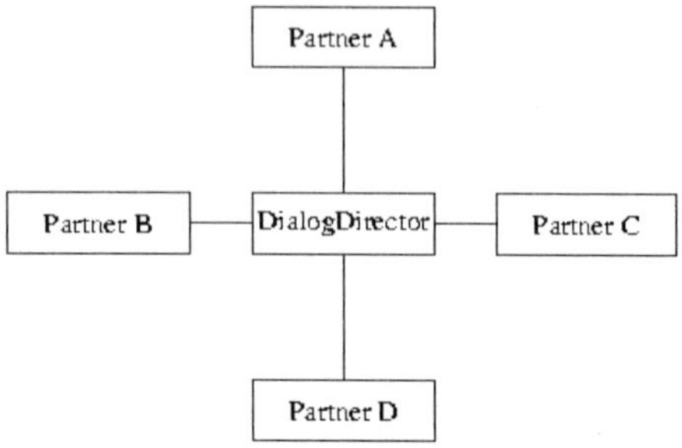

Figure 1. Mediator pattern.

Finally we must remember that not all pattern usage is preplanned [13]. In fact, many of the good practices and patterns of software design have been created long ago and they may frequently recur in software products without the developers being aware that their design solution is an identified "pattern" at all. Even more probably, the occurrence of an anti-pattern may be unknown to the developer. Again the experience data stored in the pattern library could be used, provided that the pattern (or anti-pattern) embedded in the design can be recognized. It is therefore useful to detect all the recurring patterns in the design, regardless of their origin, and to apply the information in the pattern library to predict the quality effects of the detected patterns.

5. The Maisa approach to quality prediction

Maisa (Metrics for Analysis and Improvement of Software Architectures) is an ongoing research project for developing methods and tools for automatically analyzing the software architecture and for predicting some central quality factors based on this analysis [17]. At present the quality factors that are examined are size, complexity and predicted performance, but the concept is suitable for various kinds of other quality factors as well. Some measures (such as design size measures) can be directly computed from the original UML diagrams. For more complex measures such as performance prediction, we need small extensions to UML to allow user provided information such as execution times and branching behavior; this can be accomplished by using annotations, such as UML stereotypes, tagged values and constraints [5].

In the Maisa project, the strategies used for quality prediction rely on two basic ideas: pattern discovery and hierarchical measures. In the following sections, we study each of these ideas in more detail. Section 6 then presents some industry examples of measuring and predicting product quality based on these measures.

5.1. Pattern discovery

The analysis in Maisa is based on discovering patterns from the UML diagrams that describe the software architecture. While the original purpose of design pattern collections has been to encourage designers to reuse the patterns as components of the software under development, we should not rely on the developer to provide information of the patterns embedded in the architecture. Instead we wish to discover all patterns and anti-patterns automatically from the software design, irrespective of their origin, and to evaluate their quality effects. In fact, some common patterns are very general and they may not be sufficiently well defined in a high-level design. Therefore pattern discovery may result in finding also patterns that are in fact not intended as such at all, or in failing to find patterns because of inadequate level of detail in the diagram. By interaction with the tool, the user can choose which patterns to look for and afterwards each finding can be approved or discarded by the user. The pattern discovery method is based on considering pattern mining as a constraint satisfaction problem [17]. The method that we use, AC-3, is described in more detail in [12].

In order to evaluate the quality effects of the embedded patterns, the pattern library must contain the necessary information for quality calculations. The quality calculations may also involve use case related parameters that must be provided by the user. Moreover, historical information about the usage and relevance of the patterns must be collected and maintained in the pattern library to improve the accuracy of the predictions. This type of data has previously not been included in pattern libraries, but it would add value even to the traditional use of the libraries as sources for reuse. At present, we are working on a suitably flexible structure for such an enhanced pattern library.

In practice each pattern covers only part of the entire UML diagram, but even detecting a single anti-pattern (or unsuitable use of a design pattern) may pinpoint a crucial problem. Some elements may be part of several patterns, while some parts do not belong to any pattern. Hence quality prediction of the entire system is not entirely covered by the pattern mining approach, but depending on the comprehensiveness of the pattern library we may gather useful information of the potential pitfalls of the architecture.

5.2. Hierarchical quality evaluation

Many quality measures are hierarchical in the sense that the measure for the entire system can be computed as a function of the measures of its subsystems, taking into consideration the sequencing and nesting structure of the architecture [8]. Typical examples of hierarchical measures include size metrics such as the number of classes, complexity measures such as the McCabe cyclomatic complexity measure [14], and performance measures such as response time [18].

We assume that the software is presented as a collection of UML diagrams. Some of these typically form a hierarchy representing the same view (e.g., a hierarchy of class diagrams), while others represent different views of the software (e.g., class diagrams for the logical view, and interaction diagrams for the process view). Quality prediction may require combining data from several diagrams of different kinds. For example, a use case diagram may describe a set of possible actions and their probabilities, and a set of activity diagrams may describe possible flows of control in more detail, annotated with the resource requirements of the activities. To obtain an average response time of the software, we need to compute the weighted sum of the response times of the use cases, while the response time of each use case in turn is computed from the execution times of the activities of the activity diagram (for details, see [18]).

While many software quality factors may be described using a single number (e.g., McCabe's complexity measure, software size measured in lines of code or in function points) some quality factors such as performance require using several numbers. To predict performance, the user typically wants worst case and best case predictions, and often also the performance for some typical cases within the domain [22]. This may require interactive use of the tool, where the user gives parameter values for each of the interesting cases, after which the tool computes the required predictions. Similarly, we may want to study the software on various level of detail, and our measuring tool should produce measures for the entire system as well as smaller subsystems (such as subdiagrams, or classes).

Metric	Per project	Per diagram			Per class		
	avg	min	max	avg	min	max	avg
NOA (nr of associations)	62	14	30	20.7	0	7	1.09
NOC (nr of classes)	57	15	26	19.0			
NOMA (nr of all methods)	5	0	5	1.7	0	2	0.09
NOOB (nr of objects)	0						
NOAttr (nr of attributes)	47	0	26	15.7	0	7	0.82
DIT (depth of inheritance tree)		1	3	2.0			
NOI (nr of interfaces)	0	0	0	0			
NOM (nr of public methods)	5	0	5	1.7	0	2	0.09

Table 1. Metric results for the CASE tool architecture.

6. Examples of pattern-based measurement

At present, the Maisa tool has been tested both with small artificial examples and with example cases of industry level software. Our first example studies the high-level design of an industrial CASE tool consisting of three class diagrams. The architecture of the CASE tool was examined with Maisa, and Table 1 presents some size metrics of the diagrams (see [7] for details of the metrics).

Maisa produces size metrics for the entire architecture (or project) and separately for each diagram and each class (where appropriate). At the high-level design phase the architecture contains 57 classes but only 47 attributes and very few methods. This is typical of high-level design diagrams where only the most important attributes and methods are included. However, this has some implications when searching for design patterns, since typically design patterns are defined using code level concepts. As an example, an association is a design level concept that can be presented at the code level in many different ways. High-level diagrams typically do not contain this level of detail, and in order to detect patterns in high-level diagrams, we need to relax the rules describing some of the patterns.

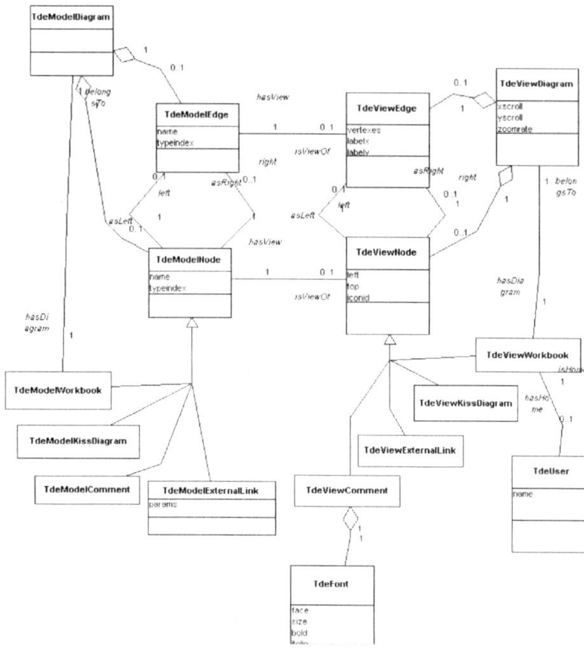

Figure 2. Design diagram for part of the CASE tool.

But if we relax the rules too much, we may not be able to distinguish between related patterns. Another problem with more relaxed rules is that we may find false positives, i.e., pattern candidates that are not real pattern instances. The possibility of false positives increases with higher level diagrams. In these cases the user must interactively select the correct instances from those detected by Maisa.

The diagram in Figure 2 is one of the design diagrams for the CASE tool architecture. It has just a few attributes or methods and, in consequence, only some of the basic pattern elements such as referencing attributes and derived attributes can be found in it. These are detected in the same way as the more complex patterns. As a result, Maisa found 41 instances of the *Derived Attribute* pattern element, but no other patterns.

As a second example, the diagram in Figure 3 shows part of the class diagram for the Maisa tool itself. In principle, the enclosed area in the picture could quite well represent the *Factory Method* or even part of the *Abstract Factory* pattern [9]. When using Maisa to search for *Factory Method* instances from this class diagram, we found four correct instances of the pattern. The following two descriptions give the name of the pattern role on the left and the name of the corresponding diagram element on the right (note that all the methods and elements in the example are not in Figure 3):

Product = CElement
ConcreteProduct = CClass
ConcreteCreator = CClassDiagram
Creator.FactoryMethod() = CDiagram.NewElement()
Creator = CDiagram

and

Product = CElement
ConcreteProduct = CState
ConcreteCreator = CStateDiagram
Creator.FactoryMethod() = CDiagram.NewElement()
Creator = CDiagram

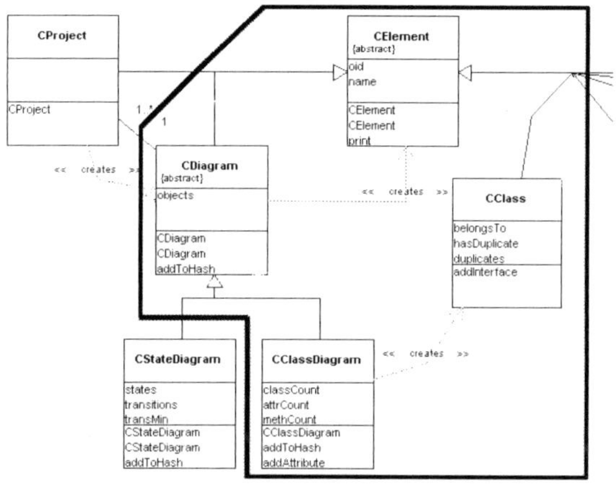

Figure 3. Pattern instance found in the class diagram of Maisa.

If the NewElement method is not included in the diagram or the CClass instance is not used as a return value, these instances will not be found. If we define the methods too loosely, Maisa finds twelve instances, eight of which are incorrect. (Actually the classes depicted here are not even supposed to form *Factory Method* instances. This will, however, become evident only when we use actual program files as basis for our measurement. The diagram classes are containers rather than factories.)

Our third example considers hierarchical evaluation of quality metrics, which is particularly important in performance evaluation. The (extended) activity diagram in Figure 4 shows a simple use case for an Internet shopping system. Execution times of the activities are presented as annotations over the corresponding nodes the activity diagram. (The units are not explicitly specified, but typically they would be milliseconds.) A lower limit for the execution time can be computed by selecting a path consisting of the fastest subroutines and using the minimum execution times for each node. In the minimum case the user buys nothing and hence the node *buy products* is not entered at all; the minimum execution time is 1530 units (= 450 + 800 + 280). This lower limit assumes that no product is bought and also that every other activity occurs as quickly as possible, which is clearly unrealistic. A more realistic lower limit would be the average execution time for the minimum case which is 3250 units (= 800 + 2000 + 450).

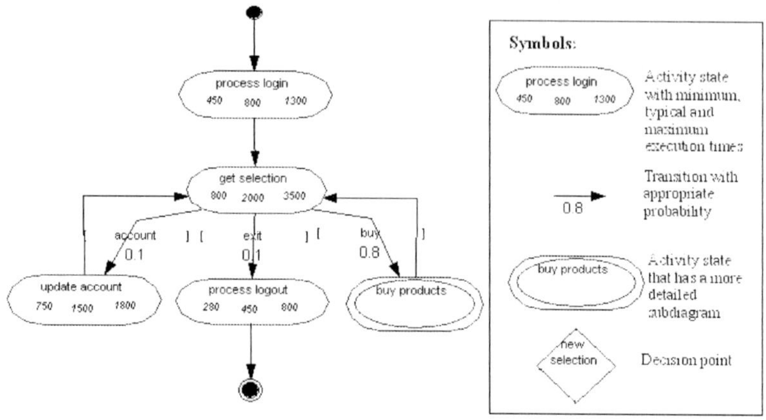

Figure 4. Shopping system activity diagram with annotations.

To obtain execution times for use cases where the customer buys at least one item, requiring the activity *buy products*, we need an execution time for this node. The node has been expanded in Figure 5 and its total execution time is computed from the execution times of the nodes in the subdiagram. For the case where the customer buys one item and pays by account, we get a total average execution time of 4625 units (= 800 + 2000 + 1375 + 450). The value 1375 for the node *buy products* results from the path through the diagram in Figure 5 where one product is purchased and paid by account. (Note that the number of products is represented by the branching structure of the node *new selection*.) Finally, to compute the execution time for a typical case we use the respective branching probabilities to weight the execution time for each path. According to the branching probabilities of Figure 5, an average customer buys four items. Half of the customers pay by account, 40 per cent use a credit card and 10 percent pay by invoice. The average execution time of the typical case is 6079 units (= 800 + 2000 + 0.1*1500 + 0.8*3855 + 0.1*450), where again the value 3855 is the average execution time for the *buy products* subdiagram.

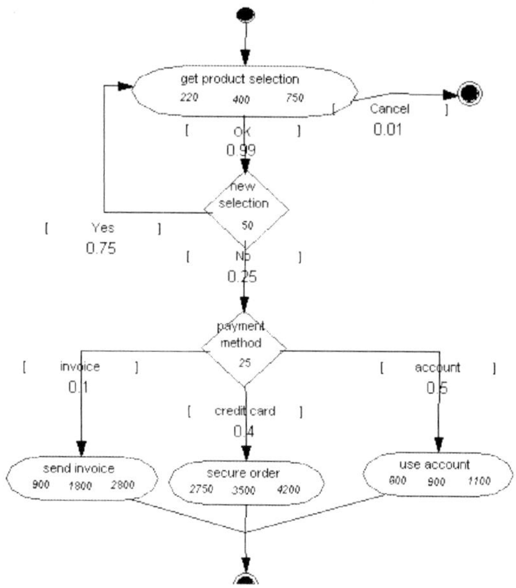

Figure 5. Subdiagram for activity "buy products".

7. Conclusion

In this paper we have considered the possibilities of measuring software design quality and predicting product quality based on the design patterns embedded in the architecture. By discovering recurring patterns and anti-patterns in the architecture and using previously recorded knowledge of their quality effects, we expect to arrive at reasonably accurate predictions of the final product quality already during the design phase. The success of the method depends heavily on the comprehensiveness of the pattern library, and particular care must be taken that both successful and unsatisfactory attempts of pattern usage are stored in the library, with adequate detail to refine our understanding of the scope and effects of the patterns. In particular, most of the published design patterns have been class diagrams, and as such not useful for performance prediction. It seems possible that performance related patterns are more domain specific than most design patterns; certainly the performance effects of patterns should be evaluated with the intended application domain in mind.

The tool developed in the Maisa project produces both simple metrics for software size and complexity [16] as well as more complex predictions of performance, based on a collection of published patterns [9]. Our next task is to augment the pattern library with specific patterns of our industrial partners, along with experience of pattern usage that will serve as the basis of quality prediction. We are confident that an extensive selection of such domain specific patterns will emerge as the users gather experience of the gains of including their own patterns in the library.

Bibliography

[1] V. Basili, L.C. Briand, and W.L. Melo, "A validation of object-oriented design metrics as quality indicators", IEEE Transactions on Software Engineering 22, 10, 1996, 751-761.

[2] V.R. Basili and D. Weiss, "A methodology for collecting valid software engineering data", IEEE Transactions on Software Engineering 10, 16, 1984, pp. 728-738.

[3] B.W. Boehm, J. R. Brown, H. Kaspar, M. Lipow, G.J. MacLeod, and M.J. Merritt, "Characteristics of Software Quality", North-Holland Publishing Company, 1978.

[4] G. Booch, "Object Oriented Design with Applications", Benjamin/Cummings, 1991.

[5] G. Booch, J. Rumbaugh, and I. Jacobson, "The Unified Modeling Language User Guide", Addison-Wesley, 1998.

[6] W.J. Brown, R.C. Malveau, W.H. Brown, H.W. III McCormick, and T.J. Mowbray, "Antipatterns: Refactoring Software, Architectures, and Projects in Crisis", John Wiley & Sons, 1998.

[7] S.R. Chidamber and C.F. Kemerer, "A metrics suite for object-oriented design", IEEE Transactions on Software Engineering 20, 6, 1994, pp 475-493.

[8] N. Fenton and S.L. Pfleeger, "Software Metrics: A Rigorous and Practical Approach", International Thompson Computer Press, 1996.

[9] E. Gamma, R. Helm, R. Johnson, and J. Vlissides, "Design Patterns: Elements of Reusable Object-Oriented Software", Addison-Wesley, 1995.

[10] H. Kabaili, R.K. Keller, F. Lustman, and G. Saint-Denis, "Class cohesion revisited: an empirical study on industrial systems", in Proceedings of the Fourth International ECOOP Workshop on Quantitative Approaches in Object-Oriented Software Engineering, Cannes, France, June 2000.

[11] P.B. Kruchten, "The 4+1 view model of architecture", IEEE Software 12, 6, 1995, pp. 42-50.

[12] A. Mackworth, "Consistency in network of relations", Artificial Intelligence 8, 1, 1977, pp. 99-118.

[13] R. Martin, "Discovering patterns in existing applications", in J.O. Coplien and D.C. Schmidt, editors, Pattern Languages of Program Design, Addison-Wesley, 1995.

[14] T.J. McCabe, "A software complexity measure", IEEE Transactions on Software Engineering 2, 4, 1976, pp. 308-320.

[15] J.A. McCall, P.K. Richards, and G.F. Walters, "Factors in software quality;" Technical Report RADC TR-77-369, Rome Air Development Center, 1977.

[16] L. Nenonen, J. Gustafsson, J. Paakki, and A.I. Verkamo, "Measuring object-oriented software architectures from UML diagrams", in Proceedings of the Fourth International ECOOP Workshop on Quantitative Approaches in Object-Oriented Software Engineering, Cannes, France, June 2000.
[17] J. Paakki, A. Karhinen, J. Gustafsson, L. Nenonen, and A.I. Verkamo, "Software metrics by architectural pattern mining", in Proceedings of the International Conference on Software: Theory and Practice (16th IFIP World Computer Congress), Beijing, China, August 2000.
[18] C.U. Smith, "Performance Engineering of Software Systems", Addison-Wesley, 1990.
[19] C.U. Smith and L.G. Williams, "Performance engineering evaluation of object-oriented systems with SPE-ED", in R. Marie et al., editor, Computer Performance Evaluation: Modelling Techniques and Tools, Springer-Verlag, 1997.
[20] C.U. Smith and L.G. Williams, "Software performance antipatterns", in Proceedings of the Second International Workshop on Software and Performance (WOSP'2000), Ottawa, Canada, September 2000.
[21] C.U. Smith and M. Woodside, "Performance validation at early stages of software development", In E. Gelenbe, editor, System Performance Evaluation: Methodologies and Applications. CRC Press, 1999.
[22] A.I. Verkamo, J. Gustafsson, L. Nenonen, and J. Paakki, "Design patterns in performance prediction", in Proceedings of the Second International Workshop on Software and Performance (WOSP'2000), Ottawa, Canada, September 2000.

Software Process Assessment Through Metrics Models

Authors: Dr. S. Ravichandran
P Mohammed Shareef

Abstract

Achieving gains in software quality require the use of software measurement and the desire to make metrics driven process improvements. Software measurement has been a successful approach in evaluating and predicting process capability. Reliable process capability can be attained by applying a various type of Software metrics and models using various data collection and analysis techniques. This write-up narrates some experiences on metrics data collection and analysis used to drive quantifiable results in a software organization for assessing and managing the software process for development and maintenance.

1. Software Process Assessment

The software process improvement is defined as the set of planned and systematic activities and methods employed to continuously enhance the capability of the software development processes. . The data collection and analysis of software metrics is playing a major role in the software process capability assessment and its management. Data captured through planned and structured data capturing techniques and methods, from daily activities, experiences, software parameters and lessons learned, and the routine analysis in order to provide guidance in improving current and subsequent efforts is said to be process assessment and management software process. The above two definitions are the basis for the software process capability improvement and getting quantifiable beneficial in the following areas:

- Increased software reliability and early and accurate prediction size and effort estimation
- Decreased costs for development and maintaining software.
- Reduced development time and increased productivity
- More accurate estimation, prediction of costs and resource loading in projects.
- Guidance for accurate schedules and risks for future software efforts.
- Quantitative project management with predictive capability
- Decreased defect and residual defect densities

The approach of SSI Technologies is measurement of critical elements of software activities during its entire development life cycle activities both on process and product, the metrics techniques are applied for assessing the process capability assessment and process management.

This paper describes the data collection and analysis made from experience gained in projects execution for assessing the software process capability assessment and management (only few selected baseline parameters are indicated as example).

Also, the focus on the measurement effort required for various type of projects are outlined along with few metrics as sample case studies for detailed explanation.

2. Development Environment

SSI Technologies is a dedicated global software development and consulting service provider offering cutting edge IT solutions in the key areas of Telecom, Healthcare, Banking, Insurance and Financial Services and E-business and E-Commerce. A division of SSI Limited, the leaders in emerging technologies training in India, SSI tech provides sustainable software services to varying client needs through a component-based and muti-tier architecture approach.

SSI Tech specializes in designing, developing, implementing, re-engineering and supporting complete IT solutions for Banking, Healthcare, Insurance, Telecom industries and Financial and E-business and E-commerce services. The following are the product offerings from SSI Technologies:

- Develop new applications for customers that are flexible, reusable and reliable, using our component libraries.
- Re-engineer existing solutions by deploying existing functionality as components in an n-tier architecture.
- License components from our repository for plug and use with existing business applications.
- Build incremental solutions using component architecture that will inter-operate with existing systems.

The solutions developed by SSI Tech are structured to fulfil the following objectives:

- Ensure faster time to market products
- Facilitate quicker response to changing business and customer needs
- Reduce cost of ownership to the customer
- Ensure language, tool and hardware independence
- Ensure interoperability with existing systems to protect customer's current investments
- Ensure Internet readiness.
- Ensure Customer Delight.

3. Metrics Process at SSI Technologies

3.1 Responsibilities:

Responsibilities for performing different activities defined as per SSI Technologies Quality Management Process are given below:

1. The Quality Coordinator who is attached to project is responsible for reviewing project metrics.
2. The Process Metrics Group at the organizational level is responsible for collating and issuing organizational metrics and suggests process improvements.
3. The Project Coordinator ensures that project data are entered into the Metrics Database.
4. The Process Metrics Group Coordinator is responsible for collating and presenting project metrics and metrics analysis for discussion during meetings of the Process Metrics Group.
5. The software engineering manager and quality coordinator must authorise the use of metrics that are not documented in the procedure. Any such metrics must then be submitted for inclusion in this procedure so that subsequent projects may potentially benefit from them.

3.2 Metrics Process: Development Project

An overview on the metrics process for a development project followed at SSI Technologies is briefly named below:

3.2.1 The Project Coordinator ensures that project data are entered into the Metrics Database, at least at the end of each phase of the project. The Quality Coordinator verifies that project data are available in the Metrics Database at the end of each phase of the project. For maintenance projects project data are entered into the Metrics Database, at the end of each calendar month. SSI Technologies metrics database essentially contains information obtained from weekly activity report of project team members, defect data and project information viz. Size, effort, schedule, no. Of requirements and its changes, control charts and others.

3.2.2 The Project Coordinator ensures that project data are entered into the Metrics Database, at least at the end of each phase of the project. The Quality Coordinator verifies that project data are available in the Metrics Database at the end of each phase of the project. For maintenance projects project data are entered into the Metrics Database, at the end of each calendar month. SSI Technologies metrics database essentially contains information obtained from weekly activity report of project team members, defect data and project information viz. Size, effort, schedule, no. Of requirements and its changes, control charts and others.

3.2.3. Following are the data from development; projects are input into the Metrics Database.

- ❑ Estimated as well as actual, effort and duration for project activities
    - Estimated as well as actual, effort and duration for requirements specification, design, coding, all test phases and test planning (all test phases)
    - Estimated as well as actual, effort for project management, quality assurance, configuration management, defect prevention activities, training, and other project activities
    - Estimated as well as actual, effort for all work product reviews
    - Initially identified number of requirements
    - Number of requirements added or changed during development
    - Number of defects recorded during and after development
    - Number of defects detected during requirements, design, coding, during testing, and after system testing categorized by source and severity
    - Estimated and actual size of the project in KLOC and SSIT Feature point
    - Estimated and actual number of reviews

3.2.4. Based on the data, metrics in Table 1 is calculated for projects.

3.2.5. The Process Metrics Group (PMG) meets at monthly intervals to analyse these project metrics and establish as well as revise if necessary, organization software process capability baselines for metrics after the careful analysis on process capability. The PMG coordinator collates the metrics for presentation during the PMG meetings.

3.2.6. Data collected from projects, metrics calculated from this data and process capability baselines decided upon by the Process Metrics Group are maintained in the Organization Process Database. The Process Database is accessible to all staff through a central repository named as "Knowledge Master".

3.2.7. Project plans use the organization process capability baselines to arrive at the following quality goals for the software being produced by the project.

- ❑ Effort variance for the project
- ❑ Schedule variance for the project
- ❑ Residual defect density (Post system test defects/KLOC)

To achieve the required product purity, project plans record the following quality goals for the review and testing processes followed by the project

- ❑ Number of defects to be detected by requirements specification, design, code review and testing

The Project coordinator also records Upper and lower control limits for the Quality Goals on the baseline value, in their project plan.

3.2.8. The lower and upper control limits are arrived at using the following formulae.

Mean = Average of the select project metrics

Standard Deviation (σ) = $\sqrt{[n \sum x^2 - (\sum x)^2 / n (n-1)}$

Lower Control Limit (LCL)

LCL = (Mean-3σ) if σ is less than 10% of Mean
LCL = (Mean-σ) if σ is more than 10% of Mean
Upper Control Limit (UCL)
UCL = (Mean-3σ) if σ is less than 10% of Mean
UCL = (Mean+σ) if σ is more than 10% of Mean

3.2.9. The PMG Coordinator will identify the organizational baselines control limits are set based on 3σ and σ control limits. While revising the organizational baselines, the PMG coordinator aims and focuses on ensuring the revision of σ baselines to 3σbaselines.

3.2.10. The Project Coordinator and Quality Coordinator monitor the quality goals for the project against actual data during project assessment meetings. Based on findings suitable corrective and preventive actions are decided upon, recorded and tracked to closure by the Project Coordinator.

3.2.11 Feedback from project assessment meetings and from meetings of the PMG is handled according to the *Corrective And Preventive Action Procedure* of SSI Technologies.

Table 1 - Baseline metrics for development projects

Metric	Equation
Schedule Variance	(Actual duration - Planned duration)/Planned duration
Effort Variance	(Actual effort - Planned effort)/Planned effort
Size Variance	(Planned size - Actual size)/Planned size
Requirement stability Index	Number of requirements changed, added or deleted / Total number of requirements
Defect density	Total Number of defects detected / size
Residual defect density	Number of defects found after system testing / Size in KLOC
Productivity	LOC per person-day (Software size / Total effort)
Effort distribution (%)	
SRS	Effort for SRS*100/ Total project effort
Design	Effort for Design*100/ Total project effort
Code	Effort for Code*100/ Total project effort
Test planning	Effort for test planning*100/ Total project effort
Testing	Effort for testing*100/ Total project effort
PM	Effort for project management*100/ Total project effort
QA	Effort for Quality Assurance*100/ Total project effort
Project Training	Effort for Training*100/ Total project effort
CM	Effort for CM activities *100/ Total project effort
DP	Effort for DP activities *100/ Total project effort
Support	Effort for support*100/ Total project effort
Others	Effort for any other project activities*100/ Total project effort

Defect distribution (%)	
SRS	Number of Requirements category defects / Total Number of defects
Design	Number of Design category defects / Total Number of defects
Code	Number of Code category defects / Total Number of defects
Documentation	Number of Doc category defects / Total Number of defects
Others	Number of Others category defects / Total Number of defects
Process efficiency (%)	
SRS review efficiency	Number of *Requirements* category defects detected by SRS review/ Total Number of *Requirements* category defects
Design review efficiency	Number of *Design* category defects detected by design review/ Total Number of *Design* category defects
Code review efficiency	Number of *Code* category defects detected by code review/ Total Number of *Code* category defects
Test efficiency	Number of bugs found up to and including system testing / Number of bugs found during and after testing
Defect Removal Efficiency	Number of defects found until and including system testing / total Number of defects

4. Metrics Process: Maintenance Project

4.1 A maintenance Project in SSI Technologies collects the following metrics for quantitative process and project management:

- Duration of maintenance
- Number of help desk calls received
- Total time and total effort to process help desk calls
- Number of problem reports received
- Total time and total effort to process problem reports
- Total effort spent on any other maintenance activities
- Total effort spent on Configuration Management, Training and other miscellaneous activities like Project Management, Release, Defect Prevention, Clean Up activity etc.

4.2. The quantitative quality goals for the project is based on the organization process capability and are mentioned in the maintenance plan of the project and defined as follows:

- Average effort and time to clear a Help Desk Call
- Average effort and time to clear a Problem Report
- Average maintenance effort per month per KLOC (person-days)
- Average number of problem reports per month per KLOC (person-days)
- Load factor (Ratio of total effort spent against the total effort available)*100 – If load factor is more than a percentage set by the organization, it is considered as exceeding the Burn Out Ratio leading to causal analysis and revisiting of effort.

Metric	Equation
Average effort to clear a Help Desk Call/Problem Report (Person days)	Total effort to clear help desk calls (Problem Report) / Total number of help desk calls (Problem Report)
Average time to clear a Help Desk Call/Problem Report (Days)	Total time to clear help desk calls (Problem Reports) / Total number of help desk calls (Problem Reports)
Average maintenance effort per month per KLOC (person-days)	Total maintenance effort / (Maintenance activity duration in months * Software size in KLOC)
Average number of problem reports per month per KLOC (person-days)	Total number of problem reports / (Maintenance activity duration in months * Software size in KLOC)
Load Factor	Actual Maintenance effort per month / Total available effort per month

Table 2 - Baseline metrics for maintenance projects

4.3 Case Study: Development Project

The following is the metrics data obtained from a communication software project developed at SSI Technologies for its one of the clients. The organizational base line parameters for these metrics (what was prevailing at that time) is also given for comparison (refer Table 3)

Table 3- Metrics for Development Project

Sl. No	Metric Type	Organizational baseline Parameters	Actual data from a development project	Variance %
1	Schedule Variance	8.5 %	16.5 %	94.12 (positive)
2	Effort Variance	10.5 %	18.5 %	76.19 (positive)
3	Defect Density	12.8 per KLOC	11.4 per KLOC	10.94 (positive)
4.	Productivity	42.5 LOC/ person day	41 LOC / person day	3.53 (negative)
5.	Requirements Stability Index	0.6	0.52	133.33 (negative)
6.	**Effort distribution (%)**			
	a. SRS	8	6	25 (negative)
	b. Design	31	29	6.45 (negative)
	c. Code	11	21	90.91 (positive)
	d. Test Planning	29	13	55.17 (negative)
	e. Testing	21	31	47.62 (positive)
7.	**Defect Density distribution (%)**			
	a. SRS	4.9	8.2	67.35 (positive)
	b. Design	71.3	74.3	4.20 (positive)
	c. Code	20	15	25 (negative)
	d. Testing	1.4	2.5	78.57 (positive)

8.	**Additional Metric (Customer Complaint Response Time)**			
	Customer Complaints handled during Acceptance Test a. Below 5 days b. 1-5 days c. 5-10 days d. 10-15 days e. 15-20 days f. Above 20 days		 3 6 35 46 10 4	

Graphical representation of various metrics data obtained compared with organizational baseline parameters is given below for understanding (Fig.1 to 4)

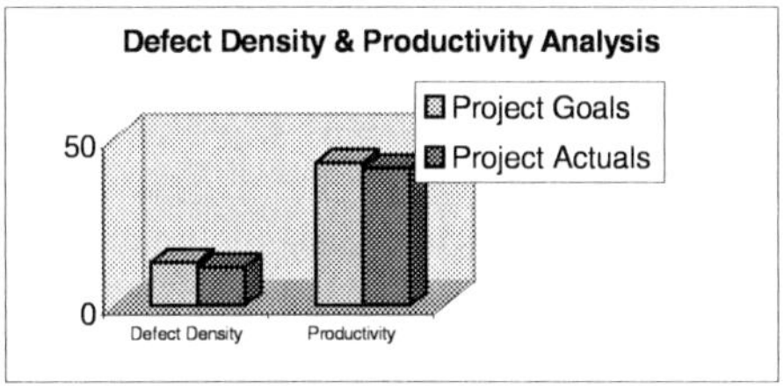

Fig. 1

Defect Density measured in LOC/Person day

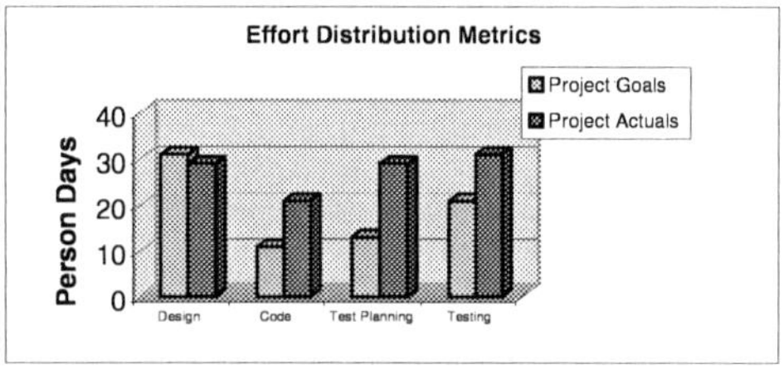

Fig. 2

Defect Productivity measured in KLOC/Person day

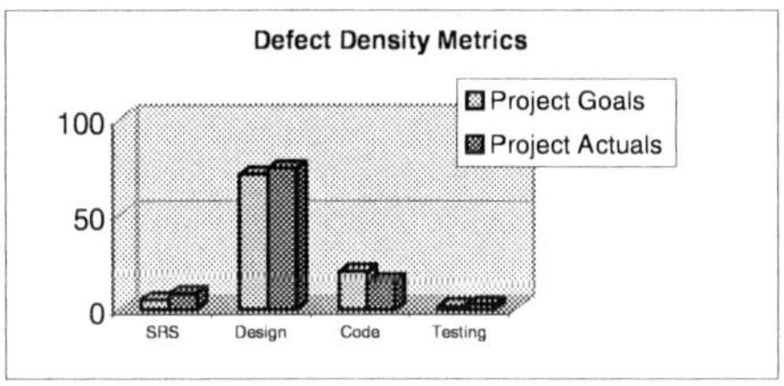

Fig. 3

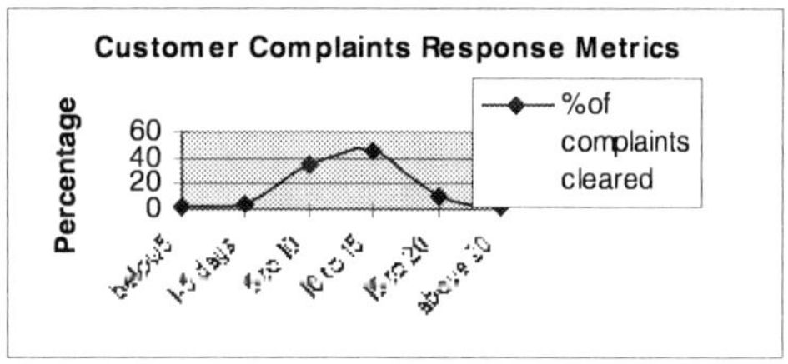

Fig. 4

4.3.1 Analysis

A quick analysis on the above project metrics data compared with organizational baseline parameters defined at that time are furnished below:

- Schedule variance is increased to almost double the defined baseline parameter. Effort variance is increased by 76% than the defined baseline parameter. Defect density and productivity level attained close to the defined baseline parameters. Requirements stability index is reduced by 13% compared to baseline parameters. Effort distribution (%) has significantly increased in design and testing phases and reduced by 55% during test-planning activity. Defect density distribution (%) is reduced by 25% in coding phase and almost doubled in testing and SRS phases.
- Additional metrics collected on response time to handle customer complaints serious concerns are listed below (refer Table 3):
  Category (c) 5 – 10 days 35 complaints
  Category (d) 10-15 days 46 complaints

4.3.2 Conclusions

The following are the conclusions made after the detailed analysis by process metrics group:

- The increases in effort and schedule variances were due to reduced stability of the requirement specifications. Requiement Stability Index (RSI) for the project was 0.52.The complexity of the project has led to increase in distribution of effort (person days) in the design and testing phases.
- Increase in the defect density distribution (person days) during SRS and testing phases seems to be due to defect leakages in reviews at different phases. Due to the complexity of some problems during customer support and prioritisation of issues necessitated for more response time handling customer complaints.
- Productivity level and defect density was attained closely to the organizational requirements although the variances are seen in effort, schedule, and requirements stability index. This could be due to more effort and time put in activities.

4.3.3 Process Improvement Strategies

The following practices were adopted to improve the process capability and its management (these recommendations were considered based on some more metrics data obtained from other similar projects)

- Training of the personnel for effective reviews at various phases of software development cycle was recommended and implemented.
- Although requirement stability index was found to be less in this case certain amount of schedule adjustment should have been made while tracking and monitoring the project activity. It was concluded by the project that the present project tracking tool applied for this project is not that effective therefore a new integrated project management and control tool was recommended for the evaluation and implementation for the company wide activities, that can effectively track the work in progress, with online reporting and enhancing predictive capability for the Project coordinator
- The prioritisation of handling customer complaints has been ensured by changing the process of help desk calls by numbering the complaints and evidence of discussion with the customers in prioritising the issues as accepted by them.

4.4 Case Study

The following is the metrics data obtained from a maintenance software project developed at SSI Technologies to one the leading stock exchanges in India. This product is successfully running the stock exchange since 1996. The organizational base line parameters for these maintenance metrics is given based on the data collected in the year 2000 with the comparison (refer Table 4)

Table 4 – Metrics for Maintenance Project

Sl. No	**Metric Type**	**Organizational baseline Parameters**	**Actual data from a maintenance project evaluated: Jan - Dec 2000**	**Variance %**
1.	Average effort to clear a Help Desk Call (Person days)	2.02	0.03	98.51% (negative)
2.	Average time to clear a Help Desk Call (Days)	3.54	1.62	54.23% (negative)
3.	Average effort to clear a Problem Report (Person days)	6.096	2.00	67.19% (negative)
4.	Average time to clear a Problem Report (Days)	6.503	2.00	69.24% (negative)

5.	Average maintenance effort per month per KLOC (person-days)	0.04629	0.0088	89.98% (negative)
6.	Load Factor (%)	47.46	20.581	56.63% (negative)

Graphical representation of various metrics data obtained compared with organizational baseline parameters is given below for understanding (Fig.1 to 6)

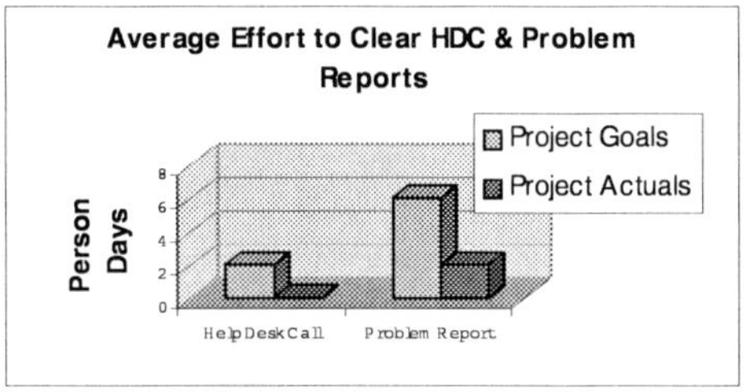

Fig.1

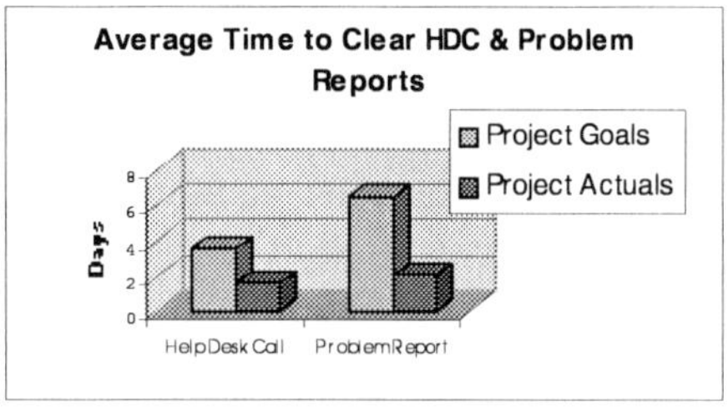

Fig.2

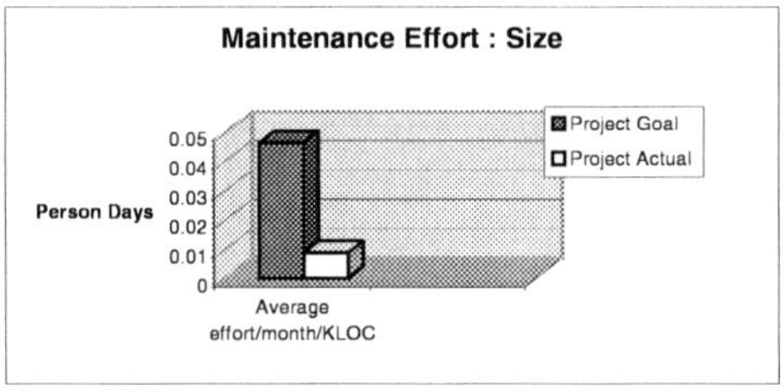

Fig.3

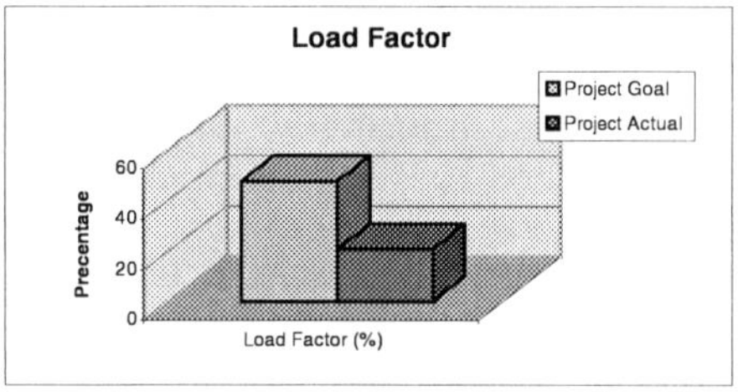

Fig. 4

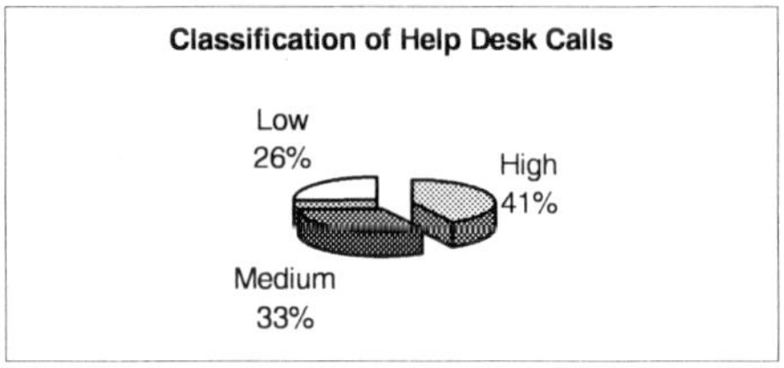

Fig.5

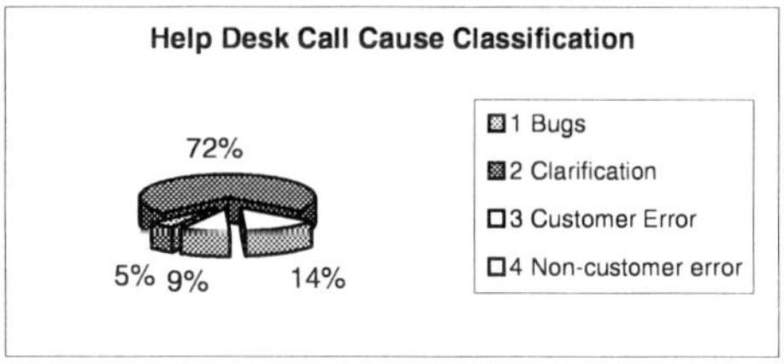

Fig.6

4.4.1 Analysis

A detailed analysis on the above maintenance project metrics data compared with organizational baseline parameters defined are furnished below:

- On analysis of variance results, the entire project actual to the baseline goals is showing negative variance. Further, average of all the baseline parameters are found to be operating below the lower control limits for the entire project baselines.
- In the period of analysis, the project actual did not exceed the upper control limit boundary. 72% of the HDC were clarifications or queries from the customer or representatives. 14% of the calls were related to customer mistakes or errors committed. Hardware, network, etc. problem accounted to 9% of the Help Desk Calls (HDCs) and only 5% of the calls were related to bug fixing and patch release.

4.4.2 Conclusions

The following are the conclusions made after the detailed analysis by process metrics group:

- The lower effort required to clear a help desk call was found to be below the Goal (to the effect of more than 95% from the goal) and the lower control limit, mainly because of the fact that the product was found to have stabilized over a period of operation and predominately the calls were of simple query resolutions. Further, the only two patch releases were accounted in the whole year, even after Year 2000 conversion. No calls were observed for the months October to December 2000.

- Based on the above scenario, and accounting the number of patch releases made by the project, the time taken for clearing an help desk call was found to be negative with respect to the baseline. It was found to be less 50% from the baselines.
- One problem report was raised in the project during the complete year and has resulted in a patch release, which was main reason for the lower effort in clearing problem reports. The effort for clearing problem report was found to be more than Help Desk Call, because of priority but still the about 65% less than the goal. Since the severity of the problem reported was medium, the time for fixing the problem report was less which was less than the project goal. The time taken for clearing the report was found to less than 65% from the goal.
- Despite a having huge of size of 1100KLOC, the average maintenance effort per month per KLOC (size) was found to less than 85% of the goal. This mainly contributed to the fact the number of help desk calls for the complete year was 43 and majority being the queries and clarifications. The effort required for these and patch releases made were very less compared to the goal. In-spite of shared resources being utilized for the project and total available effort estimated per month being 44 person days, the load factor for the project was found to be less than 55% from the goal. This substantiated with the fact that no help desk calls or problems reports were raised three months.

4.4.3 Process Improvement Strategies and Suggestions

The following practices were adopted to improve the process capability and its management (these recommendations were considered based on some more metrics data obtained from other similar maintenance projects)

- Proactively conduct customer and their representative training sessions, periodically to educate new representatives, so as reduce the number of frequent enquires and increase productive time of the customer during trading sessions.
- To arrive at an interim baseline for these projects that can use for the effort estimation of similar projects. To re-estimate the effort requirement for the project based on the new interim baselines, which is more suitable for similar projects. This estimation could be used for continuing the maintenance activities.
- From the analysis, since the product has already stabilized, no problem reports were raised. The metrics usage of this baseline parameter was less and may be re-looked by PMG based on the other similar maintenance projects trend.

Acknowledgement

Authors wish to record their sincere thanks to Mr. K.Shriniwas, CEO and Mr. K.S.Suresh, Chairman of our organization for their support and engorgement for carrying out the above work. Acknowledgement is also due to our colleagues from Quality Assurance department who are involved in the ongoing effort, including Mr. P Karthik and Mr. M Hariharan. We also like to record our sincere thanks to Mr. V. Kanann, SPI Consultant of KPMG – India for his assistance and guidance for completing this work successfully.

Should you test the code before you test the program?

Keith Paton

Abstract

Suppose a software development manager is considering whether or not to add automatic code inspection to the current development process. The paper shows what properties of the current process to measure, and how to use these measurements in order to make a rational decision. Let P1 denote the process whose steps are {write code, test program against requirements, find faults, fix faults} and P2 be the process P1 augmented by the single step {test code against guidelines}. The fractional effort actually saved by adopting P2 rather than P1 is given by dfic, where d, f and i are measurable properties of the process P1, and c is the efficiency of the automatic code inspection tool employed. Over a wide range of realistic values for these quantities, automatic code inspection will save more than 10% of the effort devoted to the process P1 defined above.

The paper makes realistic assumptions about the salaries of software developers and the cost of the machinery needed to carry out automatic code inspection; typical net savings given by automatic code inspection in the first year are some 10,000 US dollars per developer.

1. Introduction

Parnas [13] suggested that software projects should be managed by evaluating software products. Thus, every software product should be evaluated before being used at any later stage in the development process. This is to ensure that any faults in the product are detected as early as possible; Boehm [2] has pointed out that the longer a fault stays in a software system the more expensive it is to remove. This leads to a principle of software development:

Principle of Alternating Activity:
Every construction activity is followed by an evaluation of the product just constructed.

Now consider a software development process defined by products and activities as shown below

Table 1: Products and activities in a software development process.

Products	Activities
• requirements	1. construct the requirements
• code (e.g. in source and header files)	2. evaluate the requirements (by inspection)
• program (e.g. an executable file)	3. construct the code (from the requirements)
• test cases	4. construct the program (from the code)
	5. evaluate the program (by testing it)

The list on the right breaks the principle of alternating activity but the notation does nothing to warn us of this. As soon as we tabulate the list in two columns, one for construction and one for evaluation, the inconsistency becomes obvious; the gap in row 2 column 2 tells us that something is wrong.

Table 2: Software development process as a table.

Construction	Evaluation
1 construct the requirements	2 evaluate requirements (by inspection)
3 construct the code (from the requirements)	
4 construct the program (from the code)	5 evaluate the program (by testing it)

In work at IBM, Fagan [4, 5] showed how to fill this gap, using a technique that has since become known as Fagan-style *code inspection*. Here the code is inspected by at least three people to check that the code does what the requirements call for and that it satisfies relevant coding guidelines. Although Fagan showed [4, 5] that such code inspection was cost-effective, the technique has been slow to catch on. Many developers have explained to me that they find the cost of such manual code inspection doubles the cost of writing the code and they believe that this extra cost is not recovered in lessened cost at later stages. This is why they do not practise manual code inspection. The same developers point out that many of the checks for coding guidelines required in Fagan-style code inspections can be automated.

In fact several automatic tools [15] already exist to check that code satisfies guidelines of the type called for in Fagan-style code inspection. This paper explores the conditions under which such tools will be cost-effective in augmenting a development process whose activities are {*write code, test program against requirements, find fault, fix fault*}.

Section 2 defines failures and faults and illustrates several types of fault. Section 3 shows that several types of code fault can be detected automatically as breaches of so-called coding guidelines. Section 4 discusses the economics of the technique. In the language of testability, we are asking the question

> *Should you test the code against the coding guidelines*
> *before you test the program against the requirements?*

We define four measurable properties of the software development process and show how the effort saved depends on these values. Section 5 shows that, over a wide range of realistic values, you will save effort by testing the code against the guidelines before you test the program against the requirements.

2. Faults and Failures

Programs fail because of three main types of fault, namely

- Requirements faults
- External code faults
- Internal code faults

We discuss these individually below.

2.1 Requirements faults

Sometimes the requirements themselves are at fault. Table 3 below shows three types of such fault. These examples are obvious but when such faults occur in practice they are often more subtle and better disguised. Finding faults in requirements is discussed in [14].

Table 3: Some requirement faults

#	Requirement	Fault	Associated failure
1	for x >= 0 return sin x; for x <= 0 return cos x	Inconsistent at x = 0	No program could be built to satisfy these requirements
2	for x > 0 return sin x; for x < 0 return cos x	Incomplete at x = 0	The behaviour of the program for x = 0 is not defined, so we cannot know whether the program behaves properly on an input of x = 0
3	Sort an arbitrary collection of *n* numbers in time O(*log n*)	Impossible	No program could be built to satisfy these requirements

2.2 External code faults

Sometimes the code fails to carry out what the requirements call for and this can only be detected by looking at the code and the requirements together. Table 4 below shows three types of such fault.

Table 4: Some external code faults

#	Requirement	Code	Associated failure

1	Write the squares of the numbers in the file input.dat in the file output.dat	fq=fopen("input.dat","w");
		fp=fopen("output.dat","r");
		// etc.
			The data file input.dat will be destroyed

2	int total(int x, int y) returns the sum of its arguments	Int total(int x, int y)
		{
		return x-y;
		}
			Wrong answer

3	Speed(distance d, time t) returns the speed when a particle covers distance d in time t	Speed(distance d, time t)
		{
		return t/d;
		}
			Wrong answer; modelling fault

2.3 Internal code faults

Sometimes the code fails to carry out what the requirements call for but this can be detected by looking at the code by itself. Table 5 below shows three types of such fault.

Table 5: Some internal code faults

#	Code	Fault	Associated failure

1	Void cf(char *name, char *name2)
	{
	char buffer[132];
	FILE *fp=fopen(name,"r");
	if(fp){
	FILE *fq=fopen(name2,"w");
	if(fq){
	while (fgets(buffer,132,fp)){
	fputs(buffer,fq);}}}
	}
		The file pointer should have been released before leaving the function.	If the function is called too often the program will run out of file handles and crash.

2	#include <stdio.h>
	int main(void)
	{
	int i=7;
	// contravenes ISO undef 18
	i = ++i + 1;
	printf("i=%d\n",i);
	return i;
	}
		The code is illegal and the program behaviour is undefined but the ISO standard does not require the compiler to issue a diagnostic for this.	Anything can happen

3	float total(float a[], int n)
	{
	float sum=0.0;
	for (int i=1;i<=n;i++){
	sum+=a[i];}
	return sum;
	}
		The use of the bounds 1,n breaks the C idiom that arrays run from 0 to n-1.	This function will return the wrong answer when the array has previously been filled according to the C idiom

3. Mechanically Checkable Coding Guidelines

For each of the three types of internal code faults described above we can devise a coding guideline that warns programmers not to commit this fault. Table 6 shows these guidelines.

Table 6: Example guidelines to prevent some intrinsic code faults

#	Guideline
1	A function that executes fp = fopen(..) for a local fp must execute fclose(fp) or export fp.
2	Do not modify the value of a variable twice between sequence points.
3	Do not set the control variable to other than 0 or test it with <= in the for control loop.

Many guidelines as precise as these appear in the literature [2, 6, 7, 8, 9, 10, 11, 12]; breaches of such guidelines can be detected with automatic tools already on the market. A list of such tools appears in [15].

4. Economics of Automatic Code Inspection

This section describes how to decide rationally whether or not to try automatic code inspection.

4.1 Benefit of Automatic Code Inspection

This sub-section explains what to measure about the existing software development process in order to estimate the benefit that automatic code inspection might bring. Figure 1 decomposes the effort spent in software construction. Tasks appear in the rows; each task is decomposed in the rows immediately indented from it. The task at the top is *build and debug code*, the task being decomposed in the rows that follow. The value E on the far right indicates that the effort consumed by this task is E units; it can be measured in any appropriate unit.

Rows 2 and 3 break the task *build and debug code* into two sub-tasks, *build code* and *debug code*. The value *Ed* on the far right indicates that the effort devoted to *debug code* is *Ed*. It is assumed that the effort is exactly decomposed, i.e. the *E* in row 1 is exactly accounted for by the *Eb* and the *Ed* in rows 2 and 3, which is to say that $b+d=1$. Thus, *d* denotes the effort consumed by the sub-task *debug code* as a fraction of the effort consumed by the whole task.

Rows 4, 5, and 10 break the task *debug code* into three sub-tasks, as shown. The value *Edf* indicates that the effort devoted to the sub-task *find faults* is *Edf*. Thus, *f* denotes the effort consumed by the sub-task *find faults* as a fraction of the effort consumed by the task *debug code*.

Rows 6, 7 break the task *find faults* into two sub-tasks, distinguishing between the *external* faults and the *internal* faults. The value *Edfi* (marked as ←) indicates that the effort devoted to finding internal faults is *Edfi*. Since the internal faults are by definition those that can be detected by looking at the code in the absence of the requirements, the value of *Edfi* is the **maximum** effort that can possibly be saved by adopting automatic code inspection.

However, this effort will be saved in practice only if the tools are 100% efficient, i.e. they catch all internal faults. We allow for this in rows 8, 9 by breaking the task *find internal faults* into two sub-tasks, distinguishing between the faults caught and the faults missed by the automatic tools in use. The value *Edfic* (marked as ←←) indicates that the effort devoted to finding internal faults that can in practice be caught by automatic tools is *Edfic*. Thus, the effort **actually** saved by using automatic tools is *Edfic*, and the fractional effort **actually** saved is therefore *dfic*.

Index	Task	Effort	
1	Build and debug code	E	
2	Build code	Eb	
3	Debug code	Ed	
4	Run tests	Edt	
5	Find faults	Edf	
6	Find external faults	Edfe	
7	Find internal faults	Edfi	←
8	Find internal faults **caught** by tools	Edfic	←←
9	Find internal faults **missed** by tools	Edfim	
10	Repair code	Edr	

Figure 1: Effort diagram for Software Construction

To sum up, you can predict how much you will save by adopting automatic code inspection tools just by multiplying the values of these four fractions:

Table 7: Key fractions for use in deciding whether to adopt automatic code inspection

d	The fraction of the total effort devoted to **debugging the code**
f	The fraction of the debugging effort devoted to **finding the faults**
i	The fraction of the fault-finding effort devoted to **finding internal faults**
c	The fraction of the internal fault-finding effort devoted to finding those faults that are **in practice caught by automatic tools.**

This paper offers some guidance on the values of the last two, *i* and *c*. Hatton [6] reports from several large studies that 50% of all program failures were caused by internal faults. We shall therefore adopt a value of 0.5 for *i*. (This assumes that the effort required to find a typical **external** fault is much the same as that required to find a typical **internal** fault.)

Automatic tools to catch internal faults have been under development for many years and collectively they have wide coverage of the faults that really occur in practice. We shall therefore adopt a value of 0.8 for *c*. (The tools overlap in coverage, so we can get wider coverage by using two or more in parallel. This assumes that the effort required of a human to find a typical fault **caught** by the tools is much the same as that required to find a typical fault **missed** by the tools.)

The values of *d* and *f* are likely to vary from place to place. Table 8 shows the value of *dfic* for *i=0.5, c=0.8* and a wide range of realistic values of *d* and *f*.

Table 8: Effort saved by employing automatic code inspection tools.

Find fraction (f)	**debug fraction (d)**			
	0.8	0.6	0.4	0.2
0.8	**.256**	**.192**	**.128**	.064
0.7	**.224**	**.168**	**.112**	.056
0.6	**.192**	**.144**	.096	.048
0.5	**.160**	**.120**	.080	.040

Places where the effort saved exceeds 10% are in bold face. Managers of software development can use this table to decide whether to go further with the analysis.

Table 8 shows effort saved as a percentage. Let us now assume that the loaded cost of a software developer is 150,000 US dollars per annum and each developer spends 50% of his/her effort in writing and debugging code. Then we can create a further table showing the gross benefit of automatic code inspection in US dollars for each year of operation.

Table 9: Gross benefit of automatic code inspection per person per annum in US dollars.

Find fraction (f)	debug fraction (d)			
	0.8	0.6	0.4	0.2
0.8	19,200	14,400	9,600	4,800
0.7	16,800	12,600	8,400	4,200
0.6	14,400	10,800	7,200	3,600
0.5	12,000	9,000	6,000	3,000

4.2 Cost of Automatic Code Inspection

Automatic code inspection is low-cost but not free. The costs include

- The one-time purchase price of the tools
- Cost of an annual service contract
- The cost of applying the tools to inspect the code
- The cost of false alarms, i.e. examining code that is wrongly labelled as faulty
- The cost of any auxiliary software to control the process of automatic code inspection

As an example of how to calculate costs, we show below the cost of automatic code inspection for a 10-member work group. We assume that all code is to be analysed **after every successful compilation**; to ensure that this does not interfere with other work we assume that the analysis takes place on a dedicated machine connected to the network.

Table 10: First-year costs of automatic code inspection in US dollars (for a 10 person work group)

Item	Assumption	Cost
Purchase Price	Buy three code inspection tools	3000
Cost of applying tools	Buy one dedicated machine	1000
False alarms	Adjust tools to suppress these	
Extra software to control automatic code inspection	Buy extra software	3000
Total		7000

Analysing code after every successful compilation ensures that faults are detected as early as possible. If it is required merely to analyse every day the code that has changed that day then the dedicated machine could be dispensed with and all the code analysed on some existing machine overnight. This change would save $1000 in the first year. (All amounts are in US dollars.)

In subsequent years the cost is that of the service contract, say $1400 for the 10-person work group.

4.3 Cost-Benefit Analysis

Table 9 in section 4.1 showed the gross benefit of automatic code inspection per person per annum. The software development manager is likely to be more interested **in the net benefit per person in the first year**. The cost per person in the first year is $700, so the net benefit per person in the first year is obtained by subtracting this $700 from the gross benefit per person shown in table 9.

Table 11: Net first-year benefit of automatic code inspection per person in US dollars.

Find fraction (f)	debug fraction (d)			
	0.8	0.6	0.4	0.2
0.8	18,500	13,700	8,900	4,100
0.7	16,100	11,900	7,700	3,500
0.6	13,700	10,100	6,500	2,900
0.5	11,300	8,300	5,300	2,300

The software development manager may also be interested **in the net benefit per person in the subsequent years**. The cost per person in **subsequent years** is $140, so the net benefit per person is obtained by subtracting $140 from the gross benefit per person shown in table 9.

Table 12: Net subsequent-year benefit of automatic code inspection per person in US dollars.

Find fraction (f)	debug fraction (d)			
	0.8	0.6	0.4	0.2
0.8	19,060	14,260	9,460	4,660
0.7	16,660	12,460	8,260	4,060
0.6	14,260	10,660	7,060	3,460
0.5	11,860	8,860	5,860	2,860

5. Discussion

This section discusses questions raised by many colleagues over the years.

5.1 How can automatic code inspection help with requirements?

Books on requirements [14] stress that requirements should be complete but this is really a counsel of perfection. Whenever the customer specifies the requirements, he is likely to leave out some items that he would have put in if he had remembered them. Here is an example. The task is to read a list of pairs of file names and copy the first named file to the second named file. An important but often unstated requirement is that the program must work just as well for a list of $n+1$ pairs as it does for a list of n pairs. However, if we do not close files then there must always be an n such that the program will work for n but fail for $n+1$. Automatic code inspection that files are opened where they are closed will detect such a fault in the requirements.

5.2 How can automatic code inspection help with design?

Lakos [10] has described several principles and guidelines for software design in terms of relations between classes and relations between classes and files. Many of these can be checked from the code itself using automatic code inspection.

5.3 How can automatic code inspection help with testing?

As explained in the body of the paper, automatic code inspection finds faults that would otherwise have to be found during debugging after a failed test. This saves effort during testing.

5.4 Isn't automatic code inspection too obtrusive?

A well-designed automatic code inspection system runs silently in the background at time intervals chosen by the user, e.g. after every successful compilation, at the end of the day. It makes its presence felt only as required by the user, e.g. when a severe fault has been detected.

5.5 Doesn't automatic code inspection raise too many false alarms?

A well-designed automatic code inspection system can be configured by the user to suppress messages about faults that the user has confidence are not serious.

5.6 Doesn't pair programming make automatic code inspection unnecessary?

In the development method known as extreme programming [1, 9], programmers work in pairs and the second member is always reviewing the code written by the first; hence pair programming provides one form of continual manual code inspection. In extreme programming, a fault is something that makes the program behave improperly on a test case; if all the tests pass, then the code is deemed to contain no faults.

Automatic code inspection can contribute value to extreme programming; to see this, consider the example of 5.1 again. The task is to read a list of pairs of names and copy the first named file to the second named file. The customer's **stated** requirements call for the program to work for a list of size up to 10. However, if we do not close files properly then there must always be an n such that the program will work for n but fail for $n+1$. Certainly, the extreme programmer wrote a program that satisfied the requirements; however, automatic code inspection discovered something very valuable, the fact that the program will eventually fail when more thoroughly stressed than envisaged by the developer. Thus, automatic code inspection added some value to the development process.

5.7 Is automatic code inspection limited to finding faults?

Siy and Votta [16] have pointed out that manual code inspection is valuable in finding code that is not wrong but "just" hard and therefore costly to maintain. Some of the constructions that make code hard to maintain can be automatically detected using tools.

5.8 If you generate code automatically, surely you don't need any form of code inspection, automatic or manual?

When the code is automatically generated, that code need not be inspected, but there is still a place for inspection; the appropriate product to inspect is **the last software product that is hand-generated**. In building systems with UML [17], this last software product is the system description in UML; the rules of inspection would be different but the principle is the same.

6. Conclusion

We have supposed that a software development manager is considering whether or not to add automatic code inspection to the current development process. As an example, let P1 denote the process whose steps *are {write code, test program against requirements, find faults, fix faults}* and let P2 be the process P1 augmented by the step *test code against guidelines*. We have shown that the fractional effort saved by adopting P2 rather than P1 is given by *dfic*, where *d, f* and *i* are measurable properties of the process P1, and *c* is the efficiency of the automatic code inspection system employed. Over a wide range of realistic values for these quantities, an automatic code inspection system will pay for itself in the first year of operation.

We have made realistic assumptions about the salaries of software developers and the cost of the machinery needed to carry out automatic code inspection. Typical net savings given by automatic code inspection **even in the first year** are some $10,000 US dollars **per developer**. The analysis is conservative; automatic code inspection can detect not only faults due to missing requirements but also faults that never surface due to missing tests. However, we have not taken account of such benefits.

7. References

[1] Beck, K., "Extreme Programming Explained", Addison-Wesley, 2000.

[2] Boehm, B.W. "Software Engineering Economics", Addison-Wesley, 1983.

[3] Cobb, L., "Code Analysis using Code Check", Abraxas Software, 1985.

[4] Fagan, M.E., "Design and Code Inspections to Reduce Errors in Program Development", IBM Systems Journal, 15,3, 1976, pp 182-211.

[5] Fagan, M.E., "Advances in Software Inspections", IEEE Transactions in Software Engineering SE-12, 7 (July) 1986, pp 744-751.

[6] Hatton, L., "Safer C", McGraw-Hill, 1995.

[7] Henricson, M. and Nyquist, E., "Industrial Strength C++", Prentice-Hall, 1997.

[8] Jeffries, R., Anderson, A., and Hendrickson, C., "Extreme Programming Installed", Addison-Wesley, 2001.

[9] Koenig, A., "C Traps and Pitfalls", Addison-Wesley, 1989.

[10] Lakos, J. "Large Scale C++ Software Design", Addison-Wesley, 1996.

[11] McConnell, S. "Code Complete", Microsoft Press, 1993.

[12] Meyers, S., "Effective C++", Addison-Wesley, 1992.

[13] Parnas, D.L. and Clements, P.C., "A Rational Design Process: How and Why to Fake it", IEEE Transactions in Software Engineering SE-12, 2 (February) 1986, pp 251-257.

[14] Somerville, I. and Sawyer, P., "Requirements Engineering", Wiley, 1997.

[15] Spuler, D. "C++ & C Tools", Prentice-Hall, 1996.

[16] Siy, H. and Votta, L. "Does the Modern Code Inspection Have Value?", International Conference on Software Maintenance, Florence, 2001.

[17] Mellor, S. "Automatic Code Generation from UML Models", http://www.projtech.com/pdfs/autocg-1.pdf

CoWTeSt: A Cost Weighted Test Strategy

F. Basanieri, A. Bertolino, E. Marchetti

Abstract

In this paper we present CoWTeSt (COst Weighted TEst STrategy), an original strategy for selecting and prioritarising test cases. Cowtest supports managers to schedule and make cost estimates of the testing stages since the early phases of development. The derivation of test cases is based on the software analysis and design documentation, and uses the UML-based methodology UIT, Use Interaction Test. We report about the application of the proposed strategy to a real case study with some preliminary results.

1. Introduction

One difficulty in project management is to evaluate the cost or required effort of a planned testing phase; this evaluation might be (and is often) done in terms of number of necessary test cases. In this paper will we present Cowtest (Cost Weighted Test Strategy). The advantage of this method is that it helps to decide which and how many test cases should be executed since the early phases of the software development process, well in advance of the coding phase. Cowtest thus represents a practical help for managers to support test planning and to evaluate the impact of the testing phase on the cost of the final product.

In particular, it is possible to apply the proposed method in two ways: if a certain resource investment is fixed for a testing phase, it helps not only to estimate how many test cases to execute, but more importantly to prioritise them and pick those that are judged more useful to assure quality, stability and to evidence problems of the developed product. On the other hand, if the testing stopping rule is given by the coverage of a fixed percentage of functionalities (e.g., 90% test coverage), Cowtest helps to evaluate from the very first stages the cost of such a target and consequently choose the most suitable test cases, as for the previous case.

In our approach we adopt UML, the Unified Modelling Language, that is the emerging graphical notation to model, document and specify OO systems along all the phases of the software process. In literature there are many studies about using UML for design, but only few regarding its usage for testing [1], [2], [4]. We opportunely decided to base our test strategy on UML, so that its application can descend directly from the analysis of the diagrams already developed for the analysis and design phases. Therefore this strategy can be adopted by industries already using UML with little additional effort.

Cowtest supports the organization of the test cases. To derive them, we use a UML-based methodology, called the Use Interaction Test (UIT) method. This has already been presented in [1].

The paper is organized as follows: in Section 2 we give the basic knowledge required for the application of the UIT methodology. Then in Section 3 we describe the details of the Cowtest strategy and present in Section 4 and 5, respectively, a case study and the results obtained applying the method. The conclusion are drawn in Section 6.

2. Background

2.1. UML diagrams

UML [6], [7] is a graphical modelling language to visualize, specify, design and document all the phases of a software development process. It is rapidly becoming the *de facto* standard notation for analysis and design of object oriented software and systems.

UML is based on several types of diagrams, that are graphs differently describing all the aspects, features and phases of a software product. In the following we mention only the diagrams used in our methodology.

Use Case Diagram (UCD): consists of use cases (UCs), actors and their associations. A use case is the representation of a functionality (a specific use) provided by the system. The actor, that can be a system or a person, is an external user that interacts, through associations, with the system, to realize a specific functional requirement. This diagram can be defined in different phases of software development: in the analysis phase, to develop a preliminary design of functional system requirements; in the design, to describe thoroughly all the specific functionalities of the subsystems involved; in the implementation phase, to define the software architecture and the components of the final product. Moreover, the UCD can describe the system at different levels of abstraction, following the incremental development of the system through subsequent refinements and improvements.

Sequence Diagram (SD): shows a number of objects and the messages passed between them, realizing the functionality described in a use case. The realization of a certain functionality through the dynamic collaborations is called a *scenario* and is described by the set of messages exchanged between objects. Also the SD is used at different levels of abstraction and granularity according to the characteristics of the involved objects.

Class Diagram (CD): shows the static structure of the system through the representation of classes with their attributes and methods. Although UML is a language, and as such it does not impose a specific design procedure, an object in a SD often derives from a class in a CD, because it represents one of its possible instantiation in a particular system behaviour realization, which is a scenario.

2.2. Use Interaction Testing

The contribution of this paper is a general strategy to draw and prioritise between a general "universe" of potential test cases. This strategy interacts with a method that derives the (unorganised) test cases from the UML diagrams. The method to derive the tests is the Use Interaction Test (UIT) methodology, and has already been presented in [1]. UIT is an innovative method to derive integration test cases, at different integration or abstraction levels, exclusively based the UML design diagrams. Therefore the main advantage is that it can be already applied in the early phases of the software process, like analysis and design, without additional formalization effort and only using the already existing diagrams in association with background design information.

The construction of Test Cases in UIT is largely inspired by the Category Partition method [5], that is a well-known method to construct functional tests from the specifications. Its partitioning of the input domain of the function to be tested is a standard approach to functional testing, based on the idea that, for the classes of equivalence defined, one can select one or few tests representative of the whole class behaviour.

In our method we analyse one or more SDs relative to a selected Use Case. The integration testing goal is verifying that objects (components, classes, subsystems) interact correctly to perform the required functionality. These interactions are described by the messages that the objects in a SD exchange with each other and so they are exactly the items to be tested. Thus, each object inside a SD is considered a Test Unit, in the sense that it can be separately tested and represents a possible use of system. For each of these Test Units we derive the relevant Settings and Interactions Categories that are, respectively, environment parameters (or state variables) and messages coming from other Test Units. In this phase we need the related Class Diagram to capture information about parameters values and messages definition. Then a Test Specification is derived finding for each identified category of a Test Unit all the possible values and constraints. Then, observing the temporal ordering of SD messages, it is possible to find the Message Sequences, i.e., a set of messages exploited by objects to define and elaborate specific functionalities. Inside each Message Sequence, we can find a set of Interactions (messages of this sequence) and Settings (attributes that affect the messages) categories. Finally, an executable Test Case is constructed from a Test Specification, taking each of every possible choices, for each involved category.

We report below an example of one test case, generated from the example we will describe in section 4.

The test case is defined for OrigCallSetupUseCase and represents the first test case we can derive from "OrigCall" SD (see Figure 2). Here it is possible to distinguish the InteractionsCategories (e.g. *receiveQ931Msg* or *doMediaFacility*) defined by messages and SettingsCategories (e.g. *pBuffer, len, connKey*) depicted by all the attributes involved in these messages. The test case can be executed considering one of the possible value, taken from its Test Case Specification, of each Settings Categories involved.

```
TEST CASE 1
        receiveQ931Msg(pBuffer, len, connKey, NEAREND)
                pBuffer
                len
                connKey
                NEAREND
        Q931Msg elaboration [Li+1.TestCase1..4]
        [if (Fast Start or Tunneling) perform Media Restriction]doMediaFacility
        elaboration of message FAREND [Li+1.TestCase6..7]
        sendQ931Msg(pBuffer, len, connKey, FAREND)
                pBuffer
                len
                connKey
                FAREND
```

Figure 1: A UIT derived Test Case

Note that the description of the test cases at this level actually remains abstract and can be considered as the specification of test classes. The real executable test cases will be derived instantiating the involved categories values.

3. Proposed strategy

In Section 2.2 we outlined the method UIT to derive the test cases from the UML diagrams. In this paper we want to provide a wider strategy for selecting among the many test cases found by UIT, according to various possible industrial needs. Knowing both the typology and the number of test cases to execute, since the early analysis or design phases, would really be a good result, both for planning different testing activities and for estimating the effort required. Indeed, without a strategy that can discriminate among the many (thousands, or even millions) possible tests, a test derivation method such as UIT, or analogous methodologies, risks being not helpful and too wasteful.

Therefore here below we describe the identified steps of a systematic method for test cost planning and test cases selection and organization in view of software project cost exigencies and estimated risks, which we called Cowtest. The strategy is described in steps, divided into two groups (corresponding to Sections 3.1 and 3.2). In the former group, we put those steps necessary to build the basic structure (a weighted tree) used for test derivation; in the second group, we put the steps for test case selection in view of different project exigencies.

3.1. Weighted tree derivation

In this section we describe the necessary steps for preparing the basic structure used to apply Cowtest.

1. UCDs and SDs organization

Starting from the main UCD, describing the system functionalities at a very high level, each UC can contain in turn other Use Cases, since, to obtain a complete system functionality, it is generally necessary to execute several actions realizing lower level functionalities. We assume therefore that this criterion is applied to develop a more detailed specification of system functionalities and organize the UCDs in a sort of hierarchical tree.

For each Use Case at the lowest level of the hierarchy, one or more SDs can then be derived, which describe the objects interactions, and exchanged messages, used to realize the Use Case scenarios. As for the UCs we organize these diagrams in the tree in the appropriate position. An example of the obtained structure so far is in Figure 2.

2. Deduce the critical profile

Considering each level of the resulting tree, we annotate every arc with a value representing in a sense the "importance" of the associated node (be it a UC, or a SD scenario) with respect to the other nodes at the same level. The importance is explicitly expressed assigning a significance weight to the representing node of the tree (see Figure 3). The weight values belong to the [0,1] interval and must be assigned in such a manner that the sum of the weights associated to all the children of one node is equal to 1.

The weight should be as high as critical is the functionality represented by the associated node (UC or SD). Several criteria for assigning the importance factor could be developed, for example, evaluating which are the parts, or the functionalities of the system, that will be more significant with respect to usage frequencies, architectural (hw/sw) roles, development complexity, and so on. Generally the knowledge necessary to assign the proper arc's weight is present in the industrial realities but oftentimes it is not explicitly formalized. Here therefore we are requiring the effort to express in quantitative terms the intuitions and the information about the peculiarity and importance of the system functionalities that must be developed or integrated, considering that such "weight" should correspondingly affect the testing stage.

3. Test case derivation

From the SD, using the UIT method [1] ,the test cases are identified by a combination of all possible choices of variables (or parameters or environmental states) for all message sequences identified in the diagram, as describe in Section 2.2. As in the previous steps we associate to each SD the derived set of test cases. The resulting structure is therefore a tree, in which the root is the main Use Case diagram and the leaves are the SDs with associated test cases at different integration levels.

3.2. Test cases selection and prioritarisation

We depict in this section the steps necessary for selecting the test cases according to the different project needs. Considering the tree developed following the steps described in the above section, the strategy can be applied at different levels of integration. We introduce the concept of *integration stage*:

- The *first integration stage* is represented by the main UC and the SDs (if any), which are children of this node (hence they are at level 2 of the tree).
- The *i-th integration stage* is represented by the UCs positioned in at *i-th* level of the tree and every SDs, children of these nodes, situated at *i+1*-th level.

We decide to consider in the *i-th* integration stage the SDs at level *i+1,* because they represent the interaction between the different components that realize the functionalities described in the UCs at *i-th* level of the tree.

As previously said, it is first of all necessary to define the integration stage we are interested in. The weights assigned to each node contribute to define a relative importance factor, in terms of how risky is that node and how much effort should we put to test it, for each element belonging to the integration stage considered.

In fact considering every node, from the root down to the elements belonging to the integration stage considered, the product of all the nodes weights on the complete path from the root to this node represents its final weight. The final resulting weight associated with each leaf of the tree becomes therefore an element of discrimination for choosing amongst the tests to execute.

We consider now two different situations that can occur in test case selection. The first is the case in which a certain test budget is available, or a fixed number of test cases must be executed. In such a case, with Cowtest, we derive the most suitable distribution of the test cases among the functionalities developed. Regarding the budget, it could be expressed in terms of effort required, man/hours or simply money available: further budgeting consideration is outside the scope of the present paper, we want just to give an idea of how to use the methodology proposed. In our case we consider that we can select on the basis of the leaves weights the number of test cases feasible with respect to the available budget.

The second situation considered is that a certain percentage of functionalities must be covered. In this case by Cowtest we define which are the functionalities to be prioritarily covered and the minimum number of test cases to develop.

In the next section we describe the application of the Cowtest strategy to test selection in the two situations.

3.2.1. Fixed number of tests

In this section we consider the case in which a fixed number of test cases, *NT,* is planned for the testing phase. Cowtest is therefore useful to find a clever distribution of these *NT* test cases among the different functionalities designed.

For each SD, that represents a leaf of the building tree, we use its relative weight, *nw*, corresponding to the chosen integration stage as previously described, for deriving the number of test cases, *nt,* to select among all those associated to the SD. In particular, as many times the final weight is not an integer value, we use for each SDs the following formula:

$$nt = \lfloor nw * NT + 0.5 \rfloor$$

Therefore it is possible to know the number of test cases to plan for each leaf/SD. Using the set of tests associated to each SD (as derived per the UIT methodology) it is possible to choose the tests to be executed and implement them.

In particular associating to each SD a value representing the effort or the cost (for example in terms of man/hours, required budget) it is also possible to calculate the total amount of effort/cost to be scheduled for the testing phase. It is in fact sufficient to multiply the number of test planned for each SD times an average cost and sum all the obtained values (clearly deciding the average cost of test cases is not banal).

Another orthogonal application view of the proposed method is considering a certain budget, *B*, planned for the testing. If no information is available about the cost of the single test cases belonging to the set associated with a SD, the "relative cost" *b* of this SD can be derived using the following formula:

$$b = nw * B$$

The typology of the tests to execute will be selected among the set of tests associated to the SD according to the budget *b* calculated. Otherwise, if the cost of a test case belonging to the set associated to the SDs is available, then it is possible a more appropriate distribution of the total budget.

3.2.2. Fixed coverage

In this section we consider the case in which a certain percentage of functional test coverage (e.g. 90%) must be reached. In this case the proposed methodology can drive the functional choice, highlighting the most critical system functionalities and properly distributing the test cases. Moreover it is possible to distribute, as explained in the previous section, the amount of budget required for reaching the established coverage.

Following the steps described in the previous section for each SD that represents a leaf of the building tree, we consider its final weight, *nw*, calculated for the chosen integration stage.

Considering the coverage to be reached, *C*, the selection of the functionalities to be tested can be easily derived ordering in decreasing manner the *nw*100* values and summing them, starting from the heaviest one, until *C* is reached. In this manner the test effort is focused on the most critical system functionalities, avoiding to devote important test resources towards those less "important".

It must be noticed that before using the weight for test selection it is necessary to normalize to 1 the selected leaves weight in such a manner that their sum is equal to 1. In particular setting *NW=C/100*, the resulting final weight, *nwf*, for each selected SDs hence is:

$$nwf = nw / NW$$

As shown in Section 3.2.1, having fixed the number of test cases to execute, it is possible to distribute them using the *nwf* values. In orthogonal manner the weight can be also used to derive the number of test cases to be planned. In fact considering the minimum value among the *nwf*, called for simplicity *nwf_min*; multiplying each *nwf* for the factor *f = 1/nwf_min*, and summing the obtained values, the minimum number of test cases required to reach the prefixed coverage, *C*, can be calculated.

In Section 5 some examples are shown.

4. Case study

We present an example from a case study in which we applied Cowtest to a real project provided by a Telecommunication software developer. We consider here only a little part of the analysed system, named SK. In Figure 2 the main functionalities of SK are shown: network access management, network resources management and call management. We analyse in detail the "Call Management" subsystem, that is the part of system that handles all the phases of a Call, that could be defined as a connection between two terminals (PC, GSM phones, IP phones...).

The CallManagement UC can be divided into four sub-UCs:

1 Setup, that is the phase in which caller and receiver are identified and localized,
2 Connect, in which the partners, after their connection, can communicate with each other;
3 Release, in which one of the users involved in the connection decides to terminate the call;
4 Event Management, used to manage all events and signals related to the calls.

Moreover, in the Setup UC the management of a call is divided in two parts: the originating and terminating side, where respectively, the operations and functionalities of caller and receiver are performed. In the same way, the Connection UC is divided in two different behaviours: the connection and the disconnection, describing the two different events that can occur during a call connection phase.

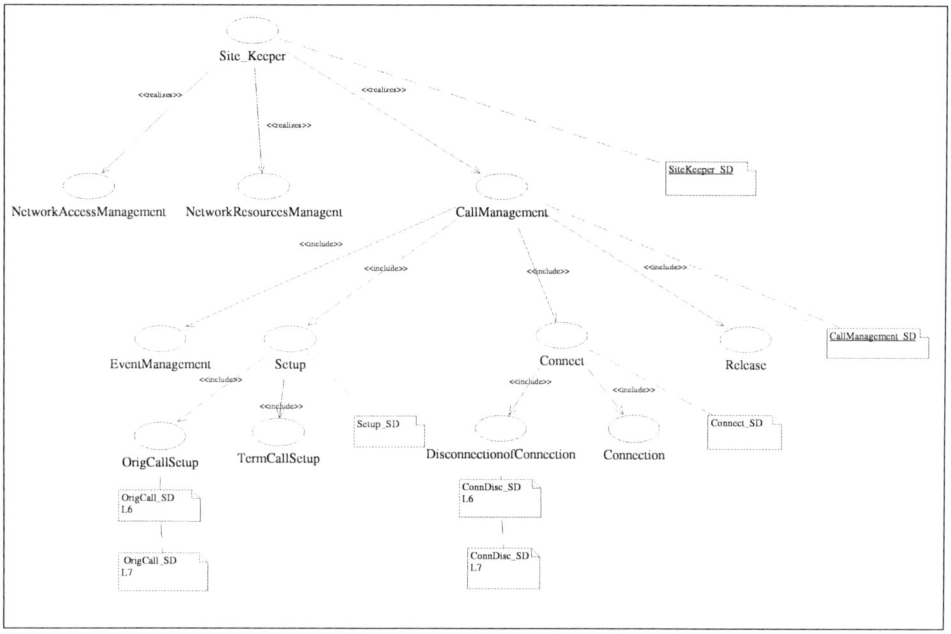

Figure 2: SK main Use Case Diagram

All these functionalities represent the possible call scenarios and so they can be linked to a SD; in Figura 2 we can see the complete tree with all UCs and SDs involved.

A SD describes one of the subsystem functionalities. Each functionality can be realized inside a software component, like modules or packages, or obtained by the interactions of several different components. In the first case we have only a SD, a tree leaf, where objects are the implementation classes of the component that realizes the functionalities. Whereas in the second case, we have more than one levels of SDs such that, the SDs at lowest level are those that realize in detail the described functionality through different actions and the SDs at a higher level represent the integration among all the sub-functionalities to realize the behaviour of the (sub)system as a whole. As shown in Figure 2, there are different levels of integration: SDs linked to the lowest UCs, like "Events management" or "Setup", describe the realization of UCs in detail using specific software components of the system; the SDs at higher levels, like "CallManagement_SD" or "SiteKeeper_SD", are those that describe the interaction among subsystems realizing the main functionalities.

In this manner the test cases can be developed both to verify the integration between different system parts and to investigate on the specific interactions between implementation objects.

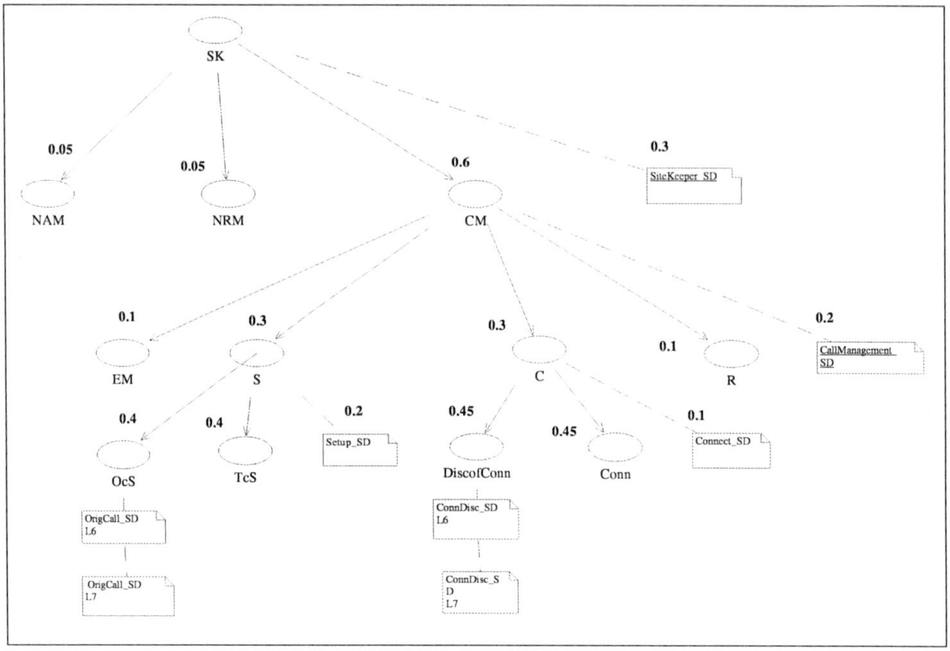

Figure 3: Annotated Cowtest tree

5. Results

In this section we report some results of the presented case study. Applying the methodology described in Section 3, we obtained the annotated tree shown in Figure 3. As already observed, the leaves weights, their critical profile, can be used in different manner depending on the project needs.

We report in Table 1 some results for the situation that the number of test cases is fixed. The weights distribution as well as the number of test case (*NTest*) are redistributed and assigned using the formulas shown in Section 3.

The table is organized in the following manner: the first and the second columns hold respectively the level of integration stage and the name of all tree leaves, that can be UCs or SDs. Note that the names with the suffix *NDchild* (not defined child) are not really present in the tree. They are necessary for representing the part of the tree not yet implemented at the integration stage considered. The third column shows the leaves critical profile. Considering a fixed number of tests to be executed equal to, say, 500, the remaining columns are divided in two parts showing, respectively the relative weight and the final tests number with respect to the selected integration stage.

Note that increasing the integration stage the relative weights and the assigned number of test of each nodes suffixed with NDchild, are redistributed among their children giving a more complete view of the critical functionalities profile.

We report in Table 2 some results obtained for the situation that a functional coverage is fixed. We consider the fourth integration stage and several coverage degrees. The weights distribution as well as the number of test case (NTest) are redistributed and assigned using the formulas shown in Section 3.

Table 1: Distribution of test case at different integration stages

Int-Stage	Leaves names	Critical profile	2nd Stage/NTest		3rd Stage/NTest		4th stage/NTest	
1st Stage	SK	1						
	SK_SD	0.3	0.3	150	0.3	150	0.3	150
	SK_NDchild	*0.7*	-	-	-	-	-	-
2nd Stage	NAM	0.05	0.05	25	0.05	25	0.05	25
	NRM	0.05	0.05	25	0.05	25	0.05	25
	CM	0.6	-	-	-	-	-	-
	CM_SD	0.2	0.12	60	0.12	60	0.12	60
	CM_NDchild	*0.8*	*48*	*240*	-	-	-	-
3rd Stage	EM	0.1			0.06	30	0.06	30
	S	0.3			-	-	-	-
	S_SD	0.2			0.036	18	0.036	18
	S_NDchild	*0.8*			*0.144*	*72*	-	-
	C	0.3			-	-	-	-
	C_SD	0.10			0.018	9	0.018	9
	C_NDchild	*0.90*			*0.162*	*81*	-	-
	R	0.1			0.06	30	0.06	30
4th Stage	OcS	0.4					0.072	36
	TcS	0.4					0.072	36
	DiscofConn	0.45					0.081	41
	Conn	0.45					0.081	41

The table is organized in the following manner: the first and the second columns hold respectively the name of all the tree leaves and the their relative weights at the fourth integration stage. The remaining columns are divided in two parts showing, respectively, the normalized weight and the minimum number of tests with respect to the fixed coverage percentage.

Table 2: Weights normalization at different coverage percentages

Leaves names	4th Stage weights	70%coverage *nwf*/MinNtest		80%coverage/ *nwf*/MinNtest		90%coverage/ *nwf*/MinNtest		100%coverage/ *nwf*/MinNtest	
SK_SD	0.3	0.413	5	0.354	5	0.137	6	0.3	17
CM_SD	0.12	0.165	2	0.141	2	0.126	3	0.12	7
DiscofConn	0.081	0.111	2	0.95	2	0.085	2	0.081	5
Conn	0.081	0.111	2	0.095	2	0.085	2	0.081	5
OcS	0.072	0.1	1	0.085	2	0.076	2	0.072	4
TcS	0.072	0.1	1	0.085	2	0.076	2	0.072	4
EM	0.06			0.071	1	0.063	2	0.06	4
R	0.06			0.071	1	0.063	2	0.06	4
NAM	0.05					0.052	1	0.05	3
NRM	0.05					0.052	1	0.05	3
S_SD	0.036							0.036	2
C_SD	0.018							0.018	1
Total		72.3%	13	84.6%	17	94.6%	23	100%	59

6. Conclusions and future work

In this paper we have presented the Cowtest method and showed its application to a real case study. This example is referred to a simple part of the system with few developed functionalities; therefore the number of possible integration stages is not representative as well as the planned number of tests. However, the obtained results are quite good and encouraging. We are going to validate the complete strategy in an industrial context for the test planning of a complex system with lot of functionalities involved.

Those familiar with Musa's SRET [3] approach should have noticed some similarities between it and Cowtest. In particular, these two methods share a quantitative approach for test cases selection and prioritarisation.

We are developing a tool to automate the Cowtest approach application. In particular, one of the main tool feature will be the integration of Cowtest with a commercial UML design tool so as to allow the smooth integration of the test planning phase with the design stage.

Acknowledgements

The authors wish to thank Ericsson Lab Italy for providing the case study (and the problems to solve!), and more particularly Giovanni Nucera and Gaetano Lombardi for the insightful discussions and nice availability.

References

[1] Basanieri, F., Bertolino, A., "A Practical Approach to UML-based Derivation of Integration Tests", in QWE2000 conference proceeding, Bruxelles, November 20-24, 3T.

[2] Hartmann, J., Imoberdof, C., Meisenger, M., "UML-Based Integration Testing", in ISSTA 2000 conference proceeding, Portland, Oregon, 22-25 August 2000.

[3] Musa, J,D, "Software-Reliability Engineered Testing", in QWE1996 conference proceeding, S. Francisco, USA, May 21-24, 2Q2.

[4] Offutt, J., Abdurazik, A., "Generating Test from UML Specifications", in UML conference proceeding , Fort Collins, CO, October 1999.

[5] Ostrand, T.J., Balcer, M.J., "The Category Partition Method for Specifying and Generating Functional Tests", Communications of ACM, 36(1), June 1998, pp. 676-686.

[6] Rumbaugh J., Jacobson I., Booch J. "The unified Modeling Language Reference Manual", Addison Wesley, 1999.

[7] UML Documentation version 1.3 Web Site. On-line at http://www.rational.com/uml/resources/documentation/index.jsps/

The impact of quality assurance and metrics in real projects

Martin Wenger

Abstract

This empiric report shows the role of quality in the software development of a complex large-scale project in the financial area. The project's progress is presented from the point of view of the quality assurance.

The analysis of the business process in the Retail Office uncovered high potential of optimisation in bank-internal operations, whose improvement represents direct benefits for the clients of the bank and for account executives. The business process will be automated by an IT solution to be developed. The interfaces to an existing host system, which had grown over time, had to be created and new technologies had to be built and introduced in a data processing centre. The change of the paradigm from host development to modern methods in software engineering was completed, which implicated big expenditure for the change.

With the help of the magic square model the project's progress and the causality between the dimensions costs, time, function range and quality are explained. During the project the parameters change to the disadvantage of the quality. The software producers must learn to deal with the lack of quality and recover it. As a possible improvement quality assurance can be appointed to an external, neutral consultant. During the quality measurement simple metrics are to be used, in order to be able to be understood by a heterogeneous team and in order to be communicated by the quality-manager.

Quality assurance often leads to interhuman conflicts which have to be mastered additionally. The use of quality assurance must be pointed out to all people concerned with the project: the developer team profits from the certainty of a "second look" and from the security that other colleagues check their work before the customer could be dissatisfied. An additional use for the developers is in delegating the laborious testing. The software producer and all the software users not only get the chance of financial savings but also the chance to better meet the needs of the customers and of the market since errors can already be detected in the development phase.

1. Introduction

The Real Time Center AG (RTC) is an IT-service company covering with the standard software IBIS® and a comprehensive range of services all a bank needs for the outsourcing of computer competence. It offers a product portfolio in the financial sector ranging from software development, the operation of data processing to products and services for client/server systems. The client/server section supplies the banks with a universal support that covers the whole bandwidth of IT disciplines such as software installation and -distribution, network operation, version- and configuration management, user administration, server operation, support and training.

The data processing and outsourcing functions are used by six banks (BEKB, BLBK, BKB, BCJ, AKB, and Migrosbank) and further service providers in the financial area (EVD, Bank Coop, RBA, SwissBankers, Atag Asset Management).

2. Situation

2.1. The problem – a customer's view

Within the functions of the Retail Office (open accounts, modify accounts etc.) and the clerks' readiness to inform, it was found that the workflows in the front office are expensive, labour intensive, not customer friendly and incorrect. The main problem was the fact that the front desk created forms and papers for the back office. Therefore the entire process was neither fast nor efficient enough for the satisfaction of the customer's requirements. The customer orientation and increase of the ability to inform are the main attention of the banks. The process must be improved in order that

- the customer is served immediately (after termination of the interaction with the customer all administrative activities are completed and the transaction is finished when the customer leaves the bank) and by this the turn-around time in the bank is shortened,
- all data are entered only once and
- the registration of data is simple and standardized in order to increase the data-quality.

2.2. Proceeding

To resolve these problems the business processes were analysed as a first step and a concept for the improvement of the situation was developed. The suggested process modification was verified for adequacy with organizational measures. Finally the software KUBA ("Kundenberaterapplikation"; account executive application) was ordered for automation and support of the business process. The six banks as the principal clients of the data processing centre united and formed the project group for KUBA. One of the banks was nominated as the lead bank to be equipped first with the new solution.

2.2.1. Goals of KUBA

The goals of the system 'KUBA' ("Kundenberaterapplikation") are:

- Data acquisition once only at the workstation of the account executive with quick and simple processes
- drastic reduction of the number of forms for customers by the use of standard texts
- high ability to inform (customer information system)
- development based on the existing infrastructure
- standardisation of the operational procedures
- acceleration of the clerks' main processes (less rework)
- completion of the business transaction quickly (max. 10 minutes) after customer service
- Increased data quality

KUBA automates as a common base for all banks the main operational sequence with the possibility of flexibly adapting the individual specialities of each bank. The same client specific software is uniformly operated in the processing centre and can be configured for different looking user interfaces and each bank's individual procedures.

2.3. Specifications and basic conditions

2.3.1. Integration of existing systems

To avoid specialized point-to-point connections a communication bus (Tuxedo) was selected and implemented. The following figure shows how for example five applications lead up to $n*(n-1)/2 = 10$ point-to-point connections.

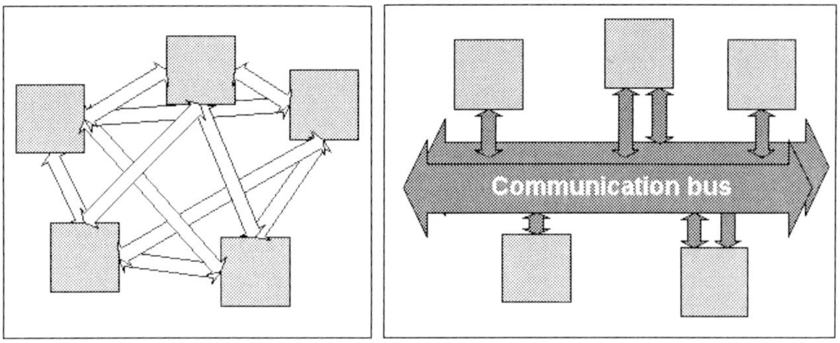

Figure 1 - Communication bus

Table 1 - Existing legacy systems

Name	Description
IBIS-Basic-System (Host)	Universal financial application Based on different transactions for several user interfaces (GUI and non GUI) and applications.
IBIS-PFS	Data management system for clients / persons (such as business partners etc.)
IBIS-UPS	System to check signatures

2.3.2. Integration of the new architecture

As an outsourcing partner RTC had to renew the IT architecture and therefore had to start an architecture project. The use of the new architecture was defined as a mandatory requirement of the development of KUBA. The architecture project was started before the application project and both had to be integrated in order to form one unit. The new architecture is based on the n-tier allocation (see also Figure 2 in accordance to [16]). Since there was no experience within the areas of performance, ideal distribution and configuration of the system, all possible versions of architecture were left open for evaluation and test.

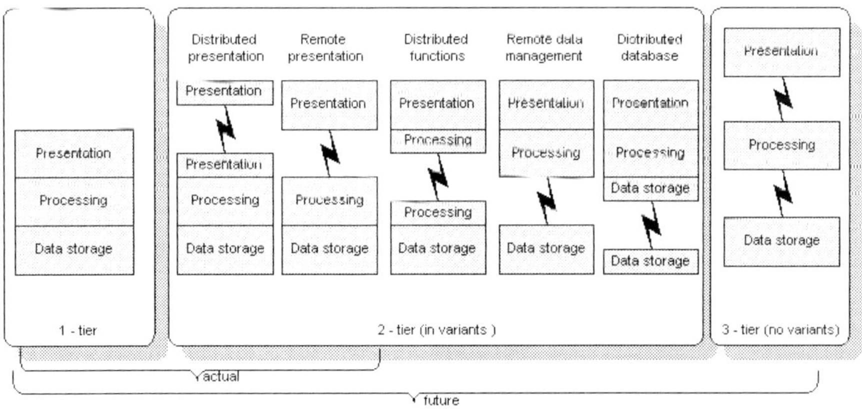

Figure 2 - n-tier architecture

Table 2 - n-tier architecture

Description	Advantages & Disadvantages
1 tier monolithic application	Advantage of low complexity Disadvantages of poor ability to reach data and the lack of flexibility.
2 tier Splitting in two parts, many possibilities exists (see figure 2)	Commonly used model in database oriented applications. Potential disadvantages in flexibility and scaling.
3 tier All three layers can be separated	Advantage of good flexibility, specialised allocation of resources (computers) and easy ways of extensions. Disadvantages of complexity.

The application of the communication bus and the 3-tier architecture help to uncouple and integrate the legacy systems in the project and is used as base architecture for all further projects.

2.4. Team building and necessary knowledge

For the accomplishment of the various functions, the high requirements and the broadly strewn knowledge a heterogeneous team had to be built with

- employees from more than twelve internal units,
- technical representatives from the six banks, as well as
- more than five external consultants.

Roles	knowledge necessary
End users Front office clerks Members of data maintenance 1st-level-supporter **Supporters and Trainers** 2nd, 3rd-level-supporter Trainers (KUBA, Operating, ...) **Developers (Host, Middleware, Clients)** Analyst Designer Programmers **Testing** QA-Management Q-Manager Tester **Operating** Operators of applications (IBIS, PFS, UPS, ...) Technical Operators (Host, Client/Server, Unix, NT, Oracle,..) System operators (Installation, Distribution, ..) Network operators **IT-Architect** **Project managers** technical professional **Top Management** **Representatives of the banks** **Consultants** Developers Middleware (Tuxedo) Quality assurance Auditors	• business processes • existing technical components and hardware • existing platforms and operating systems • existing applications • GUI-Tool • GUI-platforms (SAL 2, Browser) • server-platforms (NT, Unix) • IT-Management • basics of object oriented methods • GUI-Tool paradigm • application programming (JAVA) • system programming (C/C++) • communication bus (TUXEDO, SGL*Net, RMI) • Databases (Oracle) • host programming (COBOL, C) • host database (DMS, RDMS) • host Tools (z.B. PROPIP) • existing host transactions (TPs) • middleware (TUXEDO, RMI) • security • test-scripts (tcl, jacl) • test-tools • database technology • transaction monitors • networks / communication etc.

Figure 3 - Roles and knowledge

2.5. Chronology of the project's progress

The preliminary study on the project was concluded at the end of 1997. The results were the customer requirements for the system KUBA serving as basis for all further work.

Up to June 1998 a visual prototype (with screens) was developed with the method RAD (rapid application development) in close co-operation with the banks. All necessary source documents (like interfaces to the legacy systems, individual design documents, rules, flows, dependencies etc.) were developed.

One year after the start of the project the company APP management consulting Ltd (APP; www.app.ch) was assigned the function of the external quality assurance. APP is specialised in Quality Assurance in IT-projects since more than 10 years and has a comprehensive QA-method proven in wide areas of practice. APP built up and institutionalised project-accompanying quality assurance in autumn 1998. The results (quality assurance plan, inspection scheme, test architectures) of the preparatory work corresponded to the common practices and theories of the quality assurance [1][2][7]. The members of the existing host-based quality acceptance were trained in the techniques of the project-accompanying quality assurance. During the project a tool (Testdirector by Mercury) for managing test-cases and tracking of defects was introduced.

3. The role of the quality

3.1. The magic square

What happens during the process of software development (software production [4][5][8])?

Management or the clients determine the timelines and the budget of a project. These parameters are normally put in contracts and fixed. With the progress of the project time gets short and development of the functions is not finished.

1) The timelines must be kept and the pressure in the project increases. Faults and errors arise or one tries to jump the process model (short cuts outside of planning). This leads to a decline in quality and an increased error rate.
2) With the sinking quality the costs rise because of additional work on elimination of errors.
3) In order to meet the deadlines the range of functions is reduced ("we will deliver this in the next release").

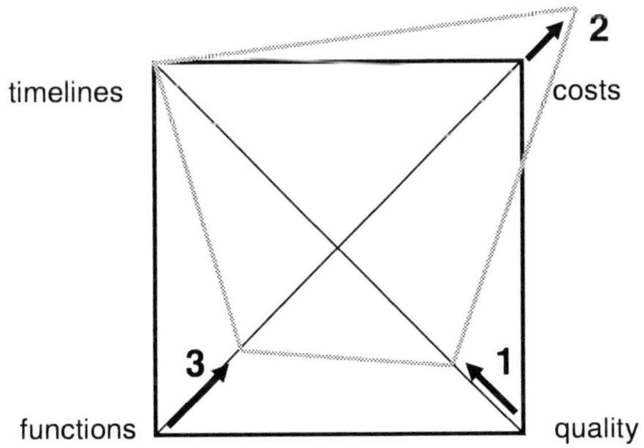

Black: plan
Grey: effective

The worst possible case is:

- Hardly any functions,
- costing the full budget
- with poor quality
- but in time!

Figure 4 - the magic square

3.2. The course of errors in the project

The number of errors found in KUBA after 8 months amounts to about one thousand. This is a normal situation in software production. Quality assurance in the project KUBA functioned, because every error that is found and removed by the development team will not be found by the customer.

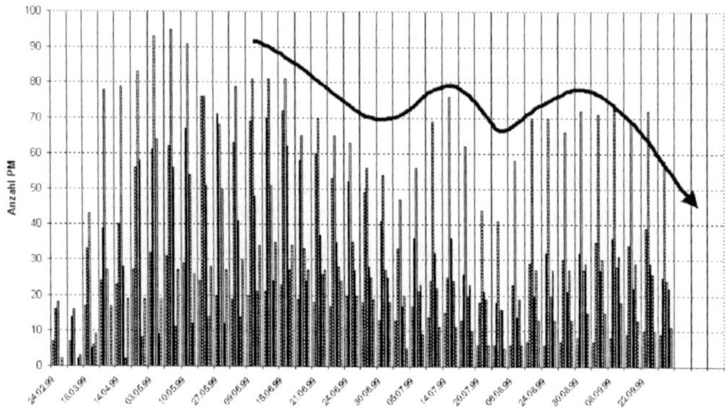

Figure 5 - Statistics of all problem reports

Classification of problem reports:

- Fatal error
- High error
- Medium error
- Small error
- Questions
- Changes

Priority to resolve:

- Immediately
- High priority
- Normal queue
- Low priority
- Next release

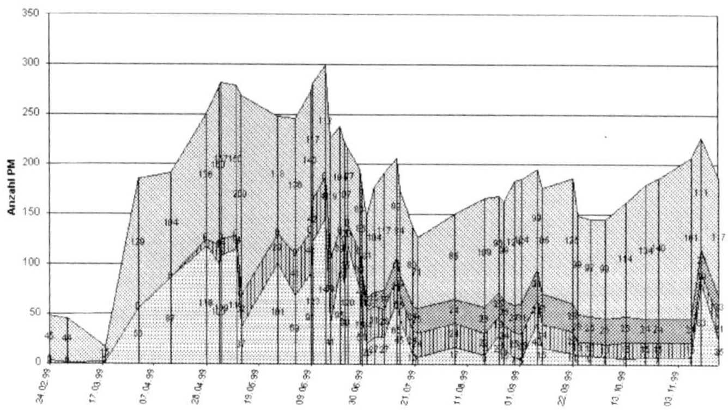

Figure 6 - Statistics of open problem reports

Possible status of problem reports:

- In progress
- Open
- Rejected
- In test

The errors found in all tests (HW/SW-integration, system-generation, functional, performance, degradation, data security) were filed as problem reports and classified. They were periodically analysed by means of the above statistics. The problem reports as a common component of communication in the team has proved to be useful. They do have a certain potential for conflict in disputed or not assignable cases.

For unmistakable communication of the errors and problem-reports in this heterogeneous team the simple way of classifying the errors – without the use of too theoretical models and metrics [9] - worked out satisfactorily.

Conclusion: Software metrics have to be as simple as possible in order to be communicated and understood.

The rate of elimination of errors was enormous. The duration of development and testing cycles amounted to 8 months. This leads to an errors elimination rate of 5.6 errors per working day.

Table 3 - error elimination rate

Item	Number
Period of quality assurance	8 months = 240 days = 160 working days
Number of errors	1000
Eliminated errors	900
Error elimination	5.6 errors / working day

Is it possible to minimize the high rate of errors? The first rule is not to produce errors or to produce at least the same error only once [3]. It is approved that it is impossible to write an error free software [1].

Not the end users of software products must learn to live with errors but the software producers.

3.3. Quality assurance – an improvement

How can software producers get the quality of their software products under control? A practical and simple approach is to appoint an external, neutral Quality Assurance Consultant. The tasks of this role are to control and assure quality in large-scale IT-projects.

The quality assurers /consultants

- check the results by a „second look" and
- to judge them in the sense of a „second opinion".

The software producer expects an overall check of his project and the results. Therefore the quality consultant must detect problems and suggest the necessary steps to resolve the problems in order to fully support the software developers in reaching their goals and the goal of the customer.

3.3.1. Phases of quality assurance

Carrying out Quality Assurance consists of basically two phases: Building up Quality Assurance and Carrying out Quality Assurance tasks.

- The Quality Assurance tasks must be laid down in close co-operation between the quality consultant and the project manager in the course of defining the goals and the work methods of the project and the quality of the system to be built. With this co-operation the two parties build up a close relationship and mutual confidence. The consultant and the project manager become the colleagues. This limits the required neutrality of the quality assurer and he finds himself in a tightrope walk between confidence and independence.
- In the second phase – carrying out Quality Assurance tasks – tests [6], reviews, audits [1][2] etc. are executed to measure the quality. If measurement and analysis show in this phase that the quality is insufficient; the quality consultant will be regarded as a policeman or even used as a scapegoat. The discrepancies in the project and the dissonance in the team grow [13]. The relationship between the quality consultant and the project manager usually cools off if the quality consultant does his job right and relentlessly uncovers all errors.

Conclusion: Project management and Quality Assurance have to respect each other, as without quality assurance good quality cannot be achieved and without quality it is not possible to achieve the project targets.

Conflict potential and other 'soft' factors occur in all teamwork, however they must be considered particularly in the work of quality assurance. When several parties are involved in a development effort, conflicts of interest are inevitable. The area of system development and installation is particularly susceptible to conflicts [13].

3.3.2. Benefits of quality assurance

It is important to communicate the benefits of quality assurance to all people involved in the project.

- The development team profits from the security of a "second look" and the certainty that other colleagues check the work again, before the customer could be dissatisfied. An additional advantage for the developers is in delegating the laborious testing work, whereby in accordance with development methodology unit tests remain however in any case the responsibility of the developers.
- Apart from financial savings, the software producer and the entire company get the chance to meet the requirements of the customers and of the market better since errors can be already detected in the development phase.
- The end users will thank the software producer for hassle-free software, likewise the managers of training and support. In the software industry unfortunately the banana methods apply still too often: to harvest green and let them ripen at the customer's!

3.3.3. Chances

The project KUBA caused changes which had to be mastered by the software producer:

- The new architecture and the change of paradigm from host development to modern methods in software engineering had to be treated.
- The application KUBA is not just transaction-oriented but includes the entire business process.
- The culture of open communication and tolerance of errors, as well as close co-operation with external consultants and many employees in a heterogeneous team had to be recognized, accepted and learned to be handled [12][13].

A special aspect in the project was the „change management". Very often comments were heard that some things had not ever been made in such a way and that the new ideas were simply wrong or could not be produced. But if in project work everything stays the same, as it was before then it's really daily business rather than a project.

Each modification, independently of whether it is viewed as positive or negative and regardless by what or whom it is caused, means loss of confidence, of security and of control to all involved [10]. Implementing changes requires intellectual and mental energy and is usually related to occupational and private risks [11][14].

The changes caused by KUBA at the software producer are in progress and show success already. Holding the changes and preventing relapses into old habits in all areas of the change is the way to continued success [10].

4. Final Conclusion

What are the lessons learned from the project presented? In this sense the following points are worth mentioning:

- All projects have a history which has to be taken account of. Software projects are usually based on a potential for optimisation detected by the analysis of the business processes. Quality assurance gains significance and gets often the additional role of the integrator with interfaces to legacy systems. In this context quality assurance becomes a central role, because the new networked systems hardly allow direct, fast and accurate error finding any more (or not yet?).
- The quality of software must be always treated from the customer's point of view: What quality factors are crucial for his business? [15]
- Projects of software development are important for companies and can't be regarded on their own. A heterogeneous know-how is required to be achieved only by the interaction of several people and parties. The employees and their knowledge in developing software are the critical success factors [15]. If everyone uses the newest methods and technologies the quality of the employees is crucial to the success of business.
- The requirements on teamwork are increasing. The culture of criticism, frankness and the admission to errors must be established. Conflicts earn respect and are no sign of unprofessional behaviour. Most organizations for system development have bad conflict resolution abilities [13]. The ability to accept criticism as a personal skill is to be trained and promoted in the team. Coaching as a further neutral instance beside the quality assurance would create a good remedy so that the conflicts can be discussed and settled without provoking a project stop.
- Quality assurance must start as early as possible and continue over all parts and phases of the project, and not just in final testing. In order to measure and control the quality in general QA should be part of the project-management and projects should to be planned and managed using the methods of risk management.

In this way quality assurance can be extremely successful in supporting the reaching of business-goals keeping under control the four dimensions timelines, costs, function range and quality.

5. References

[1] Wallmüller, Ernest, "Software-Qualitätssicherung in der Praxis", Carl Hanser Verlag, München, 1990

[2] Frühauf K, Lideweg J., Sandmayr H., "Software-Projektmanagement und Qualitätssicherung", vdf Hochschulverlag AG ETH Zürich, Zürich, 1999

[3] Malik, M.o.M., "Darf man Fehler machen?", Letter on Management 6/95, S.86-93, 1995

[4] Prof. Dr. Schönsleben, Paul und Dr. Specker, Adrian, "Von der Softwareentwicklung zum Softwareunternehmen", iomanagement Nr. 6, 1999, S.90-96

[5] Paulk, Mark Cc, "The capability maturity model guidelines for improving the software process", et al., 1995

[6] Myers, G.J., "Methodisches Testen von Programmen", Oldenbourg Verlag München Wien, 1989

[7] Software Engineering Standards, ANSI/IEEE-Standards 729, 730, 828, 829, 830

[8] Moore, James W., "Software Engineering Standards, A User's Road Map", IEEE Computer Society, 1998

[9] Möller, K. H., Paulish D. J., "Software Metrics", Chapman & Hall, 1993

[10] Häfelfinger, Kurt, "Grundsätze für ein erfolgreiches Change Management", Management & Qualität 6/99, 1999, S.58-61

[11] Senge, Peter, "The Dance of Change", Doubleday, New York, 1999
[12] de Marco, Tom and Lister Timothy, "Wien wartet auf dich – Der Faktor Mensch im DV-Management", Carl Hauser Verlag München Wien, 1991
[13] de Marco, Tom, "The Deadline", Dorset House Publishing Co., Inc, New York, 1997
[14] Fopp und Schiessl, "Business Change als neue Management-Disziplin", Campus, 1999
[15] Prof. Dr. Yoshinori, Iizuka, "2nd World Congress for Software Quality", Japan, 2000
[16] Edward, Jeri, "3-tier Client/Server at work", John Wiley&Sons, Inc., New York ,1999

Maximising customer satisfaction

Ton Dekkers

Abstract

"We boldly go where no man has gone before". We want to announce new products and services and use matching supporting information systems. All this more rapidly than before and with higher quality. Thinking about quality in IT projects, you will come automatically to the question: "what is then the result or product of quality?" The answer is very simple: Customer satisfaction. This means a good product, working as expected and produced well, in other words just fit for purpose is not good enough. We need a structured approach like Quality Tailor-Made (QTM) to maximise customer satisfaction.

1. Introduction

When an information system is developed, the customer view is leading. The information system (IS) should reflect the user requirements, the business needs. Information Technology (IT) has no reason for existence as independent activity; IT has to support the core business of the company that wants to use IT. Information Technology is just a tool to attain the goals. An information system should meet not only the requirements specified, but also the implicit requirements and all other expectations. To get to this, the end-user has to be aware that he or she has to provide all necessary information to the developer. On the other hand the developer should be aware that it is difficult to think about all the things that could be important for the system. So the challenge of the developer is to help getting the requirements clear and to assure the user gets the right solution for his needs from the technical point of view. The developer has to keep in mind: the solution is not a highly sophisticated state-of-the-art information system, but a system fit for purpose that also meets the expectations of the user. And not to forget the solution has to fit within the time and money constraints. The user has to be aware to set the scope of the system or the project in such a way that it is possible to develop a system within budget. Here you are, the twofold human-centered software quality perspective: developer's (personal) challenge versus end-user awareness.

2. Customer satisfaction

A customer reference model is used to understand from which customer satisfaction can be assessed. The model expresses the customer satisfaction using four key related components. As shown in the figure, the model components are:

- Business requirements (arisen from new or changed business strategy).
- Functional design (transformation of the requirements including quality levels, development criteria and constraints).
- Development process (process capability and people competence).
- Quality aspects (the human factor, the expectations).

This model represents optimal result if all its components maximise their contribution to customer satisfaction. For example, customer satisfaction is achieved when the product

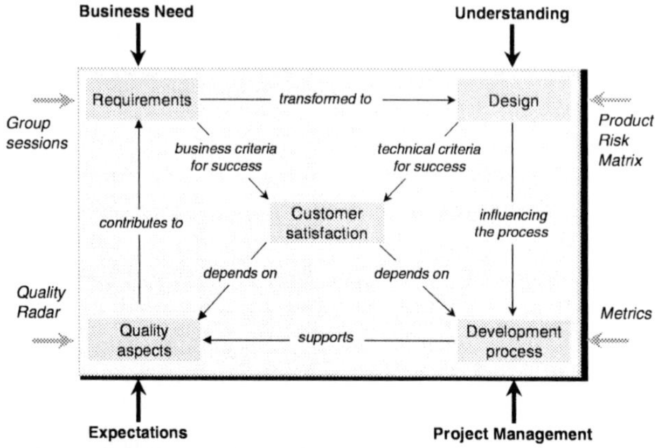

(information system) matches the needs. Only that is not possible when the requirements are not transformed accurately into the design. The design not only reflects the projection of the requirement on the development environment. It also influences directly the development process, the project organisation and competence of team members involved. The right process execution will deliver trustworthy product quality.

The left triangle (Requirements, Customer satisfaction and Quality aspects) reflects the product area. The customer can't be satisfied when the IS is not functioning in the right manner and is not is not doing it in the way he expected it to do. The right triangle (Design, Customer satisfaction, and Development process) reflects the process area. The customer will not be satisfied when it is not produced well; he expects the information system to be delivered in time and within budget. The customer wants value for money.

Software Control has looked for an approach to be able to manage all the aspects mentioned before and during the project. For us, Quality Tailor-Made is the approach to maximise customer satisfaction. QTM is no new development method; QTM does not commit to replace existing tools, standards and so on. No, it is just a practical approach that helps to find out what's important to do and to think off in a project. All in relation to the focus of the customer. The message of QTM is: consider automation projects not only from the point of view of time or money, but by choosing an approach which keeps in mind the explicit and implicit requirements of the customer. What do we need to do to satisfy the customer? What are the risks? What threatens the project? What can go wrong?

3. Quality Tailor-Made

3.1. Risk Areas

Looking at the customer satisfaction model it is obvious the risks can be split into risks related to the deliverable product and risks related to the process to get to the product. Analysing the triangles in the model we can recognise two kinds of risks in the product area: risks in the functionality and risks related to quality aspects. In the process area two types of risks can be distinguished: risks in relation to internal planning and control of the project organisation internally and those in relation to the outside factors.

Briefly, the risk in respect of the product: the right system is not built. The risk in respect of the process: the system is not built right. To get customer satisfaction you need to take care of both, product and process.

When you analyse the activities of a project leader in detail, you can categorise these activities in five steps. These steps are aimed at eliminating the risks on the product and in the product development. These five steps will be considered for all four risk areas: Functional Requirements, Quality Aspects, Planning & Control and Outside factors.

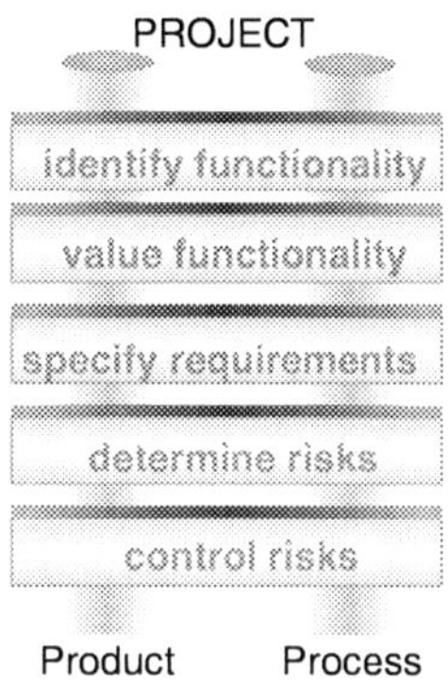

The first step is to *identify*: what do we really want? In this step we will try to identify all possible aspects within the four risk areas respectively. When we *value* the objectives, a selection will be made from all aspects that are relevant for this specific project. There is always a hierarchy in the properties. From properties that are considered to be important, the requirements must be *specified* in detail. For instance, if response time of the system is important, criteria for response time must be laid down, and quantitative aspects like the percentage tolerance must be set.

There are still two more steps to go. Now the requirements have been made explicit, we have to *determine* which risks there are. And finally the risks must be *controlled*: measures should be taken.

Summary: in five steps the needs will be defined, valued and worked out in demands and wishes, after which the risks will be mapped and measures taken to cover these risks.

QTM matrix

The QTM matrix is created when we match the four risk areas (Functional Requirements, Quality Aspects, Planning & Control and Outside factors) and the five steps (Identify, Value, Specify, Determine and Control):

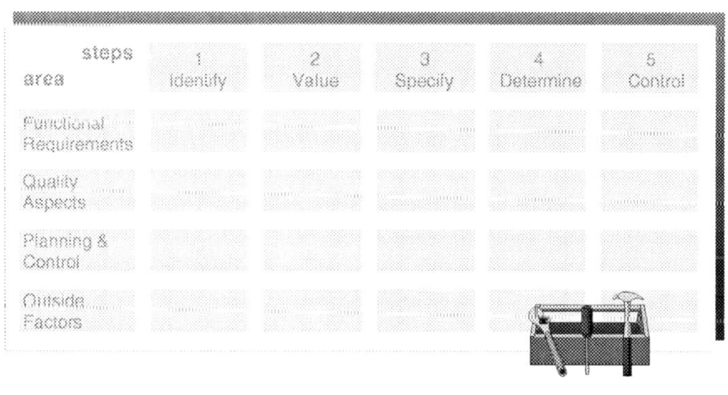

For a project carried out using this method, each cell of the matrix contains specified actions. It is possible that a certain cell is not filled up, but in that case there is a well thought out reason: you choose consciously to take no action, you are aware that you take a risk.

Looking at how projects are executed: they are all focused on controlling the process in terms of time and budget. Of course, in these methods Functional Requirements and Quality Aspects are also important, but the main goal is still: finish the project within time and budget. The quality (of the deliverables) plays second fiddle. In practice the system delivered (on time) often does offer most of the functionality required. The system is fit for purpose but does not meet the all expected quality. Conclusion: the customer is not satisfied.

QTM will help you to find the right balance between attention for process and product. The QTM matrix addresses the relevant issues regarding customer satisfaction in a structured way to ensure optimal result in each area. Take care you get the demands and wishes well mapped, determine the risks and the consequences of those risks. When you know the consequences, you can decide how much time and money you want to spend to eliminate or control the effects of the risks.

3.2. Functional Requirements

The Functional Requirements comprise all that the information system should offer in order to support the business process: the IS should at the least be fit for purpose. QTM supports this row in the QTM Matrix with a characteristic approach.

- *Step 1: Identify functionality*
  The needs of the various users will be identified in group sessions. The result of these sessions is a total vision that represents the view of all of the users.
- *Step 2: Value functionality*
  The importance of the functions will be valued from the point of view of relevant stakeholders:
  - the business: how important is the function for the business process?
  - the user: which functions are important for operational tasks?
  - the administrator: which functions are necessary to manage and maintain the system?
- *Step 3: Specify functionality*
  The user(s) specifies the main functional aspects so the developer can form a good picture of the system that should be built. In group sessions the requirements drafted and checked on feasibility (technical and budget).
- *Step 4/5: Determine and control risks*
  After the specifications are drafted, the (standard) risks are considered: the consistency of the requirements (several translations depending on the development method) and quality of the data (reliability, actuality and conversion). Risks and measures to control these risks come together in the Product Risk Matrix. This Product Risk Matrix is also used to control risks related to quality aspects and will be explained later.

3.3. Quality Aspects

When talking about Quality Aspects all "other" properties of the information system are included. Aspects that can be seen as the Human factors of the system. The right attention to the quality aspects makes the information system more than just fit for purpose.

Getting clear what the system should do is challenging. Even more challenging is to find out what stakeholder (customers) expects the IS will reveal this functionality. QTM fills in the activities in the row quality aspects of the QTM Matrix by using (international) Standards, tools and group sessions.

Step 1: Identify

It is very difficult to start identifying without any reference. With functionality you can fall back on your business but identifying quality is another story. In this case we can use an international standard like ISO-9126 [3], Quint II [4] or Tmap® [5]. These standards give you a list of attributes (and definitions) that helps you to define and to decide about quality.

Step 2: Value

When valuing, all attributes from the chosen list that are relevant for the required information system will be investigated. We use the same point of view used when checking Functional Requirements: Business Importance, User Importance and Administrator Importance. Each party has a different view of the system and has different (sometimes conflicting) interests. Sometimes, there are even more parties that have specific requirements e.g. Accountancy and Security. The number of "customers" of the system extends, and each "customer" expects to get what he wants and what he needs to do his job.

Because it is difficult for the user to indicate on a list of quality attributes what is important is almost impossible. In short, choices about properties and valuing are not so easy.

QTM uses a tool to value the properties: the Quality Radar. In this tool you identify your set of quality aspects, you define a proposition for each quality aspects and you link quality aspects to defined stakeholders. The user (stakeholder) always gets two propositions from which he must choose. By making a choice with the required information system in mind, the stakeholder indicates the importance of the "other" properties of the system. The result is the Quality Radar. In the figure is a radar shown from the user point of view using Quint II as a reference.

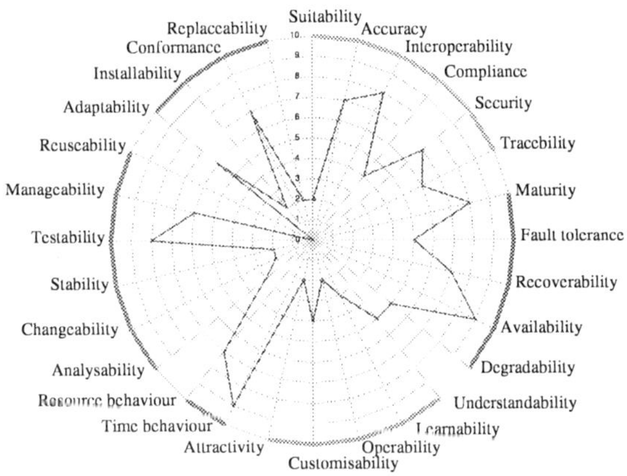

These radars enable discussions by stakeholders about the properties, why are they important and why are some of the quality attributes more important than others. The Quality Radar is a powerful communication tool: it gives a good basis to discuss the system and leads to greater involvement of users and other parties.

Step 3: Specify

The (most) important properties must be specified. If "Availability" is considered to be important, the user must define concrete requirements, e.g.: "the information system must be operational five days per week, eight hours a day". The properties must be defined such that during the project the system can be checked that it will meet the requirements.

By "Operability" we mean the users want an easy to handle information system. This requires for example uniform screen layouts, not only within the system, but also common with other existing systems.

Step 4 and 5: Determine and Control

When the properties are known in detail, the developer has a good understanding of what should be built. Further, he has to think about what kind of risks he runs in developing the system? Is the requirement a certain transaction should be completed within two seconds feasible? Is it easy to accomplish, or is it a problem - due to the way the transaction is defined, the performance of the network, etc.? If it is a problem, measures must be taken to meet the specified requirements.

Once we have determined the risks, the question remains: what are we going do about it? How do we control the risks? Depending on the exposure (likelihood versus consequences) various types of measures are possible:

- preventive, the occurrence of risks can be prevented;
- detective, the occurrence of risks will be signalled;
- corrective, possible causes will be removed and
- repressive, the consequences will be suppressed.

3.4. Product Risk Matrix

An essential part of QTM is the direct coupling of measures to products. In the Product Risk Matrix you position the risks directly to deliverables. So it easier to define concrete measures and the results will be visible on the right moment. In the Product Risk Matrix the columns reflect the possible product risk areas (Functional Requirements and Quality Aspects) and the rows, chronologically represent the deliverables of the project.

Product Risk Matrix	Functionality				Quality Aspects						
	consistent definitions	quality of data	inefficiency in the project	exceeding of the budget	standard screen lay-outs	context related help sceens	at least 50 users in one session	authorisation of transactions > 50k	screen changes < 0.5 seconds	couple to financial admin.	data definitions as in business model
Organization Model								✓			
AO procedures								✓			
System Architecture			✓				✓			✓	
Overview functions	✓										
Overview data	✓	✓								✓	✓
Function / Data Matrix	✓										
Man Machine Interface					✓	✓					

The list of deliverables (products and intermediate products) is directly related to the development method used. This list varies depending on development method and the implementation of the method in an organisation, but it is always possible to draw up a list of deliverables. This list does not contain only documents or coding; for instance a "prototype" is also a kind of intermediate product. Mind that products like "Functional System Design" are too generic; the matrix works better when products comprise smaller logical units, such as function structure, data model, user interface and AO description. Only those products that describe the information system will be included in the matrix (system documentation), not the project documentation (like plans, phase reports, etc.).

Getting to the Product Risk Matrix the project already passed the steps: Identify, Value, Specify and Determine. This resulted in a limited number remaining risk areas on the horizontal axis of the Product Risk matrix. For these risk areas the concrete requirements are known. Next we mark (√) in the Product Risk Matrix in which (intermediate) product at the earliest point where we can check that the requirement for the (intermediate) product is met. By these marks the requirements are linked to the deliverables of the project. By defining the measures at the appropriate time step five: control is filled in.

The Product Risk Matrix is the basis for the specification of product related measures. In the matrix concrete measurable requirements are linked directly to physical system products.

The project leader can take appropriate measures based on a risk analysis. The (intermediate) products will be used early in the project to ensure specified properties of the end product.

3.5. Project strategy

Ultimately QTM leads to a project quality strategy. Based on the Product Risk Matrix the project approach should be adjusted. Briefly, after defining the definitive list of deliverables the strategy must be defined, while the measures must be specified in a quality plan and/or a risk plan:

- Lay down product standards: requirements will be seen in at least one deliverable.
- Schedule reviews, checks and test activities;
- Decide on the techniques to be used, dependant upon the products to be reviewed, the way those products will be reviewed and which techniques fit best.

Choices should be made based on the Product Risk Matrix that shows the total overview of the risks and the relation to (intermediate) products: at which moment and by whom it will the checks be executed, on which (intermediate) product, and what will it cost? Decisions can be made, together with all participants on the basis of a cost / benefit analysis: do we take this measure or not? It is the responsibility of the project leader to decide if it is more efficient to combine test activities, to add additional products and so on.

3.6. Process Control

The development process usually starts with a drawing a plan. In this plan the goals for the project are set and the milestones in the process. Making this plan the RADAR method is also very useful. The projectleader identifies the issues that are important for the project, e.g. development platform, organisation, schedule, resources, securityplan, qualityplan, etc. With the stakeholders the issues are valued and specified.

The most important items in this area for stakeholders are Time and Money: when is it finished and what will it cost? The availability of metrics helps us to estimate effort. Effort can be expressed in time or in money. We can do this on account of the correlation between functional size and effort [7, 8, 6]. Another main variable of effort is the development platform and the available tools. The collective noun for all effort-related variables is productivity attributes.

After that the projectleader should perform a risk analysis (determine) and define the appropriate measures to attend to the risks (eliminate). At the end all of this should be reflected in the projectplan.

4. QTM in practise

4.1. Introduction

. Most approaches give the best result when it is implemented completely. The ideal situation is of course when you introduce QTM at the start of a project. This will avoid some inefficiency during the project. Then you can fill in the activities in all the cells of the QTM matrix tuned in on the wanted situation. In practise however some of the stages of project are already carried out when Software Control (SC) is asked to participate. When the customer realises the result of the project is not meeting the expectations (functionality, quality aspects and process control) action should be taken. The power of QTM is that it is useful at that time as well. This we will show with two cases in practice.

4.2. A governmental department

By order of a governmental department CS was asked to do all quality assurance during the project. We proposed to implement quality assurance based on QTM.

The first thing we did was to find out the status of the project. The primary stakeholders were the (end-) users, operations (functional and technical) and exploitation. Their main interest was functionality, reliability (including availability, exclusivity and integrity) and the aspects operation, performance and maintainability. Next to product control we also had to do quality assurance on the process and to participate in drawing up the test strategy. Although the last issue is integrated in QTM, the principal wanted this to be seen as a separate activity.

The interviews with participants made clear that there were already documents describing the functional requirements in very concrete terms. Also identification and valuing of the quality aspects was available. All the documents were checked on relevance and actuality using review techniques and questionnaires.

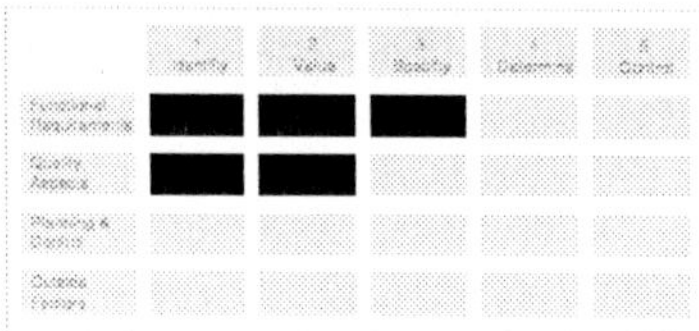

Based on the outcome of the interviews we assumed that sufficient attention was paid to the black-coloured cells, functionality and quality aspects. As you can see all other cells were not yet (completely) filled in. On the process side there was only a draft version of a project plan. This was nice because it was still possible to integrate the quality assurance in the project plan. This is crucial: the quality plan must be integrated in the project plan otherwise you cannot guarantee the quality of the product and process. In other words then you are not sure you can get to customer satisfaction.

The project plan should cover the main activities that were necessary to realise the IS: building and testing. To assure quality we agreed upon some basic standards: development method (organisational standard with project specific adjustments), project management (approach IQUIP), change management (change control and findings register of IQUIP) and Tmap® [5] for testing. Now we had the starting-points for the project.

In the interviews and questionnaires some of the issues that came up for discussion were already related to possible risks and specialities we should think of during the realisation of IS. In addition to that we initiated several risk analysis sessions to determine all tricky issues and risks. We created a risk register were we keep up the risks, the exposure, the responsible person and possible measures.

Now we had sufficient input to produce the product risk matrix for this project. When all participants agreed upon the content of the matrix, we started to describe in a quality plan all actions to be taken to assure quality of product and process and the measures to control the risks. Scheduling of the activities and the availability of the required people was included in the project plan. The quality activities should fit in the schedule of the project but also the milestones in the project depend on the quality activities: a two-way dependency.

To have an idea of the kind activities that were defined in this project we will give some examples. Roughly you can categorise the activities in three sections: product and process support (preventive measures), checking and test activities (detective measures) and finding control (corrective measures). In detail:

- Product and process support:
  - additional standards: standards for development, GUI, communication and interfaces;
  - product review: procedure and criteria;

- configuration management: procedure and control;
- change management: procedure and control.

- Checking and testing:
  - overview of deliverables, standards and the acceptance criteria;
  - testing according to Tmap®.
- Finding control:
  - register and procedure.

Although the project is not yet finished, all participants are very pleased about how thing go and how the risks are controlled. We are still on schedule and most of the people involved are confident that the project will end within budget and will meet the expectations.

4.3. A food distributor

In this case CS was requested to do quality control. The design and the realisation of the wanted information system were put out to contract on a fixed price base. In practise it means quality control is product control. Also in this project we used QTM as a starting point.

The first thing to do was again to find out the status of the project. As primary stakeholders were defined the (end-) users and operations (functional). Their main interest towards our job was getting a system fit purpose working as expected.

We held interviews with participants about the starting-points, the way the contractor worked, the status of the deliverables and the expectations of the user (both explicit and implicit). Based on the outcome we coloured the QTM matrix. The row functionality was (partly) handled by user and contractor. The process control was the responsibility of the contractor. As you can see in the figure no attention was paid at that time to the quality aspects. So we started with the identification of the quality aspect. There were no standards defined neither by the user organisation nor by the contractor organisation. On practical reasons we agreed upon using the Quint II standard [5]. At that time this was the only standard supported by the Quality Radar Tool. We used the tool as described in 3.3 to value the quality aspects. The result of the radar and discussions thereafter helped to define the acceptance criteria. Based on these criteria we developed a tailor-made checklist for product control.

When we started to compose the Product Risk Matrix we did not restrict the risk analysis to just the product. Although it was not the scope of the agreement we are included the process in the analysis. On the product we determined risks basically in the areas of correct transformation of requirements to design and transformation of design into programs. The fixed price and the tight schedule created a situation that to many things needed to be done at the same time. To control these risks in functionality we initiated inspections and group reviews in the project. The group reviews helped to improve communication and assured developing the right information system. This helped us to keep documents consistent.

The conditions in the contract were the reason project control was primarily on budget and time. The contractor focussed on developing an information system. The Risk Analysis also produced several risks related to the process. Although these risks were passed on to the stakeholders (users and contractor) limited action was taken. The user organisation was not capable (budget) and not sufficient flexible to address these risks. The contractor had difficulties to change things because of the contract.

Other major risks identified were involvement and culture in the user organisation. Not all users had participated in defining requirements and the organisational changes. Although all participants fully agreed on product quality, the cultural aspects and the merger that was initiated by the user organisation caused the information system is not implemented.

5. Customer Satisfaction

In the case we illustrated how to use QTM in a project, even when the project is already started. Back to the customer satisfaction model. In this model we marked in each area the most important item out of the cabinet of instruments we have available in QTM: group sessions, quality radar, product risk matrix and metrics. Depending on the situation you put on instruments that are relevant and contribute to the control of the determined risks. The instrument in QTM you always must use is the product risk matrix: this helps you the keep up with requirements, risks, deliverables and activities. In this matrix come all items together that influence and determine customer satisfaction. We have control over product and process, over quality, time and money.

Using quality tailor-made we offer **maximum customer satisfaction**.

6. References

[1] KoM, Boeters, Andre, Noorman, Bert, "Kwaliteit op Maat", Kluwers Bedrijfswetenschappen, Deventer, ISBN 90-267-2579-5, 1997.

[2] Dekkers, Ton, "Quality Tailor-Made", in ESCOM/SCOOPE conference proceedings, Munich, April 2000.

[3] Dekkers, Ton, "Quality Tailor-Made", in Quality Week Europe conference proceedings, Brussels, November 2000.

[4] ISO/IEC 9126, Information Technology - Software product quality, characteristics and metrics, International Organization of Standardization, 1997-1998

[5] Quint II, Zeist, B. van, Hendriks, P., Paulussen, R., Trienekens, J., "Kwaliteit van softwareproducten", Kluwers Bedrijfswetenschappen, Deventer, ISBN 90-267-2430-6.

[6] Tmap®, Pol, Martin, Veenendaal, Erik van, "Structured Testing of Information Systems", Kluwer, ISBN 90-267-2910-3, 1998.

[7] IFPUG (International Function Point User Group), "Function Point Counting Practices", IFPUG

[8] Dekkers, Ton, "Van functiepuntanlyse naar integrale functiepuntanalyse", IQUIP, 1994

Modelling Software Quality Through Organisational Position and Software Role: A Pilot Study

Maria Sverstiuk, June Verner

Abstract

Over the last 30 years, many software quality models have been defined. Because there has been little empirical validation of these models, we are left with a number of unanswered questions. How do managers, developers, and users really perceive software quality? Is there an overarching view of quality that colours their view of software quality attributes? Does their role with a particular software product make a difference to their view of software quality? Does their major job function also colour their attitude? In short, we want to better understand what is meant by the term "software quality" and to analyse perceptions of what constitutes software quality from the perspective of different groups of professionals involved with both software development and software use. In order to investigate these aspects of quality we conducted a survey of 300 professionals asking them to rank the importance of 17 software quality attributes.

The results of our study show different patterns for our respondent groupings. Although our respondents may discuss the same quality attributes, they appear to have different views of the importance of these attributes. While some of the software quality attributes appear to be important to all professionals regardless of their job function or software role, there are differences in software quality priorities for different professional and user groupings. Analysis of our results shows that the overarching view of software quality taken by most of our respondents is a "user view".

1. Introduction

Quality is defined as "a distinctive inherent feature"; as "a degree of excellence"; as well as "a degree of conformance to a standard (as of a product or workmanship)" [17]. Being "a degree" of something implies the relative nature of the concept. The multifaceted nature of "quality" is behind a number of unresolved issues that directly impact the quality of software products. A review of the existing research shows that it is common to view software quality not as an absolute measure, but in terms of trade-offs [5]. Ideally, we would like every software system to possess the highest measure of quality for each software attribute. However, in reality, everybody involved with a software system, from developers to managers and users, has to compromise and focus on the quality factors most important to them. Because managers, technical personnel and customers differ in their views of what constitutes a quality product the differences in their perceptions and the impact of these perceptions on software product development require greater understanding. The relative nature of quality suggests that software quality needs be defined from many points of view, depending on the role the person plays in the development process and on the type of system being developed ([1], [4], [16]). Garvin, [5] noted differences in quality perceptions in a quality framework where he identified five main overarching views of quality: (1) transcendental, (2) product, (3) user, (4) manufacturing, and (5) value-based views.

The main objective of our research is to analyse perceptions of the constitution of software quality from different points of view. Our study is a step in the direction of achieving a more complete picture of software quality and a broader perspective of software quality using statistically validated results. A better understanding of software quality priorities will lead to better communication between the different parties involved with the system. Managers and developers should understand what aspects of software quality are important to them, and to users, so that they can ensure that developers of the system implement the most important features.

2. Related Research

A number of studies have analysed software quality factors and presented tradeoffs in matrix form (e.g., [8], [11], [13]). Glass [8], basing his work on Boehm et al's [2] quality model, analyzed the relationships between software quality product factors and provided a chart representing tradeoffs in achieving desired quality attributes. Glass [8] also prioritised software quality attributes within the software development lifecycle stages and provided a correlation matrix showing those quality attributes that reinforce each other, and those attributes that have no effect on the other quality attributes. McConnell [11] also looked at the relationships between Boehm et al's [2] software quality attributes and, based on experience, derived a quality factor correlation matrix. Shumskas [14] also presented a version of Boehm et al's [2] software quality attributes and included a matrix showing not only positive and negative attribute correlations, but also those quality relationships that are application dependent. Perry [13] (based on his intuition), summarized relationships between the quality factors in Boehm et al's [2] model as inverse, neutral, and direct. He notes that there are lifecycle aspects of software quality factors that we must consider, where the quality factor should be measured, and where the impact of poor quality is realised.

In a later section, we extend our discussion and compare our results with the earlier research.

2.1. Unanswered Questions

Because there has been so little empirical validation of the suggested software quality models [15] our literature review has left us with a number of unanswered questions. How do we think about software quality? What are different groups' mental models of software quality? Are there differences in the groups' overarching views of software quality? Do the software quality attributes correlate with each other as individual authors' experiences suggest? If the mental models of different groups of people truly are different, we need to know so that we can understand how best to communicate unambiguously. How can we possibly meet software quality requirements if we have little understanding of the mental models held by the people who manage, develop and use software?

Our pilot survey was conducted in order to gain insight into software users, software development practitioners' and IT managers' cognitive models of software quality. This will allow us to explore software quality in order to draw conclusions based on the experiences of a number of different groups of people.

In the next section we focus on the method of study and follow this with a discussion of our experimental results and our conclusions.

3. Research Method

We developed a survey that includes questions covering our respondent's overarching software quality views, job function, their relationship to a specific software product that they recently used, and a set of questions asking the respondent to rate the 17 software quality factors. We distributed the survey via email to the employees of the University of Pennsylvania Wharton School Computing Department, to the graduate and undergraduate students of the Drexel College of Information Science and Technology, and to recent graduates of the Wharton Executive MBA program. Such a distribution guaranteed us respondents with different technical backgrounds.

Our questionnaire was mainly based on the Boehm et al. [2] software quality model because, even today, it is still one of the most heavily cited quality models in the literature. We asked the respondents to rank, on a seven point likert scale, the importance of seventeen software quality attributes from the perspective of their job, with reference to a software system with which they are familiar. A score of one is given to an attribute that has no relevance to the respondent, and a score of seven to an attribute with great importance. Definitions of each quality attribute, based on those given in the original Boehm et al model [2], were included in our questionnaire. Though we did not make any changes to the original definitions, we do wonder if some definitions should be updated due to the changes in technology since the mid-seventies. In a separate question, we asked respondents to identify their role in relation to the software they are assessing, that is, manager, user, or developer. We also presented respondents with the list of Garvin's [5] definitions of quality and asked them to identify which view most closely coincides with their own view of "software" quality.

4. Results

The survey return rate was 56%, with 305 responses. Our respondents had backgrounds that varied from corporate and technical management, and software development, to casual users of software. The respondents were employed in a number of different industries: manufacturing (9%), banking (10%), education (25%) and computer-related areas (37%). Table 1 shows the distribution of our respondent's software roles. We were interested in three "software roles" with respect to the evaluated software: manager, user, and developer. Though 22% of our respondents occupy managerial positions (see Table 2), in fact, only 10% had managerial responsibilities for the software they evaluated. Seventy-seven percent of respondents identified themselves as users of the software they were assessing; 6% of the respondents were developers of the software. This gave us a group of respondents whose roles spanned all main categories: manager, developer and user and allowed us to compare their perceptions.

Table 1. Respondents' roles with respect to the evaluated software

	Frequency	Percent
Manager	29	10
User	234	77
Developer	17	6
Total	280	92

We identified four "job functions": 1. corporate/technical manager, 2. data administrator/application developer, 3. IS/MIS/DP/IT staff, and 4. other non-technical personnel. Table 2. shows the distribution of the respondents' job functions. A particular job function might not always coincide with the respondent's responsibility concerning the software system that the respondent focussed on, in the questionnaire responses.

Table 2. Respondents' job function

Job Function	Frequency	Percent
Corporate / Technical Manager	67	22
Data Administrator / application developer	19	6
IS/MIS/DP/IT Staff	72	24
Other non-technical	147	48
Total	305	100

Table 3. shows the distribution of "software role" within each "job function". As mentioned earlier though 22% of our respondents occupy managerial positions, only 10% had managerial responsibilities for the software they evaluated. The majority of respondents identified themselves as users of the software that they assessed. Twenty four percent of our respondents were both managers by function and by their software role; 15% of the IS staff were managers of the software they assessed and 4% of them participated in the development of this software.

Table 3. Distribution of the user roles by job function

Job Function \ User Role	Manager	User	Developer
Corporate / Technical Manager	24%	70%	6%
Data administrator / application developer		74	26%
IS/MIS/DP/IT Staff	15%	81%	4%
Other	2%	94%	4%

As the main goal of this study is to explore the differences in the software quality attribute priorities within our different professional groups we divided our sample into groups in three different ways:

- by the respondent's role with regard to the evaluated software (either developer, user, and manager, see Table 1; and
- by job function (i.e., corporate/technical managers, data administrator/application developer, IS/MIS/DP/IT staff and non-technical (other), see Table 2; and,
- by Garvin's [5] overarching quality view (transcendental, product, user, manufacturing and value).

With these groupings, we can identify how the ratings of software quality attributes changes with differences in roles and job function.

Figure 1 shows means for all 17-quality attribute rankings for the three software role groups. For this data set, there are three significant differences (< 0.5) in responses from the groups. These are shown with a '**' on the X-axis of Figure 1. This figure shows that there are many similarities in the groups' perceptions: for example, correctness and accuracy were consistently ranked as most important across all three role groups. Robustness was next most important for managers, and developers, while usability came next for users. Respondent perceptions of adaptability and accessibility were also very similar across software roles. However, portability though scored as important by developers and users was seen as less important by managers. On the other hand, for developers communicativeness was much less important than for managers and users. Differences were also observed for testability and interoperability; these attributes were more important for managers and developers than for users.

The attributes ranked highest by users include usability, adaptability reusability and accuracy. Developers ranked accessibility, efficiency, interoperability, maintainability, and testability higher than the other groups while managers ranked all the other attributes highest.

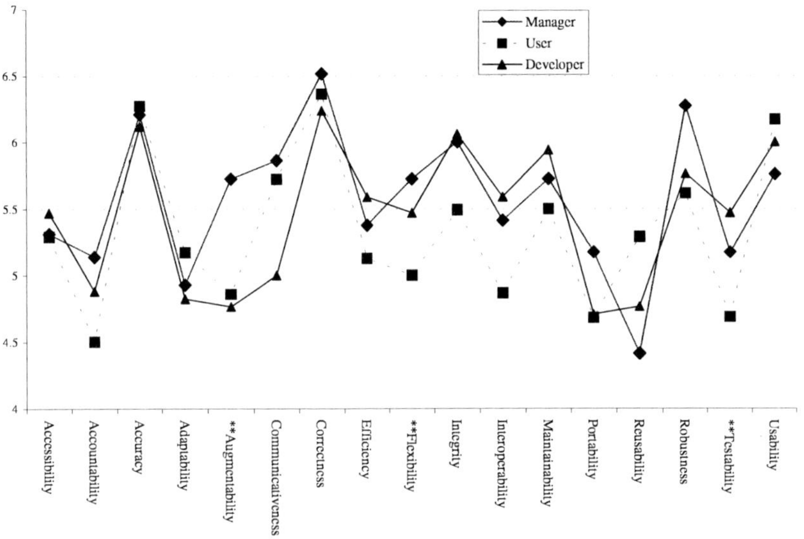

Figure 1. Quality Attribute Means by Software Role

Figure 2, displays overall similarities and differences in perceptions of the software quality attributes, by job function, and shows that actual job function makes quite a difference in the ratings when compared with our earlier software role. Corporate/technical managers exhibit the most noticeably different quality preferences when compared with other professional groups. As Figure 2 shows they rated almost all the quality attributes lower in importance than the other groups except for accuracy, communicativeness, correctness, and robustness; both of which were rated similarly to the other groups. There are many more significant differences in responses for these job function groups (12 out of 17). Again significant differences < 0.05 shown with '**'. As Figure 2 shows, respondents whose job function has to do with software in either an IS/MIS/DP/IS staff role or as data administrator/application developers, rate quality attributes higher than the other two respondent groups. The mean ratings here are quite a different from the mean ratings shown Figure 1. Figures 1 and 2 together show that both the software role taken by the respondent with regard to software, and the respondent's job function impact differently on quality attribute percepetions. However, for a comprehensive study of how the overlaps between job function and software role affect attitude differences more data would be required.

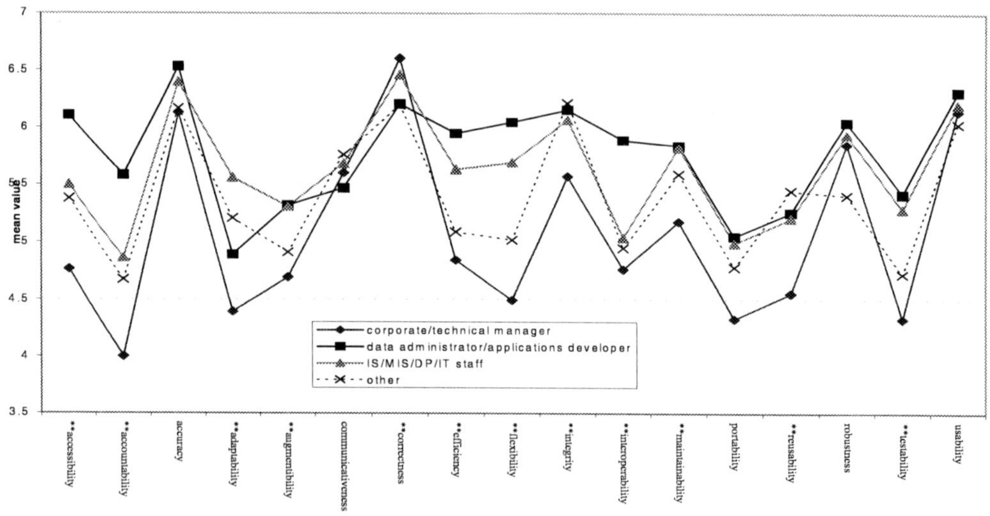

Figure 2. Quality Attribute Means by Job Function

When we consider the overarching view of software quality taken by our respondents we note that 36% of our respondents were not comfortable taking a single view of quality; 29% preferred to combine two views of quality, 5% three views and 2% four or five views. Figure 3 shows our results for quality view by software role and job function.

The majority of our respondents, 58%, have a **user view** of software quality, i.e., that it is a measure of how well software product characteristics meet the users' needs. Eighty one percent of corporate/technical managers, 100% of data administrator/application developers, 81% of IS/MIS/DP/IS staff and 84% of "other" take this view of quality. When categorized by software role, 69% of managers, 86% of users and 82% of developers take a user view of software quality.

The **trancendental view** that software quality can be recognised but not defined, taken by only 4% overall of our respondents is made up of 4% of the corporate/technical managers, 8% of the IS/MIS/DP/IT staff, and 7% of "other". When categorized by software role, a transcedental view is taken by 8% of managers, 6% of users, and 6% of developers.

The **product view**, that software quality is a context-independent measure of software product internal and external properties, is taken by 16% corporate/technical managers, 11% of data administrator/application developers, 18% IS/MIS/DP/IS staff and developers take a product view of software quality 18% "other". When categorized by software role 38% managers, 14% users and 18% developers take a product view.

The **manufacturing view**, that software quality is a measure of how cost efficient the product development process was, is taken by 10% of our respondents. A manufacturing view is taken by 8% of the corporate/technical managers, 21% of the data administrator/application developers, 16% of the IS/MIS/DP/IS staff and 16% of "other". When categorized by software role 14% managers, 14% of users and 24% developers take a manufacturing view of software quality.

The **value view**, that software quality is a trade off between the cost of software development and how much a customer values certain software features, is taken by 16% of our respondents. A value view of software quality is taken by 27% of the corporate/technical managers, 16% of the IS/MIS/DP/IS staff, 14% of the data administrator/application developers, and 28% of "other". When categorized by software role 24% of managers, 23% of users and 29% of developers take a value view of software quality.

These results show that a user view of quality i.e., how well the software product meets users needs is the most prevalent view taken of software quality (58%). The other views of quality are less common; the user view is followed by the value view at only 16%, the product view at 12%, the manufacturing view at 10%, and the transcendental view at 4%.

When we consider software roles 69% of managers, 86% of users and 82% of developers take a user view of quality. The next most common view taken by this categorization of respodents viewa are: managers-product view 38%, users-value view 23%, and developers-value view 29%.

When we consider job function 81% of corporate/technical managers, 100% of data administrator/application developers, 81% of IS/MIS/DP/IS staff and 84% of "other" take the user view of quality. The value view is next most popular, with 27% corporate/technical managers, and 28% of "other" choosing this view The IS/MIS/DP/IS staff are alittle different with 18% taking a product view. Figure 3 below shows both job function and software roles by overarching software quality views. This figure shows very clearly that the user view is the main software quality view.

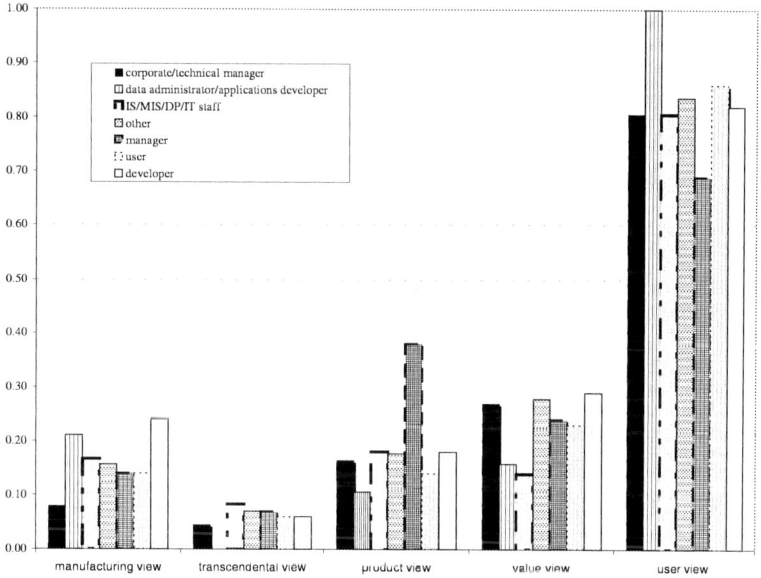

Figure 3. Quality View by Software Role and Job Function

We next compare the 17 software quality attributes within the five overarching quality views see Figure 4, below.

We find that respondents who take a transcendental view of software quality, i.e., that "software quality can be recognised but not defined" rate almost all the quality attributes lower than do respondents who take other views. This groups' perception of software quality will most likely make it difficult for software developers to deal with them. If this group cannot define quality, have to see the product first to know if quality is there, and rate the majority of quality attributes lower than other groups, software development becomes problematic. This is an interesting result but needs further research with additional data. In contrast respondents who take a manufacturing point of view tend to rate the quality attributes highest of all. Not only do they want to measure how cost efficient the development process is, they also want a high level of quality for their money. We may assume that these respondents are interested in development efficiency/quality tradeoffs. The value and user views give very similar ratings for the software quality attributes.

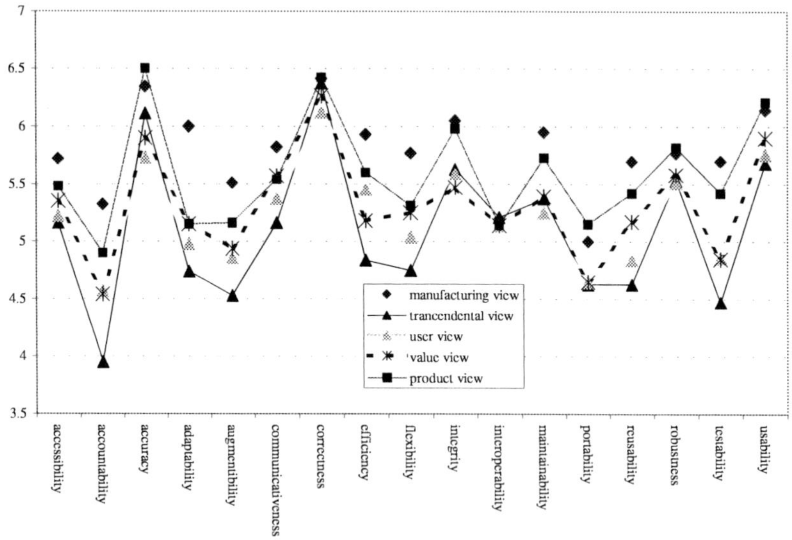

Figure 4. Software Quality Attributes by Overarching Quality View

While the main purpose of our study is to explore our respondents' prioritisation of software quality attributes, we also compare the results of our derived software quality attribute relationships with the results of earlier studies. We show a matrix, similar to that of the earlier research, see Table 4. A "**" in our matrix symbolises correlations at the 0.01 level (two tailed). The authors of the prior research do not completely agree with each other on all interrelationships between software quality attributes ([7], [8], [11], [13], [14]). For instance, Perry [13] disagrees with Gillies [7] on the correlation between Portability and Testability; our results are consistent with Perry [13] as we found a positive correlation between *portability* and *testability*. Though overall, our results are mostly agree with Perry's [13] findings there is one noticeable difference. When we analyse the relationship of *efficiency* with the other attributes, our results did not match any of the earlier work. Although all authors report that efficiency has a negative effect on all other quality factors our results did not support this as efficiency was positively correlated with all software quality attributes. In fact, we did not get any negative correlations at all.

	Efficiency	Reliability	Testability	Portability
Correctness	0.105	0.169**	0.089	-0.018
Efficiency	1	0.185**	0.422**	0.05
Integrity	0.355**	0.173**	0.322**	0.132**
Usability	0.9	0.087	0.148**	0.211**
Maintainability	0.307**	0.156**	0.572**	0.337**
Testability	0.422**	0.232**	1	0.406**
Flexibility	0.421**	0.106	0.563**	0.402**
Portability	0.05	0.073	0.406**	1
Reusability	0.253**	0.163**	0.308**	0.409**
Interoperability	0.27**	0.155**	0.35**	0.371**
Adaptability	0.383**	0.05	0.458**	0.351**
Accuracy	0.189**	0.431**	0.247**	0.073
Reliability	0.185**	1	0.232**	0.073
Accessibility	0.382**	0.361**	0.394**	0.194**
Accountability	0.439**	0.227**	0.436**	0.225**
Augmentability	0.304**	0.374**	0.513**	0.366**
Communicativeness	0.149**	0.285**	0.291**	0.217**

Table 4. Software quality attributes correlations

4. Conclusions

No matter how we categorise our respondents by job function, software role, or by overarching quality view, accuracy and correctness are the software quality factors rated as most important. Usability follows for most groups although our software role group "managers" rates communicability as more important than usability. If we consider our results in more detail, we find that when we compare our respondents by (1) job function with (2) software role, we see a number of differences in our results. When job function is the grouping variable, we see many more significant differences in quality attribute rankings. This indicates that what the role of the respondent is, in the organisation, makes a greater difference to the importance placed on software quality attributes, than does their own personal interactions with software (software role).

The overarching view of quality taken by most professionals, no matter what their job function is that of "user view" i.e., concern with how well software product characteristics meet the users' needs. Respondents who take a transcendental view of quality, and rate the majority of software quality attributes lower than the other "view" groups, will probably make it difficult for software developers to provide them with (what in their view is) a quality product. This group cannot define quality, and have to see the product first to know if quality is there. This makes it problematic for our data administration/software development group given that not a single respondent in that group viewed software quality as transcendental. This is an interesting result but needs further research with additional data.

When we consider quality attribute tradeoffs we find that our results agree with those of Perry [13] except for the direction of the efficiency relationships. Given that this is a pilot study this result needs further investigation with both more data and with a different set of questions. How much the respondents'view of quality is impacted by rapid changes in technology and how the definitions of quality factors in the older models might need to be changed should be further investigated

Our study has perhaps shed some light on attitudes to software quality but there is much more work that needs to be done. To discover more about software quality we need to investigate the structure of software quality attributes within Garvin's overarching quality framework. This will allow us to find out, for the various groups involved with software and its development, what differences an overarching quality view makes to their cognitive mappings of the software quality attributes.

References

[1] Arthur, L. J. Measuring Programmer Quality, John Wiley and Sons New York 1985

[2] Boehm, B.W., Brown, J.R., and Lipow, M. (Eds.), (1976), "Quantitative Evaluation of Software Quality", Proceedings of the Second International Conference of Software Engineering, pp. 592-605.

[3] Cerpa N. and Verner J.M., "Practitioners' Views of Software Quality", The International Journal of Computing and Engineering Management, Vol. 4, No. 3, September-December 1996, pp. 1-15.

[4] Deutsch, M. S and Willis, R. R. Software Quality Engineering Prentice-Hall Englewood Cliffs NJ (1988).

[5] Garvin, D. "What Does "Product Quality" Really Mean?" Sloan Management Review, Fall 1984, pp25-45.

[6] Gentleman, W.M., "If software quality is a perception, how do we measure it?", The Quality of Numerical Software: Assessment and Enhancement, Ronald Boisvert, ed., Proceedings of IFIP WG2.5 Working Conference 7, Oxford, UK, 7-12 July 1996, Chapman & Hall, London, p.32.

[7] Gillies, A. Software Quality Theory and Management, 2nd Ed., London: International Thomson Computer Press, 1997.

[8] Glass, R.L. "Building Quality Software", Prentice Hall, 1992

[9] Kitchenham B., Pfleeger S.L., "Software Quality: The Elusive Target"., IEEE Software, January 1996, pp.12-21.

[10] Kusters, R.J.; van Solingen, R.; Trienekens, J.J.M., "User-perceptions of embedded software quality", Eighth IEEE International Workshop on Software Technology and Engineering Practice incorporating Computer Aided Software Engineering, p.184-97, 1997

[11] McConnell, Steve. Code Complete: A Practical Handbook of Software Construction. Redmond, WA: Microsoft Press, 1993.

[12] Nance, K.L., Strohmaier, M., " End user perception and software quality assessment", Journal of International Information Management vol.6, no.1, p.1-8, 1997.

[13] Perry W.E. "Quality Assurance for Information Systems: Methods, Tools and Techniques", QED Technical Publishing Group, 1991.

[14] Shumskas, A. F. "Software Risk Mitigation" in Schulmeyer, G. Gordon and James I. McManus, ed. Total Quality Management for Software. 1992: NY, Van Nostrand Reinhold. pp. 190-220.

[15] Verner, J.M., Moores, T.T. and Barrett, R., "Software Quality: Perceptions and Practices in Hong Kong", in Achieving Quality in Software (eds) S. Bologna and G. Bucci Chapman and Hall 1996, pp. 77-88.

[16] Wallmuller, E., Software Quality Assurance: A Practical Approach, Prentice-Hall Englewood Cliffs NJ 1994.

[17] Webster's Third New International Dictionary, Unabridged, Copyright 1993 Merriam-Webster, Incorporated.

[18] Wilson, D. N. and Hall, Tracy, "Perceptions of Software Quality: A Pilot Study". Software Quality Journal, 7 pp. 67-75, 1998

Adapting Software Development Process for Customer Requirements and Personnel Capability

Makoto Nonaka, Kyota Kanno, Soichi Matsushita, Motoei Azuma

Abstract

Producing a software product with sufficient quality within estimated cost is an important issue for software projects. It is necessary that a process be designed and adapted for the project, as customer requirements and other constraints are specific to each project. Based on the measured capability of human resource, development efforts must be estimated accurately, for each defined process.

We set our research goal on a software process design and adaptation support system. This paper describes a conceptual model for software process design support in a formal manner. As it requires measurement of process and product data for process design and adaptation support, its support system must be implemented. This paper also describes an experiment for measuring personal capability using product and process metrics, and architecture of the support system.

1. Introduction

In order to produce a software product with sufficient quality within estimated cost, a well-defined software process must be applied. When a process that uses rigorous methods is applied, a high-quality software product is expected. However, more activities that use rigorous methods are applied to the process, the more development efforts are needed. If a software team develops a product with excessive quality that the customer did not require, with over schedule and budget, it must become a failure project. Therefore, a process must be designed to meet customer requirements, schedule, and other constraints.

Once a process is designed, it must be adapted to changes in customer requirements and constraints during a project. As customer requirements may change frequently while the software project, a process must be adaptable for their changes. By measuring process data and tracking a project, we can find which activity to be adapted and how to do it. In order to measure and analyze process data, a measurement support system must be implemented.

It is important for successful project management to estimate development effort accurately. In order to estimate development effort based on the designed process, primary factors that have a large influence on development effort must be identified. As COCOMO II [1] states that personnel of high capability contribute to effort 1.85 times as much as one of poor capability. We regard personnel capability as a major factor of development effort. By measuring personnel capability, development effort can be estimated with high accuracy.

There are well-known technologies such as ISO/IEC 9126 series [2][3] as software product quality model and metrics, CMM (Capability Maturity Model) [4] as a process improvement and assessment model, PSP (Personal Software Process) [5] and TSP (Team Software Process) [6] as process measurement and analysis models, and COCOMO II [1] for effort estimation model. Though these technologies are effective for their specific purposes and scopes, we tried to unify and apply these technologies for improving process design and adaptation support.

Our major goal is to support software process design and adaptation with measured resource capability. In clause 3, a conceptual model for process design and effort estimation with measured resource is described. As a trial for measuring personnel capability, an experiment is described in clause 4. In order to measure process data during a project, the architecture of support system and its prototype is described in clause 5.

2. Approach

As process design and adaptation support is a major issue for our research, the mechanism for process design and adaptation must be clarified. In order to apply it to practical software project, resource measurement and its support system are important. In the following sections, we describe our approaches for process design, resource measurement and estimation, and a support system.

2.1. Process design

When considering process design for customer requirements, it is important to define quality requirements precisely. We regard quality requirements as a major factor for process design. For instance, if a customer regards changeability and adaptability as important characteristics for the software product, developers have to introduce activities for customisation into high-level design phase and another activities for modulation into detailed level design phase. On the other hand, if customer requires another functional requirements without any change in quality requirements, additional efforts must be required but the same process can be applied. This is the reason why we regard quality requirements as a major factor for process adaptation.

We apply the QFD (Quality Function Deployment) [6] concept to process design for quality requirements. The original QFD method converts customer demands into product characteristics and features. In our approach, customer quality requirements are converted into process activities. Quality requirements are specified based on ISO/IEC 9126 [2] software product quality model. After all of quality requirements are specified, required activities are derived from quality-activity relationship table. In clause 3, we represent the concept of process design method in a formal manner.

2.2. Resource measurement and estimation

In order to estimate development effort with accuracy, personnel capability must be measured. In COCOMO II [1], programmer capability and other cost drivers are evaluated and rated in the subjective method. Though it is useful to estimate development effort at initial stage of a project, personnel capability can be evaluated by measuring personal process and product data. Using the PSP method, a developer's process data is recorded and his process and product metrics such as productivity, defect density, and appraisal/failure rate, are measured. These metrics can be applied to measuring personnel capability.

We regard developers' knowledge amount as one important aspect of personnel capability. However, there is no way to measure it directly. In substitution for measuring it, we measure product and process metrics with PSP forms. These metrics imply developer's knowledge amount to be compensated for the project. With these data, personnel capability can be measured and development efforts can be estimated more accurately. In clause 4, we discuss the method for measuring with these metrics and an experiment result.

2.3. Support system

In order to measure such process and product data through a project, a support system must be implemented to measure data and to support process design and adaptation. It is also important for developers to integrate development tools into the support system and to measure process data semi-automatically. As development tools may be used in distributed environments, the support system must provide the method to communicate with each tool. In order to separate development tools from the support system, we designed flexible architecture of the system and implemented its prototype. These are described in clause 5.

3. Conceptual model for process design

In this clause, we describe a conceptual model for process design and adaptation in a formal manner. First, quality requirements model is described with ISO/IEC 9126 quality model. Then some constraints are described with the model. Finally, the concept of process design and adaptation method is described.

3.1. Quality requirements

In order to adapt a software process to customer requirements, they must be precisely described. ISO/IEC 9126 quality model is suitable for this purpose, because it is defined mainly from a customer's viewpoint. ISO/IEC 9126 defines six quality characteristics such as functionality, reliability, usability, efficiency, maintainability and portability. These characteristics are divided into sub characteristics. We use ISO/IEC 9126 quality characteristics categorization as quality requirements for defining quality requirement items.

Quality requirements can be defined as a set of quality requirement items. It is described as follows.

$$QR = \{ q_i \mid 1 \leq i \leq N \} \quad (1)$$

where
QR is customer quality requirements,
q_i is a quality requirement item,
N is number of quality requirement items.

Each q_i is classified by ISO/IEC 9126 quality sub characteristics. According to the weight for its importance, customer gives weight for each q_i. We represent a weighted value for q_i as qw_i.

3.2. Constraints

After a process is designed, quality of a software product with the process can be estimated with historical data. When designing a process, a final software product quality must satisfy the customer quality requirements criteria. In a formal manner, the following formula must be satisfied.

$$QR \leq \hat{Q} \quad (2)$$

where
$\hat{Q}$ is estimated quality of a final software product with historical data.

$\hat{Q}$ is also represented in the same form as formula (1). In general, the more activities and more methods that are rigorous are introduced into a process, the more efforts must be spent on the project. Available efforts are limited by the customer required delivery date. In addition to the previous constraint, a process must be designed to meet effort limitation. The following formula must be satisfied.

$$E \geq \hat{E} \quad (3)$$

where
E is an available effort, and
$\hat{E}$ is an estimated effort that is derived from a defined process and other factors.

3.3. Activity and script

A process can be modelled as a subset of pre-defined activities that is available for projects. An activity is a phase or a step such as planning, design, or coding, as defined in ISO/IEC 12207 [9]. The relationship between a process and activities are modelled as follows.

$$P \subset A \qquad (4)$$
$$A = \{ a_j \mid 1 \leq j \leq M \}$$

where
a_j is an activity,
A is a set of activities that is defined in advance, and
P is a process, which is a subset of activities.

When a developer enacts an activity, a script is used in order to guide the developer. Each activity has multiple scripts to achieve it, according to scripts rigorousness. We use the symbol $S_{j(k)}$ as a script with rigorousness k for an activity a_j. A sample script for design phase from PSP is shown in table 1. This is a relatively rigorous script as many design templates are to be used.

Table 1. a sample script for design phase from PSP

Phase	Scripts
Design	- Review the requirements and product an external specification to meet them. - Complete Function Specification and Operational Scenario Templates to record this specification. - Produce a design to meet this specification. - Record the design in Functional Specification, Operational Scenario, State Specification, and Logic Specification Templates as required. - Record in the Defect Recording Log any requirements defects found. - Record time in Time Recording Log.

3.4. Quality-activity relationship table

In order to satisfy a quality requirements item q_i, some related activities must be done. For instance, if a customer sets priority on suitability for a software product, prototyping and design review activities must be done with importance. This relationship is arranged into quality-activity relationship table (Table 2). It is originally proposed by Sakurai [7]. In Table 2, quality requirements characteristics are listed on the left side, and phase and activities are listed on the top of the table. We use the relationship model as a main tool for process design support.

Before using this table, the relationship between quality requirement items and activities are defined and rated. A correlation between an activity and a quality requirement item is evaluated subjectively. We use a symbol r_{ij} that represents the correlation between a quality requirement item q_i and activity a_j. For example in Table 2, we can see that there is a strong correlation between suitability and prototyping, system design review, and detailed design review.

3.5. Script selection

At requirements definition phase, each quality requirement item q_i is weighed by setting a value to qw_i. In order to select a script $S_{j(k)}$ that is suitable for q_i, rigorousness k is determined with its relative importance against all of quality requirements. It is calculated with the quality-activity relationship table and the following equation

Table 2. Quality-activity relationship table

QUALITY REQUIREMENTS	PHASE	requirements definition			system design						high level design			detailed level design					
	quality sub characteristics \ activities	prototyping	terminology standardization	use of figure and table	structured design	test case design	protocol standardization	terminology standardization	user interfaces standardization	design review	structured design	test case design	data format standardization	structured design	component reuse	test case design	module simplification	module independency	design review
functionality	suitability	8	3	3	2			3		7	2	4		2					7
	accuracy		5	5	3			5		7	3			3		2			7
	interoperability						7			3			7						3
	compliance						8		8	2			5						2
	security									2									2
reli-ability	maturity					3				2					2				2
	fault tolerance									2									2
	recoverability																		
usa-bility	understandability	4							3	2		2							
	learnability								3	2		2							
	operability									2		2							
effici-ency	time behaviour					2				2									2
	resource behaviour					2				2									2
maintain-ability	analysability							3									3	2	
	changeability																2	3	
	stability																2	3	
	testability												4				4	4	
portability	adaptability						3												
	installability						3	3					3				2	2	
	conformance						3				4								
	replaceability												3					3	

$$k = \frac{m_j}{\sum_i qw_i} \times qw_i \times r_{ij} \qquad (5)$$

where

m_j is an adjustment constant.

By calculating required rigorousness for each activity a_j, a script candidate for the activity is determined. With this method, a process that meets quality requirements is designed by selecting suitable scripts.

3.6. Quality estimation

After a process is designed with the method described above, quality of a final software product can be estimated with historical process data. Estimated quality can be modelled as a function of a designed process as described in the following equation

$$\hat{Q} = f(P). \qquad (6)$$

The function for quality estimation can be modelled with statistical analysis based on historical data.

3.7. Development efforts estimation

Development efforts are estimated based on product size, a defined process, and measured personnel capability. There are two approaches to estimate efforts; statistical approach based on regression analysis, like COCOMO II, and constructive approach, such as work breakdown structure. As our method select a script for every activity, constructive approach is suitable. Effort can be estimated by totalling up estimated effort for each activity a_j.

Effort estimation is modelled in an abstract model as the following equations

$$\hat{E} = \sum \hat{T}_i$$
$$\hat{T}_i = f(Size, P, RC) \tag{7}$$

where

$\hat{T}_i$ is an estimated effort for an activity a_i,

Size is an estimated component size which is produced with related activities, and

RC is measured resource capability, especially for personnel.

Effort $\hat{T}_i$ for an activity a_i is estimated based on historical process data. With applying multivariate analysis, an estimation model may be derived.

3.8. Process Adaptation

We described a conceptual model for process design as mentioned above. With this method, a process is designed at launch phase of a project. However, as the project progresses, the designed process must be adapted to changes in customer requirements and project status. When quality requirements are changed after launching the project, the process can be adapted using quality-activity relationship table in Table 2. Degree of project progress is also a factor for process adaptation. Therefore, process data must be measured during the project.

The details of process adaptation are not described in this paper, and it is a future work of our research to define them.

4. Personnel capability measurement and estimation

As stated in formula (7), effort estimation based on measured personnel capability is required to design a process. When focusing personal work such as components development, studying time is not a small portion of overall development time. If the time can be estimated accurately, development efforts estimation accuracy must be improved.

As an experiment, we made a small experiment to see the correlation of studying time and developer's knowledge amount. Developers' knowledge amount is one of important aspects of personnel capability. As there is no way to measure it directly, substitution metrics must be applied. We measure number of compensated API (Application Programming Interface) that a developer used on a project for the first time and studying time for the API. Number of API metric is countable from products automatically. These metrics imply developer's knowledge amount to be compensated.

PSP offers a set of forms to record development process data. We made a slight extension on it in order to record the time for studying how to use the API. Table 3 is a sample process data using the form. A studying time field is added to the original PSP time recording log. When a developer studies the usage of an API, studying time and related component name are recorded on the form. With this form, studying time and work time are recorded separately.

Table 3. a sample time recording log

Date	Start	Stop	studying time	interruption time	work time	phase	component name
11/20	12:40	12:57	2	3	12	design	
	12:57	12:59	0	0	2	design review	
	12:59	13:05	0	0	6	code	DataSet
	13:05	14:55	22	20	68	code	LinkedList

In the experiment, we have two subjects develop five programs development tasks. Figure 1 is a scatter chart and regression lines for each subject. Each development task is represented with a point on Figure 1. From these data, studying time for each subject can be estimated with the regression line. Two equations for studying time estimation are derived (Table 4). Thought there is only a very small data set, we found that studying time and number of compensated API has a strong correlation for each subject.

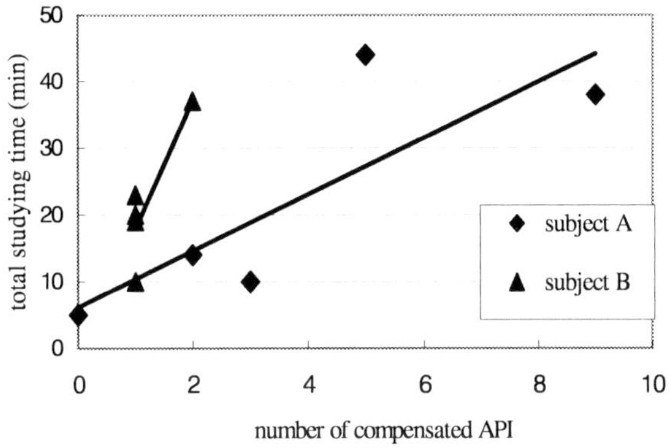

Figure 1. correlation of studying time and number of compensated API

Table 4. Studying time estimation models for each subject

Subject	Studying time estimation model	Correlation
A	Y = 4.2X + 6.1	0.82
B	Y = 19.0X – 1.0	0.85

With these results, we could also find the efficiency for knowledge acquisition. Subject B is about five times as effective as subject A for acquiring knowledge of studying the usage of an API. This implies that subject B is more capable than subject A. In fact, subject B has much experience than subject A. By analyzing other process metrics that was recorded during their development projects, the relationship between personnel capability and product and process metrics can be modelled.

Though there is only a very small data, we assume that studying time can be estimated using this method. If studying time is estimated, development efforts can be estimated more accurately.

5. Support System

Measurement and analysis support is essential to design and adapt a process to changes in customer requirements and project status. In order to measure developers' process and product data, we are developing a support system for measurement and analysis. As most developers do not want to record their process data for development activities by themselves, it is important to measure them semi-automatically by the support system.

Development tools and metrics are independent for organization; the support system must be adaptable to an operational environment. We define architecture that can measure process data semi-automatically and connect any tool into the support system. In the following section, an overview of the support system architecture is described.

5.1. Architecture and components

Figure 2 is architecture of the support systems. In order to make the system adaptable for an operational environment, we separate a common framework and components that is specific for the operational environment. We define a framework system called Process Enact Engine and four key components: Listener, Recorder, Measure, and Process Model. These components must be developed in order to meet the operational environment. As the templates for these components are provided as abstract classes, only specific lines of code are to be added to them.

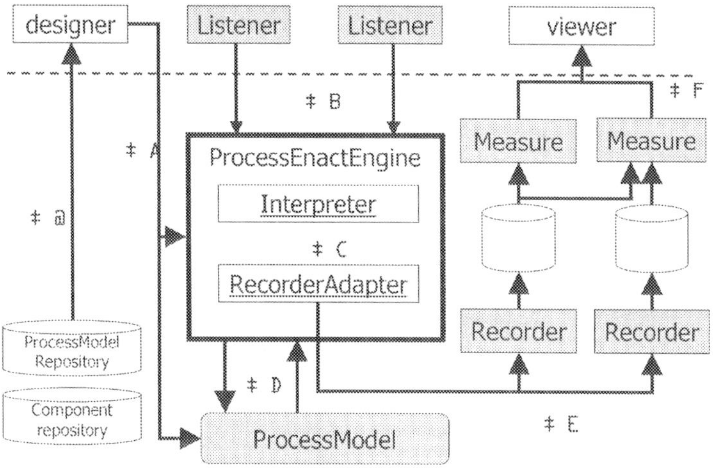

Figure 2. Architecture of process design and adaptation support system

Listener component acquires events from development tools and communicates to Process Enact Engine. It is developed for each development tool that is connected to the support system in order to support communication between tool and Process Enact Engine. With this component, application events that are generated from the tool such as user operation or checking in action to repository are hooked.

Recorder component converts the hooked events into meaningful data and stores it into database. In order to filter out the required data from raw data, the conversion rule must be defined and implemented within the component.

Measure component calculates a value with defined metrics from the data that is stored by Recorder components and generates its representation. Process Model component represents a structure and definition of process.

5.2. Prototype implementation

In order to validate design correctness and feasibility of the proposed architecture, we developed a prototype system. We use Java (JDK1.3) for a base model and user interfaces, and CORBA (Common Object Request Broker Architecture) for communication between each component. We developed over 40 classes. We verified feasibility of the architecture design by implementing it.

6. Conclusion and current status

We introduced a conceptual model for process design and described it in a formal manner. Though it is an abstract model, the mechanism for process design support is clarified. With measuring product and process data, we showed a method to measure a developer's knowledge amount and a result of an experiment. With this method, more accurate effort estimation is expected. Finally, we described architecture of the support system and implemented a prototype system. With the support system, process and product data are measured independent of development tools.

Now we are refining them and planning to apply them to a practical software development project. With this application, we will be able to refine these models by analyzing practical process and product data.

7. References

[1] COCOMO II Model Definition Manual Version 1.4, University of Southern California, 1997.

[2] ISO/IEC 9126 Information Technology - Quality characteristics and guidelines for their use, International Organization for Standardization, 1991.

[3] ISO/IEC DIS 9126-1 Software Engineering - Software product quality - Part 1: Quality model.

[4] Paulk, M.C., Weber C.V., Garcia S.M., Chrissis M.B. and Bush M., "The Capability Maturity Model: Guidelines for Improving the Software Process", Addison-Wesley, Reading M.A., 1993.

[5] Humphrey, W.S., "A Discipline for Software Engineering", Addison-Wesley, Reading M.A., 1995.

[6] Humphrey, W.S., "An Introduction to the Team Software Process", Addison-Wesley, Reading M.A., 1999.

[7] Akao, Y., "Quality Function Deployment", Productivity Press, 1990.

[8] Sakurai, M. and Murakami, "Theory and Practice for Software Price Decision", Chuo-keizaisya, 1998.

[9] ISO/IEC 12207 Information Technology - Software Life Cycle Process.

Factors in Software Quality for Advanced Computer Architectures

S. Khaddaj and G. Horgan

Abstract

A quality model links together and defines the various software metrics and measurement techniques that an organisation uses which when measured, the approach taken must be sufficiently general for hybrid hardware and software systems. In this work factors in software quality that should be taken into account when using parallel architectures will be considered. We start by identifying the metrics and measurement approaches that can be used. Many of the quality factors would be applied in similar way for serial and parallel machines, however a number of factors will be investigated which are relevant to the parallel class. A major example will be the lack of suitable performance metrics, which affect the cost/benefit factors. Portability and usability are other major problems that need to be taken into account when considering all the relevant factors that affect quality for the new environment.

1. Introduction

There are a number of requirements that need to be met by a quality model, in order for confidence to be gained that the model correctly captures quality requirements, and correctly reflects how well those requirements have been met. A quality model links together and defines the various software metrics and measurement techniques that an organisation uses which when measured, the approach taken must be sufficiently general for hybrid hardware and software systems.

In the last few decades there have been substantial improvements in computer performance, due not only to advances in hardware but also to innovations in computer architectures, that is, how the computer is designed and organised to carry out its computational tasks. A major development that has affected the computer performance is parallel architectures, wherein the processors are replicated and organised such that they can act in unison on one application. The general acceptance of this technology has been slow for a number of reasons, including the wide differences of the available parallel architectures, which mean that there is no unifying software/hardware environment. It is also widely accepted that software/hardware development can be ad hoc and evolutionary. As a result, engineering environments may start off with poor quality. As the software development evolves so quality should improve.

In this work factors in software quality that should be taken into account when using parallel architectures will be considered. We start by identifying the metrics and measurement approaches that can be used. A major example will be the lack of suitable performance metrics, which affect many quality factors such as the cost/benefit factor. Performance metrics for parallel algorithms are tied to the target parallel architecture, and there are as many of these as there are parallel architectures. Portability is another major problem; Changing computer architecture usually requires the rewriting of programs or readapting to a particular architecture and to a particular parallel software system. Usability is also important since it is harder and more time consuming to program and use parallel systems when compared with serial systems.

2. Quality modeling

Quality is a multidimensional construct reflected in a quality model, where each parameter in the model defines a quality dimension. It comprises implicit and/or explicit attributes. There are a number of views and opinions that need to be considered when defining and measuring quality. These views and opinions are referred to as Essential Views, and are determined by examining an individual's expected use of the product, their experiences in developing or using similar products. By concentrating on removing conflicts of opinion between the Essential Views, a consensus can be reached as to what properties constitute quality, and how quality should be measured.

The properties that constitute the 'explicit and / or implicit attributes' of quality form a set of Key Quality Factors and a set of Locally Defined Factors [1][2]. The Key Quality Factors (KQFs) represent global quality criteria, i.e. factors that are required of all products, and their list of properties is static. The Locally Defined Factors (LDFs) represent local quality criteria, i.e. additional factors identified by the Essential Views, and are appropriate only to the current product being developed. In this way, the KQFs represent a common set of criteria that can be used for cross-project comparisons, whilst the LDFs retain the ability to allow local tailoring. The LDFs are not a replacement for the KQFs. Instead, they define additional quality criteria. Their identification and inclusion is entirely the responsibility of the Essential Views. If the different views agree that additional criteria are required, then the additional criteria form the LDFs. In this work we only consider Key Quality Factors and for the rest of the paper they are referred to as simply Quality Factors.

2.1 Quality Factors

In total, eight Quality Factors are defined. These are Performance, Scalability, Cost/Benefit, Usability, Portability, Robustness, Correctness, and Reliability. Many quality factors would be applied in similar way for serial and parallel systems, as mentioned earlier we are mainly concerned with those specifics to parallel systems. Thus, many factors will not be included, such as Security, which is defined as the ability of a product to be defended against unauthorised use, Maintainability which is defined as the ability of a product to be modified, and Timeliness which is defined as the ability of a product to meet delivery deadlines. If a product is delivered late, then it may have good quality aspects, but customers may rightly consider it to be of lesser quality than products delivered on time [1].

Parallel processing offers the possibility of an increase in speed and memory beyond the technological limitations of single-processor systems. The performance of parallel systems can be varied and complex and users need to be able to understand and correct performance problems. Using parallel techniques it is possible to achieve higher throughput, efficiency, performance, and other advantages. Although parallel execution time, concurrency, scalability, and speed-up have been proposed in the literature as performance metrics, the use of speed-up dominate the literature. The notion of speed-up was initially used to estimate the performance benefit of a multiprocessor over a uniprocessor [3]. Later, speed-up has been proposed as a metric to estimate the performance of parallel and distributed algorithms [4] and parallel processor architectures [5]. The most common definition of speed-up is the ratio of the execution time of the best known serial algorithm to the execution time of the parallel algorithm on a given number of concurrent processors. The execution time corresponding to a parallel execution is the longest of the CPU times required by any of the concurrent processors.

A general, commonsense definition of performance is presented in [6] wherein he defines performance as an indication of how well a system, already assumed to be correct, works. In general, the performance metric for parallel systems must reflect the program, the machine, and the implementation strategies for it depends on each one of them. However, while the parallel execution time, speed-up, and efficiency serve as well known performance metrics, the key issue is the identification of the parallel processing overheads which sets a limit on the speed-up for a given architecture, problem size, and algorithm.

Every problem contains an upper bound on the number of processors, which can be meaningfully employed in its solution. Additional processors beyond this number will not improve solution time and can indeed be detrimental. This upper bound provides an idea as to how suitable a problem is for parallel implementation: a measure of its scalability. For scalability, we look for the ability to handle large numbers of processes and large or long-running programs on increasing number of processors.

Cost / Benefit is defined as the ability of a product to satisfy its cost/benefit specification. The Costs and Benefits involved in a product's creation, should be a major consideration [7][8]. If the costs are high, and the benefits of its development are low, then there is little point in developing the product.

Usability is defined as the ability of a product to be used for the purpose chosen. It is a factor that is also considered important in other models [9] [10]. If a product isn't usable, then there is little point in its existence. To be useful, a tool should have adequate documentation and support, and should have an intuitive easy-to-use interface. On-line help is also helpful for usability. Adequate functionality should be provided to accomplish the intended task without putting undue burden on the user to carry out low-level tasks.

Because of the short lifespan of high performance computing platforms and because many applications are developed and run in a distributed heterogeneous environment, most parallel programmers will work on a number of platforms simultaneously or over time. Programmers are understandably reluctant to learn a new performance tool every time they move to a new platform. Thus, we consider portability to be an important feature.

For robustness, we expected the product to crash infrequently and its features to work correctly. Research tools are not expected to be as robust as commercial tools, but if the tool has been released for public use, considerable effort should still have been invested in debugging it and on error handling.

Correctness is defined as the ability of a product to meet and support its functional objectives. Other models also include this factor [11]. If software doesn't meet its objectives, then it may be reliable and it may be delivered on time, but no one will use it. Reliability is defined as the ability of a product to reproduce its function over a period of time, and is also included in other approaches [12].

No other factors are included in the Quality Factors list. People tend to resist plans, which evaluate many quality factors, due to limited resources or tight schedules. Based on previous research, the number of key factors should be kept between three and eight [13]. The Quality Factors set were chosen for their obvious importance for the particular system. However, it is accepted that only empirical validation across a large number of projects can determine the completeness of this set.

2.2 Relationship Chart

The first step of the conflict removal mechanism is implemented by use of a Relationship Chart [9]. The chart displays graphically the relationships between quality criteria as a first stage towards measuring the criteria, and provides the basis for constraints on what can be achieved. In the Relationship Chart, each criterion is listed horizontally and vertically. Where one criterion crosses another, the relationship between those criteria is specified. The relationships for the Quality Factors are fixed. Figure 1 shows the Relationship Chart for the discussed earlier Quality Factors.

By considering these relationships, checks can be made as to the feasibility of requirements. For example, users may state that a reliable product is required, that is both scalable and portable. The relationships between Reliability and Portability, and Portability and Scalability are set to Neutral. Therefore, it is acceptable to state a requirement for a reliable product that is also portable. Similarly, the relationship between Portability and Usability is set to Direct so it is also acceptable to state that a product be portable and usable. As a result, it is an acceptable requirement for a product to be reliable, usable and portable. Note that the Relationship Chart is only a tool and it is still necessary to check the detail of what is being asked.

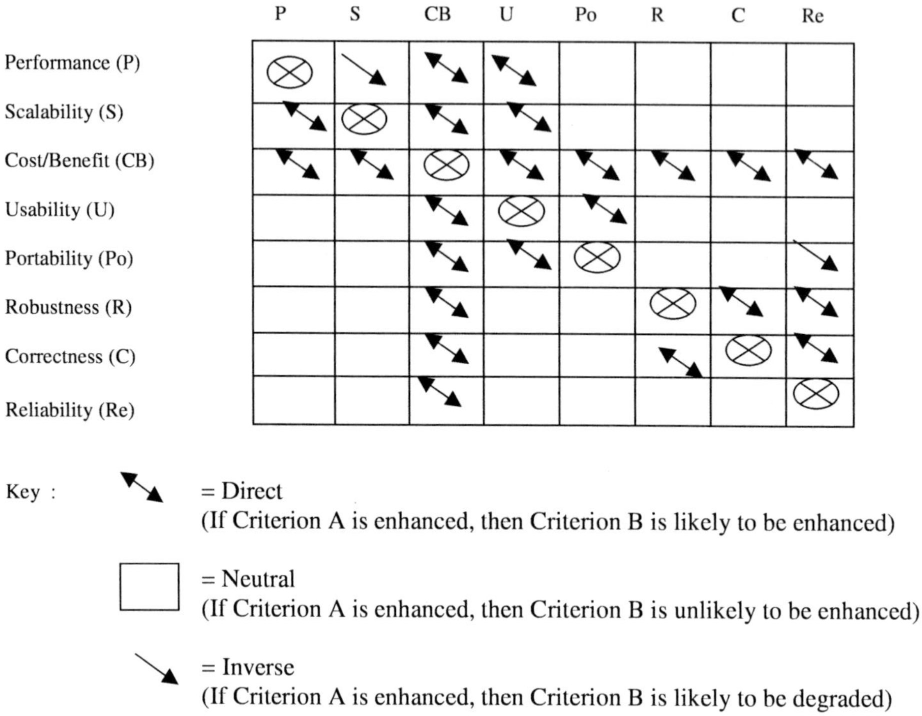

Figure 1 The Relationship Chart

2.3 Polarity Profile

The second step in producing a consensus view of quality, is to set the required goals for each criterion, based on the relationships identified in the Relationship Chart. In other approaches, a pie chart is used to represent quality goals [14]. There is a need to ensure that anyone can understand the graphical format chosen quickly and easily, particularly when it is considered that some essential views may belong to individuals with little technical background. There is also a need to illustrate over-engineered criteria (I.e., criteria that has exceeded its requirements), since further improvements in these areas will have little effect on the overall quality of the product. Such criteria cannot be shown easily using existing pie chart techniques.

The solution chosen, therefore, is to use a Polarity Profile [9]. For each criterion, a range of values exists. The Required Quality of a criterion is defined as a single value on a horizontal line. The Actual Quality achieved is also defined as a single value on the same line. The advantage of using a Polarity Profile is that its format can be easily understood by anyone. Further, it is easy to determine whether or not a criterion has been over-engineered, since its Actual Quality value will be further advanced along the line than its Required Quality value. Figure 2 shows an example Polarity Profile. As can be seen, both Scalability and Robustness have been over-engineered, since their Actual Quality values exceed their Required Quality values The criteria listed in the Polarity Profile are the same criteria as listed in the Relationship Chart.

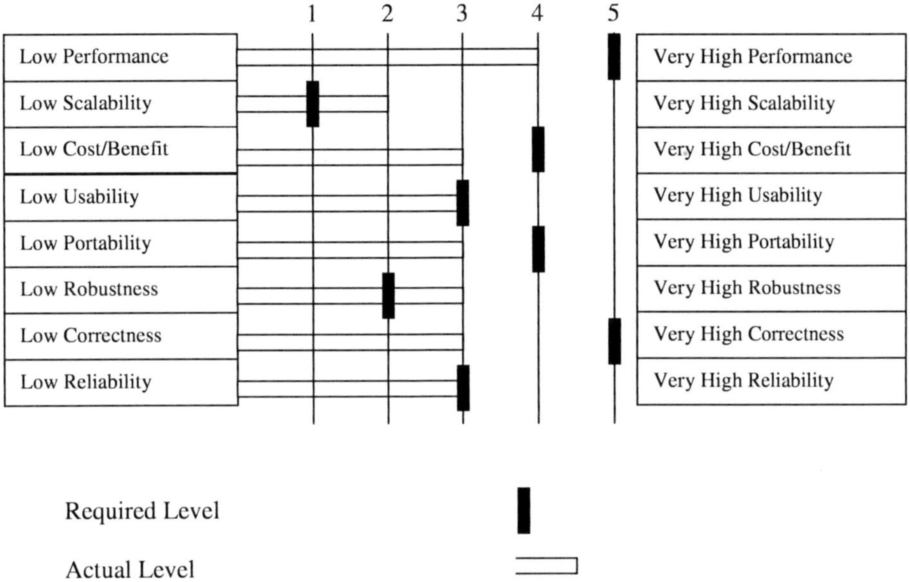

Figure 2 An example Polarity Profile

Each organisation will use different metrics and metric approaches to measure different quality attributes. These metrics may be similar, identical or entirely different to those used by other organisations. In order to identify the Required Quality for each criterion in the Polarity Profile, the expected properties of that criterion need to be expressed using metrics. The same metrics should be used to identify the Actual Quality for that criterion. There is a need, therefore, for Conversion Mechanisms, which convert the results of metrics used to measure the quality of a criterion. However, For each criterion, the Conversion Mechanism will probably be unique to each metric used. Since different organisations may use different metrics, no single Conversion Mechanism will be suitable in all cases. The Conversion Mechanisms used, therefore, should be agreed between the Essential Views.

3. Conclusions

In the approach presented in this paper individual quality views can be combined, view conflicts can be removed. It allows the specification of benchmarks against which achieved quality levels can be measured, and provides guidance for building quality into software for parallel systems. The feasibility of quality goals is controlled by the use of a Relationship Chart and a Polarity Profile. Since one cannot apply the constraint of having to define upfront the final requirements of a system [15], the approach is not static; if project personnel changes occur, or project requirements change, the Relationship Charts and Polarity Profiles can be updated to reflect these changes. Currently, a set of formal guidelines has yet to be finalised for identifying the Essential Views, despite their importance to the approach. For each occasion that the approach is used, time is required to identify the Essential Views and for those views to derive a consensus of opinions.

4. References

[1] G. Horgan, "Construction of a Quality Assurance and Measurement Framework for Software Project, PhD Thesis, 2000.

[2] G. Horgan, S. Khaddaj, P. Forte, "An Essential Views Model for Software Quality Assurance", ESCOM-SCOPE 99, pp. 387-396.

[3] David J. Kuck. The Structure of Computers and Computations, Vol. 1. John Wiley and Sons, New York, 1978.

[4] S. Ghosh and M-L. Yu. An Asynchronous Distributed Approach for the Simulation and Verification of Behavior- Level Models on Parallel Processors. IEEE Transactions on Parallel and Distributed Systems, 6(6):639-652, 1998.

[5] M. Manwaring, M. Chowdhury, and V. Malbasa. An architecture for parallel interpretation: performance measurements. In Proceedings of the 20th EUROMICRO Conference, pages 531-537, Liverpool, UK, 1994.

[6] D. Ferrari. Computer Systems Performance Evaluation. Prentice-Hall Inc., Englewood Clis, New Jersey, 1978.

[7] Elbert, C., "The Road to Maturity : Navigating Between Craft and Science", IEEE Software, November / December 1997, pp. 77-82.

[8] Turnball, P. D., "Effective Investment in Information Infrastructures", Information and Software Technology, April 1991, pp. 191-199

[9] Gillies, A. C., "Software Quality : Theory and Management", Chapman and Hall, 1992, pp. 1-33, 92-93.

[10] Dromey, R. G., "A Model for Software Product Quality", IEEE Transactions on Software Engineering, February 1995, pp. 146-162

[11] Fenton, N. Software Metrics : A Rigorous Approach. Chapman and Hall, 1991, pp. 42-62.

[12] Kitchenham, B., "Towards a constructive quality model.", Software Engineering Journal, July 1987, pp. 105-113.

[13] Miyoshi, T. and Azuma, M., "An Empirical Study of Evaluating Software Development Environment Quality", IEEE Transactions on Software Engineering, May 1993, pp. 425-435.

[14] Pfleeger, S. L., "Lessons Learned in Building a Corporate Metrics Program.", IEEE Software, May 1993, pp. 67-74.

[15] Butter, M., "Object Disorientation", Business Computer World, February 1998, pp. 107.

Data Analysis of Software Requirements Risk

Norman F. Schneidewind

Abstract

In order to continue to make progress in software measurement, as it pertains to reliability, we must shift the emphasis from design and code metrics to metrics that characterize the risk of making requirements changes. By doing so we can improve the quality of delivered software because defects related to problems in requirements specification will be identified early in the life cycle. We developed an approach for identifying requirements change risk factors as predictors of reliability problems. Our case example consists of twenty-four Space Shuttle change requests, nineteen risk factors, and the associated failures and software metrics. The approach can be generalized to other applications with numerical results that would vary according to application.

1. Introduction

While software design and code metrics have enjoyed some success as predictors of software quality attributes such as reliability [2, 3, 4, 5, 6, 7, 8], the measurement field is stuck at this level of achievement. If measurement is to advance to a higher level, we must shift our attention to the front-end of the development process, because it is during system conceptualization that errors in specifying requirements are inserted into the process and adversely affect our ability to maintain the software. A requirements change may induce ambiguity and uncertainty in the development process that cause errors in implementing the changes. Subsequently, these errors propagate through later phases of development and maintenance. These errors may result in significant risks associated with implementing the requirements. For example, reliability risk (i.e., risk of faults and failures induced by changes in requirements) may be incurred by deficiencies in the process (e.g., lack of precision in requirements). Although requirements may be specified correctly in terms of meeting user expectations, there could be significant risks associated with their implementation. For example, correctly implementing user requirements could lead to excessive system size and complexity with adverse effects on reliability or there could be a demand for project resources that exceeds the available funds, time, and personnel skills. Interestingly, there has been considerable discussion of project risk (e.g., the consequences of cost overrun and schedule slippage) in the literature [1] but not a corresponding attention to reliability risk.

Risk in the Webster's New Universal Unabridged Dictionary is defined as "the chance of injury; damage, or loss" [11]. Some authors have extended the dictionary definition as follows: "Risk Exposure=Probability of an Unsatisfactory Outcome*Loss if the Outcome is Unsatisfactory" [1]. Such a definition is frequently applied to the risks in managing software projects such as budget and schedule slippage. In contrast, our application of the dictionary definition pertains to the risk of executing the software of a system where there is the chance of injury (e.g., crew injury or fatality), damage (e.g., destruction of the vehicle), or loss (e.g., loss of the mission) if a serious software failure occurs during a mission. We use risk factors to indicate the degree of risk associated with such an occurrence.

In addition to the relationship between requirements and reliability there are the intermediate relationships between requirements and software metrics (e.g., size complexity) and between metrics and reliability. These relationships may interact to put the reliability of the software at risk because the requirements changes may result in increases in the size and complexity of the software that may adversely affect reliability. We studied these interactions for the Space Shuttle. For example, assume that the number of iterations of a requirements change -- the "mod level" -- is inversely related to reliability. That is, if many revisions of a requirement are necessary before it is approved, this is indicative of a requirement that is hard to understand and implement safely -- a risk that directly impacts reliability. At the same time, this complex requirement will affect the size and complexity of the code that will, in turn, have deleterious effects on reliability.

2. Objectives

Given the lack of emphasis in measurement research on the critical role of requirements, we were motivated to investigate the following issues:

- What is the relationship between requirements attributes and reliability?
- What is the relationship between requirements attributes and software attributes like complexity and size?
- Is it feasible to use requirements attributes as predictors of reliability?
- Which requirements attributes pose the greatest risk to reliability?

This paper is organized as follows: research approach, risk factors, results, and conclusions.

3. Research Approach

By retrospectively analyzing the relationship between requirements and reliability, we were able to identify those risk factors that are associated with reliability and to prioritize them based on the degree to which the relationship was statistically significant. In order to quantify the effect of a requirements change, we use various risk factors that are defined as the attribute of a requirement change that can induce adverse effects on reliability (e.g., failure incidence), maintainability (e.g., size and complexity of the code), and project management (e.g. personnel resources). Several examples of risk factors are shown in the section *Risk Factors*.

Table 1 shows the Change Request Hierarchy of the Space Shuttle, involving change requests (i.e., a requests for a new requirement or modification of an existing requirement), discrepancy reports (i.e., reports that document deviations between specified and observed software behavior), and failures. We analyzed categories 1 versus 2 with respect to risk factors as discriminants of the categories.

Table 1: Change Request Hierarchy

Change Requests (CRs)
1. No Discrepancy Reports (i.e., CRs with no DRs)
2. (Discrepancy Reports) or (Discrepancy Reports and Failures)
2.1 No failures (i.e., CRs with DRs only)
2.2 Failures (i.e., CRs with DRs and Failures)
2.2.1 Pre-release failures
2.2.2 Post-release failures

In previous research we had done a finer grained analysis using the categories (*CRs with no DRs*) vs. (*CRs with DRs only*) and (*CRs with no DRs*) vs. (*CRs with failures*) [9]. The categories (*CRs with DRs only*) and (*CRs with failures*) are subsets of 2 above. In this research we find that different and more accurate results can be obtained by combining the subsets into one set 2 because a larger sample size is obtained for 2.

3.1. Categorical Data Analysis

Using the null hypothesis, H_o: A risk factor is *not* a discriminator of reliability versus the alternate hypothesis H_1: A risk factor is a discriminator of reliability, we used categorical data analysis to test the hypothesis. A similar hypothesis was used to assess whether risk factors can serve as discriminators of metrics characteristics. We used the requirements, requirements risk factors, reliability, and metrics data we have from the Space Shuttle "3 engine out" software (abort sequence invoked when three engines are lost) to test our hypotheses. Samples of these data are shown below.

- Pre-release and post release failure data from the Space Shuttle from 1983 to the present. An example of post-release failure data is shown in Table 2.

Table 2

Failure Found On Operational Increment	Days from Release When Failure Occurred	Discrepancy Report #	Severity	Failure Date	Release Date	Module in Error
Q	75	1	2	05-19-97	03-05-97	10

- Risk factors for the Space Shuttle *Three Engine Out Auto Contingency* software. This software was released to NASA by the developer on 10/18/95. An example of a partial set of risk factor data is shown in Table 3.

Table 3

Change Request Number	SLOC Changed	Complexity Rating of Change	Criticality of Change	Number of Principal Functions Affected	Number of Modifications Of Change Request	Number of Requirements Issues	Number of Inspections Required	Manpower Required to Make Change
A	1933	4	3	27	7	238	12	209.3 MW

- Metrics data for 1400 Space Shuttle modules, each with 26 metrics. An example of a partial set of metric data is shown in Table 4.

Table 4

Module	Operator Count	Operand Count	Statement Count	Path Count	Cycle Count	Discrepancy Report Count	Change Request Count
10	3895	1957	606	998	4	14	16

Table 5: Definition of Samples

Sample	Size
Total CRs	24
CRs with no DRs	14
CRs with (DRs only) or (DRs and Failures)	10
CRs with modules that caused failures	6
CRs can have multiple DRs, failures, and modules that caused failures. CR: Change Request. DR: Discrepancy Report.	

Table 5 shows the definition of the Change Request samples that were used in the analysis. Sample sizes are small due to the high reliability of the Space Shuttle. However, sample size is one of the parameters accounted for in the statistical tests that produced significant results in certain cases (see *Results* section).

The Mann-Whitney test for difference in medians between categories was used in the analysis because no assumption need be made about statistical distribution; in addition, some risk factors are ordinal scale quantities (e.g., modification level). Furthermore, because some risk factors are ordinal scale quantities, rank correlation was used to check for risk factor dependencies.

4. Risk Factors

One of the software maintenance problems of the NASA Space Shuttle Flight Software organization is to evaluate the risk of implementing requirements changes. These changes can affect the reliability and maintainability of the software. To assess the risk of change, the software development contractor uses a number of risk factors. The risk factors were identified by agreement between NASA and the development contractor based on assumptions about the risk involved in making changes to the software. This formal process is called a risk assessment. No requirements change is approved by the change control board without an accompanying risk assessment. During risk assessment, the development contractor will attempt to answer such questions as: "Is this change highly complex relative to other software changes that have been made on the Space Shuttle?" If this were the case, a high-risk value would be assigned for the complexity criterion. To date this *qualitative* risk assessment has proven useful for identifying possible risky requirements changes or, conversely, providing assurance that there are no unacceptable risks in making a change. However, there has been no *quantitative* evaluation to determine whether, for example, high risk factor software was really less reliable than low risk factor software. In addition, there is no model for predicting the reliability of the software, if the change is implemented. Our research addressed both of these issues.

4.1. Space Shuttle Flight Software Requirements Change Risk Factors

The following are the definitions of four of the nineteen risk factors that are statistically significant with respect to predicting reliability. The details of the findings are shown in the *Results* section. In many instances, there was insufficient data to do the analysis. The names of the risk factors used in the analysis are given in quotation marks.

Complexity Factor

o Number of modifications or iterations on the proposed change; "mods".
  - How many times must the change be modified or presented to the Change Control Board before it is approved?

Size Factor

o Number of lines of code affected by the change; "sloc".
  - How many lines of code must be changed to implement the change request?

Requirements Issues Factor

o Number of possible conflicts among requirements (requirements issues); "issues".
  - Will this change conflict with other requirements changes (e.g., lead to conflicting operational scenarios)

Performance Factor

o Amount of memory space in full words required to implement the change; "space".
  - Will the change use memory to the extent that other functions will not have sufficient memory to operate effectively?

5. Results

This section contains the results of performing the following statistical analyses shown in Tables 6. 7, and 8, respectively. Only those risk factors where there was sufficient data and the results were statistically significant are shown.

a. Categorical data analysis on the relationship between *CRs with no DRs* vs. *((DRs only) or (DRs and Failures))*, using the Mann Whiney Test.

b. Dependency check on risk factors, using rank correlation coefficients; and

c. Identification of modules that caused failures as a result of the CR, and their metric values.

5.1. Categorical Data Analysis

Of the original nineteen risk factors, only four survived as being statistically significant (alpha $\leq .05$); seven were not significant; and eight had insufficient data to make the analysis. As Table 6 shows, there are statistically significant results for *CRs with no DRs* vs. *((DRs only) or (DRs and Failures))* for the risk factors "mods", "sloc", "issues", and "space". We use the value of alpha in Table 6 as a means to prioritize the use of risk factors, with low values meaning high priority. The priority order is: "issues", "space", "mods", and "sloc".

The significant risk factors would be used to predict reliability problems for *this set of data and this version of the software*. Whether these results would hold for future versions of the software would be determined in validation tests in future research. The finding regarding "mods" does confirm the software developer's view that this is an important risk factor. This is the case because if there are many iterations of the change request, it implies that it is complex and difficult to understand. Therefore, the change is likely to lead to reliability problems. It is not surprising that the size of the change "sloc" is significant because our previous studies of Space Shuttle metrics have shown it to be important [10]. Conflicting requirements "issues" could result in reliability problems when the change is implemented. The on-board computer memory required to implement the change "space" is critical to reliability because unlike commercial systems, the Space Shuttle does not have the luxury of large physical memory, virtual memory, and disk memory to hold its programs and data. Any increased requirement on its small memory to implement a change comes at the price of demands from competing functions.

In addition to identifying predictive risk factors, we must also identify thresholds for predicting when the number of failures would become excessive (i.e., rise rapidly with the risk factor). An example is shown in Figure 1 where cumulative failures are plotted against cumulative issues. The figure shows that when issues reach 286, failures reach 3 (obtained by querying the data point) and climb rapidly thereafter. Thus, an issues count of 286 would be the best estimate of the threshold to use in controlling the quality of the next version of the software. This process would be repeated across versions with the threshold being updated as more data is gathered. Thresholds would be identified for each risk factor in Table 6. This would provide multiple alerts for the quality of the software going bad (i.e., the reliability of the software would degrade as the number of alerts increases).

Table 6: Statistically Significant Results (alpha ≤ .05). CRs with no DRs vs. ((DRs only) or (DRs and Failures)) Mann Whiney Test			
Risk Factor	**Alpha**	**Median Value** CRs with no DRs	**Median Value** (DRs only) or (DRs and Failures)
issues	.0076	1	14
space	.0186	6	123
mods	.0401	0	4
sloc	.0465	10	88.5
issues: Number of possible conflicts among requirements. space: Amount of memory space required to implement the change. mods: Number of modifications of the proposed change. sloc: Number of lines of code affected by the change.			

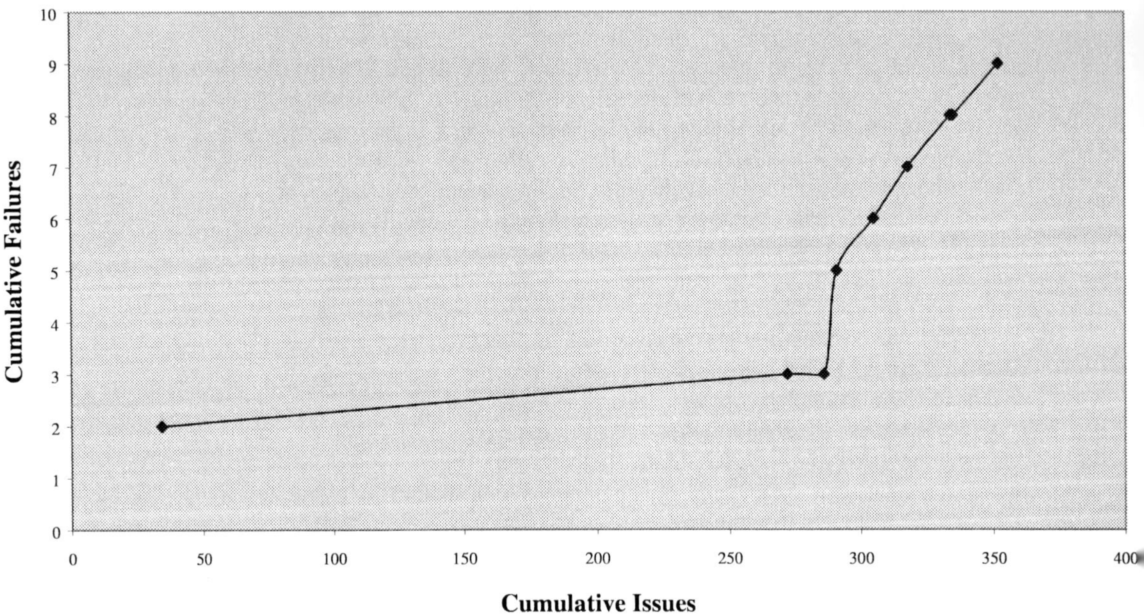

Figure 1. Failures vs. Issues

5.2. Dependency Check on Risk Factors

In order to check for possible dependencies among risk factors that could confound the results, rank correlation coefficients were computed in Table 7. Using an arbitrary threshold of .7, the results indicate a significant dependency among "issues", "mods", and "sloc" for *CRs with no DRs*. That is, as the number of conflicting requirements increases, the number of modifications and size of the change increase. In addition, there is a significant dependency among "space", "mods", and "issues" for *(DRs only) or (DRs and Failures)*. That is, as the number of conflicting requirements increases, the memory space and the number of modifications increase.

Table 7: Rank Correlation Coefficients of Risk Factors

	CRs with no DRs			
	mods	sloc	issues	space
mods		.370	**.837**	.219
sloc	.370		**.717**	.210
issues	**.837**	**.717**		.026
space	.219	.210	.026	
	(DRs only) or (DRs and Failures)			
	mods	sloc	issues	space
mods		.446	.363	**.759**
sloc	.446		.602	.569
issues	.363	.602		**.931**
space	**.759**	.569	**.931**	

5.3. Identification of Modules that Caused Failures

Table 8 shows modules that caused failures, as the result of the CRs, had metric values that far exceed the critical values. The latter were computed in previous research [10]. A critical value is a discriminant that distinguishes high quality from low quality software. A module with metric values exceeding the critical values is predicted to cause failures. Although the sample sizes are small, due to the high reliability of the Space Shuttle, the results consistently show that modules with excessive size and complexity lead to failures. Not only will the reliability be low but this software will also be difficult to maintain. The application of this information is that there is a high degree of risk when changes are made to software that has the metric characteristics shown in the table. Thus, these characteristics should be considered when making the risk analysis.

Table 8: Selected Risk Factor Module Characteristics

Change Request	**Module**	**Metric**	**Metric Critical Value**	**Metric Value**
A	1	change history line count in module listing	63	558
A	2	non-commented loc count	29	408
B	3	executable statement count	27	419
C	4	unique operand count	45	83
D	5	unique operator count	9	33
E	6	node count (in control graph)	17	66
All of the above metrics exceeded the critical values for all of the above Change Requests.				

6. Conclusions

Risk factors that are statistically significant can be used to make decisions about the risk of making changes. These changes impact the reliability and maintainability of the software. Risk factors that are not statistically significant should not be used; they do not provide useful information for decision-making and cost money and time to collect and process. The number of requirements issues ("issues"), the amount of memory space required to implement the change ("space"), the number of modifications ("mods"), and the size of the change ("sloc"), were found to be significant, in that priority order. In view of the dependencies among these risk factors, "issues" would be the choice if the using organization could only afford a single risk factor. We also showed how risk factor thresholds are determined for controlling the quality of the next version of the software.

Statistically significant results were found for *CRs with no DRs* vs. *((DRs only) or (DRs and Failures))*.

Metric characteristics of modules should be considered when making the risk analysis because metric values that exceed the critical values are likely to result in unreliable and non-maintainable software.

Our *methodology* can be generalized to other risk assessment domains, but the specific risk factors, their numerical values, and statistical results may vary. Future research will involve applying the methodology to the next version of the Space Shuttle software and identifying the statistically significant risk factors and thresholds to see whether they match the ones identified in this research.

7. Acknowledgements

We acknowledge the technical support received from Julie Barnard, Boyce Reeves, and Patti Thornton of United Space Alliance. We also acknowledge the funding support received from Dr. Allen Nikora of the Jet Propulsion Laboratory.

8. References

[1] Barry W. Boehm, "Software Risk Management: Principles and Practices", IEEE Software, Vol. 8, No. 1, January 1991, pp. 32-41.

[2] Taghi M. Khoshgoftaar and Edward B. Allen, "Predicting the Order of Fault-Fault-Prone Modules in Legacy Software", Proceedings of the Ninth International Symposium on Software Reliability Engineering, November 4-7, 1998, Paderborn, Germany, pp. 344-353.

[3] Taghi M. Khoshgoftaar, Edward B. Allen, Robert Halstead, and Gary P. Trio, "Detection of Fault-Prone Software Modules During a Spiral Life Cycle", Proceedings of the International Conference on Software Maintenance, November 4-8, 1996, Monterey, California, pp. 69-76.

[4] Taghi M. Khoshgoftaar, Edward B. Allen, Kalai Kalaichelvan, and Nishith Goel, "Early Quality Prediction: A Case Study in Telecommunications", IEEE Software, Vol. 13, No. 1, January 1996, pp. 65-71.

[5] D. Lanning and T. Khoshgoftaar, "The Impact of Software Enhancement on Software Reliability", IEEE Transactions on Reliability, Vol. 44, No. 4, December 1995, pp. 677-682.

[6] John C. Munson and Darrell S. Werries, "Measuring Software Evolution", Proceedings of the Third International Software Metrics Symposium, March 25-26, 1996, Berlin, Germany, pp. 41-51.

[7] Magnus C. Ohlsson and Claes Wohlin, "Identification of Green, Yellow, and Red Legacy Components", Proceedings of the International Conference on Software Maintenance, November 16-20, 1998, Bethesda, Maryland, pp. 6-15.

[8] Niclas Ohlsson and Hans Alberg, "Predicting Fault-Prone Software Modules in Telephone Switches", IEEE Transactions on Software Engineering, Vol. 22, No. 12, December 1996, pp. 886-894.

[9] Norman F. Schneidewind, "Investigation of the Risk to Software Reliability and Maintainability of Requirements Changes" (submitted for publication).
[10] Norman F. Schneidewind, "Software quality control and prediction model for maintenance", Annals of Software Engineering, Baltzer Science Publishers, Volume 9 (2000), May 2000, pp. 79-101.
[11] Webster's New Universal Unabridged Dictionary, Second Edition, Simon and Shuster, New York, 1979.

Using software metrics and evolutionary decision trees for software quality control

Peter Kokol, Vili Podgorelec, Maurizio Pighin

Abstract

Reliability is one of the most important aspects of software systems of any kind (embedded systems, information systems, intelligent systems, etc.) The size and complexity of software is growing dramatically during last decades and especially during last few years. Various methods can be used to achieve the software reliability i.e. software reliability engineering, fault tolerance, testing strategies, fault tree techniques, simulation, machine learning and software metrics. We have used several software complexity metrics together with a fractal software metric as the attributes for learning evolutionary decision trees. In this way one should be able to estimate whether a software module is dangerous regarding the probability of containing software faults. The aim of this paper is to present the α *metric together with decision trees as a fault predictive approach used to foresee dangerous software modules, which identification can largely enhance the reliability of software.*

1. Introduction

Reliability is one of the most important aspects of software systems of any kind (embedded systems, information systems, intelligent systems, etc.) The size and complexity of software is growing dramatically during last decades and especially during last few years. The systems consisting of hundred of millions lines of code are not a rarity any more, and the demand for highly complex hardware/software systems is increasing more rapidly than the ability to design, implement and maintain them. When the requirements for and dependencies of computers increase, the possibility of crises from failures also increases. The impact of these failures ranges from inconvenience to economic damages to loss of lives - therefore it is clear that software reliability is becoming a major concern not only for software engineers and computer scientists, but also for the "society" as a whole.

Various methods can be used to achieve the software reliability i.e. software reliability engineering (SRE), fault tolerance, testing strategies, fault tree techniques, simulation, machine learning [19] and software metrics.

1.1. Software metrics and reliability

Software development is a complex and complicated process in which software faults are inserted into the code by mistakes during the development process or maintenance. It has been shown that the pattern of the faults insertion phenomena is related to measurable attributes of the software, especially with the software metrics. For example, a large software system consists of various modules and each of these modules can be characterized in terms of attribute measures – it would be quite useful to be able to construct "dangerous module" prediction models based on these measurable attributes.

This project was partially supported by the grants: Ministry of Science of Slovenia – Project INCOMPETENT J2-0514-0796-98; Italian-Slovenian bilateral project "New Software Metrics for Real World Applications"; USA-Slovenian bilateral project "Physical Based Software Complexity Metrics".

1.2. Weaknesses of traditional software metrics

Although the software metrics are becoming more and more recognized in software engineering, many weaknesses remain. Some of them concerning software design are:

- The software is written in different programming languages ranging from "old fashioned third generation languages" FORTRAN, PASCAL or COBOL, trough fourth generation languages, spreadsheets and data base systems to fifth generation languages like PROLOG, LISP, etc. Still worse for some systems the source files have been lost, only the machine/executable code did remain. But the conventional software metrics are language dependent. We have to use (or even design) a different metric or at least a different tool for each programming language, again another metric for a program written in an assembler language and worse using traditional software metrics we are not able to asses the complexity of object or executable code.
- Software can be represented in many forms: requirements, specification, documentation, help files, requirements, user interfaces, etc. and all that representations can be manifested in very different appearances: written text, graphical, symbolic, formal languages, etc. To be able to assess the complexity of such a system in a holistic manner it is not enough to measure just the source code of the software, all other forms and artifacts have to be assessed – unfortunately no such metric does exist.
- To be able to track the progress of the software development process we have to measure the software during various stages like requirements engineering, architectural design, implementation and maintenance using a single metric – again no such metrics does exist.
- Normally software designers aren't metric's experts and while the output of a traditional complexity metric is a number, usually without any "physical" meaning and unit it is hard for them to interpret the assessed results. Is the number large or small? What is the unit? What does the measured number imply about complexity, reliability, effort already spent, effort needed for maintenance, quality, etc.?

1.3. Software metrics and complexity

The majority of experts in the computing field agree that complexity is one of the most relevant characteristics of computer software. For example Brooks states that computer software is the most complex entity among human made artifacts [20]. There are three possible, not completely distinct, viewpoints about software complexity:

- the classical computational complexity [22, 23],
- traditional software metrics, and
- recent "science of complexity" [21, 2, 7, 9].

Recently two attempts have been made to use the science of complexity in the measurement area. In her keynote speech at FESMA conference 1998 Kitchenham [1] argued that software measurement or estimates and predictions or assumptions based on them are infeasible. This is because software development, like in management science and economics, is a complex, non-linear adaptive system and inaccuracy of predictions is inherently emergent in such systems. As a consequence it is important to understand uncertainty and risk associated with that. Kokol et al [5-10] in their papers represent the similar view but their conclusion is that one not only has to understand the principles and findings of science of complexity but can use them to assess and measure the software more successfully, for example with the employment of so called α metric. This metric is based on the measurement of information content and entropy and it is known that the entropy is related to reliability – and thereafter α metric is a very viable candidate for software reliability assessment and software fault prediction.

1.4. The Aim and Scope of the Paper

The aim of this paper is to present the α metric and the employment of α together with decision trees as a *fault predictive metric* used to foresee dangerous software modules. Identified modules can be re-designed or tested and maintained more cautiously and any other special care can be devoted to these modules. In such manner the reliability can be largely enhanced.

In the second chapter some weaknesses of traditional software complexity metrics are enumerated. Next a physical background of α metric and some results of its use are presented. A study based on the analysis of 217 modules of a software system is presented in the last part of the paper together with concluding remarks. It is showed how α metric can be used together with other software complexity measures to induct a decision tree for the identification of potentially dangerous software modules. Decision trees are built with evolutionary algorithms, what increases their prediction power; the brief description of evolutionary approach in inducting decision trees is also provided.

2. Physical background

Both computer programs and natural language texts (human writings in the following text) can be in general classified as means for communicating. Communication can be defined as [14] *the interaction between systems or parts of a system using a prearranged* ***code,*** and the human communication as [15] *the organized behavior among a human group, according to a shared cultural and semantic* ***code***. It is clear from both of the above definitions that the **code** is crucial for effective communication, however it is not always so obvious that the code is in general complex, offering physical, perceptive, syntactic, semantic, pragmatic and cultural aspects in accordance with the characteristics of the environment shared by the communication systems. In general we can argue that the code is embodied in the communication language (or simply the language in the text that follows). There are many more or less related definitions of language [15], but an interesting view has been pointed out by a Slavic linguist Jakobson, building on the theories of de Saussure [13]. He argued that all languages share certain structures and rules that allow some combinations and forbid others. Without such structures and rules the words have no inherent meaning (i.e. "oo" occurs in "soothe" and "cool").

Another aspect necessarily associated with human writings and communication is the concept of meaning [16]. Like for the definition of language there are many different definitions of meaning, but we are only interested in the relation meaning – information in this paper. In that context [15] **meaning** is mainly subservient to implicit knowledge i.e. formerly acquired and organized **information.**

Many different quantities [3] have been proposed as measures of complexity to capture all our intuitive ideas about what is meant by complexity. Some of the quantities are computational complexity, information content, algorithmic information content, the length of a concise description of a set of the entity's regularities, logical depth, etc., (in contemplating various phenomena we frequently have to distinguish between effective complexity and logical depth - for example some very complex behavior patterns can be generated from very simple formula like Mandelbrot's fractal set, energy levels of atomic nuclei, the unified quantum theory, etc.- that means that they have little effective complexity and great logical depth). Li [17] relates the complexity with difficulty concerning the system in question, for example the difficulty of constructing a system, difficulty of describing the system, etc. It is also well known that complexity is related to entropy. Several authors speculate that the relation is one to one (i.e. algorithmic complexity is equivalent to entropy as a measure of randomness) [12] but [17] shows that the relation is one to many or many to one depending on the definition of the complexity and the choice of the system being studied.

Using the assumption that meaning and information content in text is founded on the correlation between language symbols one of the meaningful measures of complexity of human writings is entropy as established by Shannon [11]. Yet, when a text is very long it is almost impossible to calculate the Shannon information entropy so Grassberger [12] proposed an approximate method to estimate entropy. But entropy does not reveal directly the correlation properties of texts so another more general measure is needed. One possibility is to use Fourier power spectrum, however a method yielding much more quality scaling data was introduced recently. This method, called ***Long-range correlation*** [4] is based on the generalization of entropy and is very appropriate for measuring complexity of human writings.

3. Long-range correlations

Various quantities for the calculation of long range correlation in linear symbolic sequences were introduced in the literature and are discussed by Ebeling [18]. The most popular methods are dynamic entropy, scaling exponent $1/f^{\delta}$, higher order cumulates, mutual information, correlation functions, mean square deviations, and mapping of the sequence into random walk. It is agreed by many authors [18, 4] that the mapping into random walk is the most effective and successful approach in the analysis of human writings.

Long-range power law correlation (LRC) has been discovered in a wide variety of systems. As a consequence the LRC is very important for understanding the system's behavior, since we can quantify it with a critical exponent. Quantification of this kind of scaling behavior for apparently unrelated systems allows us to recognize similarities between different systems, leading to underlying unification. For example LRC has been identified in DNA sequences and natural language texts [4, 18] - the consequence is that DNA and human writings can be analyzed using very similar techniques.

3.1. Calculation of the long-range power law correlation

In order to analyze the long-range correlation of a string of symbols the best way is to first map the string into a Brownian walk model [4]. Namely, the Brownian walk model is well researched and publicized and the derived theories and methodologies are widely agreed and in addition easy to implement with the use of computer. There are various possibilities to implement the above mapping [6]. In this paper we will use the so-called CHAR method described by Schenkel [4] and Kokol [6]. A character is taken to be the basic symbol of a human writing (Figure 3). Each character is then transformed into a six bit long binary representation according to a fixed **code table**. It has been shown by Schenkel that the selection of the code table does not influence the results as long as all possible codes (i.e. we have 64 different codes for the six bit representation – in our case we assigned 56 codes for the letters and the remaining codes for special symbols like period, comma, mathematical operators, etc) are used. The obtained binary string is then transformed into a two dimensional Brownian walk model (Brownian walk in the text which follows) using each bit as a one move - the 0 as a step down and the 1 as a step up.

An important statistical quantity characterizing any walk is the root of mean square fluctuation F about the average of the displacement. In a two-dimensional Brownian walk model the F is defined as:

$$F^2(l) \equiv \overline{[\Delta y(l,l_0)]^2} - \left[\overline{\Delta y(l,l_0)}\right]^2$$

where

$$\Delta y(l, l_0) \equiv y(l_0 + l) - y(l_0)$$

l is the distance between two points of the walk on the X axis

l_0 is the initial position (beginning point) on the X axis where the calculation of *F(l)* for one pass starts

y is the position of the walk – the distance between the initial position and the current position on Y axis

and the bars indicate the average over all positions l_0.

The *F(l)* can distinguish two possible types of behavior:

- if the string sequence is uncorrelated (normal random walk) or there are local correlations extending up to a characteristic range i.e Markov chains or symbolic sequences generated by regular grammars [17], then

  $$F(l) \approx l^{0.5}$$

- if there is no characteristic length and the correlations are "infinite" then the scaling property of *F(l)* is described by a power law

  $$F(l) \approx l^{\alpha} \text{ and } \alpha \neq 0.5.$$

The power law is most easily recognized if we plot *F(l)* and *l* on a double logarithmic scale (Figure 3). If a power law describes the scaling property then the resulting curve is linear and the slope of the curve represents α. In the case that there are long range correlation in the strings analyzed, α should not be equal to 0.5.

The main difference between random sequences and human writings is purpose. Namely, the writing or programming is done consciously and with purpose that is not the case with random processes, thereafter we anticipate that α should differ from 0.5. The difference in α between different writings can be attributed to various factors like personal preferences, used standards, language, type of the text or the problem being solved, type of the organization in which the writer (or programmer) works, different syntactic, semantic, pragmatic rules etc.

4. Evolutionary decision trees

Inductive inference is the process of moving from concrete examples to general models, where the goal is to learn how to classify objects by analyzing a set of instances (already solved cases) whose classes are known. Instances are typically represented as attribute-value vectors. Learning input consists of a set of such vectors, each belonging to a known class, and the output consists of a mapping from attribute values to classes. This mapping should accurately classify both the given instances and other unseen instances.

A decision tree [26] is a formalism for expressing such mappings and consists of tests or attribute nodes linked to two or more sub-trees and leafs or decision nodes labeled with a class which means the decision (figure 1). A test node computes some outcome based on the attribute values of an instance, where each possible outcome is associated with one of the sub-trees. An instance is classified by starting at the root node of the tree. If this node is a test, the outcome for the instance is determined and the process continues using the appropriate sub-tree. When a leaf is eventually encountered, its label gives the predicted class of the instance.

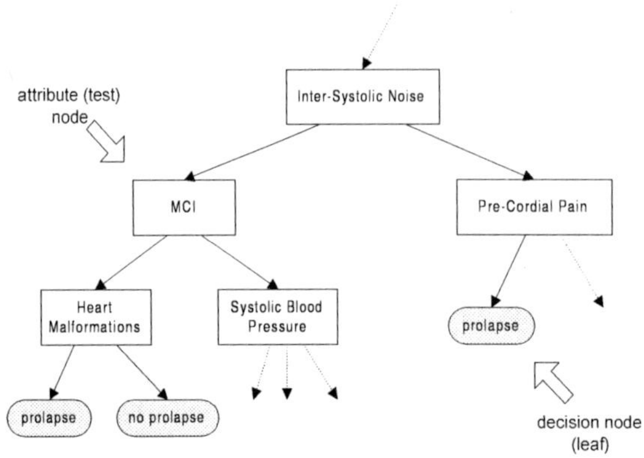

Figure 1. An example of a decision tree.

Evolutionary algorithms are adaptive heuristic search methods which may be used to solve all kinds of complex search and optimization problems. They are based on the evolutionary ideas of natural selection and genetic processes of biological organisms. As the natural populations evolve according to the principles of natural selection and "survival of the fittest", first laid down by Charles Darwin, so by simulating this process, evolutionary algorithms are able to evolve solutions to real-world problems, if they have been suitably encoded. They are often capable of finding optimal solutions even in the most complex of search spaces or at least they offer significant benefits over other search and optimization techniques.

As the traditional decision trees' induction methods contain several disadvantages we decided to use the power of evolutionary algorithms to induct the decision trees. In this manner we developed the evolutionary decision support model that evolves decision trees in a multi-population genetic algorithm SAEDT: self-adapting evolutionary decision trees [25]. Many experiments have shown the advantages of such approach over the traditional heuristic approach for building decision trees, which include better generalization, higher accuracy, possibility of more than one solution, efficient approach to missing and noisy data, etc.

4.1. SAEDT algorithm

When defining the internal representation of individuals within the population, together with the appropriate genetic operators that will work upon the population, it is important to assure the feasibility of all solutions during the whole evolution process. Therefore we decided to present individuals directly as decision trees. This approach has some important features: all intermediate solutions are feasible, no information is lost because of conversion between internal representation and the decision tree, the fitness function can be straightforward, etc. The problem with direct coding of solution may bring some problems in defining of genetic operators. As decision trees may be seen as a kind of simple computer programs (with attribute nodes being conditional clauses and decision nodes being assignments) we decided to define genetic operators similar to those used in genetic programming where individuals are computer program trees [27].

For the selection purposes a slightly modified linear ranking selection was used. The ranking of an individual decision tree within a population is based on the local fitness function:

$$LFF = \sum_{i=1}^{K} w_i \cdot (1 - acc_i) + \sum_{i=1}^{N} c_i \cdot attr(t_i) + w_u \cdot nu$$

where K is the number of decision classes, N in the number of attribute nodes in a tree, acc_i is the accuracy of classification of objects of a specific decision class d_i, w_i is the importance weight for classifying the objects of a decision class d_i, $attr(t_i)$ is the attribute used for a test in a node t_i, c_i is the cost of using the attribute of $attr(t_i)$, nu is number of unused decision (leaf) nodes, i.e. where no object from the training set fall into, and w_u is the weight of the presence of unused decision nodes in a tree.

According to this local fitness function the best trees (the most fit ones) have the lowest function values – the aim of the evolutionary process is to minimise the value of LFF for the best tree. A near optimal decision tree would classified all training objects with accuracy in accordance with importance weights w_i (some decision classes may be more important than the others), would have very little unused decision nodes (there is no evaluation possible for this kind of decision nodes regarding the training set) and would consist of low-cost attribute nodes (in this manner the desirable/undesirable attributes can be prioritised).

Crossover works on two selected individuals as an exchange of two randomly selected sub-trees. In this manner a randomly selected training object is used to determine paths (by finding a decision through the tree) in both selected trees. Then an attribute node is randomly selected on a path in the first tree and an attribute is randomly selected on a path in the second tree. Finally, the sub-tree from a selected attribute node in the first tree is replaced with the sub-tree from a selected attribute node in the second tree and in this manner an offspring is created which is put into a new population.

Mutation consists of several parts: 1) one randomly selected attribute node is replaced with an attribute, randomly chosen from the set of all attributes; 2) a test in a randomly selected attribute node is changed, i.e. the split constant is mutated; 3) a randomly selected decision (leaf) node is replaced by an attribute node; 4) a randomly selected attribute node is replaced by a decision node.

With the combination of presented crossover, which works as a constructive operator towards local optimums, and mutation, which works as a destructive operator in order to keep the needed genetic diversity, the searching for the solution tends to be directed toward the global optimal solution, which is the most appropriate decision tree regarding our specific needs (expressed in the form of LFF). As the evolution repeats, more qualitative solutions are obtained regarding the chosen fitness function. The evolution stops when an optimal or at least an acceptable solution is found or if the fitness score of the best individual does not change for a predefined number of generations.

4.1.1. Self-adaptation by information spreading in multi-population model

The multi-population model consists of three independent populations, one main population and two competing ones. First population is a single decision tree, initially induced in traditional way with the C4.5 algorithm [26], and the decision trees in the other two populations evolve in accordance with the evolutionary algorithm, described in the previous section. The best individual from the main population, which serves as the general solution, is competing with the best individuals from other populations in solving a given problem upon a training set. When it becomes dominant over the others (in the sense of the accuracy, sensitivity and specificity of the classification of training objects) it spreads its "knowledge" to them. In this way the other solutions become equally successful and the main population has to improve further to reclaim its dominance. This can be done by adjusting the local fitness function – for this purpose the weights used for the LFF is modified:

$$\forall i, i \in [1..K]: w_i = w_i + (1 - acc_i) * rand(av)$$

where av is the adaptation value and $rand(av)$ is random value from $[0,av]$.

One global fitness function (different from the local ones – those used in the evolutionary process to evaluate the fitness of individual decision trees) is used to determine the dominance of one population over another. It is predetermined as a weighted sum of accuracy, sensitivity and specificity (look at the results in the next section) of the given solution, together with the cost of chosen attributes:

$$GFF = w_{acc} \cdot (1 - acc) + w_{sens} \cdot (1 - sens) + w_{spec} \cdot (1 - spec) + \sum_{i=1}^{N} c_i \cdot type(t_i) + w_u \cdot nu$$

where the last two parts are the same as in the local fitness function and acc is the accuracy of classified training objects, $sens$ is the sensitivity of classified training objects, $spec$ is the specificity of classified training objects, w_{acc} is the importance weight of accuracy, w_{sens} is the importance weight of sensitivity, and w_{spec} is the importance weight of specificity.

5. Fault prediction using decision trees and α metrics

To test the usability of decision trees and fractal metrics α in predicting potentially dangerous modules and in this manner designing reliable software we performed a study in a real world environment. We tested a software system consisting of 217 modules representing more than 200000 lines of code.

First the modules have been identified either as OK or DANGEROUS by applying the model developed by Pighin [24]. The purpose of this model is to use the software complexity metrics to define complexity risk thresholds. The modules are divided into two classes – bellow and above some fault threshold value (5 faults in our case).

A set of 168 attributes, containing various software complexity measures, have been determined for each software module and the α coefficient has been calculated for each software module. From all 217 modules 167 have been randomly selected for the learning set, and the remaining 50 modules has been selected for the testing set. Several decision trees have been induced for predicting dangerous modules. In the figure 2 an induced decision tree is presented as an example. The results of classification using induced decision tree is presented in tables I-III.

Table I. Classification results on learning set (number of software modules).

	Classified as OK	Classified as DANGEROUS
OK	108	11
DANGEROUS	4	44

Table II. Classification results on testing set (number of software modules).

	Classified as OK	Classified as DANGEROUS
OK	30	6
DANGEROUS	4	10

Table III. Results of induced decision tree for predicting dangerous software modules.

	learning set	testing set
accuracy	91.02	80.00
sensitivity	91.67	71.43
specificity	90.76	83.33

Table IV. Results using only α metric as a fault predictive method.

	testing set
accuracy	70.0
sensitivity	66.7
specificity	72.7

```
alpha
 |--[<0.63233] OK
 |--[>=0.63233] signif_di_commento
    |--[<1480.04000] StrCtrl_linee
    |  |--[<44.55000] OK
    |  |--[>=44.55000] DANGEROUS
    |--[>=1480.04000] istr_di_selezione
       |--[<3.79900] DANGEROUS
       |--[>=3.79900] funz_param_formali
          |--[<19.16200] DANGEROUS
          |--[>=19.16200] signif_di_commento
             |--[<3026.50800] OK
             |--[>=3026.50800] DANGEROUS
```

Figure 2. Evolutionary induced decision tree for predicting potentially dangerous software modules.

Above facts showed the usability of decision trees together with various software complexity measures and α metric in software fault prediction. The Table IV shows that the accuracy, when only α metric is used, is about 70% - that means that 70% of modules are correctly classified. When α value is used together with other complexity measures to build the decision tree, the accuracy is increased to 80%, which represents a big improvement, especially regarding the fact that both the sensitivity and the specificity increase.

One of the most interesting characteristic of the induced decision tree (figure 2) is that alpha has been chosen as the most important attribute (root node). This fact shows that α metric is actually useful in predicting dangerous software modules. The combination of α metric with some other software complexity measures as the attributes for decision trees proved to be very successful.

Another important fact is the size of the induced decision tree. As it is very small, regarding the number of possible attributes, it can be concluded that the induced decision tree is highly generalized and is not biased to over-fitting.

6. Conclusion

In the paper we present the use of evolutionary decision trees as a fault predictive approach. We show that the α metric as an attribute together with other software complexity measures can be successfully used to induce decision trees for predicting dangerous modules (modules having a lot of undetected faults). Redesigning such modules or devoting more testing or maintenance effort to them can largely enhance the quality and reliability, making the software much safer to use. In our future studies we would like to use more advanced text mining methods to even better assure the reliability of software.

References

[1] Kitchenham, B., "The certainty of uncertainty", Proceedings of FESMA (Eds: Combes H et al), Technologish Institut, 1998, pp. 17-25.

[2] Morowitz, H., "The Emergence of Complexity", Complexity 1(1), 1995, pp. 4.

[3] Gell-Mann, M., "What is complexity", Complexity 1(1), 1995, pp. 16-19.

[4] Schenkel, A., Zhang, J., Zhang, Y., "Long range correlations in human writings", Fractals 1(1), 1993, pp. 47-55.

[5] Kokol, P., Kokol, T., "Linguistic laws and computer programs", Journal of the American Society for Information Science 47(10), 1996, pp. 781-785.

[6] Kokol, P., Brest, J., •umer, V., "Long-range correlations in computer programs", Cybernetics and systems 28(1), 1997, pp. 43-57.

[7] Kokol, P., Podgorelec, V., Brest, J., "A wishful complexity metric", Proceedings of FESMA (Eds: Combes H et al), Technologish Institut, 1998, pp. 235 - 246.

[8] Kokol, P., "Analysing formal specification with alpha metrics", ACM Software Engineering Notes, 24(1), 1999a, pp. 80-81.

[9] Kokol, P., Podgorelec, V., Zorman, M., Pighin, M., "Alpha - a generic software complexity metric", Project control for software quality : proceedings of ESCOM-SCOPE 99, Shaker Publishing BV, 1999b, pp. 397-405.

[10] Kokol, P., Podgorelec, V., Zorman, M., "Universality - a need for a new software metric", International workshop on software measurement, 1999c, pp. 51-54.

[11] Shannon, C.E., "Prediction and entropy of printed English", Bell System Technical Journal, 1951, pp 30, 50.

[12] Grassberger, P., "Estimating the information content of symbol sequences and efficient codes", IEEE Transactions on Information Technology, 1989, pp. 35, 669.

[13] Gibbs,W.W., "The Profile of Claude Levi-Strauss", Scientific American 278(1), 1998, pp. 24-25.

[14] Young, J.Z., "Programs of the Brain". Oxford U.P., Oxford, 1978.

[15] Francois, C. (ed.), "International encyclopaedia of systems and cybernetics", K.G. Saur, Munchen, 1997.

[16] Parkinson, G.H.R. (ed.), "The Theory of Meaning", Oxford U.P., Oxford, 1982.

[17] Li, W., "On the Relationship Between Complexity and Entropy for Markov Chains and Regular Languages", Complex Systems 5(4), 1991, pp. 381 – 399.

[18] Ebeling, W., Neiman A., Poschel T., "Dynamic Entropies, Long-Range Correlations and Fluctations in Complex Linear Structures", Proceedings of Coherent Approach to Fluctations, World Scientific, 1995.

[19] Lyu, M.R. (ed.), "Software Reliability Engineering", Computer Society Press, 1995.

[20] Brooks, P.F., "No silver bullet: essence and accidents of software engineering", *IEEE Computer* 1987, 20(4)10-19, 1987.

[21] Pines, D. (Ed.), "Emerging syntheses in science", Addison Wesley, 1988.

[22] Cohen, B., Harwood, W.T., Jackson, M.I. "The specification of complex systems", Addison Wesley, 1986.

[23] Wegner, P., Israel, M. (Eds.), "Symposium on Computational Complexity and the Nature of Computer Science", Computing Surveys 27(1)5 - 62, 1995.

[24] Pighin, M., Kokol, P., "RPSM: A risk-predictive structural experimental metric", Proceedings of FESMA'99, Technologish Institut, 1999, pp. 459–464.

[25] Podgorelec, V., Kokol, P., "Self-adapting evolutionary decision support model", Proceedings of the 1999 IEEE International Symposium on Industrial Electronics ISIE'99, Bled, Slovenia, IEEE Press, 1999, pp. 1484-1489.

[26] Quinlan, J.R., "C4.5: Programs for Machine Learning", Morgan Kaufmann, 1993.

[27] Koza, J.R., "Genetic Programming: On the Programming of Computers by Natural Selection", MIT Press, 1992.

Author affiliations

Abran, Alain; abran.alain@uqam.ca; Université du Québec a Montréal; Canada
Abts, Chris; cabts@sunset.usc.edu; USC-CSE; USA
Angelis, Lefteris; lef@csd.auth.gr; Aristotle University of Thessaloniki; Greece
Armour, Frank; frank_armour@ams.com; American Management Systems; USA
Azuma, Motoei; azuma@azuma.mgmt.waseda.ac.jp; Waseda University; Japan
Bailey Clark, Elizabeth; Betsy@Software-Metrics.com; SMI; USA
Balla, Katalin; balla@iqsoft.hu; IQSOFT Ltd.; Hungary
Basanieri , Francesca; basa@rep1.iei.pi.cnr.it; IEI-CNR ; Italy
Bell, Gary; bellgaa@sbu.ac.uk; South Bank University; United Kingdom
Bemelmans, Theo; t.m.a.bemelmans@tm.tue.nl; Technical University Eindhoven; The Netherlands
Bertolino, Antonia; bertolino@iei.pi.cnr.it; IEI-CNR ; Italy
Beyers, Craig; craig_beyers@ams.com; American Management Systems; USA
Bobkowska, Anna; annab@eti.pg.gda.pl; Technical University of Gdansk; Poland
Boehm, Barry ; boehm@sunset.usc.edu; University of Southern California ; USA
Britton, Carol; c.britton@herts.ac.uk; University of Hertfordshire; UK
Brown, A. Winsor; awbrown@sunset.usc.edu; University of Southern California; USA
Bundell, Gary; bundell@ee.uwa.edu.au; Uni of WA; Australia
Cantone, Giovanni; cantone@info.uniroma2.it; Universita' di Roma Tor Vergata ; Italy
Catherwood, Bill; bill_catherwood@ams.com; American Management Systems; USA
Chulani, Sunita; sunita@us.ibm.com; IBM Research; USA
Coleman, Gerry; gerry.coleman@dkit.ie; Dundalk Institute of Technology; Ireland
Cooper, Maggie; maggie@soi.city.ac.uk; City University; United Kingdom
Daily, Kevin; qpi@improveqpi.co.uk; Improve QPI Ltd; UK
Davidson, Gary; davidson@us.ibm.com; IBM Software Group; USA
Dekkers, Ton; dekkerto@iquip.nl; IQUIP Informatica; Netherlands
Desharnais, Jean-Marc; desharnais.jean-marc@uqam.ca; SELASM; Canada
Donzelli, Paolo; p.donzelli@palazzochigi.it; Presidenza del Consiglio dei ministri ; Italy
Dumke, Reiner; dumke@ivs.cs.uni-magdeburg.de; Otto-von-Guericke-Universität Magdeburg; Germany
Evanco, William; William.Evanco@cis.drexel.edu; Drexel University; USA
Fabrizi, Stefano; fabrizi.stefano@insedia.interbusiness.it; Banca d'Italia; Italy
Ferris, Jane; Jferris@maths.dit.ie; Dublin Institute of Technology; Ireland
Foltin, Erik; foltin@ivs.cs.uni-magdeburg.de; Otto-von-Guericke-Universität Magdeburg; Germany
Forselius, Pekka; pekka.forselius@kolumbus.fi; STTF; Finland
Foss, Tron ; tron.foss@bi.no; Norwegian School of Management; Norway
Gustafsson, Juha; gustafss@cs.helsinki.fi; University of Helsinki; Finland
Horgan, Gerard; gmhorgan@hotmail.com; Nexis Ltd; UK
Jenkins, John; j.jenkins@mdx.ac.uk; Middlesex University; United Kingdom
Kammelar, John; john.kammelar@ecsoft.nl; ECsoft; Netherlands
Kanno, Kyota; kyota@azuma.mgmt.waseda.ac.jp; Dept. of IMSE, Waseda University; Japan
Kaposi, Agnes; agnes@kaposi.demon.co.uk; Kaposi associates; UK
Khaddaj, Souheil; s.khaddaj@kingston.ac.uk; Kingston University; UK
Kirsopp, Colin; ckirsopp@bmth.ac.uk; Bournemouth University; UK
Kokol, Peter; kokol@uni-mb.si; University of Maribor; Slovenia
Kusters, Rob; R.J.Kusters@tm.tue.nl; Technical University Eindhoven; The Netherlands
Leszkowicz, Bob; bobl@us.ibm.com; IBM Software Group; USA
Loconsole, Annabella; bella@cs.umu.se; Umeå University; Sweden
Marchetti, Eda; e.marchetti@iei.pi.cnr.it; IEI-CNR ; Italy
Martinez, Antonio; amartinez@inf-cr.uclm.es; University of Castilla-La Mancha; España
Mateos, María Dolores; lolimatcri@terra.es; UCLM; Spain
Matsushita, Soichi; so1@azuma.mgmt.waseda.ac.jp; Dept. of IMSE, Waseda University; Japan
Maxwell, Katrina; kmaxwell@datamax-france.com; Datamax; France

Meli, Roberto; roberto.meli@dpo.it; DPO Srl; Italy
Miranda, Eduardo; eduardo.miranda@lmc.ericsson.se; Ericsson Research Canada & Université du Quebec a Montréal; Canada
Moore, Darrell; darrellm@us.ibm.com; IBM Software Group; USA
Myers, Margaret ; myersm@richmond.ac.uk; Richmond, the American International University in; UK
Myrtveit, Ingunn; ingunn.myrtveit@bi.no; Norwegian School of Management; Norway
Nawrocki, Jerzy; Jerzy.Nawrocki@put.poznan.pl; Poznan University of Technology; Poland
Nenonen, Lilli; lnenonen@cs.helsinki.fi; University of Helsinki; Finland
Nonaka, Makoto; nonaka@azuma.mgmt.waseda.ac.jp; Dept. of IMSE, Waseda University; Japan
O'Connor, Rory; roconnor@compapp.dcu.ie; Dublin City University; Ireland
Oligny, Serge; oligny.serge@uqam.ca; Université du Québec a Montréal; Canada
Paakki, Jukka; paakki@cs.helsinki.fi; University of Helsinki; Finland
Page, Andy; whitley.nicola@virgin.net; City University; United Kingdom
Paton, Keith; paton@total.net; Paton System Design; Canada
Piattini, Mario; mpiattin@inf-cr.uclm.es; University of Castilla-La Mancha; España
Pighin, Maurizio; pighin@dimi.uniud.it; University of Udine; Italy
Podgorelec, Vili; vili.podgorelec@uni-mb.si; University of Maribor; Slovenia
Polo, Macario; mpolo@inf-cr.uclm.es; UCLM; Spain
Procaccino, Drew; jdproc@aol.com; Drexel University; USA
Qureshi, Shoaib; shoaib.qureshi@philips.com; Philips Research Labs; United Kingdom
Ravichandran, S.; drravis@ssi-technologies.com; SSI Technologies; India
Rollo, Tony; trollo@compuserve.com; CIT; UK
Ruiz, Francisco; fruiz@inf-cr.uclm.es; UCLM; Spain
Rule, Grant; PG_Rule@compuserve.com; Software Measurement Services Ltd.; UK
Rus, Ioana ; irus@fc-md.umd.edu; Fraunhofer Center Maryland - University of Maryland; USA
Sakellaris, Evangelos; vaggelis@si.gr; Singular International; Greece
Santhanam, P.; pasanth@us.ibm.com; IBM Research; USA
Schmietendorf, Andreas; a.schmietendorf@telekom.de; T-Nova, Development Centre Berlin; Germany
Schneidewind, Norman ; nschneid@nps.navy.mil; Naval Postgraduate School ; USA
Shareef, Mohammed; shareef@ssi-technologies.com; SSI Technologies; India
Stamelos, Ioannis; stamelos@csd.auth.gr; Aristotle University of Thessaloniki; Greece
Stensrud, Erik; erik.stensrud@ieee.org; Stensrud Consulting; Norway
Stutzke, Richard; Richard.D.Stutzke@saic.com; SAIC; USA
Sverstiuk, Maria; sverstim@drexel.edu; Drexel University; USA
Symons, Charles; charles_symons@compuserve.com; Software Measurement Services Ltd.; UK
Trienekens, Jos; J.J.M.Trienekens@tm.tue.nl; Technical University Eindhoven; The Netherlands
Tron, Foss; tron.foss@bi.no; Norwegian School of Management; Norway
Vaughan, Lori; lori.vaughan@trw.com; TRW; USA
Verkamo, A. Inkeri; verkamo@cs.helsinki.fi; University of Helsinki; Finland
Verner, June; june.verner@cis.drexel.edu; Drexel University; USA
Victor, David; dmv@algorithm-n-blues.co.uk; Plex Computer Services Ltd; UK
Virtanen, Pentti; Pentti.Virtanen@sci.fi; Turku Centre for Computer Science; Finland
Ward, Robert; rob.ward@qsm-consulting.com; QSM; UK
Warwick, Jon; warwick@sbu.ac.uk; South Bank University; United Kingdom
Wenger, Martin; martin.wenger@app.ch; APP management consulting Ltd; Switzerland
Westwood, Peter; pwestwoo@istar.ca; Westwood Technology Management; Canada
Wojciechowski, Adam; Adam.Wojciechowski@put.poznan.pl; Poznan University of Technology; Poland
Woodings, Terry; terry@ee.uwa.edu.au; Uni of WA; Australia
Wright, Terry; terywright@mmv.gov.au; Multimedia Victoria; Australia